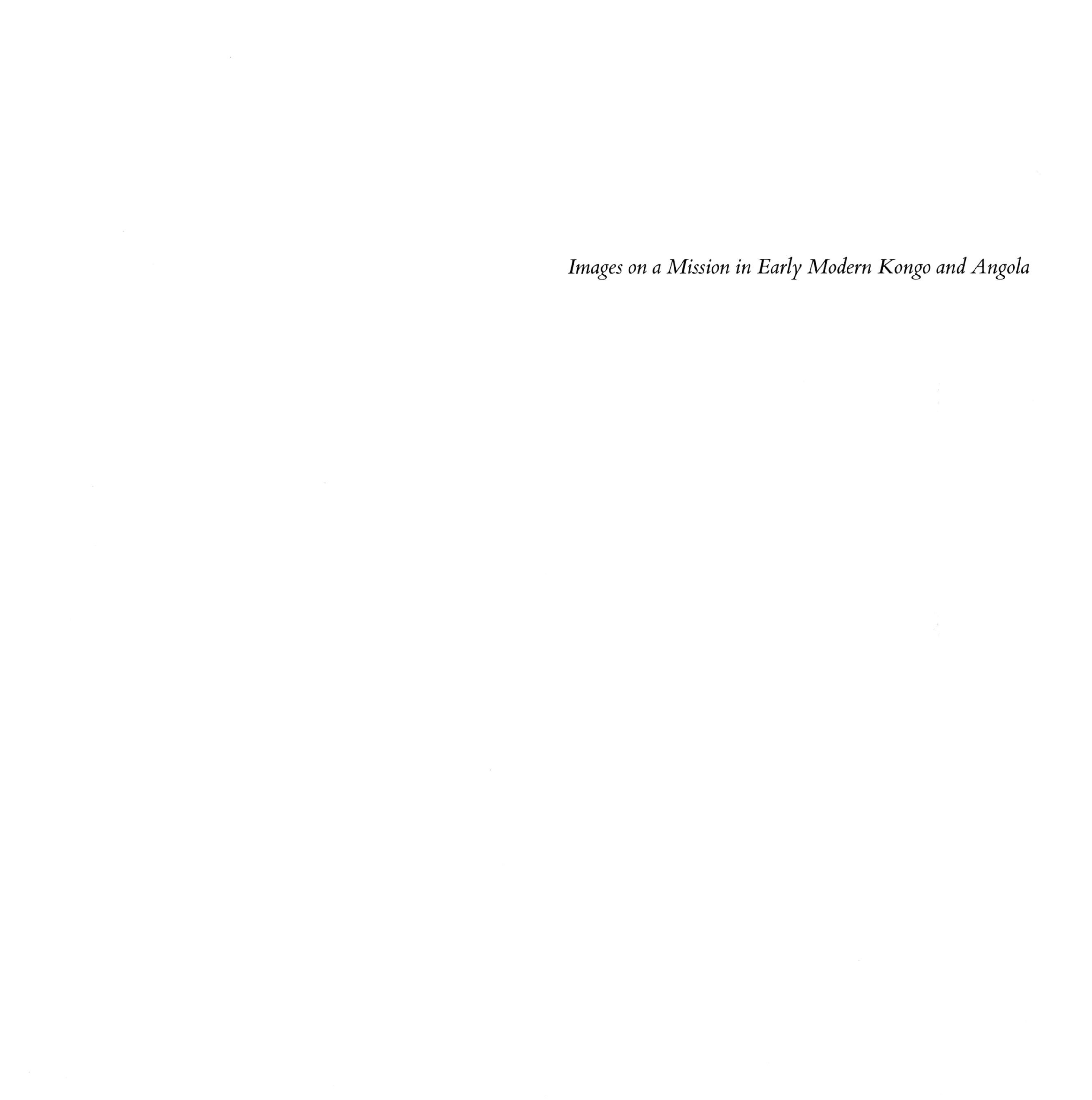

Images on a Mission in Early Modern Kongo and Angola

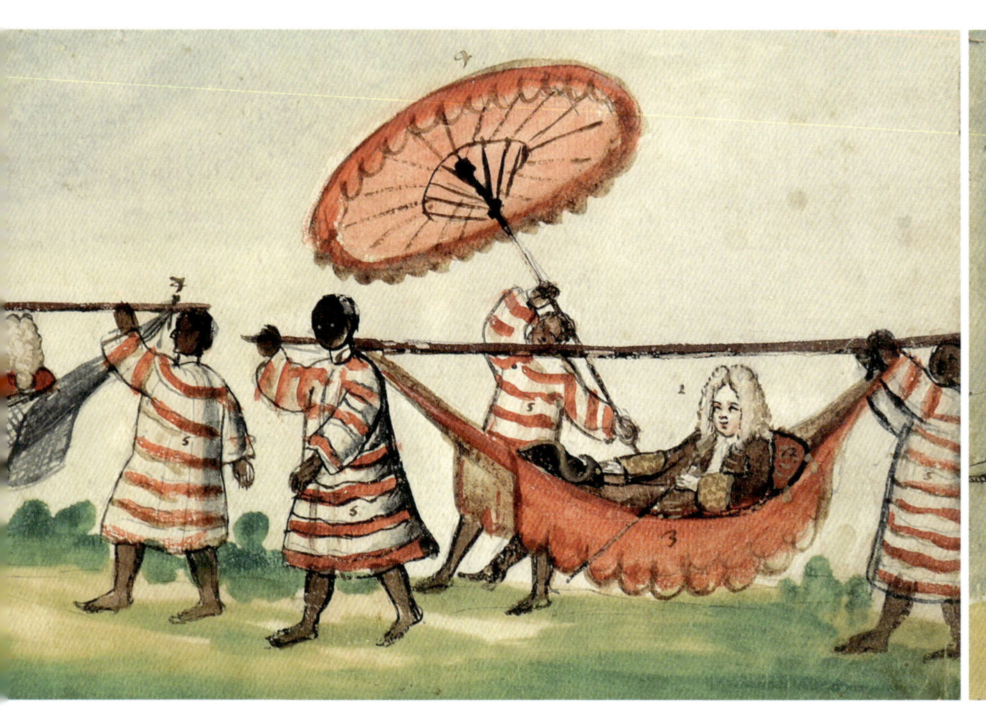
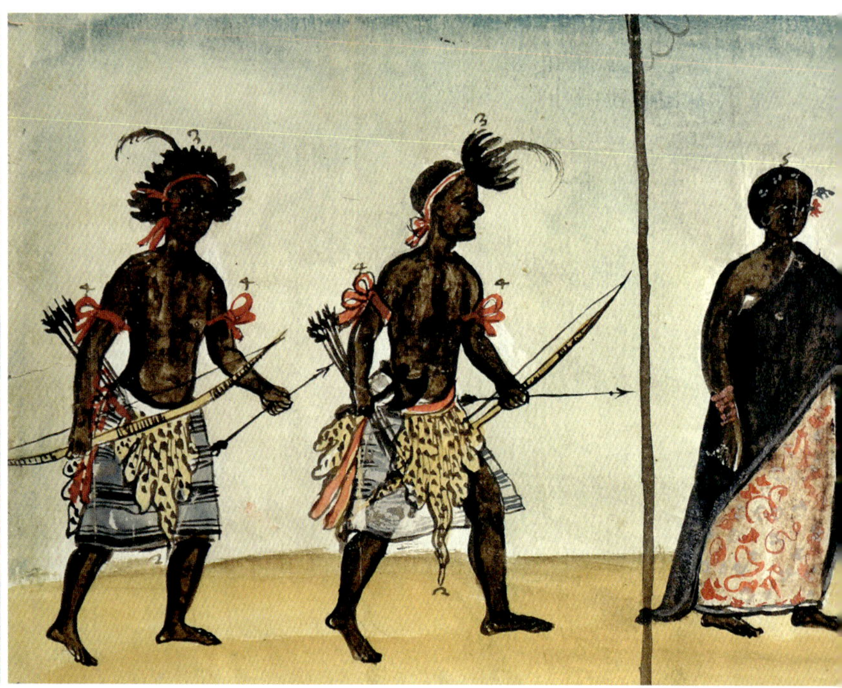

CÉCILE FROMONT

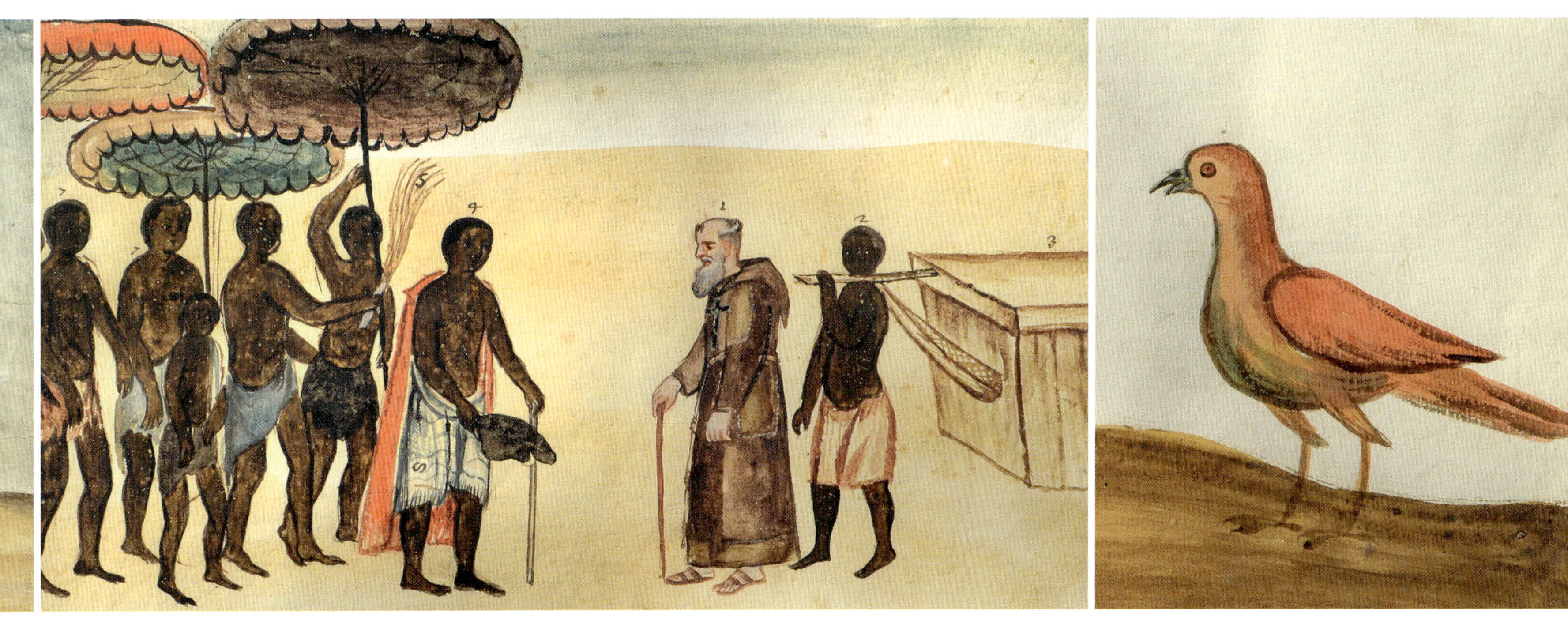

Images on a Mission in Early Modern Kongo and Angola

The Pennsylvania State University Press
University Park, Pennsylvania

Published with the assistance of the Frederick W. Hilles Publication Fund of Yale University.

Publication of this book has been aided by a grant from the Millard Meiss Publication Fund of CAA.

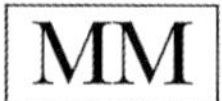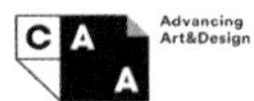

LIBRARY OF CONGRESS CATALOGING-IN-PUBLICATION DATA

Names: Fromont, Cécile, author.
Title: Images on a mission in early modern Kongo and Angola / Cécile Fromont.
Description: University Park, Pennsylvania : The Pennsylvania State University Press, [2022] | Includes bibliographical references and index.
Summary: "Presents and analyzes a set of unpublished images from seventeenth- and eighteenth-century Kongo and Angola created within the Capuchin Franciscan mission to the region"—Provided by publisher.
Identifiers: LCCN 2021061073 | ISBN 9780271092188 (cloth)
Subjects: LCSH: Capuchin art—Kongo Kingdom—17th century. | Capuchin art—Kongo Kingdom—18th century. | Capuchin art—Angola—17th century. | Capuchin art—Angola—18th century. | Capuchins—Missions—Kongo Kingdom—History—17th century. | Capuchins—Missions—Kongo Kingdom—History—18th century. | Capuchins—Missions—Angola—History—17th century. | Capuchins—Missions—Angola—History—18th century.
Classification: LCC N7989.6.C6 F76 2022 | DDC 255/.36096751/1401—dc23/ eng/20220208
LC record available at https://lccn.loc.gov/2021061073

Printed in Korea by Tailored Group
Book design & typesetting by Garet Markvoort, zijn digital
Published by The Pennsylvania State University Press,
University Park, PA 16802–1003

The Pennsylvania State University Press is a member of the Association of University Presses.

It is the policy of The Pennsylvania State University Press to use acid-free paper. Publications on uncoated stock satisfy the minimum requirements of American National Standard for Information Sciences—Permanence of Paper for Printed Library Material, ANSI Z39.48–1992.

In memory of Francis Fromont (1942–2014)

Contents

Illustrations

FIGURES

MAP

TABLES

Acknowledgments

This book was born of living as well as physical archives. The knowledge and advice on methods and content that many shared with me made these pages possible. My thanks go to the archivists, curators, scholars, and technicians of the Capuchin General Archives and Franciscan Museum in Rome–Bravetta, the Biblioteca del Clero and the Biblioteca Monsignor Giacomo Maria Radini Tedeschi in Bergamo, the Biblioteca civica Centrale in Turin, the Biblioteca civica Gambalunga in Rimini, the Archivio di Stato in Milan, the Biblioteca Ambrosiana in Milan, the Biblioteca Angelica in Rome, the Biblioteca universitaria Alessandrina in Rome, the Archivio dei Padri Carmelitani Scalzi in Rome, the Biblioteca universitaria Urbaniana in the Vatican, the Archivio Storico de Propaganda Fide in the Vatican, the Biblioteca Apostolica Vaticana, the Archivio Segreto Vaticano, the British Library, the Jesuit general archives in Rome, the Archives des missions étrangères in Paris, the Biblioteca Nacional in Madrid, the Biblioteca del Palacio in Madrid, the Arquivo Nacional da Torre do Tombo in Lisbon, the Biblioteca Nacional de Portugal in Lisbon, the Biblioteka Jagiellońska in Krakow, the Biblioteca Nazionale Centrale in Rome, the Arquivo Histórico Nacional de Angola, the Melville J. Herskovits Library of African Studies at Northwestern University, the Biblioteca Estense in Modena, the Bibliothèque nationale de France, the Newberry Library in Chicago, the Houghton Library at Harvard, the Beinecke Library at Yale, the Yale Center for British Art, the Arquivo Histórico Ultramarino in Lisbon, the Biblioteca da Ajuda in Lisbon, the Academia das Ciênciais in Lisbon, the Sociedade de Geographia in Lisbon, the Museu Antropológico da Universidade de Coimbra, the Metropolitan Museum of Art in New York, the Museu Nacional de Etnologia in Lisbon, the Vatican Ethnological Museum, the Afrika Museum in Berg en Dal, the Krannert Art Museum in Urbana-Champaign, the Musée du Quai Branly in Paris, the Royal Museum for Central Africa in Tervuren, and the Capuchin Provincial Archives in Florence, Genoa, and L'Aquila. I am especially thankful to Padres Giacomo Carlini and Romano Mantovi, who generously and perceptively led me to the Parma Watercolors. Fathers Servus

Gieben†, Yohannes Bache, and Luigi Martignani welcomed me to the Capuchin Central Archives in Bravetta with unfaltering kindness over the years. I also acknowledge with gratitude the Virgili and Giovanelli families as well as Dr. and Mrs. Araldi for their support of my investigations of the manuscripts in their collections over the years. To Anne and Louis-Carl Vignon, Antonella Grassi, and Alberto Savoia, my thanks.

A project that developed and grew over a decade and a half, this book has grown and changed thanks to the comments, insights, and encouragements of Suzanne P. Blier, Thomas B. F. Cummins, Esther Chadwick, Pierre de Maret, Steven Nelson, Kristina Van Dyke, Claudia Brittenham, John Thornton, Linda Heywood, Carlo Toso, Surekha Davies, Nadine Zimmerli, and the anonymous reviewers at Penn State University Press. My colleagues in the departments of art history at the University of Chicago, the University of Michigan, and Yale University; the 2014 fellows at Yale's Institute for Sacred Music and the 2017–18 fellows of the American Academy in Rome; the senior and junior members of the Michigan Society of Fellows in 2008–2010; and the patient audiences at events where I presented material from these pages—all have made the book's argument exponentially better.

Veronica Copello, Sophia Kitlinski, Nathalie Miraval, Giacomo Berchi, Francesco Giorgi, and Lolade Siyonbola have helped push the manuscript forward in key ways. Ellie Goodman, Maddie Caso, and the Penn State University Press staff, including the agile PSU Press editorial assistants, have lent their patient and generous support to this project over many years. Any coherent sentence in the book is due to Keith Monley's discerning copyediting. Emily Floyd and Sally Promey's inspired and inspiring MAVCOR online platform has allowed for a broader, richer, more ambitious project thanks to the articulation of online and print media.

Research for this volume was made possible by financial support from a Renaissance Society of America Paul Oskar Kristeller Fellowship, a Center for the Advanced Study of Visual Arts predoctoral fellowship, a Rome Prize from the American Academy in Rome, a yearlong Yale Institute of Sacred Music Fellowship, and a Michigan Society of Fellows Postdoctoral Fellowship. The Frederick W. Hilles Publication Fund and the Department of the History of Art at Yale University, as well as a Millard Meiss publication grant from the College Art Association, have contributed financially to the production of the book.

"Do not ask questions you can't answer"— Tom Cummins. "Is there another way to think about it?"—Suzanne Blier. It took me fifteen years to hear, *really*, these two pieces of advice my graduate-school advisers once gave me. The phrases stayed with me over the decades, but only in the final writing of this book did I grasp their meaning and realize the convoluted path I had taken to answer their call to action. With this realization came another lesson, this time in pedagogy: learning needs time, teaching needs patience. So let me acknowledge and thank Suzanne and Tom again for their teachings and for their patience. And I will put it in print: you were right.

Though this project started long before 2020, this is a pandemic book. Large parts of the manuscript were written while in confinement, while inventing physical and mental space for a family of five, including an infant, a school-age child, and a tween, while creating whole new curricula for suddenly online classes, while making attempts at remote schooling, while supporting undergraduate and graduate students in an unprecedented crisis, while bracing, along with my communities, against illness and death and joining them in fighting against some of the injustices we inherited from history's long shadow. This book is a far cry from what it would have been under different circumstances, but I celebrate it, shortcomings and all, as a testament to the support and inspiration I have drawn from the grit, passion, and resilience of my family, children, students, colleagues, and communities. *Nou la, nou doubout.*

Finally, and above all, thank you to my family in this world and in the realm of the ancestors. Grant, Louis, Héloïse, and Quitterie: this is for you.

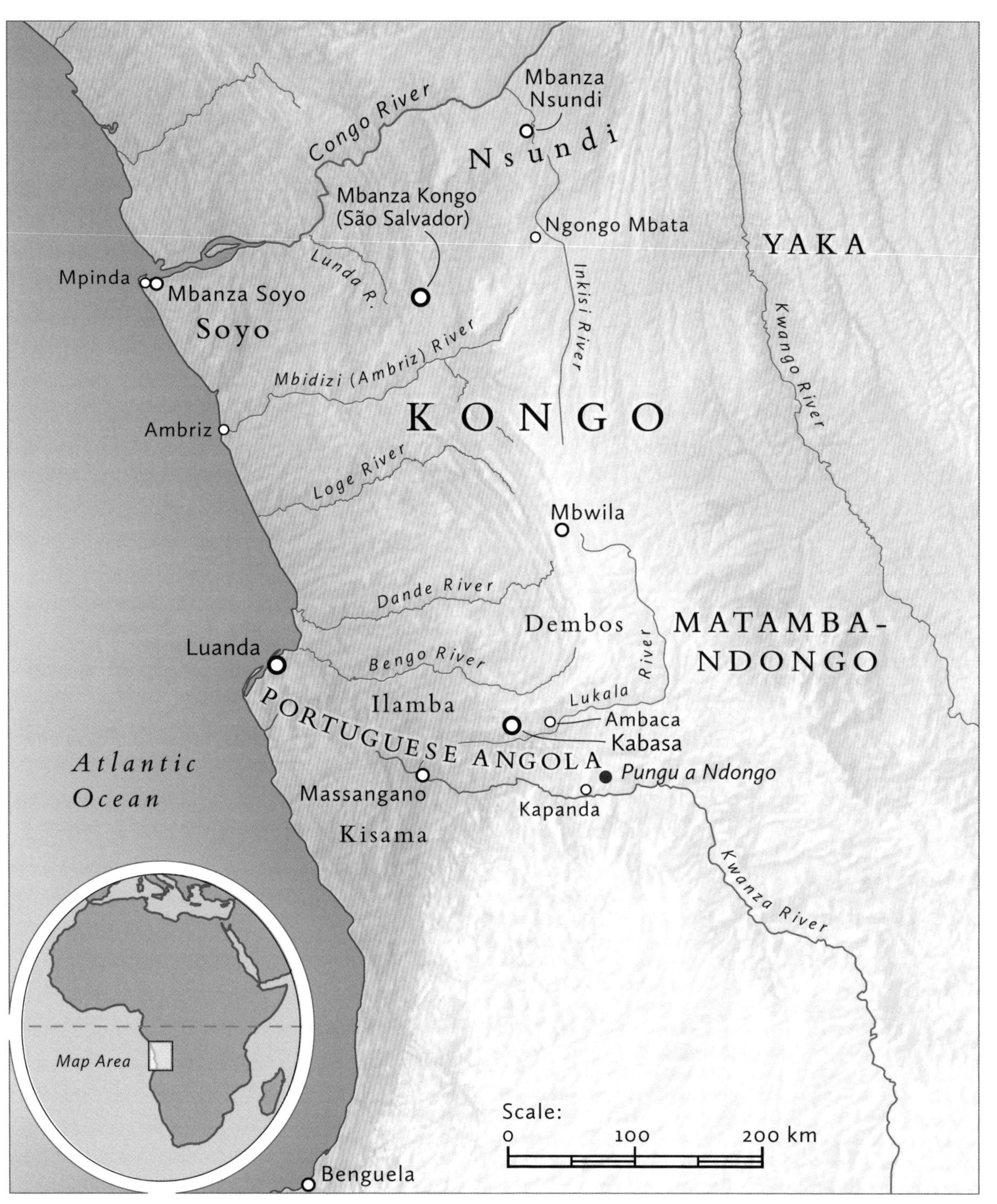

West Central Africa ca. 1700. Drawn by James DeGrand.

Introduction

On the Feast of Pentecost, May 25, 1645, twelve friars of the Franciscan Capuchin mendicant order reached the mouth of the Congo River.[1] They had sailed from Europe to central Africa to start a new mission under the auspices of the Congregation for the Propagation of the Faith, the papal institution charged with evangelization, better known as the Propaganda Fide. The ship on which they traveled, led by Genoese captain Giovanni Bernardo Falconi, set anchor for the night off the coast of Pinda, on the river's southern shore. The next morning, a vessel from the Dutch East India Company accosted the Italian crew, demanding to see a Holland-issued travel authorization to sail in these waters. The United Provinces had seized control of the Portuguese central-African *conquista* of Angola in 1641 and subsequently attempted to exercise command over the region and its coast.[2] Their foothold would be short-lived, and the Iberians would oust them in 1648.[3] But in 1645, for the nascent Catholic mission attempting to reach central-African shores, the encounter with Protestant authorities threatened disaster.

In the following days of tense negotiation, Captain Falconi reminded the Dutchmen, to no avail, that Pinda was not under their authority but that of the Catholic king of Kongo, who ruled independently over a large realm, situated to the north of what was then Dutch Angola. As the negotiations stalled, the seaman took action. He stealthily reached the shore, accompanied by two of the missionaries, to seek the help of the local ruler and vassal of the king of Kongo, Dom Daniel da Silva, who, they hoped, could save them from the heretics. As soon as they landed, one of the friars, Bonaventura d'Alessano, spotted a large cross, a bell suspended on a frame, and a church. Entering the church, he saw on its altar statues of the Immaculate Conception and Saint Anthony and an old painting of Saint Francis embracing a cross. Speechless, ecstatic, and grateful to divine providence, he could barely tear himself from contemplating the arresting sight of the African Catholic complex. He finally stepped out of the building, only to be embraced by a crowd that had gathered to welcome him to the Kongo, as elated to see him as he had

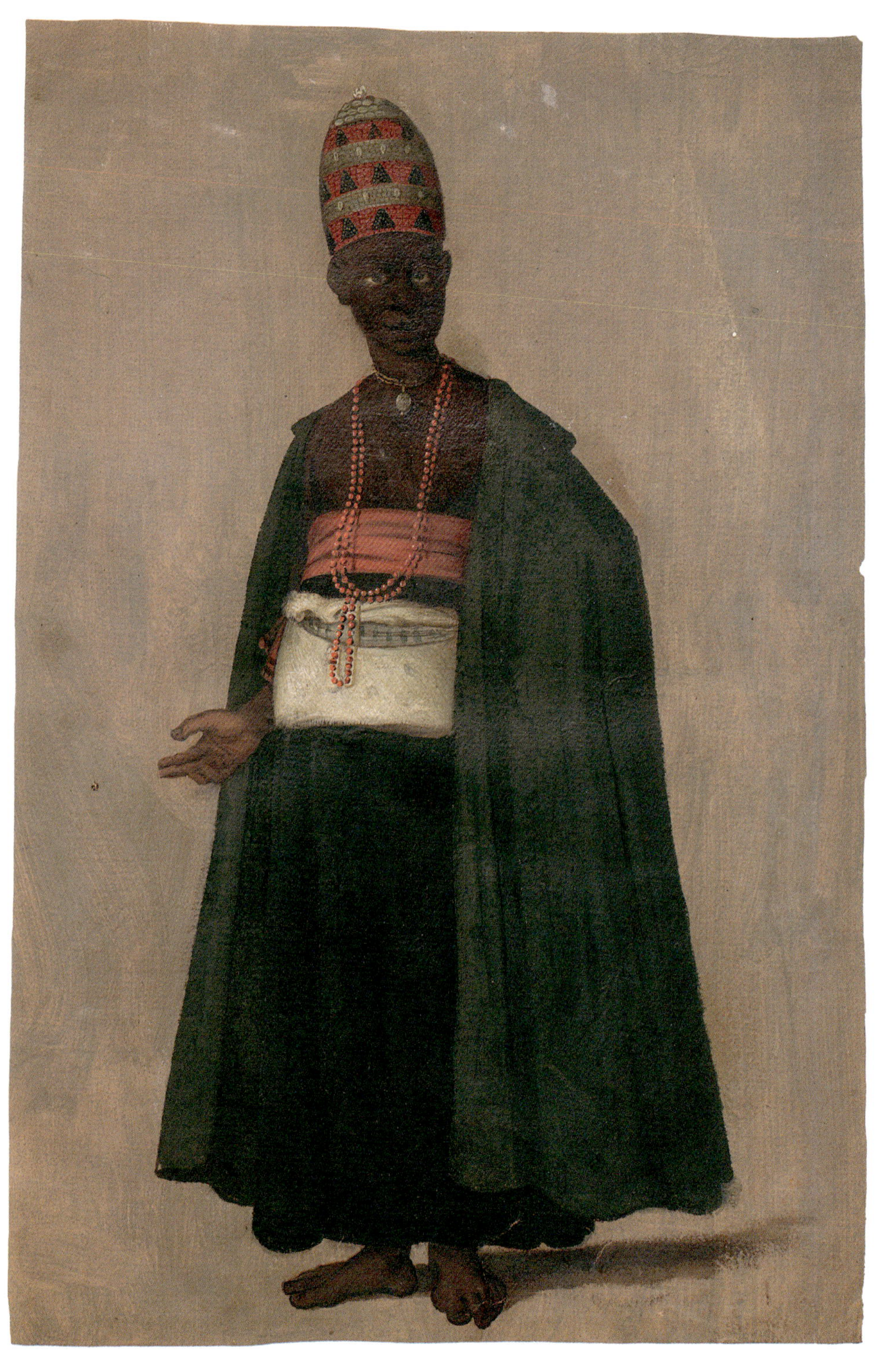

Figure 1

Albert Eckhout, *Portrait of a Kongo Ambassador to Recife, Brazil,* ca. 1637–44. Oil on paper, 30 × 50 cm. Jagiellonian Library, Krakow, Libri Picturati A 34, fol. 3. Photo courtesy of the Jagiellonian Library Photographic Services.

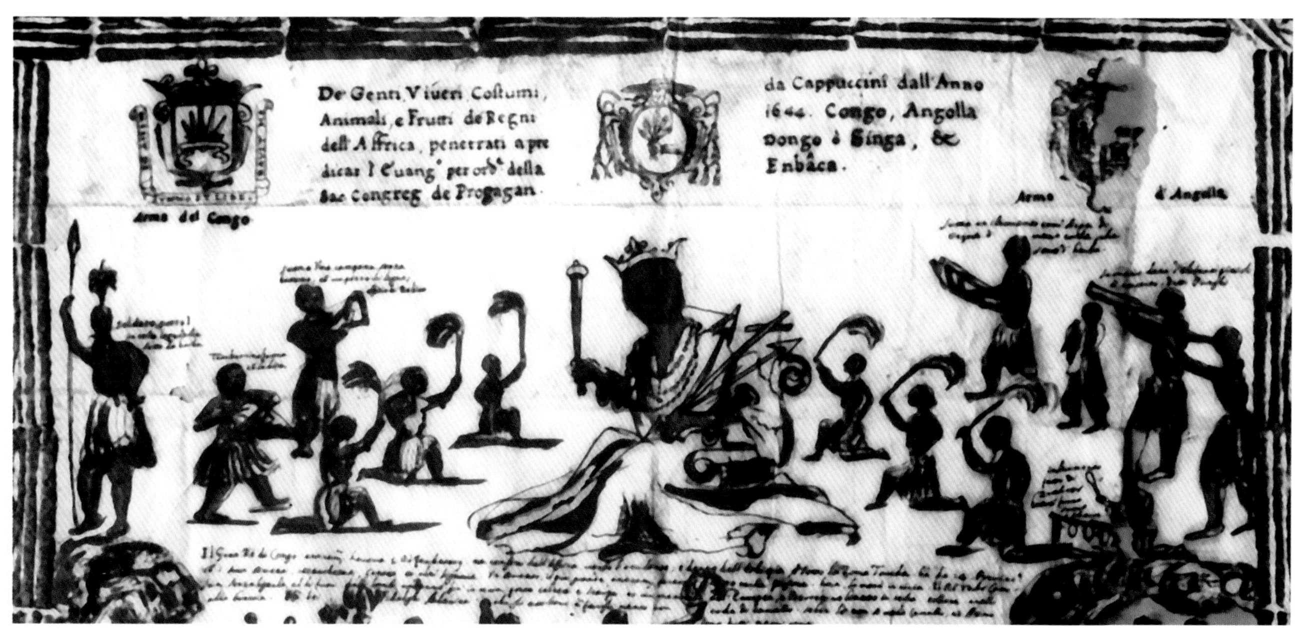

Figure 2

Unknown Capuchin artist, *King Garcia II of Kongo and His Attendants*, ca. 1652–63. Ink on paper, 73 × 40 cm (full panel). Detail from *Of the People, Victuals, Customs, Animals, and Fruits of the Kingdoms of Africa*, Franciscan Museum of the Capuchin Historical Institute, Rome, MF 1370. Photo courtesy of the Museo Francescano di Roma.

been to see the material manifestations of their attachment to Catholicism.

The locality he had reached, Pinda, served as the port for the town of Soyo, the namesake capital of a prosperous and powerful province of the Kongo Kingdom (map). It was so wealthy and mighty, in fact, that its leader, or *mani*, Dom Daniel da Silva, was at the time in open conflict with the Kongo Crown because of his increasing assertion of independence from the central authority of the king, who ruled over his large domains through the provincial governors he appointed from his inland capital city of Mbanza Kongo, also known by its Portuguese-language Christian name of São Salvador.

The *mani Soyo*, who defiantly called himself prince, soon granted an audience to Friar Bonaventura, his cloth brother, and the captain. He received them in his palace, dressed and surrounded with the sophisticated mix of imported and local items of clothing and insignia through which the aristocracy of the Kongo signified its political and religious standing as a central-African, Christian elite. He sat on a European-style chair set on a carpet, wore a European hat, and surrounded himself with attendants holding horsetail fly whisks and his ceremonial sword. Portraits of the ambassadors Dom Daniel had sent to Dutch Brazil a couple of years earlier and a drawing of the court of King Garcia II of Kongo, whom the prince without a doubt sought to emulate, bring to life the elegant spectacle his court and courtiers offered (figs. 1, 2).[4] The magnificent African Catholic ruler listened to the visitors' plea and magnanimously granted them his protection against the Dutch, saving them and the nascent Capuchin mission.[5]

Setting off for central-African shores, the friars from the inaugural group of Capuchin envoys to the region had expected to reach a distant and overwhelmingly foreign land whose souls awaited their providential arrival for their salvation. But landing in Pinda, they hardly found themselves in the position of daring apostles spearheading conversion of strange, heathen parts, following the paradigmatic—and often chimerical—narrative of Christian missions in the early modern era. Rather, the circumstances of their arrival soon reminded them that they had come to central Africa at the demand of the elite of the Kingdom of Kongo, whose independently professed Catholicism dated back more than a century and a half. They would conduct their apostolate among the inhabitants of the realm, but also among those of the neighboring Kingdoms of Matamba and Ndongo, of polities such as the Dembos, or Ndembu, and of the Portuguese (and, between 1641 and 1648, Dutch) *conquista* of Angola. These populations had for at least several decades all engaged with the commercial, religious, and diplomatic networks of the Atlantic world and with the material and immaterial novelties these networks brought to their shores. The apostolic twelve thus not only found themselves caught, at the mouth of the Congo River, in the ripples of the Thirty Years' War and in the crosscurrents of European competition for overseas control. They also stepped into a region whose worldly rulers—whether Catholics (like Dom Daniel da Silva), practitioners of local religions, or apostates (like the legendary warrior queen Njinga of Matamba, whom they would soon encounter)—selectively adopted and redeployed elements of European material, religious, and political culture and exerted independent powers on both locals and visitors from overseas.

The challenges this environment posed to the European friars' expectations and the ambivalent responses it would elicit from them already began to appear in their reports on these eventful first days in central Africa. While they clung to whatever aspect of their journey could form an exalted, heroic apostolic tale, they also quickly recalibrated their stories. On the one hand, they turned to the lexical and intellectual field of wonder as a way to make sense, both politically and theologically, of the events they experienced. Wonder, religiously linked to devout admiration for God's works and intellectually connected to the early modern European culture of curiosity, offered them a way to make sense of tribulations, interpret unexpected encounters, and process overwhelming sights. On the other hand, the early reports reveal the friars' rapid realization of the crucial role that cooperation with local people and their elite, even if often fraught, would play in the trajectory of their mission.

The Capuchin central-African visual corpus that is the subject of this book emerged at the intersection of these two trends. Its images were profoundly religious in form as well as content, bringing their providential, wondrous discoveries about local nature and culture as well as missionary praxis from central Africa to the eyes of the Church hierarchy and future missionaries back in Europe. They also pictured apostolic work in Kongo and Angola as embedded in the local fabric of power, their mission willed and supported by local authorities. Anxiety and exultation at the possibilities and risks of their endeavors ran through the corpus. Their images presented violence and peace, martyrdom and mass sacraments, predators and foodstuff, working in close concert as the warp and the weft of the mission's fabric.

Throughout the decades of their apostolate in central Africa, the friars sent to the region consistently reported similar experiences upon their arrival. Kongo and Angola challenged their preconceptions about Africa and Africans and spurred them to put pen and brush to paper to correct, with didactic images and texts, the presumptions of their hierarchy and the expectations of those who would follow in their wake. The result of their efforts was the creation of a highly idiosyncratic visual corpus. Although inspired and shaped by the intellectual and visual context of seventeenth- and eighteenth-century Europe in general and Italy in particular, the images the friars created in and about central Africa do not fit squarely into European templates of representation and interpretation of distant lands and people in the early modern period. The Capuchin vignettes about flora and fauna emulated the format of natural histories yet left ample room for other European and central-African forms of knowledge about the environment and nonhuman subjects. Their portrayal of central Africans called upon the imagery of best-selling travel literature but did not follow that genre's formulaic sensationalism or exoticism. They pictured catechization and the giving of sacraments among their African flock, but the ceremonies they described followed typically local rituals and customs rather than unfold as European-controlled and -staged events.

Unsurprisingly, the intended European readers of their works met their atypical compendia with skepticism and at times even censorship. But above all, they received them with indifference. This cold reception has kept the Capuchin central-African corpus out of public and scholarly eyes, in its own time as well as ours, in spite of its extraordinary significance. It is an unparalleled documentary source about the African continent in the early modern period. Its numerous images, derived from eyewitness experience, greatly enriches our knowledge of early modern Kongo and Angola and literally multiplies the known European-format visual record about the African continent before 1850. It also sheds light on the Capuchin missionary project, a significant facet of Christian missionary history, which has not received as much attention as the endeavors of the Jesuits or other branches of the Franciscan family.

Further, it brings to the fore a moment of sustained cross-cultural spiritual, intellectual, and material interaction between Africans and Europeans that unfolded within a sociopolitical context with few parallels in the early modern era.[6] The friars arrived and worked within populations that did not live under colonial rule but had engaged for many decades independently and in deep and transformative ways, albeit to different extents depending on the region, with Europe and the Atlantic world at large. Their activities took place in a social and political environment defined by fraught cooperation and a delicate balance of power between the friars and local populations on whom they depended in every aspect of their life, from food to security, to the ability to exercise their apostolate. The visual corpus they created in the wake of these interactions both echoed this situation and reflected on its implications. Neither projections of colonial ambitions similar to their colleagues' works about Latin America, nor tales of exalted inculturation other missionary orders retold about their Asian missions, nor exotic fantasies commonplace in travel literature, their images and writings followed a pattern of their own. Attention to the Capuchin corpus and the circumstances of its creation thus sheds light on largely overlooked dimensions to the cross-cultural transactions that shaped the early modern world.

Historical Background

The Capuchin mission to central Africa originated in a long-brewing conflict between the Kingdom of Kongo and Portugal that intensified in the late sixteenth and early seventeenth centuries. The African realm, which emerged as a centralized, powerful kingdom south of the Congo River in the thirteenth century, converted of its own accord to Catholicism around 1500, upon its encounter with Portugal. Explorers and clerics from the Iberian kingdom had reached Kongo shores in the 1480s in the course of their exploration of the Atlantic African coast in search of a maritime passage to India and of new allies for Christendom. At first cordial and mutually beneficial, the relationship between the two realms unraveled during the sixteenth century as a consequence of Portuguese participation in the transatlantic slave trade and ambitions to claim parts of central Africa as their territorial conquests. Taking advantage of a weakened Kongo recovering from the aftermaths of invasions from a bellicose group known in the historical documents as the Jaga, the Portuguese laid the foundation of their *conquista* of Angola in the city of Luanda, which they founded in 1575 at the southern edge of the African kingdom.[7] From that moment the relationship between the two realms deteriorated, with Portugal eventually attacking the Kongo's southern borders in 1622. In 1624 it recalled the bishop of Kongo, whom it controlled by rights of patronage, from São Salvador to Luanda.[8]

As a response to these multivalent assaults, the Kongo maneuvered to assert broader independence from Portugal in the conduct of its spiritual affairs. It welcomed Jesuits, who did not respond to the Portuguese Crown, starting in 1619.[9] The kings of Kongo also asked the papacy to dispatch clerics who did not hail from Portugal. The pope answered positively, designating Spanish friars of the Capuchin order for the task in 1618. However, the geopolitical situation resulting from the union of the Crowns of Portugal and Spain between 1580 and 1640 and the Thirty Years' War delayed the departure of the missionaries until 1645. From this moment Capuchins, first from Spain, then almost exclusively from Italy, maintained a thin but nearly constant presence in Kongo and neighboring polities until the departure of the last brother from Luanda in 1834.[10] In central Africa the friars acted as parish priests in regions already practicing Catholicism within the Kingdom of Kongo and Portuguese Angola and as missionaries in other areas.

The Capuchin apostolate in Kongo and Angola and the friars' relationship with their local interlocutors followed a pattern that was sharply different from that of other missionary endeavors of the early modern period. In particular, it did not fit the templates for overseas catechization that mendicants had honed since the sixteenth century in the colonial contexts of Iberian America. With the exception of a small population in Luanda, the central town of the Portuguese *conquista* of Angola, and a handful of other settlements, the Capuchins worked among peoples living in regions that remained independent from direct European control. Far from acting in concert with a colonial army and administration, they operated under the auspices of central-African rulers. They also often found themselves caught in the crossfire of European and local political and commercial interests. The situation created many occasions for clashes and conflict as the clerics endeavored to establish spiritual authority and assert their social standing as men of the Church in an environment they did not fully understand and among populations against which they held profound negative preconceptions.[11] Soon the friars learned that they could not proceed in their activities "without the consent of the people, and the secular arm of the Prince."[12]

Among the polities Capuchins visited in their central-African apostolate, the Kingdom of Kongo, whose rulers first invited them to the region, held a special place because of its declared attachment to the Catholic faith, heralded in its elite regalia and performed at all levels of its political, social, and religious organization.[13] The friars also worked in Ndongo and Matamba, the realms of the powerful Queen Njinga, whose eventful life and rule ended in a spectacular reconversion to Christianity in 1663 under the guidance of one of the friars.[14] The Capuchins were quick to claim and publicize the momentous event, which reflected positively on their missionary zeal and success, as well as on the overseas reach of the papacy, which sponsored their endeavors through the Propaganda Fide.[15] Their activities also unfolded in polities neighboring Kongo and Angola ruled by leaders with varying levels of involvement with the religious, material, and political networks of the Atlantic world, such as the Ndembu region and Kisama.[16] Forays further to the east and northeast of Kongo and Ndongo-Matamba also found them in what they deemed heathen lands, such as the realm of Makoko, around today's

Pool Malebo, whose people held only remote connections to long-distance Atlantic routes.[17] This complex and singular sociopolitical situation as missionaries under the purview of African overlords, Christian, heathen, or somewhere in between, weighed heavily on the Capuchin endeavors in central Africa and, as I argue in this book, on the mission's visual and textual production.

The Corpus Under Consideration

From their first arrival in central Africa, in 1645, to the slow disintegration of their so-called Missio antiqua between the late eighteenth century and 1834, Capuchin missionaries assiduously wrote and commented on their activities in Kongo and Angola, leaving behind a dauntingly large documentary corpus.[18] As sons and brothers, the friars wrote letters to their families. As members of a Capuchin province, they sent news of their apostolic work to their home convents. As envoys of the Propaganda Fide, they composed yearly relations for the mission's prefect, based in Luanda, who in turn summarized and transmitted them to Rome.[19] As men on an extraordinary voyage, they also kept diaries of their journeys and ventures and often shaped these memoirs into manuscripts they hoped to see published. Thousands of the pages they wrote have survived to this day in private and public archives around Europe, Africa, and beyond. The variety of their styles, purposes, and intended audiences and the geographic dispersion of the archives and collections in which they now reside make them a challenging corpus to study. They are also, because of the same characteristics, a rich source, offering a vivid and multidimensional portrait of central Africa in the seventeenth and eighteenth centuries.

In addition to writing thousands of pages, the friars created numerous images presenting the intricacies of the natural, social, and religious landscape that members of their order encountered in central Africa. They pictured scenes and individual elements they saw in the Christian Kingdom of Kongo, in the Kingdoms of Matamba and Ndongo, in Portuguese Angola, and in several other locations in the broader region. Their paintings and drawings, and the prints eventually produced after them, featured detailed everyday scenes, examples of flora or fauna isolated and labeled, and thorough views of missionary life, all captioned with words of advice and admonition. Most of the images belonged to a coherent set of primarily visual manuscripts that were, as I demonstrate in this book, intended as practical guides for the edification of future missionaries. The group consists of four distinct but related works: a large panel now in the Museo Francescano in Rome that I date to the 1650s (plate 1); a once-bound set of sixty-seven paintings likely created in the 1670s that I call the Parma Watercolors (plates 2–68); and two versions of the same practical guide composed around 1750, Friar Bernardino d'Asti's "Missione in prattica," held in Turin and the Vatican (plates 69–72, figs. 19, 44, 58, 60, 73, 77, 78, 92–96). This book reproduces much of this largely unpublished corpus, including the totality of the extant Parma Watercolors and of the plates in the Vatican "Missione in prattica." A large number of the Turin paintings appear in these pages; the full manuscript is available as an online gallery on the Turin Civic Library website.[20] I have created an image collection paired with an essay and translation of the Parma Watercolors texts on the

Material and Visual Culture of Religion website to complement this book's documentary and illustration program.[21]

Puzzlement and *Poesis*

For centuries these illustrated manuscripts, as well as related material also considered in this volume, lingered untouched in public and private repositories. Interest in central Africa's Catholic past that arose in the twentieth century, in the wake of renewed missionary and then scholarly inquiries on the region, only brought faint attention to a small number of them. Some have appeared since then as illustrations or cover designs for historical scholarship, without direct analysis.[22] Others have been published as curiosities.[23] Overall, the heterogeneous set has left modern scholars as perplexed and indifferent as its own contemporaries, and it has been the object of little scholarship.

Curiosity and perplexity also marked my own initial encounter with the images of the Turin "Missione in prattica" as a graduate student interested in the visual and material culture of Africa and the early modern Atlantic world. I first approached the vignettes with enthusiasm and eagerly planned to make them the focus of my doctoral dissertation. Excitement soon faded into frustration. The images of the "Missione in prattica" were rich, exceedingly rare documents in need of scholarly attention but proved opaque to my attempts at analysis informed by a training in African and colonial Latin American art history. I found that their European format left little to no room to investigate African voices. The relationship they illustrated between locals and foreigners did not depict consistent power asymmetries or situations of oppression and resistance that would lend themselves to an analysis of subaltern agency. Their few depictions of African material culture did not open the door either to a sustained study of central-African expressive culture. So I, too, put them to the side and turned my attention to other sources.

A few years later, in Italy, as I conducted research on the Christian arts of the Kongo, the friars with whom I worked in the archives led me to an unknown set of paintings that I would call the Parma Watercolors.[24] This encounter and the promise it held of new avenues to approach the Capuchin images renewed my interest. After studying the watercolors in person, I realized that I had come across the central opus of a distinctive body of work. A majority among the extant Capuchin vignettes from central Africa produced between 1650 and 1750 formed, I now understood, a coherent group of didactic images, with shared format, subject matter, and goals. Complementary paintings, drawings, and prints from the same circles fell into place as related but peripheral productions. I wrote about these findings and derived key insights from the analysis of the corpus in my dissertation and several later publications.[25]

Yet much about this group of closely related images continued to baffle. Borrowing and elaborating from one another over the course of nearly a century, the images' many entanglements eluded linear interpretations. Notions of prototype and copy, drafts and corrections, did little to illuminate the extant set of paintings and related prints. In fact, in spite of years of research, of ever accumulating evidence, and of studious reckoning with an ever-growing array of hints, I could not name the friars who painted the images and wrote the texts of the Parma Watercolors, and I could only

approximate the date when they may have been painted, then glossed. What is more, the images stubbornly continued to defy the templates of analysis and the modes of interpretation on which I had trained to rely as a student of early modern visual culture. They did not fit within the categories or respond to the analytical tools scholars usually brought to bear on early modern European approaches to and representations of non-European locales and peoples. Savagery, exoticism, hybridity, subaltern resistance, and colonial projections played little to no role in a visual corpus that persisted in eluding interpretation.

Years later still, instead of putting the documents to the side once more, I chose, in writing this book, no longer to see these unanswered questions, this categorical and interpretative resistance of the corpus, as obstacles to analysis or causes for puzzlement but to take them as points of departure. I realized that rising to the many challenges the corpus posed required me to move, as art historian Suzanne Blier once suggested, "beyond, through, behind, and under both customary and new theoretical frames."[26] Leaving behind the search for individual authors and turning my attention beyond narrow dates, I sought alternate ways to discern the corpus's sources and map the course of its coming into being. Eventually, it was the Capuchin vignettes themselves that set my path. I took my cue from the permeability they demonstrated between pictured and real worlds at the time of their reception as Franciscan images. Following the order's precepts of emulation of saintly examples in imitation of Christ, the Capuchin visual works invited their intended viewers to immerse themselves in the world within the images through iconographic, compositional, and narrative elements. Breaking through and looking under the familiar frames that led to frustration and puzzlement, I found new direction in exploring the parallel permeability between real and pictured worlds at the time of the vignettes' inception. *Poesis*, I realized, the process through which the set of images took its form, could be interpreted as holding authorial agency.[27] The European painters and etchers responsible for the lines and washes of the images put their art at the service of a narrative voice that preceded the image's visual texts and determined their form.[28] The great landscape print that serves as a guide through most of the book (fig. 41), and the many other vignettes picturing dialogue between friars and central Africans, functioned as self-aware images, pointing back to their *poesis*. The encounters and dialogues between friars and central Africans they represented appeared within their frames as both subjects of their narratives and the actual sources of the discourses they documented and participated in shaping.

This take on the images considers authorship expansively, as characterized by the sources and course of the corpus's creation and thus by the explicit and implicit, featured and disavowed, entanglements of the immediate and deep-rooted social, intellectual, and visual interactions that led to its construction. Though images of European format and made by European hands, the Capuchin central-African vignettes, I argue in this book, were products of the encounters between the friars and central Africans and as such were cross-cultural creations that were not images *of* but images *from* central Africa and created by central Africans in dialogue with the European friars.

The disconnect between the Capuchin central-African images' European form and their cross-cultural dimension begs for deeper investigation of the barely visible or outright invisible heterogeneity of other early modern European images of non-European topics. That visual productions such as the ones under consideration in these pages did not appear to their original European viewers or to later European scholars as mixed points to two moments when the role of Others—in this case, Africans—in their construction was overlooked. The first belongs to the early modern period, when the construction and reception of the documents consciously or unconsciously ignored or silenced their non-European sources.[29] The second lies in our contemporary moment of interpretation, when modes of reading of the images remain blind to their cross-cultural dimension if not visible at the level of form or traceable to the identity of their makers.[30] In response, I adopt in this book a methodology that recognizes the Capuchin images, though drawn by European hands and European in style, as creations molded in a cross-cultural inception, or *poesis*. This methodology identifies and analyzes the first moment of disavowal and corrects the shortsightedness of later interpretative apparatuses.

The Pages Ahead

This book's argument weaves three interrelated threads. Frist, it presents for the first time to scholarly and public attention a set of images about Kongo and Angola in the early modern period and locates them in relation to the extant documentary record about central Africa between the sixteenth and the seventeenth centuries. It defines the corpus of Capuchin didactic images from central Africa as a singular project rooted in the veteran friars' experiences in the mission field and puts it in conversation with a wide array of contemporaneous natural-historical publications, missionary reports, and volumes of travel literature. Second, it analyzes the stories these images tell about the fraught but generative encounters and negotiations that took place between central Africans and the Italian Capuchins they hosted in their lands. It describes the emergence and analyzes the character of a novel discourse about nature, culture, and faith. A discourse that grew at the nexus of cultures in the meeting between Capuchin Reformation-era ideologies and central-African Christian and non-Christian religious thought; Italian Franciscan baroque artistic sensitivities and the predominantly conceptual, often abstract visual modes of expressions of image- and object-makers in Kongo and Angola; the European classical-infused culture of curiosity and central-African ecological, technological, and philosophical systems of knowledge and experimentation of deep local roots and broad horizons. Finally, the book makes an intervention at the level of methods in the study of early modern, apparently European images of non-European topics. Challenging approaches that consider these documents as testaments of exclusively European views and knowledge, it charts instead a method to analyze them as cross-cultural constructions.

Weaving together these three threads, this book sheds new light on the early modern Catholic missionary project, the nature of cross-cultural encounters in the seventeenth and eighteenth centuries, and the entangled histories of central Africa, Europe, and the world. More broadly, it rehearses a nuanced approach to the encounters between people, objects, and ideas that shaped the early modern world and continue to cast their long shadow into the twenty-first century.

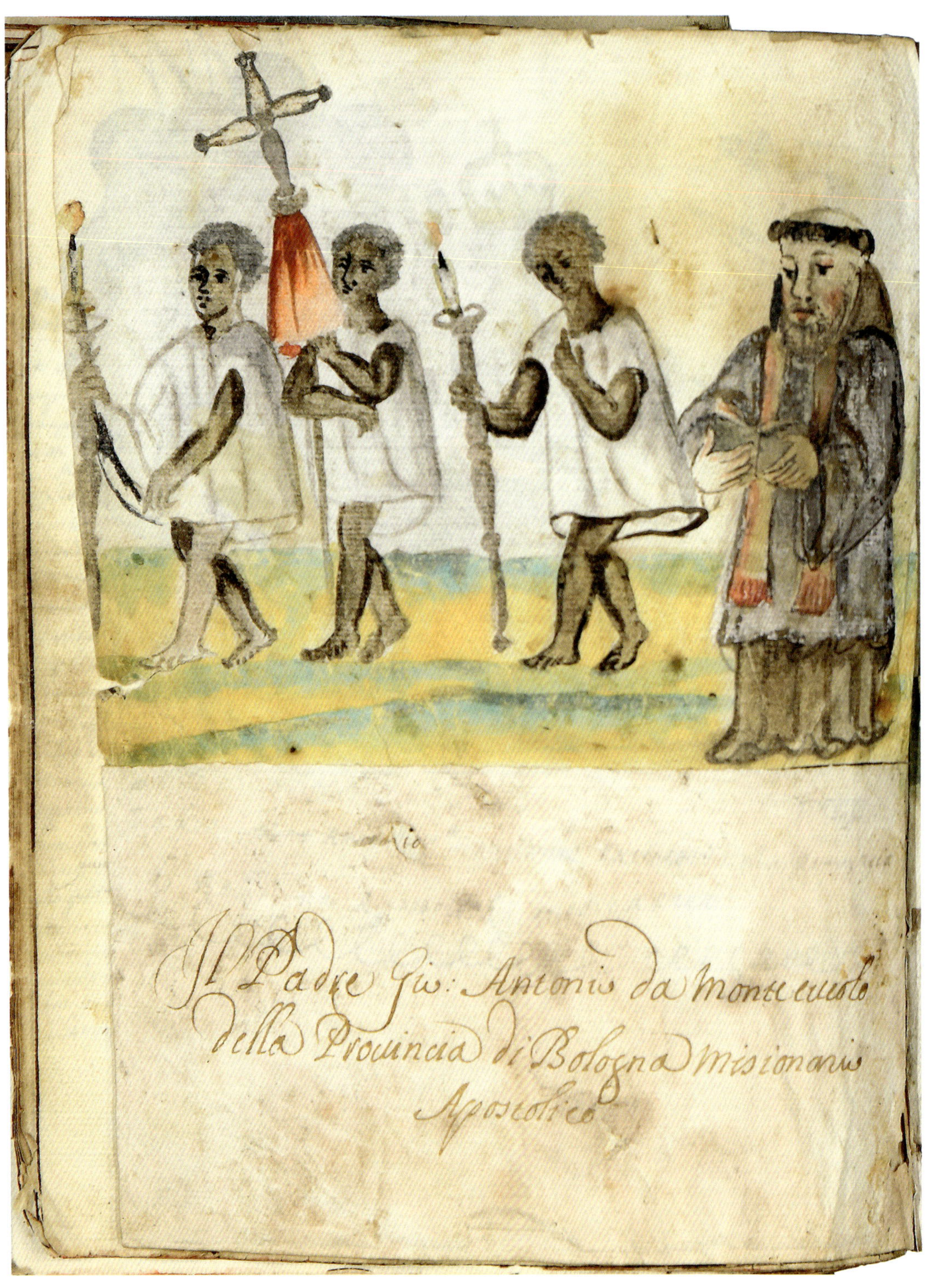

Figure 3

Giovanni Antonio Cavazzi, *Il Padre Gio. Antonio da Montecuc[c]olo della Provincia di Bologna Mis[s]ionario Apostolico*, ca. 1665–68. Watercolor and ink on paper, 17 × 21 cm (full manuscript page). From Giovanni Antonio Cavazzi, "Missione Evangelica al Regno del Congo" (the Araldi manuscript), vol. A, book ii, between pp. 201 and 211. Gallerie Estensi, Biblioteca Estense Universitaria, Modena. Reproduced by permission of the Italian Ministry for Cultural Heritage and Activities and for Tourism.

A modest friar considered of poor talent and little promise by his superiors, seventeenth-century Capuchin Giovanni Antonio Cavazzi da Montecuccolo left a monumental opus that remains to this day the essential source for the study of Kongo and Angola in the early modern period. Active for decades in west central Africa, he authored several massive manuscripts chronicling his experience as a missionary and recording the histories of several of the region's polities. He pictured himself doe-eyed, long faced, squat, and bearded in the Capuchin style on two occasions in his opus. One self-portrait shows him among a motley crew of shipwreck survivors huddled in an overpopulated canoe (fig. 4).[1] In the other, he has painted himself in liturgical garb, following three attendants dressed in white in a sequence of vignettes concerned with the funeral rites of the legendary warrior Queen Njinga of the Mbundu people of Angola, an apostate who had eventually passed away a good Christian thanks to his apostolic zeal (fig. 3). Cavazzi chose the event as the setting for a self-portrait he proudly labeled with his full name and credentials in large looping cursive: "The Father Giovanni Antonio da Montecuc[c]olo from the Province of Bologna, Apostolic Missionary." He likely considered this moment the apex of his career and, in spite of the modesty the rules of his religious order dictated, was eager to present the accomplishment to the readers of a manuscript he tirelessly worked and reworked in view of publication.

His wishes to see his pages in print would only partially come true. In 1687, nearly a decade after his death in 1678, a volume derived from his writings, the *Istorica descrizione de' tre' regni Congo, Matamba et Angola sitvati nell' Etiopia inferiore occidentale e delle missioni apostoliche esercitateui da religiosi*

CHAPTER I

"Nonsense"

Capuchin Images of Kongo and Angola Against Italian Preconceptions

Capuccini appeared in Bologna. The book, however, was a heavily edited version of the long work he had first submitted for publication more than fifteen years earlier. In between stood years of arguments between the veteran of central Africa and Italy-based editors, Church leaders, and censors. At the core of the dispute was a chasm between the two sides about the goals and format of the book and, beyond it, about the proper nature, role, and presentation of knowledge about Kongo and Angola for a European audience.

At a superficial level, the disagreement concerned the length of the work and Cavazzi's inclination toward verbose minutiae as well as his great penchant for miracles. The Holy Office under Pope Urban VIII had specifically forbidden in decrees of 1625 then 1634 the publication of writings or images presenting the lives or actions of individuals as holy or miraculous.[2] Friar Antonio Zucchelli da Gradisca, who wrote about central Africa a few decades after Cavazzi, specifically addressed the issue in the preface of his book, solemnly declaring that it was not his intent to suggest "holiness of life, praise, miracles, or similar things."[3] But the rift between Cavazzi and his hierarchy, I argue in this chapter, was deeper. Not only did the Italian editors and Church leaders show little interest in the ethnographic reports on central Africa or the exalted tales of wondrous missionary undertakings contained in the book. They also did not welcome the challenge that the manuscript offered to their misunderstandings and preconceptions about Africa, calling its contents "nonsense," opposed to "the universal taste of people."[4]

Cavazzi, like the other Capuchin authors who had traveled to Kongo and Angola, used his manuscript as a space within which to reckon in word and image with the confounding religious and social fabric of central Africa. The friars found that the inhabitants and kingdoms of the region escaped established European templates for the apprehension and description of non-European peoples and locales not only because of exotic, strange traits but also because of very familiar ones. Their mores were, in the words of one of Cavazzi's like-minded brothers, "totally opposite to our customs."[5] Yet the same friars also admitted, with much disconcertion, that central Africans' ways also reflected their decades- or centuries-long engagement with the visual, material, and religious cultures of Europe. This paradoxical impression of central Africa and central Africans is the core conundrum and formative tension at the heart of the Capuchin central-African corpus.

The Making of the *Istorica descrizione*

Cavazzi was an early member of the Capuchin central-African mission and a prolific author. Much of his palimpsestic writings and paintings have survived, spread across private and public archives in Italy and Portugal, awaiting critical edition. In addition to the *Istorica descrizione,* his works include several unpublished opera. A manuscript titled "Vite de' Frati Minori Capuccini dell'Ordine del Serafico Padre San Francesco morti nelle Missioni d'Etiopia dall'anno 1654 sino all'anno 1677" is in the public library of Évora in Portugal.[6] Another, massive, three-volume codex, the "Missione Evangelica al Regno del Congo," also known as the Araldi manuscript, is in the Biblioteca Estense di Modena.[7] Some of its contents formed an early draft of what would eventually become the *Istorica descrizione*. It is also well documented that Cavazzi lost some of his writings during his travels. In addition, he authored at least one other, now-lost or not-yet-located, seven-hundred-page draft for the 1687 book, a draft that he finished in 1671 and titled "Descrizione de' tre' grandi Regni situati nell'Etiopia inferiore, parte dell'Affrica meridionale [. . .] data in luce da P. F. Gio: Antonio da Montecuccolo."[8] A copy of the table of contents of this missing work indicates that it was an intermediary version between the Araldi manuscript and the *Istorica descrizione*.[9]

Around 1669, having heard, perhaps, of his efforts to write an account of the missions while in Luanda, the Propaganda Fide, the papal institution that oversaw the Capuchin apostolate in central Africa, commissioned Cavazzi to compose a history of his order's endeavors in central Africa. The friar, who recently had returned to Italy after fourteen years in Kongo and Angola, eagerly set to work on the commission. After two years of intense effort, in 1671 he presented the "Descrizione de' tre' grandi Regni" to the Congregation for the Propagation of the Faith, who decided later in the same year not to publish it, perhaps because of the prohibitive production cost of a volume nearly seven hundred pages long, but more likely because the contents and tone of the work had begun to raise eyebrows among the Church's establishment, as it would continue to do for another decade. Cavazzi's countryman, collaborator, and ardent supporter Bonaventura da Montecuccolo, in swift and resourceful response to the negative news, secured private funding in Bologna for the printing and in 1673 sought the Propaganda's authorization to proceed with the publication. A long negotiation ensued between Friar Bonaventura, the Propaganda, and the papal legate in Bologna, Cardinal Buonaccorsi, under whose purview the printing would take place. Finally, in 1678 the ecclesiastical hierarchy authorized the publication, with the specification that the text had to be shortened and rid of its numerous mentions of miracles. The task of editing the manuscript fell, by order of Capuchin minister general Esteban de Cesena, to Fortunato Alamandini da Bologna, a prominent member of the order who, notably, did not have direct experience of the African missions. Several rounds of revisions and approvals delayed the production until 1684, and

after three years in press, the volume, retitled *Istorica descrizione*, finally appeared in 1687.[10]

The decades-long dispute over Cavazzi's book project unfolded at many levels, with points of contention ranging from the purpose of the book to specifics of its contents. In commissioning the work, the Propaganda envisioned a publication that would provide a celebratory history of the missions they sponsored. It deemed Cavazzi's draft generally too long and, like Cardinal Buonaccorsi, specifically objected to its inclusion of what were in their view superfluous details about African rites and customs. They also frowned upon the attention it gave to wonder and miracles.

In contrast, Cavazzi and Bonaventura da Montecuccolo placed high value on both minutiae and miracles as essential to the volume's didactic role in instructing missionaries destined to central Africa. Although not an outright practical guide like other Capuchin handbooks about the region, the volume was similar in its conception, intended use, and insistence on the particularities of the central-African mission. In a letter defending the manuscript against the attempts of the Propaganda to further edit and shorten it, Friar Bonaventura pleads that "details," or "minutiae," on local mores that the ecclesiastical hierarchy judged trivial are in fact essential to the book. These details, he explains, "are included so that we understand their customs, however different they may be from ours of Italy; and if [the editors] took them out, it would falsify the title of the book,[11] and it should not say either that it describes their rites and customs as it does, and the missionaries that would be newly designated for [the mission] would not in reading this book be able to know anything about them either, and this is one of the principal reasons why [this book] is written."[12] This insistence on the role of the publication as a didactic text and the implicit description of its purpose as a salutary corrective to future missionaries' preconceptions about Kongo and Angola were two key aspects that connected the original manuscript to the Capuchin corpus of practical guides. In fact, as discussed further below, the prints Cavazzi commissioned for the book were closely related in format and style to the visual programs of these guides. Friar Bonaventura also defends with equal passion the miracles reported in the volume as the proof of God's approval of and direct involvement in the central-African mission. Editing out these signs of divine intervention would, he passionately writes, take away the "soul [*l'anima*]" of the book, belittling the divinely sanctioned work of the missionaries.

For Bonaventura, the aims and modi operandi of Cavazzi's project were clear. The volume's purpose was to convey knowledge of and from central Africa to European readers, particularly future missionaries. Detailed descriptions in words as well as images were the instruments through which to achieve this goal. Alamandini doubly disagreed. He did not think that the purpose of the book should be didactic or that a book offered the proper medium for missionary training. He concurred, however, that new missionaries destined to the Kongo needed more preparation. "Missionaries," he lamented, "leave Italy and make their way to the Congo without any knowledge of the missions, of the way to catechize, of the doubts that can occur daily in their ministry." The solution, in his view, did not lie in the circulation of printed or manuscript practical guides but rather in the opening of a seminary in Rome to train friars for the missions following the Carmelite and, above all, Jesuit models.[13]

Caught in the middle of the debate was the visual program Cavazzi had planned for his book, a program that would only in part come to the printing press, remaining a vestige of the friar's first intent. Alamandini's preface to the *Istorica descrizione* explains that Cavazzi had commissioned numerous copper plates in the early 1670s in spite of the delays he experienced in securing authorization to print his volume.[14] In 1673, shortly after Bonaventura da Montecuccolo secured financing in Bologna, Cavazzi, when he was about to leave for his second trip to central Africa, chose Capuchin artist Paolo da Lorena to produce the prints. Friar Paolo reported in a letter dated January 31, 1674, that he had completed eight of the engravings and planned to have finished the rest by Easter of the same year, although he did not indicate how many remained to be fashioned.[15] By then Cavazzi had already left for his second trip to Angola, and Friar Bonaventura remained in charge of the dealings with the artist. There is little doubt that he undertook this task with the same respect and dedication for the author's original vision that he demonstrated in defense of the text. And images, indeed, were key to Cavazzi's plans.

The Araldi Manuscript

That Cavazzi's project for the *Istorica descrizione* included a visual dimension is no surprise. The prolific author also created numerous paintings, leaving behind a complex, palimpsestic, and often puzzling oeuvre. All of the images known today to be in his hand are in the three-volume Araldi manuscript, except for the drawing of a shipwreck he appended to a letter sent to the Propaganda Fide in 1674 (fig. 4).[16] The missive reported the incident the friar experienced in November 1673 as he was on his way

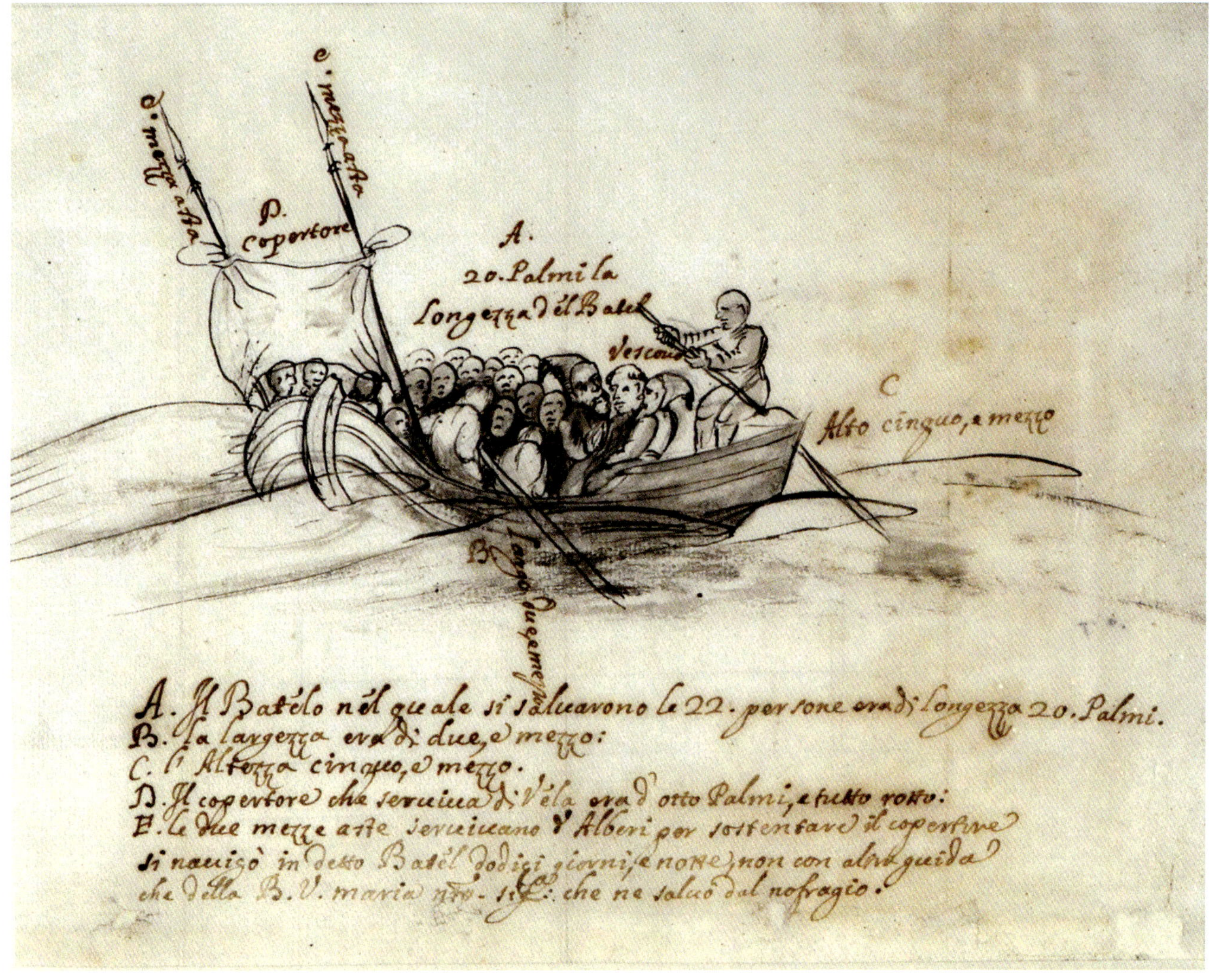

Giovanni Antonio Cavazzi, drawing of a shipwreck off the coast of central Africa included in a letter to the Propaganda Fide, 1674. Ink on paper, 20 × 25 cm. Archivio Storico de Propaganda Fide, Vatican City, SOCG (Scritture originali riferite nelle congregazioni generali) 457, fol. 375. Copyright © Archivio Storico di Propaganda Fide.

to Angola for his second mission. The ink drawing depicts the small boat on which he escaped the sinking ship with twenty-one other passengers, drifting at sea for twenty days before reaching the shores of Benguela, a Portuguese port south of Luanda. In a simple style, the friar has represented the crowded vessel, detailing the makeshift construction of the masts and sail with a mix of lines and washes. Among the passengers, Cavazzi is recognizable as the hooded friar in the center of the boat, with features similar to those of the other, earlier self-portrait in the Araldi manuscript (fig. 3). Using another type of ink, he later added lettered glosses in his easily recognized handwriting to explicate further the details of his picture. The explanatory text, the self-portrait, and the recourse to an image to make sense of and communicate extraordinary circumstances all echo corresponding features in

Cavazzi's Araldi manuscript as well as the *Istorica descrizione*. Some scholars have questioned whether Cavazzi created the paintings in the Araldi; however, these parallels, as well as the close association between text and images on the pages, the multiple versions of vignettes, and the rearrangement of the images within the codex, demonstrate that the friar was indeed the painter of the watercolors.

In 1987 Italian scholar Ezio Bassani published most of the images in the Araldi manuscript with a short critical text.[17] While an in-depth study of this important set of images is beyond the scope of this chapter, I can, from a direct study of the volumes, make some observations that shed light on the images in general and on their links with the *Istorica descrizione*'s prints in particular. The manuscript consists of three codices Giuseppe Pistoni, who rediscovered them in 1969, labeled volumes A, B, and C.[18] They include thirty-four images: thirty-two watercolors and two black-and-white ink drawings (see table 1). All but one image are in volume A, which measures 22.5 × 17.5 centimeters. Eighteen of these images appear in the volume's front matter—including a monochrome ink drawing—one is in book 1, twelve in book 2, and two in book 3. Few authors have noted the presence of the second black-and-white ink drawing, a decorated frontispiece that opens volume C (fig. 83).[19]

Previous studies have correctly, if vaguely, noted that some of the images gathered in volume A came from one or more earlier drafts, as indicated by page titles and text fragments surrounding some of the pictures in the front matter.[20] No one, however, to my knowledge, has remarked on the presence of hidden images. In fact, I observed in my study of the codex not only that several of the images were cut from previous pages and pasted into the new

volume but also that some of these glued pieces were painted on both sides recto-verso, the new arrangement obscuring one of the two sides. Backlighting the pages, I could partially decipher the hidden compositions, as outlined in table 1.

This close study of the manuscript also revealed two distinct groups of images based on the paper used. The laid lines of the paper in the main part of volume A, including, logically, all the pages in the front matter on which images were directly painted, are horizontal. The same laid wire marks left in the sheets from the paper-manufacture process are vertical in the cut-and-pasted vignettes. Images 2, 11, and 15 are three exceptions, being cut and pasted yet with horizontal lines; they also have no images on their versos. The glued-on paintings in the front matter with vertical laid lines, some of which also bear hidden images on their backs, thus likely originate from an earlier work. Their compositions preceded and inspired the more polished vignettes in the body of volume A. Cavazzi thus created, recomposed, and reordered images over time. The current state of the manuscript is that of an unfinished draft. He executed visible versions of all but one of the hidden scenes but did not finish placing his vignettes in the body of the text; they remain today gathered in the front matter.

Visual analysis nonetheless points to Cavazzi's conception of the Araldi visual program in three thematically defined groups. The first comprises full-page images in which a handful of figures appear in stark yellow-and-light-green landscapes, with short glosses within the painting itself commenting on the elements represented (1, 3, 6, 7, 10, 18, 19, 32, 33). Images 2, 11, and 15 are a second group, presenting ritual practitioners in similar yellow-and-green settings but in vignettes of a

Volume	Book	Chapter	Page	Title or description	Image cut and pasted or directly on page?	Image on the back and subject matter	Orientation of laid lines in the paper of the image	Type of background	Comparanda
A	front matter	n/a	iii	"Sacrificio de Giaghi" (Sacrifice among the Jagas)	on page itself	no, verso blank	≡	yellow-and-light-green landscape	*Istorica descrizione*, plate 33, p. 211
A	front matter	n/a	v	"Sexto Giuramento" (Sixth oath)	cut and pasted	no	≡	yellow-and-light-green landscape, smaller scale	
A	front matter	n/a	ix	"Il medemo Sacrificio. Mangia la Carne cruda. Succhia il Sangue." (The same sacrifice. [He] eats the flesh raw. [He] sucks the blood.)	on page itself	no, verso blank	≡	yellow-and-light-green landscape	
A	front matter	n/a	xii	hidden under no. 4: image depicting a scene with round building, carpet, drum, and box; see no. 10					
A	front matter	n/a	xii	"Battesimo della Regina Ginga" (Baptism of Queen Njinga)	cut and pasted	yes, hidden: drummer, tomb, and reliquary box; see no. 10	||||	grassy land and brilliant blue sky	*Istorica descrizione*, plate 43, p. 606
A	front matter	n/a	xiii	untitled: governor of Angola and his wife (the godmother of Queen Njinga)	cut and pasted	yes, hidden: child in a mortar; see no. 24	||||	grassy land and brilliant blue sky	*Istorica descrizione*, plate 43, p. 606
				hidden under no. 5: image depicting two women grinding child in mortar and another woman approaching with decorated box; see no. 24					
A	front matter	n/a	xix	untitled: Njinga orders breasts cut and beard torn	cut and pasted	no	||||	yellow-and-light-green landscape	Breast-cutting scene with three women has a parallel in Theodor de Bry's "De foeminis

Table 1 (*continued*)

Volume	Book	Chapter	Page	Title or description	Image cut and pasted or directly on page?	Image on the back and subject matter	Orientation of laid lines in the paper of the image	Type of background	Comparanda
									Monomotapani: from Lopes and Pigafetta's Latin *Regnum Congo* (1598), 14
7	A	front matter	n/a	xxi	"Primo Re di Dongo" (First king of Ndongo)	cut and pasted	no	||||	yellow-and-light-green landscape	*Istorica descrizion* plate 26, pp. 170 and 290
		front matter	n/a	xxiii	room for half-page image					
8	A	front matter	n/a	xxxii	"Lungua Strumento militare delli Giaghi" (Lungua military instrument of the Jagas)	cut and pasted	four lines of Portuguese text in blue ink, cut on top and right sides	||||		
9	A	front matter	n/a	xxxiii	untitled: Queen Njinga leading troops and a military band with bow and arrow in hand	cut and pasted	yes, hidden: perhaps prisoners	||||	grassy land and brilliant blue sky	
X3					hidden behind no. 9: image depicting a group of four people, perhaps prisoners					
10	A	front matter	n/a	xlii	untitled: Queen Njinga in front of the royal tomb and reliquary, smoking a pipe, with musicians	cut and pasted	no	||||	yellow-and-light-green landscape	*Istorica descrizion* plate 44, p. 613
11	A	front matter	n/a	xliv	three ritual practitioners working on the weather	cut and pasted	no	≡	yellow-and-light-green landscape, smaller scale	*Istorica descrizion* plate 34, p. 214
12	A	front matter	n/a	xlviii	"Della Nascita della Regina Ginga" (About the birth of Queen Njinga)	cut and pasted	yes, hidden: seated queen and probably scene of breast cutting; see nos. 6 and 26	||||	grassy land and brilliant blue sky	

Volume	Book	Chapter	Page	Title or description	Image cut and pasted or directly on page?	Image on the back and subject matter	Orientation of laid lines in the paper of the image	Type of background	Comparanda
				hidden behind no. 12: image depicting Njinga sitting and ordering breasts cut and/or beard torn; see nos. 6 and 26.					
A	front matter	n/a	il [*sic*]	"Manda Sacrificare al demonio et a suoi morti due persone" ([She] orders that two people be sacrificed to the devil and her ancestors)	on page itself (recto of 14)	yes, not hidden, no. 14	☰	grassy land and brilliant blue sky	*Istorica descrizione* background of plate 3, facing p. 32; Claude d'Abbeville *Histoire du Maragnan*, frontispiece
A	front matter	n/a	l	"Barbaro Comando della Regina executado" (Barbarous order of the queen, executed)	on page itself (verso of 13)	yes. not hidden, no. 13	☰	grassy land and brilliant blue sky	
A	front matter	n/a	lii	"Ganga ya Quibanda Sacerdote de Sacrifitii" (Ganga ya Quibanda, priest of the sacrifices)	cut and pasted	no	☰	yellow-and-light-green landscape, smaller scale	*Istorica descrizione*, plate 18, p. 102; plate 31, p. 199
A	front matter	n/a	lviii	Jagas put crucifix on the ground	cut and pasted	yes, hidden: "Manda Sacrificare al Demonio" and one figure from "Il medemo Sacrificio"; see nos. 3 and 13	‖‖	grassy land and brilliant blue sky	
				hidden behind no. 16: images depicting another version of "Manda Sacrificare al Demonio" with figure standing on a bow from "Il medemo Sacrificio"; see nos. 3 and 13					

Table 1 (*continued*)

Volume	Book	Chapter	Page	Title or description	Image cut and pasted or directly on page?	Image on the back and subject matter	Orientation of laid lines in the paper of the image	Type of background	Comparanda
17	A	front matter	n/a	lix	old man looking at textiles	cut and pasted	yes, hidden: "Singhilla": figures with arms raised; see no. 22	‖‖	grassy land and brilliant blue sky	
X6					hidden behind no. 17: image depicting an old man looking at textiles with figures with arms raised as in "Singhilla"; see no. 22					
18	A	front matter	n/a	lxiii	"Serra Liona" (Sierra Leone)	on page itself	no, verso blank	≡	yellow-and-light-green landscape	*Istorica descrizion*∙ plate 29, p. 183
19	A	1	xi	btw pages 98 and 99	"Suonatori" (Musicians)	on page itself	no, verso blank (page inserted in current binding)	≡	yellow-and-light-green landscape	
20	A	2	front	before page 1	"Primo Re di Dongho" (First king of Dongo)	on page itself	no, verso blank (page inserted in current binding)	≡	grassy land and brilliant blue sky	*Istorica descrizion*∙ plate 26, pp. 170 and 290
21	A	2	iii	btw pages 32 and 33	"guarda e osserva de Dormienti le actioni, la Regina" (The Queen watches and observes the actions of the sleepers)	on page itself (21 to 24 on a single folded sheet of paper)	yes, no. 22	≡	grassy land and brilliant blue sky	
22	A	2	iii	btw pages 32 and 33	"Singhilla"	on page itself (21 to 24 on a single folded sheet of paper)	yes, no. 21	≡	grassy land and brilliant blue sky	
23	A	2	iii	btw pages 32 and 33	servitors of the idol	on page itself (21 to 24 on a single folded sheet of paper)	yes, no. 24	≡	grassy land and brilliant blue sky	
24	A	2	iii	btw pages 32 and 33	"Comanda che si pista un Figlio e ne fa olio" ([She] orders that they crush a child and turn it into oil)	on page itself (image altered and repaired) (21 to 24 on a	yes, no. 23	≡	grassy land and brilliant blue sky	*Istorica descrizion*∙ plate 30, p. 188

Volume	Book	Chapter	Page	Title or description	Image cut and pasted or directly on page?	Image on the back and subject matter	Orientation of laid lines in the paper of the image	Type of background	Comparanda
					single folded sheet of paper)				
A	2	iii	btw pages 32 and 33	"Fatta Giaga d'Arco e Frezza arma la mano accompagnata dalli suoi soldati" ([Queen Njinga,] with bow and arrow in hand, accompanied by her soldiers, turned Jaga)	on page itself (single page bound with the folded page of 21 to 24)	yes, no. 26	≡	grassy land and brilliant blue sky	
A	2	iii	btw pages 32 and 33	"Manda tagliare le mamelle ad una sua damigella" ([She] orders the breasts of one of her young women cut)	on page itself (single page bound with the folded page of 21 to 24)	yes, no. 25	≡	grassy land and brilliant blue sky	
A	2	xvi	btw pages 210 and 211	Njinga as a Jaga walking in front of a group	on paper itself (26 and 27 are recto/verso)	yes, no. 28	≡	grassy land and brilliant blue sky	
A	2	xvi	btw pages 210 and 211	"Il Padre Gio: Antonio da Montecuc[c]olo della Provincia di Bologna mis[s]ionario Apostolico" (Father Giovanni Antonio da Montecuccolo of the Bologna province, Apostolic missionary)	on paper itself NB: a small patch of paper with writing indicates that another page was once glued on top of this page (26 and 27 are recto/verso)	yes, no. 27	≡	grassy land and brilliant blue sky	
XX	2	xvi	btw pages 210 and 211	four pages missing = 8 images	on paper itself (one bound in the middle)				
A	2	xvi	btw pages 210 and 211	Procession of altar servers	on paper itself (now facing 28)	yes, no. 30	≡	grassy land and brilliant blue sky	
A	2	xvi	btw pages 210	"Regina Ginga Donna Anna come la levarono alla sepultura"	on paper itself	yes, no. 29	≡	grassy land and brilliant blue sky	*Istorica descrizione*, plate 47, p. 718

Table 1 (*continued*)

	Volume	Book	Chapter	Page	Title or description	Image cut and pasted or directly on page?	Image on the back and subject matter	Orientation of laid lines in the paper of the image	Type of background	Comparanda
				and 211	(Queen Njinga Donna Anna, as they took her to the tomb)					
31	A	2	xvi	btw pages 210 and 211	"La Regina Donna Barbara chiamata Cambo sua morta [*sic*] e sepultura" (Queen Donna Barbara, called Cambo, her death and sepulture)	on paper itself	no, verso blank	≡	grassy land and brilliant blue sky	
32	A	btw 2 and 3	n/a	unpaginated	"Num custos fratris mei sum ego?" (Am I my brother's keeper? [Genesis 4:9])	on paper itself	no, verso blank	≡	yellow-and-light-green landscape	
33	A	3	iv	btw pages 36 and 37	"Sacerdote che parla al leone" (Priest who speaks to the lion)		no, verso blank	≡	yellow-and-light-green landscape	
34	C	frontispiece			Immaculate Conception above Capuchins and central Africans			‖‖		*Istorica descrizione* frontispiece; see Paolo da Lorena design in Carna, *Città di rifugio*, 4.

smaller scale. The third set gathers scenes that Cavazzi described, for those not cut and pasted, with texts outside of the picture frame. These vignettes depict episodes of the origins and life of Queen Njinga, setting individual characters and crowds in grassy lands under brilliant blue skies (4, 5, 9, 12, 13, 14, 16, 17, 20–31). Image 8, glossed "Lungua military instrument of the Jagas," is an outlier (fig. 5). It is not only conspicuously black and white, in contrast to the vivid colors of the rest of the paintings, but the figure it features is much larger in scale than most other characters elsewhere in the manuscript. In fact, the Portuguese text in blue ink at the back of the image indicates that this vignette does not come from one of Cavazzi's Italian drafts but from another type of document. A tantalizing possibility may be that of an exchange with António de Oliveira de Cadornega, whose images (discussed in chapter 2 below) bear some stylistic resemblance to the Lungua drawing. In any case, the borrowed image shows that the friar's practice of freely compiling text from a number of sources, cited or uncited, also extended to images.

Looking past the unfinished arrangements of the vignettes in the front matter, it is easy to grasp the general direction of Cavazzi's reckoning about his visual program for the "Missione Evangelica." The Njinga vignettes from the third group (4, 5, 9, 12, 13, 14, 16, 17), currently in the front matter, would have gone to enrich others on the life of the queen already included in book 2 (20–31). The full-page paintings about the Jaga (1, 3, 18), in turn, would have joined the illustrations for book 1 (alongside 19) or book 3 (alongside 32 and 33), whose text focuses on the awe-inspiring group.[21] The remaining seven images in the front matter are either extras or the beginning of another thematic set, as well as the odd black-and-white Lungua player. First, paintings 6 and 7 are already featured in book 2 as respectively 26 and 20. Then 2, 11, and 15, all with horizontal laid lines, may have been cut from a discussion of ritual practitioners. Missing completely from the front matter are illustrations of Kongo, Portuguese Angola, and Capuchin missionary work.

Even as an unfinished project, the Araldi images are extraordinarily significant. They provide a rare view of central Africa in the seventeenth century from an eyewitness perspective and are made all the more noteworthy by their production on the African continent itself. They not only seize elements of the region's material environment but also articulate local oral histories and traditions in images that are both descriptive and narrative. By extension, unlike the stereotypical views of Africa deployed in many early modern illustrated volumes, the images of the *Istorica descrizione*, although printed in Italy, drew from firsthand experience.

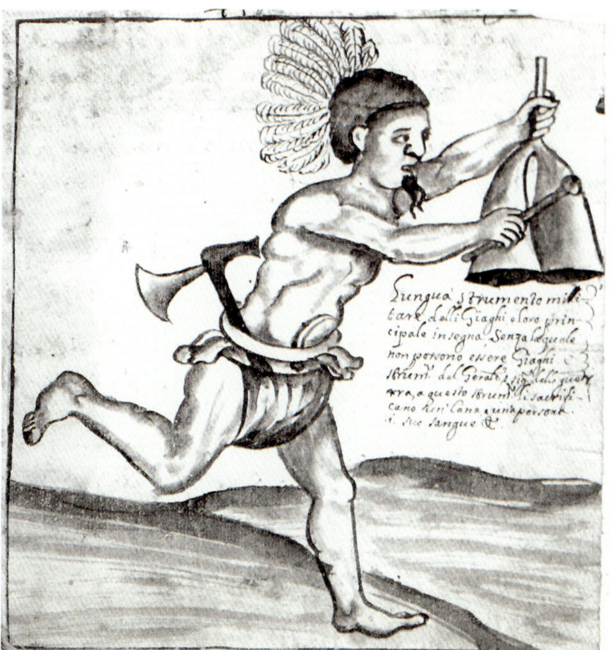

Figure 5

Giovanni Antonio Cavazzi, "Lungua military instrument," ca. 1665–68. Ink on paper, 17 × 21 cm (full manuscript page). From Giovanni Antonio Cavazzi, "Missione Evangelica al Regno del Congo" (the Araldi manuscript), vol. A, front matter, p. xxxii. Gallerie Estensi, Biblioteca Estense Universitaria, Modena. Reproduced by permission of the Italian Ministry for Cultural Heritage and Activities and for Tourism.

Fifteen of the prints from the 1687 volume indeed partly or fully derive from images in the Araldi manuscript (see table 2).

Cavazzi's Plates for the *Istorica descrizione*

Where did the designs for the remaining *Istorica descrizione* prints come from? Images from the very popular 1591 *Relatione del reame di Congo*, a publication famous Italian cosmographer Filippo Pigafetta edited from Portuguese merchant Duarte Lopes's eyewitness account of central Africa, inspired in whole or in part seven of the illustrations (table 2).[22] The renowned, several-times reedited volume was the only source on Kongo and Angola published in Europe before the Capuchin texts, and was a key reference not only for Cavazzi—who cites the Italian edition—but also for the maker of the book's

Table 2   Images from the *Istorica descrizione*

Total prints		*51*
Signed by Fortunato Alamandini	3, 4, 5, 6, 7, 9, 10, 12	8
Linked to the Araldi		15
Derived predominantly from the Araldi manuscript	frontispiece, 26,★ 29, 33, 43, 44, 45, 47	8
Derived partly from the Araldi manuscript	3, 16, 18, 28, 30, 31, 42	7
Linked to the Parma Watercolors		*33*
Predominantly similar to the Parma Watercolors	2, 8, 10, 11, 12, 13, 14, 15, 20, 21, 23, 24, 25,★ 30, 37	15
Partly similar to the Parma Watercolors	16, 17, 18, 34, 40, 42	6
Possibly derived from missing Parma Watercolors	3, 4, 6, 7, 9, 16, 17, 19, 36, 38, 41, 46	12
Derived from Lopes/Pigafetta in whole or in part	*5, 6, 7, 22, 23, 27, 28*	*7*
In foldout format	map and landscape print	2

★appears twice

vignettes, as well as for Alamandini.[23] A copy of the 1597 or 1598 Latin edition of the *Relatione* was in Luanda in the 1670s, available to Cavazzi.

Thirty-three of the *Istorica descrizione* images bear close kinship with paintings in the Parma Watercolors (plates 2–68).[24] The two works were separate projects, albeit conceived and implemented within a close-knit circle of Capuchin veterans of the central-Africa missions. Similar designs and compositions appear in both the watercolors and the prints, perhaps because one inspired the other. Yet, because of the operation of the Capuchin central-African milieu in which ideas, texts, and images changed hands fluidly, without emphasis on individual authorship, it is more accurate to think of the similarities as deriving from their origins in the common reckonings of a handful of friars at work picturing nature, culture, and faith in Kongo and Angola in the 1660s and 1670s. Drafts of manuscripts and images circulated frequently among this small group of missionary-authors who worked, traveled, and may have met each other between Luanda, Brazil, and Italy.[25] Cavazzi, for instance, not only used the same compositions from one manuscript to the next, and from manuscripts to print editions, he also included images featured in the works of his colleagues. The *Istorica descrizione*, for example, includes a fish associated with a 1648 sketch by Serafino da Cortona (see figs. 29, 31), and a range of vignettes directly linked to the Parma Watercolors, such as depictions of a potato plant (figs. 6, 7) and a funerary ceremony (figs. 8, 9).

Table 2, which lists the book's illustrations, indicates the sources for their designs, fleshing out the sphere of visual exchange at the core of the central-African Capuchins' early visual endeavors.

Still, some of the *Istorica descrizione*'s illustrations do not have identifiable precedents. It is likely that they derived from images that would have featured in the Parma Watercolors but are now lost. Indeed, most images from the *Istorica descrizione* not in the current Parma Watercolors collection easily fit in the lacunae in the watercolors' numbering. The book's pineapple (fig. 103), for instance, likely belongs in the midst of the Parma Watercolor fruit series as folio 34, between the cola nut (plate 20)

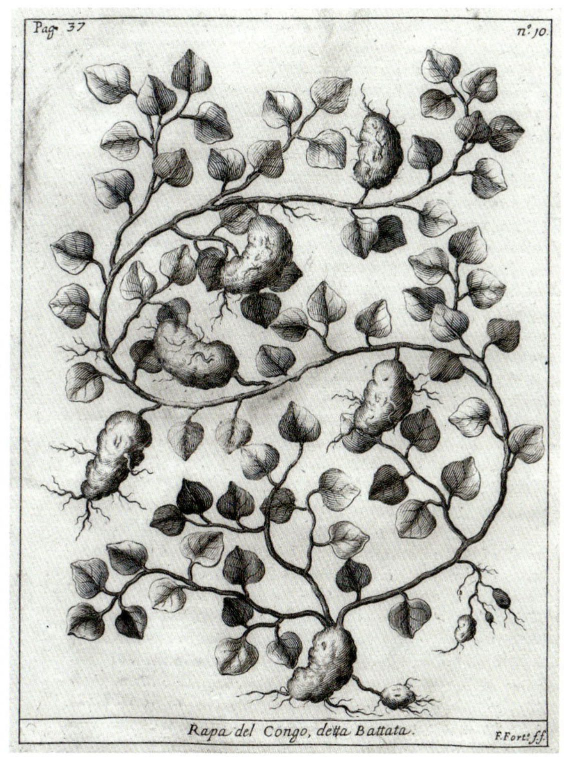

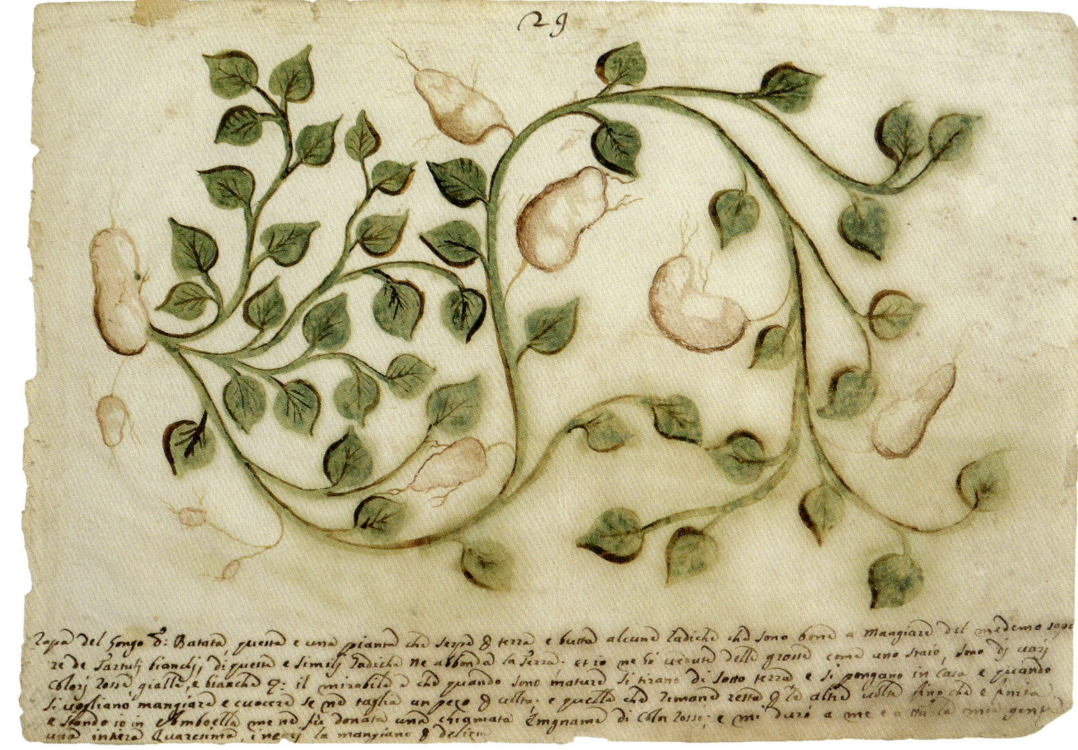

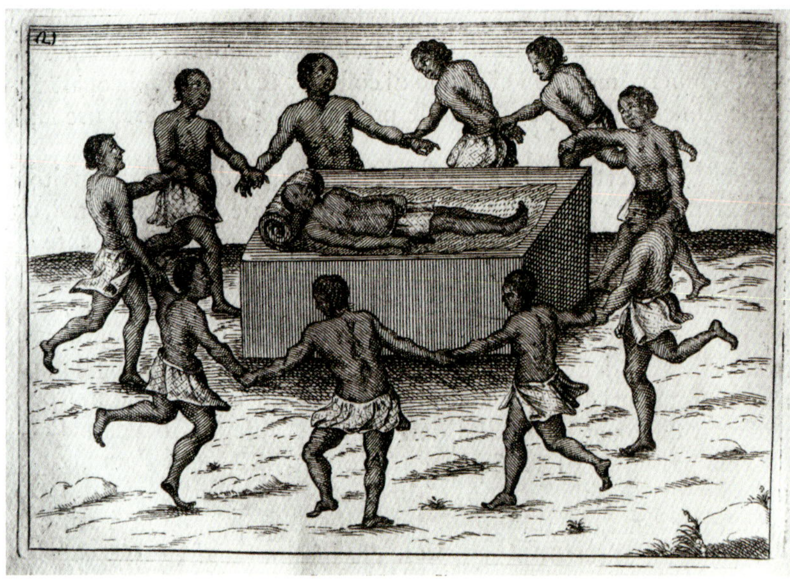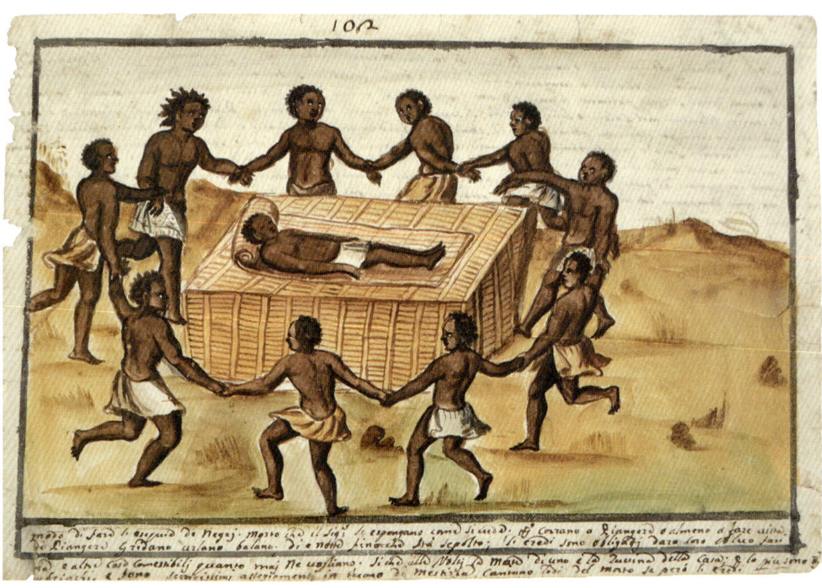

and the banana (plates 21, 22). Similarly, some of the prints Cavazzi commissioned for the *Istorica descrizione* that do not have extant sources bear close stylistic similarities with the Araldi manuscript. Cavazzi may have composed them first for one of his manuscripts or made them specifically for the published volume.

The Propaganda and other Italian revisers of the *Istorica descrizione* may have complained about Cavazzi's editing skills, but the plates he planned for the volume demonstrate, on the contrary, great effort at synthesis and at creating uniform compositions. Although drawn from more than one source, all the plates have a common orientation, format, and style that either Cavazzi or Bonaventura and Paolo da Lorena deliberately devised. They reworked, in particular, the images drawn from the Araldi manuscript, using a template close to that of the Parma Watercolors, that is, a horizontal

orientation with figures involved in an activity and set between a ground occupying about half of the frame and a thin sky. The editing process also summarized into a single print scenes depicted across several watercolors—for instance, in the consolidation of apostolic activities appearing on folios 96 and 97 (plates 61 and 62, and likely a missing one featuring a seated friar) into a single print, number 40 of the *Istorica descrizione* (fig. 10). Engravings representing ritual practitioners also combined imagery from several paintings into a single frame.[26] The large landscape print Cavazzi commissioned is similarly a composite (fig. 41), mixing elements from various sources within the Capuchin corpus. It features a friar under a leafy canopy, as seen in ministry scenes (plates 61–63, 70 top, 71 bottom; figs. 44, 95). Its trees and spare grounds echo those seen in botanical vignettes (plates 23–27, 30). The mountains in the background also close the perspective in some of the images concerned with ethnographic descriptions (plates 14, 28, 29, 47, 49, 52, 54, 56, 58).

Yet Cavazzi's efforts to prepare the images for publication did not convince Italian editor Fortunato Alamandini. In a contrived foreword to the *Istorica descrizione*, he distances himself from the volume his superiors had ordered him to edit but eventually forced him to publish without the full revisions he wished to undertake. He makes clear in this text that he finds the "many copper plates"

Cavazzi commissioned inadequate and that he publishes them only begrudgingly. He had hoped, he adamantly informs the readers, "not to be forced to include" the "numerous" engravings that the missionary had commissioned "some time ago" in the final publication, as the plates were "weak" and did not match the revised text.[27] Given the poor quality of the illustrations he inherited, a proactive Alamandini even set out to produce his own "very different" prints, eight of which would appear in

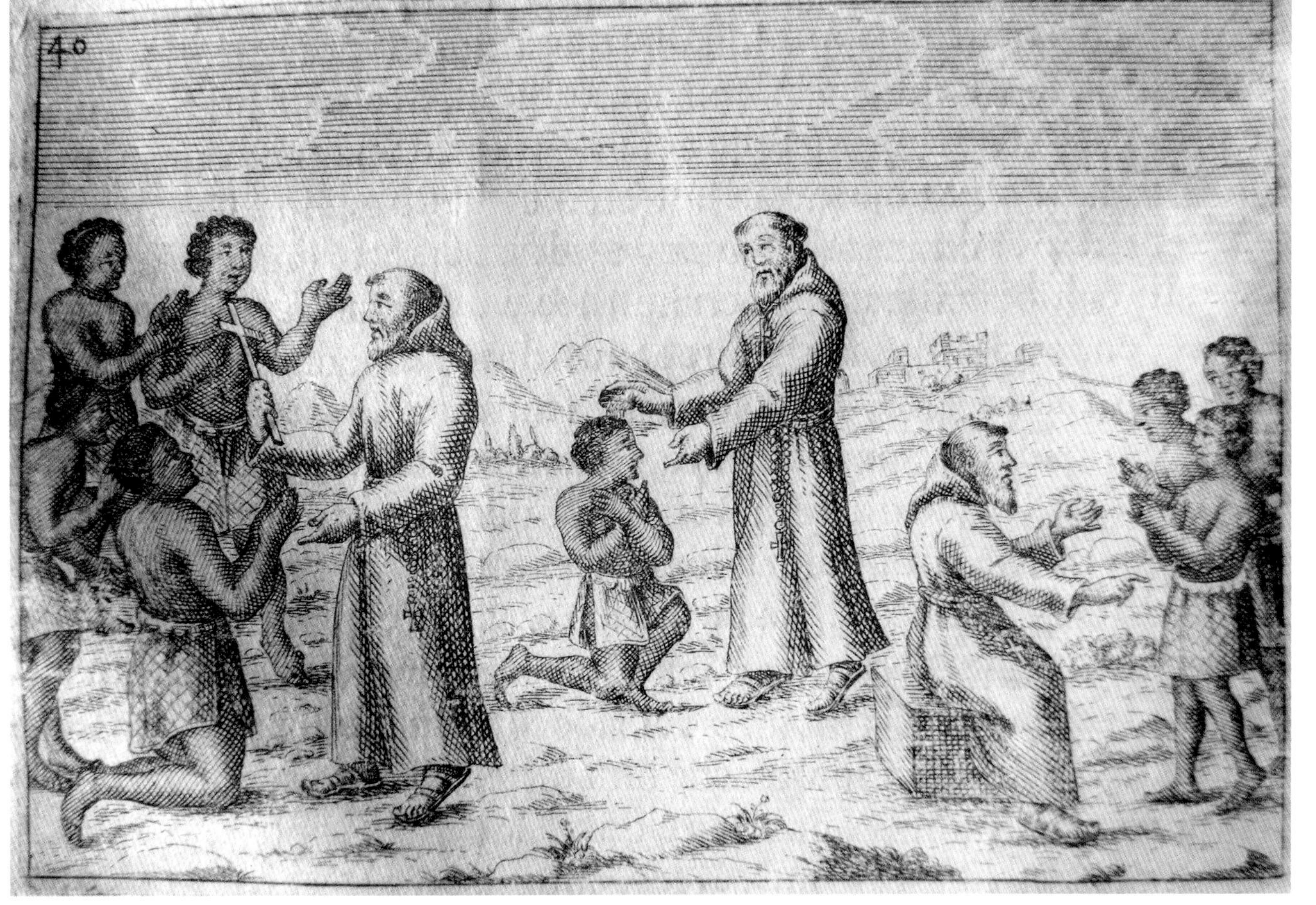

Figure 8 (opposite left)

Paolo da Lorena (attr.), *Funeral Rites*. Engraving and etching, 10 × 14 cm (plate mark). Plate 23 from Giovanni Antonio Cavazzi and Fortunato Alamandini, *Istorica descrizione de' tre' regni Congo, Matamba, et Angola* (Bologna: Giacomo Monti, 1687), 128. Bibliothèque nationale de France, FOL-H-3133. Photo: author.

Figure 9 (opposite right)

Unknown Capuchin artist, "Manner of conducting the funeral rites of the blacks," late seventeenth century. Watercolor on paper, 34 × 24 cm. Parma Watercolors, Virgili Collection, fol. 102. Photo: author.

Figure 10

Paolo da Lorena (attr.), *Friars at Work in the Mission.* Engraving and etching, 10 × 14 cm (plate mark). Plate 40 from Giovanni Antonio Cavazzi and Fortunato Alamandini, *Istorica descrizione de' tre' regni Congo, Matamba, et Angola* (Bologna: Giacomo Monti, 1687), 324. Bibliothèque nationale de France, FOL-H-3133. Photo: author.

Paolo da Lorena (attr.), *Architectural Compound*. Engraving and etching, 10 × 14 cm (plate mark). Plate 32 from Giovanni Antonio Cavazzi and Fortunato Alamandini, *Istorica descrizione de' tre' regni Congo, Matamba, et Angola* (Bologna: Giacomo Monti, 1687), 207. National Library of Portugal, Lisbon, H.G. 9174 A. Photo courtesy of the National Library of Portugal.

Paolo da Lorena (attr.), *Woman Working the Land*. Engraving, 10 × 14 cm (plate mark). Plate 2 from Giovanni Antonio Cavazzi and Fortunato Alamandini, *Istorica descrizione de' tre' regni Congo, Matamba, et Angola* (Bologna: Giacomo Monti, 1687), 27. National Library of Portugal, Lisbon, H.G. 9174 A. Photo courtesy of the National Library of Portugal.

the volume, prominently featured in the first fifty pages and proudly signed "F. Fort°. f.f." (see figs. 6, 13, 16, 18, 56, 64, 103).[28]

And indeed his vignettes stand out. They are not inserted into the text, as are the rest of the prints, but rather feature alone, each on a single page. Each presents a scene that is heavily framed, labeled, and numbered.[29] The Propaganda, however, did not support the costly commission of an entire new set of prints. Friar Fortunato had to follow the Congregation's instructions to include Cavazzi's plates without further elaborations, but still changed their order, gave each a new number at one of its top corners, and ostentatiously front-loaded his own compositions at the beginning of the book. It is also likely that he cut down the number of prints he used altogether. There are, for instance, only a few images of flora and fauna, although the topic plays a large role in the text and features prominently in the table of contents of Cavazzi's earlier draft as well as in the Parma Watercolors.[30]

The plates that remained from Cavazzi's original illustration program are the ones he had commissioned from Paolo da Lorena, whose signature appears on the frontispiece of the book as "F. Paul.ˢ a Lothar.ᵃ Cap. Sculp." (fig. 82). The name suggests that the Capuchin engraver originally came from the Lorraine province in northern Europe, but unfortunately little else is known about him, as he does not feature in the order's biographical compendia.[31] His few known works indicate that he was already an accomplished artist in 1655, when he produced the elaborate plates for Ignazio Carnago's volume on Marian cults in Milan, the *Città di rifugio* (fig. 84).[32] A few years later, Friar Paolo worked in the Piedmont region of Savoy, in the orbit of architect, polyvalent designer, and perhaps painter Giovenale Boetto.[33] He etched, for instance,

a frontispiece after Boetto's design and produced a map for Mattia Ferrerio's 1659 account of the Capuchin missions in the Alps, on the frontlines of the Counter-Reformation, the *Rationarium Chronographicum*, for Turin editor Carlo Gianelli.[34] Fifteen years later, a mature Paolo da Lorena drew from the same baroque style and catalogue of motifs to compose the frontispiece to Cavazzi's volume, which readily compares to his 1655 plates. The frontispiece to the *Istorica descrizione*, for instance, closely parallels a plate on page 450 of the *Città di rifugio* (figs. 82, 84). Paolo da Lorena thus had experience in the illustration of Capuchin themes as well as of missionary literature, albeit in European contexts. Later in his career he became more involved in visual productions dealing with overseas missions, producing, for instance, likely in the 1660s, a portrait of Cassien de Nantes, a Capuchin missionary martyred in Ethiopia in 1638.[35]

In most of the *Istorica descrizione* prints, the etcher's hand is hard to discern. His sensibilities appear most clearly, though still faintly, in the one representing a billfish (fig. 31). There, an incongruous genre scene enhances the usual template of the illustrations, a close view of a single subject against a simple background suggesting its environment. Behind the fish the silhouette of a man in a European hat appears near a small house at the top right, pole fishing from the shore while two ships sail in the background. Smaller yet similar additions feature in other images from the book. A ship sails on the horizon above the portrait of the *pesce donna* (fig. 55). A small figure holding a spyglass reclines at the bottom of a hill (fig. 11). A long-tailed rodent, a diminutive animal whose profile resembles that of a bull, and an upright, wavy snake inhabit the foreground of the second print in the book (fig. 12). These small embellishments are the only

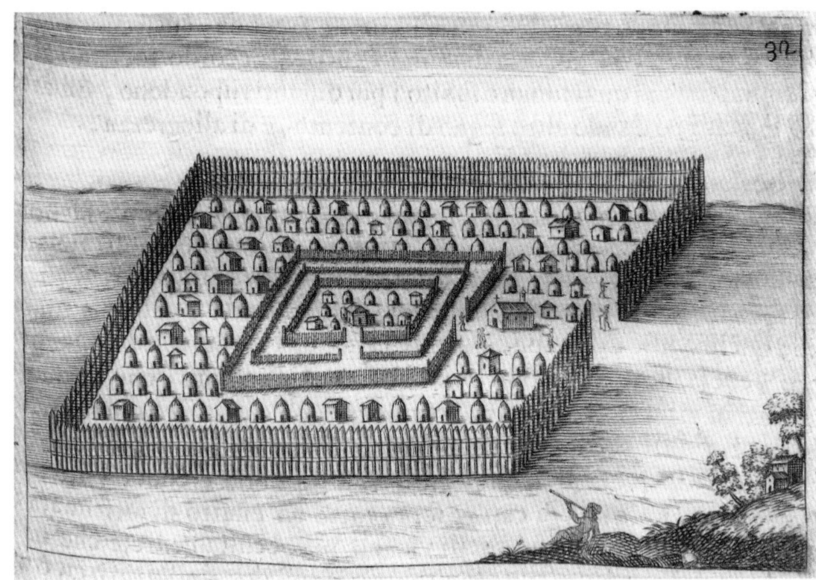 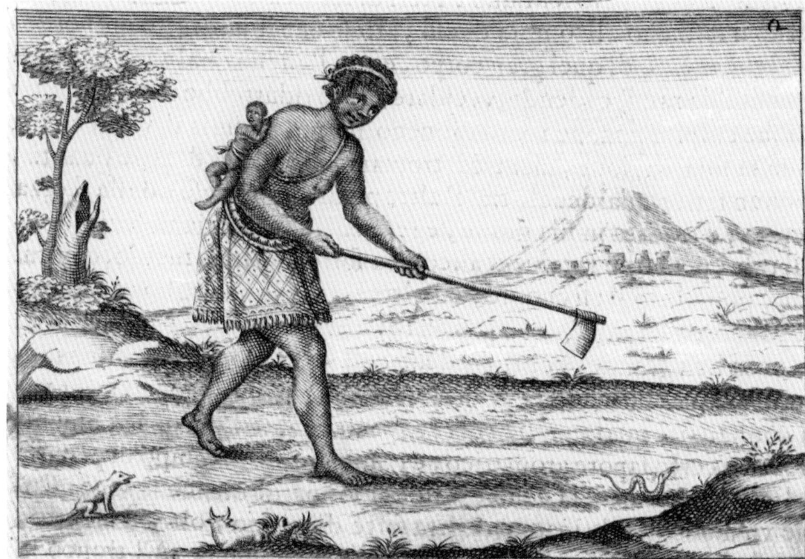

recognizable traces of Friar Paolo's hand in images otherwise closely following the templates provided to him, similar in their compositions to the Parma Watercolors. His origins in northern Europe may also have played a role in the formulation of the large landscape print, a genre associated at the time with the North of Europe (fig. 41). The *Istorica descrizione*, in a passage that must have escaped the editorial zeal of Alamandini, mentions the images that Paolo da Lorena used as templates for his engraving in the paragraphs concerning the *pesce donna*, or manatee, whose illustrations did not satisfy Cavazzi (fig. 55). The friar laments in the text that "it has not been possible to explain it [i.e., the manatee] precisely to [the maker of] the image, and while there [i.e., in central Africa] I forgot to have it painted."[36]

Cavazzi thus used as illustration for his volume four sorts of images. First, he used paintings made from nature that he commissioned while in central Africa. This commission could be the source of the Parma Watercolors. Second, he had vignettes produced in Italy under his supervision and after his own eyewitness experiences. Third, he drew plates from other sources such as Serafino da Cortona's billfish (discussed in chapter 2 below). Finally, he drew from his own repertoire of images composed for previous works such as those now in the Araldi manuscript. Notably, he also used images as sources for his text. He explains in his notes on the "abbada, ò ndemba," that he "has not seen it, except in image."[37] The set of images that served as a template for Paolo da Lorena's engravings were thus a compilation, mixing paintings made by Cavazzi himself with others gathered, copied, and formatted from other sources with the help, perhaps, of a trained artist. The compilation could have taken place either in Italy or in central Africa, where painters traveled alongside friars as part of the mission.[38]

The Parma Watercolors loom large as a parallel of or a source for the images in the *Istorica descrizione*. They were not, however, direct preliminary studies for the publication's prints but instead a broader, distinct project, possibly but not necessarily linked from the outset to Cavazzi. The friar may have had access to or could even have commissioned the Parma Watercolors during his stay in Luanda as the prefect or head of the Capuchin mission. He may have used them as inspiration for the illustration of the "Descrizione de' tre' grandi Regni," his massive, now-lost work on Kongo and Angola that predates the composition of his early version of the *Istorica descrizione*.[39] As he also continued to research and compile documents for the volume while back in Italy, he may have encountered the watercolors in the Propaganda Fide archives or some other Capuchin repository.

The sources and creation process of the prints in the *Istorica descrizione* are not entirely clear, but they inscribed themselves into Cavazzi's well-documented practices of nimble compilation and reformulation from his own works as well as that of others. The volume also formed a project in some ways parallel to, yet distinct from, that of the didactic illustrated manuscripts at the center of the corpus of Capuchin images of central Africa. Most tellingly, like them, it stood at odds with the expectations of European readers. Censors, editors, and Church hierarchy alike agreed that heavy revisions were needed before it could be fit to print.

Measuring the Capuchin Central-African Project Against Alamandini's Editing

Whether they composed watercolors or ink drawings or commissioned prints, Cavazzi and his colleagues who had worked in Kongo and Angola had a well-defined conception of the nature, form, and purpose of their images of central Africa. Fortunato Alamandini's critical views of the prints for the *Istorica descrizione* and his corrective compositions are foils against which to take stock of the idiosyncratic features of the Capuchin central-African imagery. The Italian editor, who may have had access, in addition to the engravings, to a range of other images from the Capuchin central-African orbit, including those in the Araldi manuscript and the Parma Watercolors, thought that Cavazzi's commissioned plates were unsuitable and should be replaced altogether. He set to work on his correction with the images of flora and fauna. He kept only one illustration of a fruit and four of animals from the plates Cavazzi commissioned. The print of bananas shows the fruit in profile and section, in a closely cropped view, as if set directly on the ground.[40] A manatee (fig. 55), a billfish (fig. 31), a hippopotamus, and two birds on a branch appear in similarly close-cropped frames with simple backgrounds indicating their environments, that is, respectively, sea, land, and tree.[41] They are all very similar to the corresponding watercolors (plates 11, 8, 37, and, to a lesser extent, 31).

To replace Cavazzi's plates, Alamandini created proudly signed engravings of his own, in which he presented corrected, enhanced versions of the original compositions. In what he considered improvements, he dedicated a full page to each example of flora and fauna and presented it on a mostly white background (e.g., figs. 6, 56). He began with a series of five trees. In print number 3 he has pictured what he calls a coconut palm, or "Palma del Cocco" (fig. 13). The tall plant occupies the entire page. Its trunk grows from the bottom of the frame, and its leaves fan high toward the top and almost touch its sides. The fronds and the two bundles of fruits hanging on either side of the trunk appear in sharp contour against the white background that occupies the top three-quarters of the image. Rolling hills with small shrubs occupy the lower part, their horizontal lines enhancing the vertical thrust of the coconut tree and its characteristic rings. Mountains rendered in lighter color stretch the perspective in the center, while another palm in small scale on the left of the image marks the middle ground.

In the foreground a man and a woman are hard at work on either side of the tree. The male figure, to the left, butchers a human corpse. He has already detached the head and holds firmly the arm of the lifeless body, raising his axe with his left hand to continue quartering the victim. His female counterpart, on the right, cooks a human leg on a grill, while two other limbs on the ground await their turn on the fire. The decapitation scene resembles a painting in the Araldi manuscript (fig. 14) and probably derives from one of the Cavazzi-commissioned prints that Alamandini eliminated. The human barbecue on the right comes from the widely circulating imagery of cannibalism in Brazil, such as the famous frontispiece to French Capuchin Claude d'Abbeville's 1614 publication on Maranhão (fig. 79).[42]

The format of a large tree surrounded by smaller scenes and figures repeats in prints 4 to 6. A single man drags a large palm fruit with a cord in the background of number 4. The strange, and to my knowledge fanciful, mode of carrying a passenger depicted in Lopes and Pigafetta's *Relatione del reame di Congo* (fig. 15) appears on the next illustration (fig. 16). Opposite the carrying chair, the artist has depicted a village surrounded by a round enclosure, a depiction that would feature again in Friar

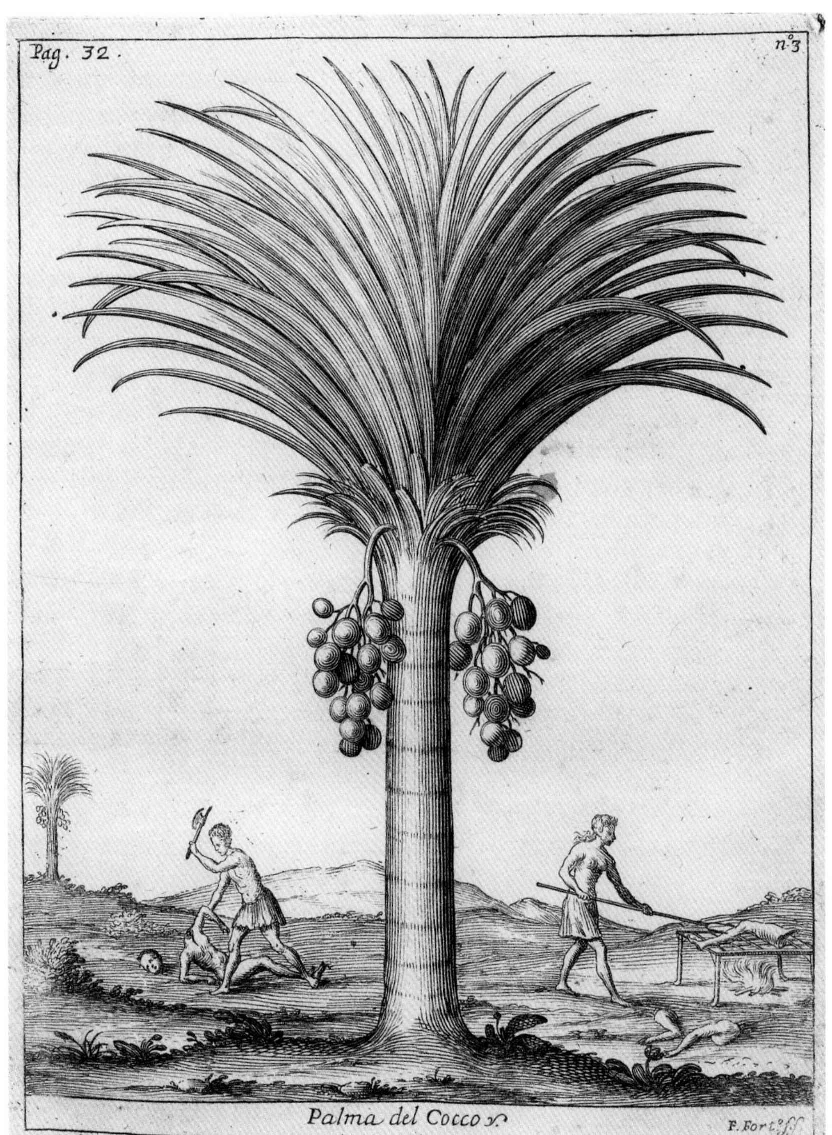

Figure 13

Fortunato Alamandini, *Palm of the Coconut*. Engraving, 19.5 × 14 cm (plate mark). Plate 3 from Giovanni Antonio Cavazzi and Fortunato Alamandini, *Istorica descrizione de' tre' regni Congo, Matamba, et Angola* (Bologna: Giacomo Monti, 1687), facing p. 32. National Library of Portugal, Lisbon, H.G. 9174 A. Photo courtesy of the National Library of Portugal.

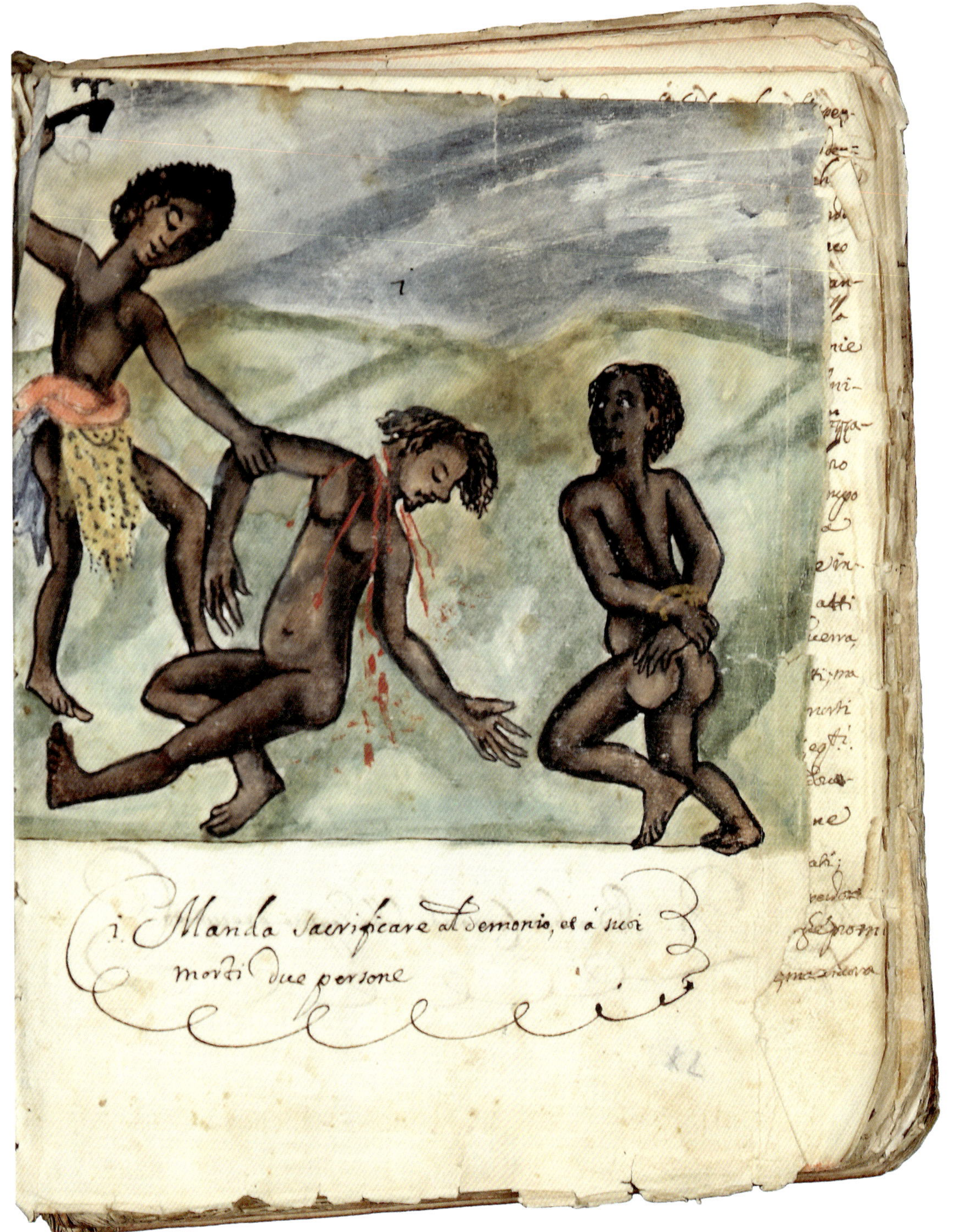

Figure 14

Giovanni Antonio Cavazzi, "[She] orders that two people be sacrificed to the devil and her ancestors," ca. 1665–68. Watercolor and ink on paper, 17 × 21 cm (page). From Giovanni Antonio Cavazzi, "Missione Evangelica al Regno del Congo" (the Araldi manuscript), vol A, front matter, p. II. Gallerie Estensi, Biblioteca Estense Universitaria, Modena. Reproduced by permission of the Italian Ministry for Cultural Heritage and Activities and for Tourism.

Figure 15 (opposite)

Natale Bonifacio (attr.), *Another way to travel*. Etching, 19.8 × 29.4 cm (plate mark). Plate 7 from Duarte Lopes and Filippo Pigafetta, *Relatione del reame di Congo* (Rome: Appresso Bartolomeo Grassi, 1591), between pp. 22 and 23. National Library of Portugal, Lisbon, RES. 495 P. Photo courtesy of the National Library of Portugal.

Merolla's 1692 publication, the *Breve, e succinta relatione* (fig. 17).[43] It recalls towns shown elsewhere in the *Istorica descrizione* and in the Museo Francescano drawing, though following an orthogonal, rather than circular, plan (fig. 11 and plate 1). Print number 6 (fig. 18) brings in Lopes and Pigafetta's zebra (fig. 33), which also inspired one of the Parma Watercolors (fig. 32 and plate 39), to the right of the "Pianta del Conde ordinaria." In the distant left, a man steps toward a statue standing in front of a large hollow tree, arms extended perhaps in prayer (fig. 64). The scene has no parallel in the Parma Watercolors or extant Cavazzi prints, but it recalls the hollow trunk of a large *Aliconde* tree featured in Merolla.[44] It is a rare period depiction of a central-African ritual figure (as discussed further in chapter 4 below). Finally, Alamandini's print number 7 shows to the left of the "Pianta del Conde straordinaria" a person in a covered hammock hanging from a pole supported by two carriers. A similar motif appeared not only in Lopes and Pigafetta but also in one of Cavazzi's own engravings and, later, in Merolla.[45]

The composition of Alamandini's vignettes makes clear the goals of the editor in the illustration program he proposed to replace Cavazzi's. His

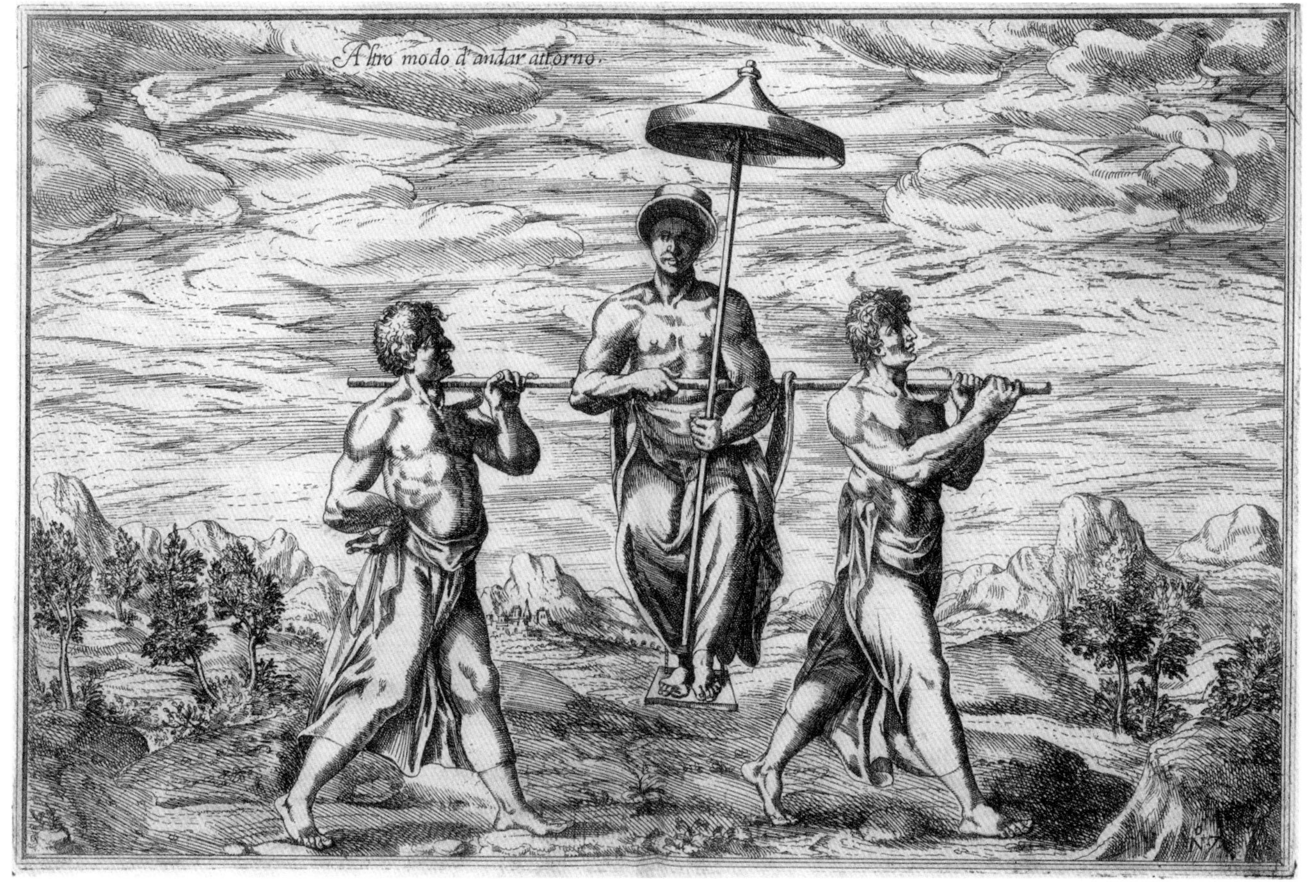

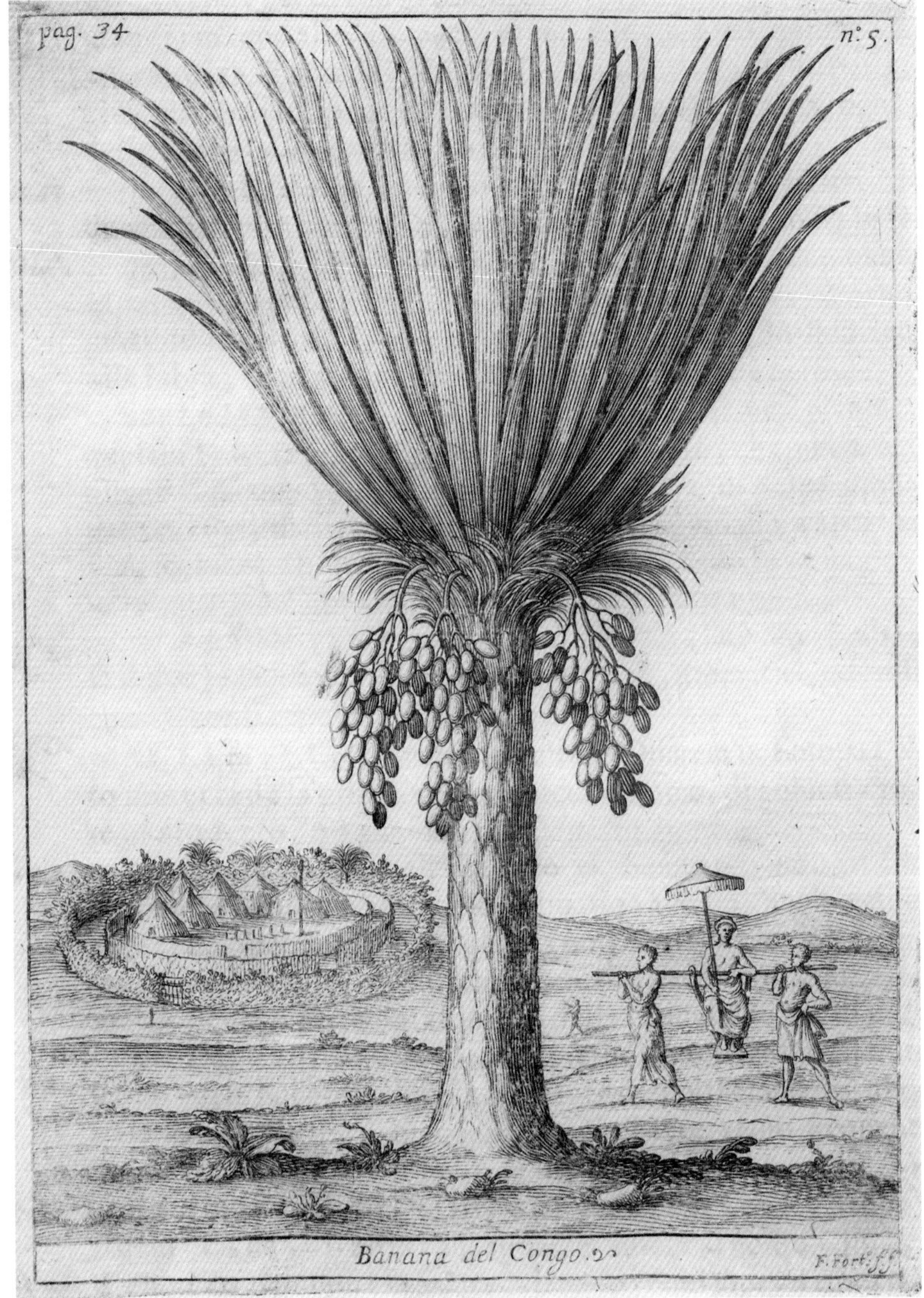

Figure 16

Fortunato Alamandini, *Banana of the Congo*. Engraving, 19.5 × 14 cm (plate mark). Plate 5 from Giovanni Antonio Cavazzi and Fortunato Alamandini, *Istorica descrizione de' tre' regni Congo, Matamba, et Angola* (Bologna: Giacomo Monti, 1687), facing p. 34. National Library of Portugal, Lisbon, H.G. 9174 A. Photo courtesy of the National Library of Portugal.

Figure 17 (opposite left)

Unknown artist, "House of Aristocrats. Knight. Lady." Engraving, 15 × 9.5 cm (plate mark). Plate 14 from Girolamo Merolla da Sorrento and Angelo Piccardo, *Breve, e succinta relatione del viaggio nel Regno di Congo* (Napoli: Francesco Mollo, 1692), facing p. 176. Biblioteca Nazionale Centrale di Roma, 6.25.H.8. Photo courtesy of the Biblioteca Nazionale Centrale di Roma.

Figure 18 (opposite right)

Fortunato Alamandini, *Ordinary Conde Plant*. Engraving, 19.5 × 14 cm (plate mark). Plate 6 from Giovanni Antonio Cavazzi and Fortunato Alamandini, *Istorica descrizione de' tre' regni Congo, Matamba, et Angola* (Bologna: Giacomo Monti, 1687), between pp. 34 and 35. National Library of Portugal, Lisbon, H.G. 9174 A. Photo courtesy of the National Library of Portugal.

full-page compositions give emphasis to uniformity. All five trees depicted look strikingly similar though of very different botanical types and thus convey the appearance of the plants with varying degrees of accuracy. The two palms and banana tree, for instance, have the same silhouette. The two other tree images, labeled "Pianta del Conde," referring to broad-leaved fruit trees from the Annonaceae family, known in Portuguese as *fruta do Conde*

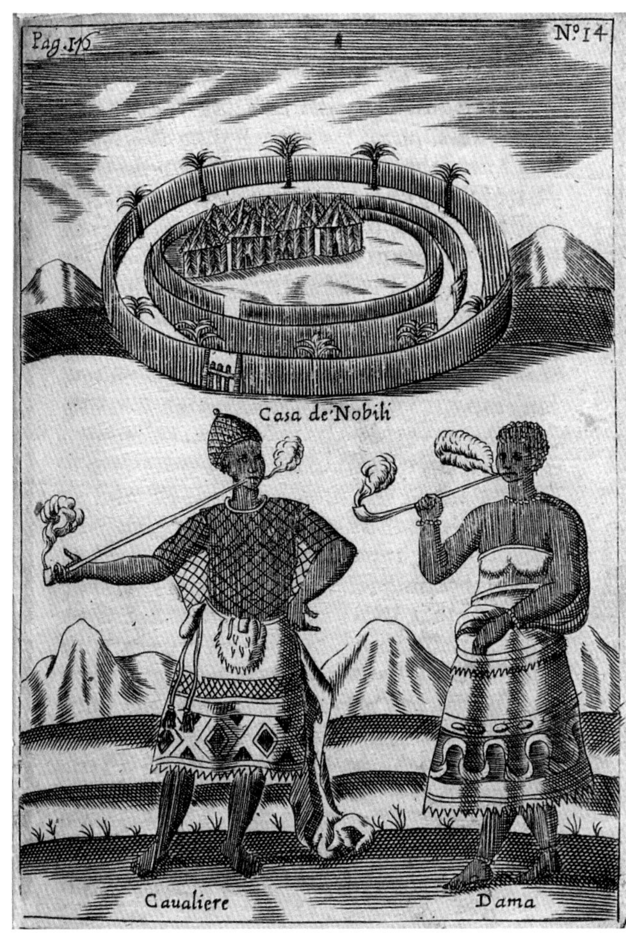

and custard apple in English, fail to describe their physical appearance.[46]

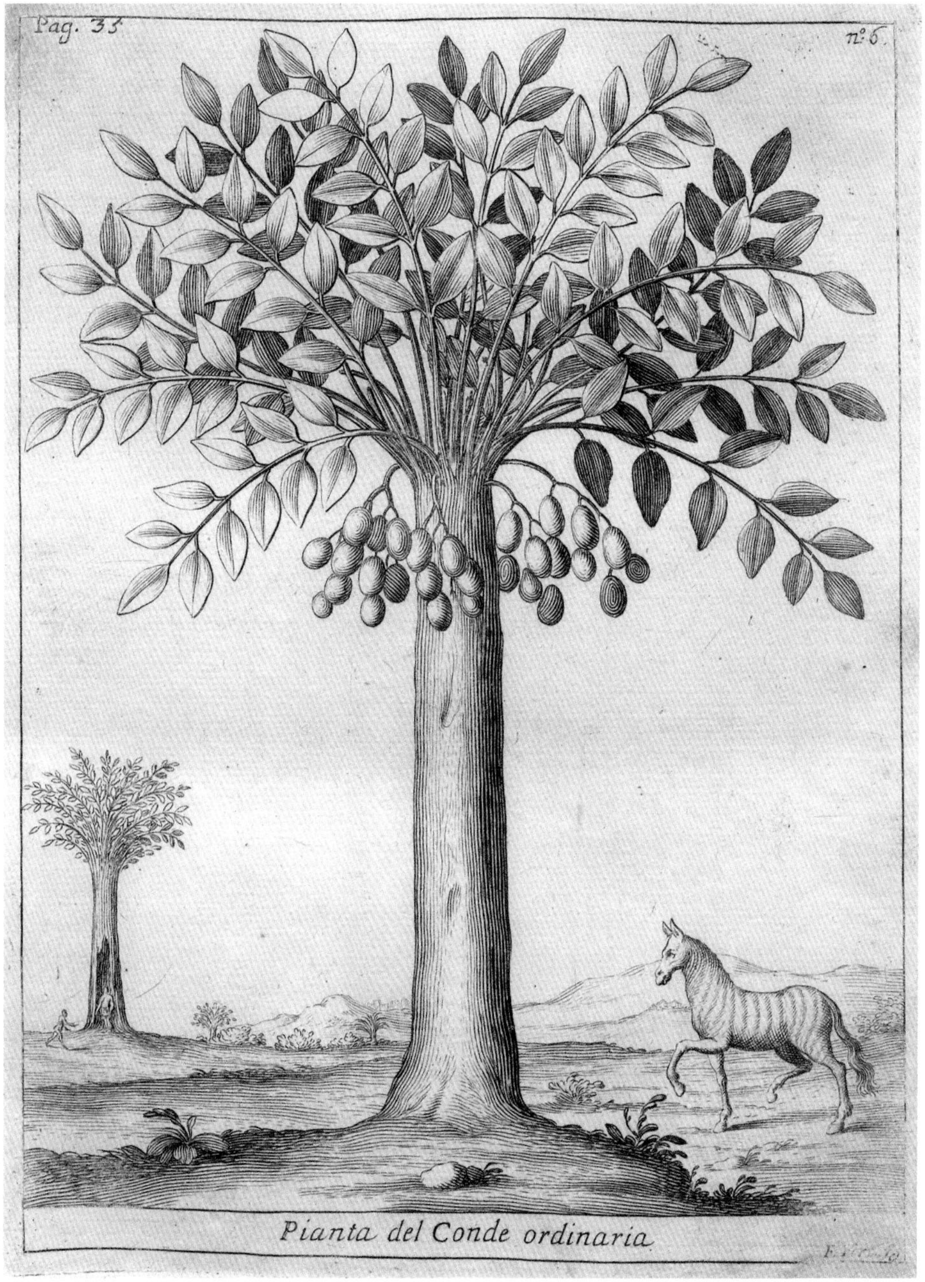

More important to Alamandini than accuracy was elegance and conformity to established visual and cultural norms for the depiction of faraway lands and peoples. He produced erudite plates that would fit with existing European templates for the depiction of non-European locales and people. He drew on multiple tools to achieve these objectives.

The first was the visual language of exoticism, framing plants with sensationalistic views of distant humanity as violent savages. Cannibalism unsurprisingly features here, as it was the preeminent foil against which the European, Christian subjects contrasted themselves in the early modern period.[47] But as the scale makes clear, cannibalism and other human activities are only backdrops to the main subject matter of the prints, exotic flora. Listing trees, plants, and animals, Alamandini offers to his readers the opportunity to increase their intellectual grasp of the world through views of newly or rarely encountered natural specimens.

His compositions emulate the format of early modern scientific illustrations in which examples of flora and fauna are presented on a blank page, deracinated, decontextualized, and made fit to travel from the four corners of the world to European centers of learning.[48] Sketched on the white page of the naturalist, plants and animals become specimens; they are no longer living organisms born from, striving in, and contributing to their environment. They are domesticated in a way that gives precedence to the gaze of the European scholarly or leisurely viewer over other perspectives on their nature and meanings. In his edited images, Alamandini suggests that the interest of the types of plants and animals observed in central Africa lay in their contribution to the reader's mental catalogue of flora and fauna rather than in the rich connections they had with local landscapes and cultures. His reworking of the figures brings information about central Africa into an epistemic realm in which distant lands, nature, and people are redefined within European templates of classification in which they feature according to their economic potential, geopolitical interest, scientific significance, or even

ability to entertain. Alamandini's program was cut short, but his emphasis on central Africa as a land distant from Europe in both its natural and social environments is clear in his combinations of scenes depicting cannibalism and palanquins within pages emulating botanical illustrations of conspicuously non-European plants and animals.

The engravings Cavazzi commissioned and the Parma Watercolors are strikingly different from Alamandini's images. In the often densely inhabited vignettes of the former, animals, plants, and, most of all, men and women appear in animated poses and anchored to their environments. If many of the scenes depicted could, and in effect probably often did, elicit readings of exoticism and savagery, they also presented within their frames a world rooted in its own time and place. For example, the same palm trees that Alamandini features alongside cannibalistic scenes appear in the Parma Watercolors as part of a description of wine tapping, enriched with a long text about the practice (plates 27–29). The Parma Watercolors of plates 28 and 29 show different techniques central Africans used to collect the nutritious sap. Climbing or felling the trees, industrious men collect the liquid into calabash gourds. The text of the vignette, in turn, explains the dexterity and knowledge the skilled seasonal activity demanded.

Like Alamandini's plates, Cavazzi's images and the Parma Watercolors make central-African people and nature available for European viewers to observe. Yet unlike them, they present Kongo and Angola as worlds of their own, and their contents unfold largely outside of European epistemic framing. What is more, central Africa appears in the vignettes as coeval with Europe. It does not dwell in a timeless, savage domain or belong to a realm that has not yet escaped its own pagan era. Rather, it is a part of the world inhabited by a cosmopolitan crowd of Portuguese and central Africans (plates 2, 3). It is a land shaken by the horrors of the Atlantic slave trade (plate 6) but also a region where Capuchin friars are humbled to be received by the great Christian king of the Kongo (fig. 87).[49] It is, as the friars tirelessly attempted to explain in their visual guides, a place where missionary work unfolds in dialogue and collaboration with lay and religious local leaders (plates 59–65).

Conclusion

The distance between Cavazzi's and Alamandini's prints not only derived from differences in experience between a friar who could draw on his firsthand knowledge of central Africa and a less-informed European armchair traveler. It also derived from diametrically different views on the construction of a proper discourse about Africa. Alamandini's images made new information on Kongo and Angola gathered during the Capuchin mission fit into preexisting or then-developing European ideas, mental projections, and conventions for the representation of faraway lands. Cavazzi, as well as the other mission veterans, in contrast, combined the European perspectives that shaped their outlook before their travels with the insights they gained in person on the mission field. Although established European patterns for the representation of Africa conditioned the friars' approach to and understanding of Kongo and Angola during their journeys, the images they eventually produced responded to these patterns in innovative ways to mobilize and communicate the knowledge they had acquired firsthand.[50] The Capuchin image-makers put to work the visual tools of seventeenth- and eighteenth-century Italy to create images presenting rich and complex views of central Africa that could serve (as I argue further in chapter 3) appropriately as proxy for lived experience of the mission and correctives for novices' misconceptions.

Too easily dismissed then and now as idiosyncratic, the Capuchin central-African vignettes in fact form a coherent and elaborate corpus. They offer representations that fell outside of the then-prevailing templates of colonial imagery or exoticism in their depictions of overseas missionary work, of mores and customs outside of Europe, and of the relationship between Europeans and the people they encountered in faraway lands. The images of the *Istorica descrizione* are a palimpsest born in a tug-of-war between the visual project Cavazzi worked at establishing from his experiences of the central-African mission and the models his religious hierarchy in Rome deemed aesthetically, theologically, and intellectually appropriate. They long stood in all their contradictions and ambivalences as the main visual testimony to the Capuchin central-African endeavors. But the now-resurfaced Parma Watercolors place them within a much broader corpus and open new avenues for the analysis of these extraordinarily significant yet little understood images.

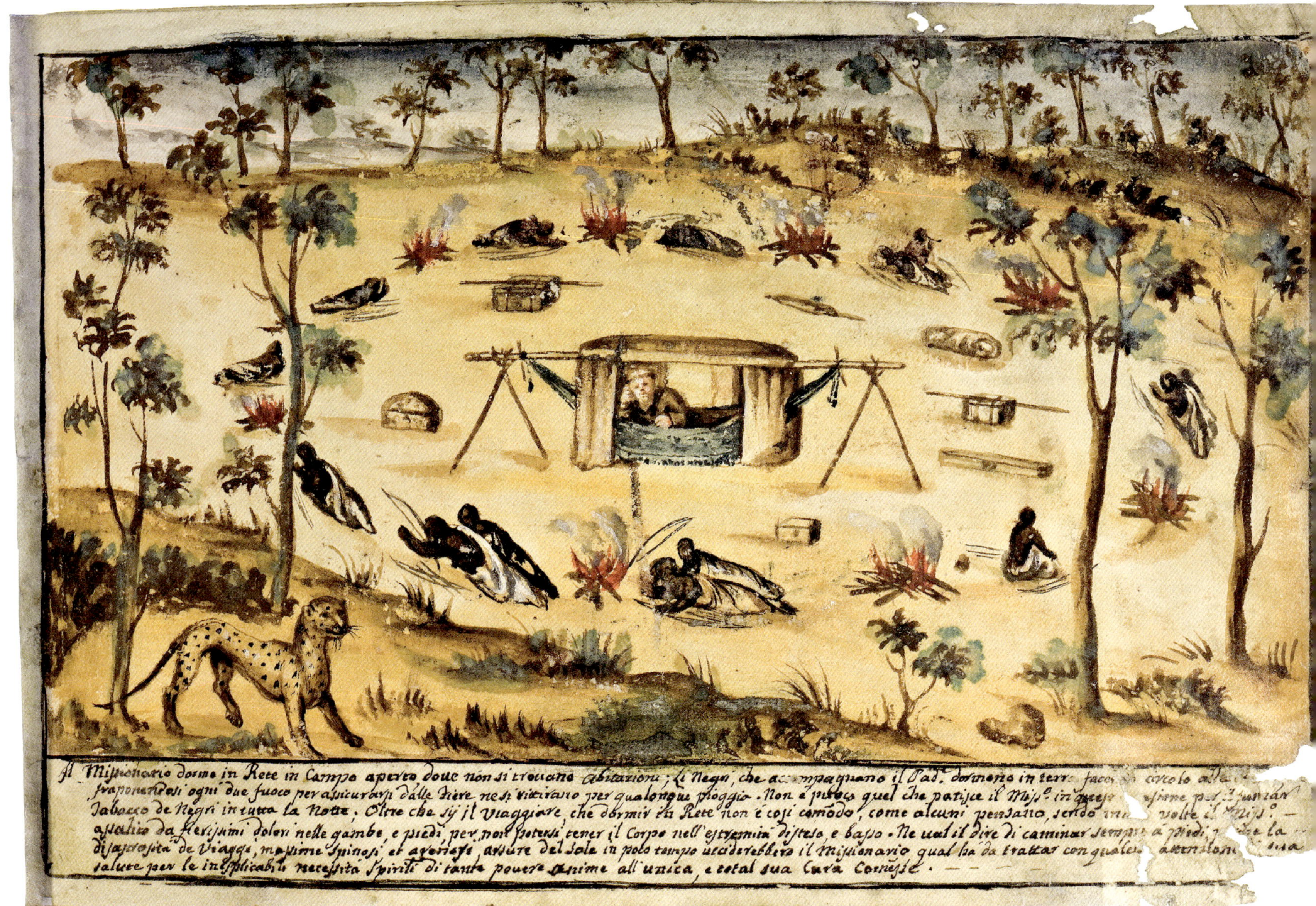

Figure 19

Bernardino Ignazio da Vezza d'Asti, "The Missionary sleeps in a Net," ca. 1750. Watercolor on paper, 19.5 × 28 cm. From "Missione in prattica," Biblioteca civica Centrale di Torino, MS 457, fol. 11r. Photo courtesy of the Biblioteca civica Centrale, Turin.

Reclining on his side in a hammock supported on trestles for the night, a friar faces a sleepless night (fig. 19). Bundles, boxes, and trunks lay on the ground next to him, and a large entourage interspersed with roaring fires forms a circle around them. Most men in the group sleep soundly on the ground of the clearing, shielded from insects by the smoke and trusting the flames to keep wild animals at bay. At the far right, one of them smokes a pipe, looking into the quiet of the night. Closer to the bottom of the page, several of his companions have raised their heads and reach for their bows and arrows. They are calling out to the seated watchman to the right, whose back is turned to a potential threat. They have spotted a leopard marking time above their circle, standing on top of a hill a leap or two away from the group. A hunt threatens to break the night's quiet, and it is unclear who will be the predator and who the prey.

The vignette makes peril look quite debonair in the guise of the almost-smiling, elegantly posed leopard. Its presence makes narrative sense in this tableau of missionary travel through what the friars called the "deserts" of central Africa. The predator seems oblivious, though, of the gathered men; it looks away from them, into the distance. It stands, in the perspectival space of the painting, close to the viewers, fully available to their scrutiny. An object of their gaze, it also shares with them an elevated view of the camp. Turned at an angle and facing out of the painting, it stares far beyond the picture's frame, deep into the viewer's space. In that position, it dwells ambiguously within the tableau and outside of it. It forms a channel, acts as an intermediary, between the pictured friar and the future missionary observing the scene, who, like it,

CHAPTER 2

Practical Guides to the Mission

The Capuchin Central–African Corpus

becomes involved in the image as both observer and participant. Looking upon the scene from the same standpoint as the leopard, the aspiring missionary finds himself face to face with the veteran friar at the center of the page. The pictured friar, in turn, returns the aspirant's inquisitive gaze with sleepy yet knowing eyes, drawing him into a vicarious journey in preparation for a future voyage, demonstrating for his sake missionary techniques and modeling a life of adventure among wondrous flora and fauna and alongside an African entourage.

This page from Friar Bernardino d'Asti's practical guide to apostolic work in central Africa, the circa 1750 "Missione in prattica," mobilizes multiple genres, inspired by multiple sources, to achieve multiple effects. It combines an array of tools toward the goals of warning future missionaries against the hindering effects of their preconceptions about Kongo and Angola and instructing them in beneficial practices for the conduct of the mission. The horseback perspective of the composition gives the manuscript's readers an unobstructed view of the bivouac and its natural setting as well as an opportunity to marvel at the splendid leopard. The beautiful beast, pictured in its most characteristic posture and in its putative habitat, steps away from a missionary caravan, lends the vignette the appeal of the exotic, the gravitas of natural history, and the thrill of a travelogue replete with tales of dangers overcome. The creator of the composition mobilized stylistic elements and visual techniques derived from this full range of genres, and mixed and merged them into an image type of its own, characteristic of the Capuchin central-African corpus. Because of this visual eclecticism, the group of images the friars created in Kongo and Angola has long remained elusive to analysis and in interpretative limbo. Scholars have known and used some of the compositions for decades but have mostly considered them as idiosyncratic and difficult to interpret.[1] In 2005–6, in the course of archival research for my doctoral dissertation, I uncovered a set of sixty-seven images, then mostly unknown and completely unpublished, that I called the Parma Watercolors.[2] Upon studying them in person, I understood that they formed the central opus among the central-African capuchin images, which emerged from this new perspective as a

coherent group. Between roughly 1650 and 1750, several friars active in the region put pen and brush to paper to create vivid, multivalent visual and textual vignettes that they hoped would disabuse their followers of their preconceptions about Africa and Africans and instruct them about attitudes and practices beneficial to what they discovered was a unique missionary field. This chapter outlines the contours of this corpus and identifies the multiple visual sources that inspired its form. It locates it within the broader network of images and writings about Kongo and Angola in the seventeenth and eighteenth centuries, as well as within the larger catalogue of manuscript instructions friars penned upon their return from central Africa to instruct novices. I argue in the following pages that in their approaches to the region and the images they composed, the Capuchins drew from the visual and cultural templates they had acquired in Italy to create a corpus of images that formed a genre of its own.

Images of Central Africa in the Seventeenth and Eighteenth Centuries

It is customary to preface studies of early modern central Africa with a celebratory note about the exceptionally large archive of historical texts penned by Africans and Europeans that document the region between the sixteenth and eighteenth centuries. In addition to this wealth of written documentation, an equally rich corpus of visual evidence has been produced in and about Kongo and Angola as a result of the interactions between Europeans and central Africans in the same period.[3] Artists from the region created objects and images that reflected their interactions with Europeans and the once-novel but soon-domesticated visual and material culture the overseas foreigners brought to African shores. Parietal art dated to the early modern period, for example, depicts musket-bearing and pipe-smoking figures and outlines the silhouettes of ships in elaborate, if only partially deciphered, commentaries on the arrival of men, materials, and practices from across the sea.[4] Central-African artists also created Christian paraphernalia, nimbly appropriating and recasting imported Catholic iconography, including some inspired by the very image of the garbed Capuchins.[5] Visual elaborations emerged in the same environment using predominantly European media and styles, but crafted in and by the encounter between central Africans and Europeans.

The earliest extant representations of central African imagery of this kind are the prints published in 1591 in Filippo Pigafetta's edition of the accounts of Duarte Lopes, a Portuguese traveler turned ambassador of the king of Kongo to Rome.[6] The Flemish-German family of engravers, editors, and publishers Theodor, Johann Theodor, and Johann Israel de Bry soon reprinted Pigafetta's text and vignettes along with supplementary illustrations of their own invention in German and Latin editions, ensuring their wide circulation.[7] Further images of the region appeared in European circles only in the middle of the seventeenth century, after a hiatus of about fifty years. They multiplied then, in the wake of the Capuchin mission, to which we owe nearly all European-style visual documents concerning Kongo and Angola before the nineteenth century.

A notable exception is the "Historia general das guerras Angolanas," a three-volume illustrated manuscript dated 1680–81 that António de Oliveira de Cadornega, a Portuguese soldier, wrote during his time in Luanda. He chronicled in volumes 1 and 2 the first century of the history of the Portuguese *conquista* and composed in the third tome a geographic and ethnographic description of Angola.[8] Of the original manuscript, volume 1 is illustrated with only one illuminated frontispiece, and volume 3 contains seventeen images. The portion of the second original volume that remains intact does not have illustrations.[9] An eighteenth-century copy of the opus, now in Paris, indicates that volume 2 once had an illuminated frontispiece and two other vignettes.[10] Cadornega had planned and in 1688 apparently started the composition of a fourth volume, the "História de Angola, a História de todas as cousas que sucederam em Angola no tempo dos governadores que governaram depois da guerra até D. João de Lencastro." He may have finished it before his death in 1690, but it has not been located yet or is no longer extant.[11] A faithful copy of the first three volumes, including their illustrations, is in Paris's National Library.[12] The full manuscript reached the printing press only in 1940, in an edition by José Matias Delgado under the auspices of Portugal's Agência-Geral das Colónias.[13]

The visual program of the "Historia general" includes pictorial frontispieces showing a range of central-African rulers in ceremonial dress, each opening a section of the narrative (fig. 20). The third tome, describing the cultural and natural environment of Angola, contains illustrations of animals, rituals, and ceremonies inserted in the body of the text. Tome 2 once contained an illuminated front page and two scenes of military activities, absent from the fragmentary original volume but present in the second tome of the Paris copy. In his frontispieces, Cadornega placed the great men and women of the region in architectural frames inspired by the de Brys' opening pages

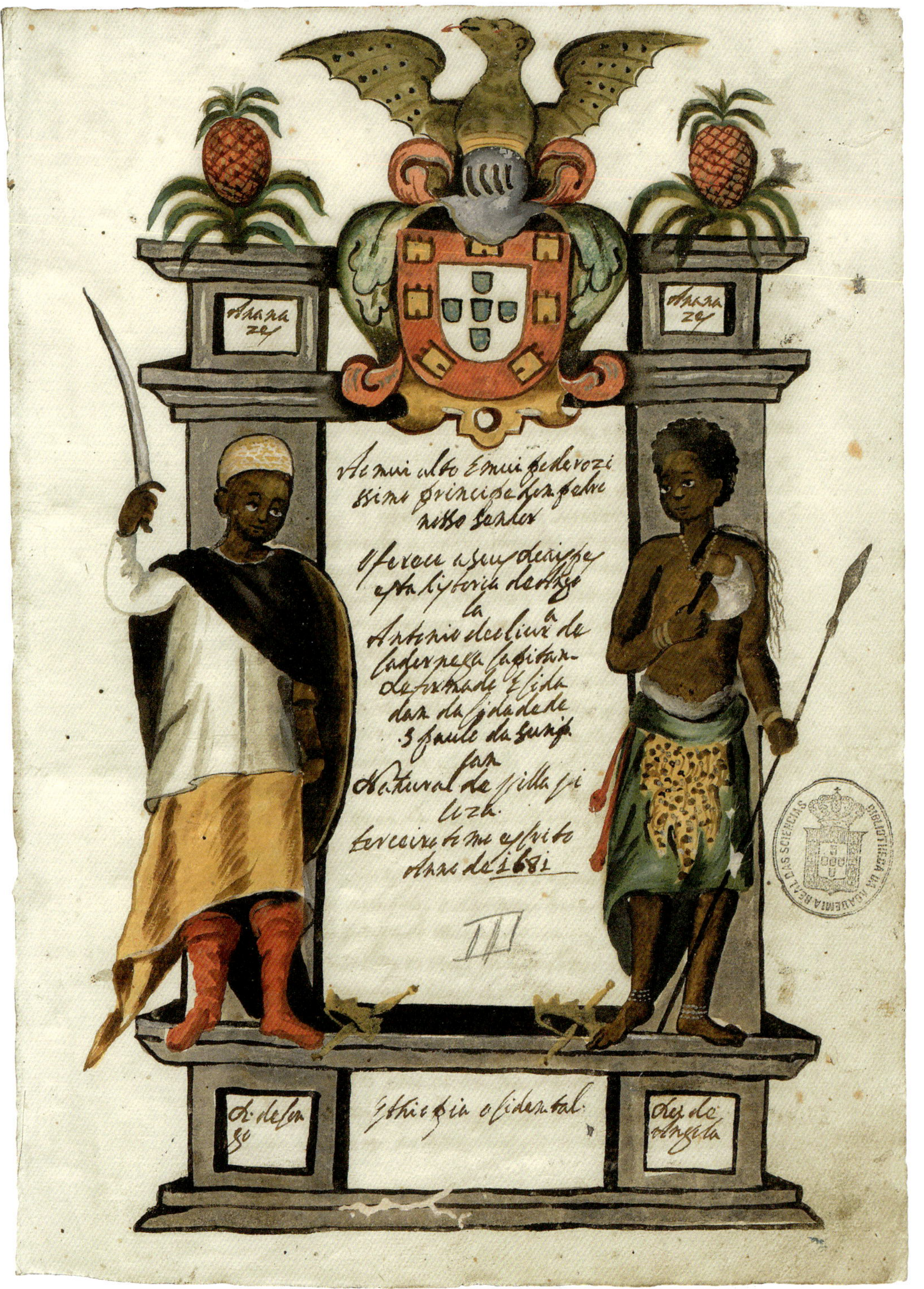

Figure 20

António de Oliveira de Cadornega, *King of Kongo and King of Angola*, ca. 1680. Watercolor and ink on paper, 30 × 20.5 cm. Frontispiece to volume 1 of Academy of Sciences, Lisbon, Manuscrito Vermelho 77. Photo courtesy of the Academy of Sciences, Lisbon.

Figure 21 (opposite)

Theodor de Bry, title page from Duarte Lopes and Filippo Pigafetta, *Regnum Congo, hoc est vera descriptio regni Africani* (Frankfurt am Main: Wolfgang Richter, 1598). Engraving, 27.5 × 18.8 cm (plate mark). General Collection, Beinecke Rare Book and Manuscript Library, Yale University, Taylor 193 1–2. Photo courtesy of the Beinecke Rare Book and Manuscript Library.

for their best-selling volumes of travel literature. They resemble in particular the template used for the 1597 German and 1598 Latin editions the de Brys produced of Duarte Lopes's account of his stay in the Kongo (fig. 21).[14] In both Cadornega and de Bry, the king of Kongo to the left wears a mix of local and foreign regalia that mark his status as a central-African Christian monarch. He faces, across the written title, a figure whose dress and attributes sharply contrast with his cosmopolitan flair. Feathers, animal pelts, and bow and arrows or a lance sketch the portrait of a central-African ruler of another type. In de Bry, that figure stands for Kongo rulers before the conversion or perhaps for neighboring heathen leaders. Cadornega explicitly labels the man on the right of his image "king of Angola," a phrase referring to the term *ngola*, the title held by the ruler of the Ndongo Kingdom.[15] The similarities between Cadornega's and de Bry's compositions are significant because, as discussed at greater length below, they provide one of an array of clues that volumes by the de Bry family, including their edition of Lopes/Pigafetta, were in Luanda in the 1670s, where Cadornega and the Capuchins could consult them.

Cadornega's vignettes demonstrate their author's careful observation and rendering of Angola's visual environment and offer an invaluable point of comparison for Capuchin images. The Portuguese soldier lived in Luanda at the time of the beginnings of the Capuchin mission, and he interacted with the friars and discussed with them their shared interest in capturing central Africa in words and images. He mentions several Capuchins by name as sources for his "Historia," reporting his conversations with friars such as Giovanni Antonio Cavazzi and Antonio Romano.[16] More generally, he held a high opinion

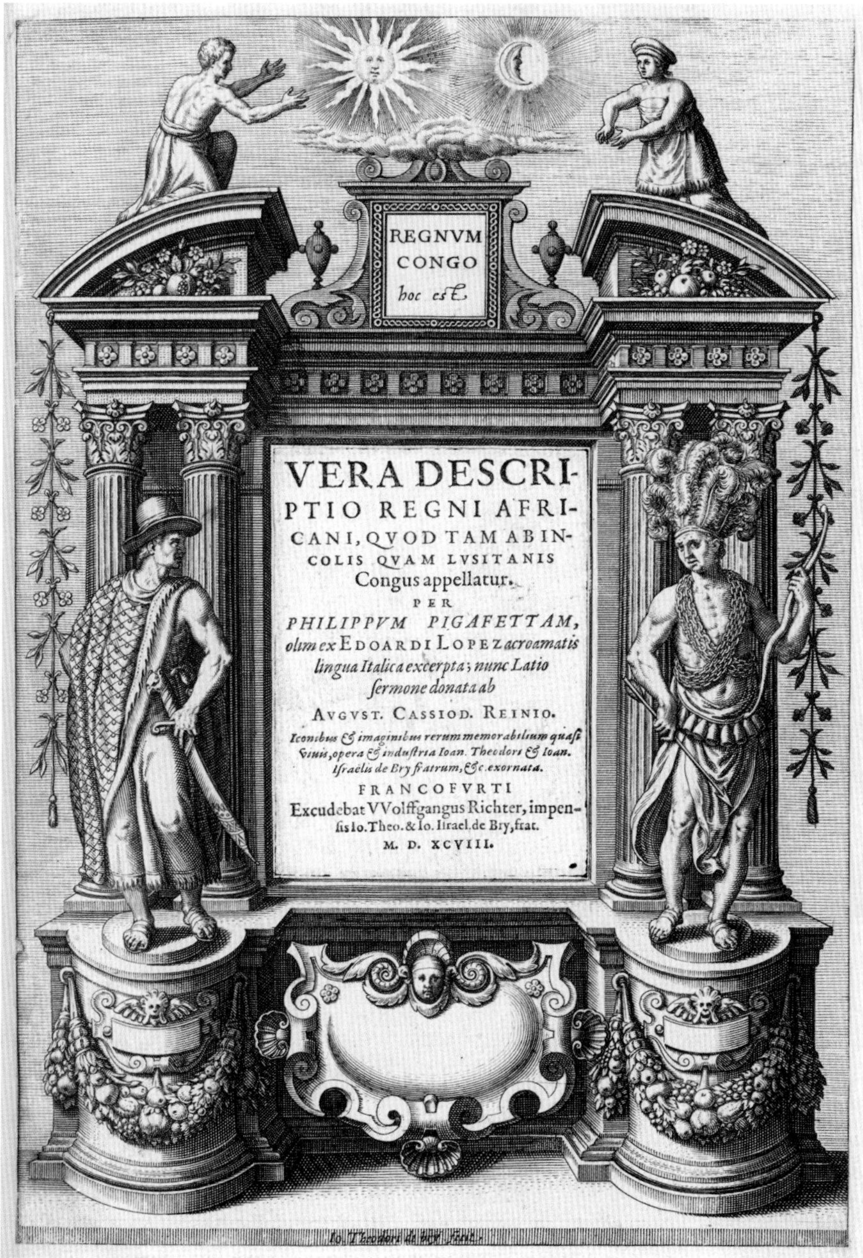

of the Italian friars, whom he called in his writings learned, charitable, and pious.[17]

It is unclear how closely the military man and the friars collaborated in their writing and painting, but Cadornega's images are great complements to and points of comparisons for the Capuchin visual accounts, particularly the Parma Watercolors. Both sets of images cover some of the same material, such as big cats, hippopotamuses, and wine tapping, which they present in similar compositions. They also address rituals involving dance and various modes of oath taking. Angolan clothing and implements shown in the Parma Watercolors and Cadornega also echo each other in many points. The lion hunter in the Capuchin corpus (fig. 22 / plate 35), for instance, wears the same spotted animal pelt tied with red bark ribbons as Cadornega's snake hunter (fig. 23). In both vignettes a fearless, muscular man approaches the dangerous beast from the left, ready to strike it with its weapon. In another example, elite men in the Parma Watercolor 70 (fig. 24 / plate 45) show the same pelts, hair adornments, and red ribbons made of bark tied around the upper arm as the leader Kafuxi of Kisama on the right side of Cadornega's illuminated frontispiece in figure 25.[18] Images in both works also share an intuitive, unsophisticated style that presents lively, detailed scenes and figures in formally simple compositions. Nevertheless, the "Historia general" differs from the Capuchin works in the scope and purpose of its illustration program. In contrast to the dozens of vignettes the Capuchins produced, the Portuguese chronicler included only a small number of images in his lengthy narrative. The paintings were illustrations for his text and did not, like the Capuchin watercolors, form a project of their own.

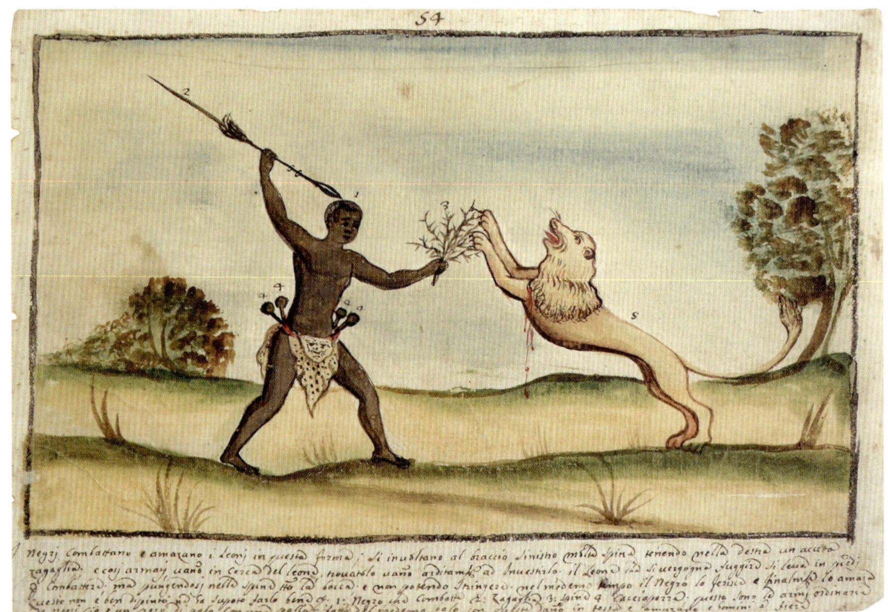

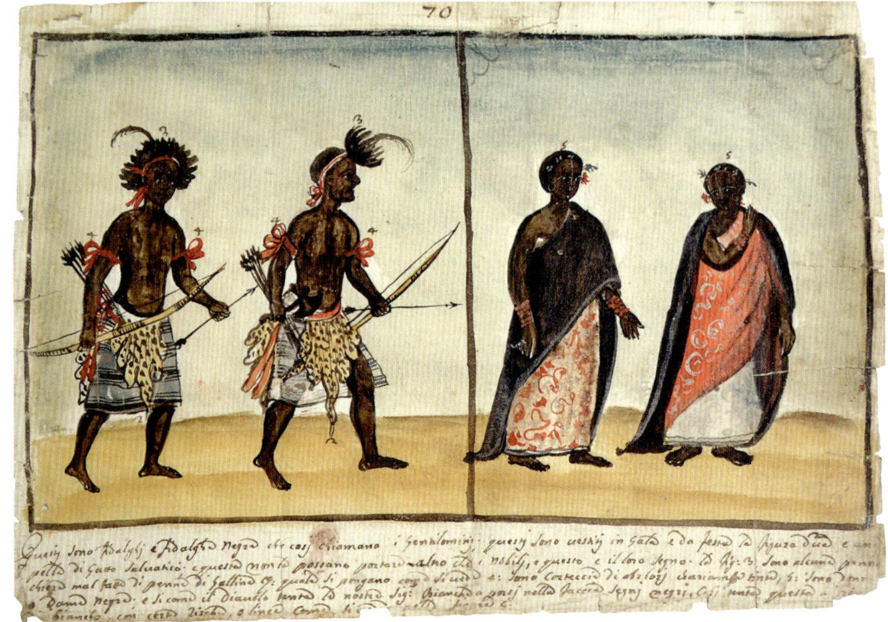

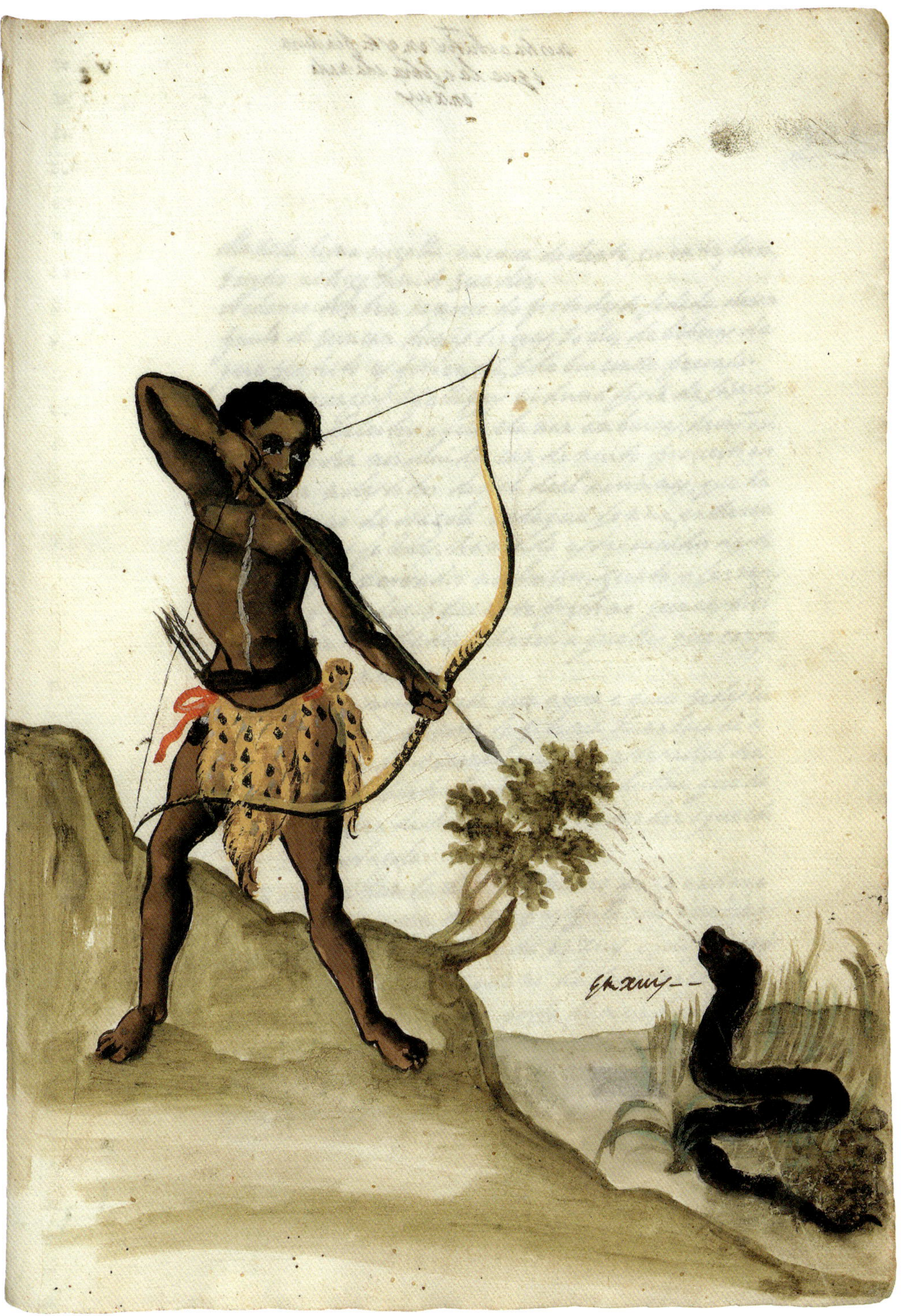

clockwise from top left

Figure 22

Unknown Capuchin artist, "The blacks fight and kill lions in this manner," late seventeenth century. Watercolor on paper, 34 × 24 cm. Parma Watercolors, Virgili Collection, fol. 54. Photo: author.

Figure 23

António de Oliveira de Cadornega, *Snake Hunter*, ca. 1680. Watercolor on paper, 30 × 20.5 cm (manuscript page). Academy of Sciences, Lisbon, Manuscrito Vermelho 78, vol. 3, between pp. 320 and 321. Photo courtesy of the Academy of Sciences, Lisbon.

Figure 24

Unknown Capuchin artist, "Black male and female aristocrats," late seventeenth century, detail. Watercolor on paper, 34 × 24 cm. Parma Watercolors, Virgili Collection, fol. 70. Photo: author.

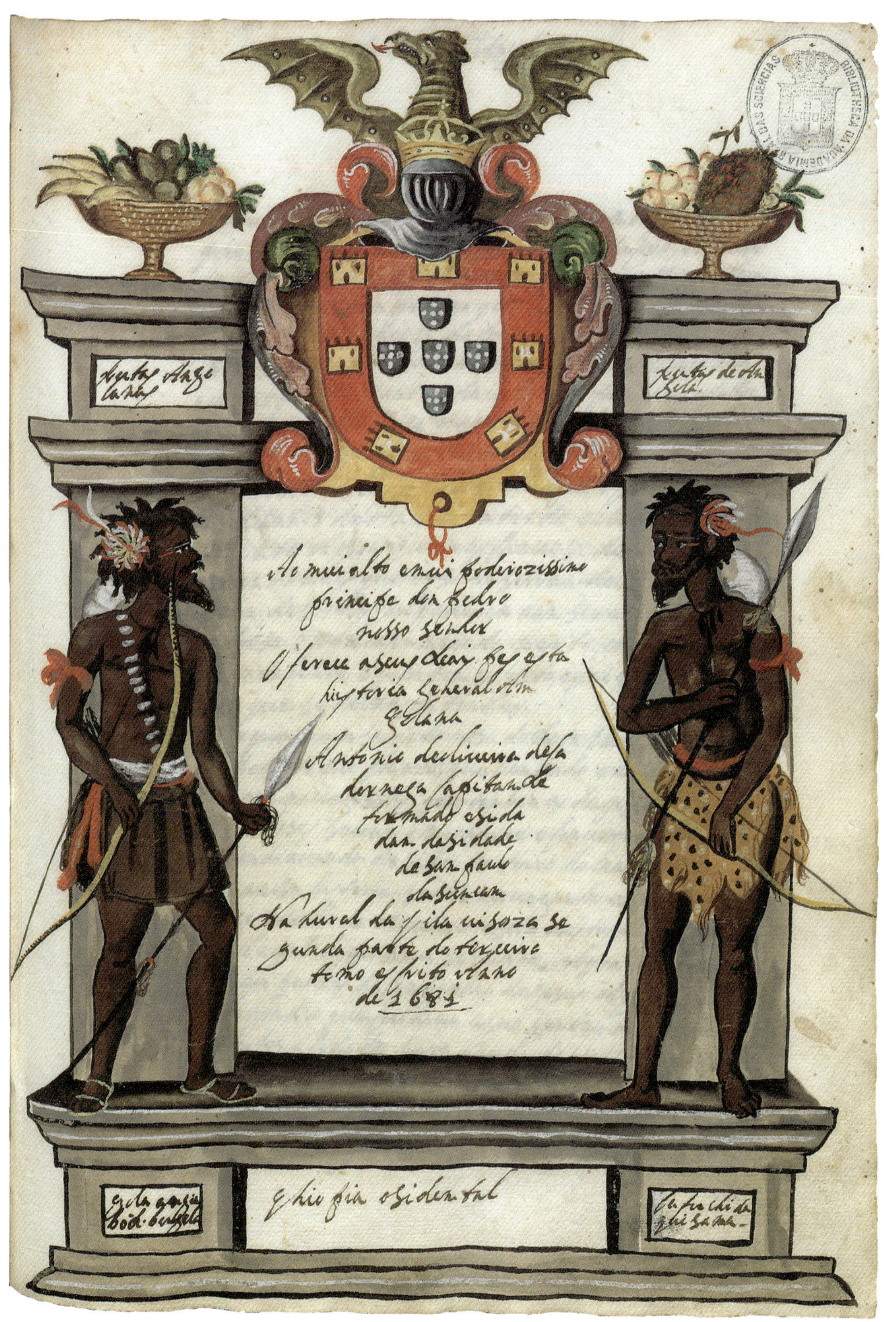

Figure 25

António de Oliveira de Cadornega, *Ruler of Benguela and Ruler of Kisama*, ca. 1681. Watercolor on paper, 30 × 20.5 cm (manuscript page). Academy of Sciences, Lisbon, Manuscrito Vermelho 77, vol. 3, between pp. 98 and 99. Photo courtesy of the Academy of Sciences, Lisbon.

The Capuchin Central-African Corpus

The vast majority of European images from and about central Africa in the seventeenth and eighteenth centuries were the work of Capuchin missionaries. Cavazzi, the author of the *Istorica descrizione*, created numerous watercolors during his stay in Kongo and Angola. The complex, three-codex "Missione Evangelica al Regno del Congo," or Araldi manuscript, which he composed between 1665 and 1668, includes thirty-three bold images retelling a historical narrative of Mdundu-speaking lands in today's Angola (table 1). Historian Giuseppe Pistoni brought the codex to scholarly attention in 1969; it had belonged to the Capuchin provincial archives in Bologna—Cavazzi's home province—until the end of the nineteenth century, when, upon the dissolution of the religious orders in Italy, it was transferred to Michaelangelo Araldi da Modena's family library. Since 2019 it has been in Modena's Biblioteca Estense.[19] Ezio Bassani published most of the images from the manuscript in 1987.[20] Some of them appeared as prints in the *Istorica descrizione* published in 1687 (see table 2).

The Araldi manuscript is an important work, but it is somewhat atypical of the Capuchin central-African corpus. Another odd image, a plan of the bishopric of the capital of the Kongo appended to a 1711 letter by Eustachio da Ravenna, operated as a planning document for the reorganization of the cathedral complex.[21] Three other sets of images of consistent style and format form the core of the strongly shaped genre the friars created over a century and a half to showcase their endeavors in Kongo and Angola and educate future missionaries about their upcoming work in central Africa. I found the earliest, a single-page ink-on-paper drawing measuring seventy-three by forty centimeters and likely dating to the 1650s, all but forgotten in the Museo Francescano in Rome (plate 1). The order's early twentieth-century historian Édouard d'Alençon recorded its presence in 1914 in what was then the Capuchin Missions Museum. His notice, which was the only published account of the image until my own mention of it in print in 2011, explained the enigmatic lack of provenance of the piece, which emerged around 1900 at an antiquary's shop in Rome.[22] The drawing has remained since then in its Capuchin depository and has received little attention. Once folded, likely to be transported, perhaps from Africa to Europe, the tall rectangular drawing presents rows of simple black ink figures interspersed with small paragraphs. The images came to the page first and remained the most important part of the composition. The writer of the text merely fit his remarks, awkwardly at times, around the drawings. A border of stamped, unevenly spaced and sometimes overlapping acanthus leaves frames both image and text. No notations appear on the back of the sheet of paper.

The large-format drawing formed an ordered compendium presenting comprehensive information on the central-African missionary environment. From top to bottom and left to right, the image-maker sketched a portrait of King Garcia II of Kongo at his court, scenes of social life, plants arranged by type and origin, the region's different polities, animals, beings of ambiguous nature, and finally missionary prowess. Short texts enriched the visuals with further information and advice. At the bottom right, the death of Friar Joris van Gheel, martyred "in odium Fidei" in 1652 by club-wielding heathens, anchored the page (fig. 26).

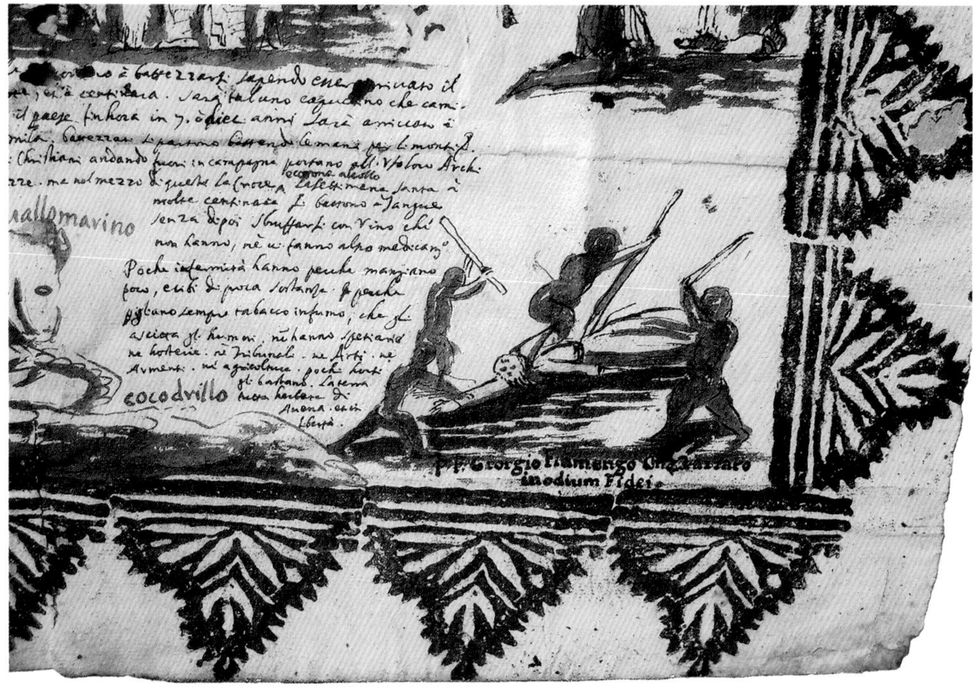

Figure 26

Unknown Capuchin artist, *Martyrdom of Joris van Gheel*, ca. 1652–63. Ink on paper, 73 × 40 cm (full panel). Detail from *Of the People, Victuals, Customs, Animals, and Fruits of the Kingdoms of Africa*, Franciscan Museum of the Capuchin Historical Institute, Rome, MF 1370. Photo: author.

The Flemish priest, who had arrived in Kongo in June 1651, succumbed to the wrath of members of an initiatory society whose ceremonies he disrupted in December 1652. The artist pictured the violent death in an expressive, dramatic scene. The friar, lying flat on the ground on his stomach, weakly lifts his face up as a muscular naked figure rendered in dark-brown wash drags him by one arm. The pointed hood of his habit still sticks up as his almost senseless body relents under the furious blows of three more dark-skinned figures. The rendering of this violent death offered the intended viewers of the drawing an enticing prospect of martyrdom and its celestial rewards. Franciscans as well as Jesuits involved in extra-European missions had produced many such images of persecution since the sixteenth century, in a period that saw a revival of the cult of martyrs.[23] In the context of this explicitly didactic compendium, the scene also functioned as a cautionary tale, depicting the risks friars lacking training or not paying heed to "salutary advice" incurred.[24]

The Parma Watercolors, discussed at length below, are chronologically the second group of images key to the Capuchin corpus. Bernardino d'Asti composed the third set a century after the Museo Francescano drawing, around 1750. His "Missione in prattica: Padri cappuccini ne' Regni di Congo, Angola, et adiacenti" offered to Italian novices a polished practical guide to apostolic work in central Africa. The pages of the codex now mounted in an album in the Turin Civic Library constitute the best known of the three iterations of Friar Bernardino's handbook.[25] They consist of an allegorical frontispiece, nineteen full-page images, each glossed with five or six written lines, and eight folios of text and a title page.[26] Two other versions of the work now belong to the Vatican Library and the Biblioteca Nacional in Lisbon.[27] Of the three, the Turin manuscript contains the largest number of images and relies the most on the visual as mode of communication for its contents. Its text addresses the reader directly, calling on "you my most estimated Reader," "my . . . brother in Religion," inviting an intimate and matter-of-fact engagement with its topic: the conduct of the mission. It is very much a practical manual, offering detail-rich views and dense admonitions "to read and observe" in a synthesized version of the Vatican's longer and more formal volume.[28]

Written in a hand similar to that of the Turin manual, the Vatican codex is primarily a text, introduced with a dedicatory image of the Virgin and a preface addressing readers while assuaging potential censors. It measures 195 × 145 mm, counts 134 pages, and, beyond the image of its frontispiece, has six plates arranged two to a page on separate folios bound in two different places in the volume, close to the written passages they illustrate; all seven images also appear in the Turin manuscript in closely related versions (plates 69–72). The clean Vatican text, complete with catchwords at the bottom of the pages, looks ready for use and perhaps publication.

The Lisbon codex, in turn, is an exact copy of the Vatican version, but in a different hand and without illustrations. It measures twenty-three centimeters in height and contains eighty-nine folios numbered in pencil. The copyist omitted the table of contents of the source volume but faithfully copied the rest, including the page numbers of cross-references, though they do not match the different arrangement of text on the pages of his volume, which he left, what is more, unnumbered.[29] Blank sheets between what would be folios 1 and 2, 33 and 34, and 72 and 73 left room for copies of the images from the Vatican codex, although the images never came to be. As indicated on its title page, the volume came from the library of the former Italian Capuchin house in Lisbon, where missionaries in transit to central Africa could consult it while waiting for the authorization to embark to Luanda directly or via Brazil, on one of the official ships linking Portugal to its African *conquista*.[30]

The text and images of the three versions clearly demonstrate that they constitute a single oeuvre. The Turin manuscript is the first version, later reworked in a fuller text in the Vatican exemplar, probably with a view to publication, with images presented as plates outside of the text. The Lisbon codex is a direct copy of the Vatican version.

Various authors have convincingly attributed the unsigned manuscripts to Bernardino d'Asti. My own research has confirmed this attribution with a comparison of the Vatican manuscript text to similar phrasings in a relation Friar Bernardino gave to the Propaganda Fide.[31]

The extant sixty-seven images of the Parma Watercolors, chronologically the second in the group of early modern Capuchin image sets, follow a template similar to that of the Museo Francescano drawing, although the current state of the manuscript does not include explicit information on its intended purpose. The folios, measuring about twenty-four by thirty-four centimeters, have stitch marks on the left side from a prior binding. No date or title appears on any of the pages, and no signatures identify the friars involved in their making. Initials that I have not been able to decipher, coupled with numbers, label each page on the recto or verso. Sometime after their painting but before the addition of the initials, all but two watercolors (plates 5, 17) received a thick black frame around the main painted part, and twenty of them a rectangular box at the bottom of the frame, inviting a caption. Text was then added to the bottom of each page, but rarely remained within the perimeter of the box and often even ran to the verso.[32] The same hand and ink that fashioned the text contributed page numbers at the top of each sheet and small digits within the paintings, referring readers to a legend in the text, although the author sometimes omitted to gloss the objects his digits labeled. In addition to the main glosses, the folios of the Parma Watercolors count two other types of inscriptions. First, the coupling of initials with numbers ranging from 51 to 188 suggests an alternative sequence for the images or a set of cross-references. The numbering yields an arrangement that does not follow a thematic scheme similar to the one produced by the numbering at the top. Second, short Portuguese captions in dark ink comment briefly on the subject matter of thirteen of the pages.[33]

While both images and text confidently describe the central-African environment from firsthand experience, different concerns in and even outright disagreement between written and visual information indicate that they do not come from a single hand. The text's writer at times has much to say about a figure, while remaining at a loss for words in front of others—for instance, in the glosses regarding aquatic animals (plates 7–10). In most cases, however, he easily recognizes the plants, animals, and practices illustrated. He fluently contributes information complementary to the images but also eagerly corrects what he perceives as errors or imprecisions in the paintings. The first-person, direct commentary presents the writer as someone working from central Africa and with robust experience of the region.

Visual syntax offers similar indication of the image-maker's familiarity with the subject matter of his images; direct knowledge of or access to very reliable sources would be essential to the production of vignettes presenting such a range of flora, fauna, and social situations. Animals, plants, and artifacts appear in great detail and, generally, accuracy, as demonstrated, for example, in the depiction of a ripe banana, with its characteristic skin of a dark yellow marbled with brown patches on folios 35 and 36, or the musical instruments on folios 72 and 73.[34] The textual and pictorial description of other little-known tropical fruit trees, such as the purple mombin (*Spondias purpurea*) on folio 39, confirms the keen eye and knowledge of painter and

writer alike.[35] The purple (or red) mombin is a small fruit of reddish or, more rarely, purple or yellow color originally from Mesoamerica, whose tree, the author describes accurately, "makes its fruits like our prunes but with a very large pit." The image presents the small tree with its characteristic reddish round fruits and small oval leaves. On occasion, text and image disagree. The writer critiques the image in plate 65, for instance, regretting that an adze was drawn instead of an axe. In vignette 15, on the other hand, the text identifies the depicted animal as a flying fish, whereas the painting shows a billfish (a case discussed further below).

It remains unclear who drew the images and who composed the text of the Parma Watercolors, although the writer was likely from Tuscany, as he fondly writes of "our Arno," a landmark of the region, and uses regionalisms in his prose. One of his Tuscan idioms on the same page, "costà," also indicates that the text and the images that preceded it were composed in Africa and destined to an intended reader in Italy. The text on folio 22 reads, "These whale bones that go *there where you are* [*costà*], which are used to make the corsets of the ladies, are [from?] the throats of the whales."[36] *Costà* is a locative adverb that refers to the location of the person whom the speaker or writer is addressing. In this example, the writer places himself at a distance from his reader, who is in Europe, where the ladies use whalebone in their corsets.[37] This places the Parma Watercolors' creation on another continent, the "here [*quà*]" mentioned throughout the text as Kongo and Angola.

Although no formal inscription dates the Parma Watercolors, clues point to the late 1660s and early 1670s as a key juncture in the history of the paintings. Folio 101 sets a firm *terminus post quem* by referring to Queen Njinga of Matamba. Both text and image describe an actual event from 1648 in which two missionaries, Buenaventura de Corella and Francisco de Veas, fell prisoners to the queen, who, against all expectations, showed them mercy and soon released them (fig. 27 / plate 66).[38] The vignette's text elaborates freely and confidently on the event. Njinga, it adds, first "ordered them to be executed" but, "by divine intervention, . . . in a sudden change, received them with benevolence and got baptized, and died a true Christian, marvelous stroke of the divine providence."[39] She had, in fact, been baptized in 1622, without, however, wholly renouncing her former religious beliefs and customs, and as far as Catholic clerics were concerned, she was an apostate.[40] "But," the text continues, "as soon as the queen died, faith failed in this kingdom, and today we are working to bring it back, but as of now, God our Lord has not yet permitted it." Queen Njinga died in December of 1663, and her sister Dona Barbara succeeded her, ruling until 1666. At her death, succession struggles erupted, and Christianity lost the brief support it had enjoyed in the last years of the formidable ruler.[41] The images were thus composed after the two friars' capture in 1648, whereas the assessment of the state of the mission places the redaction of the text at the earliest in the late 1660s,[42] and it might even postdate the 1687 *Istorica descrizione* (as I discuss in my consideration of the *pesce-volatore*, below).

The vignette also notably illustrates another key episode in Njinga lore, picturing her seated on top of a servant on all fours as she famously did in 1622 in front of the Portuguese governor of Luanda, João Correia de Sousa, who had planned to belittle her during an official audience by not offering her

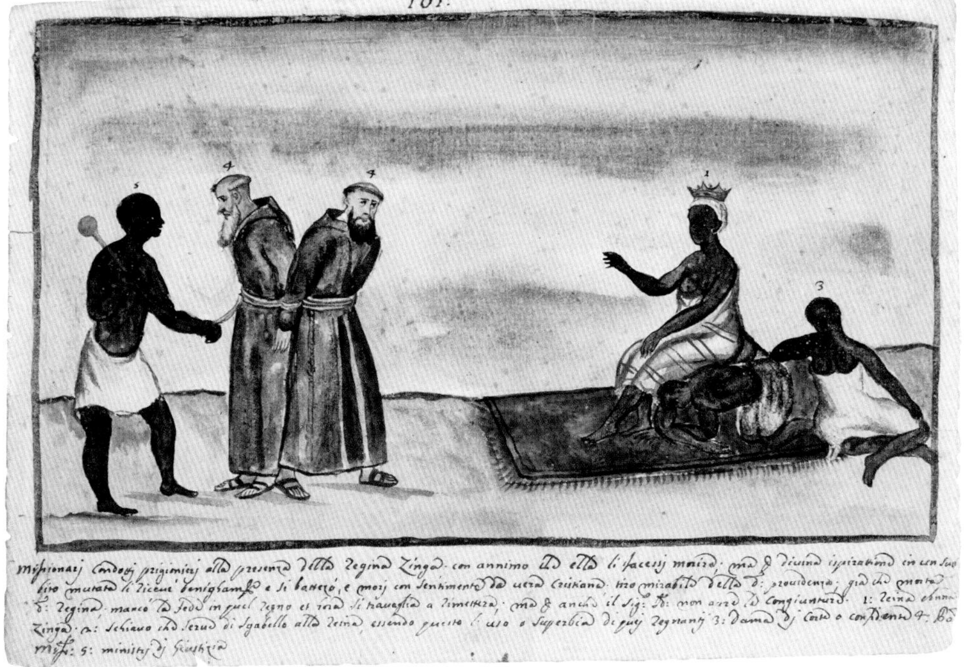

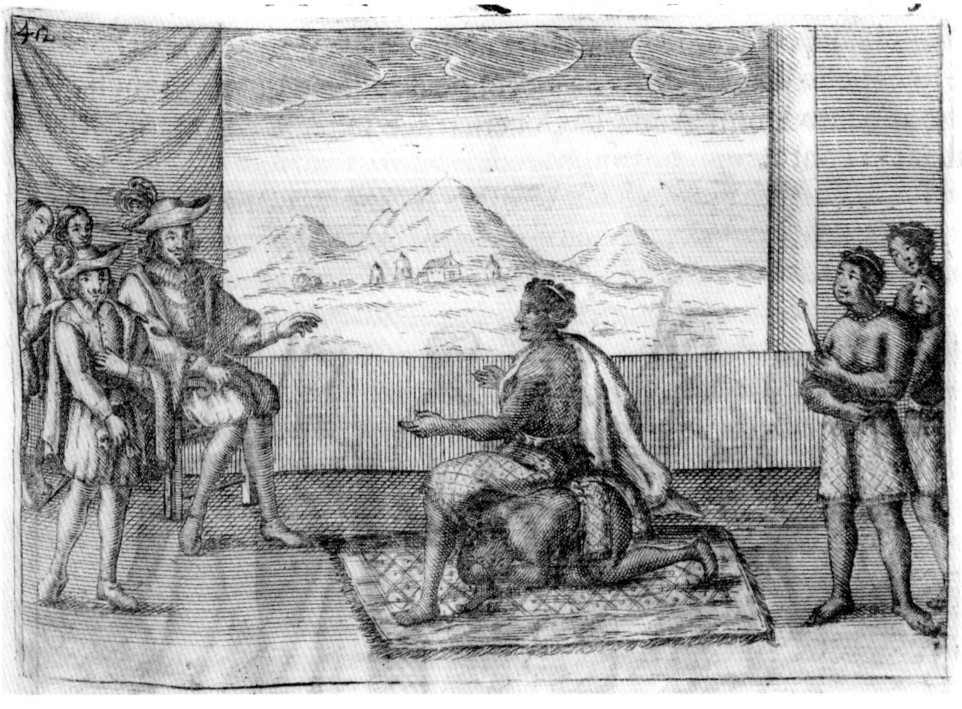

Figure 29 (opposite left)

After Serafino da Cortona, *Fish*, 1711. Ink on paper, 19 × 13 cm (manuscript page). From Filippo da Firenze, "Ragguagli del Congo" [1711]. Archivio provinciale dei Cappuccini, Florence, 81. Photo: author.

Figure 30 (opposite, top right)

Unknown Capuchin artist, "Flying Fish," late seventeenth century. Watercolor on paper, 34 × 24 cm. Parma Watercolors, Virgili Collection, fol. 15. Photo: author.

Figure 31 (opposite, bottom right)

Paolo da Lorena (attr.), *Fish*. Plate 13 from Giovanni Antonio Cavazzi and Fortunato Alamandini, *Istorica descrizione de' tre' regni Congo, Matamba, et Angola* (Bologna: Giacomo Monti, 1687), 53. Engraving, 10 × 14 cm (plate mark). Bibliothèque nationale de France, FOL-H-3133. Photo: author.

furniture on which to sit.[43] The living-chair episode, reported in the text of Cavazzi's mid-1660s "Missione Evangelica" manuscript, appeared as a print in the same author's 1687 *Istorica descrizione* (fig. 28).[44] The painter of the watercolor conflated the chair episode with the story of the friars' capture, in keeping with the Parma Watercolors' emphasis on the Capuchin mission rather than on the history of the region and of the queen, key subject matters in Cavazzi's volumes. The narrative and visual motif of the human seat is one of an array of links connecting the Parma Watercolors to Cavazzi, who, I suggest, used them or a closely related set of images in the composition of the prints for his *Istorica descrizione*.

As customary for an author of his era, Cavazzi drew from a range of sources in his writings and paintings and, when possible, sought the input of his colleagues.[45] He also encouraged others to put pen to paper. He inspired, for instance, Friar Girolamo da Montesarchio, who arrived in central Africa with the second Capuchin mission, in 1646, and remained in the region for two decades, until traveling back to Italy in Cavazzi's company for part of the trip, in 1668.[46] Friar Girolamo composed in the following year a manuscript chronicle of his experiences in Kongo and Angola, the "Viaggio al Gongho" [*sic*], now in the Capuchin Provincial Archive of Florence.[47] The date and circumstances of his travel alongside Cavazzi places him and his writings in the same circles from which the Parma Watercolors emerged. It is also noteworthy that he died in 1669 in Arezzo, where the Parma Watercolors would resurface in the twentieth century.

Another possible source or parallel for the unsigned manuscript as well as for Cavazzi's prints is Giacinto Brugiotti da Vetralla's "Infelicitá felice." The manuscript, penned in the Kongo, has not been seen in more than a century, but scholar Giuseppe Simonetti described it at enough length in 1907 to show its treatment of themes similar to those in the Parma Watercolors, such as plants, animals, and daily life.[48] Another friar, Michelangelo Guattini, also promised, although likely did not have time to compose during his short stay in central Africa, a "relation of the customs of these people and of the qualities of this country."[49] Neither of these sources, however, focused on missionary methods or dealt with Angola—rather than Kongo—as much as the Parma Watercolors and their texts.

The Parma Watercolors did not emerge from a single, discrete source. Capuchin images and writings about central Africa were complex creations, bringing together elements of multiple origins liberally and unabashedly. The Parma vignette 14, for example, also present in a print of the *Istorica descrizione*, derives from the "simple sketch" Friar Serafino da Cortona joined to a letter he wrote in Soyo on March 20, 1648, to the provincial of Tuscany. A 1711 copy of the letter and drawing provides the design, including the lettered captions about the length of the bill, "4 palms long," and the fish, "16 palms long," that appear in the printed volume's engraving (fig. 29).[50] Cavazzi or Alamandini in fact used Serafino da Cortona's written description of his encounter with the "picco" billfish for the comments on the animal in the *Istorica descrizione*. The Parma Watercolors' fish also bears close resemblance to Friar Serafino's billfish and its printed version (fig. 30 / plate 8). Thus, within the circle of Capuchin visual productions about central Africa, the Parma Watercolor painting has connections to the 1648 sketch either directly as a template or indirectly as an expression of a common set of visual solutions shared in the corpus. This common visual syntax echoes similar textual parallels. The Parma

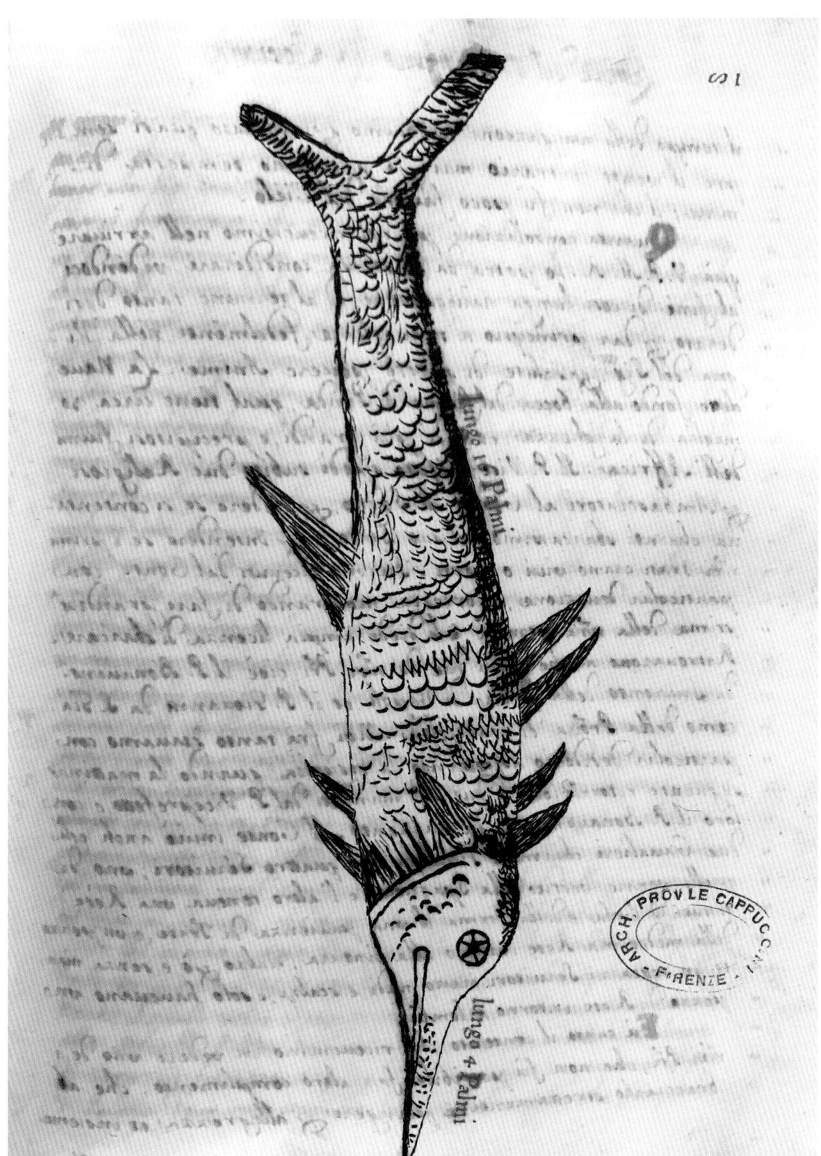

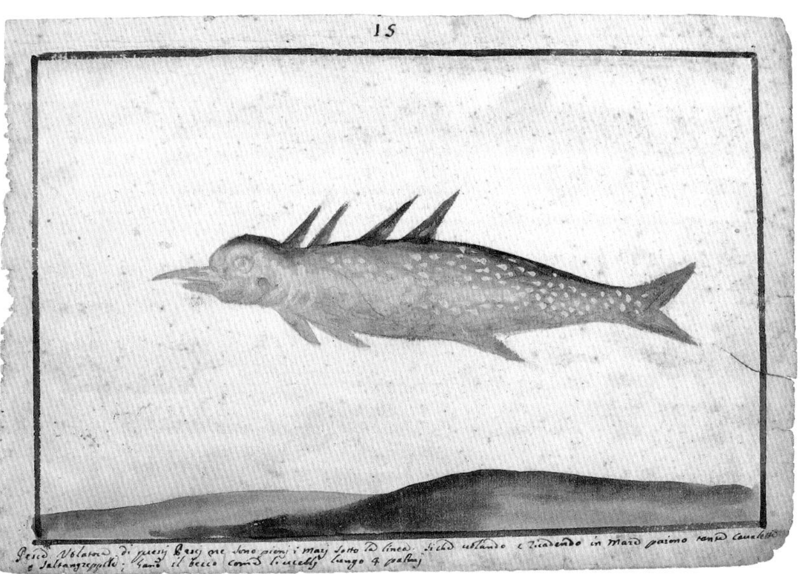

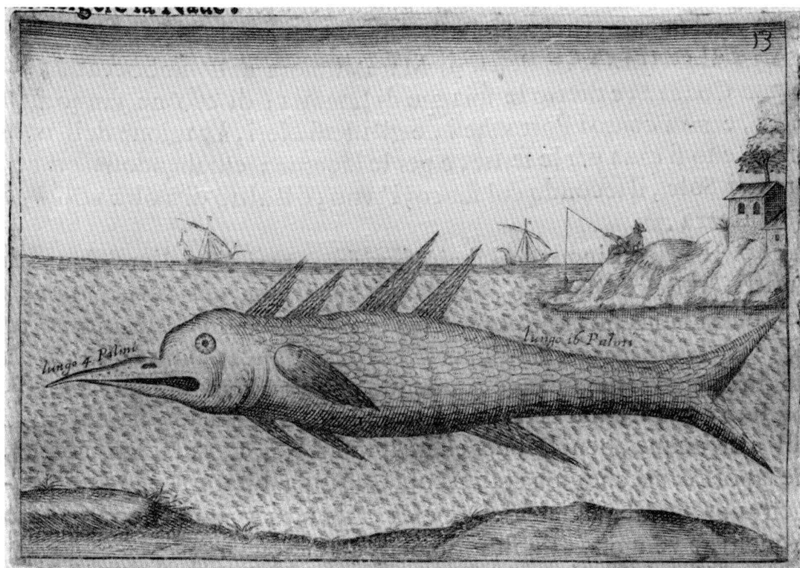

Watercolor text, for instance, identifies the animal as "pesce-volatore," or flying fish, a label derived from a misreading of the *Istorica descrizione*. The billfish print, which follows the text on the "Pico, ò PICCO," most of which is printed on a preceding page, appears near the top of its page in the 1687 book, directly above a paragraph starting with the phrase "Il Pesce VOLATORE," which looks like a title for the illustration (fig. 31). The Parma Watercolor text, by a different hand and posterior to the paintings, thus likely postdate the 1687 publication of the *Istorica descrizione*. The Capuchin central-African documents emerged from a network in which information and visual compositions fluidly circulated.

Like the Museo Francescano sheet (plate 1), the Parma Watercolors formed an ordered compendium about central Africa. The sixty-seven folios still extant are numbered from 2 to 104 and organized in thematic groupings of various length. A first set, about colonial Angola, shows the mores and customs of Portuguese and African Creoles (2 to 9). There follows a series on aquatic animals from crocodile to whale (12 to 22), then vignettes on architecture broadly conceived (23 to 27). Vegetables and fruits (29 to 36) lead to trees (37 to 46), then birds (47 to 53). Land animals (54 to 68) close the part on natural history. Vignettes 70 to 81 address mores and customs; 83 to 89 are concerned with superstitious practices. Missionary work occupies folios 90 to 101. A last section, represented by two vignettes, 102 and 104, depicts funerary practices.

Practical Guides as Genre

The dedication page of the Turin "Missione in prattica" outlines plainly the purpose of the Capuchin manuscripts and their images: "To the reader. The reason that induced me to represent and describe the organization of our missions in the Kingdoms of Congo and Angola and neighboring countries was that I observed that some new missionaries arriving in these missions, thinking that they were promoting in them major progress by reforming what until then had been practiced, did what should not be done in these kingdoms, and on the contrary caused more destruction than edification. I thus represented in this book the most essential

exercises of the mission, with a brief description underneath regarding what was depicted."[51] In the following pages, Bernardino accomplishes what he promises, depicting scenes of missionary life, from the layout of the Capuchin convent in the town of Soyo to the administration of the sacrament of Confession (plate 71), and modes of transportation and travel (figs. 19, 77, 93, plate 72). In both illustrated versions, a few lines of text under each image briefly describe the visual content. Some captions of the Vatican version cross-reference specific pages of the book (plates 107–8). Many other friars with experience of central Africa shared Bernardino's sentiment about newcomers' misunderstanding of Kongo and Angola and the need to remedy it with didactic material. They set quill and brush to paper to remedy the situation.

If the actual or planned illustrations of the three "Missione in prattica" volumes, the Museo Francescano ink-on-paper sheet, and the Parma Watercolors distinguish them, they nonetheless participated in a broader genre of practical guides in which Capuchin veterans of Kongo and Angola exposed in didactic terms the nature and challenges of apostolic work and the peculiarity of its practice in central Africa. This interest in relaying their experience and in formalizing advice on the proper conduct of what they deemed a particularly peculiar mission emerged in the very first years of the Capuchin's presence in central Africa. As early as the 1650s, Antonio de Teruel, one of the first friars of the order to work in the Kongo, wrote a "Manuale per la buona directione di quella gente" and a "Libro delli catechismi e modo d'aministrare i sacramenti." He asked the Propaganda Fide to publish both works to no avail.[52] In the same genre, Giovanni Belotti Romano (also known as da Romano) wrote in 1680 the "Avvertimenti

Salutevoli agli Apostolici Missionari, specialmente nei regni del Congo, Angola e circonvicini."[53] He explains at length, in a preface to the reader, the purpose of this practical guide, which he wrote in Bergamo upon his return from Africa, a year after finishing his more general opus, titled the "Giornate Apostoliche": "I judged [it] good (however, with advice and persuasion from our companions) to express in a small volume the present advice." If "Father missionaries" destined to central Africa studiously "ponder" those admonitions, he opines, they "will come out almost already perfected in this [apostolic] work, even before starting their laborious task, or at least enlightened in the matter, so that they will be fit to start right away with great profit for the Souls and growth of Our Christian Religion." He could himself have been so efficient, he finally laments, had he had someone to teach him.[54] Like Bernardino d'Asti half a century later, Belotti centers his concerns on the misplaced zeal of untrained novices, who were unable to grasp and accept the necessary idiosyncrasies of the central-African apostolate. In the preface for the "Giornate Apostoliche," he already notes his awareness that the methods he describes in the book could disconcert readers. For example, Italians might find particularly lenient some practices that in fact were necessary because, he explains, gentleness outdid rigor in attracting Africans.[55]

Outside Sources

To achieve their didactic goals, the friars drew from a range of sources in the creation of their images. Their mental catalogue, assembled during their formative years in Europe, broadly informed their compositions, but they also looked specifically to printed imagery as inspiration. The Capuchin library in Luanda was well stocked, and Bernardino d'Asti instructed new missionaries that it was not necessary for them to bring "books, because there is in our Luanda convent a good library."[56] Friars could also consult volumes in the city's Jesuit library, an important local resource before the Portuguese authorities put it on the market upon the dissolution of the order in 1767.[57] Although, to my knowledge, no catalogues of these collections exist, the visual production in early modern central Africa sketches a summary list of available sources. The zebra in the Parma Watercolors, for instance, derived its stripes from an illustration in Lopes and Pigafetta's *Relatione del reame di Congo* or one of its later editions by Theodor de Bry (fig. 32 / plate 39, figs. 33, 34). De Bry's frontispieces inspired Portuguese author Cadornega in the composition of his own illuminations.[58] De Bry's America series counted among the sources available to Capuchins and others in seventeenth-century Kongo and Angola. Imagery from de Bry's edition of Harriot's *Briefe and true report,* the first volume of his America series, has striking parallels with some of the Parma Watercolors. This edition, available in English, Latin, and German, contained twenty-eight copper engravings, created for the most part after eyewitness paintings by John White during his stay in the short-lived colony of Roanoke, in today's coastal North Carolina.[59] The central figure of the "Dance called *maquina mafuete*" in the Parma Watercolors is a close cognate to the figure of "The Coniuerer" in de Bry (fig. 35 / plate 48, fig. 36). The central African and the American both appear in an animated posture, left arm lifted above the head, right arm bent behind. In dramatic contrapposto, their torsos face forward, while their legs and hips point to the right, in a dynamic attitude of energetic movement. Bent left legs kicked high behind them render their

Images on a Mission in Early Modern Kongo and Angola

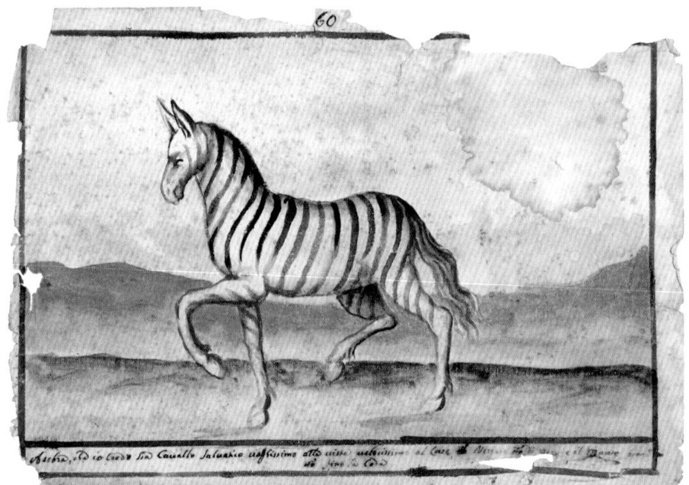

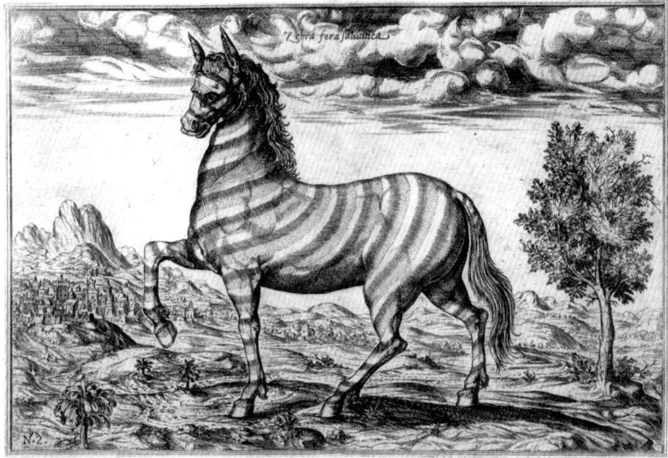

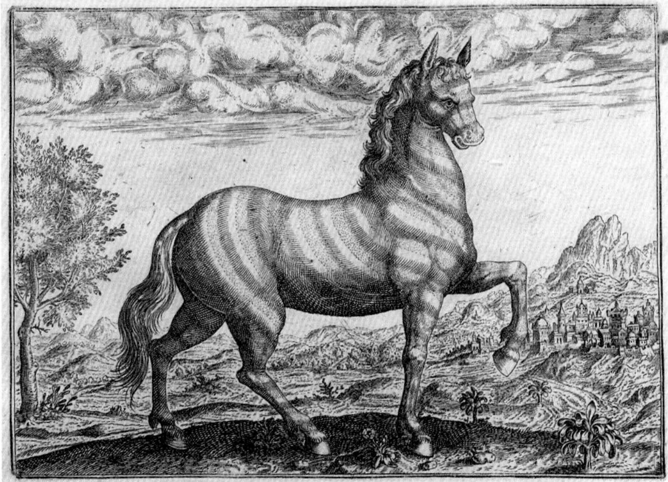

Figure 32

Unknown Capuchin artist, "Zebra," late seventeenth century. Watercolor on paper, 34 × 24 cm. Parma Watercolors, Virgili Collection, fol. 60. Photo: author.

Figure 33

Natale Bonifacio (attr.), *Zebra, savage Beast*. Etching, 20.3 × 29.8 cm (plate mark) (double page in quarto). Plate 2 from Duarte Lopes and Filippo Pigafetta, *Relatione del reame di Congo* (Rome: Appresso Bartolomeo Grassi, 1591), between pp. 30 and 31. National Library of Portugal, Lisbon, RES. 495 P. Photo courtesy of the National Library of Portugal.

Figure 34

Theodor de Bry, *Zebra*. Engraving and etching, 13.3 × 18.1 cm (plate mark). From Duarte Lopes and Filippo Pigafetta, *Regnum Congo, hoc est vera descriptio regni Africani* (Frankfurt: Wolfgang Richter, 1598), plate 9. National Library of Portugal, Lisbon, RES 500 A. Photo courtesy of the National Library of Portugal.

Figure 35 (opposite top)

Unknown Capuchin artist, "Dance called *maquina mafuete*," late seventeenth century. Watercolor on paper, 34 × 24 cm. Parma Watercolors, Virgili Collection, fol. 73. Photo: author.

Figure 36 (opposite bottom)

Gijsbert van Veen, "The Coniuerer." Engraving, 15.4 × 21.5 cm (plate mark). Plate xi from Thomas Harriot, *A briefe and true report of the new found land of Virginia* (Frankfurt am Main: Typis Ioannis Wecheli, sumtibus vero Theodori de Bry, 1590). General Collection, Beinecke Rare Book and Manuscript Library, Yale University, Taylor 194. Photo courtesy of the Beinecke Rare Book and Manuscript Library.

fast pace. The two images are strikingly similar even if the engraved version is more successful in its rendition of the human form. It articulates lower limbs and torso more convincingly than the painting, in which upper body and lower limbs appear on either side of the man's skirt as disconnected parts.

The elevated arms and the contorted body illustrate movements that European observers in the early modern period linked to lack of composure and civility. They considered measured gait and comportment, in general, and carefully calibrated gestures in dancing, in particular, important features of an educated, tempered body.[60] The English text in Harriot describes how the "coniurers or iuglers . . . vse strange gestures."[61] The Parma Watercolors gloss similarly frowns at the dance moves, for, in the friar's view, they are done not for "honest entertainment, or to show the lightness of the body and the agility of the feet, but for free license of the senses."

Bodily composure and movement were prominent concerns for the friars. They were particularly important, for example, to their oratory practices in sermons (as further discussed in chapter 3 below). They believed gestures and dramatic displays of emotions could be profoundly efficient in conveying Christian doctrine. Reciprocally, they carefully observed and ascribed significance to central Africans' bodily attitudes. The posture depicted in the *Briefe and true report* and the Parma Watercolors, and the moral judgment European observers derived from it, had deep roots.[62] A woodblock print from the Nuremberg Chronicles shows skeletons dancing in a *ronde*, kicking and waving high in a late medieval depiction of a *danse macabre* (fig. 37). Italian Renaissance images of exotic dance from around the same time as the chronicles convey strangeness

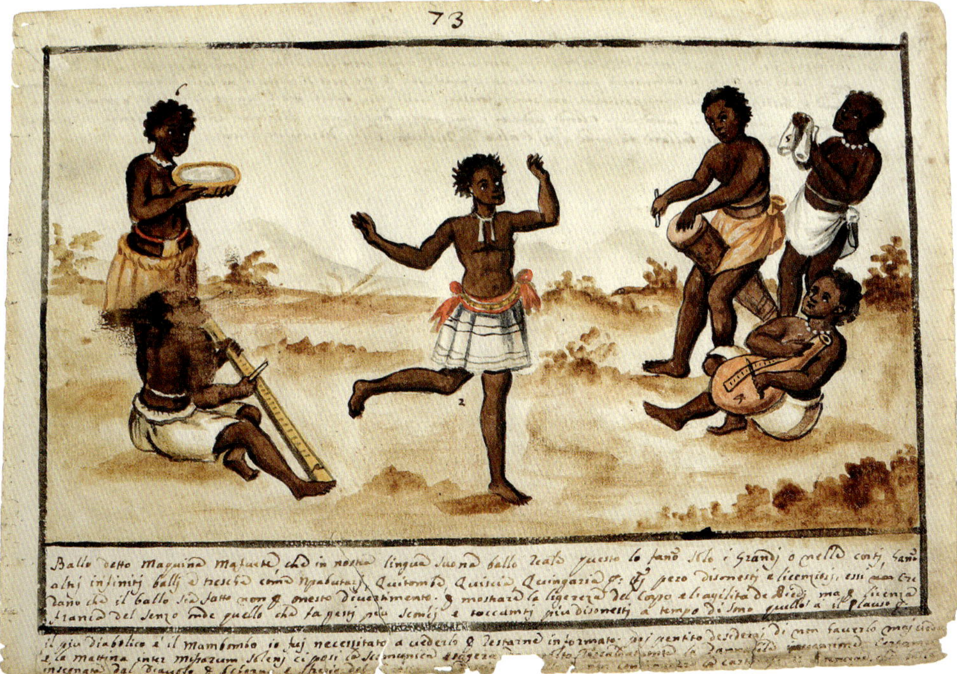

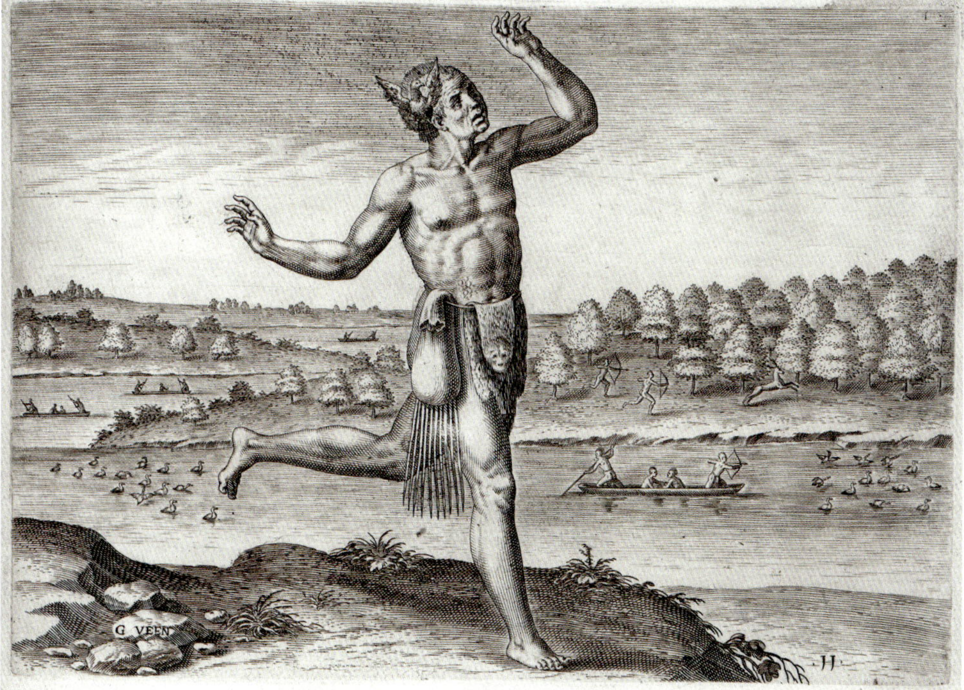

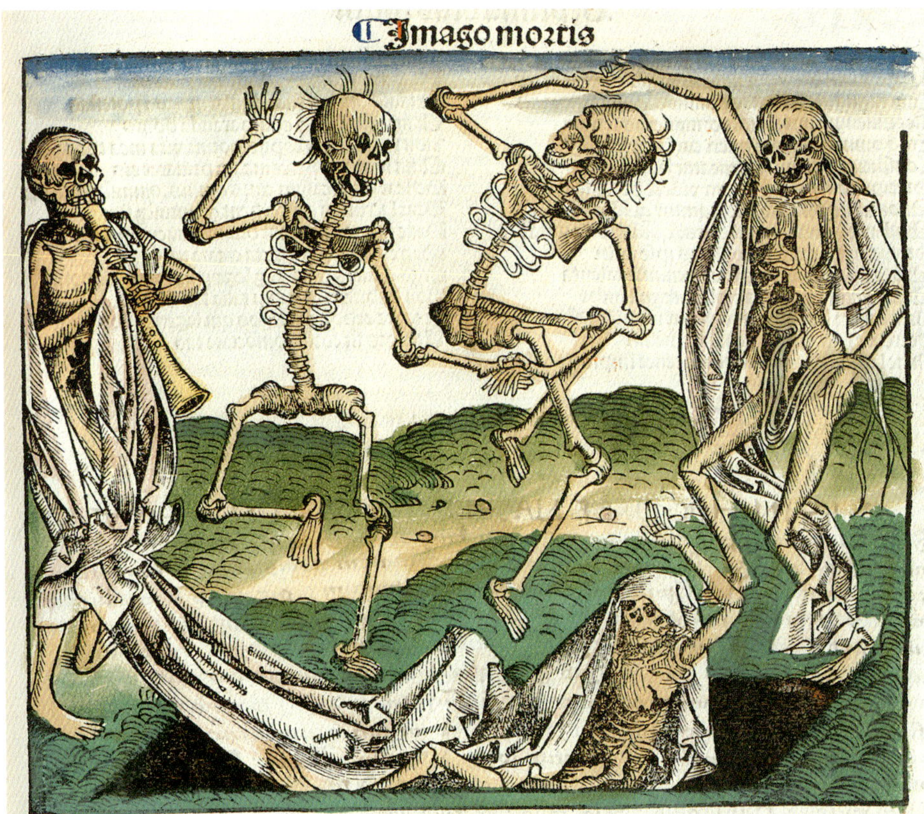

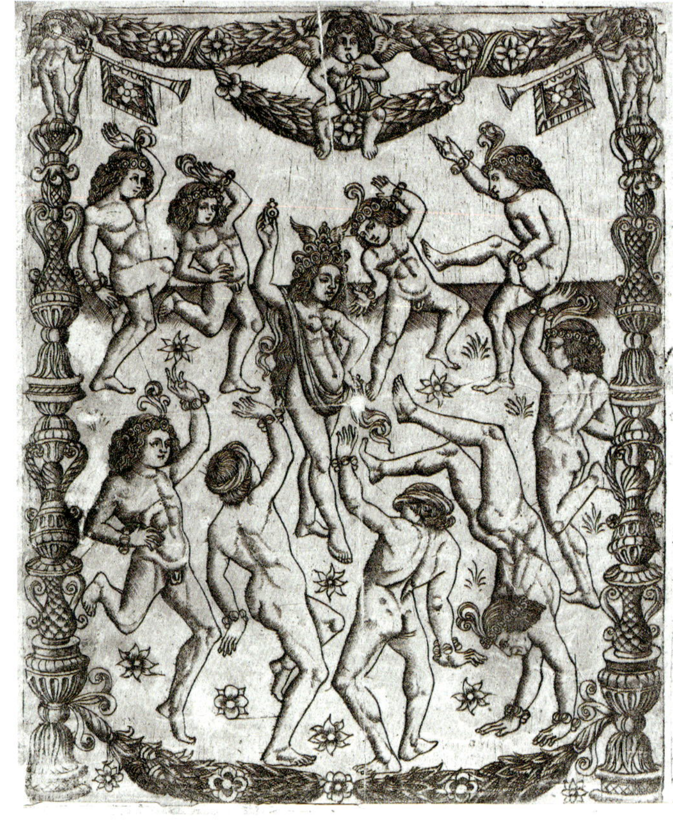

and Otherness with similarly animated dance gestures. Art historian Jill Burke has discussed two instances from quattrocento Florence featuring this very attitude, first in a frieze by Antonio del Pollaiuolo dated after 1464, second in a Florentine engraving of 1470, now in the Topkapı Museum, depicting a *moresca*, a dramatic dance staging a battle between Europeans and Africans or Moors (fig. 38).[63] In his 1508 woodcut series *Peoples of Africa and India*, Augsburg artist Hans Burgkmair depicted a child "in Gennea"—that is, Africa—in this very bodily position.[64]

The example of bodily attitudes makes clear that an array of visual sources and cultural referents flowed into the construction of the Capuchin images of central Africa. While eyewitness accounts played an important role in their composition, and their forms did not fit within—and in fact, as I argue, challenged—established templates for the representation of non-European locales and people, the Capuchins' experience of central Africa, as well as the means they mobilized to convey it visually, depended nonetheless on the mental imagery they brought with them and the books they consulted. As demonstrated in the representation of the "dance called *maquina mafuete*," the friars observed the performance and devised visual solutions to capture it on the page through deep-rooted Italian conceptions of the form and meaning of body language and comportment and their connection to morality and civility. The best-selling imagery of early modern travel literature, such as the works of de Bry from the decades leading up to the missionaries' journeys, also visibly shaped their perception and representation of Kongo and Angola.

The animated, bold gestures of the "dance called *maquina mafuete*" mark Otherness and strangeness in the same manner as the *coniuerer* or the skeletons. Yet unlike the revelers in the American and European scenes, the central-African dancer and the musicians that surround him do not dwell in a realm neatly separated from the image's viewers. A floral garland firmly encloses the dancers in the Topkapı print (fig. 38). The black hole of a wide-open grave warns viewers against joining in the corpses' jig (fig. 37). The tightly framed American conjurer nearly touches the top and bottom of the print, as if flattened on its surface. He stands on a small patch of earth floating above and in front of the broad landscape behind him. His body and the ground on which he dances block any entry viewers may have sought into the expansive, distant scenery unfolding past the dramatically foregrounded figure (fig. 36). In striking contrast, the wider view and gently sloping ground of the Parma Watercolor place no obstacles between viewers and dancers (fig. 35). Capuchin novices who formed the intended audience for the painting had an unobstructed view of the event, as they did of the scene in the image opening this chapter (fig. 19). The animated dance unfolds before their eyes, in a world that they have not yet witnessed but that already vividly appears as coeval with theirs. The vignette pictures an environment they will soon literally step into as they embark on the mission, but thanks to the images their brothers created, it is a world they can already visit virtually.

The difference in framing between Harriot's *coniuerer* and the Parma Watercolor dancer is slight but fundamental. In the American case, the engraver, who worked from an eyewitness drawing, presented the Indigenous American man in a world entirely his own.[65] With his composition, he invited viewers to see the conjurer and to ascribe significance to his comportment, prompting them to exercise a subjectivity and epistemic control over the entranced Indigenous man, whom he pictured, in contradistinction, as lacking both. I argue in the following chapters that, on the other hand, the Capuchin images connected viewers to the pictured space and created a common ground in which Italians and central Africans exercised subjectivity and participated side by side in the creation and communication of knowledge in and about Kongo and Angola. The Capuchin images show and perform knowledge-making in and of the mission as an often-fraught but nonetheless collaborative process between central Africans and European friars. This characteristic of the Capuchin central-African corpus is easily overlooked. It remained elusive even to the printmaker working under Cavazzi to turn *disegni* akin to the Parma Watercolors into prints. The plate in the *Istorica descrizione* inspired by the "dance called *maquina mafuete*" Parma Watercolor, for instance, has already lost this key dimension (fig. 39). In the print, the dancer occupies most of the frame, as does the *coniuerer*, no longer encouraging viewers to step into the scene but, on the contrary, offering himself and the contents of the image to their distant gaze. The landscape surrounding dancer and musicians has become in this context fantastical, with small gable-roof

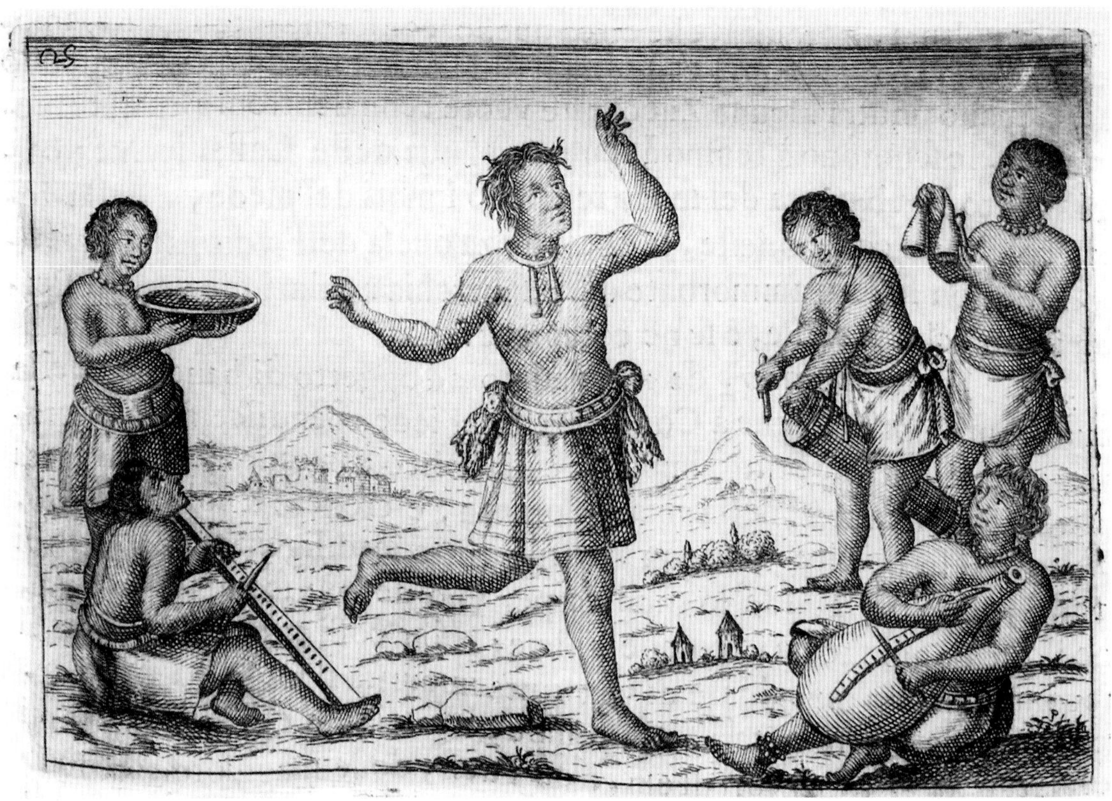

Figure 39

Paolo da Lorena (attr.), *Dance Scene*. Engraving, 10 × 14 cm (plate mark). Plate 25 from Giovanni Antonio Cavazzi and Fortunato Alamandini, *Istorica descrizione de' tre' regni Congo, Matamba, et Angola* (Bologna: Giacomo Monti, 1687), 167 and 200. National Library of Portugal, Lisbon, H.G. 9174 A. Photo courtesy of the National Library of Portugal.

constructions turning the protagonists into giants in an eerie, strange land.

Conclusion

The prints of the *Istorica descrizione* participate in the large and complex image network of the Capuchin central-African mission. Many of them emerged from the visual didactic guides the friars created to instruct future missionaries about the easily misunderstood natural and cultural environment of Kongo and Angola. To so instruct, the friars created a genre of images that remained coherent over more than a century and elaborated upon the admonitions other Capuchins penned in written form. A scene of rattling dance showcases the deep-rooted templates at play in the Capuchin perception and representation of central Africa. The friars used long-standing European iconography of exuberant bodily comportment and lack of restraint to convey what was for them the astounding spectacle of central-African dance. Yet, when compared to other European uses of the same iconography, the Capuchin central-African images created a radically different relationship between image and viewers. Instead of enclosing the depicted characters within a hermetic frame, they invited viewers to partake in the image, bringing them into dialogue and proximity with the characters and actions represented therein.

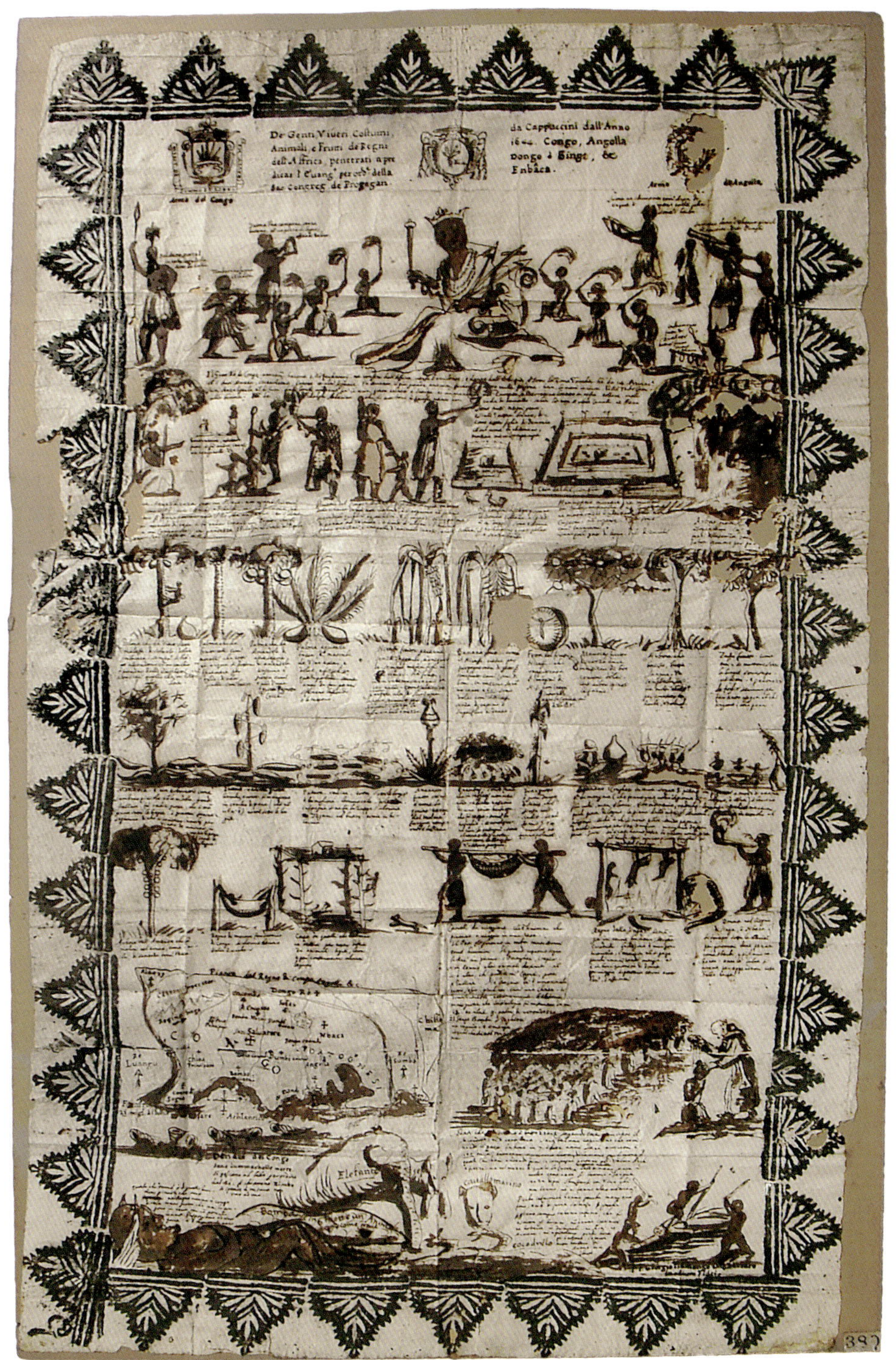

Plate 1

Unknown Capuchin artist, *Of the People, Victuals, Customs, Animals, and Fruits of the Kingdoms of Africa penetrated to preach the Gospel by order of the Sacred Congregation of the Propaganda by Capuchins since the year 1644: Congo, Angola, Dongo [Ndongo] or Singa [Njinga] and Enbâca [Ambaca]*, ca. 1652–63. Ink on paper, 73 × 40 cm (full panel). Franciscan Museum of the Capuchin Historical Institute, Rome, MF 1370. Photo: author.

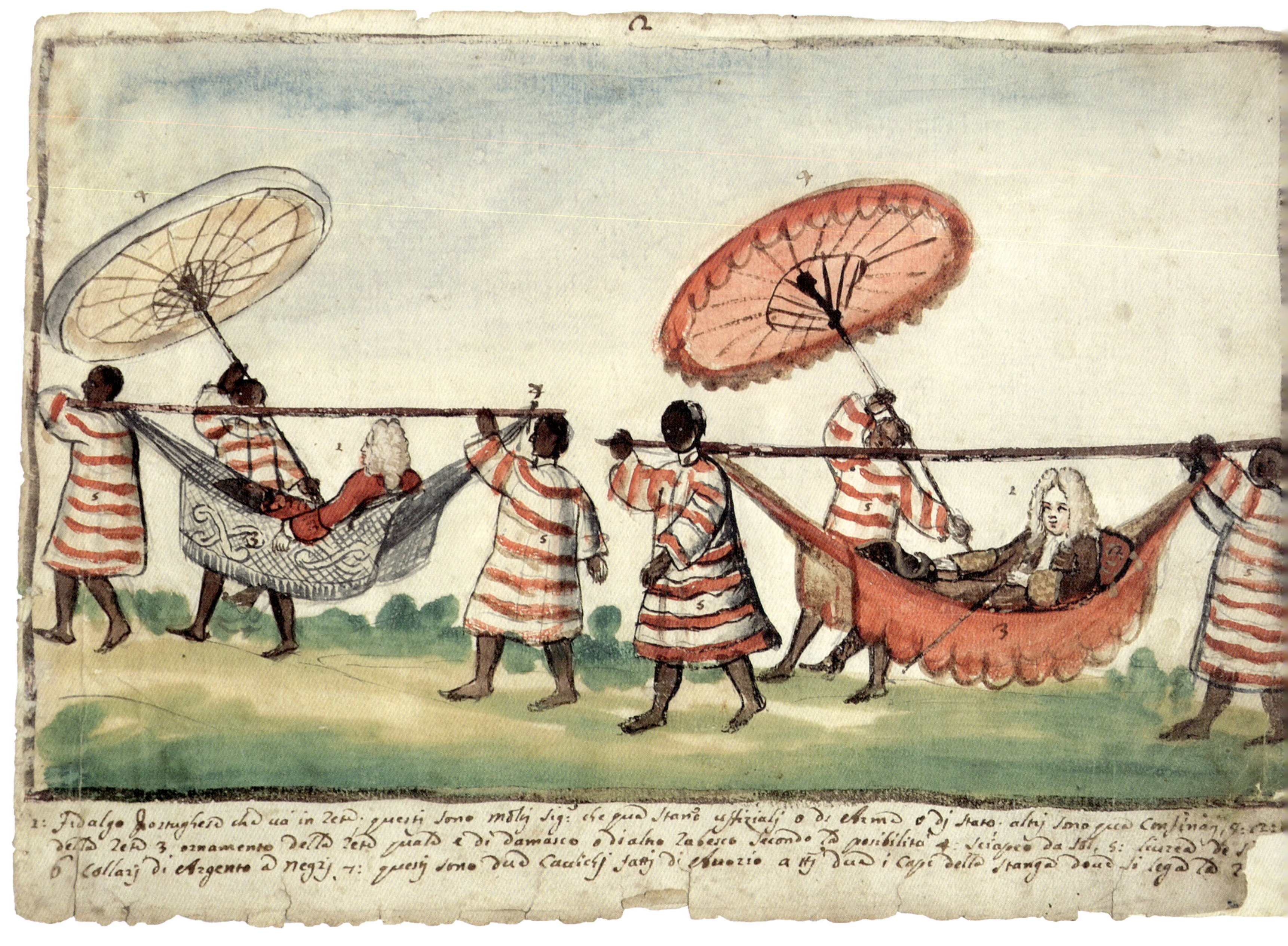

Plate 2

Fol. 2, "Portuguese aristocrat[s] traveling in nets."

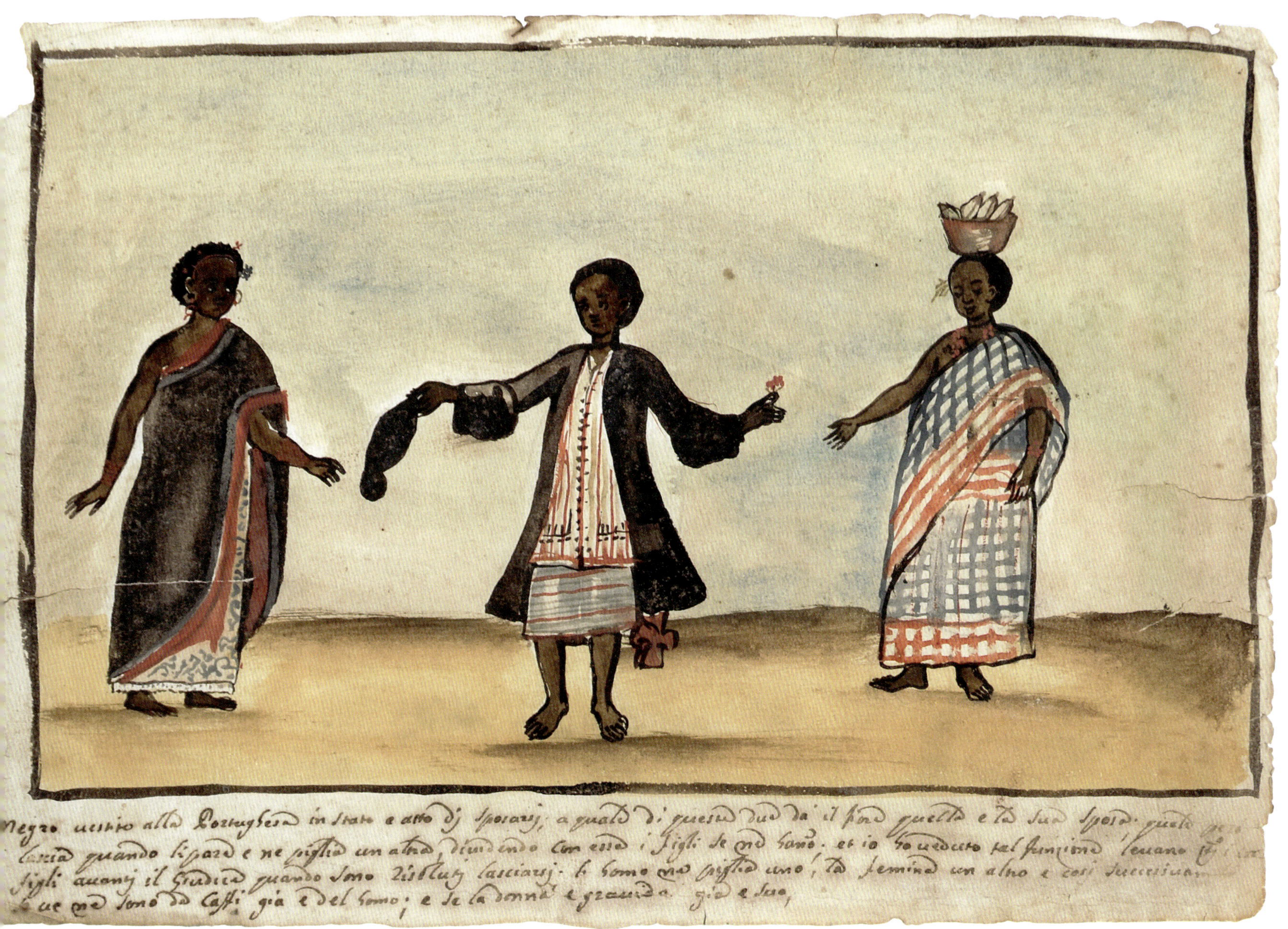

Plate 3

[Fol. 7], "Black man dressed in the Portuguese manner about to get married."

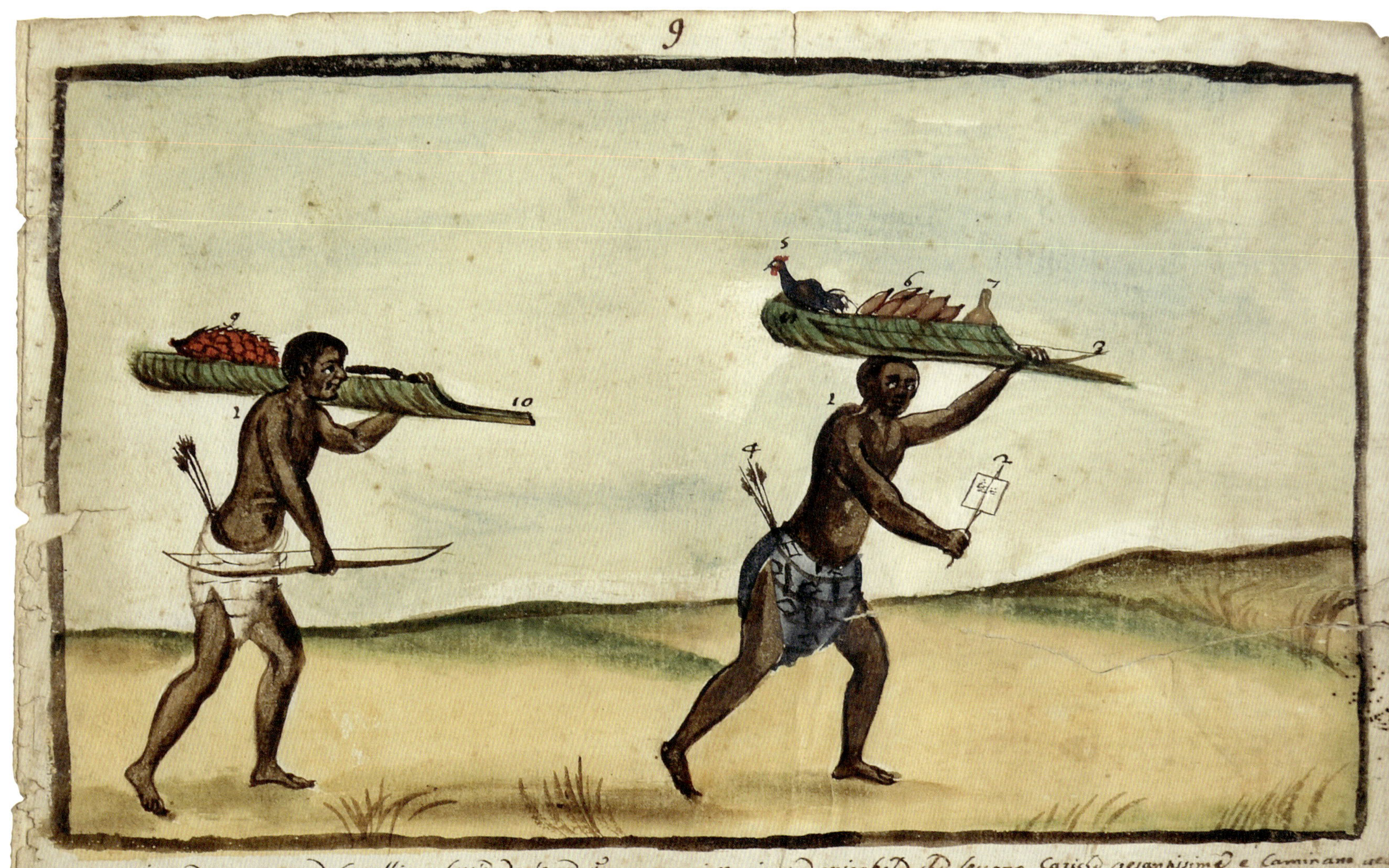

Plate 4

Fol. 9, "Carriers."

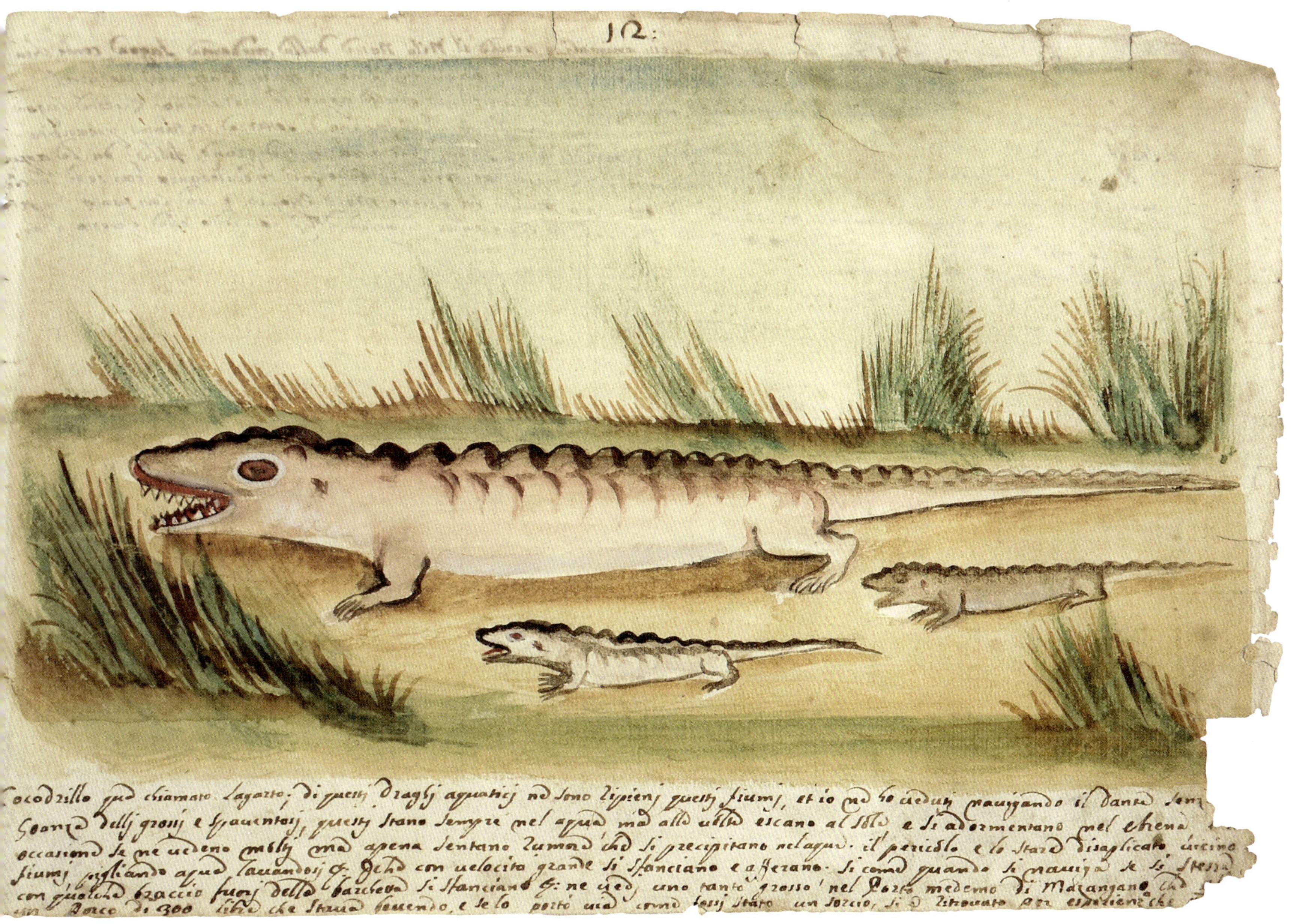

Plate 5

Fol. 12, "Crocodile, here called *Lagarto*."

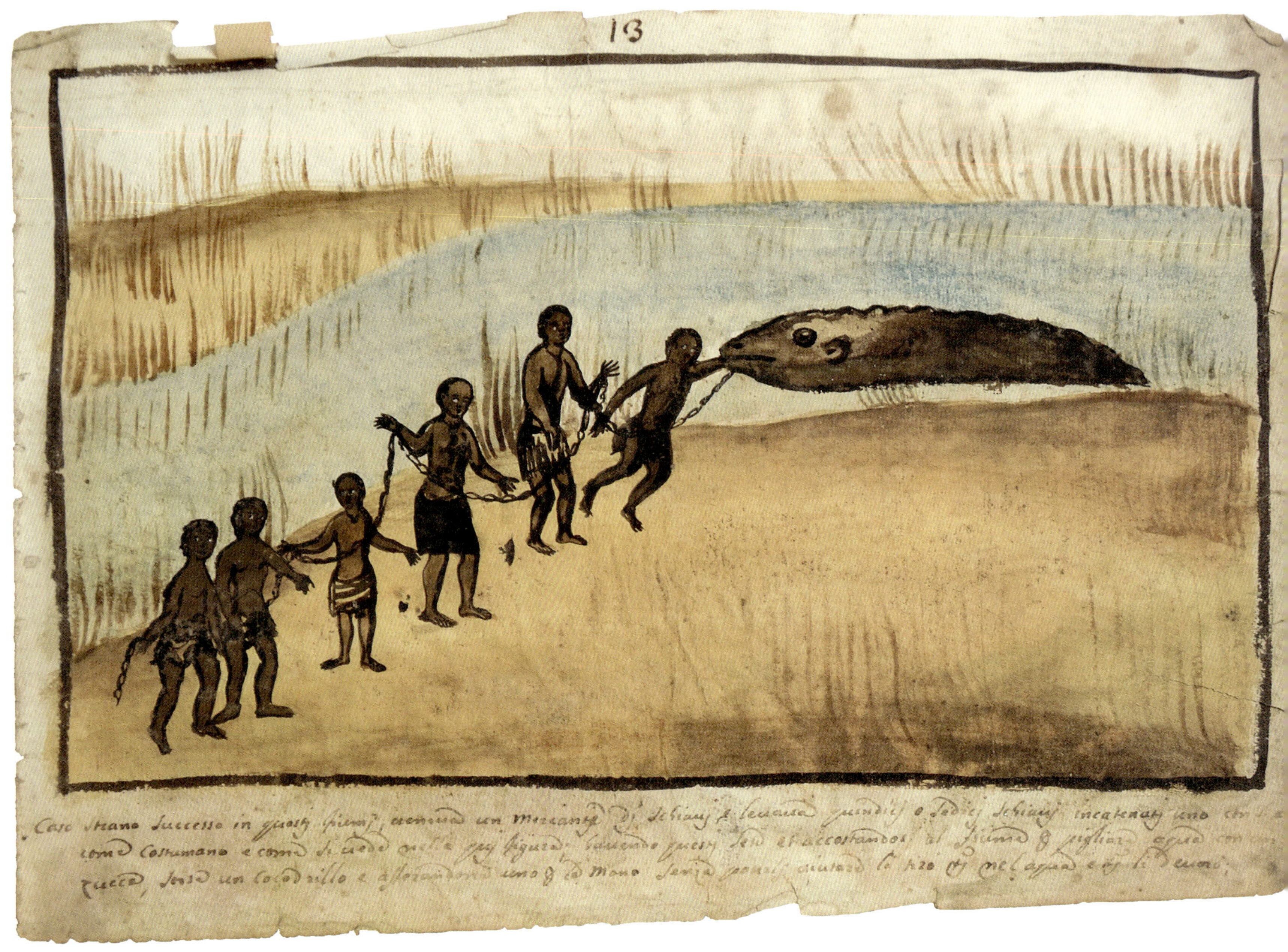

Plate 6

Fol. 13, "Strange case that occurs in these rivers."

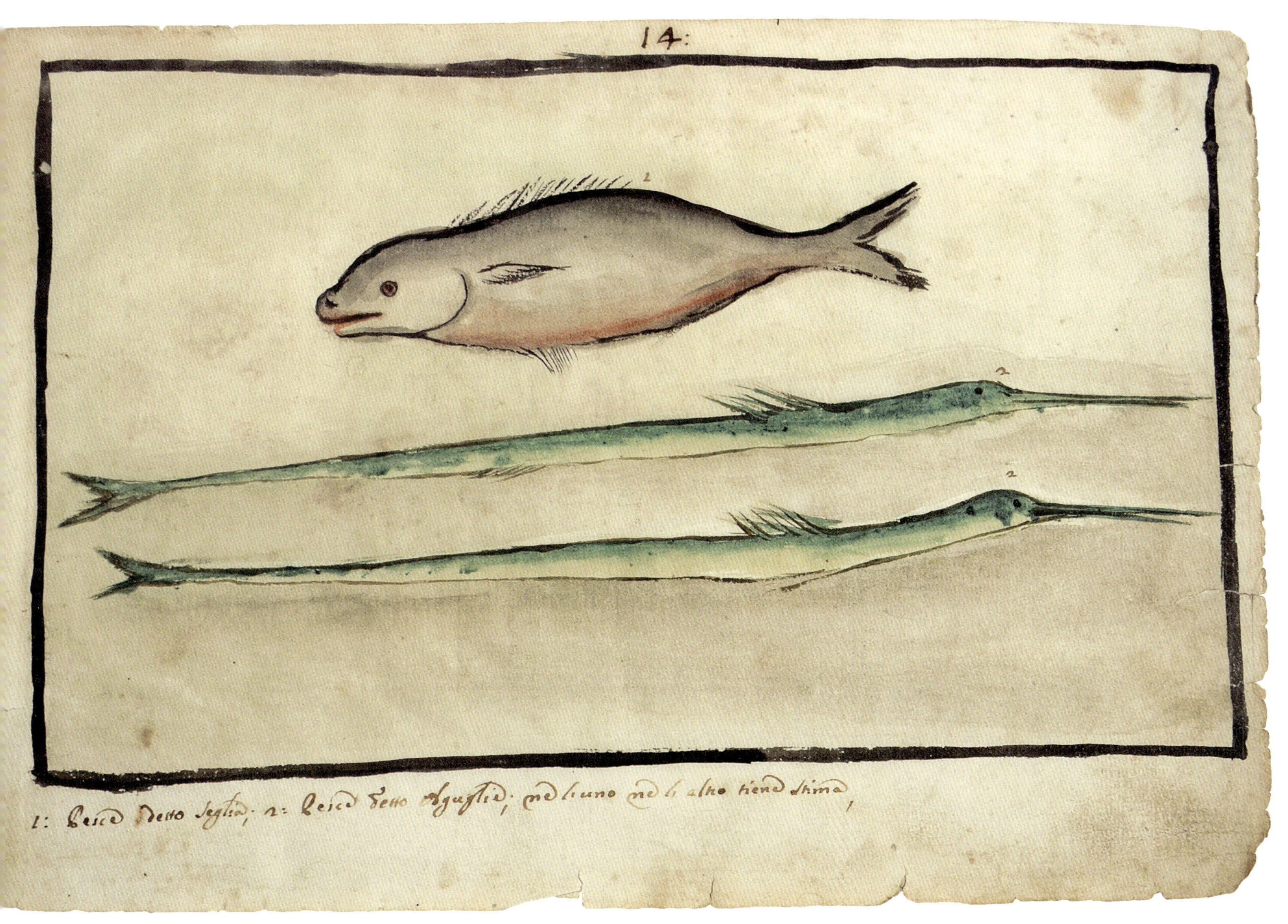

Plate 7

Fol. 14, "Fish called *seglia*, fishes called *Aguglie*."

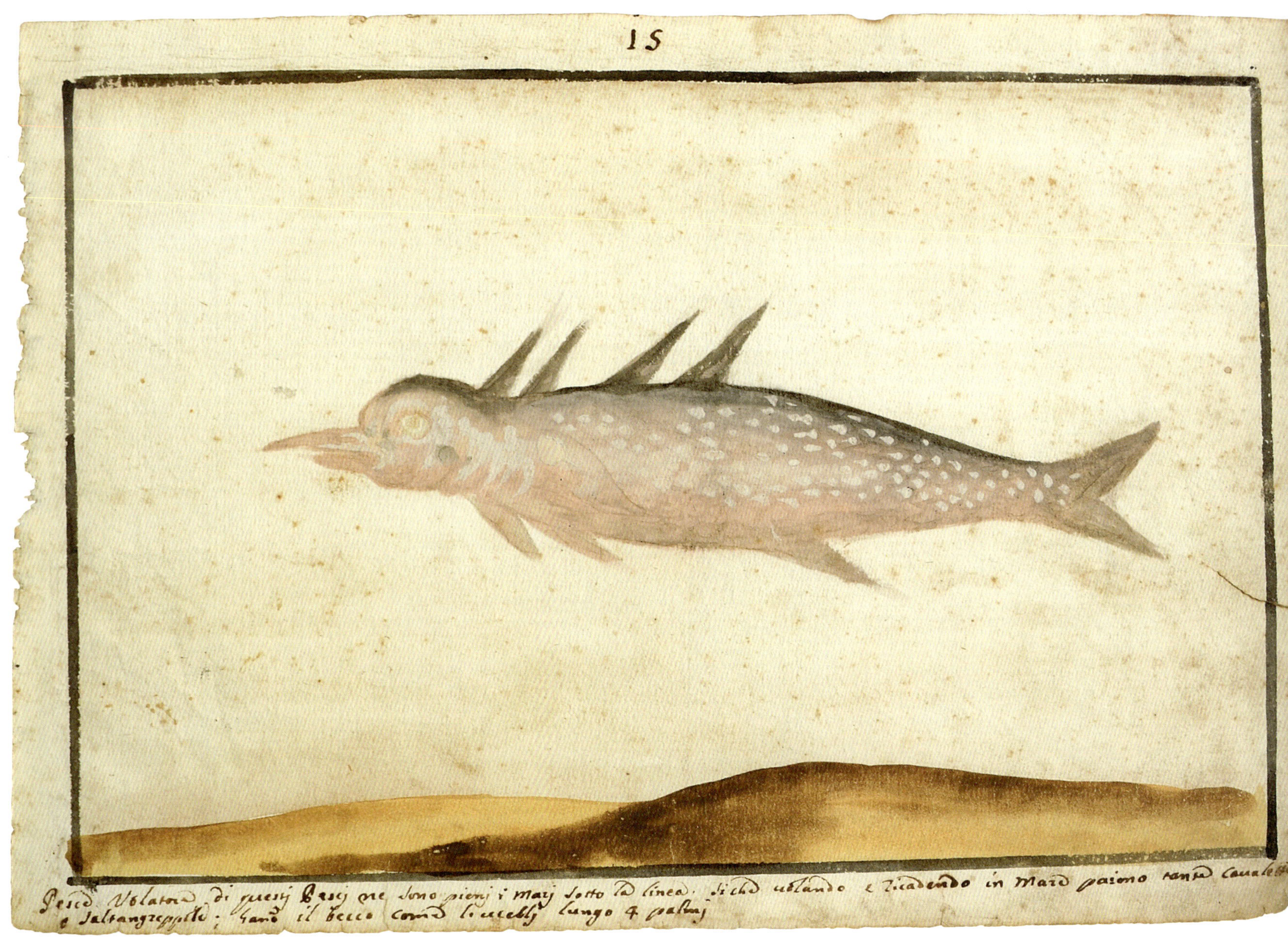

Plate 8

Fol. 15, "Flying Fish."

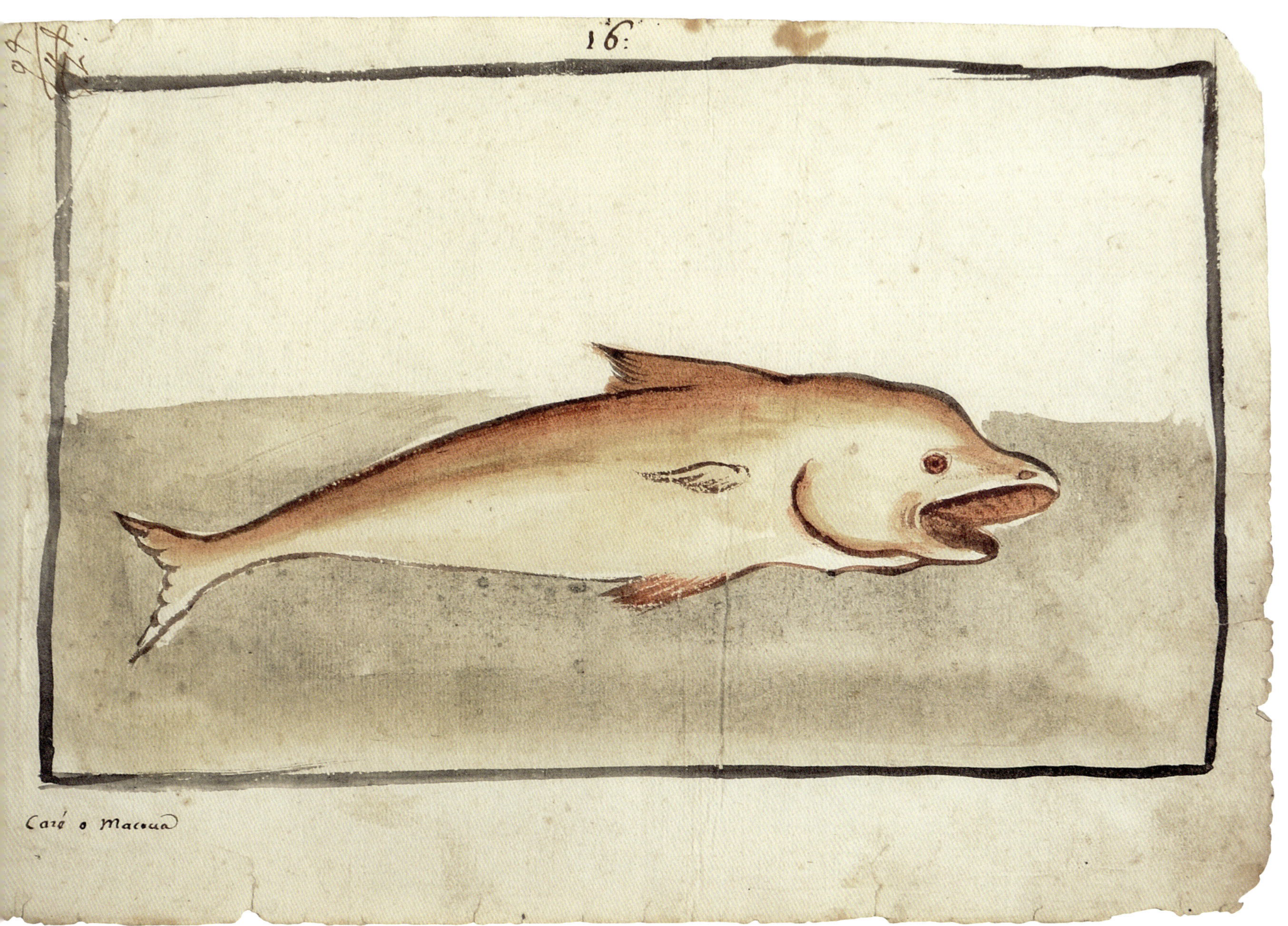

Plate 9

Fol. 16, "*Caré*, or *Macova* [fish]."

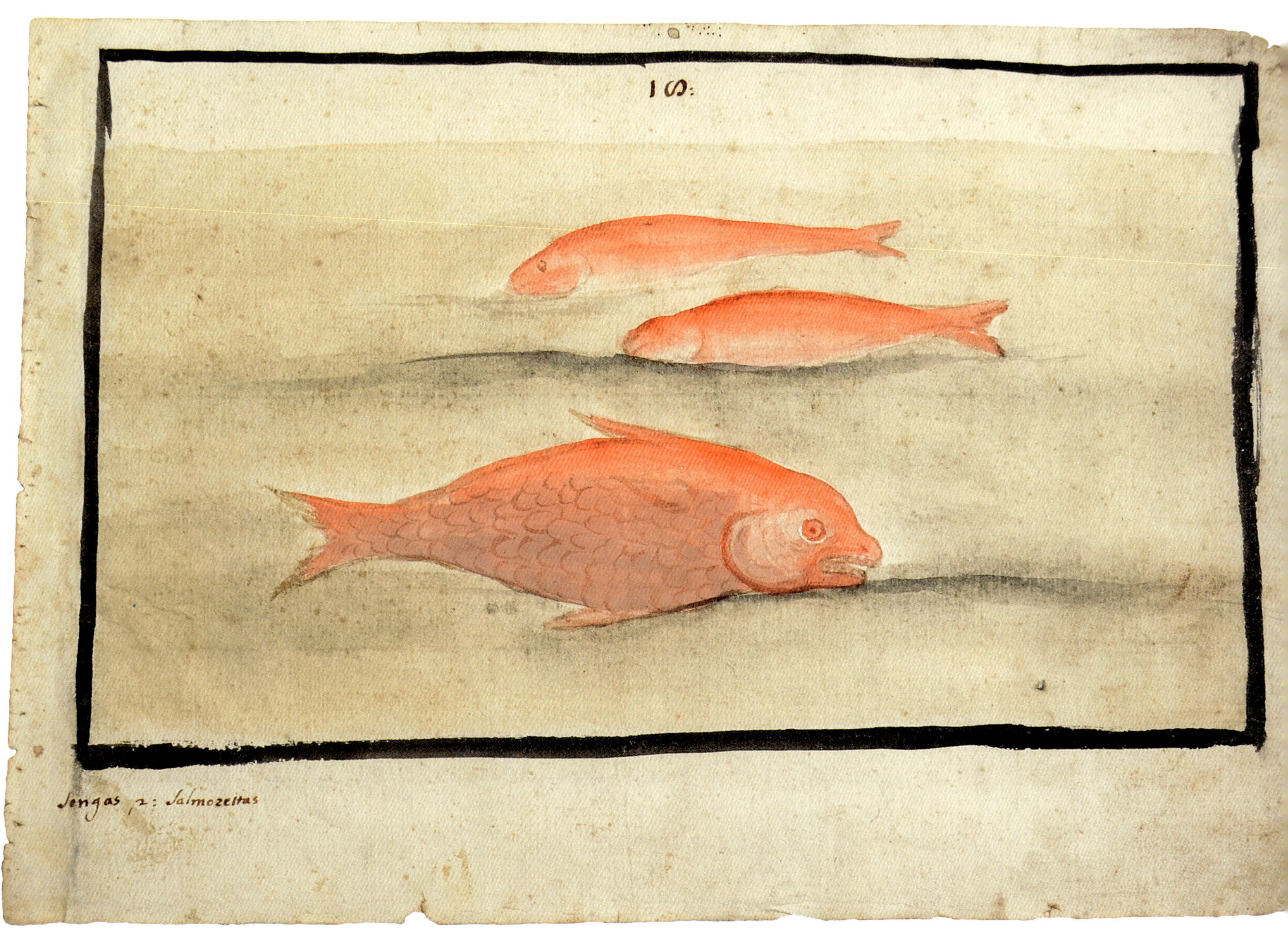

Plate 10

Fol. 18, "*Sengas*, [and] *salmorettas* [fishes]."

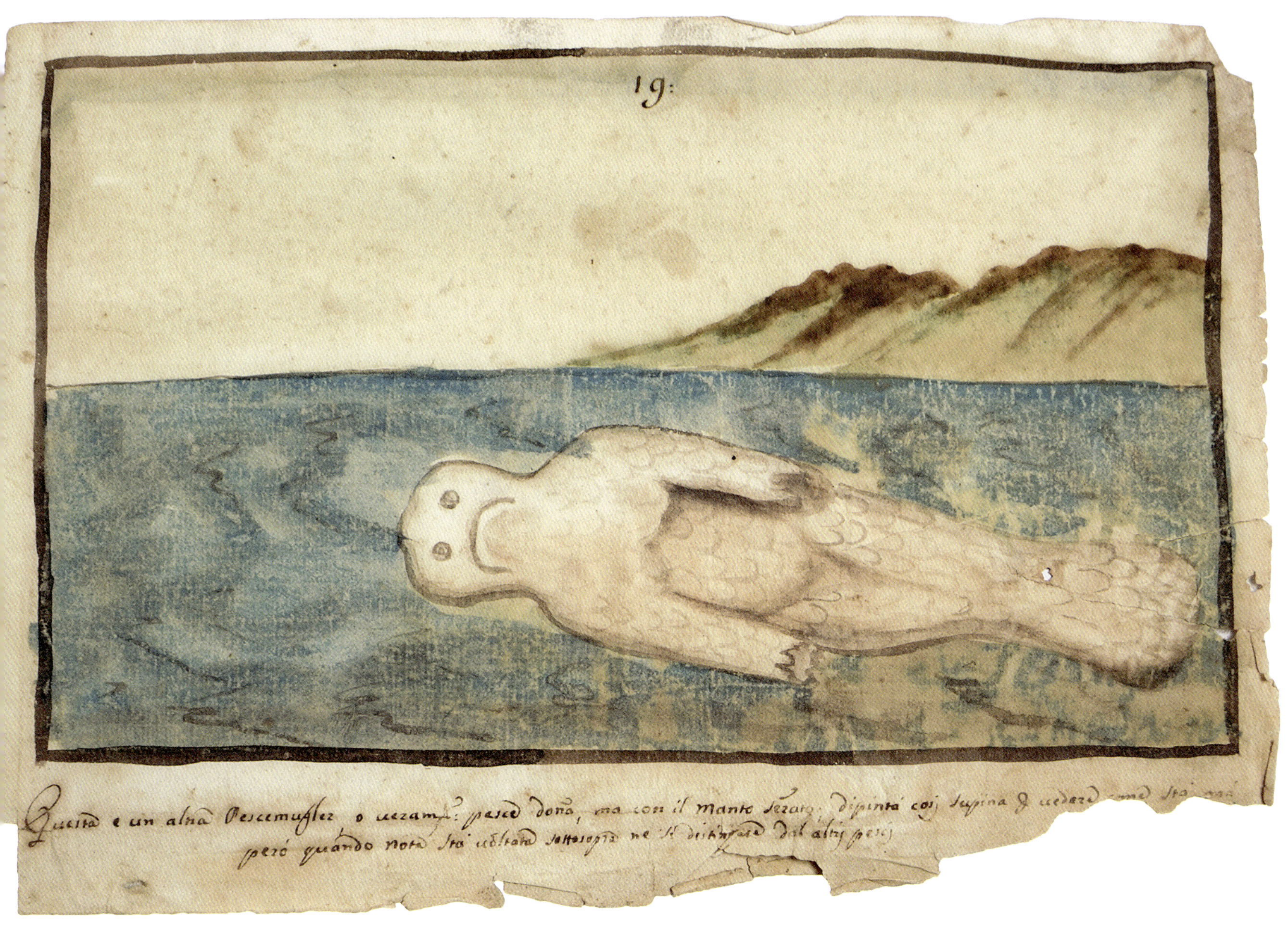

Plate 11

Fol. 19, "Another *Pescemugler* [*sic*] [manatee]."

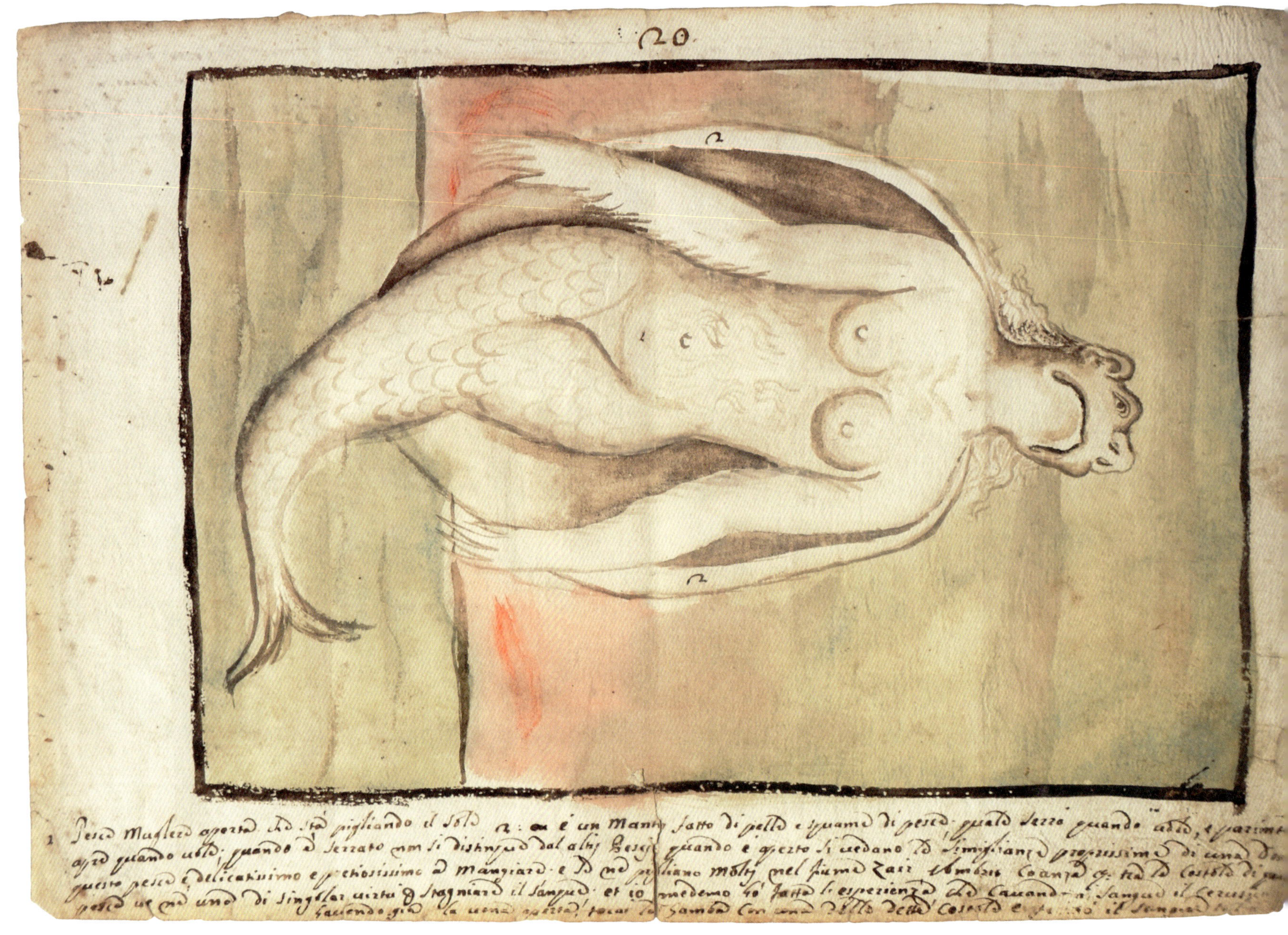

Plate 12

Fol. 20, "*Pesce Muglere* [manatee] . . . sunbathing."

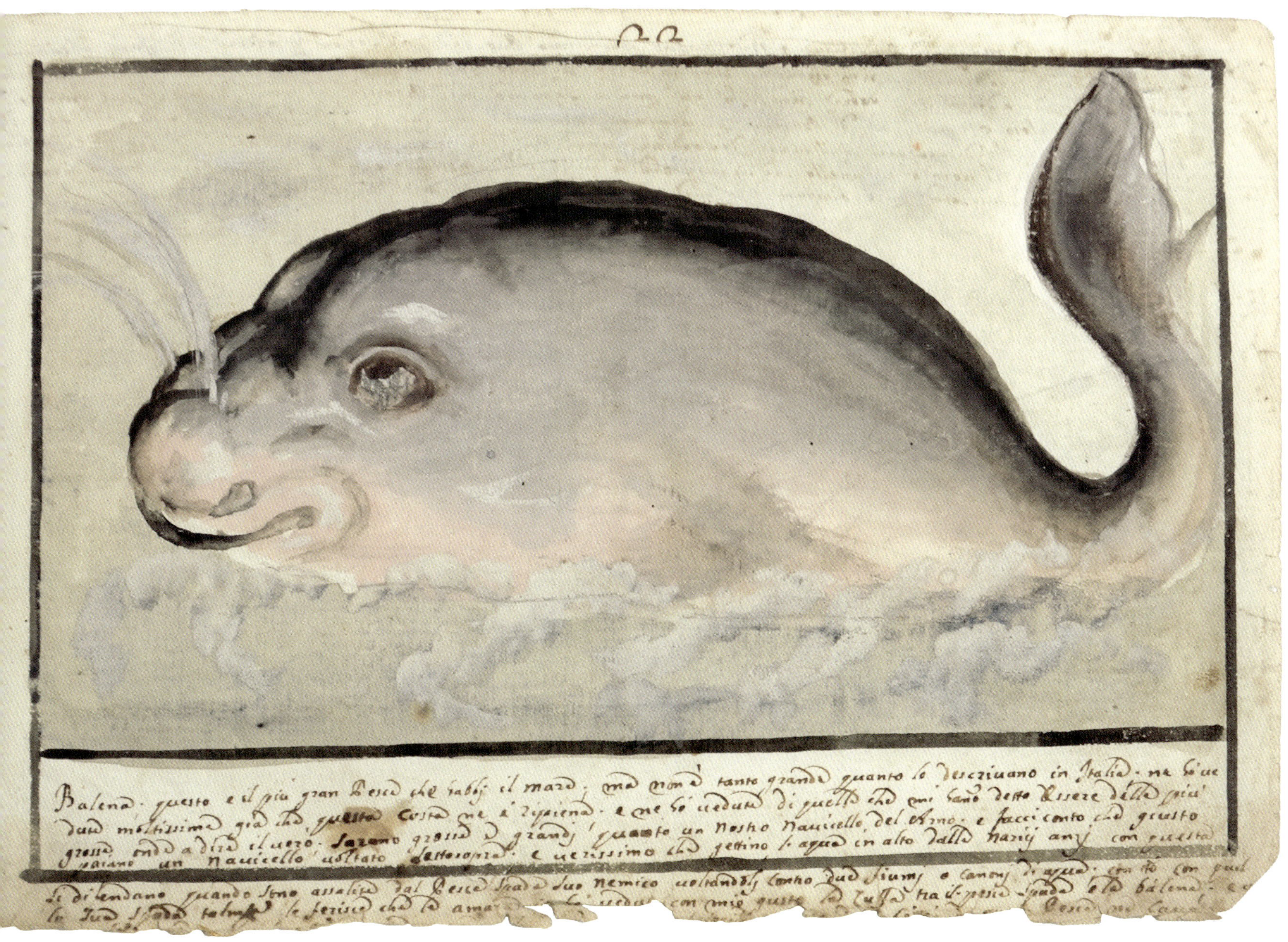

Plate 13

Fol. 22, "Whale."

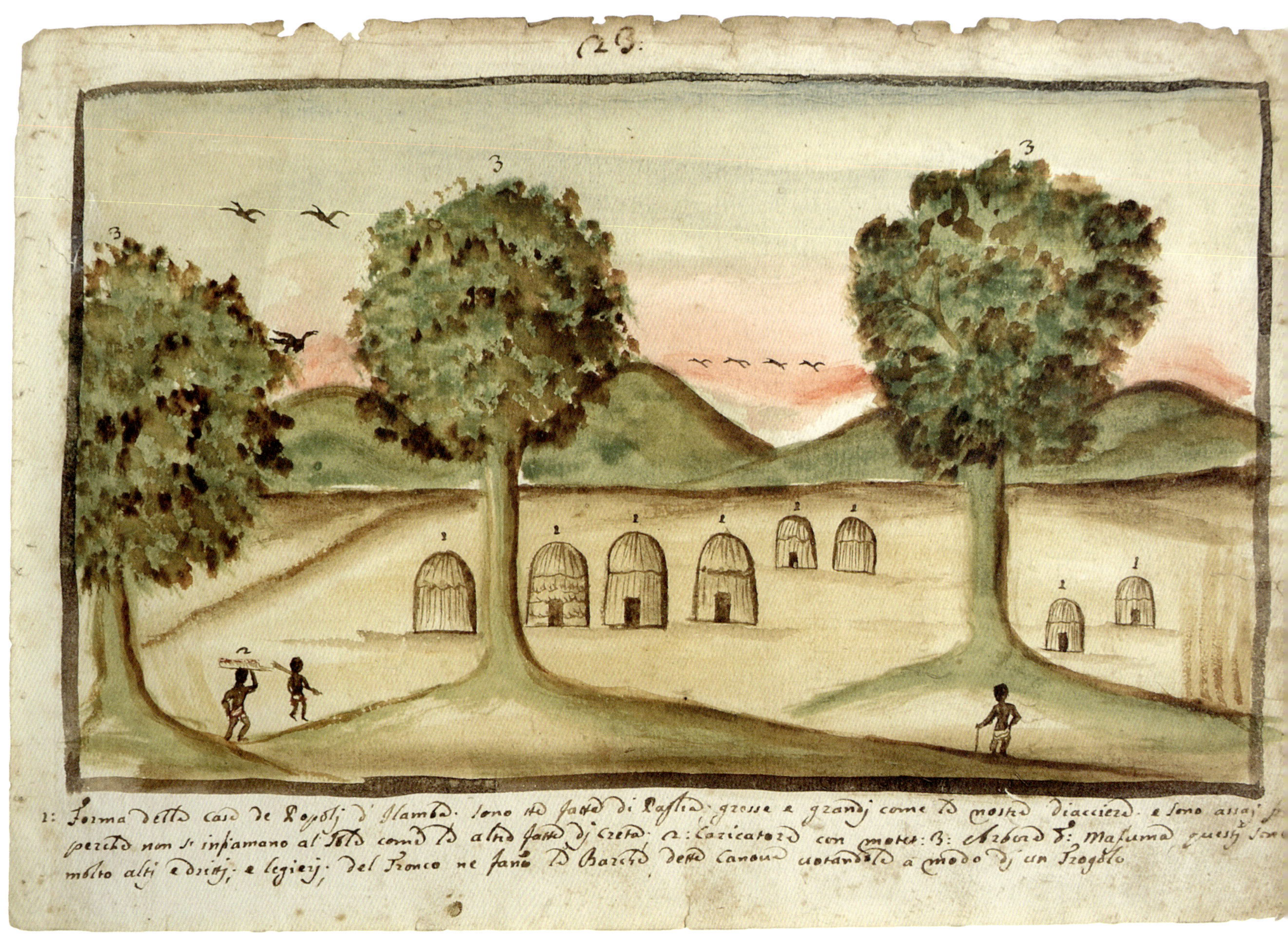

Plate 14

Fol. 23, "Houses of the people of Ilamba."

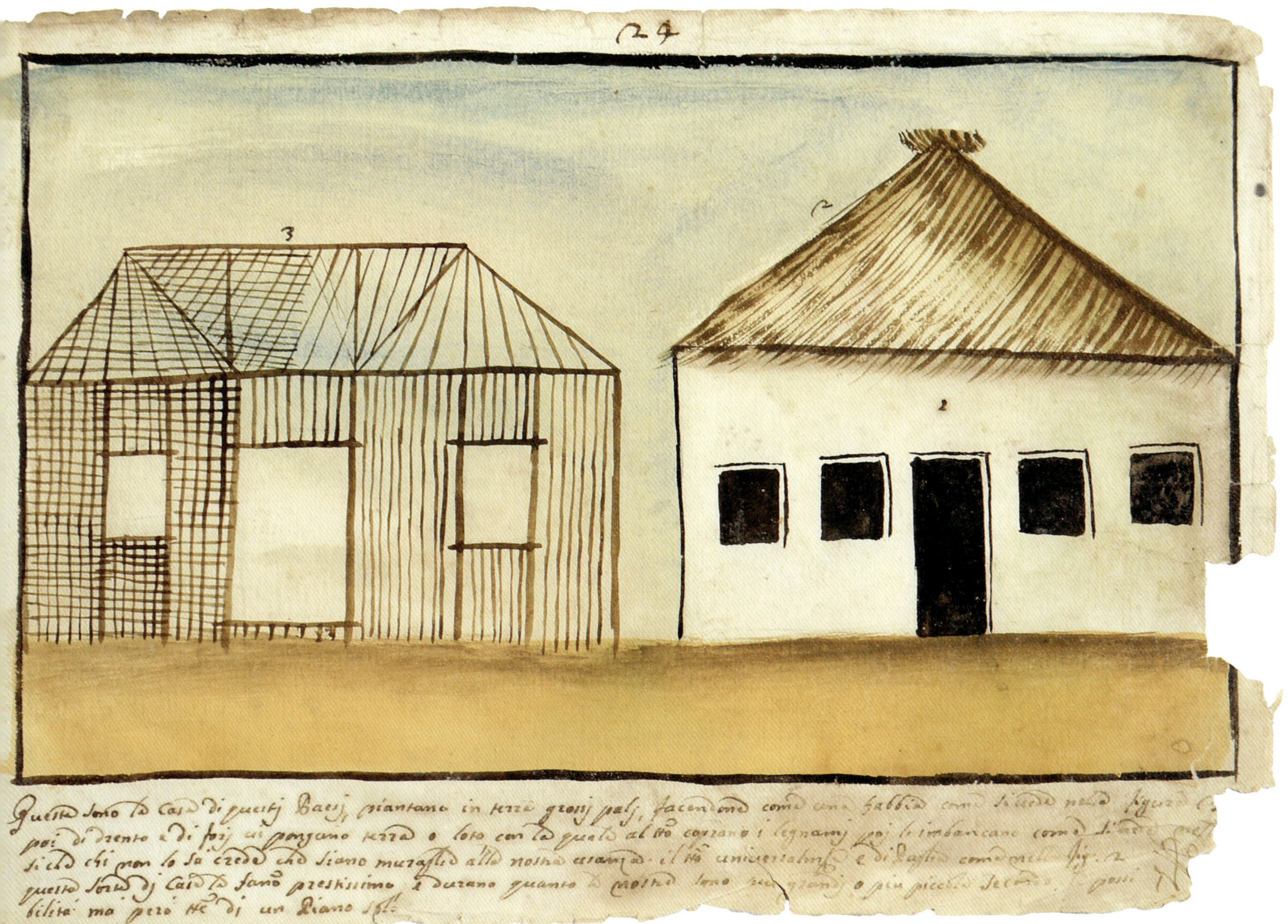

Plate 15

Fol. 24, "Houses of these countries."

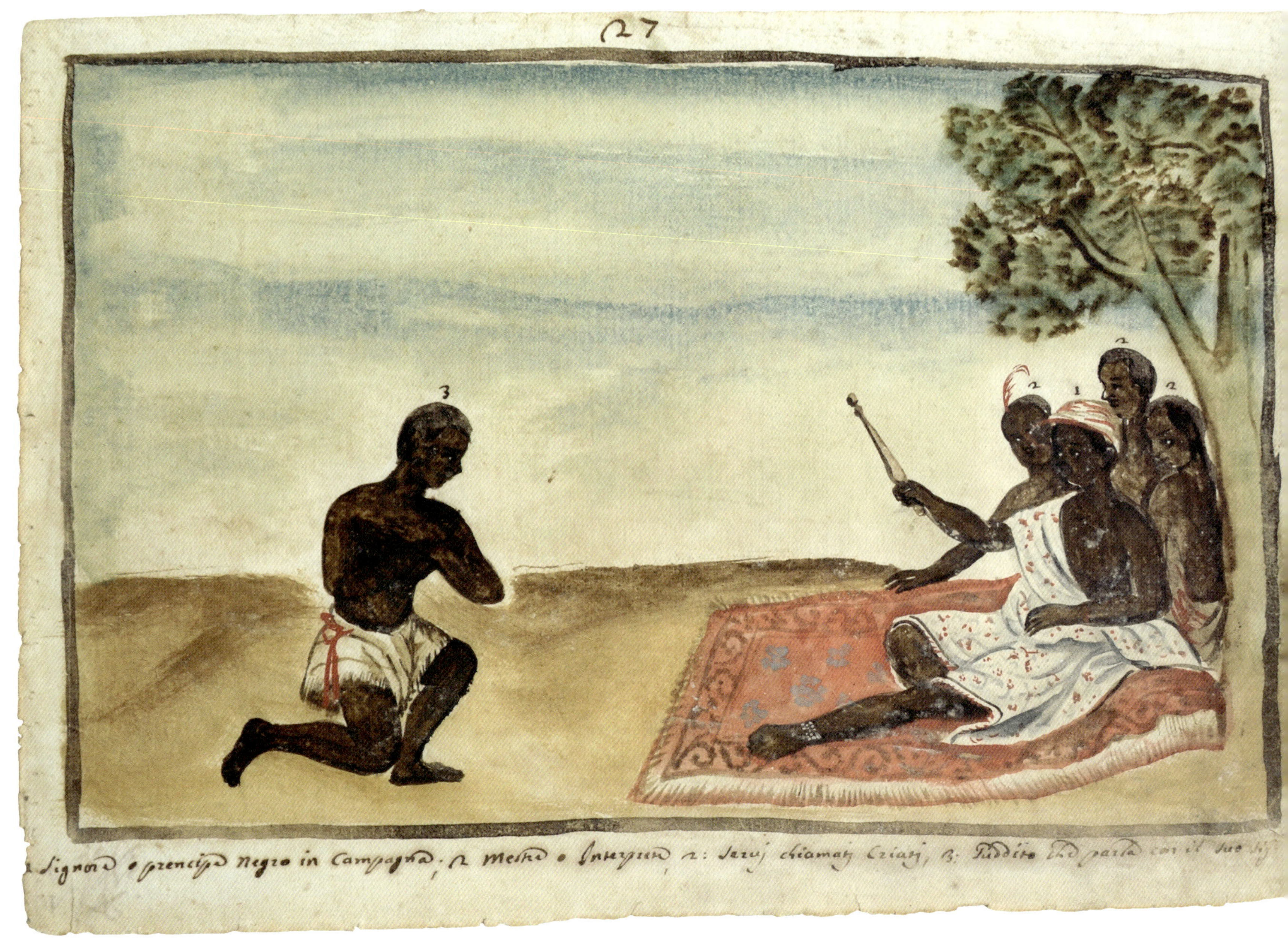

Plate 16

Fol. 27, "Black lord or prince in the countryside."

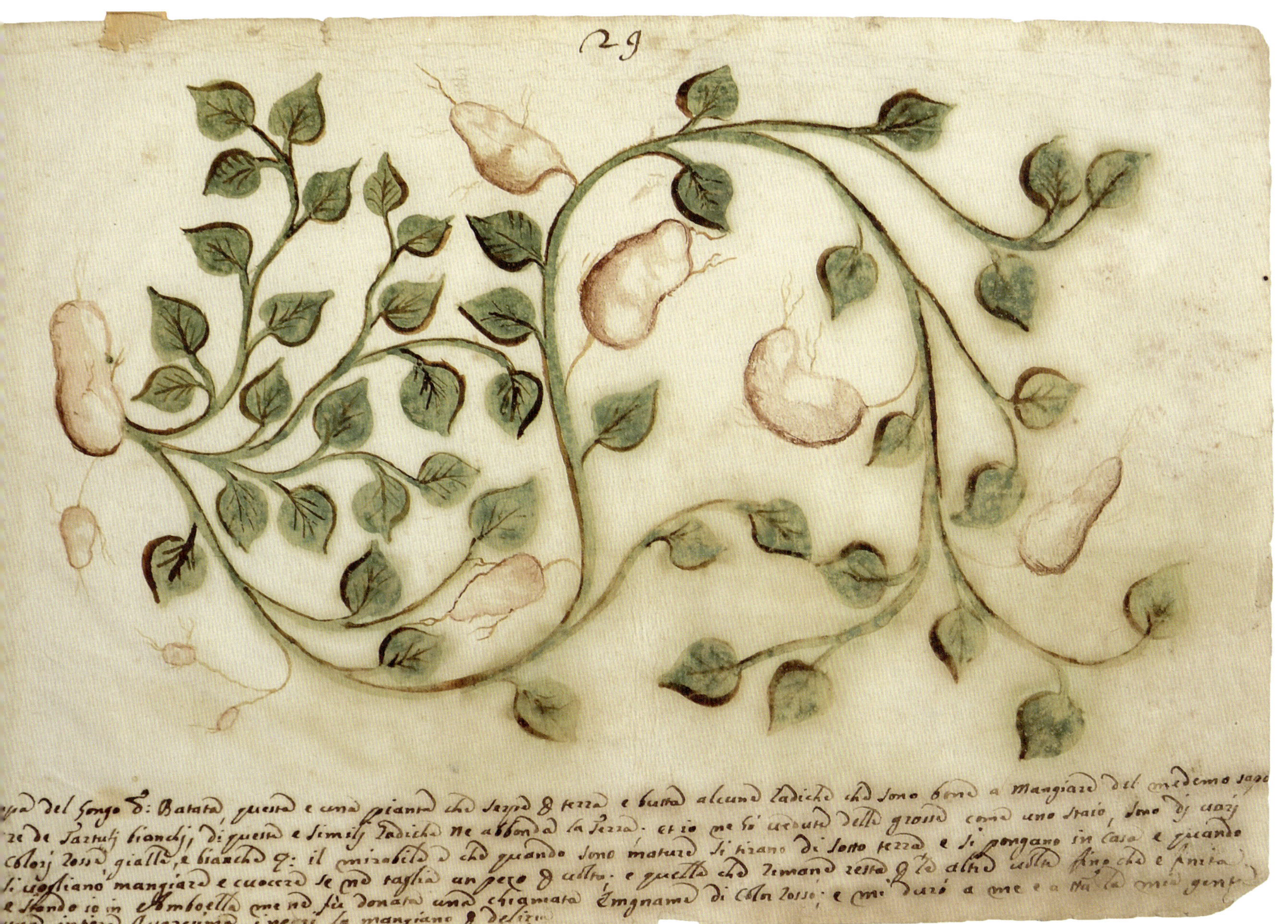

Plate 17

Fol. 29, "Turnip of the Congo, called *Batata*."

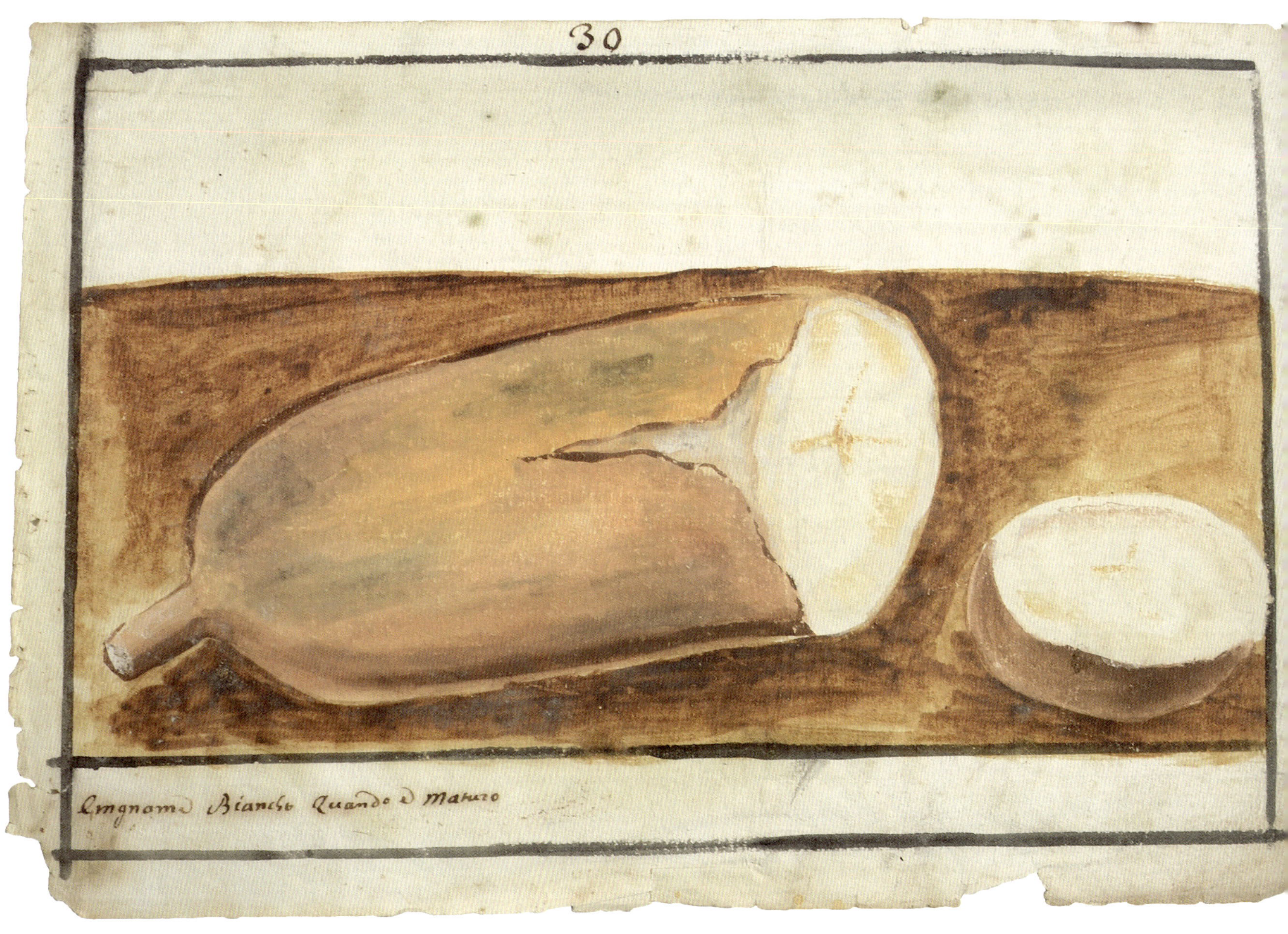

Plate 18

Fol. 30, "White yam."

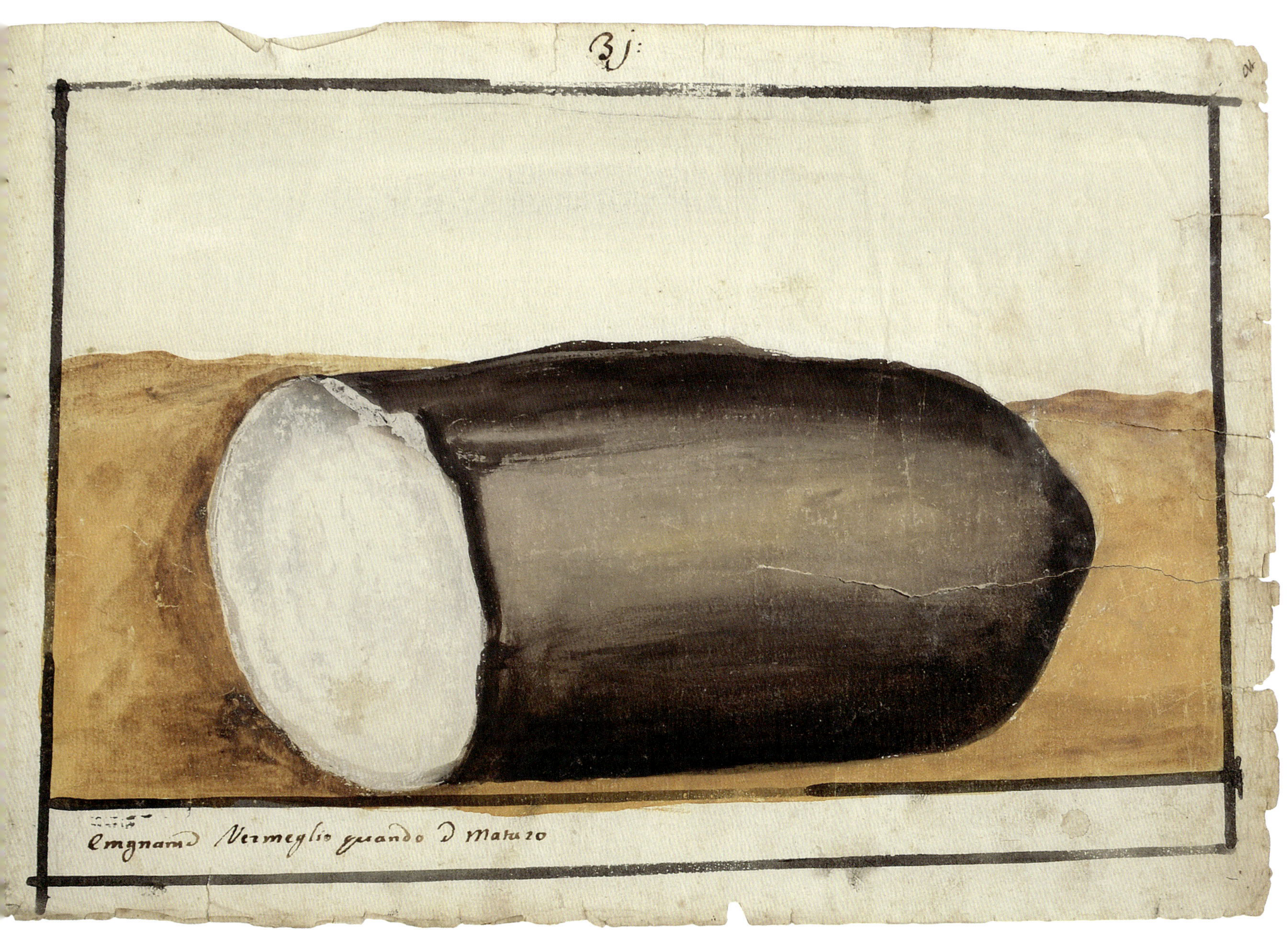

Plate 19

Fol. 31, "Red yam."

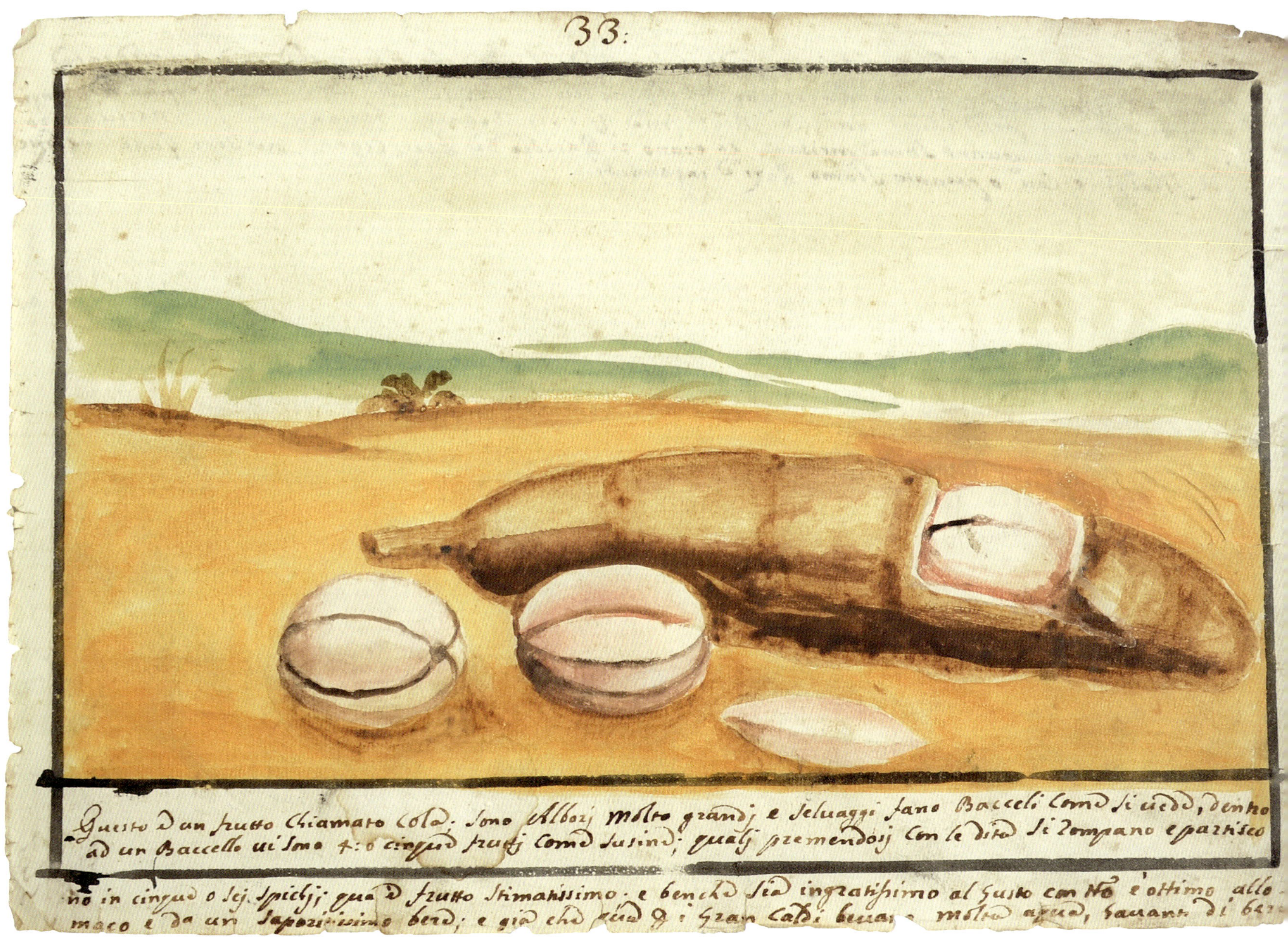

Plate 20

Fol. 33, "Fruit called cola."

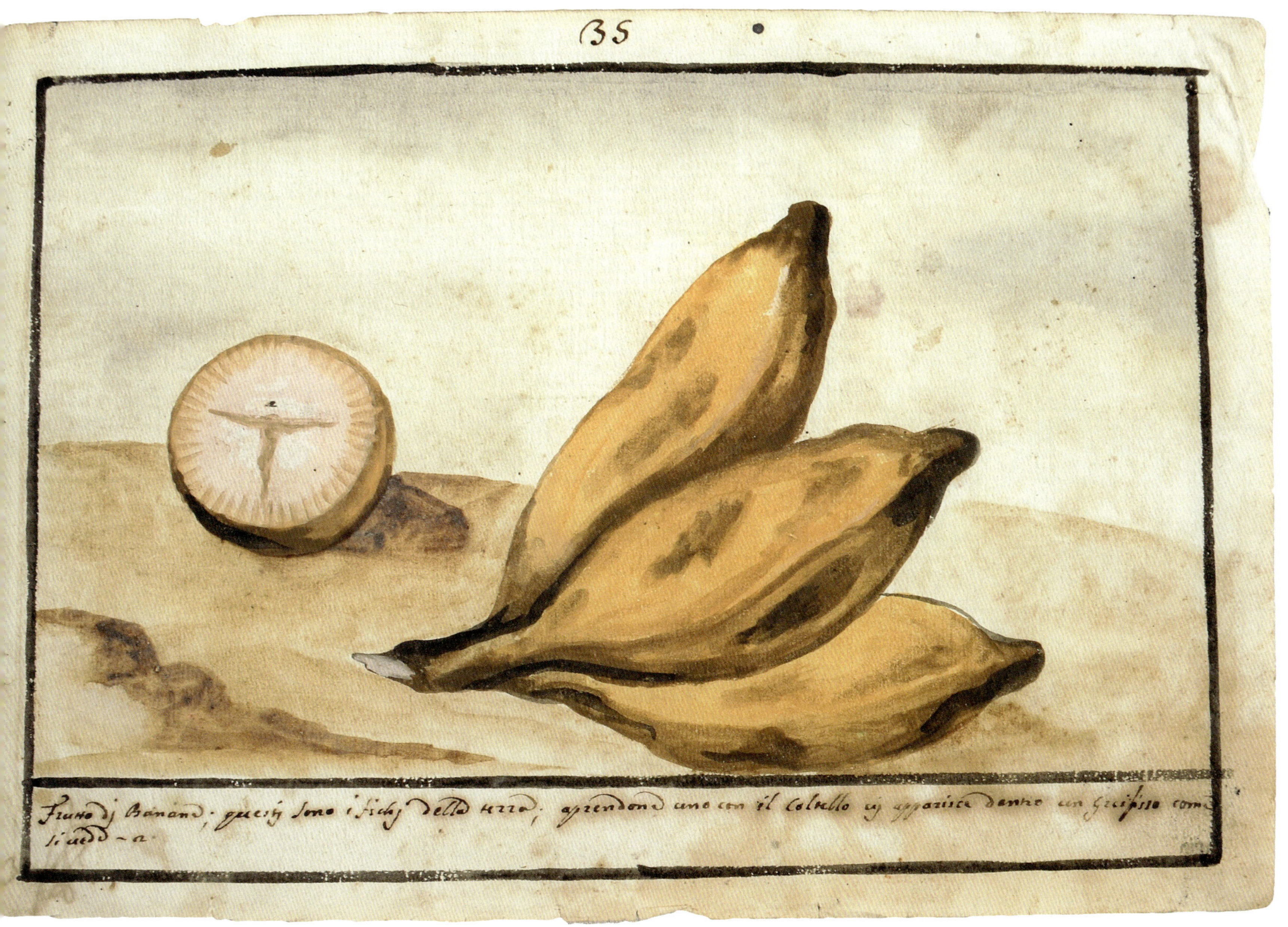

Plate 21

Fol. 35, "Fruit of a banana."

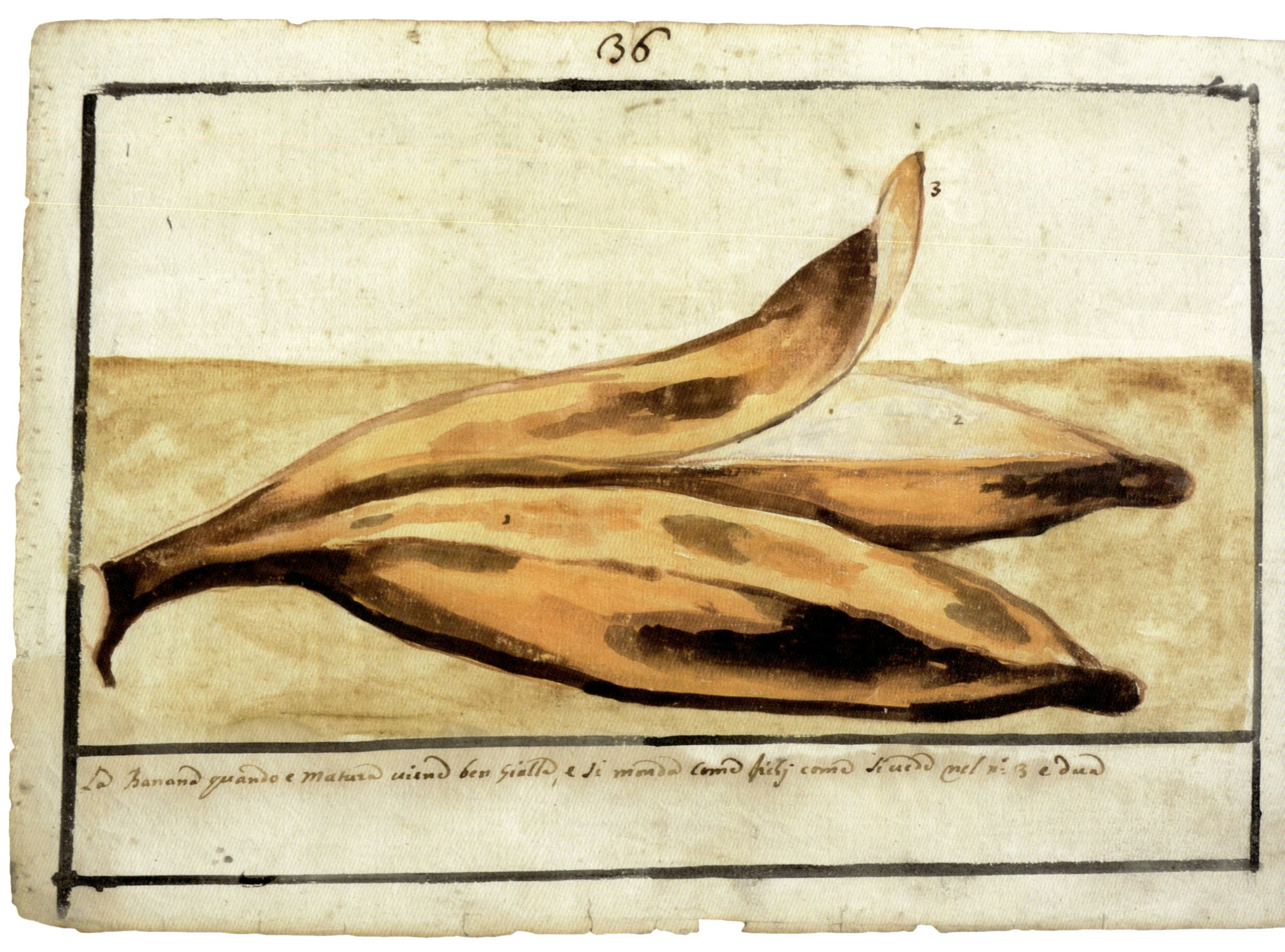

Plate 22

Fol. 36, "Banana when ripe."

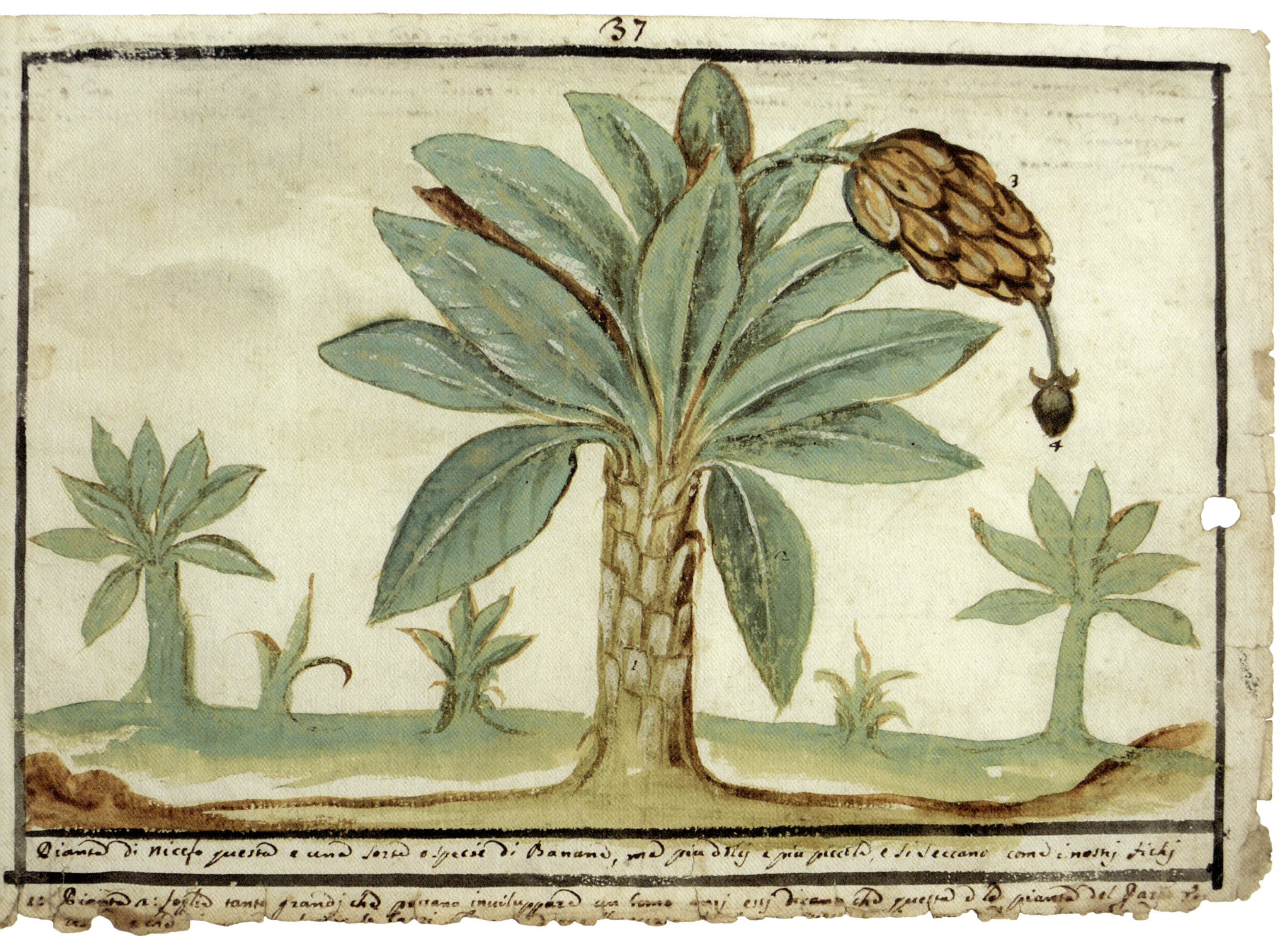

Plate 23

Fol. 37, "*Nicefo* plant [plantain]."

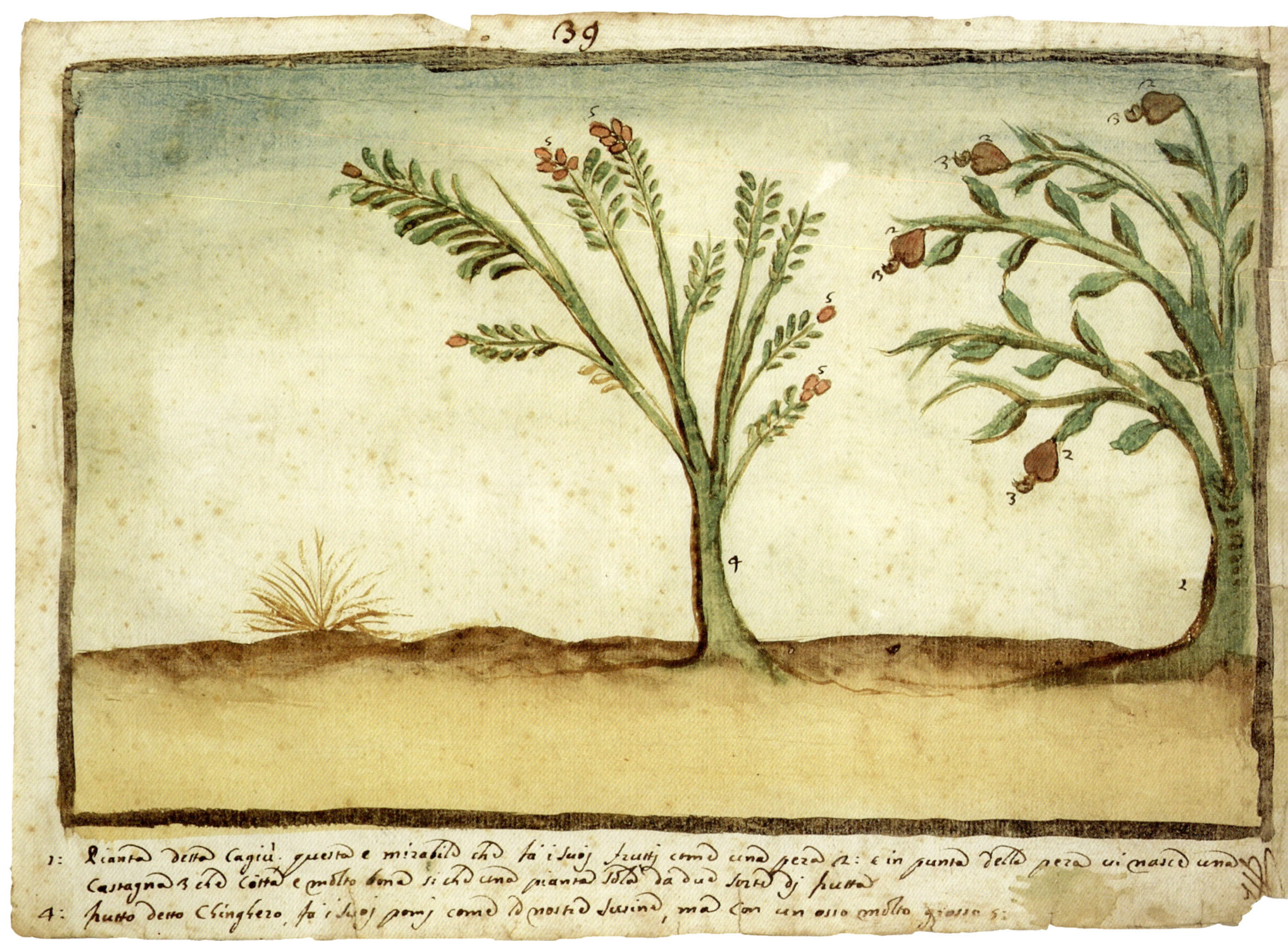

Plate 24

Fol. 39, "Plant called *cagiú* [cashew]. Fruit called *chingero* [mombin]."

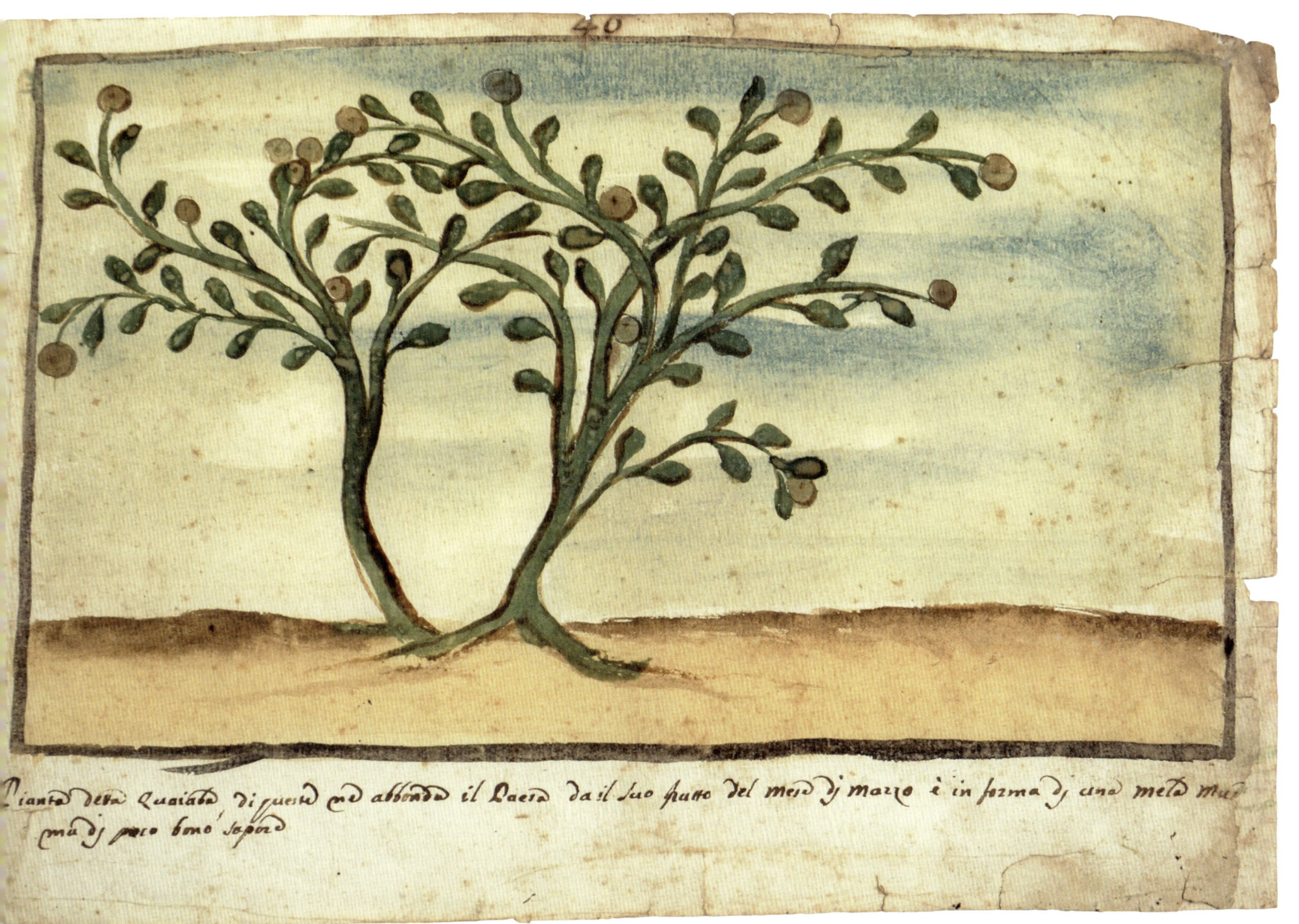

Plate 25

Fol. 40, "*Quoiaba* plant [guava]."

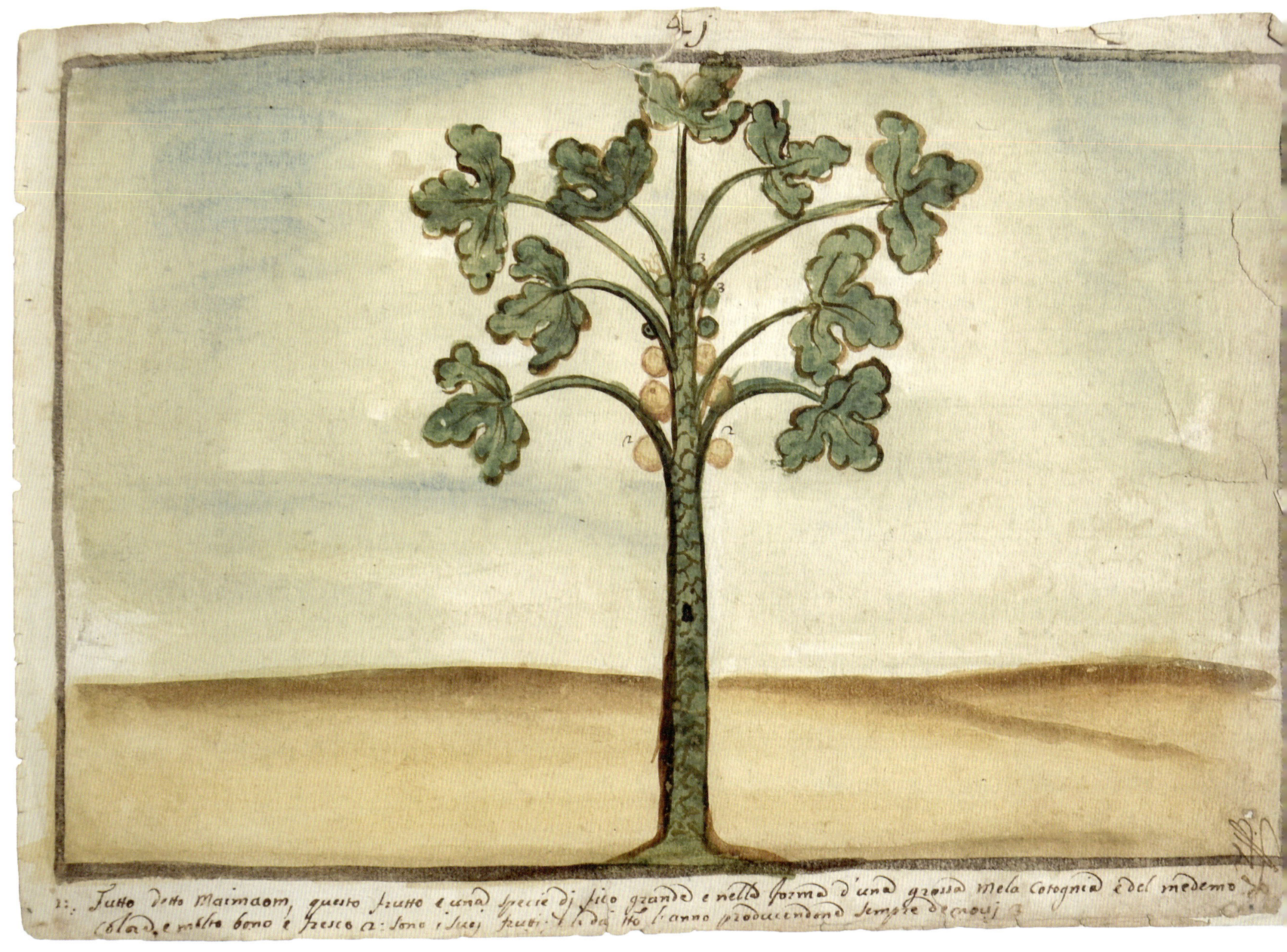

Plate 26

Fol. 41, "Fruit called *maimaom* [type of papaya]."

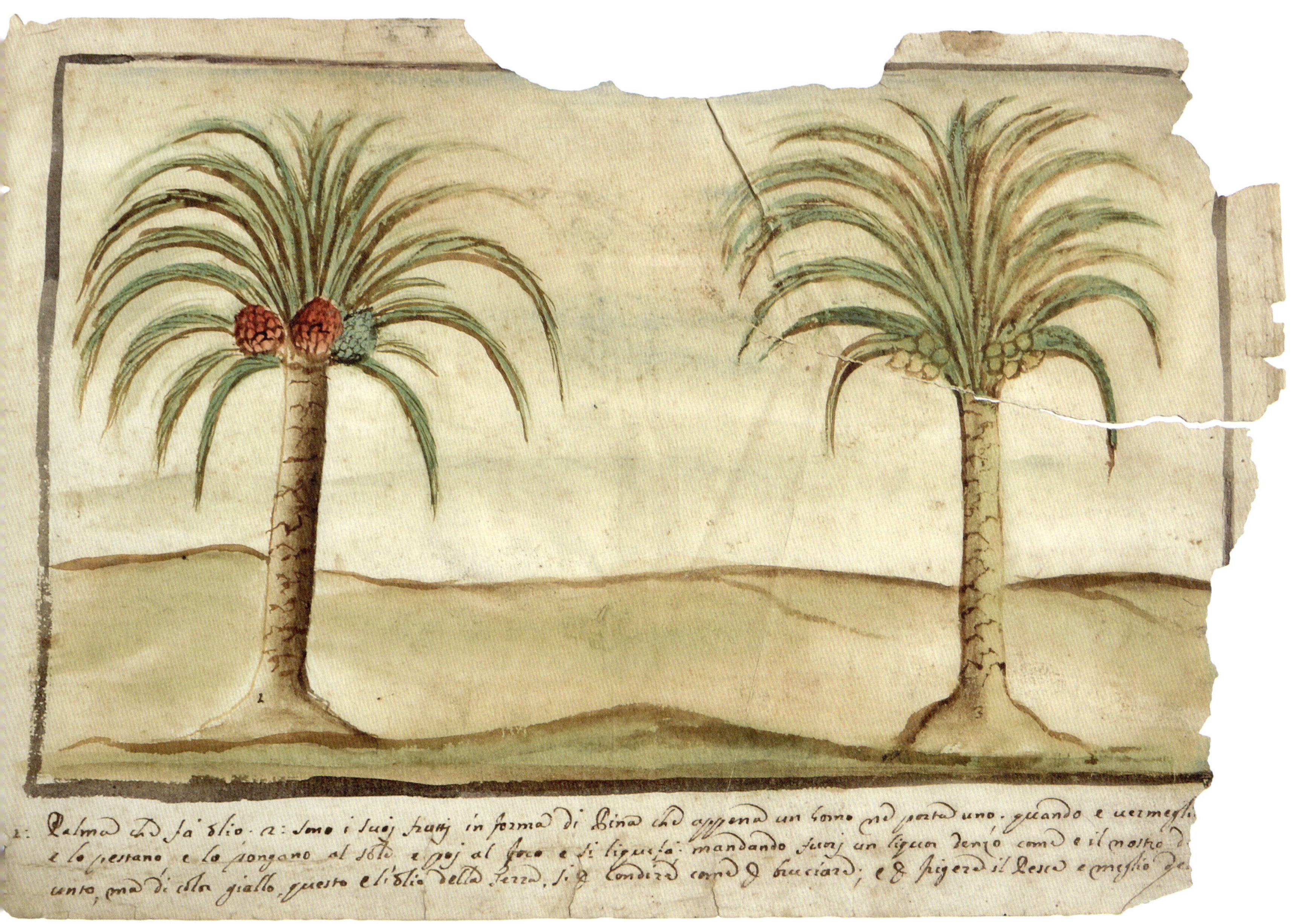

Plate 27

[Fol. 43], "Palm tree that makes oil."

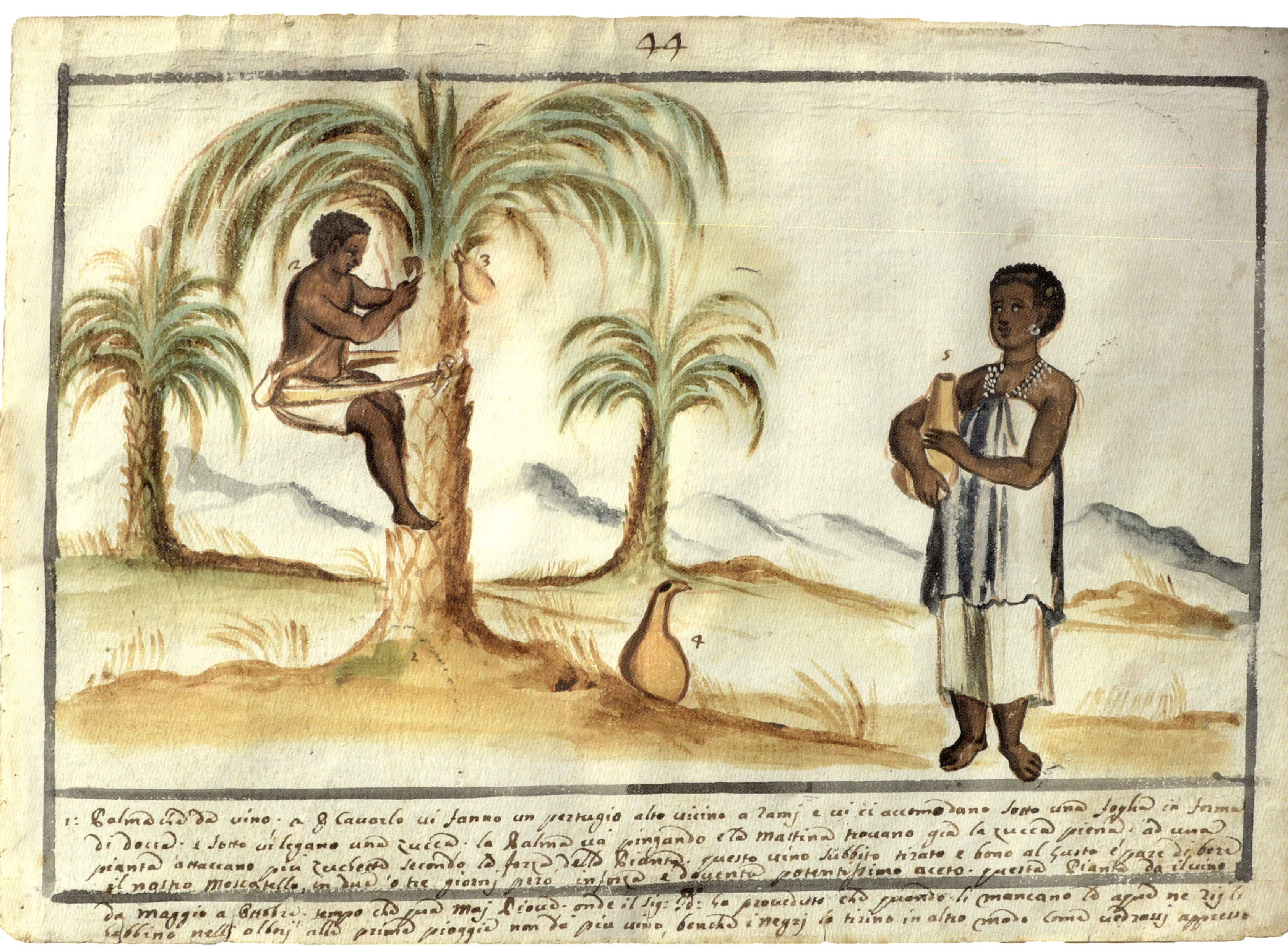

Plate 28

Fol. 44, "Palm tree that gives wine."

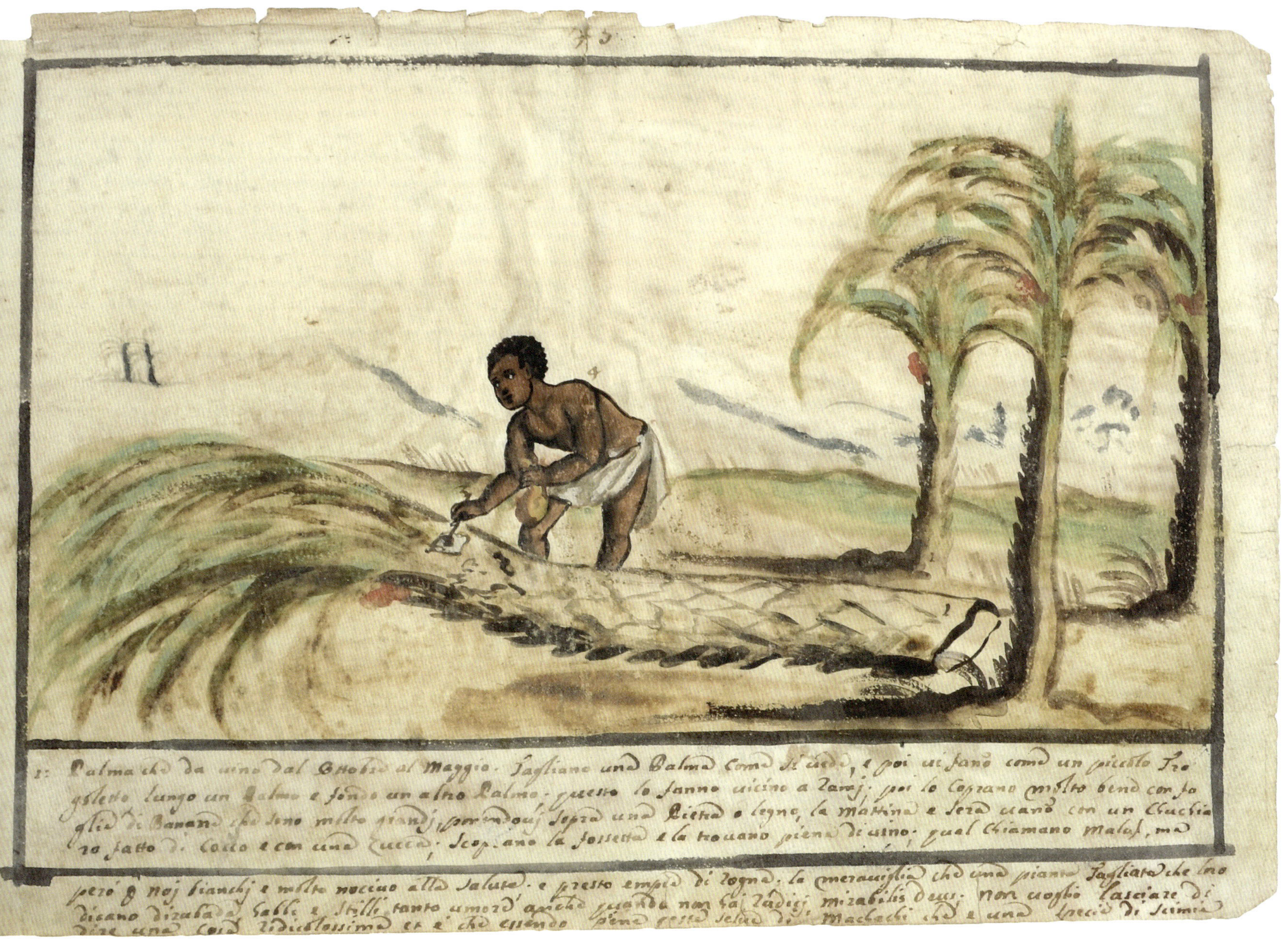

Fol. 45, "Palm tree that gives wine from October to May."

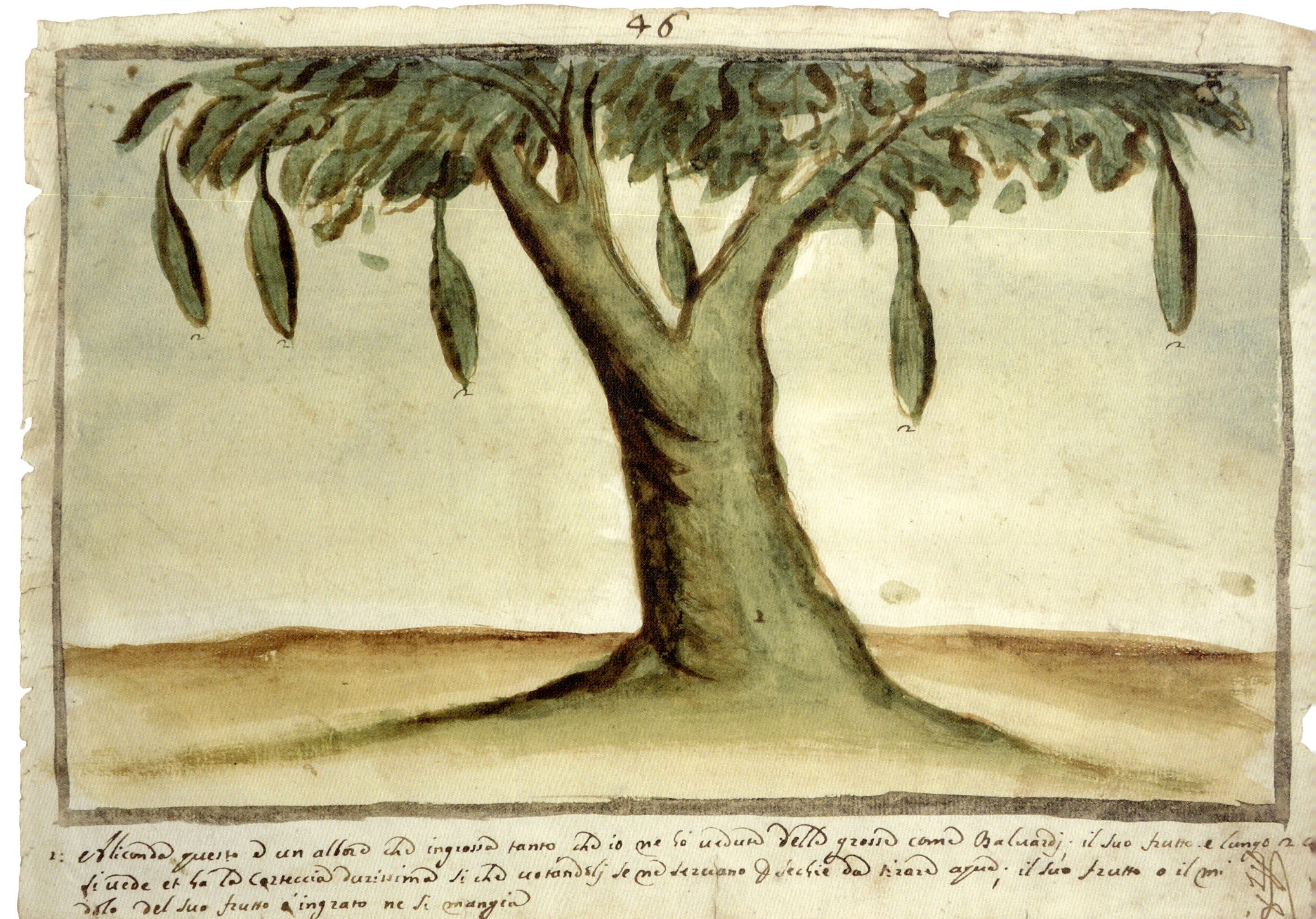

1: e' Aliconde questo è un alboro che ingrossa tanto che io ne ho ueduto della grosso como Baluardi. il suo frutto e lungo
si uede et ha la Correccia durissima si che uotandoli se ne seruano di fechie da tirare aqua. il suo frutto o il mi-
dolo del suo frutto è ingrato ne si mangia

Plate 30

Fol. 46, "*Aliconde* tree."

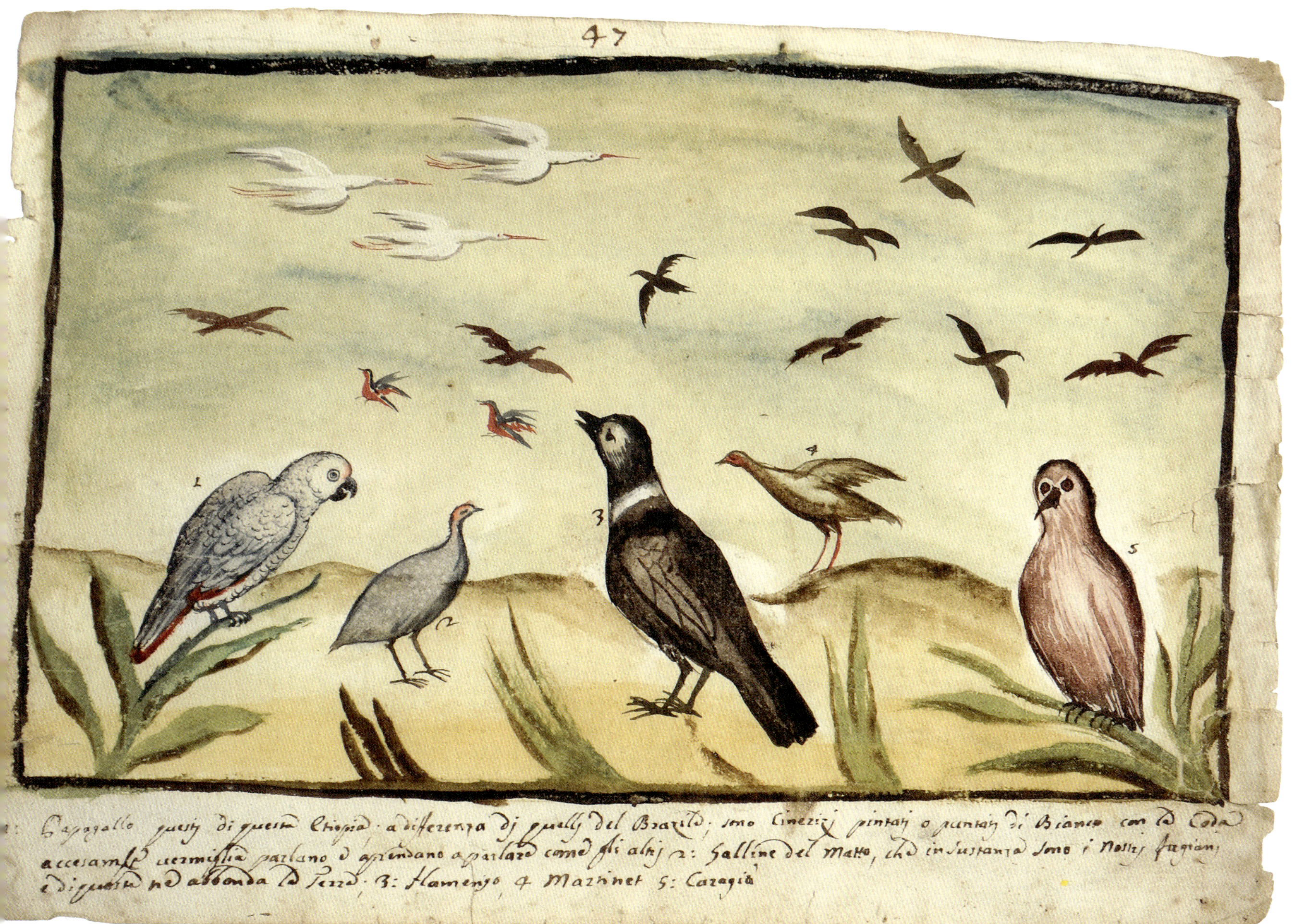

Plate 31

Fol. 47, "Parakeets. Bush hens. Flamingo. Martinet.
Caragiú."

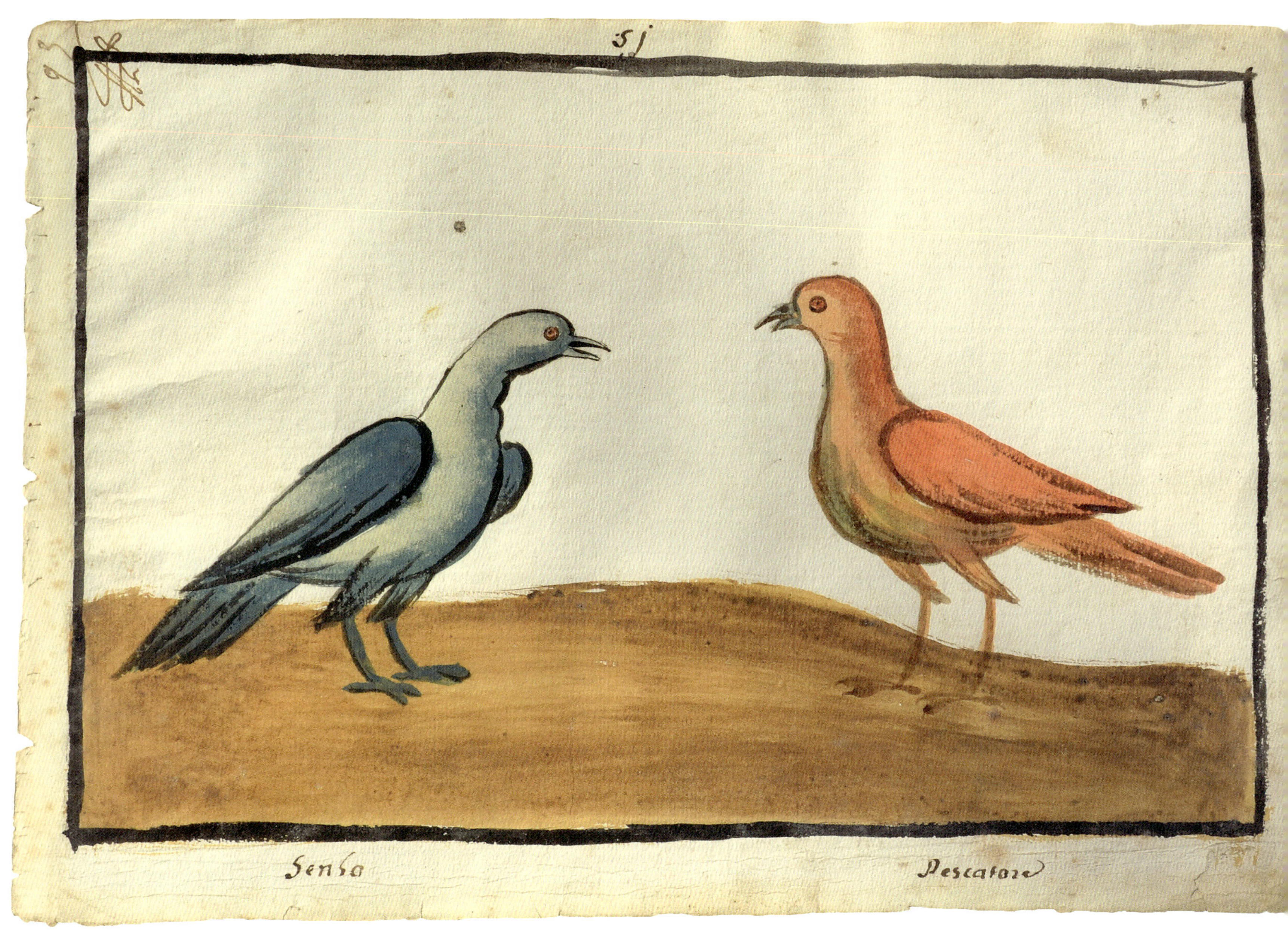

Plate 32

Fol. 51, "*Genga* [*Ganga* bird?]. *Pescatore* [fishing bird]."

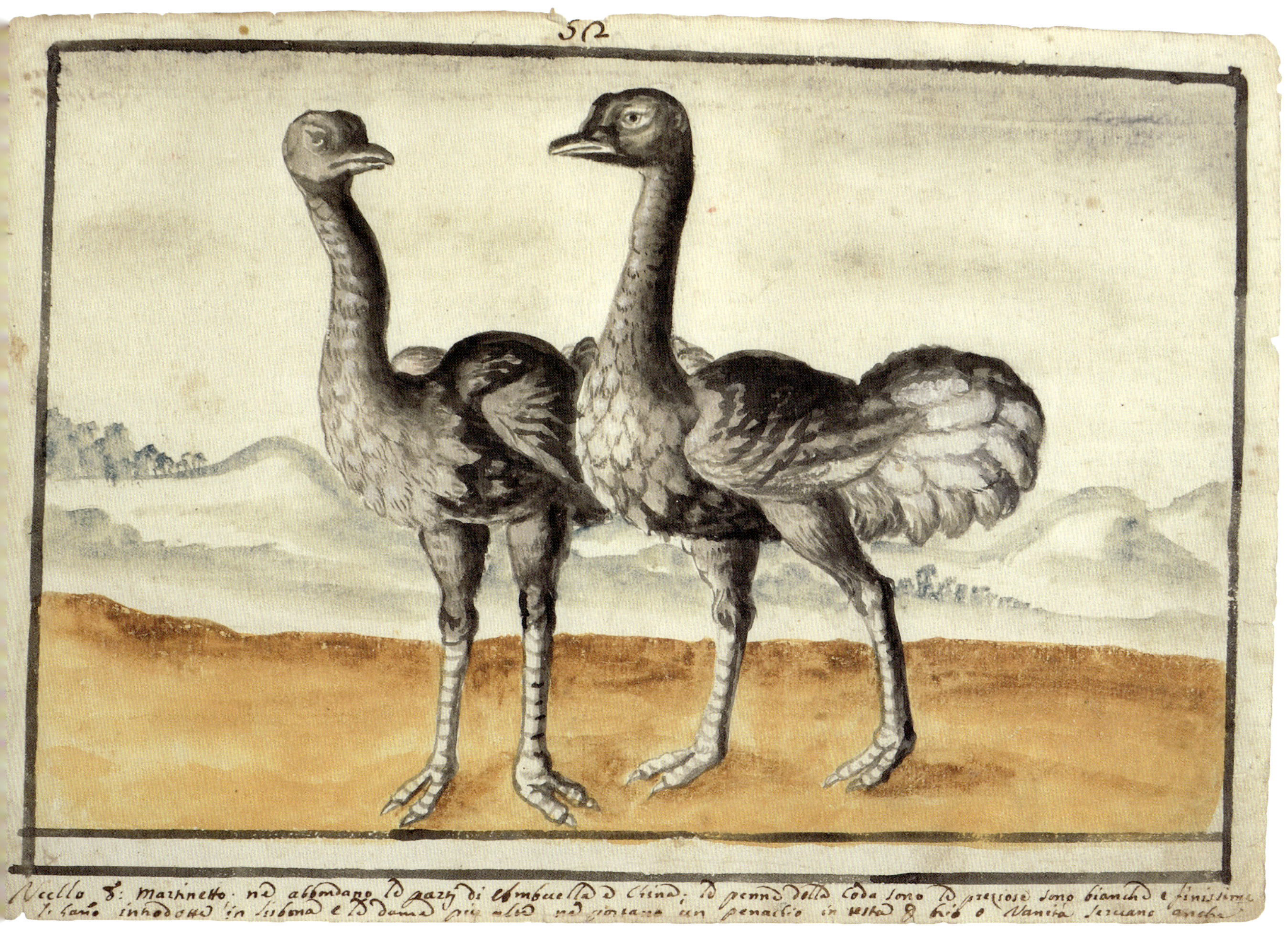

Plate 33

Fol. 52, "Bird called *martinetto*."

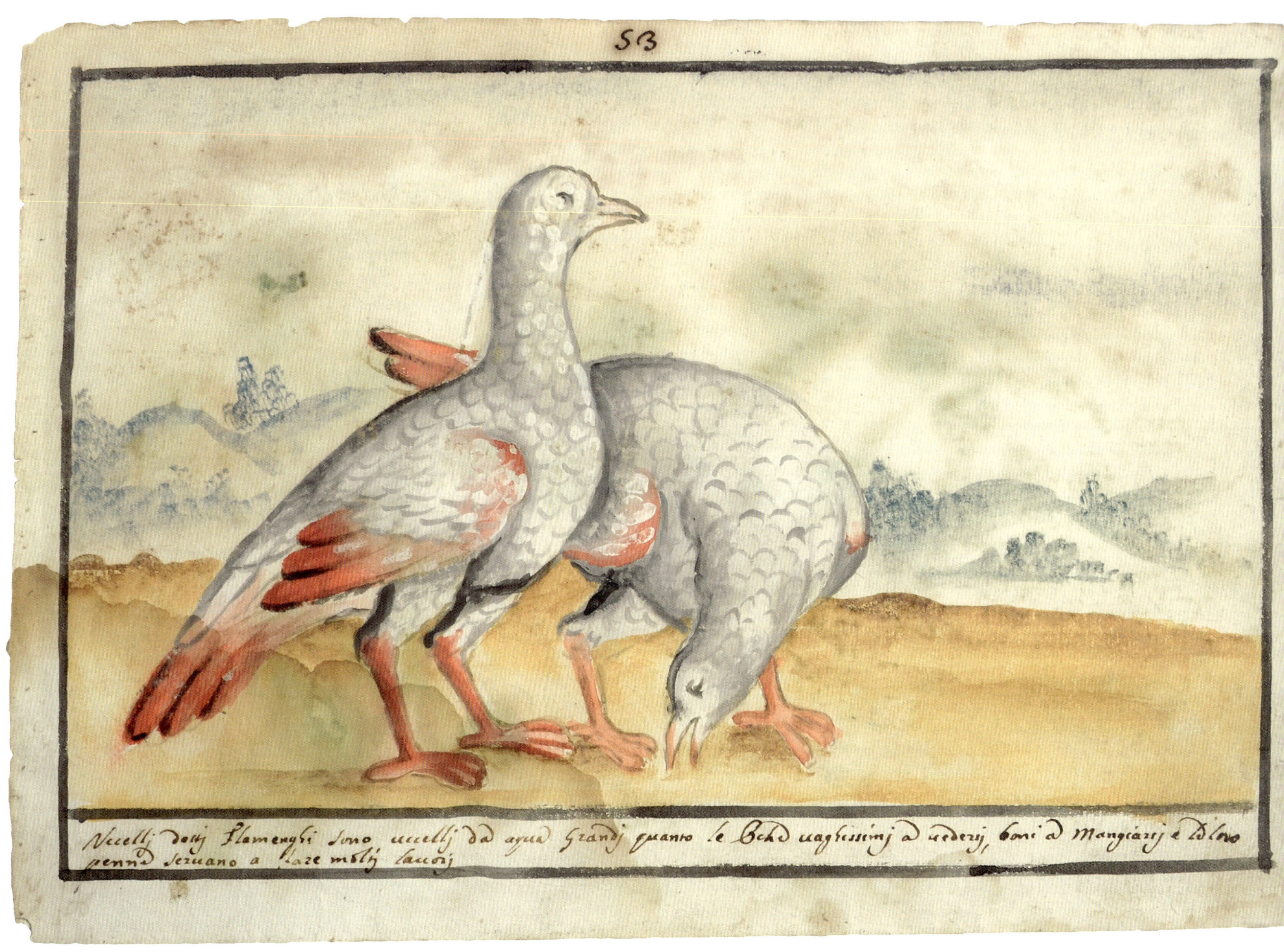

Plate 34

Fol. 53, "Birds called flamingoes."

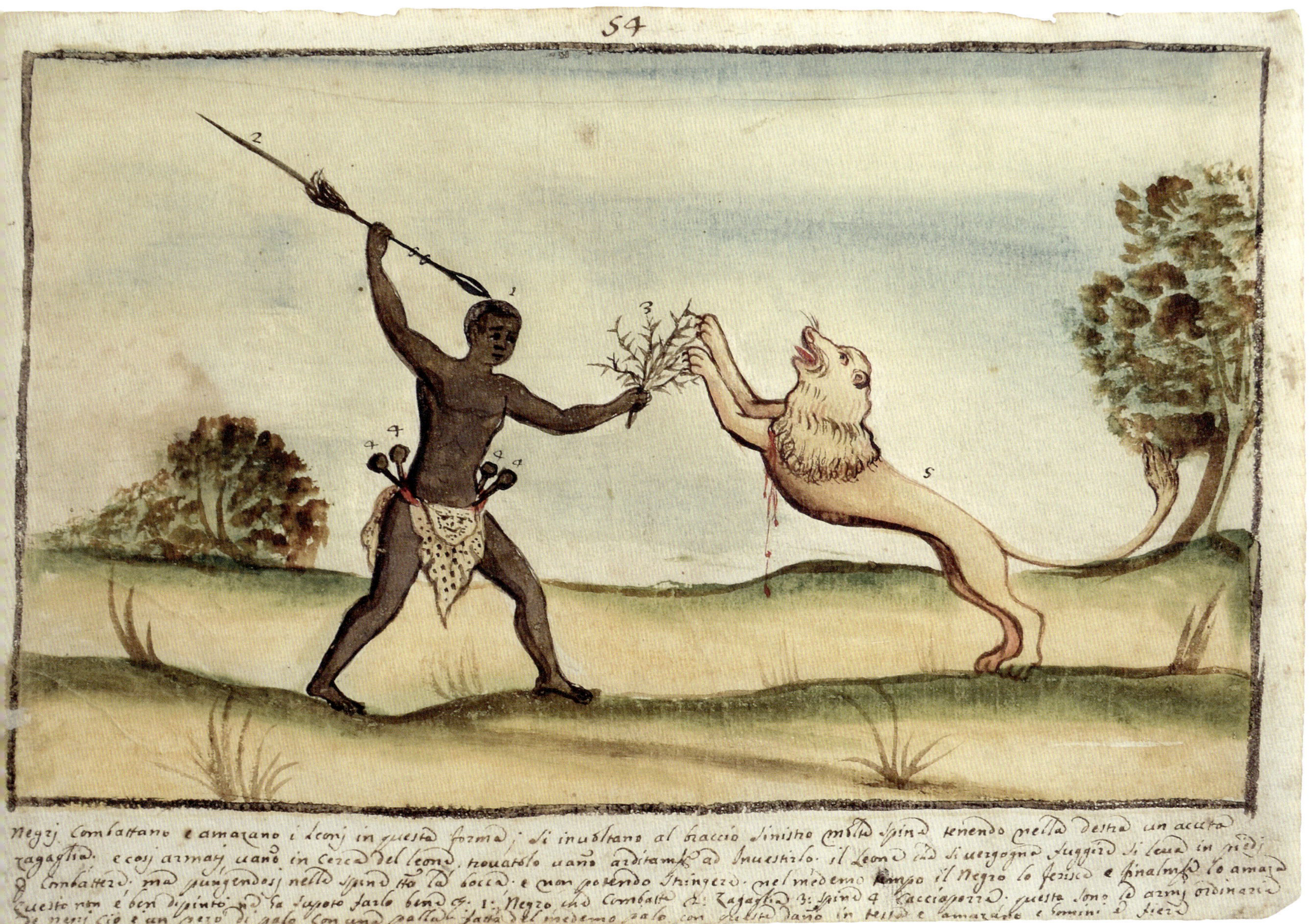

Plate 35

Fol. 54, "The blacks fight and kill lions in this manner."

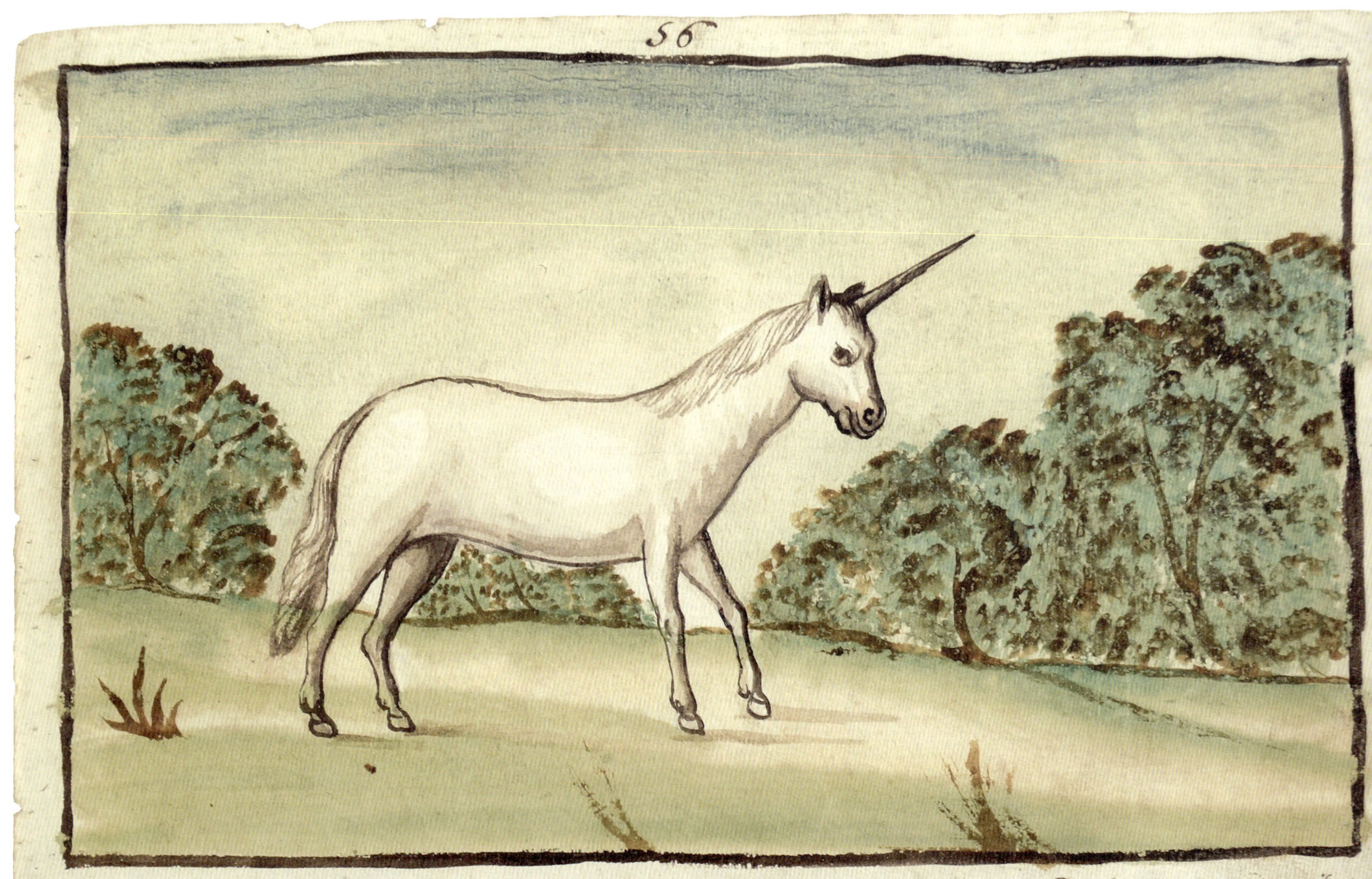

Plate 36

Fol. 56, "*Alicorno* [unicorn] here called *Bada*."

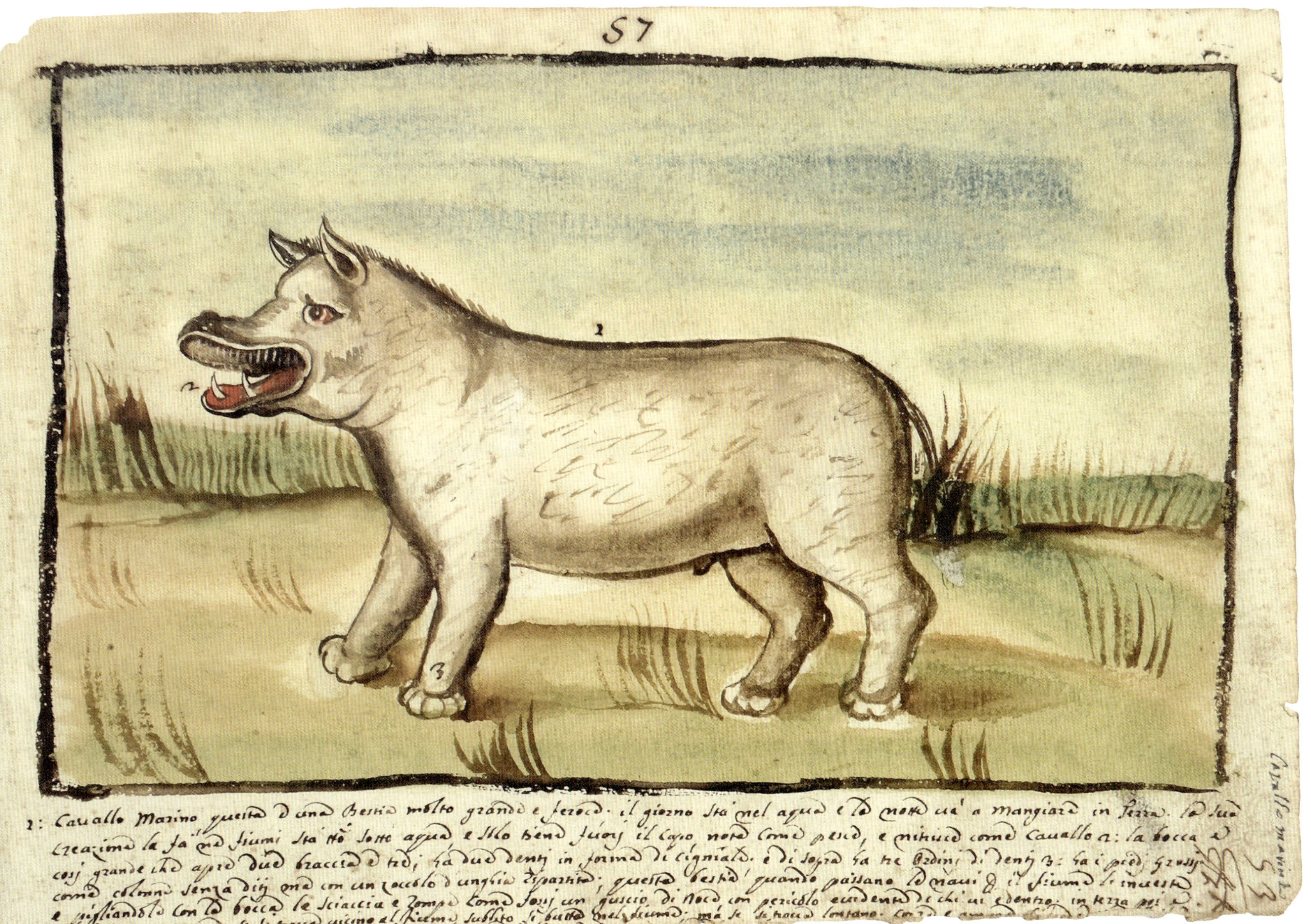

Plate 37

Fol. 57, "*Cavallo Marino* [hippopotamus]."

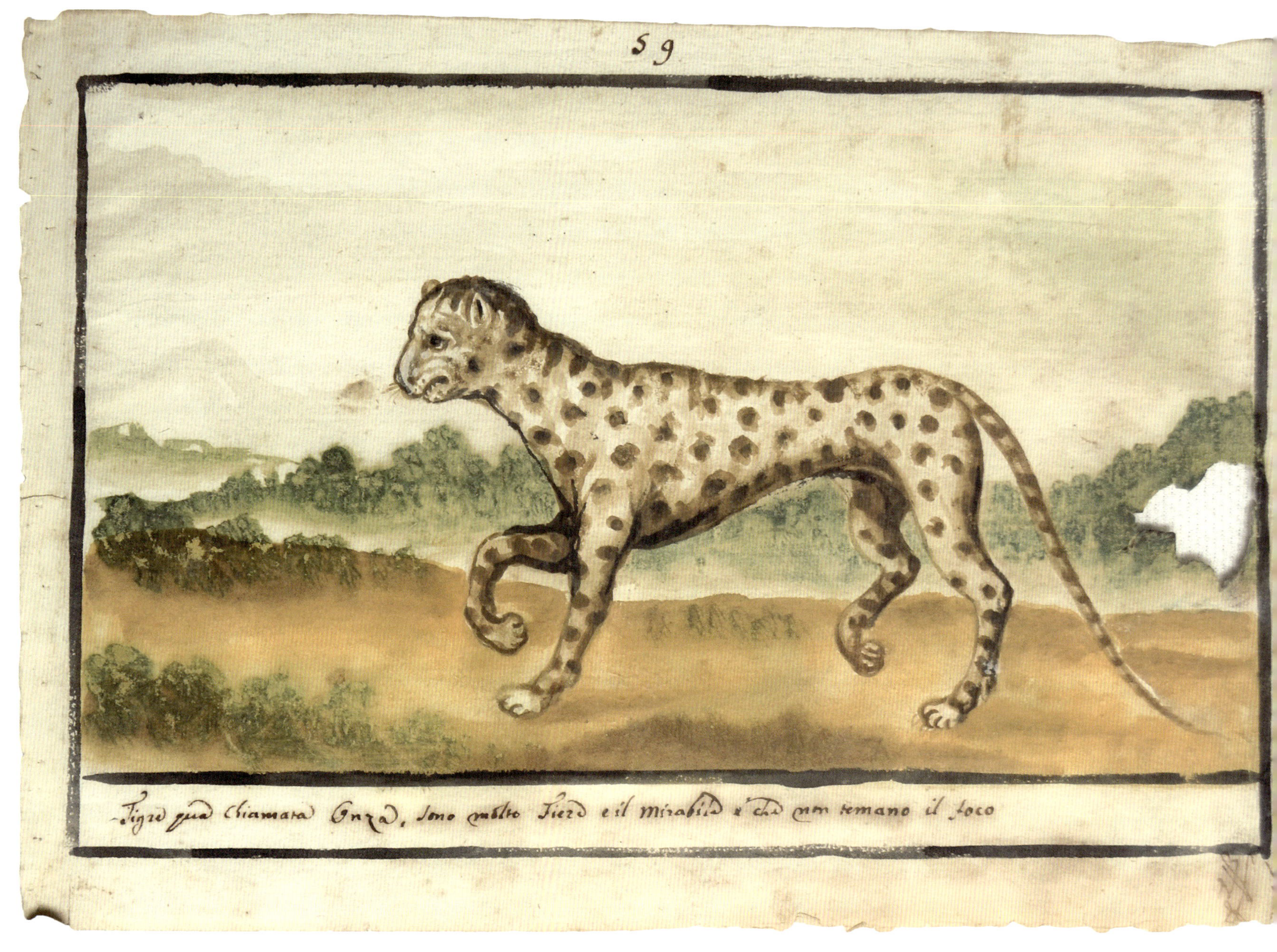

Plate 38
Fol. 59, "Tiger, here called *Onza* [ounce or lynx]."

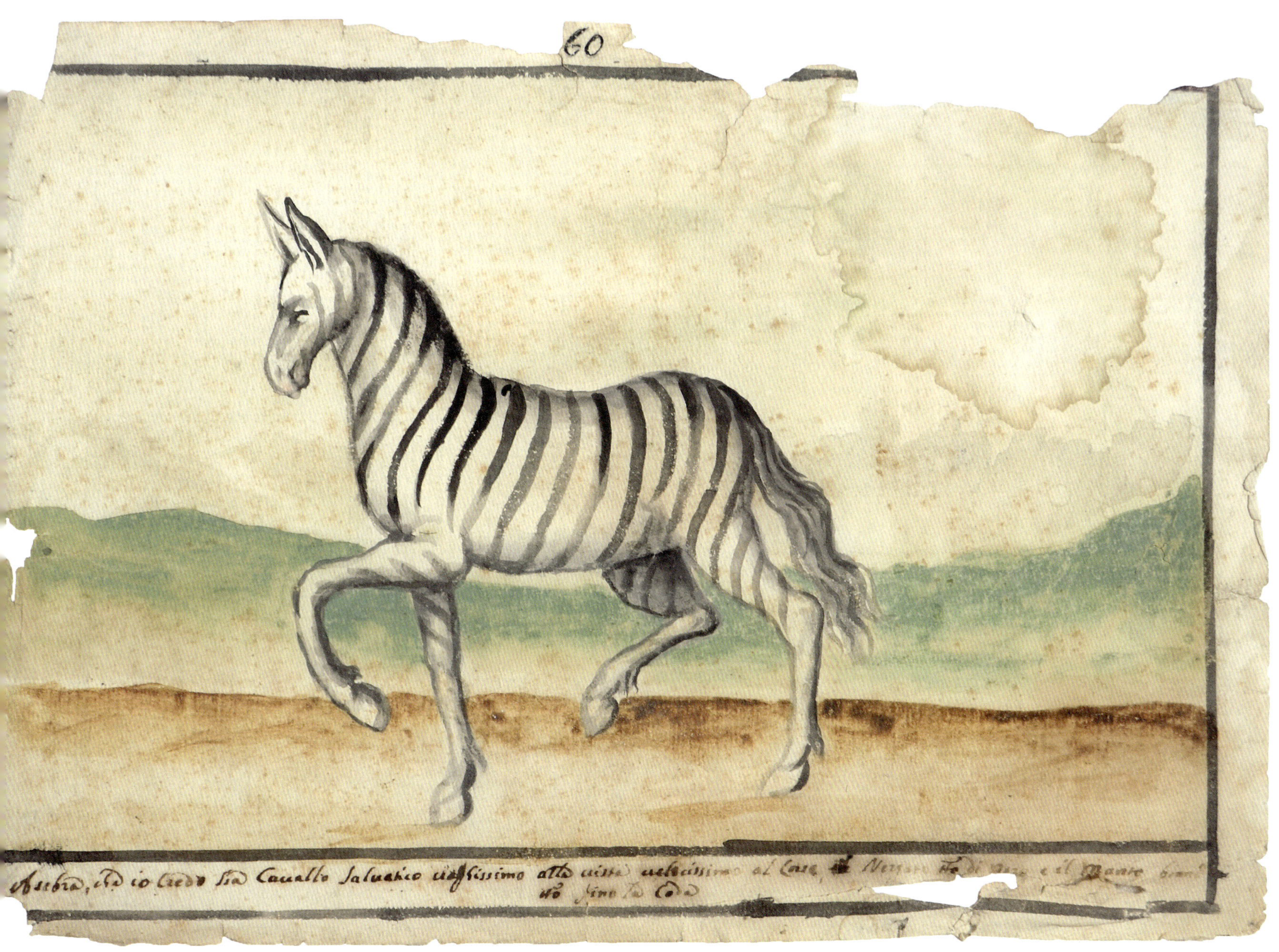

Plate 39
Fol. 60, "Zebra."

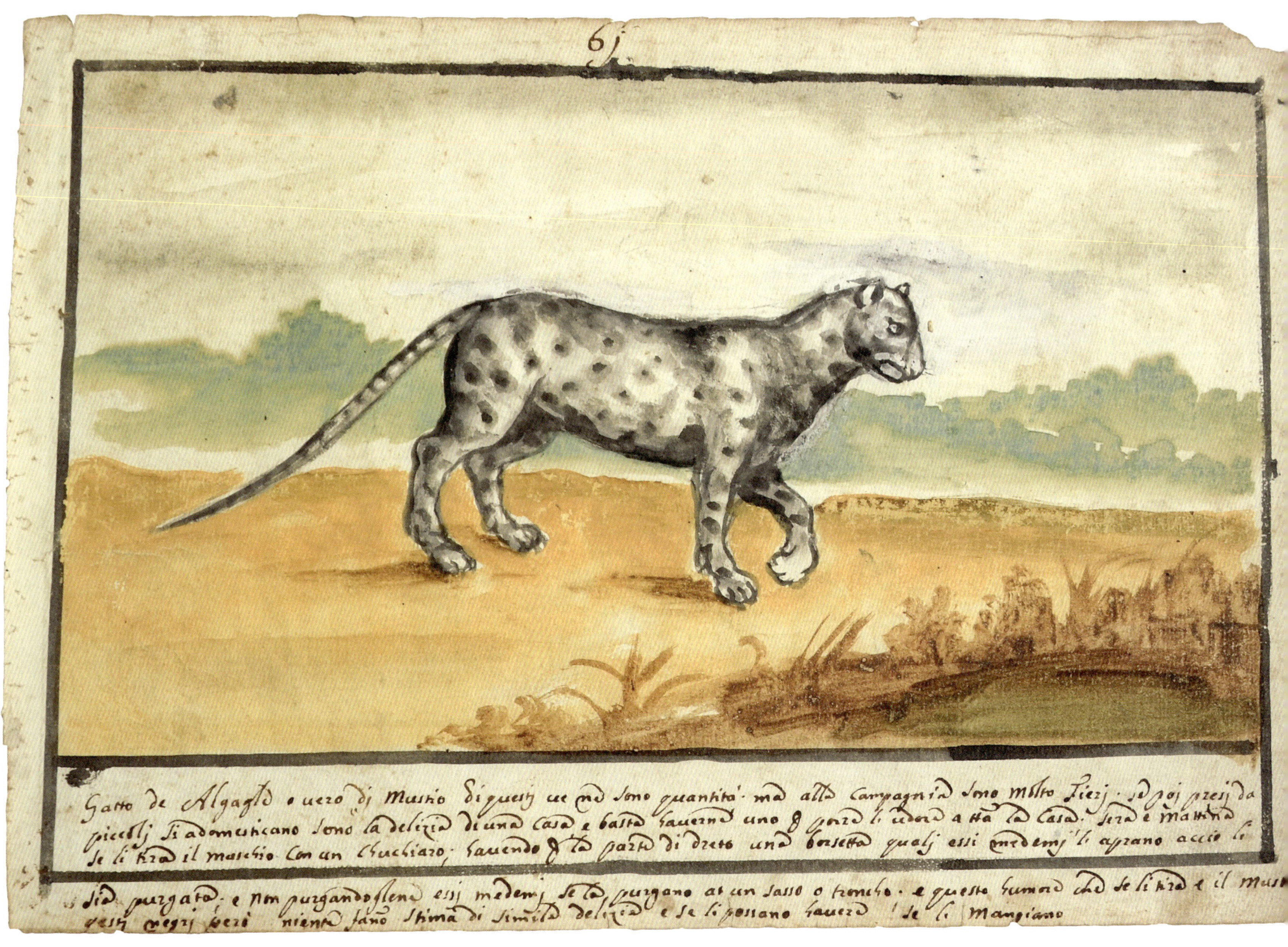

Plate 40

Fol. 61, "Civet, or musk cat."

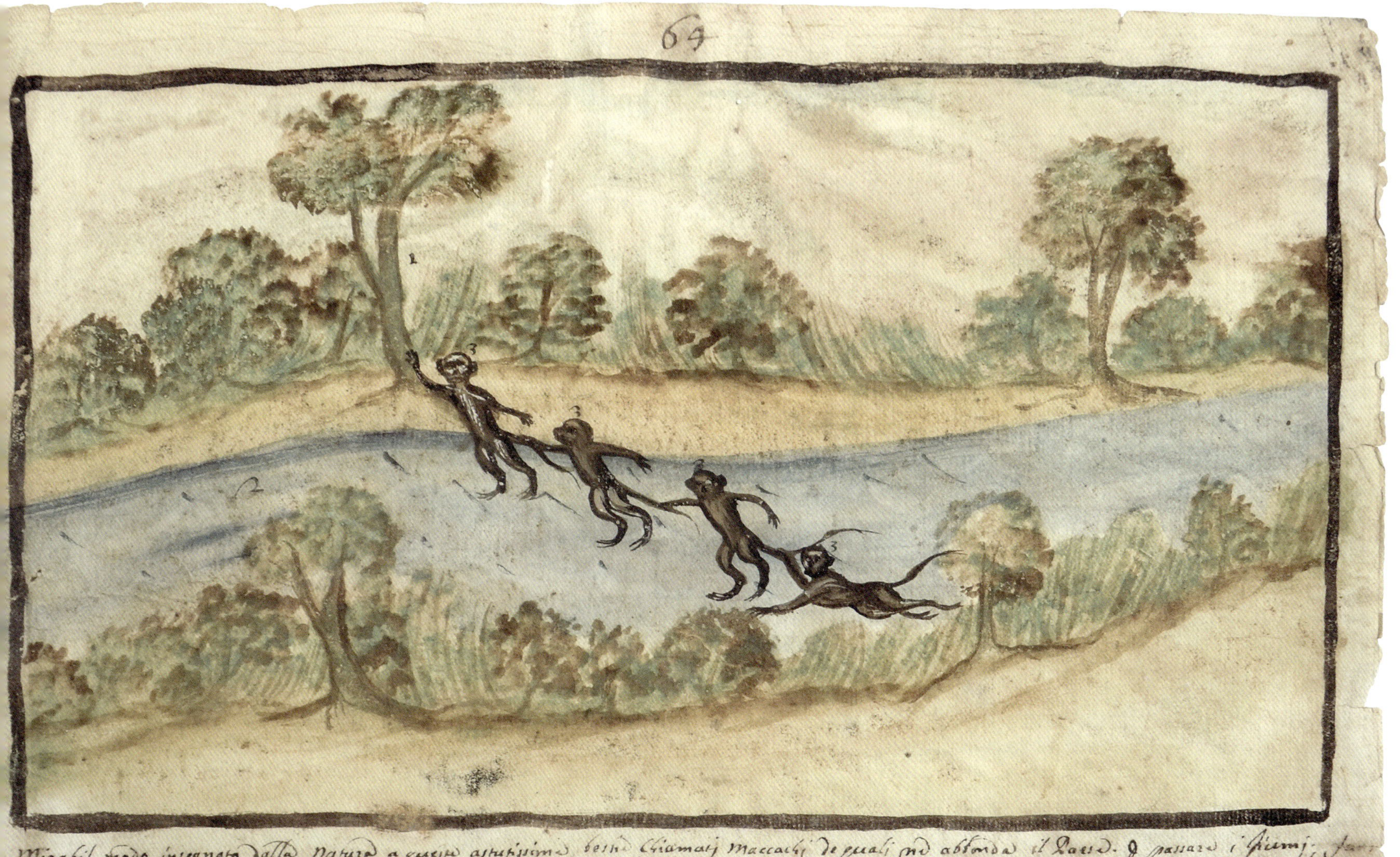

Plate 41

Fol. 64, "Remarkable way taught by nature [to] macaques
. . . to cross rivers."

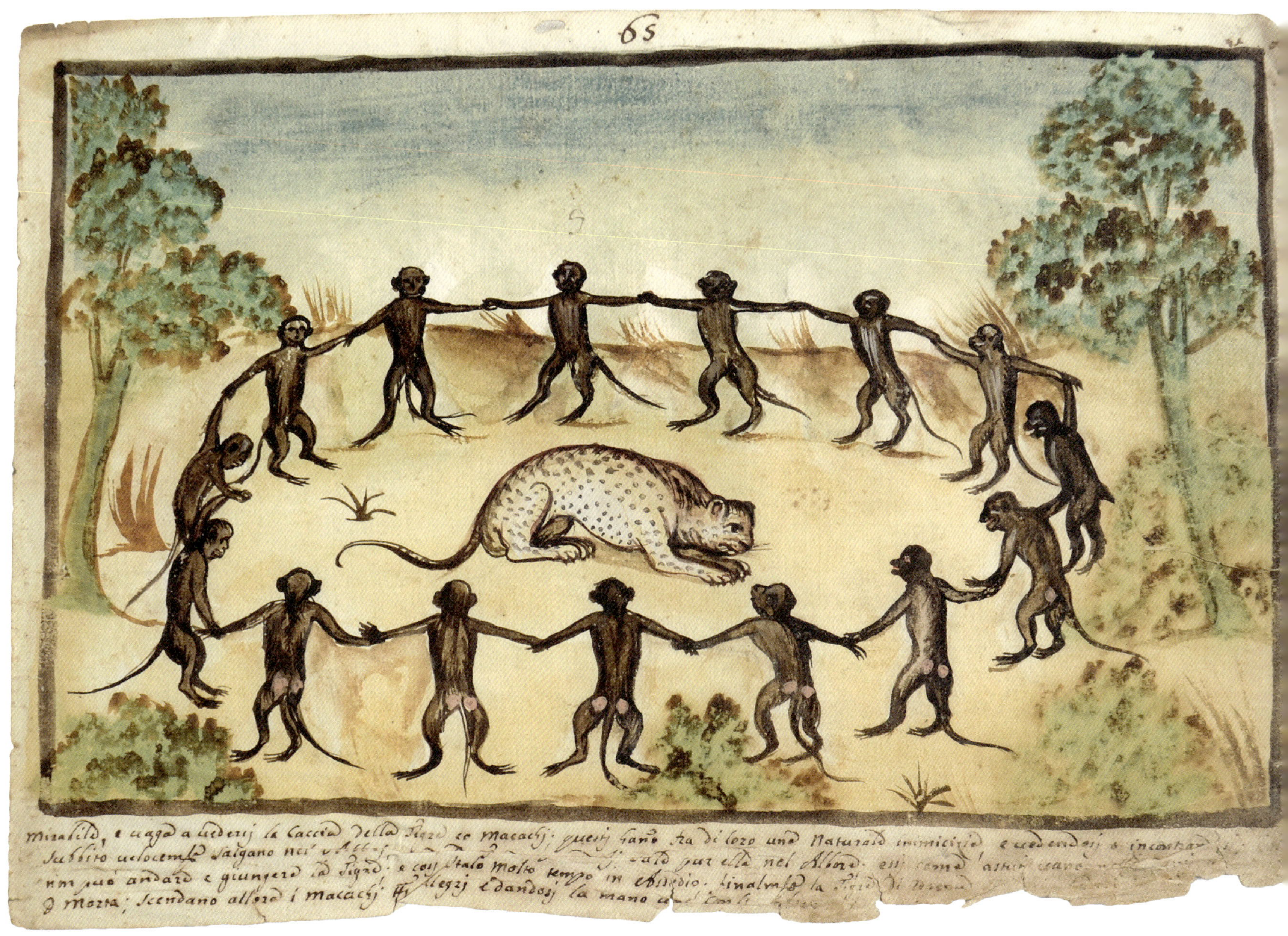

Plate 42

Fol. 65, "Remarkable . . . hunt of the tiger by macaques."

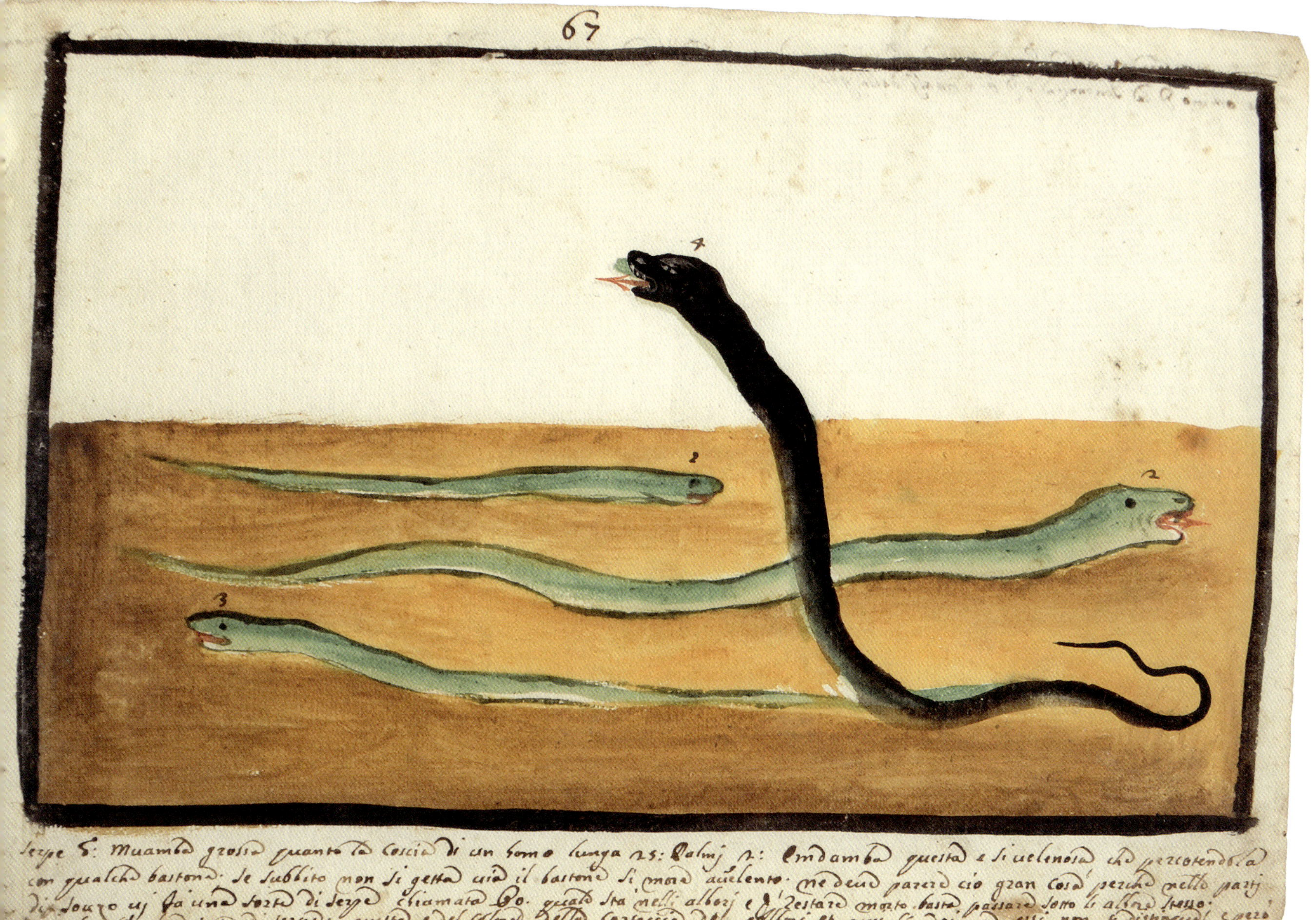

Plate 43

Fol. 67, "Snakes called *muamba . . . emdamba . . . nbambi.*"

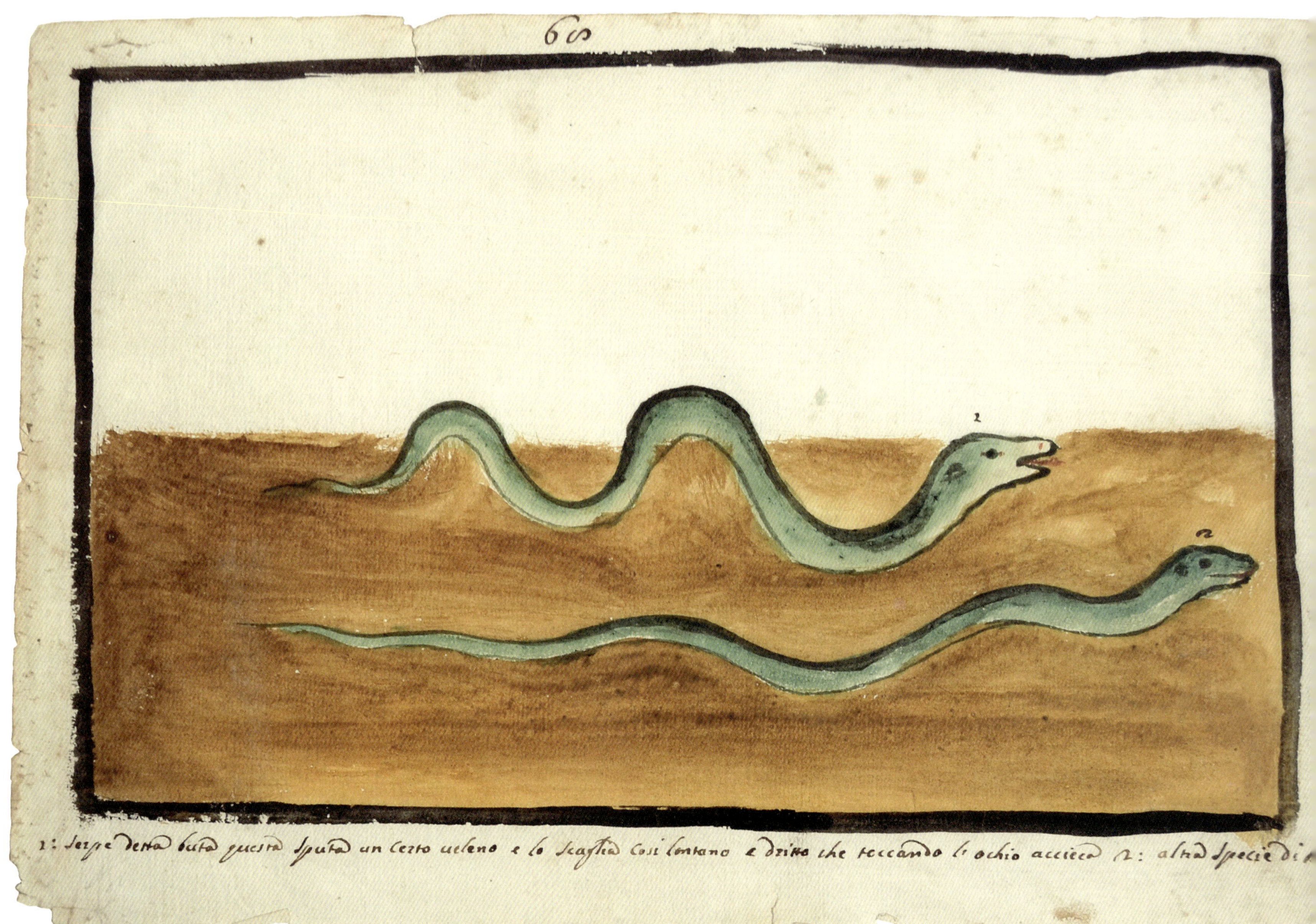

Plate 44

Fol. 68, "Snake called *buta*."

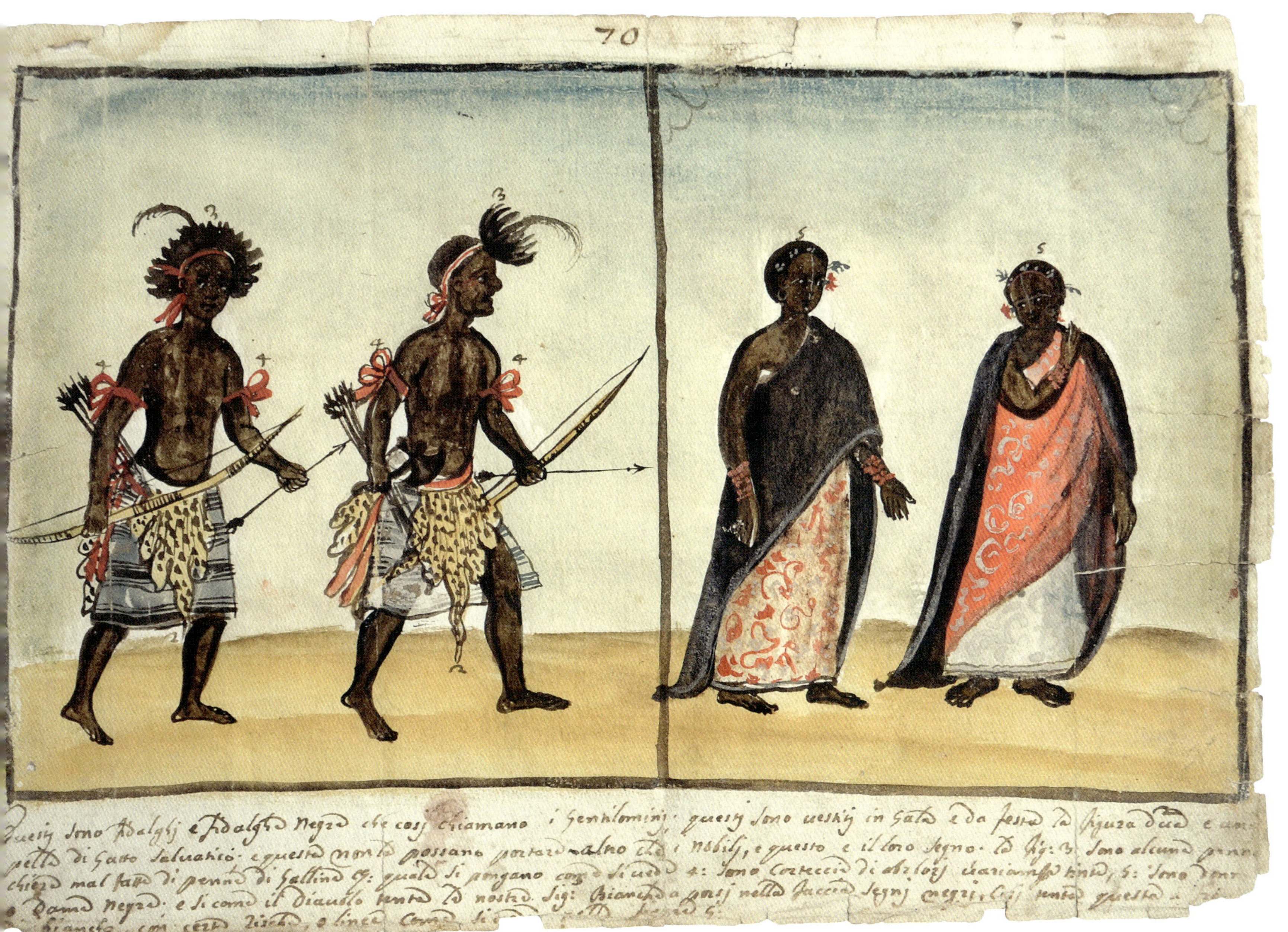

Plate 45

Fol. 70, "Black male and female aristocrats."

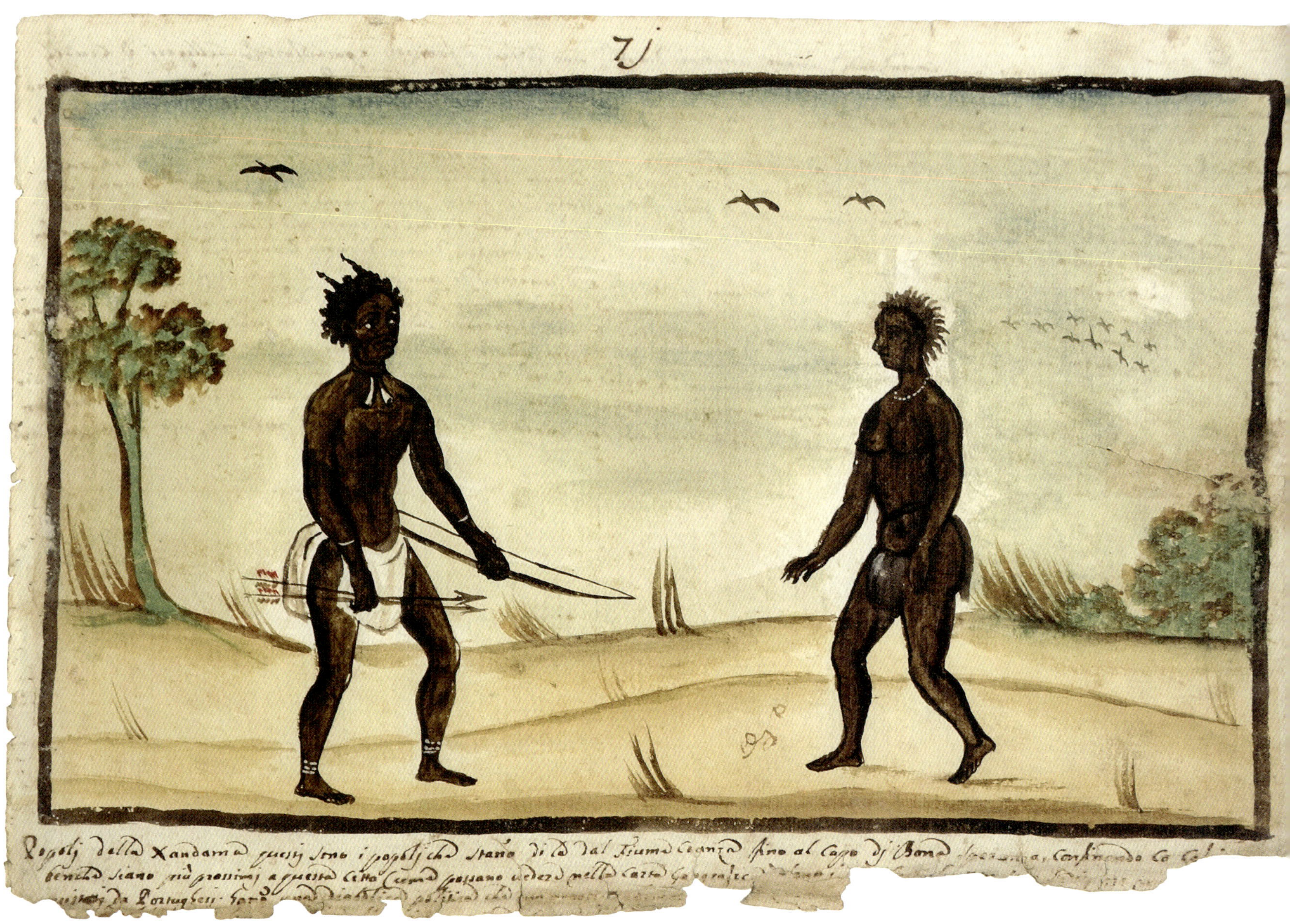

Plate 46

Fol. 71, "People of Xandama."

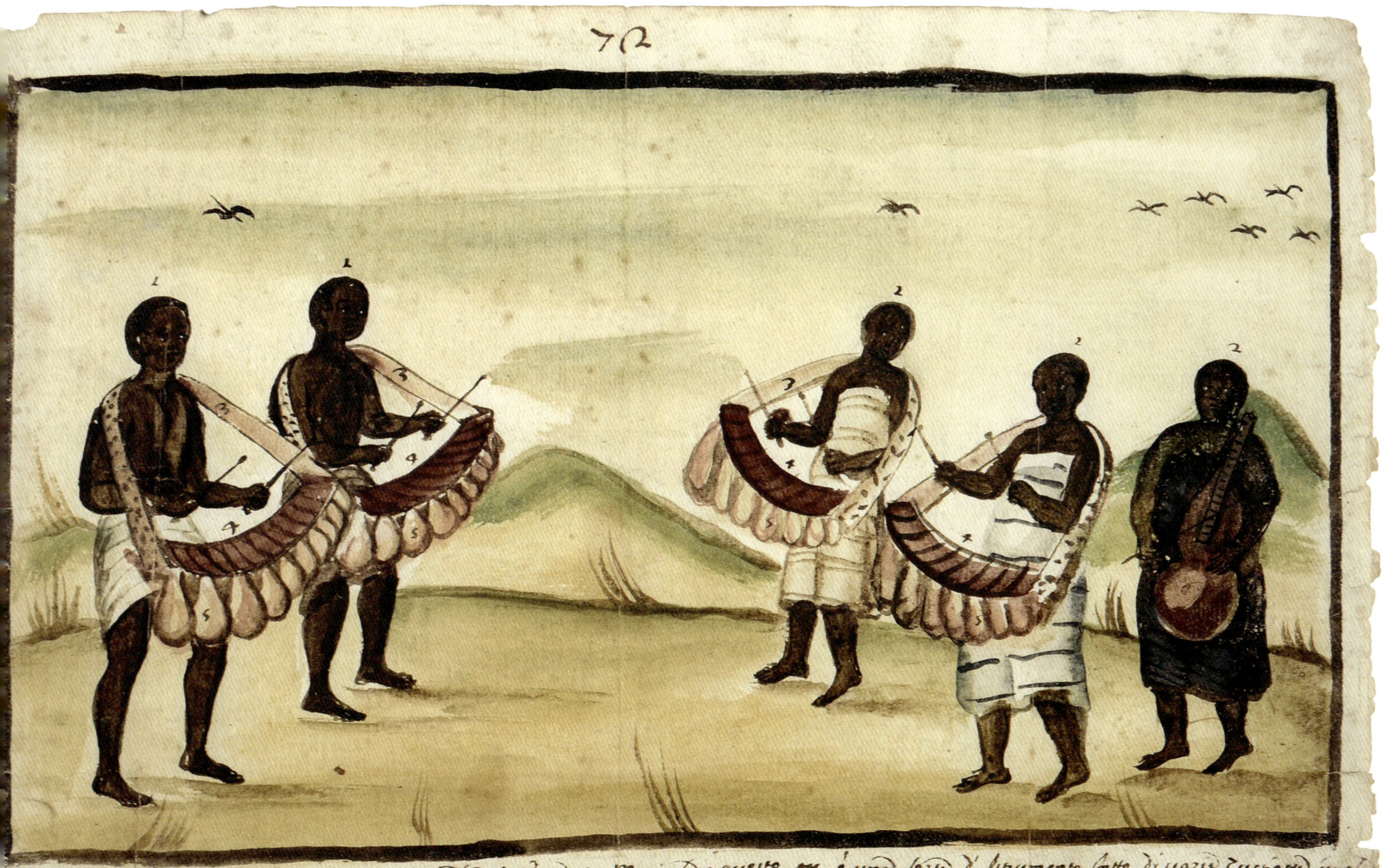

Plate 47

Fol. 72, "Black musicians."

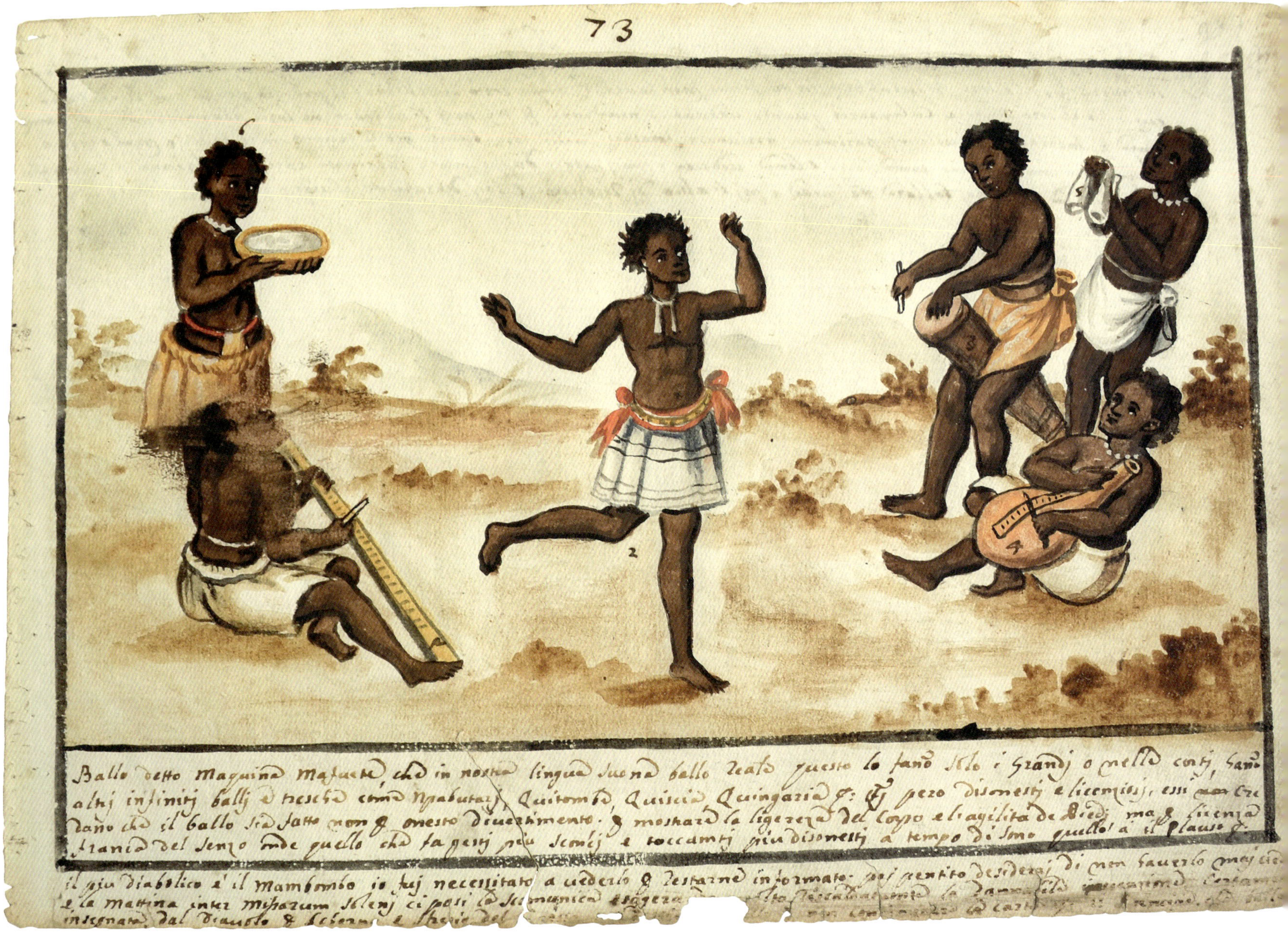

Plate 48

Fol. 73, "Dance called *maquina mafuete*."

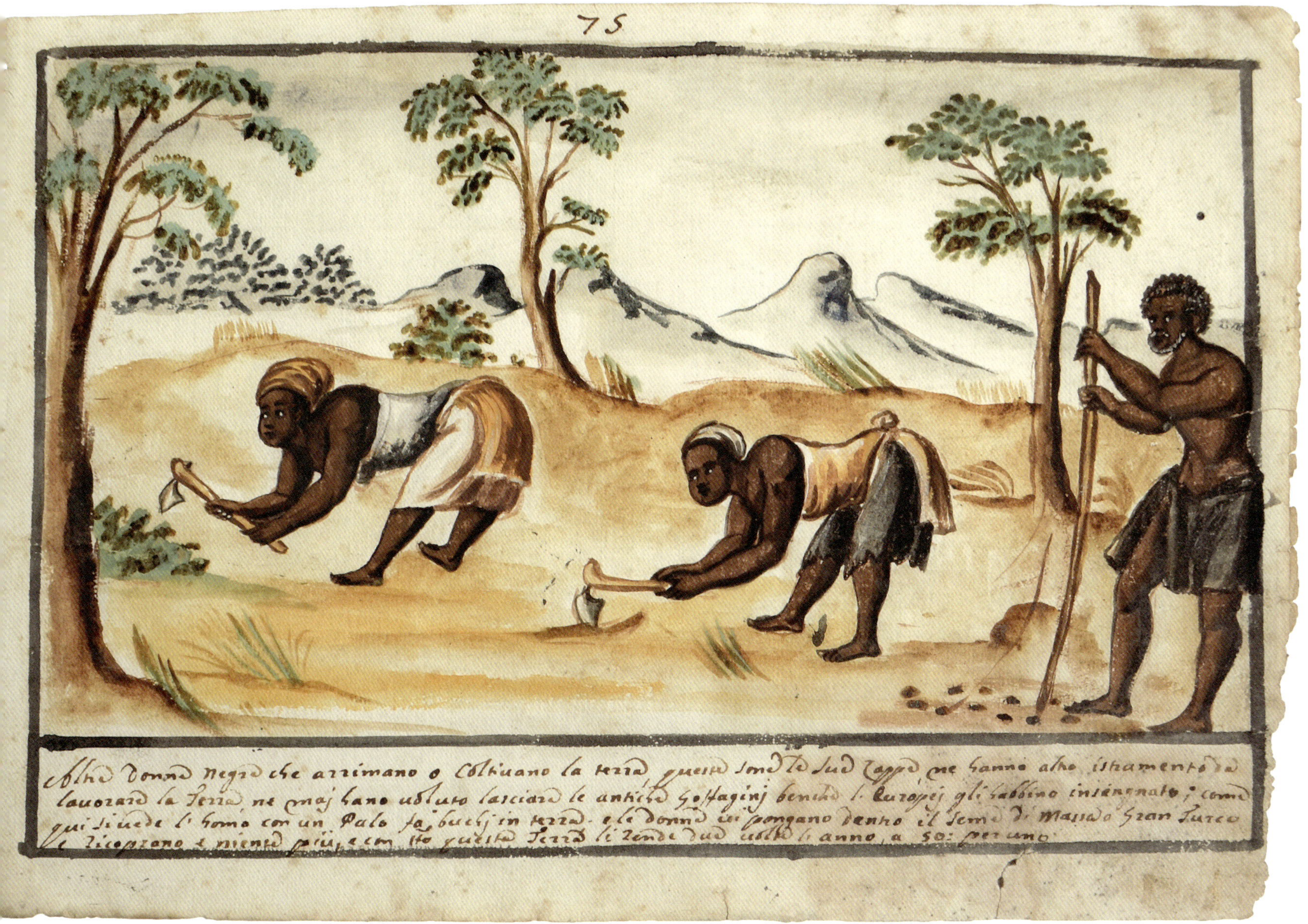

Plate 49

Fol. 75, "Other black women who . . . cultivate the land."

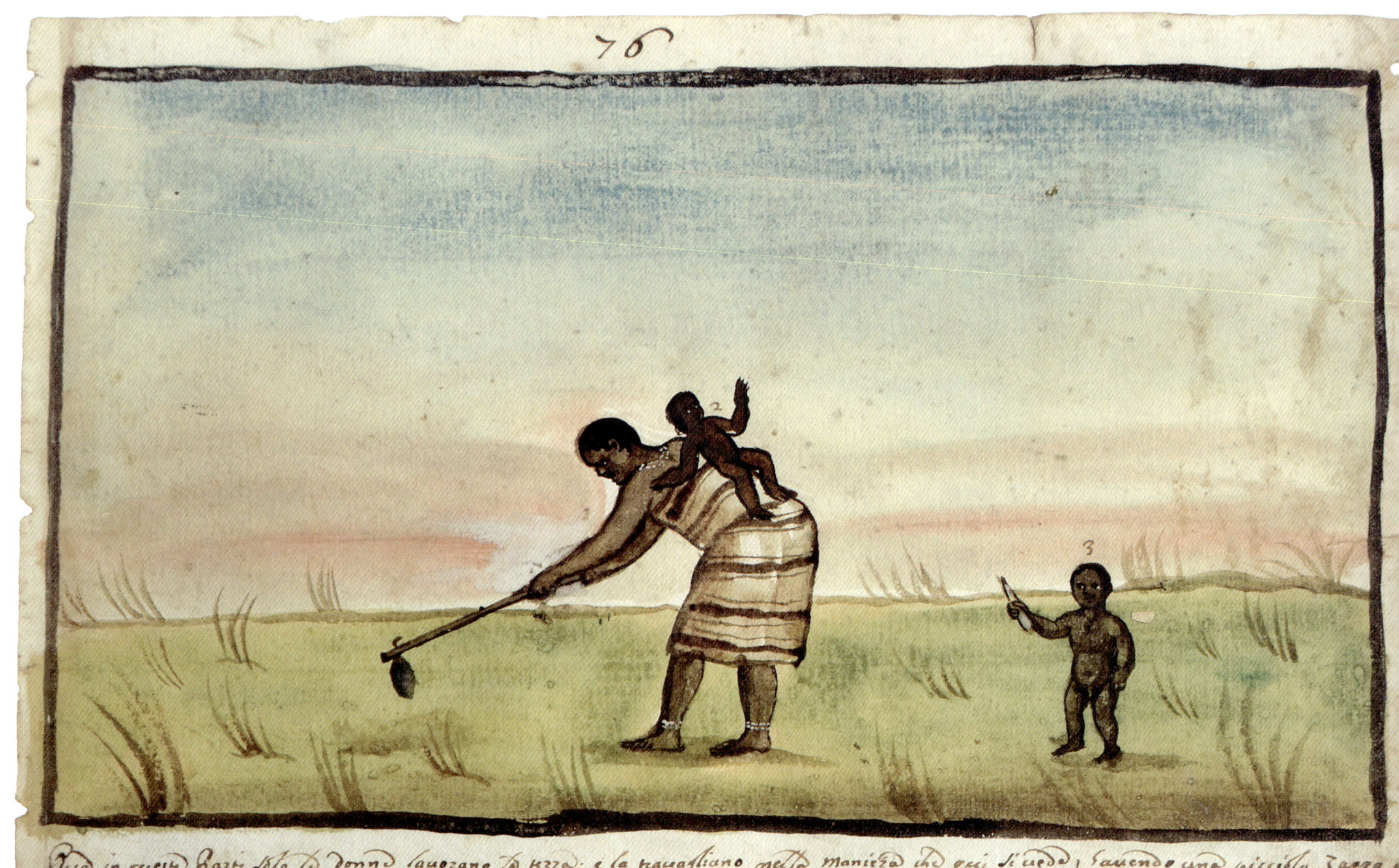

Plate 50

Fol. 76, "In these parts only women work the land."

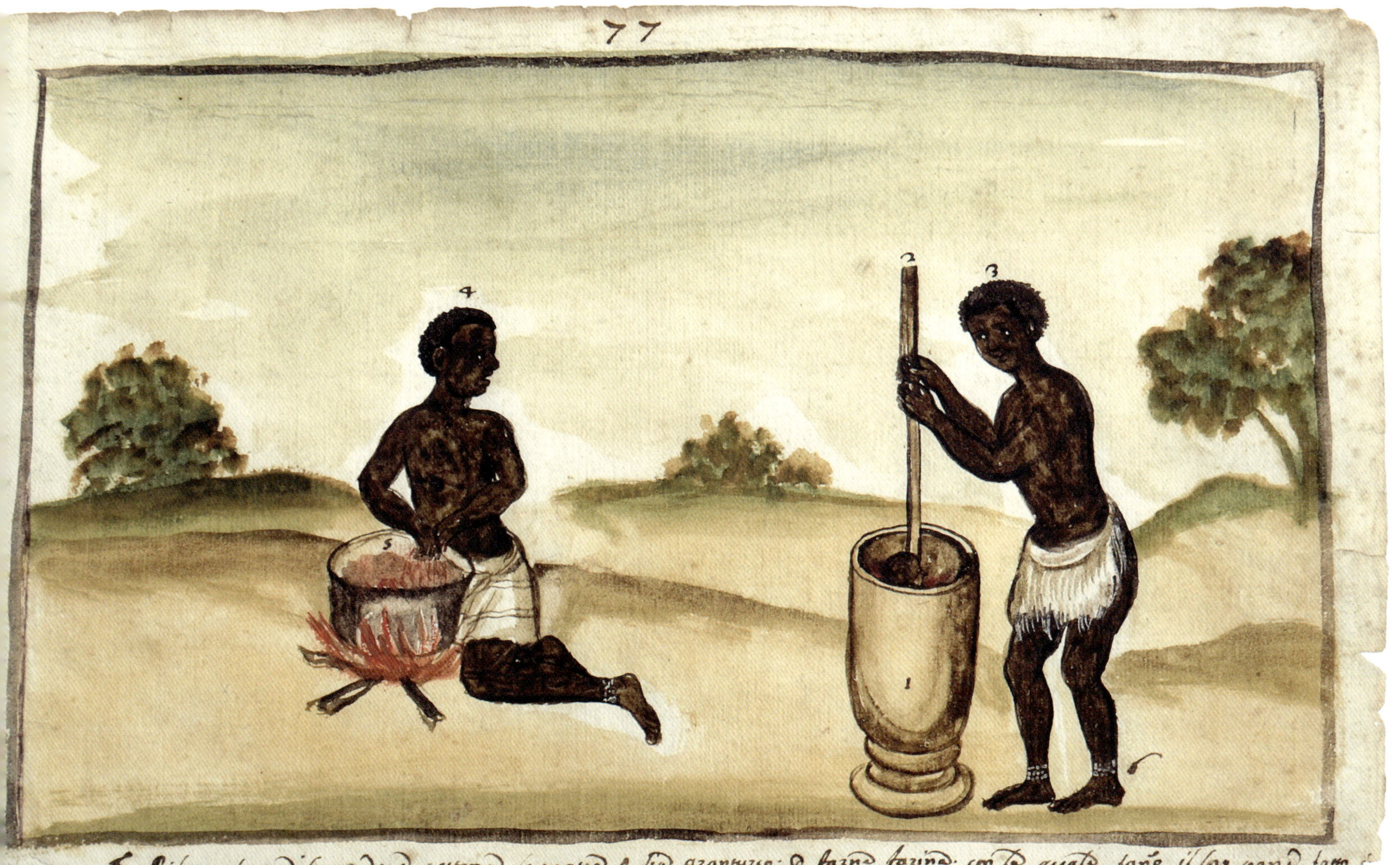

Plate 51

Fol. 77, "Mortar called *Pilaom*."

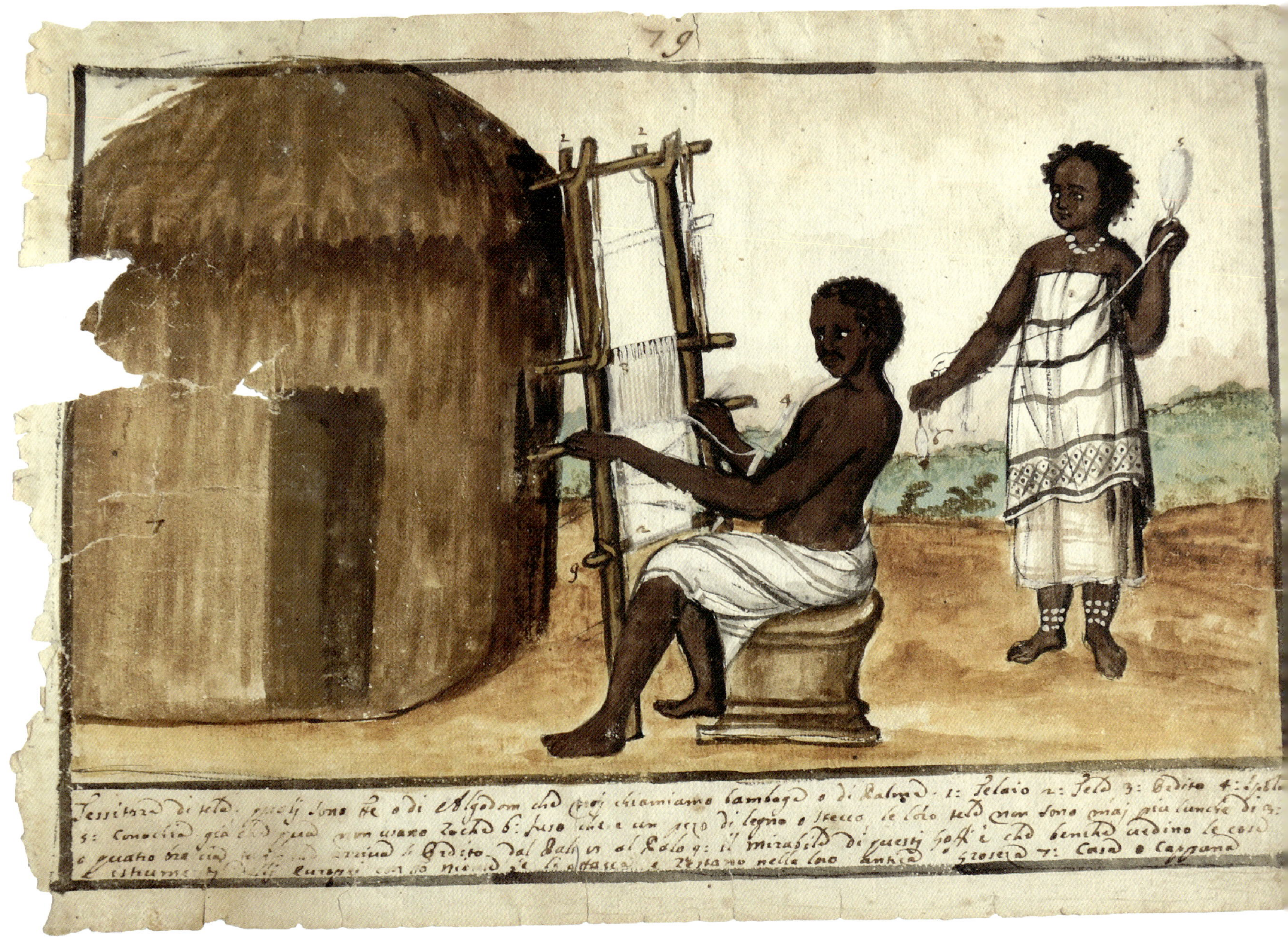

Plate 52

Fol. 79, "Weaver of cloth."

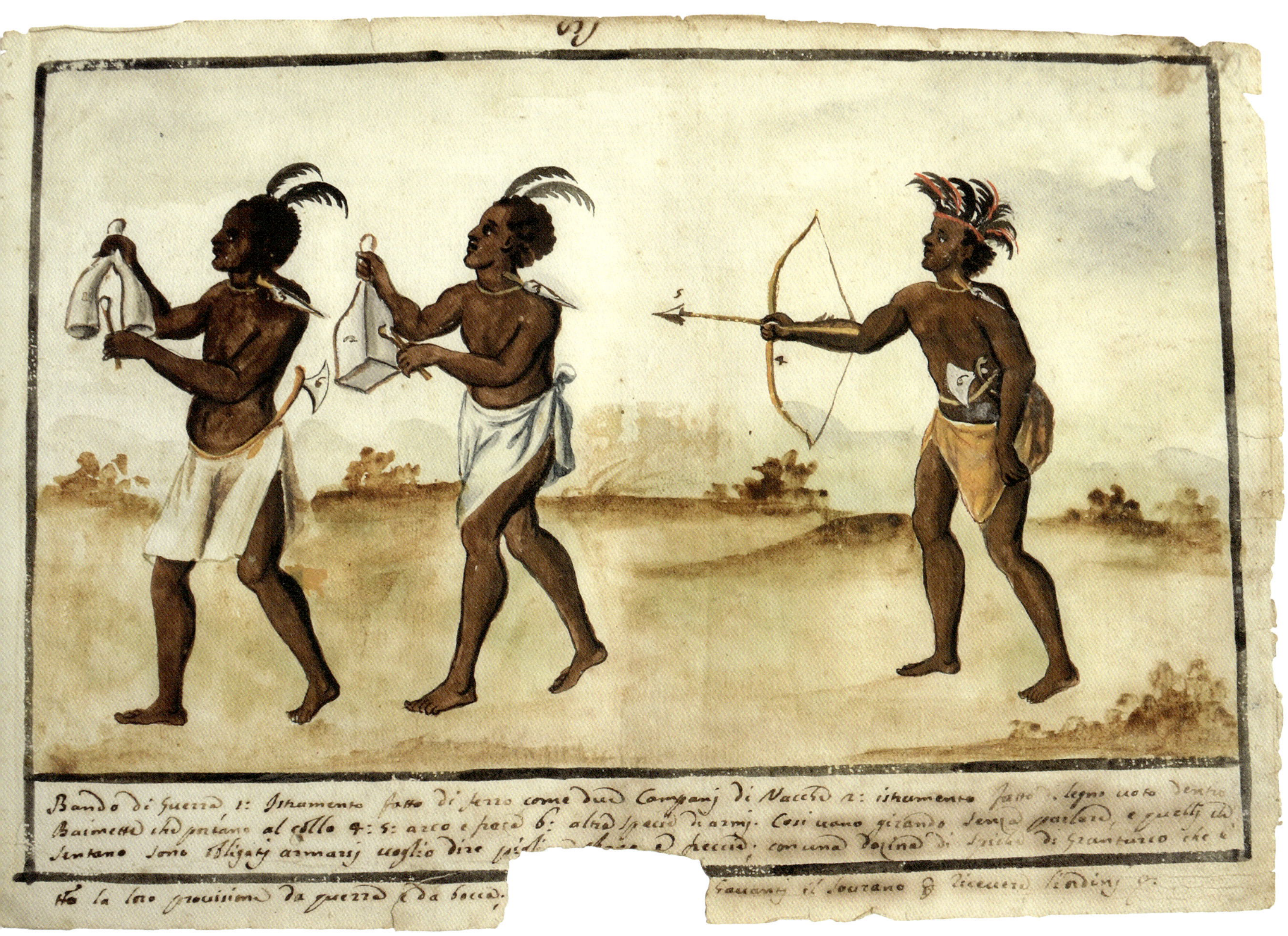

Plate 53

Fol. 81, "War band."

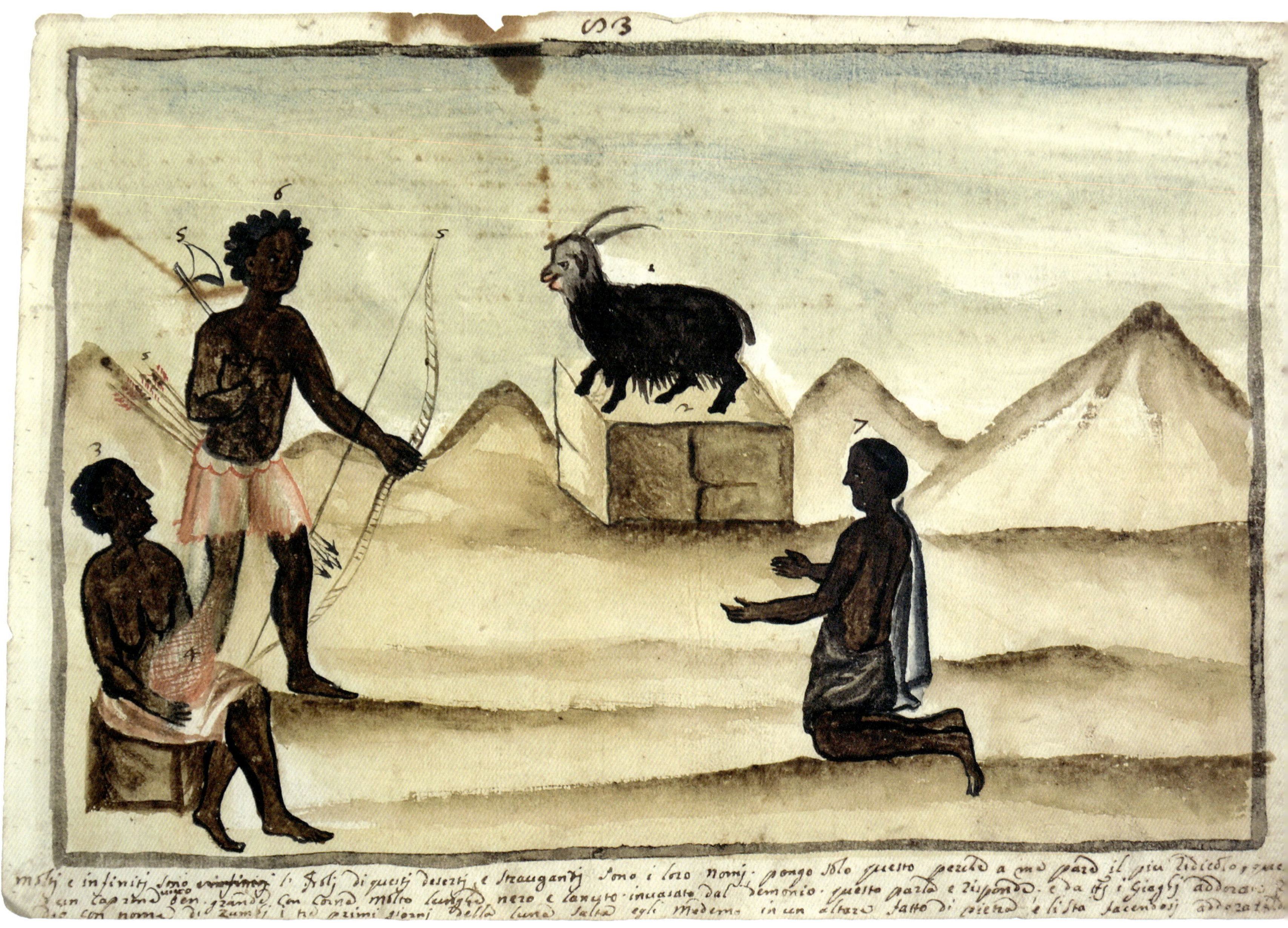

Plate 54

Fol. 83, "Many and infinite are the Idols of these deserts."

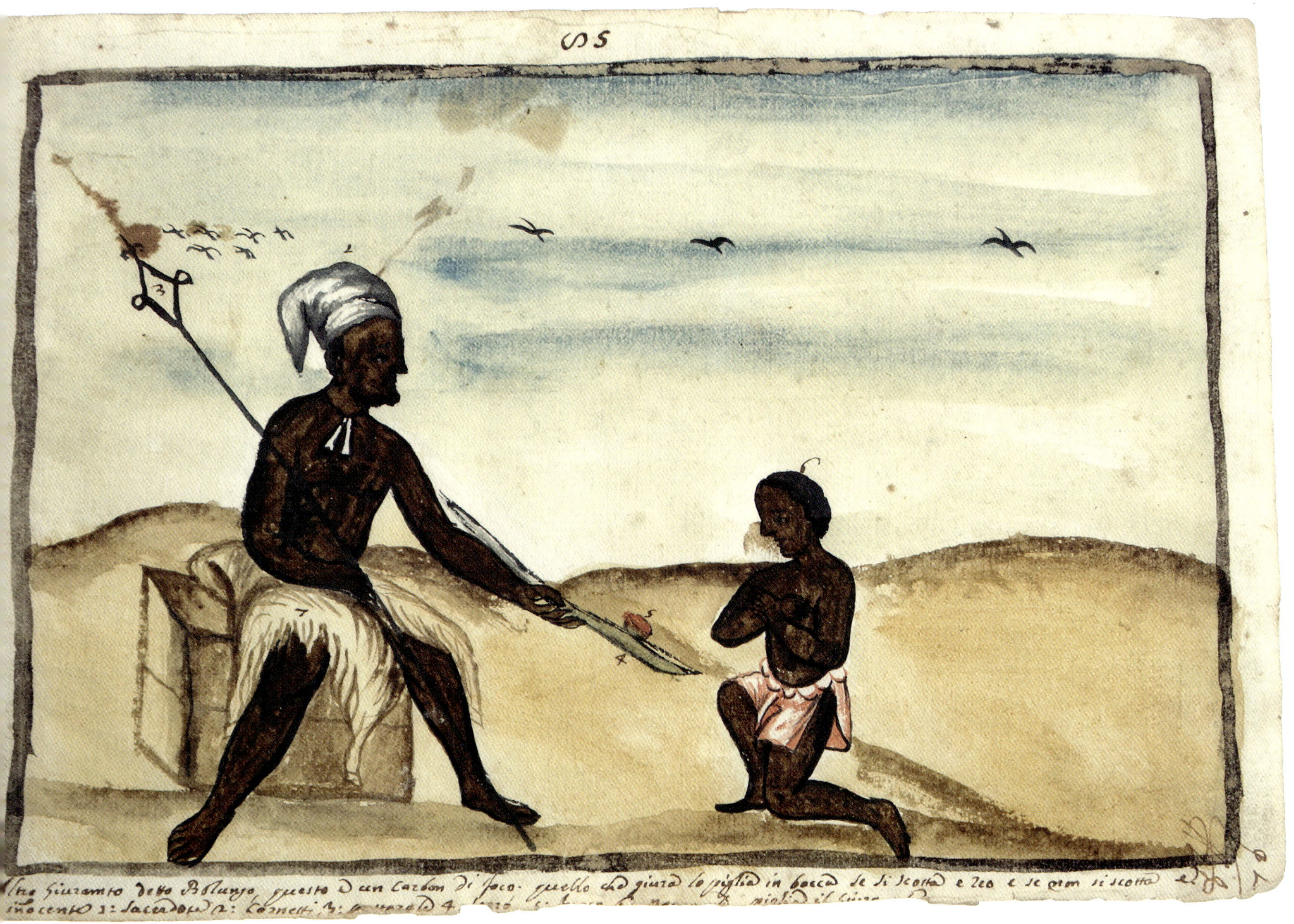

Plate 55

Fol. 85, "Another trial, called *bolungo*."

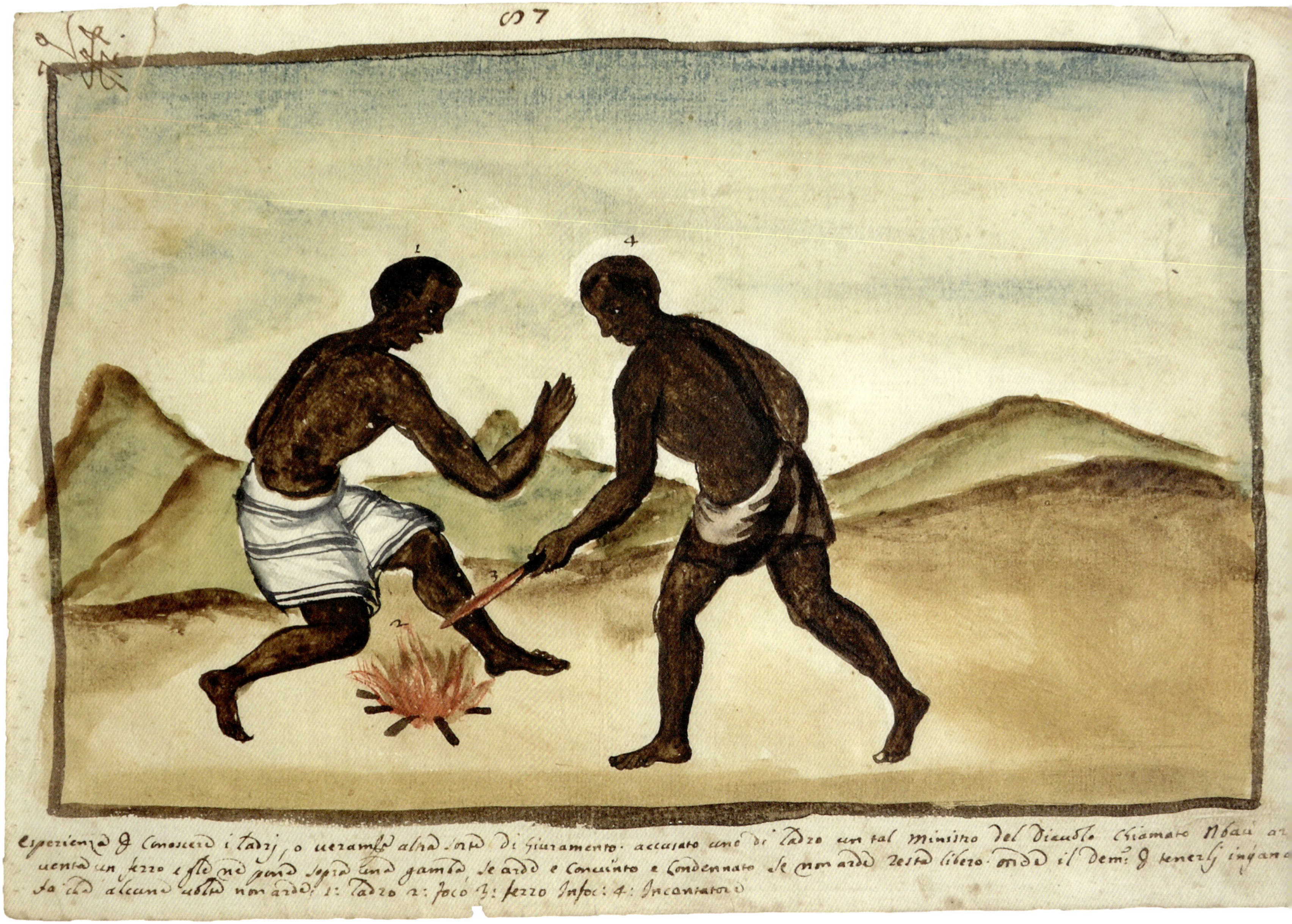

Plate 56

Fol. 87, "Experiment to expose thieves."

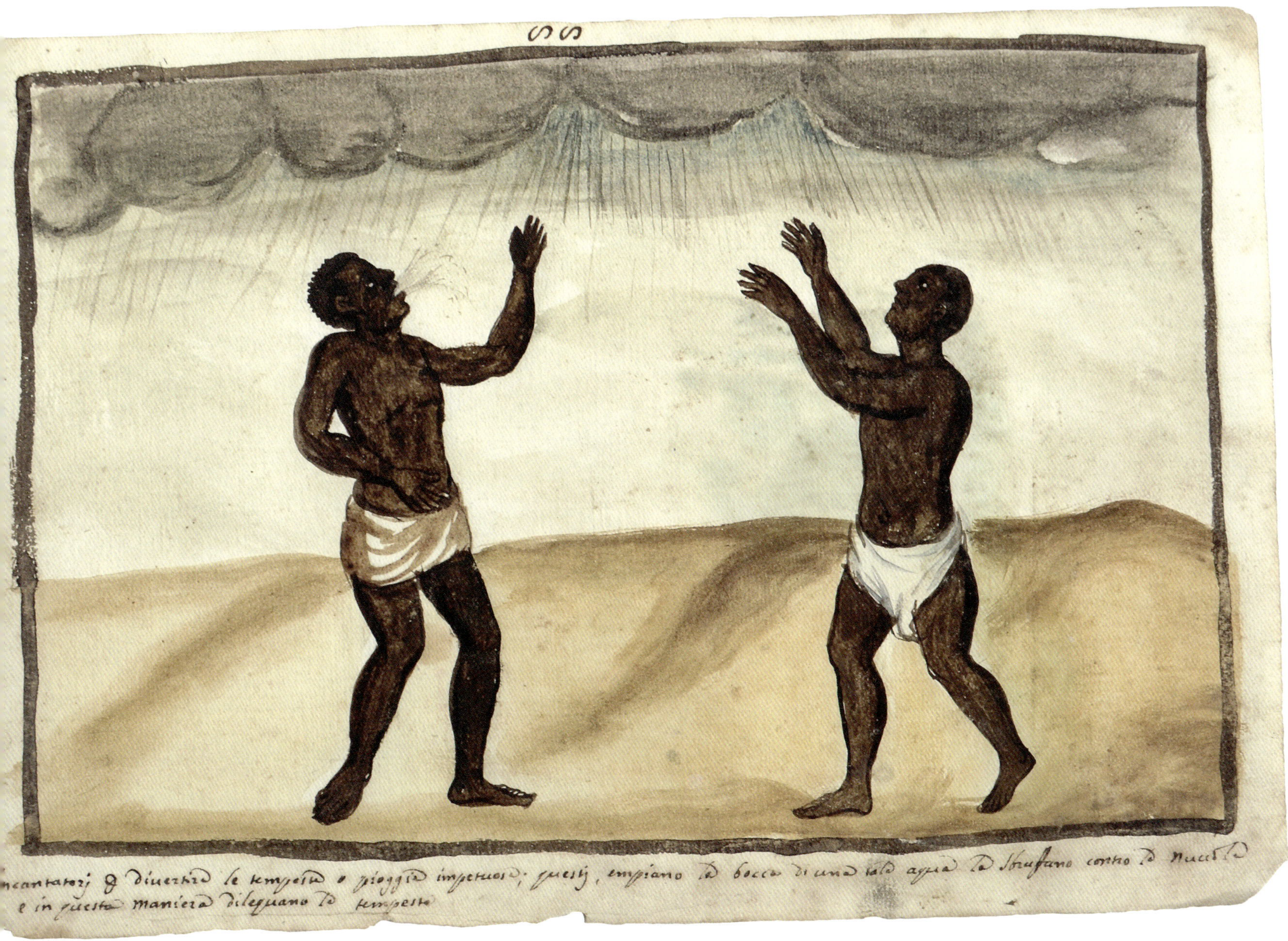

Plate 57

Fol. 88, "Conjurers to divert tempests and rains."

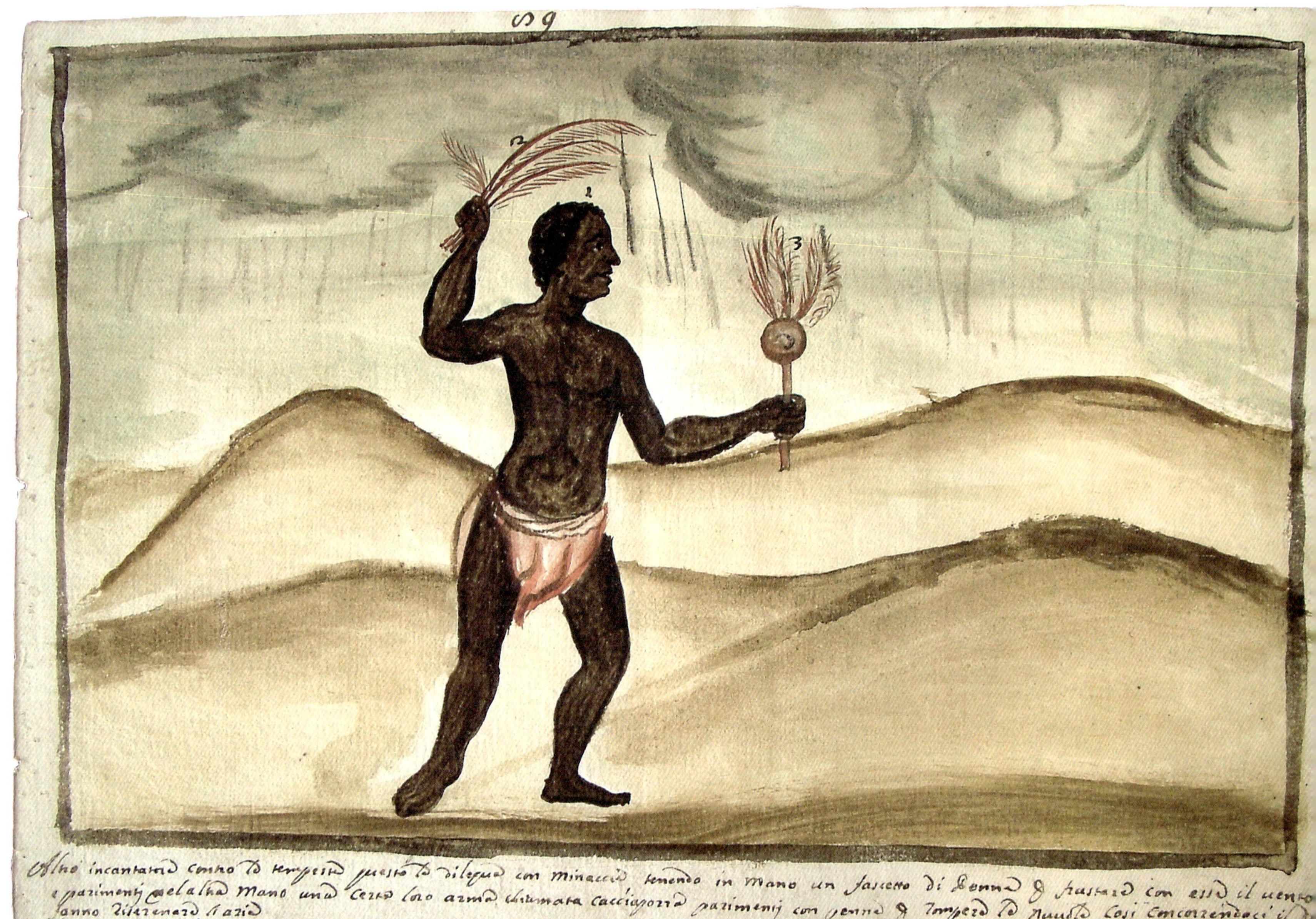

Plate 58

Fol. 89, "Another conjurer against storms."

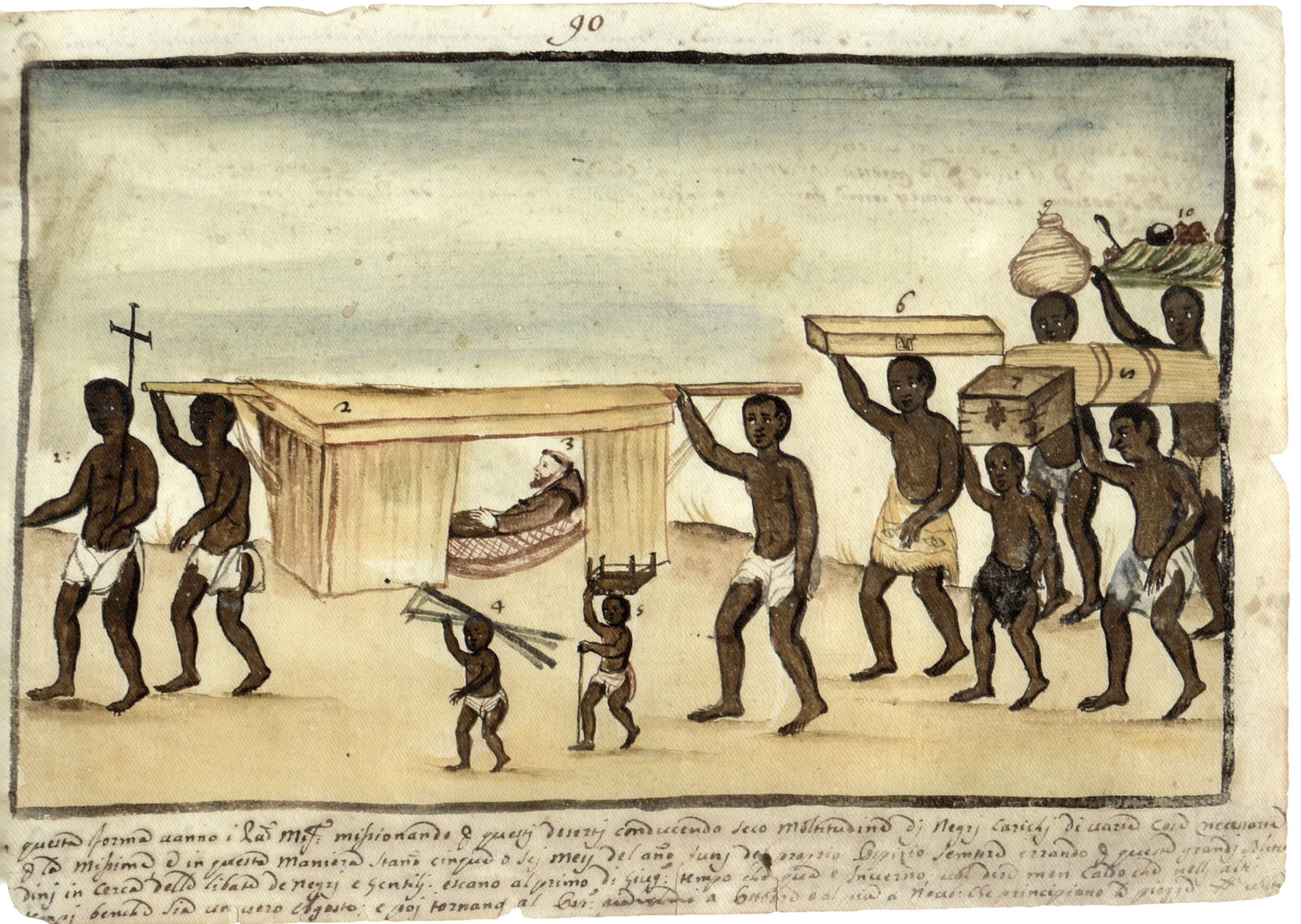

Plate 59

Fol. 90, "In this manner go the Missionary Fathers on the mission."

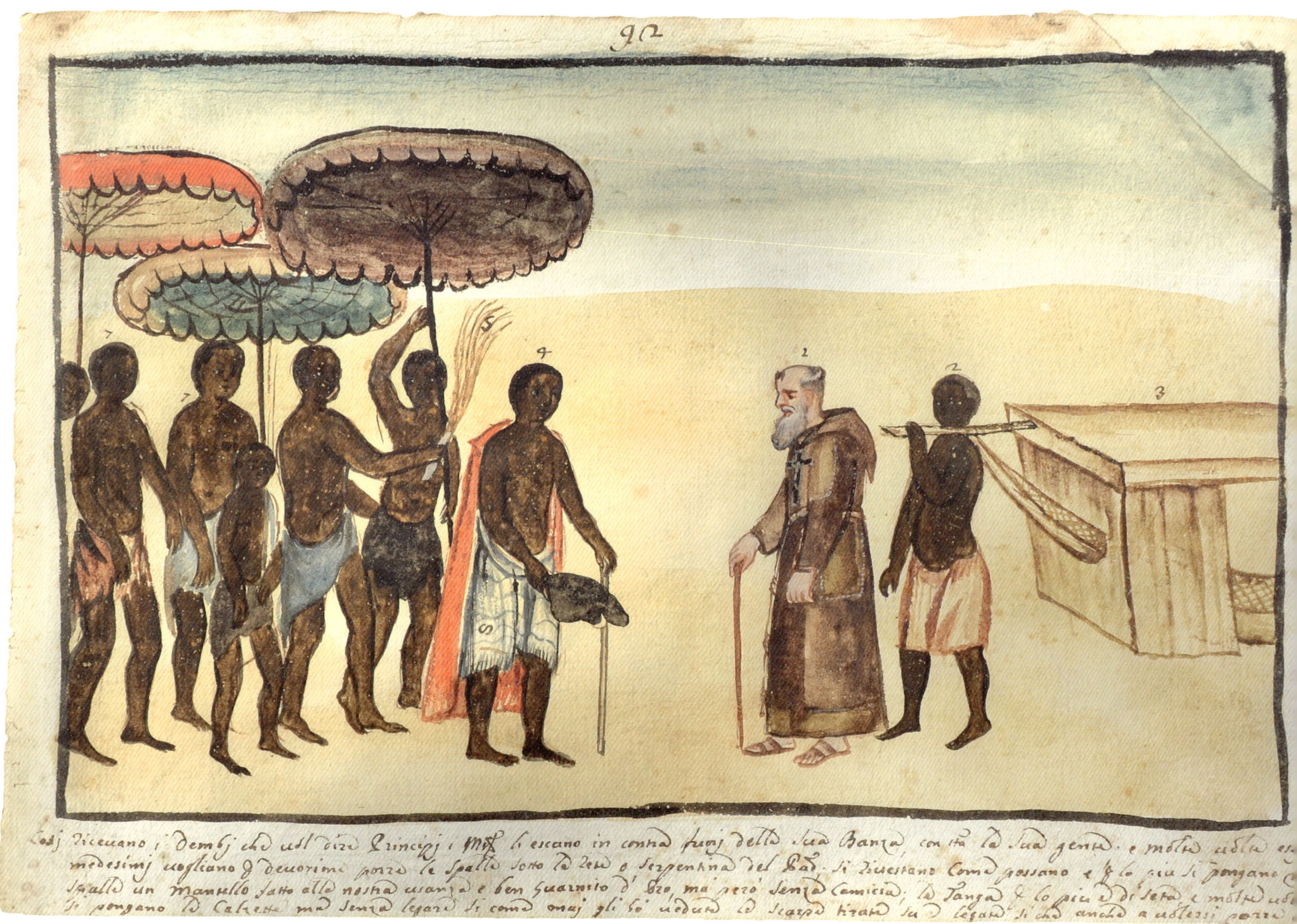

Plate 60

Fol. 92, "In this manner the Dembi [Ndembu rulers],
which means Princes, receive the Missionaries."

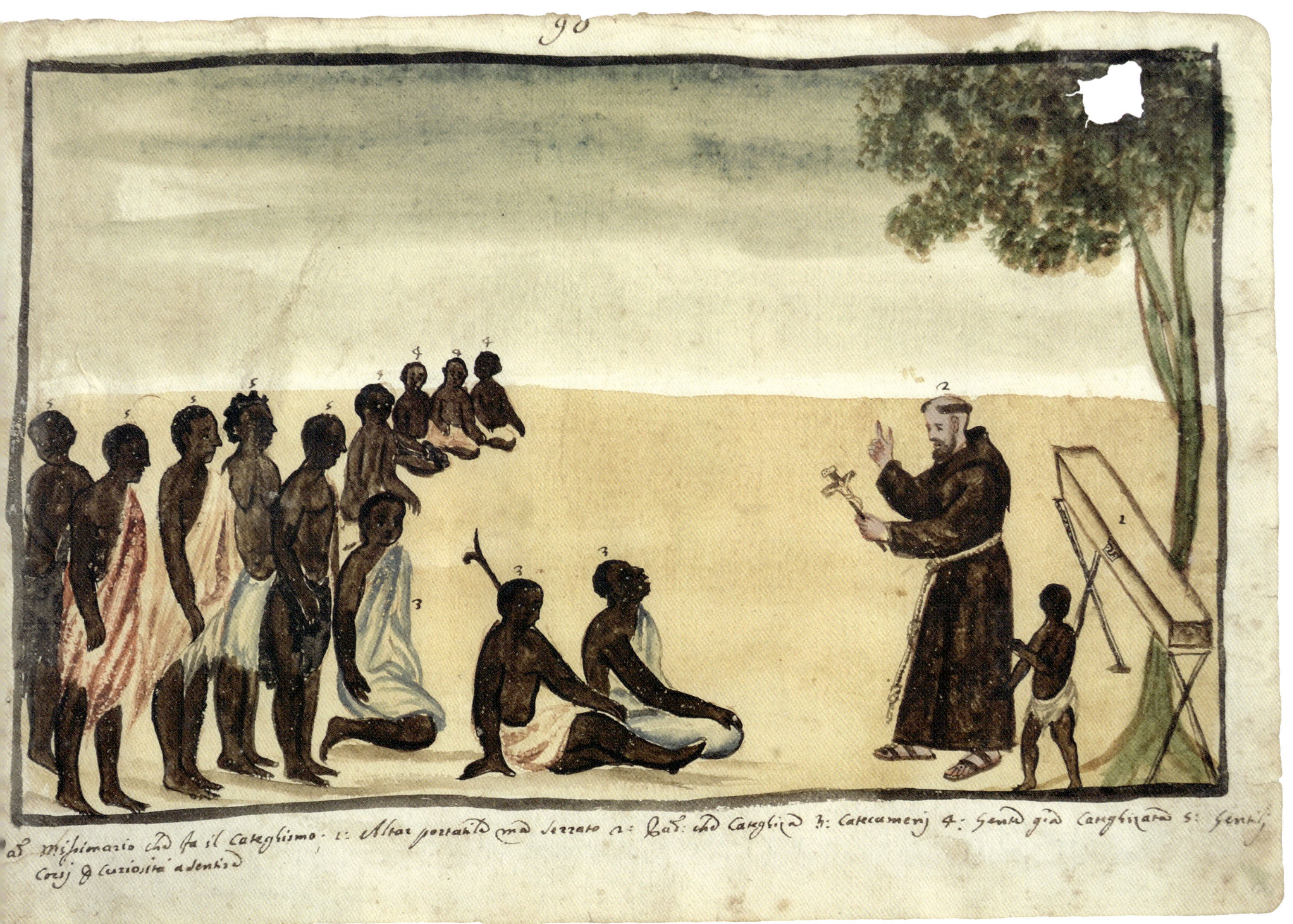

Plate 61

Fol. 96, "Missionary Father who catechizes."

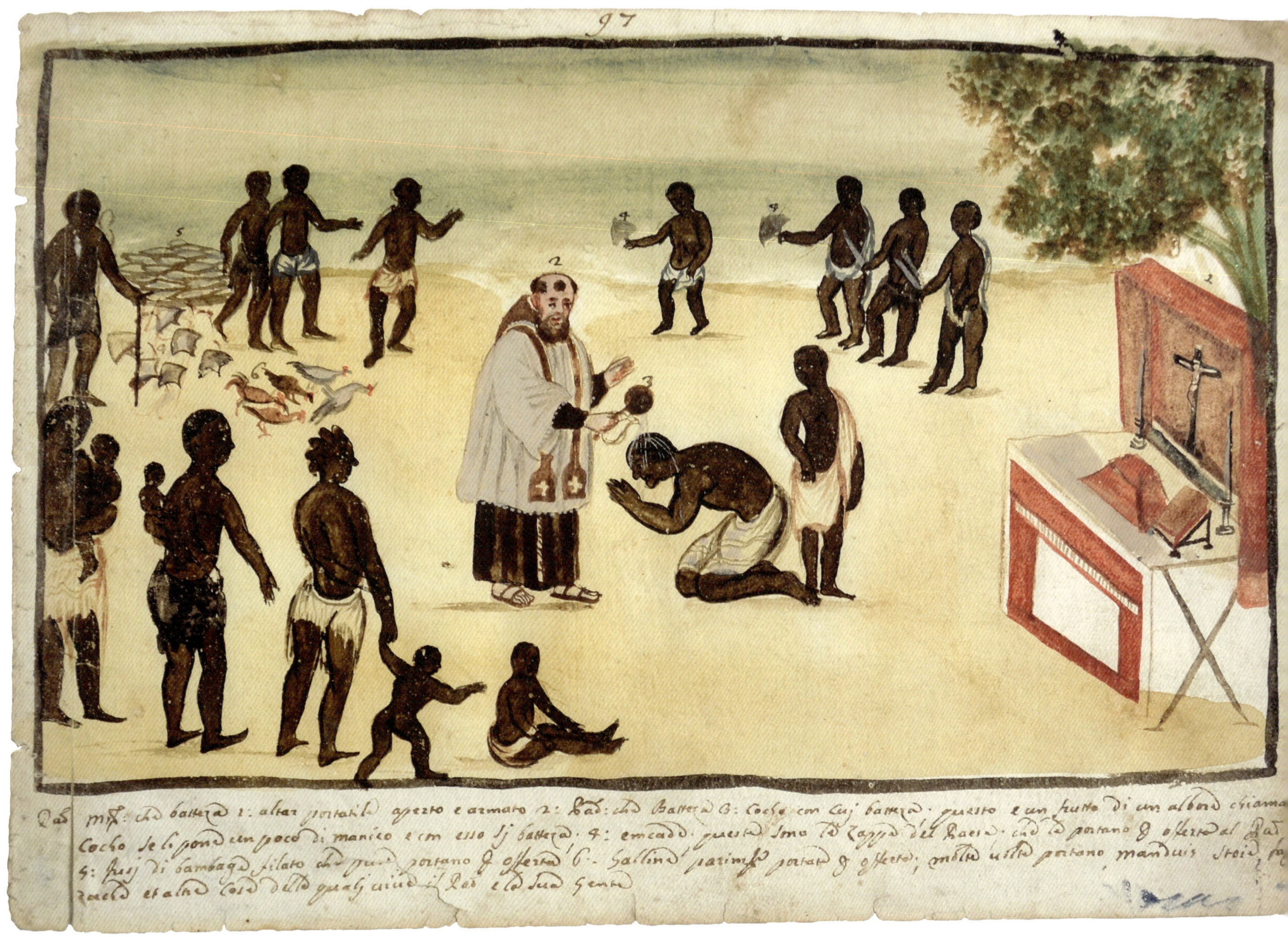

Plate 62

Fol. 97, "Missionary Father who baptizes."

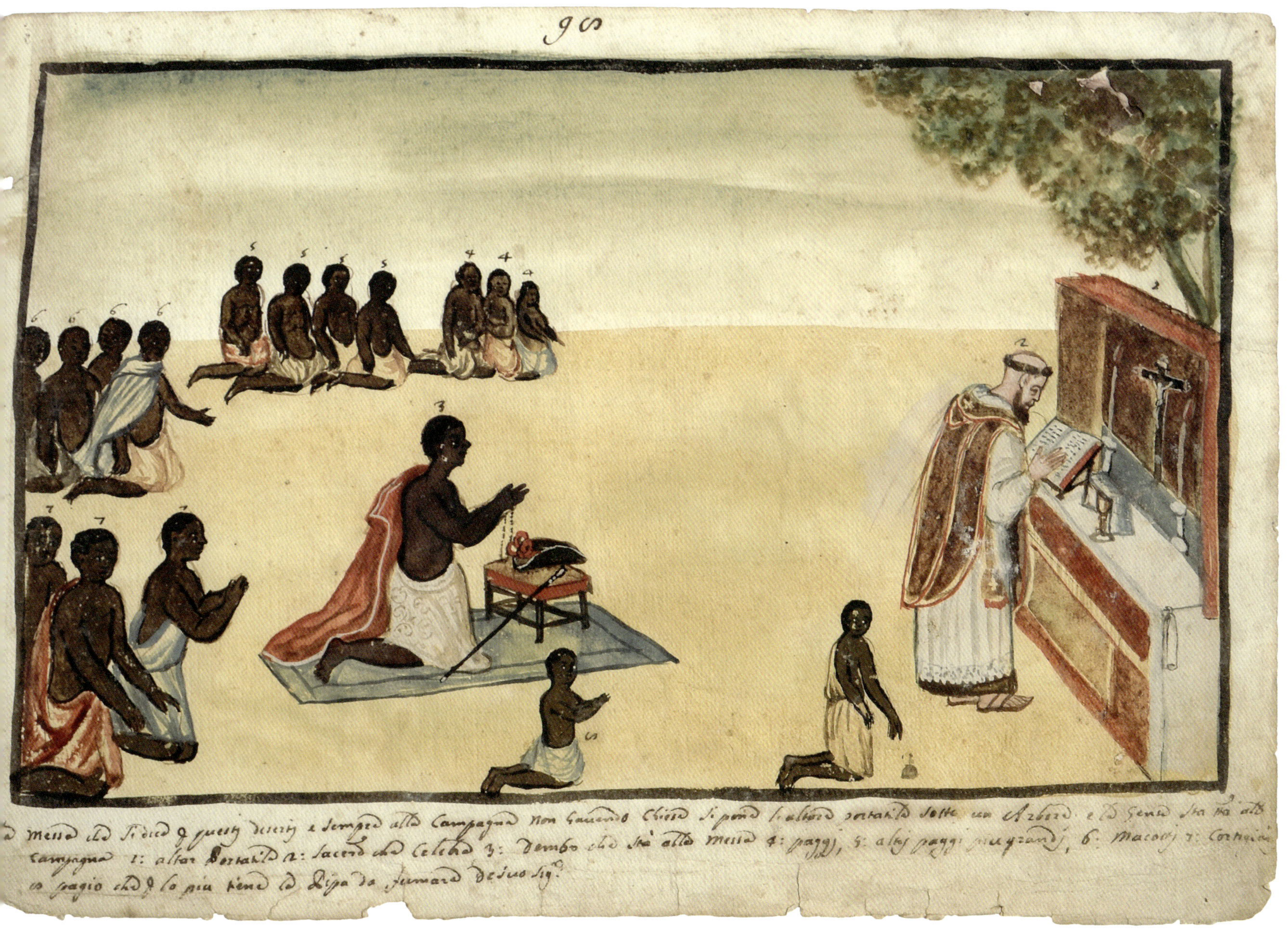

Plate 63

Fol. 98, "Mass that is said in these deserts is always in the open air."

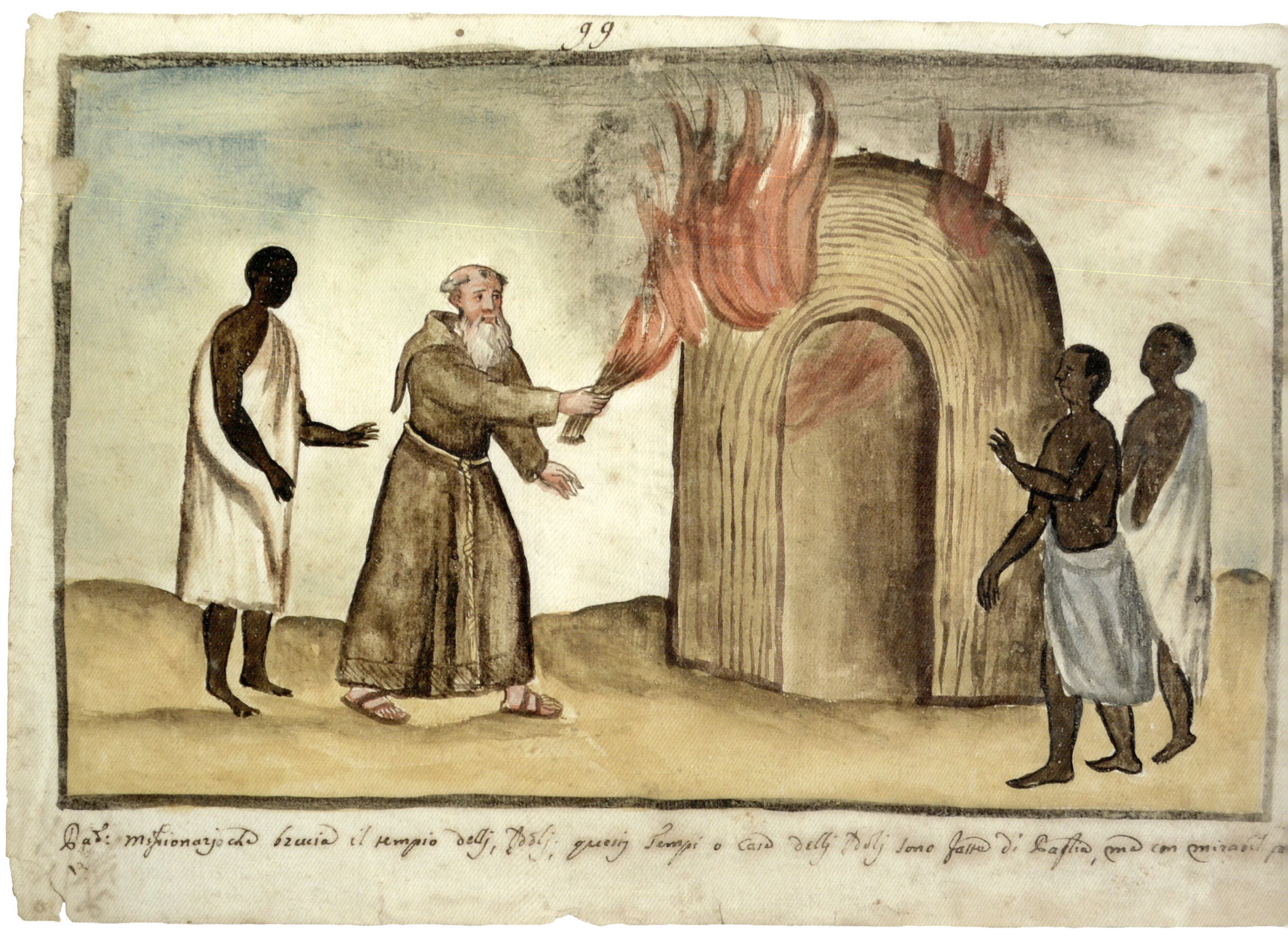

Plate 64

Fol. 99, "Missionary Father who burns the temple of the Idols."

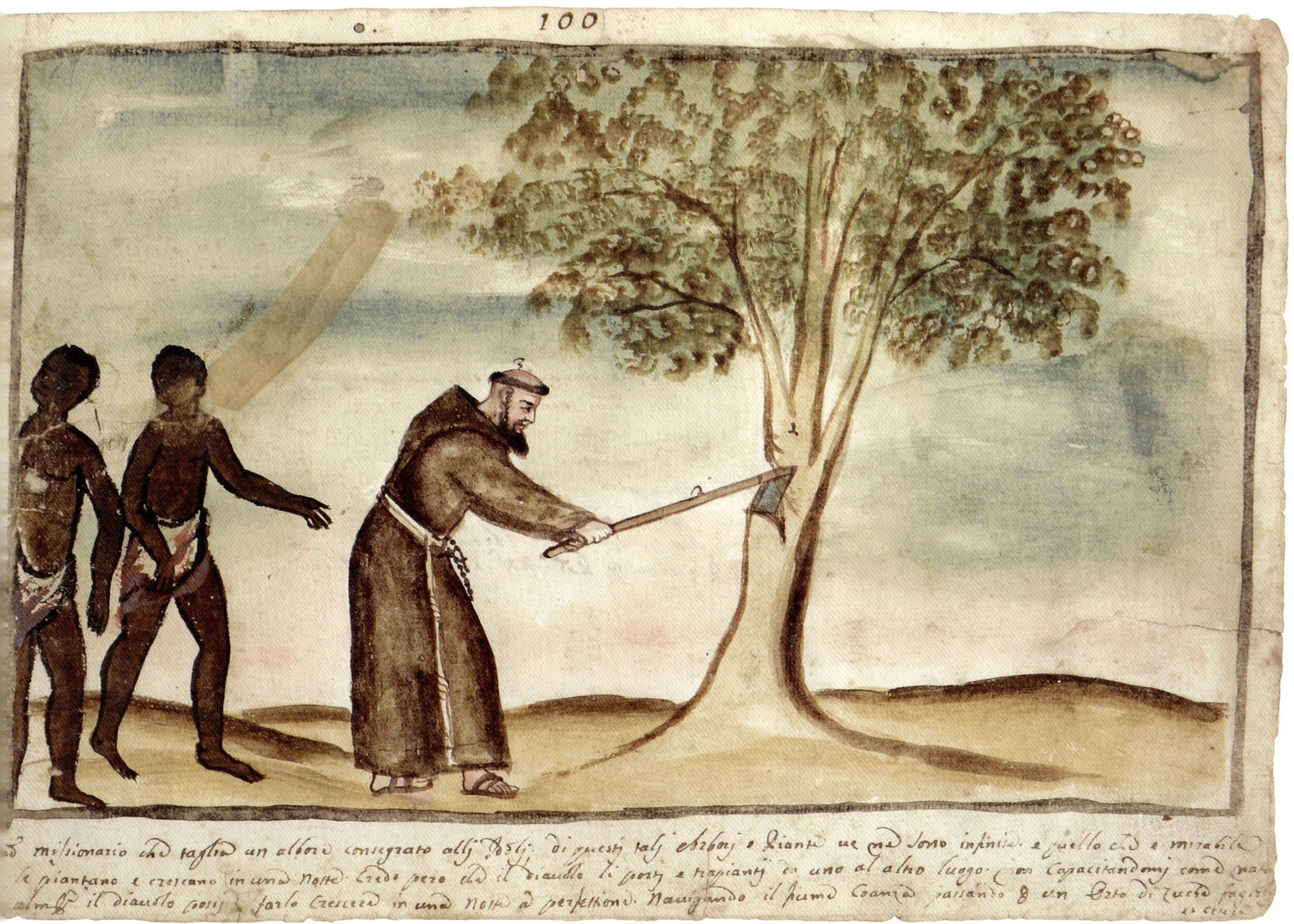

Plate 65

Fol. 100, "Missionary Father who cuts a tree consecrated to the Idols."

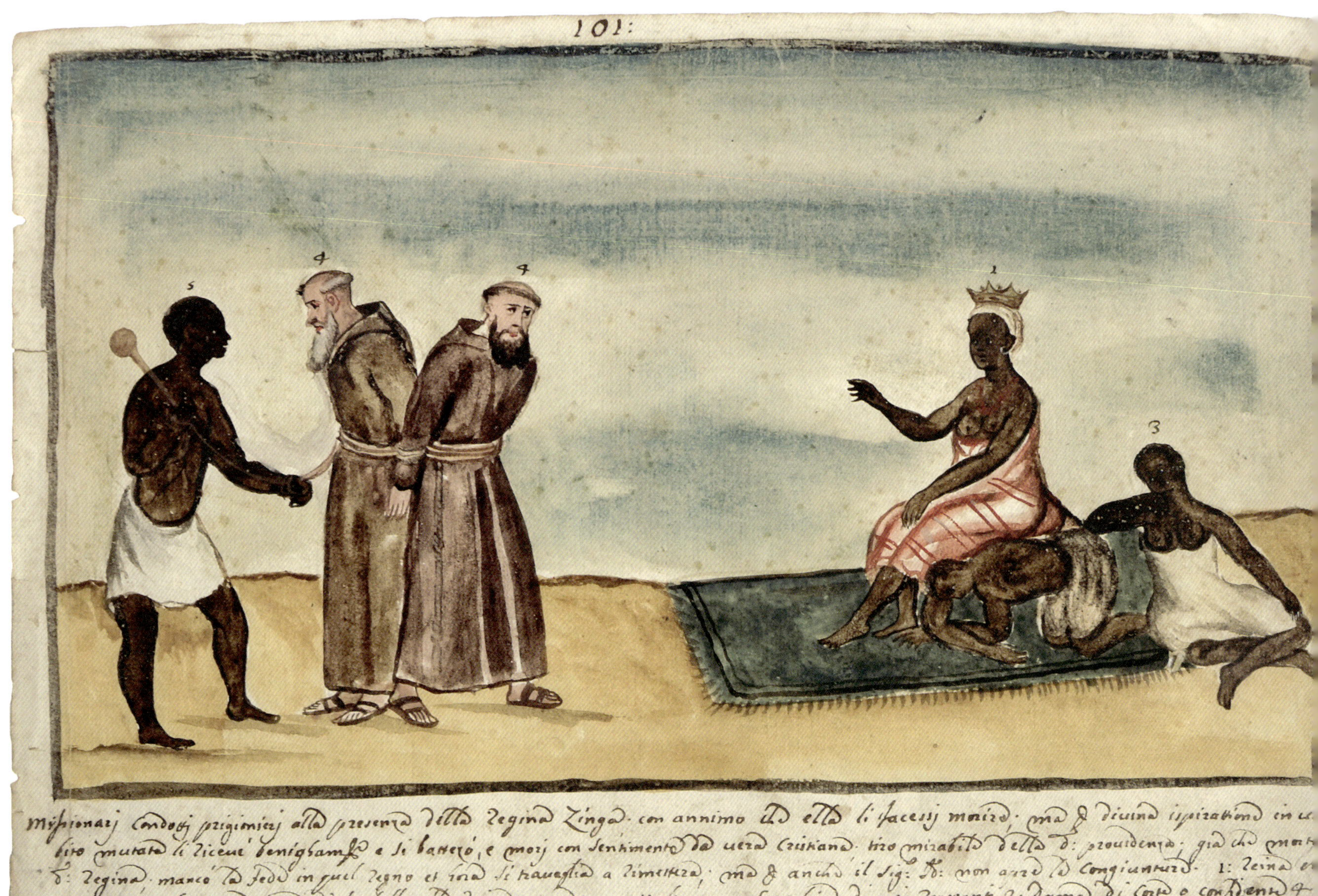

Plate 66

Fol. 101, "Missionaries taken as prisoners into the presence
of Queen Njinga."

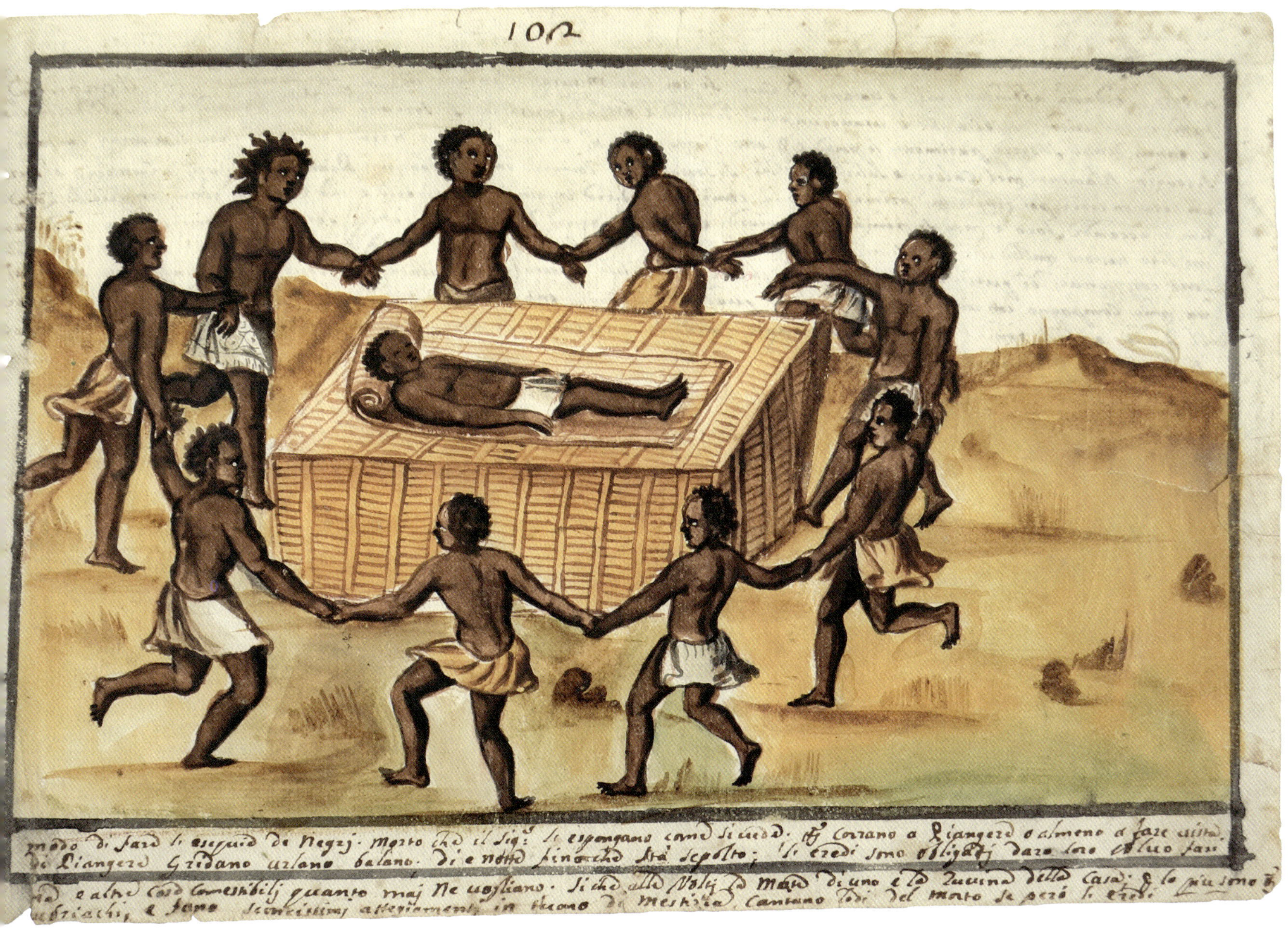

Plate 67

Fol. 102, "Manner of conducting the funeral rites of the blacks."

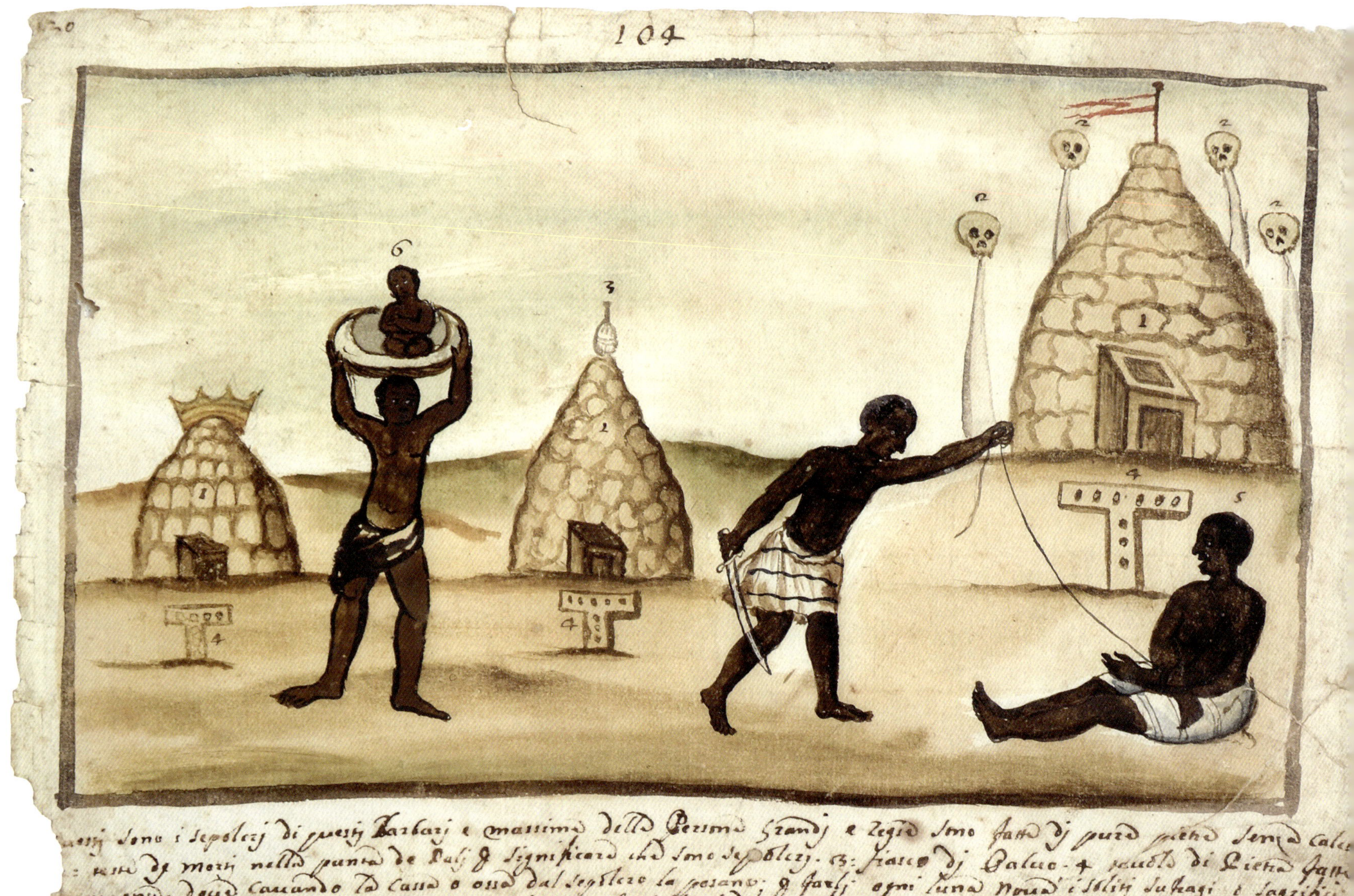

Plate 68

Fol. 104, "Sepulchers of these barbarians."

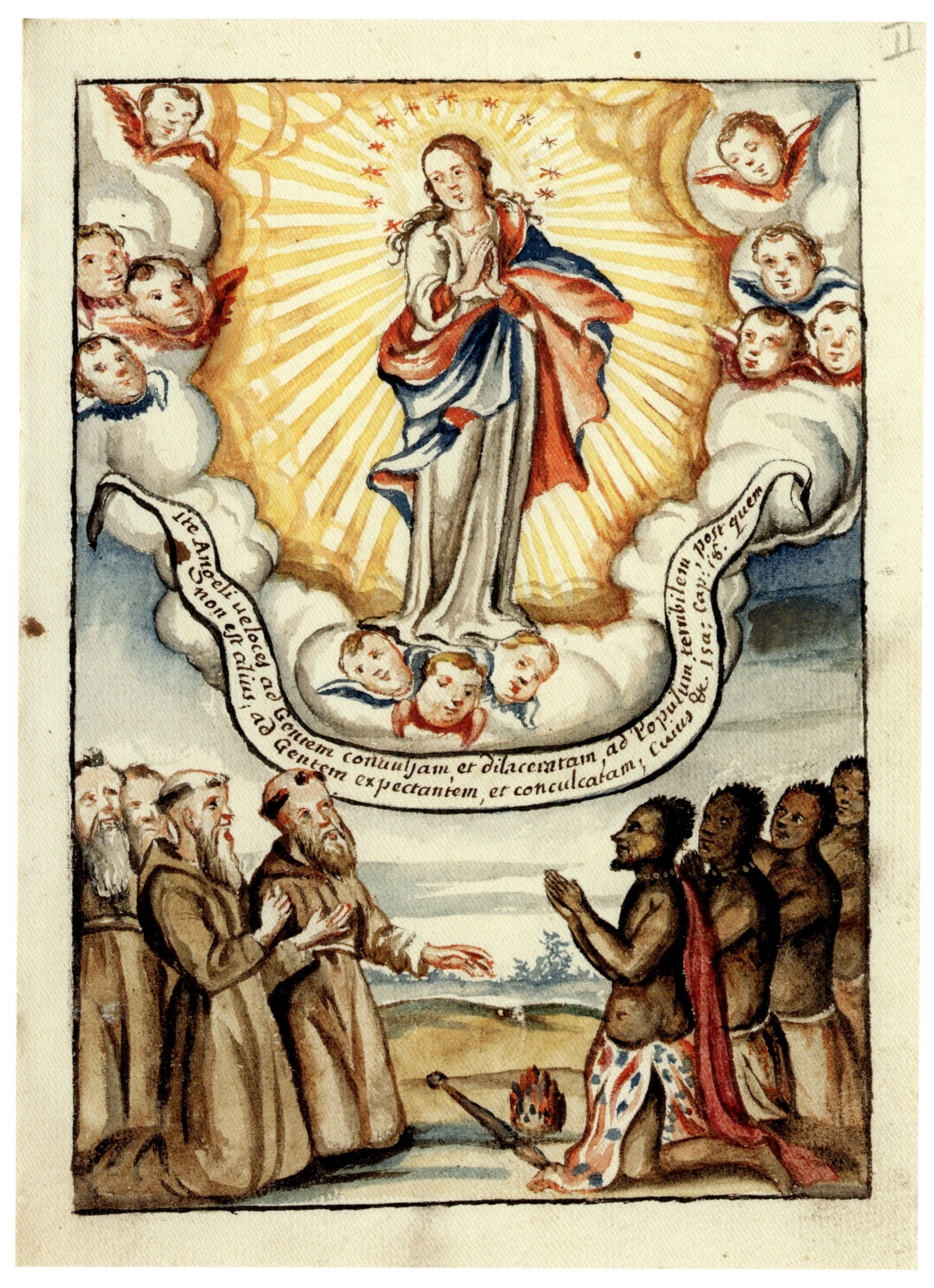
Ite Angeli ueloces ad Gentem conuulsam, et dilaceratam ad Populum terribilem post quem non est alius; ad Gentem expectantem, et conculcatam; cuius &c. Isa; Cap: 18.

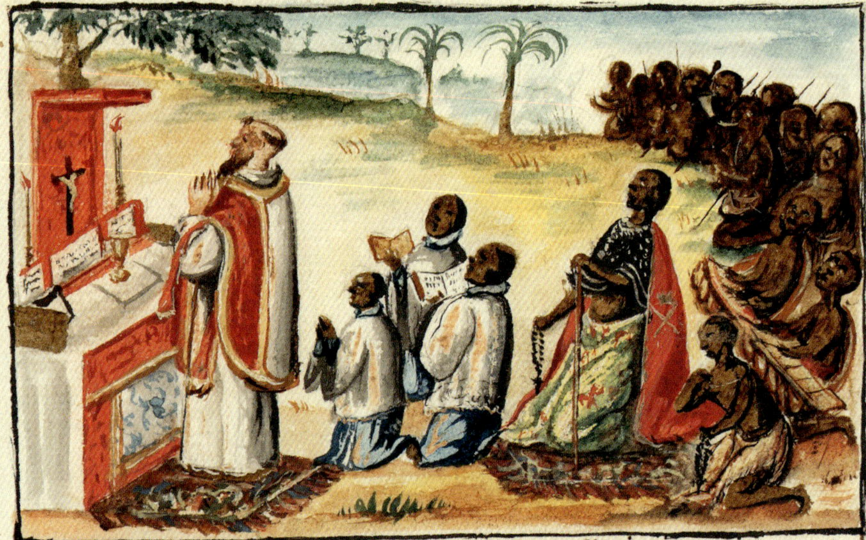

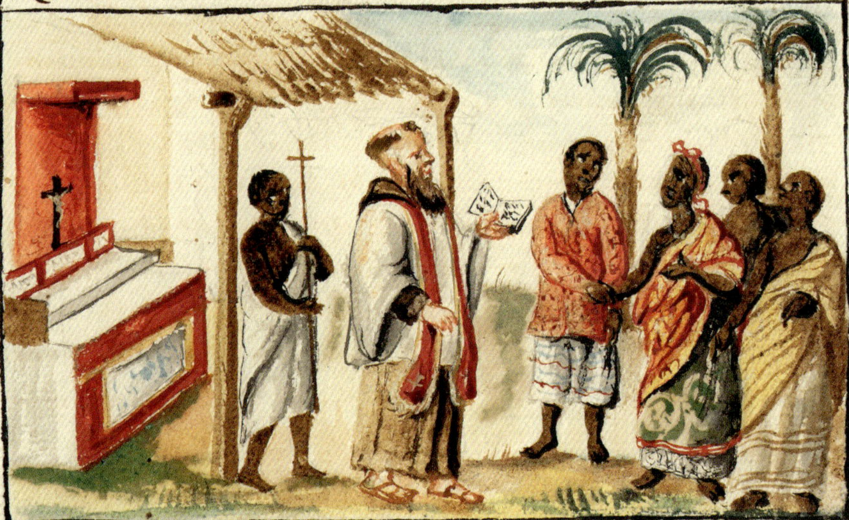

Plate 70

Bernardino Ignazio da Vezza d'Asti, "The Missionary Father sings Mass" and "The Missionary in the process of celebrating a Wedding," ca. 1750. Watercolor on paper, 19.5 × 14.4 cm (page size). From "Missione in prattica," Biblioteca Apostolica Vaticana, MS Borg. Lat. 316, p. 1, between pp. 48 and 49. © 2022 Biblioteca Apostolica Vaticana. Reproduced by permission of Biblioteca Apostolica Vaticana, with all rights reserved.

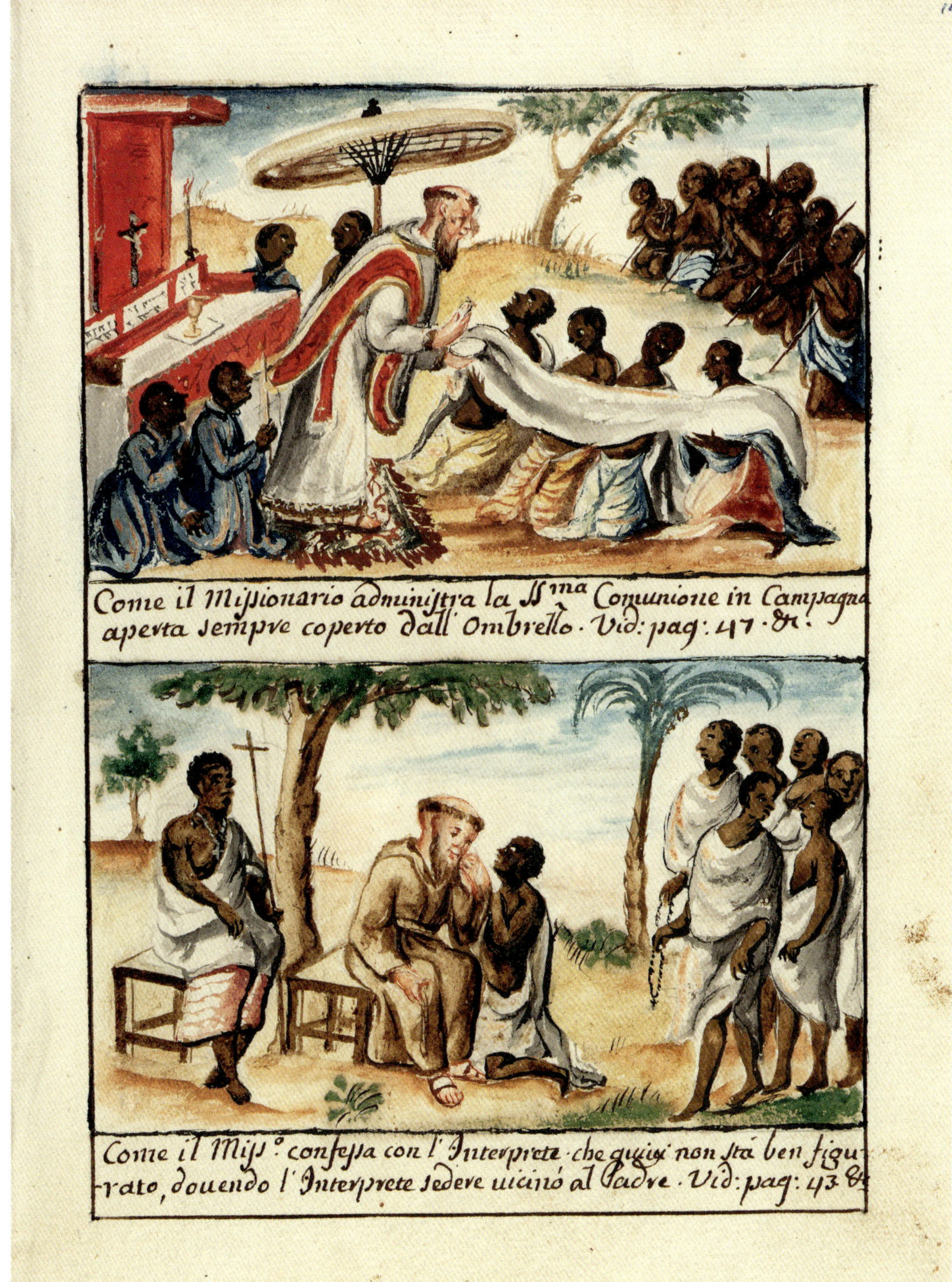
Come il Missionario administra la SS.ma Comunione in Campagna aperta sempre coperto dall'Ombrello. Vid: pag: 47. &c.
Come il Miss.° confessa con l'Interprete che quiui non sta ben figurato, douendo l'Interprete sedere uicino al Padre. Vid: pag: 43. &c

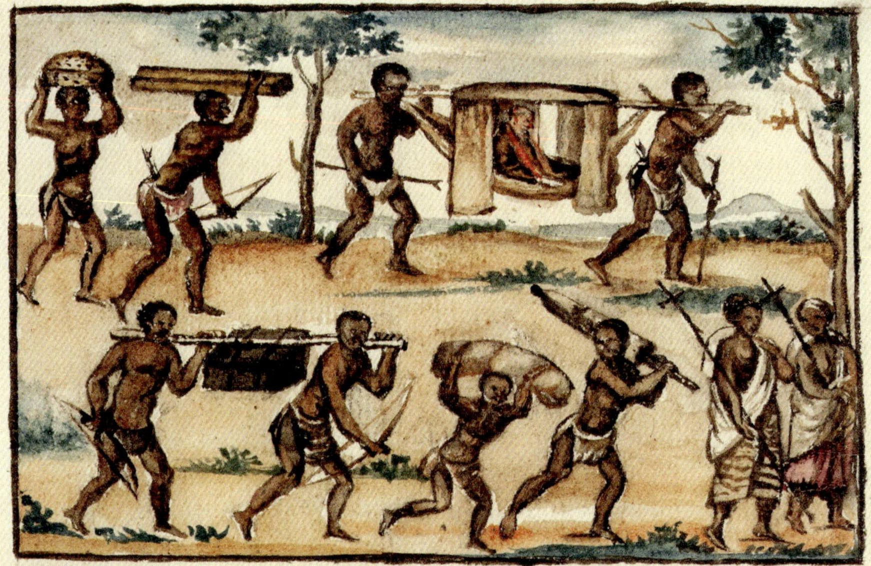

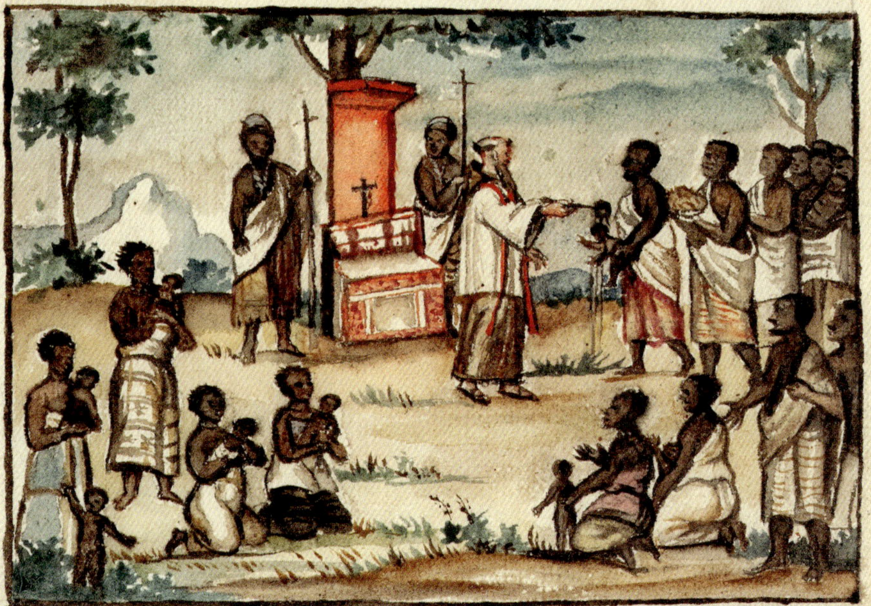

Plate 72

Bernardino Ignazio da Vezza d'Asti, "The Missionary accompanied in traveling mission" and "How the Missionary Baptizes where there is no Church," ca. 1750. Watercolor on paper, 19.5 × 14.4 cm (page size). From "Missione in prattica," Biblioteca Apostolica Vaticana, MS Borg. Lat. 316, p. 101. © 2022 Biblioteca Apostolica Vaticana. Reproduced by permission of Biblioteca Apostolica Vaticana, with all rights reserved.

Friar Giovanni Antonio Cavazzi's *Istorica descrizione* is a large and heavy volume, thirty centimeters tall and more than nine hundred pages long. Fittingly for a book presenting central Africa to intended readers in Europe, it features a map that locates its narrative and defines the contours of the territories it addresses. The cartographic notice spreads over a large folded sheet. An inscription, "Pag. I," at the top right indicates that it should be inserted in the book between the front matter and the introductory page. The map joins the many copper plates, embedded in the body of the text, Cavazzi and the book's final editor, Fortunato Alamandini, commissioned to complement the written narrative (as discussed in chapter 1 above). After poring through most of the lengthy volume, readers of the *Istorica descrizione* unexpectedly encounter a second foldout. Noticeably shorter in height than the other pages, the long strip is bound in most copies between pages 798 and 799 (fig. 40). The insert demands a change of pace and of viewing mode from studious readers who have reached this far into the long text, from armchair travelers simply leafing through the book, and even from more casual handlers, for whom the book may have opened itself at first touch to this page because of the tension the thicker foldout exerts on the binding. They free their hands, find weights to keep the pages open, carefully unfold the long strip of paper bound by one of its short sides into the spine of the book, and finally see the content of the print open up before their eyes. The format and placement of the foldout engage readers' bodies and imagination. The still-hidden print creates an experience of anticipation; the opening of the long paper, one of discovery. These features begin to build a dynamic relationship between viewers and image

that the content of the print, I argue in this chapter, strengthens through iconography, style, and narrative.

If dimensions and format make the foldout unique, many aspects of its composition and contents closely echo key features of the corpus of Capuchin central-African images to which it belongs. In this regard, the carefully composed print provides a compelling gateway for the study of the friars' central-African vignettes. It brings to the fore how Capuchin image-makers mobilized a range of visual and religious tropes to create immersive pictures of central Africa and apostolic work therein. These images presented the central-African mission and the encounters with and reckonings about nature and culture that unfolded in its course as characterized by two core dimensions. First, they

CHAPTER 3

Images and Devotion

suoi Giaghi: e soggiungendogli esso, che lasciasse partire in buonhora i Religiosi, già che non voleua vbbidirli, rispose, tenerli appresso di se per conuenienza, e per politica. Somigliante risposta hebbe da lui il P. Tomaso, allorche, presenti i suoi Sattrapi, doleuasi, ch' essendosi reso Christiano, fosse tanto restio in mantenere la fede giurata à Dio, & à gli huomini. Padre mio caro già siete informato del costume di questi Popoli, i quali caminano con le misure del Prencipe, secondando il genio di lui, per non incontrare il castigo: basta vi rammentiate dell' affronto, che vi fecero, quando nella solennità della Madre di Dio, vdendoui magnificare le grandezze di essa Vergine, osarono alzar le mani contro di voi (non ostante foste parato all' Altare) e proferirono tanti vituperij in onta di quel Santissimo Nome di Maria. Cassange insomma stà cotanto incatenato col Demonio, che se Iddio non opera vn portento della sua misericordia, scorgo disperata la di lui conuersione. Sin' ora l' hò tenuto per rinegato, adesso

non hò stimolo à crederlo mero Ateista, perche adora ciò che gli monta in capriccio, non distinguendosi hormai la formalità delle sue Idolatrie, e stimo che il sangue da lui versato in qualsiuoglia momento con tanta barbarie, e senza motiuo di giustizia, gli habbia totalmente ottenebrato l' intelletto, siche non discerna altro che le furie infernali, instigatrici delle sue enormissime azioni. Non hà molto, che mentre l' vno de' Padri Missionarj celebraua l' incruento Sacrificio, costui fece con vn colpo di manaia vccidere sù la porta della Chiesa vn pouero Nero, e fattolo in pezzi se lo mangiò tutto in compagnia di molti suoi Corteggiani, che alzauano fischiate, schernendo le nostre cerimonie; e pure poco prima haueua date buone parole à detti Padri; laonde per questo nuouo insulto essi pensano partire, & abbandonare l' infame couile; potendosi ragioneuolmente presagire, che Iddio non tarderà molto à fulminare sopra costoro la sua vendetta. L' afflizione in che viuiamo tutti, se la figuri V. P. R. Può forse numerarsi (come dicono appunto questi due Religiosi) vn solo adulto, che si sia arreso? potiamo consolarci per auuentura, che Cassange habbia attesa mai vna sola promessa? Desidera ben egli che i Padri si trattengano nel suo Chilombo per tema, che i Portoghesi non disciolgano il commercio, e gli muouino guerra (che senza dubbio sarà l' vltimo ispediente per ridurlo ne' termini del suo douere, ò leuare dal Mondo vna gran peste) mà vorrebbe, che dissimulassero ad occhi serrati, che tacessero, & aderissero alle sue sfrenatezze; condizioni, che non otterrà mai dal loro santo zelo. Amendue i Padri m' ingiungono portare à V. P. R. vn caro saluto à nome loro, supplicandola di calde Orazioni appresso la Diuina Clemenza per questo emergente di tanto rilieuo. Et io le ratifico la mia ossequiosa, & obligata scruitù.

Dal Chilombo di Polongolo à 12. di Gennaio 1663.

Paolo Carillo de Quillar.

60　Vn' altra non punto dissimile mi scrisse il mentouato P. Lodouico (in occasione di chiedermi Ostie, ouero Farina per farne, atteso
he

che il suo Superiore, distante assai più che non era io, difficilmente poteua prouuedernelo) Auuisauami, trouarsi già risoluto, & allestito alla partenza, per ritornarsene à Loanda; e che allongarebbe il camino, affine di consolarsi meco in Matamba, e vedere la Regina D. Anna Zingha, della cui sincera conuersione, e dell' affetto verso le cose di Dio volaua il grido in ogni parte.

61　A ventuno di Ottobre, portatomi l' auuiso, che questi due Reli-

PAG. 799

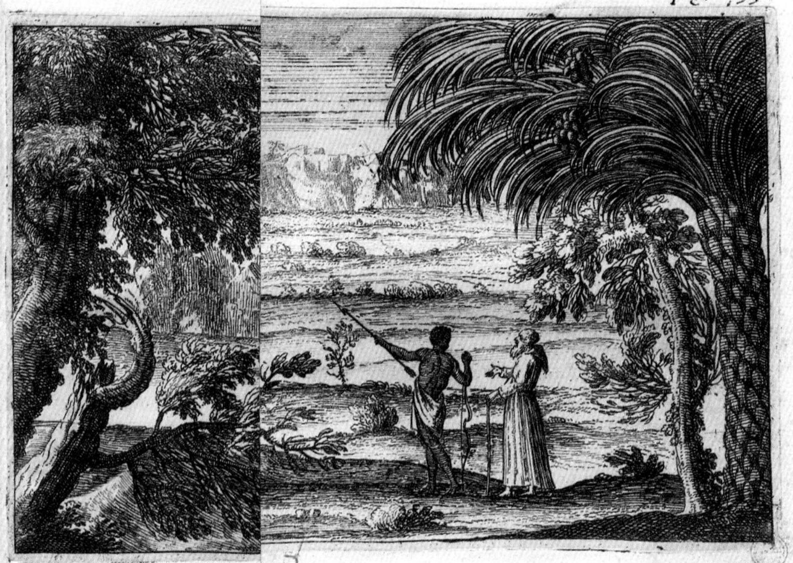

Uoarij, situate lungo la Coanza dirimpetto alle Prouincie di Lubolo, scorgesi vn' erto, e prodigioso masso di Pietra viua, che la Natura vi partorì in figura di Scoglio, e quasi hauesse hauuto in capriccio radicarlo entro il Mare, da cui ne stà lontano più di cento leghe, feceui scaturire alcune vene di Acqua (le quali secondo il saggio fattone da periti Portoghesi) vigorosamente ascendono per gl' interni meati delle Pietre, sino all' altezza di sessanta braccia sopra il liuel-

couched them as deeply religious experiences of contemplation of God's works and wonders. Second, they placed them within the Franciscan tradition of action as devotion. More than descriptive, retrospective, and distant reports on missionary activities, the Capuchin images functioned as vivid interfaces that drew their intended public into their pictured space. They achieved this permeability to viewers through three interrelated mechanisms. First, they relied on Franciscan mechanics of vision and imitation, according to which the contemplation of exemplary protagonists in images spurred devotion. Second, they used techniques of optical realism honed in the European Renaissance, and intimately entangled with Catholic piety. Third, they marshaled beliefs in the somatic effect of images articulated in early modern art theory, medicine, and philosophy.

Nature, Wonder, Art

Unfold the page. Tall trees on either side of the horizontal rectangular print frame a large open space of gently rolling hills leading up to the luminous face of the mountain range of Pungu a Ndongo, also known by its Portuguese name Pedras Negras (fig. 41). The view is labeled at its top "Maopongo o sia presidio delle Pietre," referring to the Kimbundu-language toponym of the rock formation, *matadi ma upungu a ndongo*, once the location of the capital of the Ndongo kingdom. The label also refers, with the Italian phrase for "garrison of the Stones," to the Portuguese takeover of the locale.[1] While it had long been a site of Jesuit activity, the Iberians settled it as a *presidio*, or military stronghold, in 1671.[2]

Leafy branches on the left side cast a long shadow over grass and shrubs in the foreground, forming a dark triangular space angling toward the middle of the composition. Two trunks, one straight and scaly, the other thin and curved, stand at the right edge of the image, under a tufty baldachin of palm leaves. The thinner, lighter one sprouts the upward growing branches of a broadleaf tree as well as dangling bunches akin to palm flowers or nut strings. Long, thin fronds and clusters of round fruit grow from the larger trunk, in an exuberant crown inspired by the fanlike top of palm trees. This is a fanciful canopy, however, with fruits unrealistically hanging from branches rather than the trunk, and branches multiplying far from the core of the tree, the place from which actual palm fronds emerge.

For being imaginary, the palm forms a pleasing symmetrical pendant for the broadleaf tree to the left. The two sets of trees stretch as sylvan arms embracing the long scene and placing viewers just past a forest's edge. The thick vegetation leading to the open valley echoes and transforms into a narrative feature of the image the readers' experience of anticipation and discovery upon unfolding the long print. The vegetal frame suggests a traveler's journey, walking past the edge of a dense, shady grove to stumble upon the glowing spectacle of the clearing and cliffs ahead. Similarly, in formal terms, the dense vegetation in the foreground serves, along with its shadow, as repoussoir for the light mountains pictured in the background. A large plain populated with sparse vegetation forms the middle ground, where a palm tree toward the center, some bushes, and a handful of half-bare generic plants spread out around the page give depth to the image. To create atmospheric perspective, the etcher's

Figure 40 (opposite)

Two-page spread from Giovanni Antonio Cavazzi and Fortunato Alamandini, *Istorica descrizione de' tre' regni Congo, Matamba, et Angola* (Bologna: Giacomo Monti, 1687), 798–99. 292 × 199 mm (page size). National Library of Portugal, Lisbon, H.G. 9174 A. Photo courtesy of the National Library of Portugal.

Figure 41 (overleaf)

Paolo da Lorena (attr.), *Pungu a Ndongo, or Fortress of the Pedras Negras*. From Giovanni Antonio Cavazzi and Fortunato Alamandini, *Istorica descrizione de' tre' regni Congo, Matamba, et Angola* (Bologna: Giacomo Monti, 1687), between pp. 798 and 799. Etching, 12.2 × 39 cm (plate mark). National Library of Portugal, Lisbon, H.G. 9174 A. Photo courtesy of the National Library of Portugal.

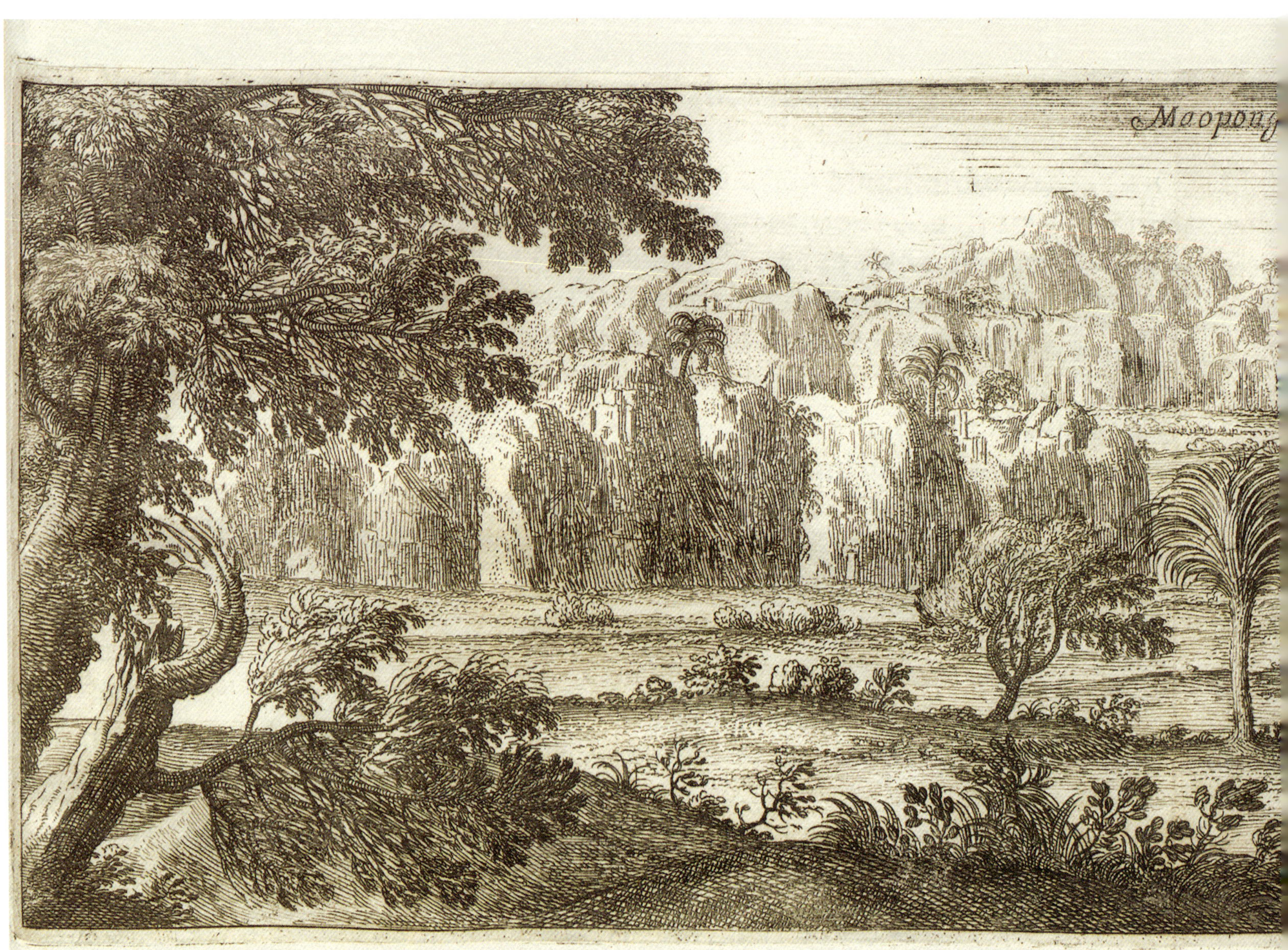
Maopou

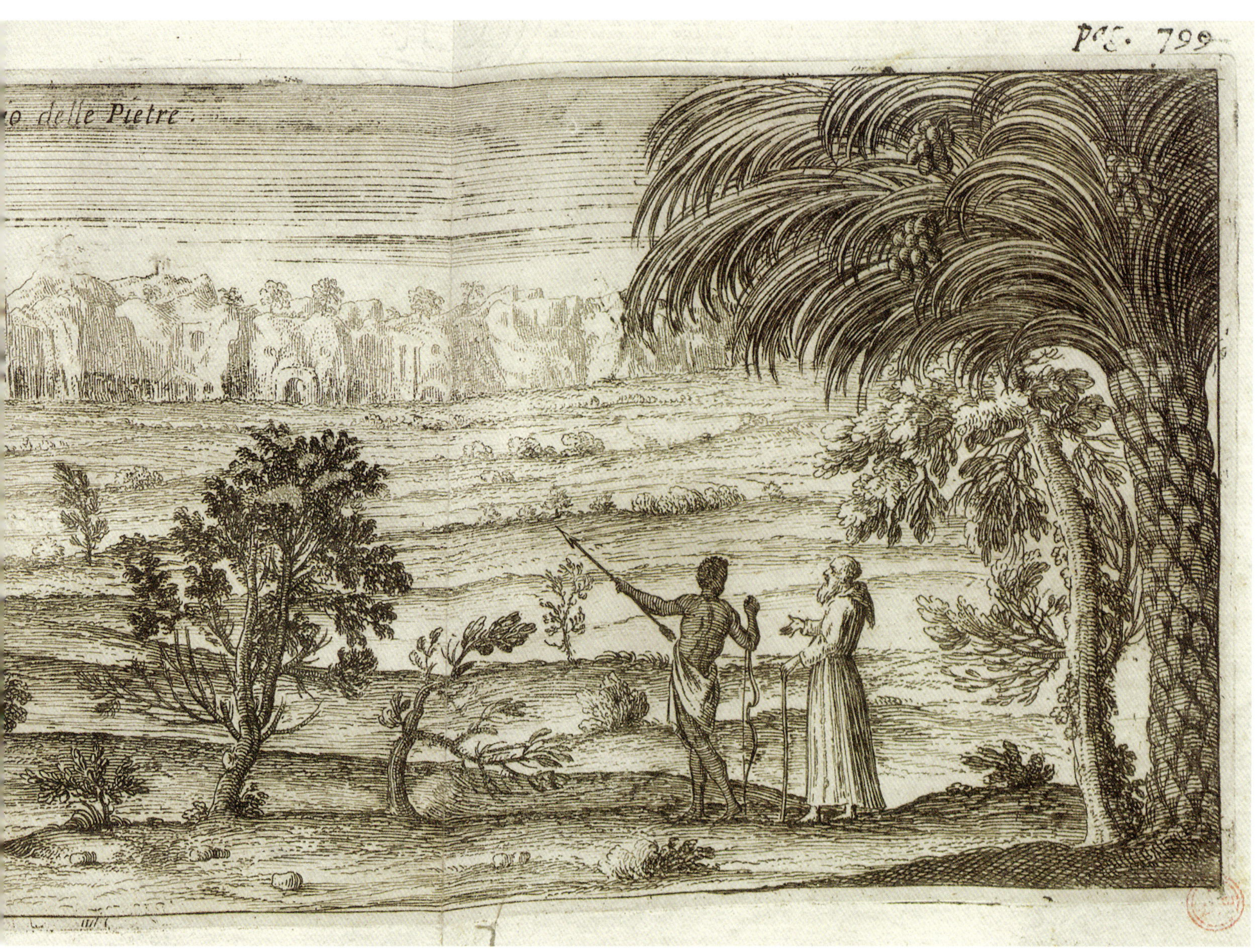
...o delle Pietre.

touch became lighter in depicting the mountains; they appear on the print in shades of gray, contrasting with the dark hue of the foreground. Although hazy, the ridge is nonetheless richly detailed. From the ground rise vertiginous cliffs of bright rock, bare, save for a handful of trees of various species growing solitarily on the escarpments. Arches and domes emerge from the rock, neither clearly man-made nor obviously wrought by nature.

"Discovering the site of Pedras Negras even from afar," writes Cavazzi's colleague and contemporary Friar Giovanni Belotti da Romano, "it appears a very delightful spectacle because of its natural shape, since it looks in fact more like an impregnable fortress, built with singular artifice, than a place composed by nature; when one sees this site of raw stones, in one part they give impressions of high towers, and in another of strong dungeons; in this part they show the semblance of prominent citadels, and in that part sublime pyramids."3

Writing about the Pungu a Ndongo rock formation upon his arrival in 1672 at the site where he would spend the first year of his central-African apostolate, Belotti verged on the lyrical: the rocks are "sublime," "delightful," "singular."4 Their shapes morph as one approaches them, challenging the distinction between natural and man-made, offering to the first-time viewer a striking multisensory spectacle. Many of his colleagues shared his awed impressions of the mountain and left equally hyperbolic descriptions, including Cavazzi. The author of the *Istorica descrizione* describes the "Maopongo Rocks" as a "prodigious mass of live rocks that Nature created in the shape of a reef" as if in the middle of the sea. He further marvels at its "springs of water," falling dozens of meters from the rocks, some brackish, others "light,

fresh, and healthy." The range, he continues, in keeping with Belotti and with the print, looks like "wonderful buildings" whose contours seem at first sight "very robust walls that some powerful monarch would have designed as fortification for a vast city." For greater magnificence "Nature worked to sketch" in the rocks "mausoleums, triumphal arches, columns, obelisks, niches, urns, gravestones, vases, and figures [*simolacri*] in so beautiful an emulation of art that I myself, having contemplated these things to my amazement, had to tell of them [*narrarle*], having myself not trusted in the past the reports of others."5 It is no doubt in anticipation of such skepticism that Cavazzi commissioned the long etching, to make the cliff and the wondrous experience of facing it for the first time more vivid to readers of his book. And in fact a keen attention to intended viewers and to the potential of images to guide their approach to and understanding of central Africa in general and its missions in particular were central concerns in the composition of Capuchins' images of Kongo and Angola. The authors of the corpus created images that used visual tools from multiple lay and religious genres, from natural-history illustrations to landscape and devotional art, in order to draw intended viewers into their pictured frames, where they could immerse themselves in the natural, cultural, and religious environment of the mission.

The spectacular landscape print of Pungu a Ndongo is particularly explicit in its intent to usher viewers into its frame and, once there, to guide their experience within its pictured space. The key to this invitation to follow in the barefoot steps of the mission's veterans is the figure of the friar standing alongside an African man at the bottom right of the print. A pendant to the "roving-artist" figures of early modern European *vedute*, the friar's presence also recalls the "wayfaring draftsmen" who suggested eyewitness authority in seventeenth-century Dutch prints.[6] It also resembles the diminutive characters populating pastoral scenes and Arcadian landscapes popular in seventeenth-century Italy as well as figures embodying the acquisitive gaze of conquest and possession in colonial images.[7]

The mendicant character successfully suggests eyewitness knowledge of a region Cavazzi had spent decades traveling, and it may well be another of his self-portraits. But the figure also plays a broader role in the image as a visualization of the friar's experience of wonderment. Mouth agape, gaze lifted up into the distance, right hand extended and palm up, the Capuchin in the print is almost an allegory of the somatic effects of wonder in the face of discovery. And this sentiment, indeed, played a large role in Capuchin approaches to novelty in central Africa, as it did for many early modern European travelers. Juan de Santiago and Antonio de Teruel, the earliest chroniclers of the Capuchin mission to Kongo and Angola, already turned to wonder to fit novelty within their own hermeneutic tradition.[8] "Truly," Spanish friar Juan de Santiago writes at the point in his narrative where the ship on which he travels enters African waters, "no part of the world has more extraordinary things to praise the Lord than the seas and lands of Ethiopia and Africa, which would appear incredible if experience did not ascertain them and rendered evident and very probable the Authorities of Saint Isidore, Aristotle, Pliny, and Berchorius and other wise authors who reported things of great wonder and monstrosity in its [i.e., Africa's] elements, animals, plants, men, and much more."[9] Narratively marking the friar's entrance into African waters,

the paragraph should nonetheless be read as a retrospective thought, summing up Juan de Santiago's experiences and the intellectual stand he took to process them, drawing from the authority of ancient knowledge and Church Fathers to make sense of wondrous novelty.

The friar's wonder at the natural world was a profoundly religious experience. In the lines before the passage above, Juan de Santiago turns to a modified Psalm 103: "How great are thy works, O Lord? thou hast made all things in wisdom; so is this great sea, which stretcheth wide its arms: there are creeping things without number, creatures great and little. There the ships shall go. May the glory of the Lord endure for ever. I will take delight in the Lord. Excellent way [*sic*] to contemplate God through the creatures, rejoicing in him and not in them."[10] The psalm offers a reading key to Friar Juan's text and to the images his colleagues crafted. In their works the Minorites presented their experiences of wonder as virtuous exercises of pious contemplation, in which they invited their readers and viewers to partake through the mediation of both words and images. Achieving the sublime and bringing to viewers visions of both the transcendent grandeur of the world and the immanence of God within it are precisely what Spanish painter and theorist Francisco Pacheco, a contemporary of Juan de Santiago, described as the goals of the Christian painter, who, he wrote, should strive to "elevate [painting] to a supreme end—the contemplation of eternal glory."[11]

Their exalted representations did justice to a central-African nature they perceived as so sublime that it seemed art itself. Girolamo Merolla da Sorrento, in his 1692 *Breve, e succinta relatione*, describes his vision of a calm stretch of the Congo River: "it rejoiced the eye to gaze at, on one or the other side of the river, two most beautiful panels [*spalliere*] of emerald vegetation that, at first glance, one would have believed were woven by the industrious hand of Pallas rather than produced by skilled [*artificiosa*] Nature, and the quiet water, augmenting the joy in our heart, looked like a long road, or ground paved with liquid crystals."[12] Woven by the hands of Pallas Athena, patron goddess of the arts, or recalling the *spalliere* panel paintings that enhanced the patrician homes of early modern Italy, nature itself is art. In the wondrous land, the line between the two blurs.[13] "It is so dazzling," Friar Marcellino d'Atri marvels decades later, upon seeing a zebra, "that it greatly delights the eyes of who sees it. . . . A painter could not have painted it better."[14]

Illusionism and immersion were key to the genre of Italian Renaissance *spalliere*, also known as "painted fables," dual and closely related effects that they achieved not only through painting techniques but also thanks to their placement in series around a room, at eye level, namely the height of the shoulder, or *spalla* in Italian.[15] These "windows," as Alberti famously described them, brought pastoral landscape, mountains, seascapes, and other vistas to the interiors of the urban elite.[16] The later Capuchin vignettes mobilized similar visual tools to bring central Africa to study rooms and libraries of the order, where novices could examine them on their way to fulfill their apostolic calling.

Optical Realism as Religious Trope

A look at the Pungu a Ndongo range as pictured in a photograph taken from a dramatic angle similar to that of the landscape print easily explains the friars' awe at the truly impressive site (fig. 42). It also to

some extent validates the etching as an apt rendering of the spectacular mountains rather than a fanciful European composition. The almost orthogonal contours of the rock formations rising above the savanna and their grid-like footprint, seen in aerial views, still evoke the elevation of fortifications and the urban plan at the center of Belotti's description and Cavazzi's image.

The friars of the central-African mission echoed in their approach to wonder and their desire to render it visually many of their lay or religious fellow travelers reporting on other equally remote and awe-inspiring corners of the world. Louis Hennepin, a Franciscan Récollet contemporary of Cavazzi who traveled with La Salle in the North American Great Lakes region, for example, expressed similar sentiments about the contribution that images could make to travel accounts. Nevertheless, the manuscript the Franciscan traveler—and suspected fibber—authored did not include images, and a map was the only illustration of its first, 1683 publication in French.[17] The later, expanded, Netherlandish editions of the account, however, featured etchings depicting some of the wonders described in the text. A foldout view of Niagara Falls in a 1697 Utrecht edition renders the multisensory spectacle of the site with a group of four men in European clothing at the bottom left of the print, arms outstretched in awe or hands over the ears to muffle the roar of the cascading waters (fig. 43). It was, according to Hennepin's introductory note to the reader, the "bookseller" who "enriched the volume with all the maps and all the engravings [*Tailles douces*] necessary to give a clear idea [*Idée nette*] of some things that are more easily understood when one has some [visual] representation of it in front of one's eyes."[18] In particular, readers would be able to see in the

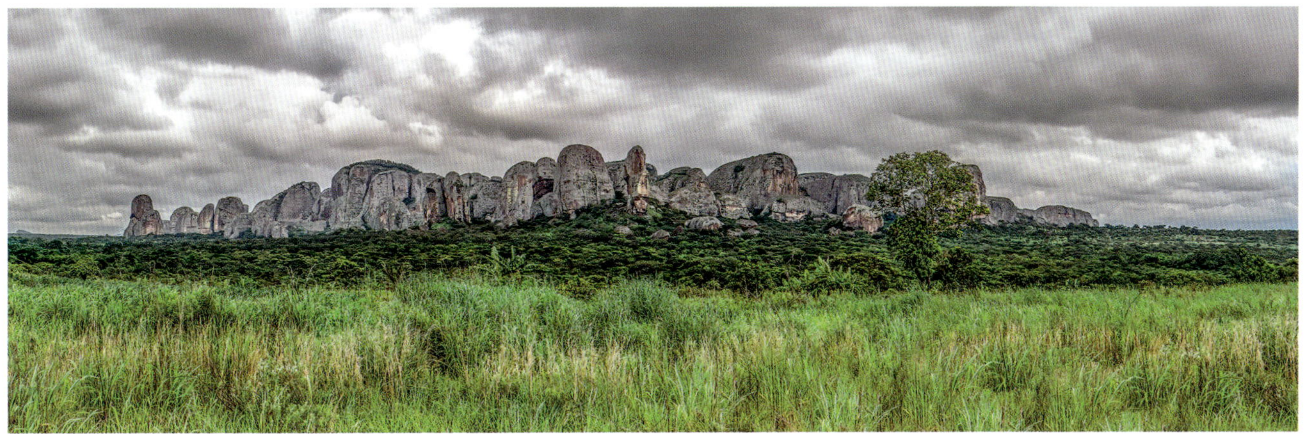

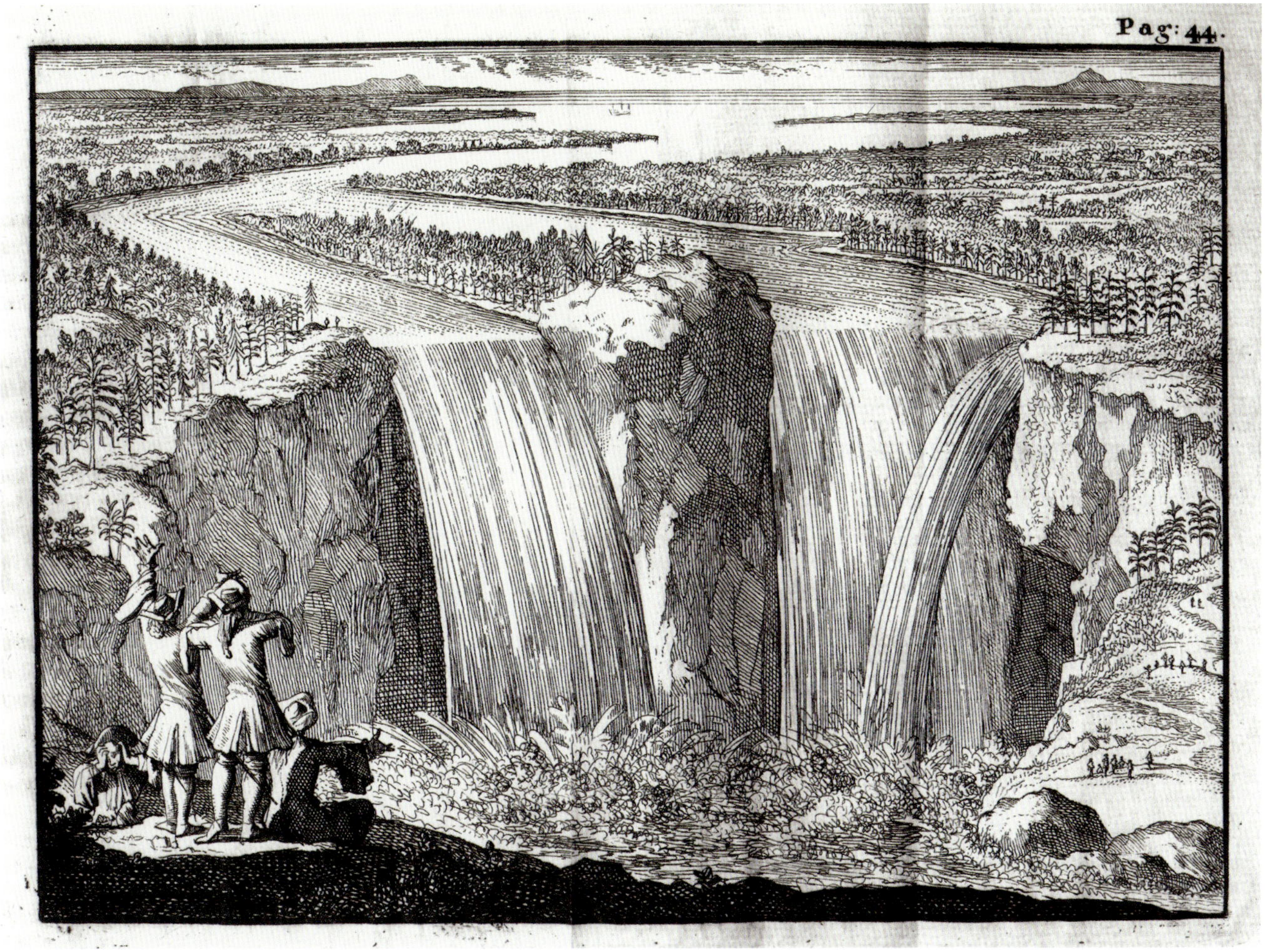

Figure 42

Nuno Miguel Ferreira de Almeida, panoramic view of the Pedras Negras (black stones) at Pungo Andongo, 2018. Digital photograph. © Nuno Miguel Ferreira de Almeida.

Figure 43

Caspar Luyken or Jan van Vianen, *View of Niagara Falls*. Etching, 125 mm × 175 mm (plate mark). From Louis Hennepin, *Nouvelle decouverte d'un tres grand pays situé dans l'Amerique* (Utrecht: Guillaume Broedelet, 1697), between pp. 44 and 45. Newberry Library, Chicago, Vault Graff 1864. Photo courtesy of the Newberry Library.

book the "great Fall of Niagara" that the friar could only describe with words, lacking, the note's author laments, the ability to capture it in a sketch. "I had often wished at the time," Hennepin writes, "to have with me skilled people who could describe [in image, he implies] this great and horrible Fall, so as to be able to give a just and well-detailed idea of it, capable of satisfying the reader, and to put him in a state of admiration of this marvel of Nature."[19] The words may be as much those of the bookmaker as those of an increasingly grandiloquent Hennepin, but they render a widely shared sentiment, seen at play in the Parma Watercolors, in Cavazzi's manuscripts, and Alamandini's printed edition. Of particular note is the clear notion of the affective as well as intellectual effect images have on viewers not only as a means for better understanding but also as a catalyst of wonder. Another Franciscan, Friar Gabriel Sagard, active among the Huron-Wendat in the early 1620s, pushed further the idea of visual images as yardsticks of successful representation, in comparing in his preface to the reader the process of writing and revising his entire written account to Apelles's painstaking working and reworking of his paintings: "Following the example of this excellent Painter [Apelles], I have freely presented to the public the sketch of my Huron journey."[20] Yet he does not include visual images in his book.

Re-creating on the page the wonder friars once experienced on the mission field was one of the goals of the Capuchin central-African paintings and prints. Whether they featured a landscape, a single plant, an African ceremony, or missionary work, for didactic purposes or to elicit awe, the vignettes all operated at some level in the documentary mode, a mode that allowed viewers trained in reading European images made in the post-Renaissance

illusionistic manner to read the painted or engraved surface as a "factual" rendering, in Panofsky's sense, of what they pictured.[21] Both simple and complex scenes in the corpus respond to the project's stated goal to document the region with a verisimilitude fit for a "practical guide." Strong compositional and visual strategies enhanced the images' claims to offer valid visual evidence. Mimetic realism was one such strategy, enhanced in some instances with seemingly accidental details, bruises and tears heightening their *effet de réel*.

The mimetic representation of people and objects drew from multiple genres, including natural-history illustrations and early ethnographic compendia such as costume books and travelogues, three types of sources the friars consulted and cited in their writings. Animals and plants appear in the Capuchin images either as protagonists of a larger scene, such as the leopard looming over an overnight camp in the Turin "Missione in prattica" (fig. 19), or, most often, as specimens isolated on a page with minimal contextualizing elements. In the Museo Francescano drawing, two rows of plants in the middle of the page showcase edible flora in this manner (plate 1). A more baroque bestiary of overlapping animals surrounds a reclining "small man" at the bottom left, maybe in reference to one of the groups of people of short stature inhabiting central Africa. This disorderly bunch, including seashells, elephant, crocodile, snake, and hardly recognizable hippopotamus (labeled "*Cavallo Marino*"), and perhaps zebra—its label maybe reads "sepra"— appear just below a cartographic sketch, in echo of cartouche decorations common at the bottom edge of early modern maps. Animals and human are nonetheless duly labeled, and some glossed with a short text, in a presentation reducing the disparity between their baroque arrangement and the orderliness of the rest of the page. The plants in the main part of the drawing are depicted more methodically. Each specimen occupies, regardless of relative scale, a similar-sized orthogonal portion of the page, making equal in height a pineapple plant and a palm tree.

The Parma Watercolors use a similar unifying scale and framing in most of their botanical and zoological images (plates 5–13, 17–44). Objects of natural history or people, when featured as illustrative of a particular trait, group, or activity, occupy a large part of the page, pushed up against the picture plane, closely and directly available to the viewers' scrutiny (plates 4, 5, 45, 46, among others). The painter has minimized the distance between pictured object and viewers, bringing the latter into the presence of the former with as little hint as possible of the contrived nature of image mediation. Specimens appear in an artificial yet observable reality, somewhat following the visual mechanics of botanical illustrations in which pictured specimens embody and transmit information about their genus, according to the belief in the knowledge-making potential of images.

Vignettes follow two different categories of templates, while still maintaining the same intent to create an observable reality. First, moments of choreographed or collective activities involving humans or animals present more-distant views—for instance, a crocodile eating shackled men, monkeys crossing a river or harassing a leopard, and people dancing at a funeral (plates 6, 41, 42, 67). Second, scenes of missionary activity center on the figure of a friar, whose presence not only suggests eyewitness authority but also invites an immersive approach from its intended Capuchin viewers, similar to that at play in the Pungu a Ndongo engraving (plates 59–65).

Illusionistic realism, the prominent mode at play in the images, contributes to other conventional and symbolic moves. As clerics and missionaries of the Counter-Reformation era, the friars were deeply invested in the rhetorical potential of images and of optical realism (as discussed further in chapter 4 below). Some of the most lifelike moments of the paintings, such as the brown-and-yellow bananas or the patched habits of the friars, served as religious tropes (fig. 49 / plate 21, plate 60). The matter-of-fact, convincing rendering of the banana, bruises and all, lends a documentary aura to a particular feature of the fruit made visible in an adjacent cross-section view, in a typical format of botanical illustrations. The transverse cut makes visible how, in the eyes of the maker of and commentator on the painting, bananas hold in their core the image of a crucifix, a feature already noted by pilgrims to Jerusalem in the Middle Ages. Here the language of scientific illustration and mimetic realism present age-old knowledge to exalt the verity of this sign of God's immanence, all the more welcome in the "deserts" of the central-African mission. The visual anecdote draws specifically on Franciscan missionary tradition by depicting bananas in the manner mendicant authors had made famous, from Niccolò da Poggibonsi in the fourteenth century to Pacifique de Provins in the seventeenth and Friar Niccoló's contemporary John Mandeville, whose narrative partly drew from the testimonies of friars of the order.[22]

The patched habits of the friars featured in the watercolors (plate 60, for instance) are a similarly polysemous detail in which realism and symbolism overlap. They certainly, at one level, picture the rugged reality of apostolic work in Kongo and Angola, but they also, and most forcefully, carry a strong religious undertone, linking the central-African missionaries to Saint Francis himself through sartorial echoes of his legendarily tattered garb. By their rules, Capuchins could only have one habit at any given time. The order's constitutions exhorted brothers "to be content with one habit, as our Holy Father in his Testament specified about himself when he said: 'We were content with one tunic, patched inside and out.'"[23] The constitutions also make explicit that the look of the saint's garb is the prototype for Capuchin habits, shaped "like those of our Father St Francis and his companions, which still exist as relics."[24] The venerated patched tunic is one of the most important relics of Saint Francis. Piously kept in the Basilica of Assisi, where the saint is entombed, it has, alongside competing habits kept in Cortona, Gubbio, and Arezzo, weathered seemingly endless controversies about and scientific investigations into its authenticity.

Franciscan Immersive Images

Attention to the visual and its devotional potential ran deep in Franciscan doctrine and manifested itself in strong ways in the order's visual culture, from sartorial choices and the practice of everyday life to the artworks the friars used and commissioned. In the Capuchin central-African corpus, the visual dimension of Franciscan devotion appears particularly clearly in images that featured friars in their composition. The motif of the Franciscan friar took the form of a garbed cleric standing under a large tree offering a canopy for his activities. It featured repeatedly in the Parma Watercolors as well as the later "Missione in prattica" of the mid-eighteenth century (plates 61, 62, 63; 71 bottom, 72 bottom, fig. 44). In these vignettes, but also in others depicting friars positioned differently, image-makers carefully constructed their scenes to invite their intended viewers—fellow Franciscans—into the pictorial space. Slightly elevated, horseback or diagonal perspectives contributed to this effect, offering a privileged line of sight and a path into the pictured space. The mirroring between readers' discovery of the foldout's contents in the *Istorica descrizione* and the two walking figures' discovery of the cliffs in the engraved landscape derived from and expanded that effect. The foldout extended into the third dimension the visual techniques through which Capuchin image-makers strove to create compositions whose pictured space reached out to viewers and invited an immersive approach to their contents.

Diagonal, leading lines of sight, horseback views, and flattened perspective are recurrent tools used in the Capuchin images to invite viewers into their frames. Strong diagonals organize the riverscape and the temple-burning scene in the Turin "Missione in prattica" (figs. 73, 93); scenes of mores and customs are generally presented from elevated viewpoints (plates 48 and 67); plan and elevation are both given space in the depiction of the Capuchin convent of Soyo ("Missione in prattica," fol. 4r). A leopard with a knowing look serves as an intermediary between a pictured friar and the picture's beholder (fig. 19). Yet more than any of the formal elements artists used to guide viewers' approach to the image, it was the figure of the friar that provided for the intended Franciscan public the most compelling gateway into an immersive experience. In the case of the landscape print, the etcher himself, Paolo da Lorena, was precisely such a Capuchin viewer of the paintings or drawings he used and reworked to produce the copper plate.[25] Stepping into the barefoot tracks of their brother in religion depicted in the print, friars like Paolo could take in the natural spectacle of Pungu a Ndongo from a diagonal angle from which he both faced the cliffs and looked toward the opening between two rows of rocky formations, where lay the path forward, beyond the mountains, to the mission post.

This invitation to embodied experience through the visual followed a well-trodden iconographic path. The mendicant of the etching stands in an attitude familiar to Franciscan representations of awe, central, for instance, to images of the order's eponymous saint. Depictions of Saint Francis receiving the stigmata on Mount La Verna routinely display him face up and with arms outstretched. Hagiographic retellings of the event such as Saint

Bonaventure's *Legenda maior*, composed around 1260–63, or the popular stories gathered in the second half of the fourteenth century in the florilegium *I fioretti*, from which sixteenth- and seventeenth-century artists routinely drew to compose images of the fateful event, describe the thirteenth-century Italian holy man receiving the stigmata in this attitude.[26] The influential accounts of the *Considerazioni sulle stimmate*, for instance, have the saint's companion Brother Leo seeing him "on his knees with his face and hands turned to the sky"[27] when the angelic crucifix from which he would receive the marks appeared in the night. As he encountered Christ, stories and images alike retell, his arms opened and stretched out in awe and rapture, his body already beginning to conform in posture to that of the crucified God. An oil-on-canvas work from the Italian Minorite milieu, Barocci's 1594–95 *Stigmatization of Saint Francis*, painted for the Capuchin church in Urbino and later circulated broadly in print form, offers one among many examples of artistic depictions of the meaningful gesture of transformative imitation (fig. 45). The rugged mountainous setting of the fateful event, Mont La Verna, inspired innumerable visual and textual depictions, like that of Barocci, and without a doubt inspired the cliff-side landscape print.[28]

Beyond simple iconographic conventions, these images of Saint Francis at La Verna, in the post-Tridentine Franciscan context, talk to the key theological concepts of *conformitas* (likeness), embodiment, and imitation. Bonaventure's canonical description of the moment Saint Francis was marked with Christ's wounds characterizes the event as an external, visible manifestation of the other, actual change taking place, that is, his inner

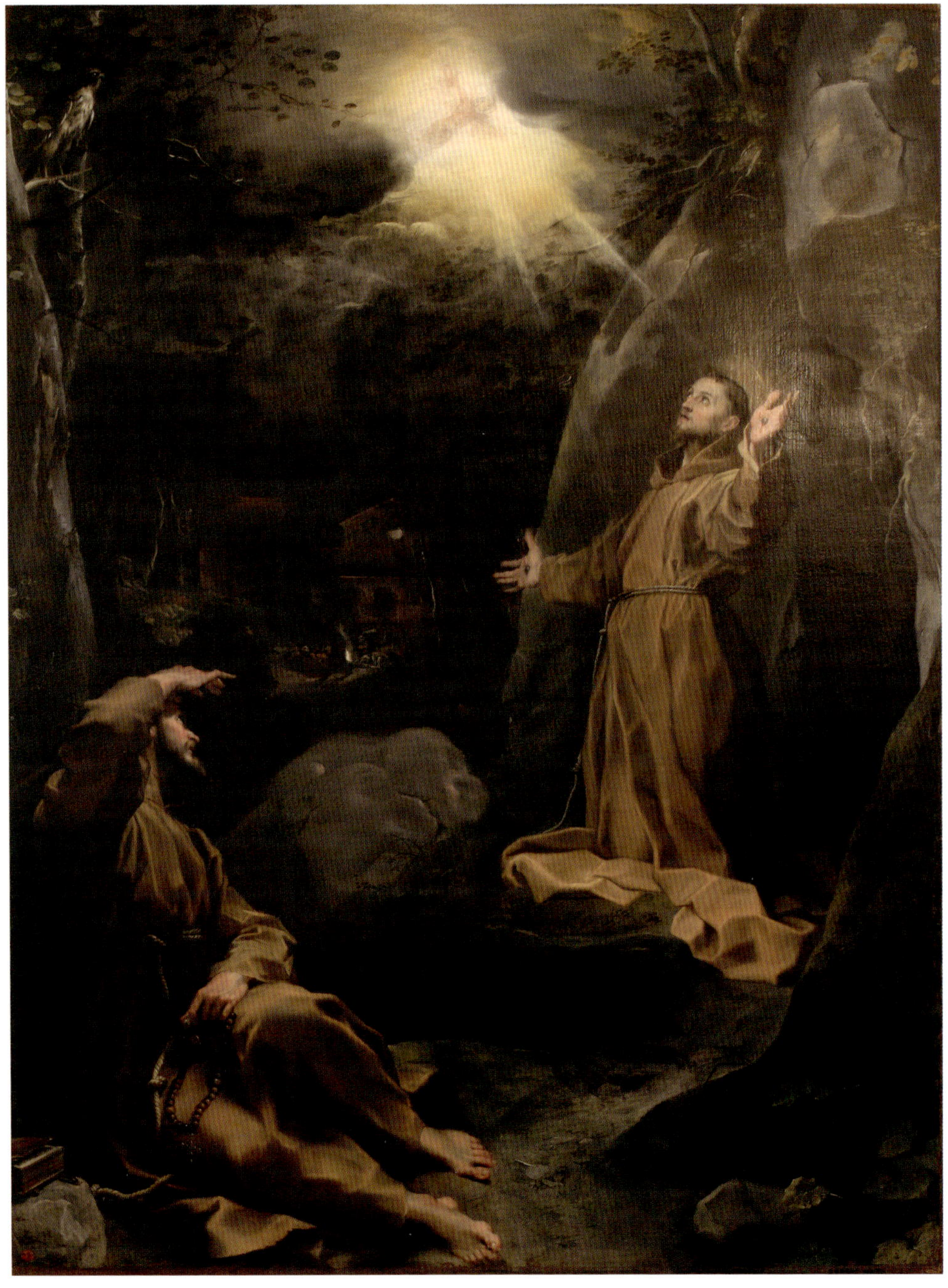

transformation into the likeness of, or *conformitas* to, Christ. "There," the Doctor of the Church explains, "he passed over into God in ecstatic contemplation and became an example of perfect contemplation as he had previously been of action."[29] The stigmata manifested the inner metamorphosis of Saint Francis as he became *alter Christus* unto the saint's body, rendering the spiritual change visible as corporeal transformation. In the same manner as God made himself visible to the world in his incarnation in Christ—a key argument in defense of images in the Catholic Counter-Reformation—Saint Francis's transformed body stood as a visible manifestation of Christ in the world.[30]

Most important here, the story of the stigmatization draws an explicit connection between emulation and likeness, making Saint Francis both exemplar and image of Christlike perfection.[31] This link took on pragmatic form in the rules of Franciscan orders—including and, as they would themselves argue, in particular the Capuchins'—which prescribed imitation of their eponymous saint in garb, mores, and actions. Friars, their constitutions explained, "are true sons of St Francis only in so far as [they] imitate his life and teaching."[32] The same focus on attentive imitation played a central role in the friars' approach to images of their tutelary saint as *alter Christus*. Paintings or prints of the holy man offered to Minorites occasions for contemplation of perfect devotion. They also served as a template to follow in the steps of their founding father.

Franciscan pictures functioned according to the modus operandi of Catholic Reformation images, that is, as media through which devotion traveled from devotees to God, the only rightful recipient of worship in Christian dogma. Central to this view of the devotional potential of pictures is an understanding of likeness as the operative link between image and prototype. These ideas about *conformitas* and *imitatio*, far from esoteric, would have been very familiar to the friars. Bartolomeo da Rinonico's *De Conformitate*, for instance, was one of the texts Franciscans were enjoined to read frequently and would regularly hear as communal reading during meals in convent refectories. It also featured among the earliest books Franciscans brought to their missions in the Americas.[33]

The crucial notion of likeness thus held particular currency in the Franciscan realm. It was the cornerstone of the founding saint's hagiography and, in conjunction with imitation, formed the principal means and goal of the friars' religious practice. *Conformitas* as the reward of imitation is both subject matter and operating mode of images of Saint Francis. They depict the holy man in action, that is, in the process of becoming (immediately in stigmatization scenes or more distantly in earlier episodes from his life) or having become *alter Christus*, while urging viewers to emulate his example. What these pictures describe is the link between inner and outer, spiritual and physical form. These ideas about vision and its impact on the soul are ultimately connected to Aristotelian and Baconian conceptions of "a tangible link between image and beholder"[34] in which the forms of seen things durably reshape the soul, in the manner of a seal's imprint on wax.[35] Such notions would, understandably, loom large in the Franciscan use of images for missionary purposes as tools to convert impressionable neophytes or deepen faith's imprint on a faltering flock (as discussed in chapter 4 below). But it is also important to underline the role the same ideas played in imagery that was crafted for and directed at a viewership of friars and that relied on

an implicit but concrete connection between prototype, image, and viewers.

To put it in other words, Franciscan images were not hermetically enclosed units, self-sufficient and impervious to the outside. Their conception and operating mode were predicated on their permeability to the world of viewers and on the generative relationship they established with them. Franciscan images stretched as open channels and connective tissue between viewers, on the one end, and God, on the other, whose presence gained sensible form through them. Viewers, in turn, projected themselves into their contents in devout exercises of contemplation. In Franciscan contexts in which imitation carried much theological and social weight, images explicitly reached out to the viewers and invited them to take part in a pious chain of imitation and likeness. Viewers of Franciscan images thus were highly trained in a particular visual approach that hinged on a nimble understanding of pictures as interfaces and as holding the power to reach beyond their frames to invite and implicate beholders into their contents.

The opening page of Friar Belotti's manuscript on the conduct of the central-African mission, the 1680 "Avvertimenti Salutevoli," deploys this Franciscan take on images in the specific context of the Capuchin apostolate in Kongo and Angola, offering the figure of a Saint Francis–like friar hovering over scenes of African catechization and baptism (fig. 46). The ecstatic friar, lifted on a cloud, faces a divine apparition toward whom he directs his gaze. The encounter is both visual and corporeal; the brother not only looks toward God but also literally breathes in his presence and words. The friar's aspiration is made visible in the drawing first in a light-colored ribbon going from God to friar

Figure 45 (opposite)

Federico Barocci, *Stigmatization of Saint Francis*, 1594–95. Oil on canvas, 360 × 245 cm. Soprintendenza per i beni Storici Artistici ed Etnoantropologici della Marche—Galleria Nazionale delle Marche, Palazzo Ducale, Urbino, Italy. Photo courtesy of the Ministero per i Beni e le Attività Culturali e per il Turismo—Galleria Nazionale delle Marche.

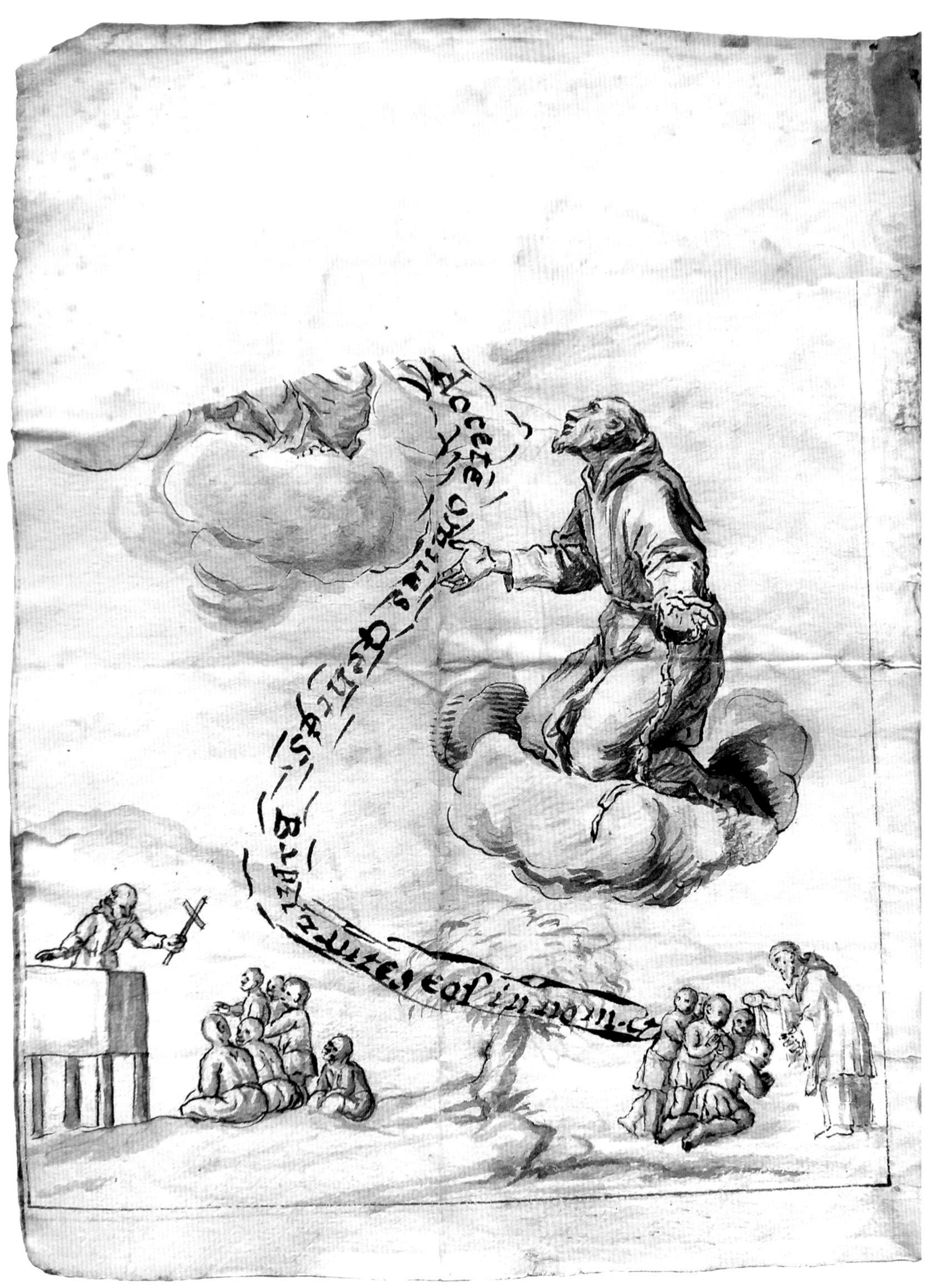

Figure 46

Giovanni Belotti da Romano, frontispiece to "Avvertimenti Salutevoli agli Apostolici Missionari, specialmente nei regni del Congo, Angola e circonvicini," 1680. Ink on paper, 16.5 × 16 cm (damaged page size). Biblioteca del Clero Collection in the Biblioteca Monsignor Giacomo Maria Radini Tedeschi, Bergamo, MS 45. Photo courtesy of the Biblioteca Monsignor Giacomo Maria Radini Tedeschi.

and from friar down to the scene below him, and then in an even more forceful and explicit written quote of Matthew 28:19, whose linear border, forming the ribbon, stretches as if inspired into the friar's breath.[36] Aspiration here is to be explicitly understood in both a biological and metaphorical sense as the friar's desire for a typically Franciscan experience of perfect devotion in the form of union with God in mind and body after the model of Saint Francis.

The standing missionary in the landscape print is obviously less exalted than the kneeling friar in the Belotti drawing, but the reference to Franciscan iconography remains compelling. Like Saint Francis, the etched cleric stands face up, gazing aloft with his right arm extended, hand open, in front of a great mountain range. In the very Franciscan context of an image made by a Capuchin printmaker after a Capuchin watercolor for a Capuchin audience, the allusion to the ecstasy on Mount La Verna is unmistakable. In fact, in the etching, as in the drawing, a short black line in the palm of each friar's hand may not directly depict a stigma but still clearly serves as yet another hint encouraging viewers to see the images at hand in chorus with Franciscan imagery. Such a reference to Saint Francis, in turn, underlines the central role of imitation and emulation in the modus operandi of the Capuchin central-African images. Hagiographic representation of Saint Francis receiving the stigmata both celebrated the divine rewards the holy man received for his assiduous imitation of Christ and invited friars to follow the example of their saint in his Christological emulation. As already noted, Saint Francis's *conformitas* derived from his actions as well as his contemplation, drawing a bridge between prayer and practice crucial to the mendicant

religious ethos of life in the world rather than removed from it, in the manner of monastic claustration. In this early modern Minorite context, then, Saint Francis's embodied experience of Christ's passion made him at once an image of God's son and an exemplar for his followers.

In the Capuchin central-African corpus of visual guides to the mission, the role-model dimension of this iconography is enlisted in images inviting novices to follow the pioneering path of the friars they feature. The parallels between study and action, between reading and transformative vision, are further reinforced in the narrative of the stigmatization from the *vita*, which retells how Saint Francis had been absorbed in reading the Passion in the Gospel before Christ appeared to him, just as the viewers of the landscape print had been concentrating on a long stretch of unillustrated text in the *Istorica descrizione* before encountering the image of the friar to project themselves into and emulate. In both cases, the visual path to action, be it the apparition and encounter with God at La Verna or in the admittedly more mundane circumstances depicted in the etching, begins as a reward for textual study and for the mental ekphrasis at work in the pious, studious minds.

Artistic Traditions of Viewer Involvement: Landscape Painting, Natural History

The fluid mutual construction of image and thought and the strong relationship between viewers and pictured space underlying early modern Catholic approaches to the visual also manifested themselves in the two other, and somewhat related, genres that influenced the making of the

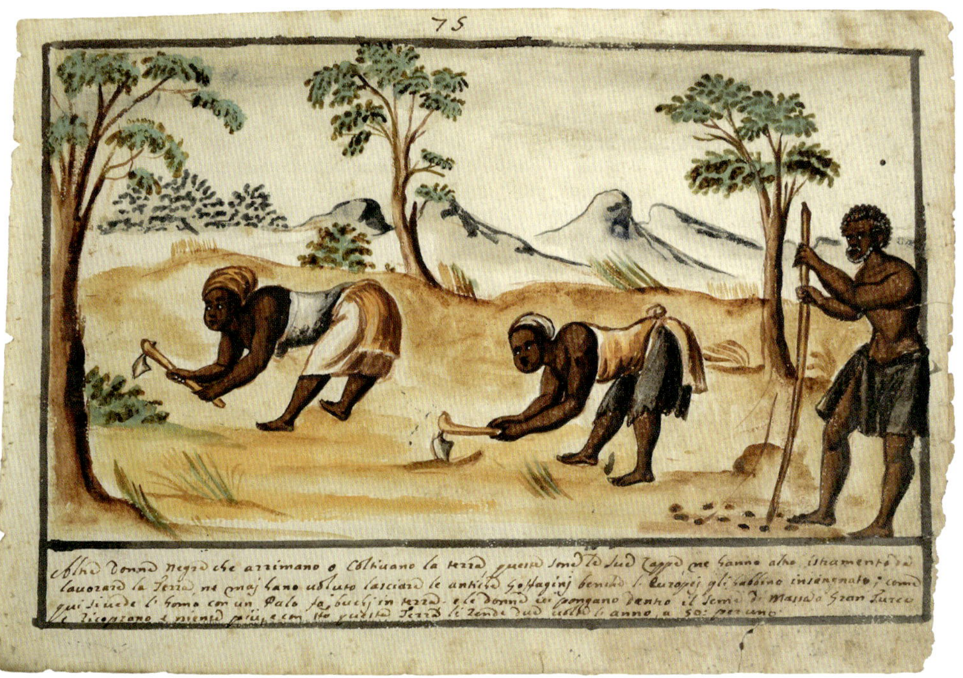

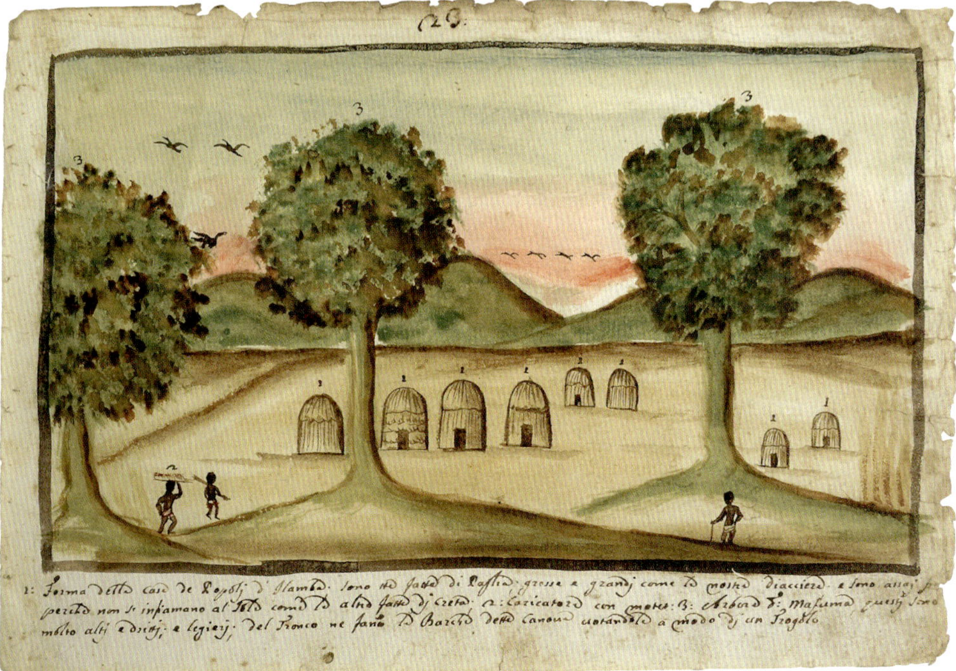

Capuchin central-African corpus: landscape and natural history. The specific painting or drawing from which the landscape print derived is no longer extant or has not surfaced yet. As discussed in the previous chapter, it belonged to the same cluster of images as the Parma Watercolors, a corpus closely related to the *Istorica descrizione* plates. The Pungu a Ndongo mountain or one resembling it appears in the background of one of the Parma Watercolors, within the manuscript's mores-and-customs sequence (fig. 47 / plate 49).[37] There, the telltale parallel ranges of bare rocks rise in the distance, behind sparse vegetation surrounding two women and an elderly man at work in agricultural activities. The vignette is an intriguing composite between landscape and ethnographic images, or perhaps an attempt at a central-African pastorale. It is unusual among the other paintings of the manuscript, which tend to present their main figures closely framed and with only minimal references to their environment. With distinct fore-, middle-, and background, and with the tall tree framing its left edge, the tilling scene is a more ambitious composition than most of the other watercolors in the set and an apt parallel to the landscape print.

Figure 47

Unknown Capuchin artist, "Other black women who . . . cultivate the land," late seventeenth century. Watercolor on paper, 34 × 24 cm. Parma Watercolors, Virgili Collection, fol. 75. Photo: author.

Figure 48

Unknown Capuchin artist, "Houses of the people of Ilamba," late seventeenth century. Watercolor on paper, 34 × 24 cm. Parma Watercolors, Virgili Collection, fol. 23. Photo: author.

Only one other page in the Parma Watercolors fully takes on the representation of an expansive landscape, the view of the village of Ilamba on folio 23 (fig. 48 / plate 14). There, a dramatic sunset or sunrise colors pink a sky populated with flocks of birds in formation. Small figures in the foreground, to the left, carry goods to the village, while a third, solitary bystander, at the bottom right, takes in the spectacle, one arm akimbo, the other resting on a cane. In a twist on formulations showcasing a European traveler, artist, or colonial administrator looking over an exotic landscape with an inquisitive and acquisitive gaze, the watercolorist here has featured instead an African man. The central-African vista shares two other features with the tilling scene and the print: a tree at the left edge and mountains rising on the horizon. Even if the rest of the vignettes only make timid references to landscapes and marine views, these genres are, along with natural-history illustrations, ethnographic scenes, and devotional images, key building blocks in the construction of the Capuchin central-African corpus. Central to all these visual types is the relationship they build between image and viewers.

A popular genre in elite Italian circles of the seventeenth century, landscape painting (and prints) served not only as a source of recreation and aesthetic pleasure but also as an instrument understood to have a strong potential to impact viewers' minds and bodies. Within a social and historical context of growing interest in tourism and travel, painted topographies rose in prominence, as did the genre of travel literature in which the Capuchin publications on Kongo and Angola to some extent participated. Seventeenth-century physician, collector, and art theorist Giulio Mancini, best known for his reflections on the Roman art market, the *Considerazioni*

sulla pittura (1619–21), wrote at length about the connections he and his contemporaries keenly perceived between painting, the construction of knowledge, and the health or illness of the body. Also the author of a guide on the art of travel, the "Modo e regola di far viaggio,"[38] Mancini considered the empirical study of the land and its topographical features crucial to the traveler's experience and a key exercise for the acquisition of knowledge, which, he opined, was the central goal of traveling itself. For the learned Roman man, who had himself traveled little, landscape painting could provide an adequate replacement for actual journeys. A well-composed *veduta*, he explained, could offer, in art historian Frances Gage's paraphrase, "a visual surrogate for forward motion in space"[39] if its composition invited, as the landscape etching in figure 41 does, movement from foreground to background. The use of repoussoir, perspective, and traveling figures are essential features for a composition to be successful in this sense. The long print in the *Istorica descrizione*, the view of Ilamba, and to some extent the agriculture scene fit this template. In Mancini's sense, gazing upon their printed lines or painted surfaces, viewers could virtually walk through the pictured Angolan lands.

The Roman physician also considered the attention that landscape painters gave to nature, particularly in their representation of foreground objects "dal vero" (from life), to hold similarities with the practices of natural-history illustrators.[40] The resulting effect on viewers also overlapped, Mancini added, as in both cases "careful naturalistic imitation demand[ed] that the beholder scrutinize the paintings as the artist had done the natural objects."[41] Artworks produced by prominent artists in Italy during the formative years of the Capuchin missions makes explicit how image-making, observation of the natural and human worlds, and the acquisition of knowledge formed a close-knit set of practices.[42] Florentine artist Jacopo Ligozzi, for instance, worked in a range of genres from landscape to botanical illustration for famed naturalist and collector of curiosities Ulisse Aldrovandi, in religious painting for the Franciscan church of the Ognissanti, and famously authored a set of gouache depictions of Turks, perhaps for the Medici or Niccolò Gaddi.[43] He also designed, at the intersection of landscape, travelogue, and devotional art, the visual program for the influential 1612 *Descrizione del Sacro Monte della Verna*. To the South, Neapolitan landscape painter Filippo Napoletano cultivated an interest in exotic human types and gathered a collection of "very beautiful curiosities of all kind."[44] Like the artists they patronized, collectors nurtured overlapping interests in natural history and landscape painting. Cassiano dal Pozzo, for example, was both a key figure in the circles of the natural-history institution the Accademia dei Lincei and a leading patron of landscapists such as Poussin and Pietro da Cortona.[45]

Cardinal Federico Borromeo, another important collector of landscape painting in Italy around 1600, who maintained interest in and correspondence with members of the Lincean Academy, explicitly connected observation of nature, lifelike representation of specimens, and landscape painting in his commentaries.[46] In the guide to his collection, the *Museaum*, the cardinal explicitly writes about how *vedute*, in his opinion, invited immersion. Paul Bril's *Seascape* of 1611, he explains, "is a view of the sea that is so soothing, peaceful, and panoramic that anyone who sees it would think that he is looking at the real thing or walking along the seacoast."[47]

Like Mancini, Borromeo readily considers paintings as spaces that viewers could penetrate and within which they could virtually perambulate. He had in his palace "painted views . . . to [him] as beautiful as open and wide views [of nature]. . . . Instead of them, when they are not had, paintings enclose in narrow places, the space of earth and the heavens, and we go wandering, and making long [spiritual] journeys standing still in our room."[48] This sentiment is in the same vein as the Capuchins' analogies between central-African nature and *spalliera* painting discussed earlier in this chapter.

Such considerations of the possibilities of armchair travel through images, painted or printed, already appeared in travel literature of the preceding century.[49] Visual or written images, André Thevet opined in his accounts of travel to Brazil of 1557, afford readers opportunities to experience faraway lands even if "it is not possible for every man to see everything sensibly during his life."[50] Considered from this angle, images in books such as the *Istorica descrizione* or in the Capuchin didactic paintings not only served to reinforce the eyewitness dimension of the written accounts they accompanied, they also offered viewers a proxy for the described experience, distant in time and space from them.[51]

What is more, for Borromeo the potential for landscapes to invite immersion from beholders also encompassed a religious dimension. It offered an opportunity to contemplate God's goodness and perfection through his creations.[52] They gave viewers, including those who could not afford to see nature for themselves, the ability to bask in God's marvelous creations, an idea very much in the *air du temps* of the seicento and articulated elsewhere, for instance, in the writings of Roberto Bellarmino, a widely read Jesuit whose works featured in

Capuchin libraries.[53] This dimension of the visual is implicit in most of the central-African vignettes but also appears very explicitly in others. The depiction of the bananas inscribed in their flesh with a holy crucifix is one of them (fig. 49). The loftily etched, marvelous white cliffs of Pungu a Ndongo, straddling the divide between natural and man-made, is another (fig. 41).

Borromeo's meditations offer an additional lens through which to approach the Capuchin central-African corpus. Beyond its didactic component as training tool for future missionaries, for whom it made central Africa already known although not yet seen, the corpus also functioned as an occasion for pious meditation on God's works, parallel to the written accounts quoted above in which friars both described and marveled at nature as art crafted by God's very hand. The Capuchin visual corpus thus drew from a multivalent understanding of the immersive potential of images, which it used toward didactic and devotional goals. At the core of the images' operating mode was the belief that they could not only make the absent present but also serve as visual substitutes from which knowledge of the not yet seen could be acquired. They made available to viewers' direct observation, for knowledge-making and pious meditation alike, the vivid likeness of faraway natural wonders, cultural practices, and missionary work depicted within their frames.

Conclusion

The Pungu a Ndongo etching invited viewers to join their brother pictured in the corner, not only in taking in the awe-inspiring natural wonder of the mountains but also in setting off to the mission. The print is both an image of the central-African apostolate and an example to follow: first, virtually, through absorption in the pictured space, and, later, in real life, by contributing to the overseas apostolate. Unfolding in the landscape print is an immersive rhetoric functioning simultaneously as an invitation to pious contemplation, a summons to take up missionary life, and an expression of the friars' belief in the spiritual and corporeal effects of the visual. This dynamic characterizes the modus operandi of the Capuchin central-African corpus at large, in which images did not function as inert records but as vivid interfaces. At work in the outreaching and permeable images was a project aimed at disabusing viewers of their preconceived ideas about Africa and missionary endeavors by plunging them into a complex and not fully resolved pictured realm replete with uncertain encounters with the unknown and generative dialogue with the Other.

Three short and plump bananas, still connected by their stem, lie unceremoniously on a bare ground (fig. 49 / plate 21). The bundle is freshly cut from its bunch; the white inside of the stem has not yet oxidized and hardened into a hard, brown stub. A brushstroke of white wash highlights the sectioned part, testifying that the ripe fruits have just been collected in time for *al vivo* observation and depiction. A caption at the bottom of the page and a cross section to the left firmly place the painting in the realm of botanical illustrations. The bananas are specimens to be observed from different informative angles that a viewer trained in the reading of natural-historical plates can synthesize into a coherent statement of about the fruits' nature and properties.

If it were not for the numbered gloss stating that "cutting [the banana] with a knife, a crucifix appears inside," some viewers of the image would certainly miss the crucial detail held in the fruit's white flesh. Exposed by the crosscut, a T-shape shadow in the pulp sketches the silhouette of a crucifix. The revelation rewards exactly the type of formal, sustained observation characteristic of early modern European scientific pursuit. The visualization technique of the cross section reveals the divine image that otherwise would have remained invisible. That the inside of the banana looks exactly like a Catholic host stamped with a cross and a radiating border hints at a further reading of the page. The fruit, emblazoned with the Christian God's image, marks nature as an agent of divine will. It is a sign of immanence, a symbol of God's benevolent presence in his wondrous creations. Franciscan viewers would recognize on the page a well-known observation about the fruit that their medieval predecessors had

CHAPTER 4

Images as Method

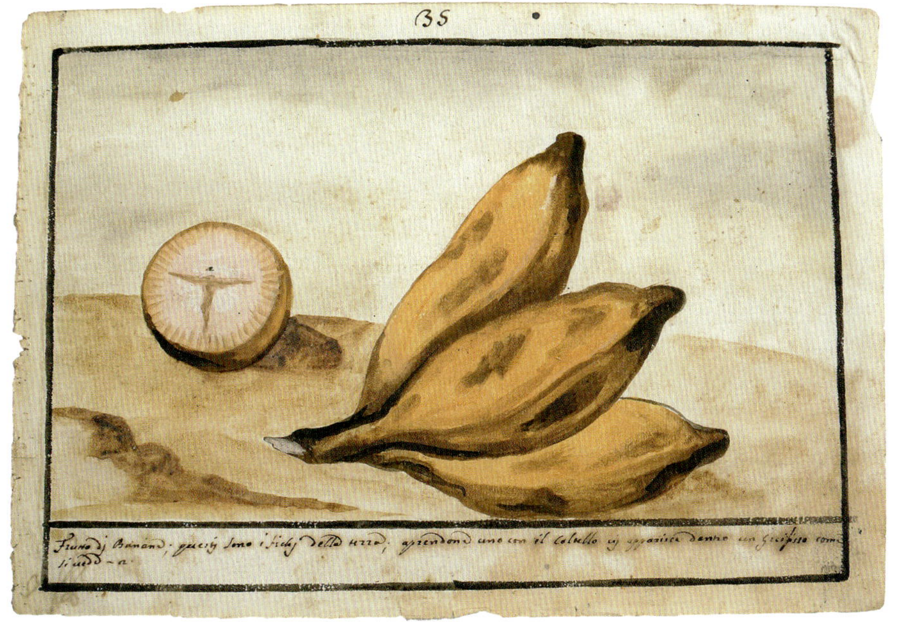

already had the opportunity to make in their travels to the Holy Land.[1]

The bananas' irregular shapes and bruised skins, however, counter the idea that the painting is merely a conceited devotional vignette or principally a synthetic scientific depiction of a specimen. Ripe and fleshy, presented as a bunch and not single fruits, they appear as they would in a market or a pantry. They are foodstuff that one can seek and consume, peeling away their patchy shells to uncover a pristine pulp. The page is at once botanical illustration, rehearsal of Minorite travel lore, pious image, and food guide. Altogether, it is a quintessential example of the multivalent operative mode of the Capuchin central-African images.

Members of a Counter-Reformation–era religious order, the friars active in early modern Kongo and Angola demonstrated a sophisticated approach to images, trusting their potential to record information, induce devotion, and convey knowledge. They drew from the visual language of natural history, the artistic conventions of naturalism, the well-trodden motifs of travel literature, and baroque Catholic imagery to create a unique set of images. Through images, they endeavored to make sense of the many wonders and dangers of central Africa. They pictured its different environments and offered frameworks to interpret the natural and social makeup of its different regions. They also used pictures to document the visual apostolic methods they developed and deployed for their pastoral work among the local Christians and heathens. Ultimately, images bore witness to the visual rhetoric the missionaries unfurled in two directions at once. On the one hand, it was aimed at the inhabitants of central Africa the friars endeavored to usher

into and retain in the Church. On the other hand, it targeted the very members of their order whom it attempted to educate in the proper conduct of a peculiar missionary field.

Visualizing Central-African Nature

The visual templates of natural history played a large role in the friars' experience, understanding, and representation of central Africa. The presentation of close-cropped, isolated, multiple views of a fruit or animal within a black frame draws unmistakable connections between many of the Parma Watercolors and botanical illustrations. The bananas in figure 49 (plate 21), for instance, are presented frontally, as a bunch, revealing their characteristic external aspect. The text provides an identification, "banana fruit," and a numbered key, oddly made of only one digit, corresponding with the number 2 written in black ink over the transverse cut of the fruit, registers a salient characteristic of the specimen. Yet, as discussed earlier, the page combines the visual language of natural history with other types of visual and knowledge-making discourses. The gloss, for instance, gives to the fruit religious significance, pointing to the crucifix held within its flesh. Formal characteristics also make the vignette a less-than-typical botanical illustration. A brown wash suggests earth against a white sky; cut and uncut bananas rest on a ground and cast shadows in a perspectival pictured space. They dwell on the page with volumetric and temporal presence, as much *nature morte* as placeless, timeless specimen plate. The natural-history images fashioned by the Capuchins do not attempt to place central-African natural environment in an abstract system of classification but rather bring, more modestly, central-African flora and fauna to European viewers' awareness, making the region's fruits and animals known to them, though not yet seen.

At the core of this difference between the Capuchin vignettes and the botanical illustrations they visually emulate are their respective intended audiences. Scientific plates addressed a loosely defined public of scholars, connoisseurs, and students, as well as merchants and, in some contexts, colonial administrators. In contrast, the Capuchin images rendered central Africa's natural environment principally for the benefit of a small, well-defined group of members of their order, originating from few places in southern Europe.[2] They only secondarily addressed a wider public, which they would in fact never quite reach.[3] If the Capuchin visual testimonies were, to borrow the words of historian of science Surekha Davies, both "ethical (tied to the personal)" and "epistemic (independent of this social context),"[4] the two aspects did not carry the same weight. Friars addressed first and foremost their brothers in religion and only secondarily an anonymous learned audience for which they needed to establish the accuracy and authority of their claims. Both the images and the texts of the Capuchin corpus were shaped to suit a largely homogeneous intended readership. Written descriptions performed translation by analogy, linking central-African plants and animals to European counterparts familiar to both writers and readers. For instance, the Parma Watercolors describe potatoes as "turnips of the Congo," bananas "the figs of this country," and flamingos "water birds as large as geese."[5] In other words, in their texts, the Capuchins used the readers' native environment and background as the operative point of reference for translation.

In their images, they referred to the background they shared with their viewers in a different way. Only in rare cases did they use analogies between faraway objects and familiar ones, such as in the case of the intriguing horselike beast the Parma Watercolors call *alicorno* (fig. 51 / plate 36). Instead, friars took as their point of departure the represented specimen itself, which they believed they could make vividly present to their intended viewers in pictured form.[6] In their visual logic, images offered a form of observable reality and as such were potent media for the transmission of information and the formation of knowledge. Capuchins shared this belief in the potential of images with their contemporary European artists and thinkers.

The "evidence of the eye" played a central role in the formation of scientific facts in early modern Europe.[7] Though the limits of description and analogy as the primary tools of scientific inquiry increasingly became evident over the course of the seventeenth century, learned minds such as the members of the Italian Lincean academy continued to have "unruffled confidence in the possibilities of scientific illustrations."[8] The Capuchins' approach to visualizing central Africa demonstrated a similar faith in images and recourse to the "evidence of the eye." The friars turned to conventions associated with natural-historical illustrations to organize and communicate what they deemed "useful" information about central-African nature. As naturalists, they created vignettes that offered distant readers opportunities for vicarious observation of the most distinctive traits of the animals and plants they wished to highlight. Also as naturalists, they both

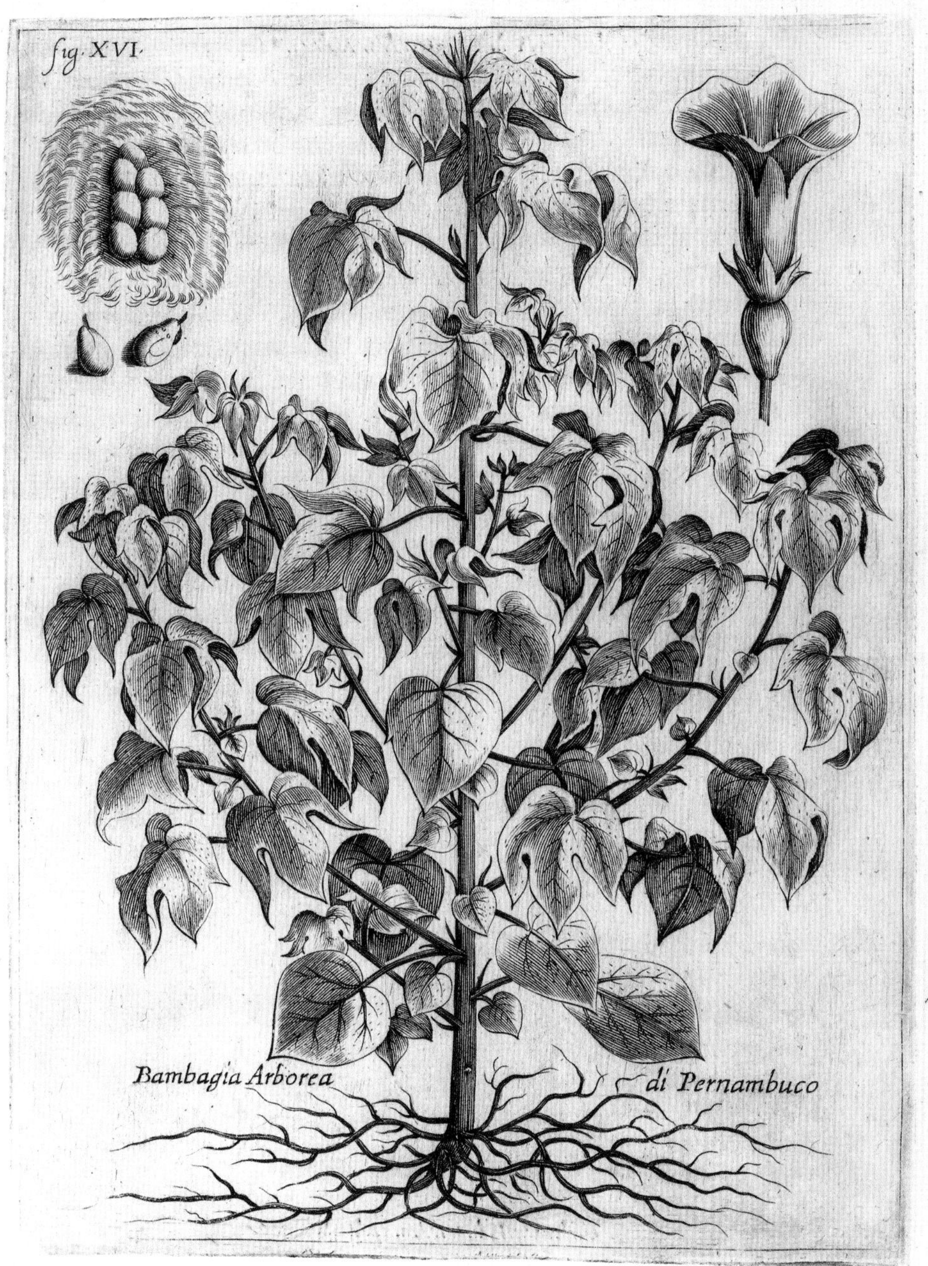

relied on and adapted the artistic conventions of naturalism to serve their epistemic goals. Illusionistic renderings of the color and shape of flora closely emulate factual observation, while manipulations of scale emphasize selected aspects. In trees, for instance, leaves and fruits, the parts essential for identification and useful for consumption, are proportionally much larger than trunks, allowing for easier scrutiny (plates 24, 26, 30). When necessary, different views of a specimen are included to convey information that would otherwise be invisible. Fruits are peeled or cut to show their flesh, animals presented in groups to demonstrate noteworthy behavior (plates 18, 19, 20, 22, 41, 42).

Some among the friars had direct connections with scientific circles and concerned themselves specifically with the production of natural-historical knowledge. Michelangelo Guattini, for instance, announced in letters to his father written from Brazil in 1667 that he was at work at collecting specimens of plants, animals, and curiosities.[9] Although the results of his efforts have not survived or are yet to be identified, some of his work, including image-making, found posterity. One of his drawings served as the basis for the cotton-plant print that appeared in the 1675 *Istoria botanica* of Giacomo Zanoni, a Bolognese botanist with whom Guattini corresponded (fig. 50). The friar had collected seeds from the plant and sent them to the learned man in 1668 while in transit through Brazil. The specimen, however, grew poorly and did not flower in Italy. The botanist relied instead on the friar's drawing for his publication.[10] It is unclear what Guattini's design might have been, but Zanoni's printed version gives an opportunity to take stock of the differences and similarities between Capuchin images of flora extant in the practical guides (including the Parma

Watercolors) and contemporaneous botanical plates. The Bolognese print shows a mature cotton plant spread over a blank page. It details the shapes and arrangement of the leaves, branches, and roots. The plant neither blooms nor bears fruit, but a flower and a cotton pod float in the top corners of the page. The flower rises vertically in the upper right corner, showing the articulation of stem, receptacle, and corolla. The pod, across the page at the top left, is open to show its seeds, two of which are also depicted detached, just below. Overall, the plant is wholly decontextualized, literally unrooted, and its component parts synthetically presented within an otherwise blank page. An aesthetic of balance, symmetry, and delicacy infuses the highly stylized plate.

In contrast, friars placed the flora they pictured in more or less summarily depicted natural or social environments. The Parma Watercolors include elements of landscape in the fore- and background to allow readers to place the species in their proper milieu. Aquatic, land, and aerial fauna appear against differentiated backgrounds rendered with either a blue wash or an earth-colored ground. Terrestrial animals stand in bushy savanna; amphibious ones, among riverine reeds. The backgrounds function as natural-historical classificatory templates but also make sense of the exotic environments by connecting habitats and species in explicit, distinct, and defined categories. This typology is as practical as it is scientific in that it conveys distinctions in the locations where missionaries might encounter given animals or plants.

Similarly, scenes of interaction between central Africans and animals or plants perform less as "Renaissance ethnography"[11] than as ways to link nature to a specific cultural environment the deciphering of which was incumbent upon the missionaries. A palm being tapped (plates 1, 28, 29), a lion being hunted (plate 35), a leopard roaming around a missionary's camp (fig. 19), and a crocodile attacking a group of enslaved men in chains (plate 6) weave together natural elements with a local human environment. Notably, two vignettes in the Parma Watercolors describe social behavior among animals (plates 41, 42). One of them shows primates harassing a leopard, and another pictures a group of monkeys collaborating to cross a river.[12] The explicit parallel drawn between the animal's *ronde* in plate 42 and the funerary ritual in plate 67 of the Parma Watercolors does not leave much to the imagination in terms of the Capuchins' uncertainties about the position of central Africans in relation to the still ill-defined category of humanity. A list of animals penned by Francesco da Pavia around 1700 explicitly rehearses the early modern trope connecting apes and Africans in a discussion of the "monos, . . . who look like wild men; . . . the Portuguese say that they are born from the union of . . . monkeys with black women."[13] A similar ambiguity underlies the representation of the reclining figure at the bottom of plate 1.

Curiosity Culture

At a broader level, the friars' compendia about central Africa participated in early modern Europe's culture of curiosity, the common thread linking scientific endeavors, travel literature, and religiously infused inquiries into the nature and shape of the world. Friars in later decades of the mission also drew inspiration from their predecessors and the images they had produced.[14] Friars such as Guattini and his colleague Serafino da Cortona, who both traveled to central Africa in the first decades of the mission, actively participated in the elite network of learned men and princes of the state or Church who sought and collected natural and man-made curiosities.[15] Guattini not only drew and collected plants but also gathered remarkable things, which he sent to his father with the explicit goal of outfitting "a room as a gallery" with all sorts of "strange things [*bizzarie*] from America and Africa."[16] What he had in mind was the production of a cabinet of curiosity, that is to say, a collection of natural or man-made objects displayed within a dedicated space. Assembling cabinets of curiosities was an elite endeavor in early modern Europe. The collections and displays of the world's natural and man-made wonders emerged and grew under the purview of a prominent political or scholarly figure for the purposes of study and pleasure, while often making political statements about the reach of its patron's influence or territorial possessions.

Guattini and his religious brother Serafino da Cortona also dispatched a range of items back to Italy as souvenirs and gifts. Guattini sent from Brazil, on his way to Angola, a chaplet made of coconut and a rosary to his mother along with other small items for his siblings.[17] Friar Serafino put in the luggage of Giovanni Francesco [da] Romano, who was on his way back from central Africa to Italy in 1654 with "an ivory cross" to send to his home convent of Cortona, "a horn of unicorn, which [he thought] real," for his superior, and a little flask made of a coconut with an ivory mouth for the nuns of the Monasterio de la SS. Trinità of his home town.[18] The very personal engagement with curios and collecting these records documented went hand in hand with an interest in wondrous

items and a keen knowledge of the Italian-elite collecting milieu. Guattini, for instance, was proud to work for Bolognese botanist Zanoni. Serafino da Cortona shared with Portuguese chronicler António de Cadornega the experience of having seen the head of a wild boar in Massangano, which he thought would garner a great price in Italy if sold to a prince who would love its "monstrosity and diversity."[19]

Friar Serafino may have had in mind figures such as Jesuit Athanasius Kircher, who gathered and organized a famed collection in Rome that may have inspired the Capuchins to begin collections in Brazil and central Africa. Guattini came from Reggio Emilia, north of Bologna, a town of illustrious scholars of natural history and collectors of curiosities. Sixteenth-century learned man Ulisse Aldrovandi, who came to be known as the father of natural history, gathered in the city a large specimen collection and founded the botanical garden where Zanoni worked. The botanist was himself the owner of a "museo di cose naturali."[20] In the next century, nobleman Ferdinando Cospi assembled the astonishing natural and man-made curiosities of the famed Museo Cospiano.[21] Both Aldrovandi and Cospi would bestow their collections on the city of Bologna.[22] These were the types of men Friar Serafino, who came from Tuscany, another center in early modern collecting, thought would be eager purchasers of the Angolan boar's head.

In fact, the collection and shipment of curiosities was a common practice among European clerics working in early modern central Africa. Historian Carlos Almeida has discussed a variety of examples in which Jesuits and Capuchins sent curious items such as snakeskins, rhinoceros horns or cups made of their ivory, zebra pelts, and a manatee's skull to their lay or religious patrons in Europe.[23] The Capuchins even had a collection in their Luanda house, holding items such as preserved skins of pelicans.[24] The curiosity of the friars about natural specimens was notorious, and intriguing items were brought to them for their inspection, such as the carcass of a prodigiously large crocodile.[25] Collecting on the mission also extended to man-made objects, which the friars occasionally dispatched or brought back with them to Italy. Andrea da Pavia returned to the Propaganda Fide with a trunk of "idols along with other varied superstitious instruments, brought with [him] from Africa"; Serafino da Cortona, as already noted, sent back a unicorn horn, an ivory cross, and a coconut shell with an ivory mouth.[26]

In spite of his great plans, it is doubtful that Guattini was able to gather a large collection or to produce a significant number of botanical illustrations besides the ones he created in Brazil on his way to Angola. He lived only a few months in central Africa, where he arrived in January 1668 and died shortly thereafter. Similarly, only one plate, the billfish discussed in chapter 2 above, remains of Serafino da Cortona's naturalist efforts. But their visions, ambitions, and the images they produced contributed to the visual economy of the Capuchin central-African mission's early years, alongside and in cross-pollination with the designs seen in the practical compendia of the Museo Francescano drawing or, later, the Parma Watercolors. Their interest in the collection of curiosities also gives a context from which to approach the inclusion of fantastical animals in the Capuchin vignettes.

Supernatural History

Against a simple background of short grass and bushes, similar to that for the other terrestrial specimens presented in the Parma Watercolors, a white horselike animal stands in profile, a single pointed horn attached to its forehead (fig. 51 / plate 36). "Unicorn," announces the gloss, "here called Bada. It abounds in this land and particularly in the Kingdom of Benguela; it runs fast and charges with the horn lowered as a lance; the said horn has miraculous virtue as antidote." The visual and written representations entangle several streams of information. On the one hand, they evoke the lore of the unicorn, a fascinating creature described in the Bible—so, in the friars' view, undoubtedly

Figure 51

Unknown Capuchin artist, "*Alicorno* [unicorn] here called *Bada*," late seventeenth century. Watercolor on paper, 34 × 24 cm. Parma Watercolors, Virgili Collection, fol. 56. Photo: author.

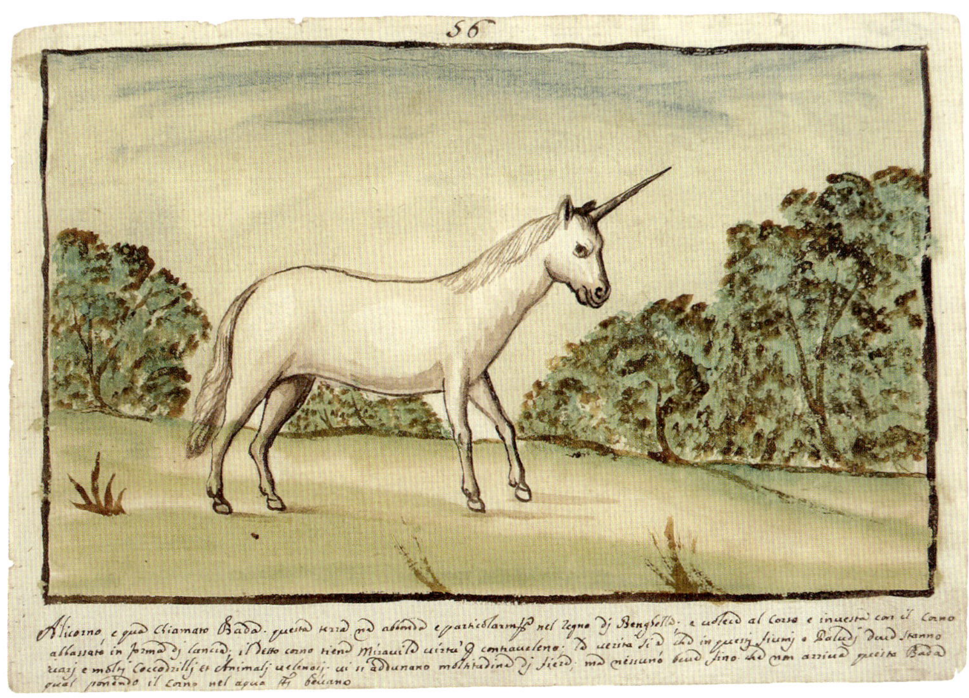

real—but yet to be clearly identified in the seventeenth century by travelers or scientists. In the 1600s few doubted the existence of the creature even if debate raged about the medicinal properties attributed to its horn.[27] On the other hand, the author uses the Portuguese word *bada* to label the animal. Abada, or Bada, was the name of the female rhinoceros famously brought to the court of Philip II of Spain via Portugal in the late sixteenth century.[28] In Portugal and its overseas possessions, the term referred to rhinoceroses at large.[29] The conflation of unicorns and rhinoceroses was hardly unusual; it had been made multiple times since 1515, when the first rhinoceros reached Rome after antiquity.[30]

At yet another level, the vignette and gloss encompass local knowledge, closely articulated with information derived from classical sources. The list of central-African animals Francesco da Pavia, another Capuchin, wrote around 1700 shows similar entanglements.[31] The missionary includes one entry for *bada* and another entry for "rhinoceros."[32] The *bada*, he explains, in a description echoing in part Pliny and Ctesias, the classical sources for unicorns, and in part what he had heard locally, was an animal similar to an antelope, but larger and with one horn on the forehead, thick at the base and two to three palms long. If the *bada* was still a virgin, he notes, the "horn [had] the same virtue as that of the unicorn."[33] There are rhinoceroses, he notes in his next entry, but few. What emerges from his description is an attempt at reconciling information about the *bada*, bringing together knowledge from the ancients with testimonies from Angola. It captures the currency the friars gave to local authority and the categorical fluidity that characterized their understanding of flora and fauna.

What Francesco da Pavia attempts to distinguish, the Parma Watercolors vignette synthesizes. In the painting and its text, the three strands of knowledge blur into the description of the "unicorn," or "Bada." It is an animal as large as a horse with a large, single horn on its head, which animals and humans alike use for protection against poison or predators.[34] The description of the rhinoceros as a horse with a horn calls to mind the parallel name *cavallo marino*, included in the Capuchin central-African context in the Museo Francescano drawing to label a large animal head, perhaps of a hippopotamus (plate 1). Composite depictions of animals were no rarities in early modern visual culture.[35] Analogy and metonymy allowed European authors and artists to describe exotica in natural-history treatises, allegories, and fantastical representations alike. In fact, historian of early modern science Dániel Margócsy has argued, in a discussion of representations of whales circa 1600, that "metonymic composition trumped firsthand observation."[36] Analogical thinking was not only a representational strategy but conditioned observation and comprehension.[37]

The presence in central Africa of many types of antelopes and other horned quadrupeds added to the complexities around the identification of the *bada* and the definition of its appearance. A plate in the edition of Friar Girolamo Merolla da Sorrento's writings about Kongo and Angola published in Naples in 1692 brings together a range of such animals (fig. 52). From the top, the "Impallancha" (Kikongo, *mpalanca*; Portuguese, *palanca*: antelope) has two spiraling horns attached to the top of its head, somewhat like André Thevet's South American Pyrassoupi.[38] The "Impanguazza" (Kikongo, *mpakassa*: buffalo) has one horn growing from its forehead and another from the side. The "Alce [elk] or Ncocco" (Kikongo, *nkoko*: gray antelope) sits on the ground, raising its hind hoof to its head to heal itself. In the accompanying text, Merolla assumes readers will know about the *ncocco*'s ability to perform that wondrous trick.[39] He also writes with the same confidence of the well-known qualities of the "*lioncorni*, which they call *Abada*, the virtues of which I do not mention, since everyone knows about them."[40] The "Abada," in the bottom left quarter of the page, has only one horn, albeit ambiguously placed on the side of its head.

The infelicities of these depictions show the hesitations of the printmaker regarding the placement, number, and shape of the horns. It is clear that the painter of the Parma Watercolors, like the maker of Merolla's print, set off to depict a unicorn he had not himself observed closely or at all. Nevertheless, through analogy, references to motifs previously circulated in Europe, and creativity, both created images that adequately reflected the Capuchins' mode of reckoning with nature and put to work their belief in the didactic role of images. Combining observations from life, previously held convictions about what they firmly believed should exist, and an imaginative stroke, the illustrations of unicorns echo those of another category of wondrous beast, the *peixe-mulher*, or *pesce-donna*, that is, woman-fish. While the unicorn kept its fantastical aura through the centuries but lost its claim at reality, the fabled *peixe-mulher* acquired a firm identity and became stably associated with the zoological species of the manatee (*Trichechus senegalensis*) at the price of shedding its most wondrous traits (figs. 53–57, plates 11, 12). In two vignettes of the Parma Watercolors, also present in the *Istorica descrizione* and in Merolla's *Breve, e succinta relatione*,

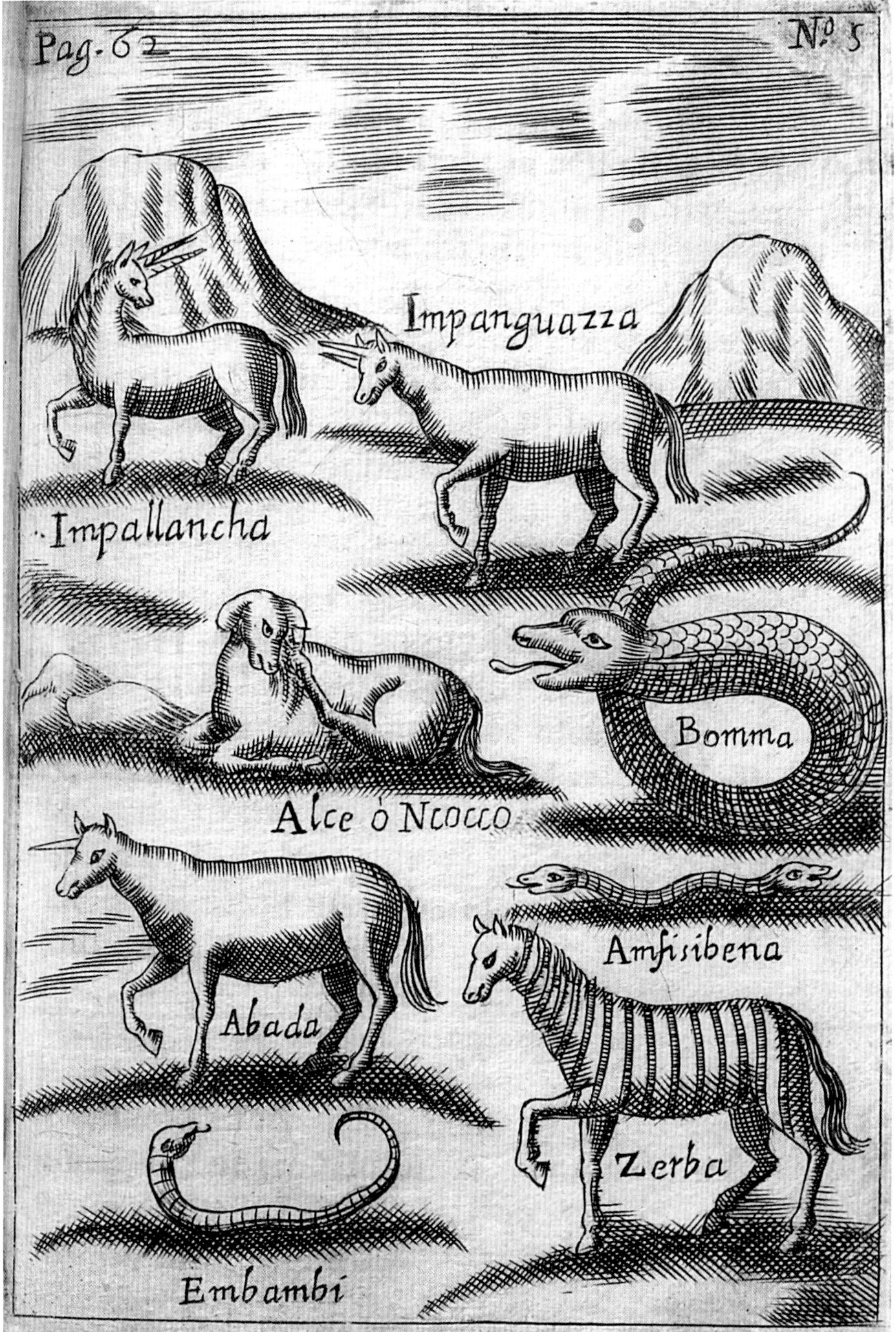

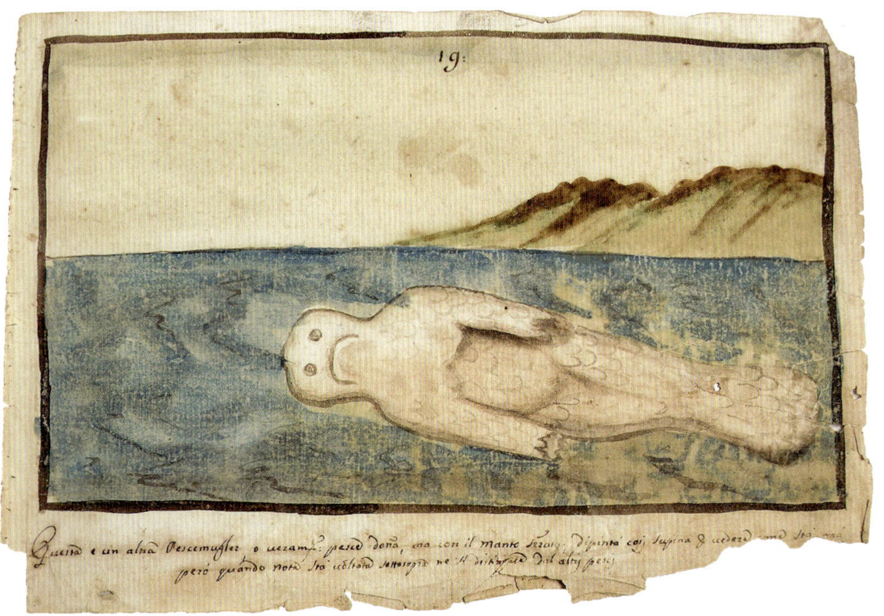

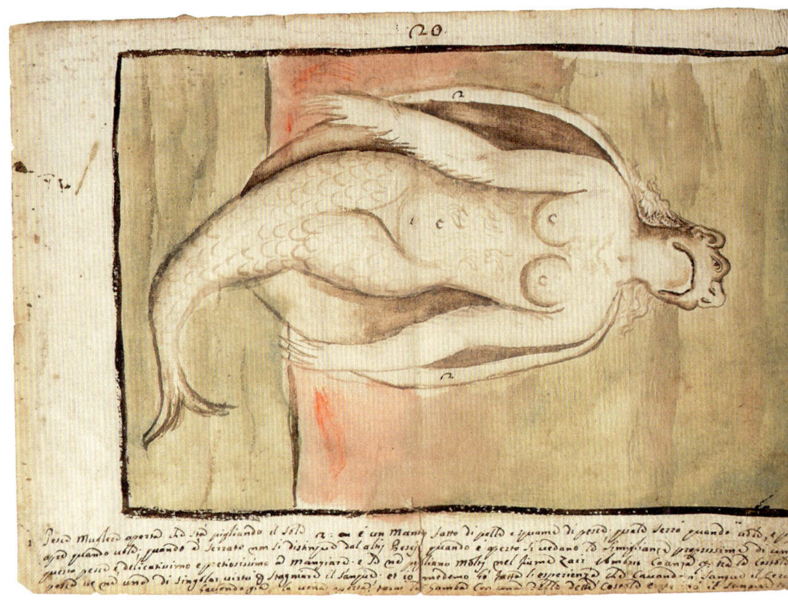

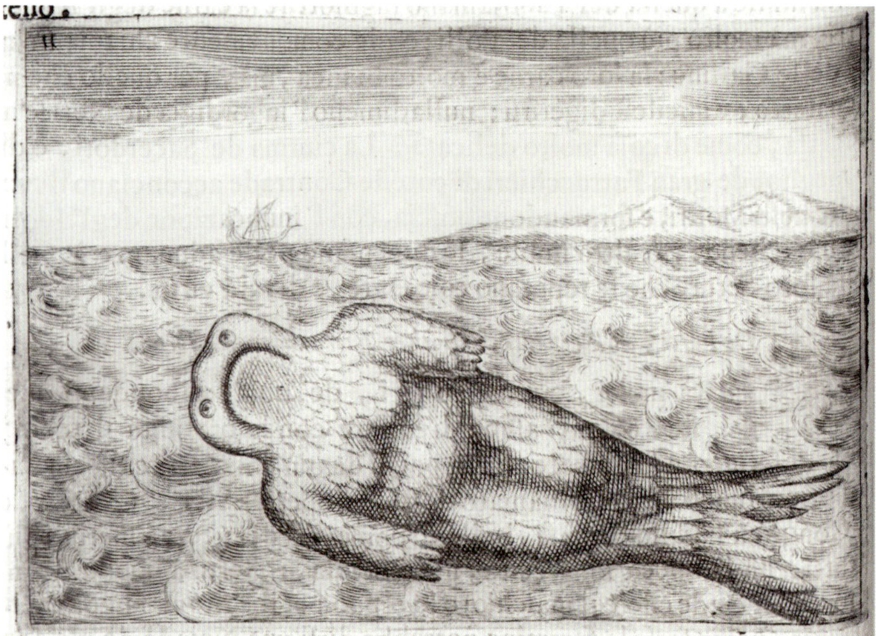

Figure 53 (above left)

Unknown Capuchin artist. "Another *Pescemugler* [manatee]," late seventeenth century. Watercolor on paper, 34 × 24 cm. Parma Watercolors, Virgili Collection, fol. 19. Photo: author.

Figure 54 (above right)

Unknown Capuchin artist, "*Pesce Muglere* [manatee] . . . sunbathing," late seventeenth century. Watercolor on paper, 34 × 24 cm. Parma Watercolors, Virgili Collection, fol. 20. Photo: author.

Figure 55 (left)

Paolo da Lorena (attr.), "Pesce Donna [manatee]." Engraving, 10 × 14 cm (plate mark). Plate 11 from Giovanni Antonio Cavazzi and Fortunato Alamandini, *Istorica descrizione de' tre' regni Congo, Matamba, et Angola* (Bologna: Giacomo Monti, 1687), 52. National Library of Portugal, Lisbon, H.G. 9174 A. Photo courtesy of the National Library of Portugal.

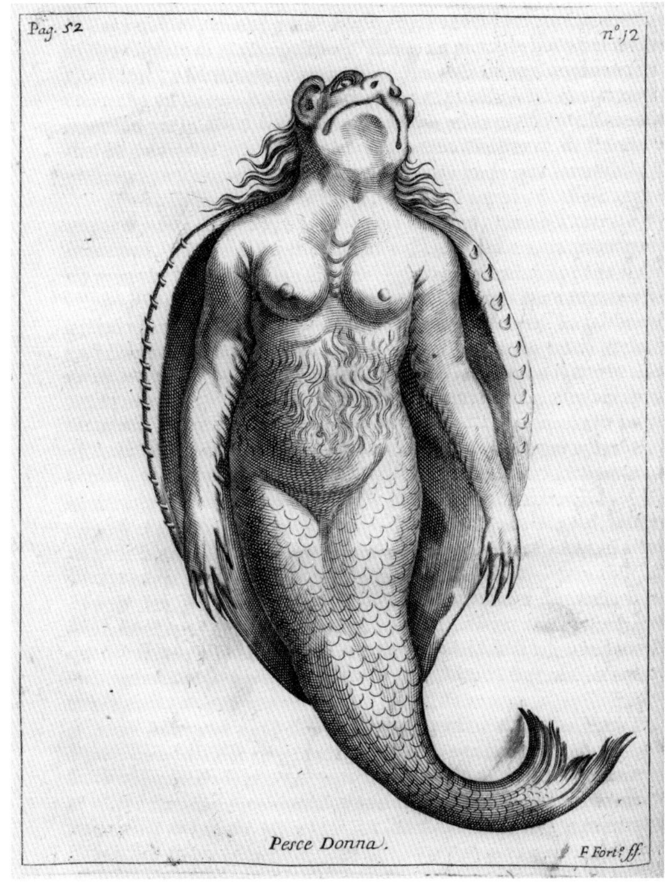

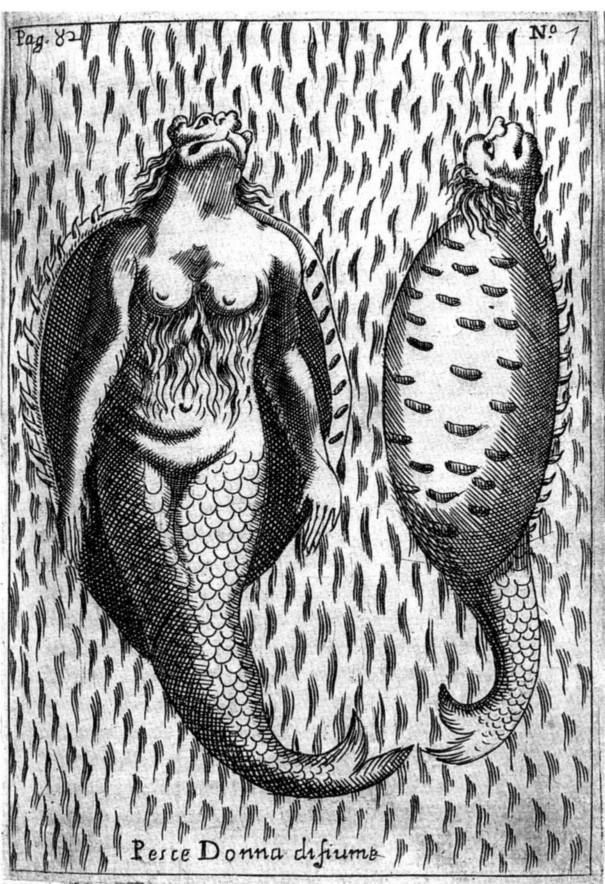

Figure 56

Fortunato Alamandini, *Pesce Donna [manatee]*. Engraving, 19.5 × 14 cm (plate mark). Plate 12 from Giovanni Antonio Cavazzi and Fortunato Alamandini, *Istorica descrizione de' tre' regni Congo, Matamba, et Angola* (Bologna: Giacomo Monti, 1687), facing p. 52. National Library of Portugal, Lisbon, H.G. 9174 A. Photo courtesy of the National Library of Portugal.

Figure 57

Unknown artist, "River Pesce Donna [manatee]." Copper-plate engraving, 15 × 10 cm (plate mark). Plate 7 from Girolamo Merolla da Sorrento and Angelo Piccardo, *Breve, e succinta relatione del viaggio nel Regno di Congo* (Napoli: Francesco Mollo, 1692), facing p. 82. Biblioteca Nazionale Centrale di Roma, 6.25.H.8. Photo courtesy of the Biblioteca Nazionale Centrale di Roma.

the *peixe-mulher* appears on its back, revealing the humanlike breasts and face from which it derived its name. Long arms ambiguously emerge from a cloak-like back, in an attempt to reconcile the rotund silhouette of the animal and the human-like limbs it was reputed to have. It also features a scaly tail that belonged to the imaginary anatomy of mermaids rather than to the smooth skin of the mammalian manatee. Hairy patches on the chest, neck, and back and a grotesque, grimacing face accentuate both its humanlikeness and its monstrosity. Hairy and scaly, beguiling and repulsive, fantastical

yet witnessed in the flesh, the *peixe-mulher* is an ambiguous beast, pictured in an equally ambiguous visual project in which direct observation, arguments of authority from a range of sources, and affective responses of awed men in an exceedingly new environment mix and merge into an idiosyncratic corpus. The fluidity between real and ideal, evidence of the eye and views of the mind, is a red thread throughout the central-African Capuchin corpus, where images are at once descriptive of local environment and prescriptive of missionary approaches to and practices in central Africa. The

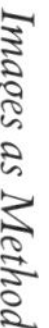

newcomers to the mission would soon discover that the peaceful, ordered apostolate the friars described in their practical guides, led by robust, respected missionaries among ruly and demure crowds, proved as elusive as unicorns. Apostolic work in central Africa revealed itself instead to be as different from the missionaries' expectations as manatees were from mermaids.

Images in the Mission

In the face of the many challenges the central-African mission met, Capuchins placed their trust in images. They not only counted on them to vividly bring central-African natural and social environment to European eyes and prepare novices for the challenges ahead. They also relied on them in their apostolic work in Kongo and Angola. In the

"Missione in prattica," Friar Bernardino d'Asti outlines the role that visual tools played in his missionary practice as he describes to future missionaries the proper use of portable altars: "In these places where there will not be a church, the portable altar of Mass can be left exposed all day to public view, to induce [*concigliar*] devotion in the people, as these altars are made with a good [*decente*] baldachin and with *riglievo* of proper perspective [*decorosa prospettiva*], all of which can be folded and unfolded with great ease."[41] Portable altars are a central feature in the vignettes describing apostolic work, where they appear alongside the friars and the local *mestres* who worked with them. The liturgical furniture appears in the images either open during ministry and for sacramental use (figs. 58, 63, plates 62, 63, 70, 71 top, 72 bottom) or neatly folded into easily transported rectangular boxes (figs. 19, 77, 92, 96, plates 59, 61, 72 top). In addition to containing the altar stone, indispensable to the liturgy of Mass, altars-in-a-box came with a range of ornaments and paraphernalia. Crucifixes, candlesticks, draperies, chalices, patens, purifier cloths, and missal provided a rich background and visually dramatic setting for the equally richly attired priests who officiated, dressed in many colorful and textured liturgical vestments. Upon reaching a destination, both friars and altars, the former in plain dress, the latter in plain boxes, would transform into bright, rich, and multisensory baroque displays for liturgical occasions. The clerics would put on their albs and chasubles trimmed with lace and colorfully embroidered.[42] The altars would unfold and present their interiors covered with decorative textiles and glittering liturgical implements: candleholders, chalices, incense burners, and so forth. In the Vatican "Missione in prattica," a friar administers Communion "in the open air"

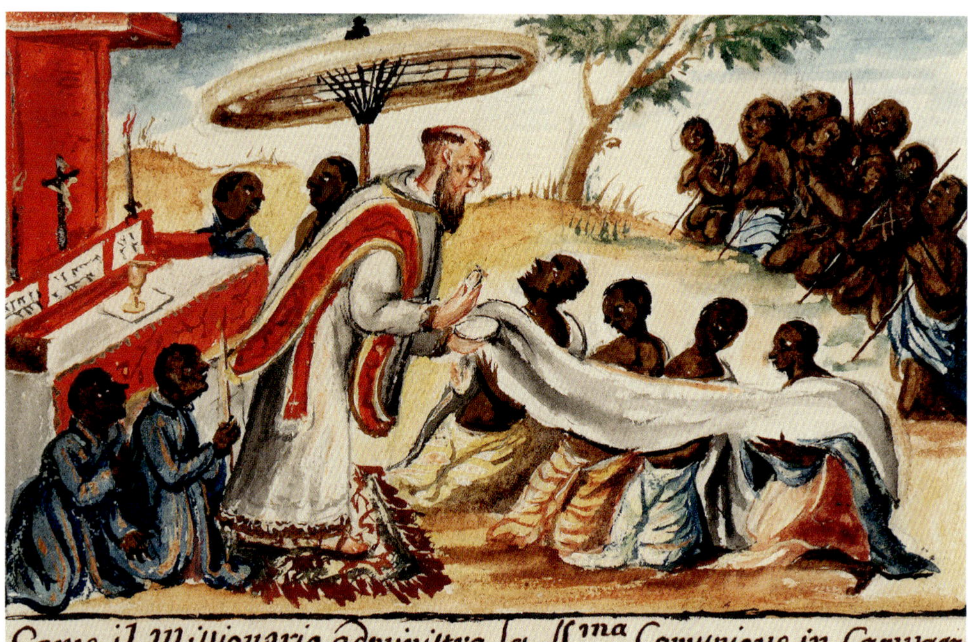

in a dazzling spectacle (fig. 58). His bright-red altar is richly outfitted with a crucifix, lit candles, a golden chalice and paten, and displays a stylized alphabetic inscription in black letters on a white background, as on an altar card. For further pomp, a colorful carpet extends on the ground in front of the altar, under the feet of the priest. The imported ground covering was a prized item among the central-African elite and spoke volumes in local terms, as did the umbrella over the friar's head, about the prestige of the cleric and solemnity of the occasion.[43]

As a central feature in the ritual drama of the liturgy and its preparation, but also through its mere presence in landscapes without churches and other visual or material markers of Christianity, the altar functioned as a key ministry tool to "induce devotion." Its furnishings dazzled viewers not only because of their visual and material richness but also thanks to the images they contained. Bernardino uses ambiguous terms in his description; "relief" (*riglievo*) and "perspective" (*prospettiva*) may refer to the spectacle of the altar as a whole or to specific parts of its visual program. In either case, they refer at least in part to the paintings, sculptures, bas-reliefs, or prints installed in the portable apparatuses that served as substitutes for churches. The visual outfit of portable altars emulated in this regard that of central-African built Catholic temples, as suggested in figure 60, where a European-style painting of the Virgin and Child pinned on the façade serves as a synecdoche for the paintings and sculptures the building held[44] (see also fig. 61). The bottom part of each portable altar depicted in the "Missione in prattica" and the Parma Watercolors has a rectangular area that may have held one of these "*riglievi*."

The visual experience Bernardino describes encompasses a temporal dimension, as he specifies that the altar should be left on view all day. The idea that images work over time is a cornerstone of Franciscan devotional practice. Friars on the other side of the Atlantic, in Mexico, also under the purview of the Propaganda Fide, reflected on the time-based effect of devotional images. An anecdote recorded in the mid-eighteenth century but concerned with an episode from 1632 retells how an image of the Virgin set up on the site of a local non-Christian cult literally caught the eye of lapsed Mesoamericans, seeped into their hearts, and eventually brought them back to the Christian faith. "They began to dedicate long periods of time gazing in amazement and spellbound at that Portrait of the Queen of Heaven and Earth," explains the friar reporting on the events.[45] The statue brought light to their souls, dissipating their errors. "Love for Mary," he concludes, "entered them through the eyes, seeing and admiring so much beauty and majesty in that wonderful image, and it wouldn't be the first time that the eyes would be the weapons that brought hearts to surrender."[46]

In Mexico, as in central Africa, the friars let devotional images work over time to change hearts and souls. The Mesoamerican example is of particular interest as a point of comparison to the central-African case because in both contexts, and unlike earlier moments in the catechization of Mexico, Kongo, or Angola, the Minorite use of the image is not linked to attempts at bridging linguistic gaps. In seventeenth-century central Africa, as in Mexico, communication between European friars and local populations adequately, if not always fluently, flowed thanks to the linguistic competence of the clerics and of the local populations. Images in both geographies did not function as replacements for words but operated independently, in a realm of their own.

The Capuchins thought about images in a broad sense and used a full spectrum of visual tools. They brought with them devotional objects. They staged Christian artworks and allegorical tableaux in theatrical displays.[47] They constructed permanent as well as ephemeral liturgical structures.[48] They used ekphrasis in preaching. Girolamo Merolla da Sorrento, active in central Africa in the 1680s, described his striking deployment of a cult image in a sermon:

The day of the Purification of Mary, always Virgin, I decided to deliver a sermon about that issue [of menstruation rituals]; and the better to move the people, I had put on the altar earlier a covered Image in relief [*di rilievo*] with a dagger in the chest, looking as if she bled from the wound. I started to talk against these young women who observed the diabolical abuse, proving that they did not only notably offend our very loving Savior but also cause no little injury to his Immaculate Mother. To better stress the point, I uncovered the Image, which the people saw all wounded and bloody, and were so moved that they began to weep.[49]

Merolla deployed in this instance a full range of visual strategies. He outfitted a statue, most likely imported, with extra props, a dagger, and fresh blood. Before the unveiling of the image, he talked about the grief Christ and the Virgin felt because of sinners. Words progressively moved from an abstract description of the moral effects of trespassing to a concrete connection between sins and physical injury suffered by Saint Mary. Finally, the mental image he created with his suggestive words took on vivid material and visual form in the statue he dramatically revealed.

A predecessor of Merolla, Friar Juan de Santiago, also explained how he counted on theatrical ministry, rather than rhetorical effects of speech, to convey the substance of doctrine when he did not yet speak the local language. "Not being able to speak in their language was of great detriment to us; however, with exterior actions, with tears and other demonstrations that Our Lord inspired in us, each one [of the missionaries] tried to convey as he could the power of the divine Word and of the doctrine, which he preached without being understood, for in the mouths of the interpreters, [the words] lost most of their substance and form." Without relying on linguistic communication or the intermediation of go-betweens, the missionaries still efficiently preached, calling, successfully, upon visual tools. As the friar further reported, "Oftentimes we experienced that the listeners were moved before the interpreter would explain to them the words in their Mosicongo language, and it happened to me once in Pinda that bringing out a pious crucifix with very simple words, I moved in a small audience more than twelve nobles." Images and visual staging, Fray Juan suggested, changed hearts and touched souls as much as or more than spoken or written words. "So we can encourage," he concluded, "those who abandon this enterprise for fear of the difficulty of the language and think that it is like preaching to the wind without hopes of any fruits."[50]

The friars did not travel to central Africa lightly. They carried with them the visual and material paraphernalia necessary for preaching and for the establishment of churches and convents where the local political and financial situation permitted. They brought to Kongo and Angola artworks and devotional objects large and small, modest and sophisticated, from elaborate paintings, sculptures, and liturgical furniture to ordinary medals, rosaries, and crucifixes. The members of the first Capuchin mission to arrive in the Kongo, in 1645, for instance, had received as a gift from a countess in Lisbon a "very beautiful painting, quite large, of the Immaculate Conception" that she had commissioned in 1641 for them to bring to the Kongo. Upon arriving in central Africa, the painting, along with a second one, of Felix da Cantalice, the first Capuchin *beato*, fell hostage to a Dutch Protestant "director" and his female consort in the coastal city of Soyo, who "displayed them both in the living room of their house, not for devotion, but purely as adornment because they were the worst sort of heretics."[51] Almost miraculously, thanks to a change of heart by the woman, the director not only returned the images to the friars but also offered them in addition two other paintings, one of Saint Francis and another of Saint Felix. The adventuresome Immaculate Conception would eventually reach its destination: the altarpiece of the Capuchin church in São Salvador, the capital of the Kongo.[52]

A few decades later, Friar Luca da Caltanisetta traveled from his native Sicily with other striking works of art. He brought a "standard of Our Lady carrying the Child in her arms" that he used in procession while entering Kongo cities for the first time. He also carried with him a life-size crucifix in papier-mâché "all bloody and exciting compassion" as well as the head and hands of a Virgin, also in papier-mâché, ready to be attached to a structure

covered with clothing to form a three-dimensional figure, a practice common in baroque-era devotional statuary.[53] In the Kongo, the Virgin wore local cloth.[54]

Capuchins did not hesitate to make use of local materials to beautify churches and altars. On the occasion of the Corpus Christi festival, Friars José de Antequera and Angel de Valencia "prepared the altar in the Church of Saint Anthony of Padua, using, instead of tapestries, branches and palms that they ordered people to bring to decorate the church as well as the streets."[55] The friars then oversaw a "solemn procession." The local ruler and aristocrats, in festive dress, carried candles at the head of the pageant. Behind them, around the Cross, the people of the town processed with flags and weapons, playing musical instruments and dancing. The two priests followed, holding the paten and the incensory. The Capuchins regularly organized these sorts of processions, which in public spaces put into ritual use imported and locally made devotional objects. The friars' written and visual descriptions suggest that the impetus for such displays and pageants came from them. They were, however, drawing largely from a well-established local Christian visual culture.

In addition to liturgical outfitting and larger artworks, the friars brought to central Africa and then widely distributed a range of devotional paraphernalia, medals, rosaries, and small crosses. Bernardino d'Asti's instructions advised newcomers to the mission to come from their province "provisioned with devotions, i.e., medals, chaplets, painted images even if very ordinary, etc."[56] Archival records describe the dispatch of tens of thousands of such objects, some of which have surfaced

Figure 59

Unknown artist, medal of
the Immaculate Conception
and Blessed Sacrament
from tomb 12 in the
Kindoki cemetery, Kongo,
seventeenth century.
Copper alloy, 30 mm ×
47 mm (with loop), 7.1 g.
Object from KongoKing
project excavations led
by Bernard Clist. Photo
courtesy of IRPA, Brussels.

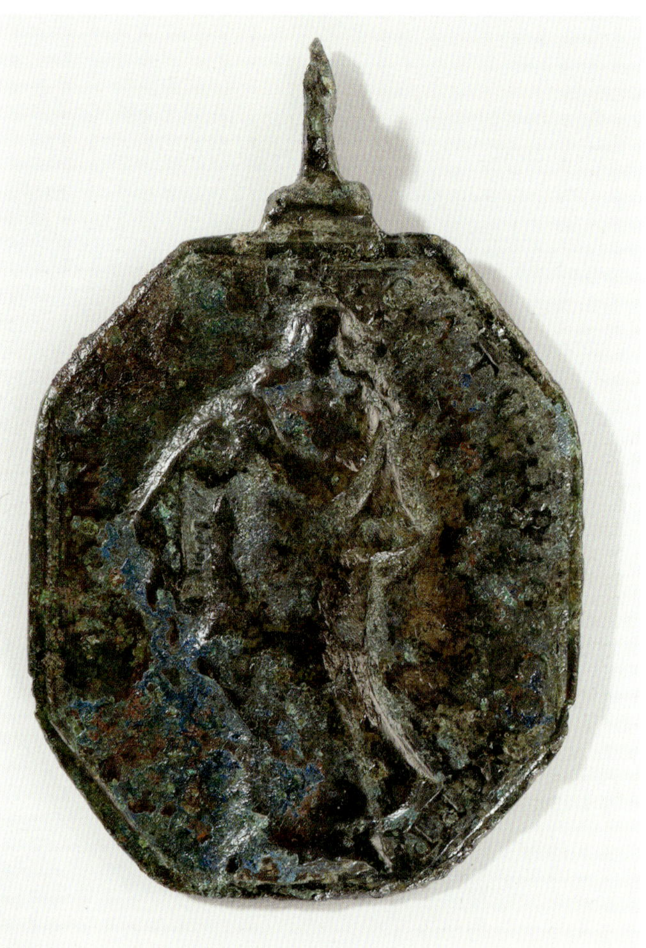
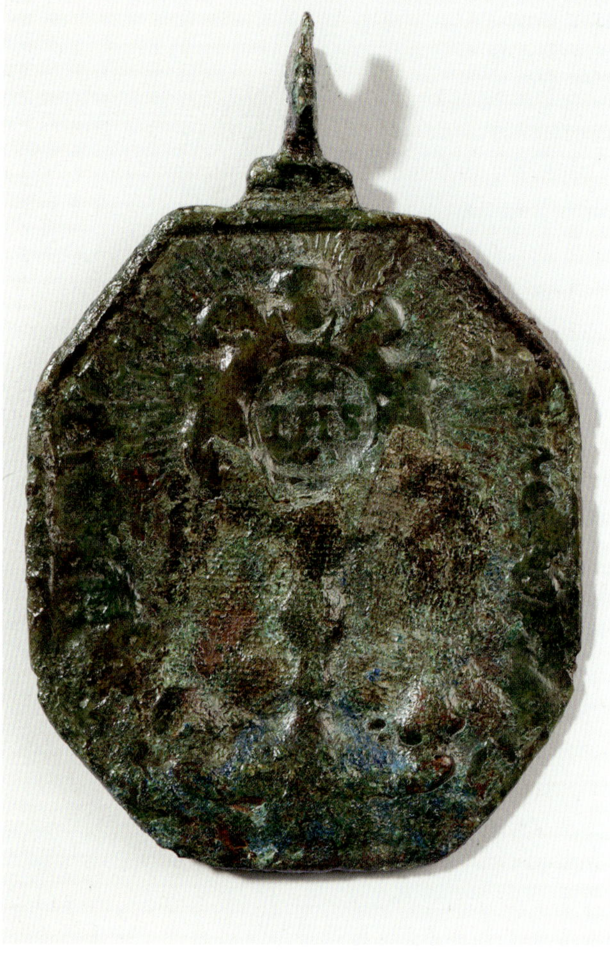

in archaeological settings in the twentieth and
twenty-first centuries.[57] For instance, the 2012–17
KongoKing project unearthed historical Catholic
paraphernalia in regions once under the purview of
the Kongo Kingdom, including many Italian medals from the plentiful Capuchin devotional cargo.[58]
The medal in figure 59, unearthed at Kindoki,
in the vicinity of the historical Mbanza Nsundi,
combines two of the friars' main devotions: the

Immaculate Conception and the Blessed Sacrament.
One side features a baroque Immaculata in swoop-
ing contrapposto and flowing drape. On the other
side, a radiating monstrance exalts the Blessed Sacrament. Recourse to images and devotional objects,
of course, was a central tenet of Capuchin ministry
well beyond Kongo and Angola.[59]

The Minorite central-African missions also produced artworks locally. Their personnel included

painters charged with the production of devotional images to outfit churches and portable altars, as well as to distribute to the local population. On January 20, 1650, in São Salvador, one of the missionary-painters, Félix de Villar, wearily composed a letter to Rome. "I have painted for every mission," he wrote, "and still there remain some paintings, and there isn't anything left to paint, because there is no more material." He continued his plea to the cardinals of the Propaganda Fide in charge of the Capuchin mission with which he had arrived in central Africa a little over two years earlier: "I have lost much of my sight, and also I suffer from a great stomach ache and kidney ache, and as a result of my ailments, I am not able to serve the Fathers in the missions. So I humbly beg that Your Most Illustrious Lordships, by the entrails of my Lord Jesus Christ, send me an order to return to my Province of Aragon." Two years would elapse before the tired missionary's wishes were granted, but he eventually returned home, where he recovered and lived for many more years. His letter stands out among the large corpus of correspondence the friars sent back to Europe, which generally extolled their suffering as a difficult but welcome part of their work. His letter nonetheless outlines how image-making was part of the Capuchin central-African missionary endeavors, with the aim to "outfit every mission."[60]

What is more, in addition to paintings and sculptures, the friars staged their own personas as a central element in their mission's visual environment. The "Missione in prattica" dedicates much space in demonstrating to its readers methods for the friars to insert themselves into existing Kongo Christian ceremonies and rituals so as to affirm their social and spiritual standing. One strategy consisted

in positioning themselves as embodiments of the Church. A vignette showing a political ceremony in the Kongo illustrates how friars created such a metonymic link between their bodies and the Church through visual and spatial continuity with sacred symbols and architecture (fig. 60). Seated on a stool with a cane in his left hand, a friar blesses with his right arm the local *mani*, or ruler, who kneels in front of him. Just behind them, a church building heralds high above the crowd a cross at the apex of its roof and a painting of the Virgin and Child on its façade. The baroque-style image shows a standing crowned Virgin similar to the one on the medal above. She carries a haloed child on her left arm and extends her right hand to the side in echo of the friar's gesture, likely to present a rosary to devout viewers (fig. 61).[61] Below the painting, a Kongo church master stands right behind the friar, buttressing the visual manifesto of Capuchin spiritual authority with his reaffirming presence as a high-status local religious leader.[62]

The central focus of the watercolor is the gesture of the ruler, who, in full regalia, kneels simultaneously at the feet of the Capuchin, the church, the monumental cross erected next to it, and the painting above them. In the image, the Church as institution to which the *mani* pays allegiance takes on cumulative and interchangeable forms. It is materialized in the building, the painting, and the crosses. It is also embodied by the friar. In other words, the watercolor outlines a visual strategy that stages the missionary as an icon in the Counter-Reform, Franciscan sense. Like the characters in the images they promoted, friars served as examples of devotion for their flock to follow, in the same manner as they themselves emulated Saint Francis. The Capuchins operated in central Africa institutionally, in

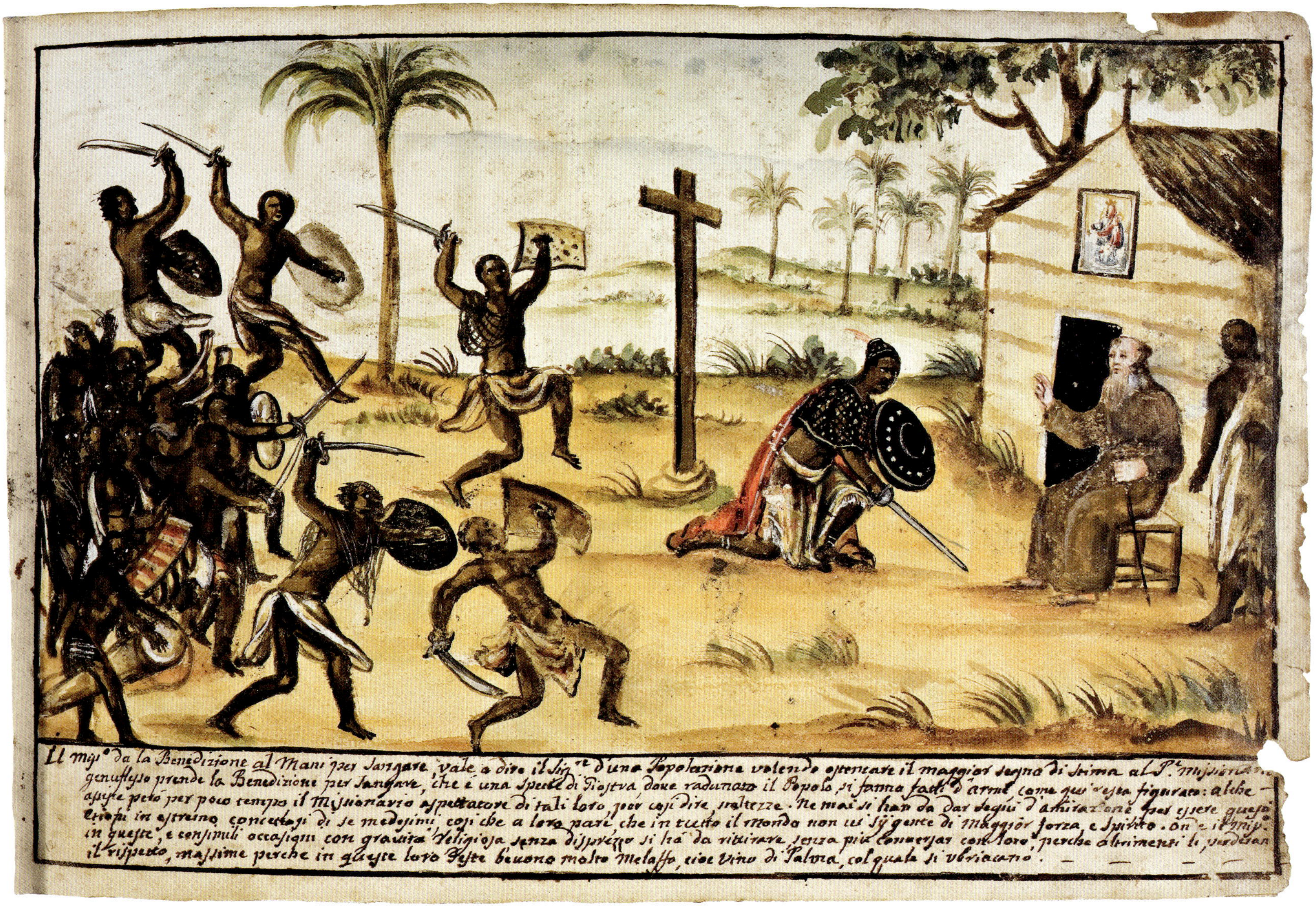

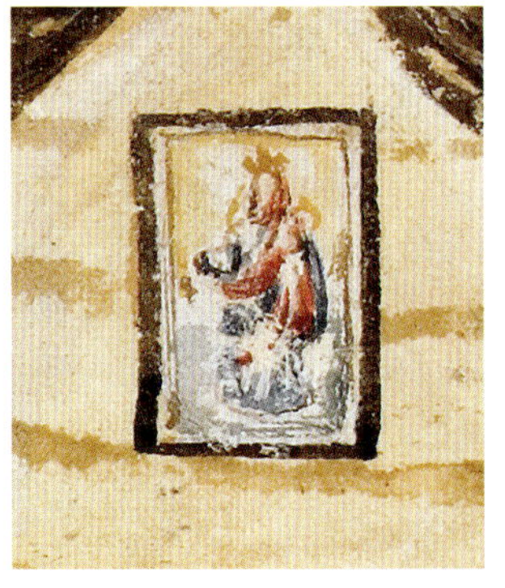

Il mis.o da la Benedizione al Mani per Jangare, vale a dire il Sig.re d'una Popolazione volendo ostentare il maggior segno di stima al P.e Missionario
genuflesso prende la Benedizione per Sangave, che è una spezie di Giostra dove radunato il Popolo si fanno fatti d'armi, come qui resta figurato: al che
assiste però per poco tempo il Missionario spettatore di tali loro per così dire scialtezze. Ne mai si han da dar segni d'ammirazione per essere questi
etiopi in estremo concettosi di se medesimi, cosi che a loro pare che in tutto il mondo non ci sij gente di maggior forza, e spirito. Onde il mis.o
in queste, e consimili occasioni con gravità religiosa senza dispprezzo si ha da ritirare senza più conversar con loro, perche altrimenti li perdesan
il rispetto, massime perche in queste loro feste beuono molto Melasso, cioe Vino di Palma, col quale si ubriacano.

their capacity as an ordained cadre of the Catholic Church available to dispense sacraments and spread the Good Word. They also acted in the region at the intersection of the visual and the spiritual in a sustained performance that made their personas sensible channels through which the faithful could connect to Christian divinity.

This mode of self-presentation proved eminently successful. Devotional figures in the form of garbed men are among the most paradigmatic objects of Kongo Christianity. Statues and pendants drawing from the Franciscan look circulated broadly in central Africa in the early modern period and continued to buttress the devotional practices of men and women of central-African origin or descent in the Americas (fig. 62).[63] Notably, the prophetic anti-Catholic Antonian movement that shook the region in the beginning of the eighteenth century had as a central tenet a Capuchin-inspired idea that closely echoed the notion of Franciscan *conformitas*. The leader of the sect, Beatriz Kimpa Vita, claimed to be Saint Anthony, one of the most important figures in Franciscanism. To embody the holy man, she emulated the ethos and ministry style of the Capuchins, from poverty and iconoclastic zeal against objects she deemed contrary to her dogma to the liturgical and administrative organization of her group. Her followers, in turn, were "little Anthonies," who emulated her and, through her, the saint.[64]

The watercolor in figure 60 summarizes key traits of the friars' pastoral methods, in which religious objects, images, and their own pious example directed central-African devotion toward the Christian God. The vignette illustrates belief in the ability of the visual to frame viewers' experiences of the sensible world and orient their spiritual practices. It functioned as a primer for missionary

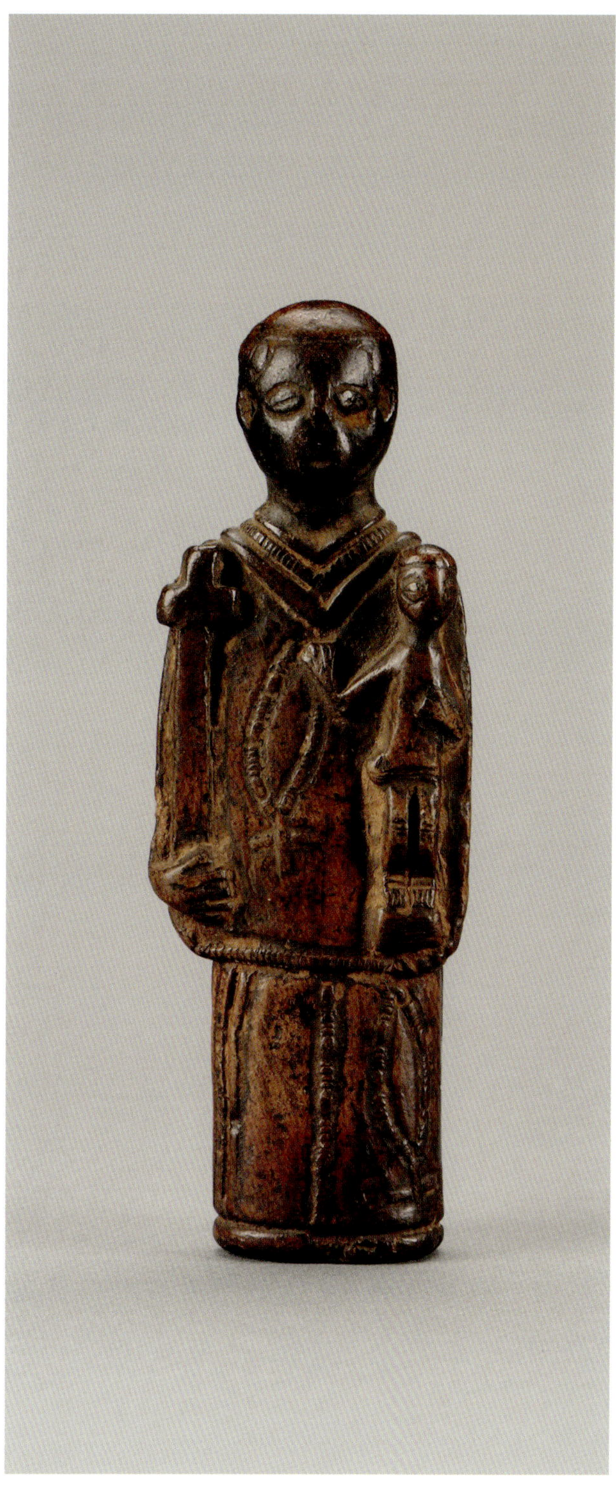

practice in two ways. First, it described for the benefit of novice missionaries the methods to use in the mission. Second, it offered the friars still in Europe an example to emulate and from which to draw pious inspiration.

Images on a Mission

Capuchin central-African images were on a mission to impress Tridentine orthodoxy onto central-African hearts and souls, but also to make a durable impact on the minds of future missionaries still in Europe. In one of the five vignettes describing missionary work still extant in the Parma Watercolors, a baptism scene unfolds in the outdoors in profuse and idiosyncratic detail for the benefit of its intended viewers (fig. 63 / plate 62). A few steps from an open portable altar set up under a tree, a Capuchin solemnly performs baptismal rites with the help of a *mestre* or local church leader. The tonsured, bearded friar has slipped over his brown habit a white alb decorated with small pompons at the hem and around the sleeves and collar. He has put around his neck a violet stole decorated with crosses

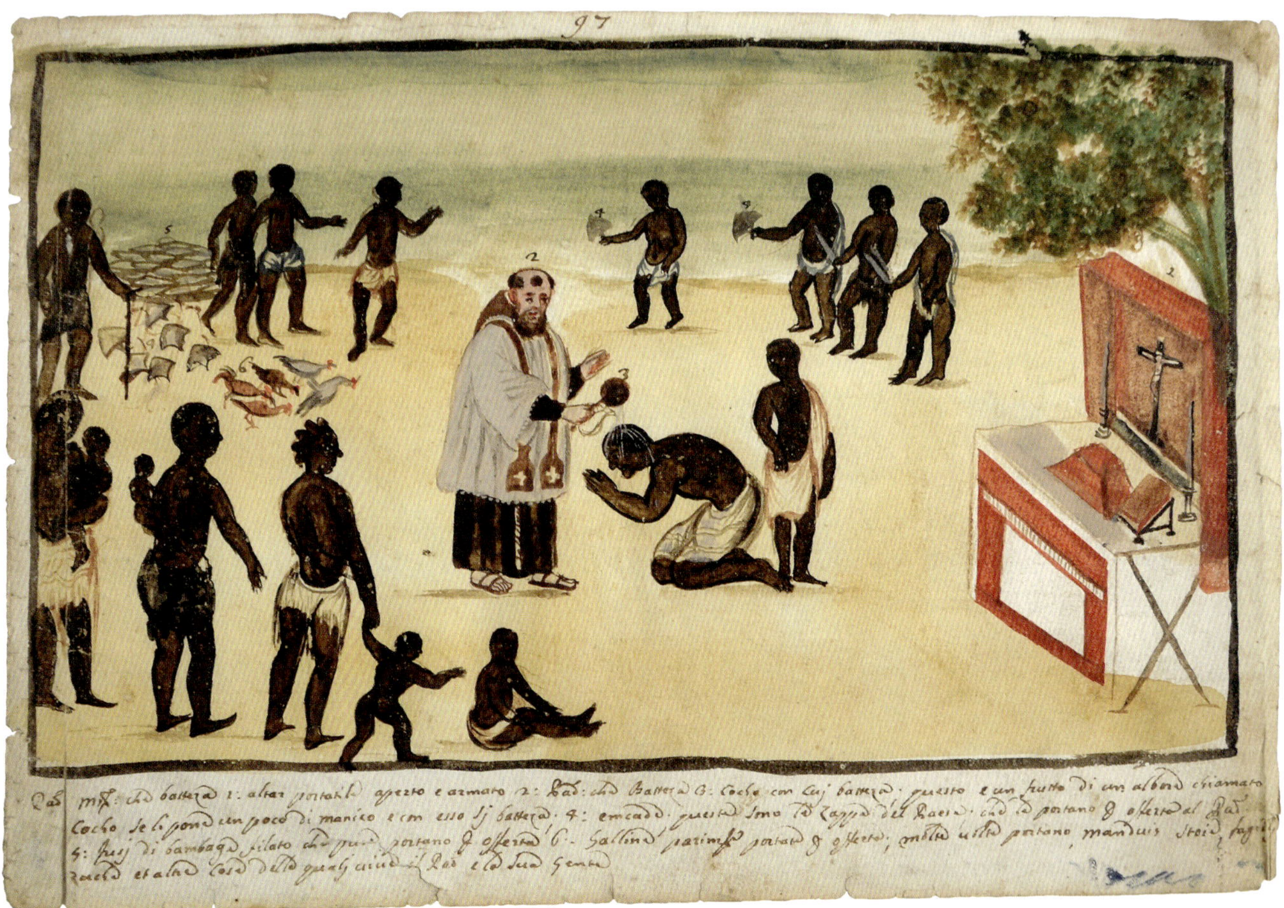

Figure 63

Unknown Capuchin artist, "Missionary Father who baptizes," late seventeenth century. Watercolor on paper, 34 × 24 cm. Parma Watercolors, Virgili Collection, fol. 97. Photo: author.

at its ends.[65] His lips are moving as he speaks the ritual formulae and pours holy water on the head of the baptizand kneeling in front of him. Hands joined and head bent, the man about to receive the purifying rite smiles softly and piously. He flinches slightly as the water touches his skin. Standing right behind him is a youth dressed in a light-colored cloth draped over his left shoulder, an attribute that suggests his role as a *mestre*, a member of the Kongo elite in charge of the transmission of Christian practices and rituals who also often served as an interpreter for the friars.[66] He looks back toward the priest and the group of adults and children observing the scene from the lower left corner of the page. The cleric, in turn, glances at the *mestre*, inviting him to translate his words for those gathered.

In the background more people approach from the right carrying semicircular or straight metallic items. A number of fan-shaped blades are gathered on the ground at the top left, next to oblong shapes that the text identifies as cotton spools but that are more likely metal ingots of a type known as *ngele*.[67] Five fowls complete the offering. The fan-shaped blades, glossed in the text as "emcade," as well as the ingots, are types of central-African iron or copper metalwork that served as currency.[68] The two types of metal objects have a long, deeply significant history in the region.[69] Plate 54 shows one mounted on a handle as an axe in the hand of an armed man. Figure 70 pictures an example in a funerary context dated 800–1000 CE.

The portable altar occupies the right side of the image. It is open in the shade of a large tree against the midday sun casting short shadows at the feet of those gathered. The main table, on folding legs, holds two long candles on sconces and a missal on a stand next to a red veil hiding a chalice and

paten. At the very back of the table a tall crucifix of dark wood holding a light-colored Christ stands in front of a dossal curtain, under a canopy that extends to both sides of the altar before folding and dropping, hanging past the table. The depiction of the front and side of the altar is unfinished but suggests a frontal made of heavy crimson drapes framing a central rectangular area, likely meant to display a painting but here left blank in the incomplete image.

The altar in fact is not only unfinished but also awkward in its realization and at odds with the rest of the image. The painter has depicted the apparatus with inconsistent perspective. A parallelogram convincingly renders the spatial projection of its rectangular table only to clash with the antependium, whose irregular sides do not follow the same recession. Is the unresolved perspectival projection a clever way for the painter to give his image a modest, unsophisticated appearance befitting the Franciscan spirit? Does it derive from an attempt to present the viewer with a clear sight of the altar's main components? Whatever the case, this area of the painting breaks the spell of immersive realism that the rest of the vignette casts, otherwise drawing viewers to take in the scene as if standing at a short distance, on elevated ground, in a privileged position allowing scrutiny and inviting absorption.

The approachable, engaging realism present in most of the image is central to its modus operandi as a didactic tool offering a descriptively rich document from which viewers may learn about central Africa. Many visible signs of revisions point to the careful construction of the detail-dense scene. The overlap of tree and altar to the right, the transformation of straight blades into semicircular ones in the hands of the men at the top right, the outline of several figures underneath the painted offerings at the top left, and the lines of a pitcher beneath the coconut asperser in the friar's hand are all traces of the multilayered creation of the painting. Together, they point to an iterative editing effort or to a reflection about the composition conducted over time. Each of the changes introduces a new level of minutia, enriching the scene with more elements characteristic of apostolic work in the central-African environment.

This concern with details and descriptive density comes out further in the color of the priest's stole and the use of the locally crafted vessel. By the time of the water rite, the purple vestment used in the first part of baptismal ceremonies should have been replaced with a white one; the image thus ostensibly presents to its knowledgeable viewers an exception to this rule that, the image argues, missionary expediency made acceptable. The incongruity and liturgical significance of the purple stole would have been evident to the clerics who were the intended viewers of the painting. Similarly, the coconut liturgical tool came in a later phase of the image composition, adding information about the material conduct of the mission. An earlier sketch still clearly visible shows the outline of a European-style beaker in the hand of the friar. The image's commentator has labeled with the number 3 the newly added instrument—"3: coconut with which [the father] baptizes"—clarifying in his usual matter-of-fact tone that it is a fruit from the coconut tree to which a handle is added for sacramental use. It is possible that the author of the text amended the image as he commented upon its content.

With such additions the image-maker (or -makers) created scenes that successfully offered viewers a rich array of information on the mission field. He attempted to construct vignettes that invited a close, immersive consideration of their contents, relying on post-Renaissance conceptions of paintings as able substitutes for the natural world. Yet in the same composition the painter deployed the artifice of naturalized illusionism in tension with moments that challenged the beholder's acceptance of the visual stratagem. The absorption of viewers stumbled, for instance, on the unfinished and unresolved altar, or on the conspicuously guileless style of the vignette as a whole. These moments in the painting are reminders of the multiplicity of visual tools the Capuchins deployed in crafting their central-African visual project, among which naturalism was but one. In the natural-historical images, as in the catechization vignettes, it served a determined purpose, in conjunction with other visual tools and genres such as natural-historical synthesis, well-trodden tropes of European lore about fantastical beasts, and a seemingly naïve style fit for a simple mendicant friar.

Conclusion

The Capuchins had boundless confidence in the multivalent potential of images. They trusted them to convey information, articulate knowledge, encourage devotion, and provide vicarious experience of nature and culture in a distant land. Their visual thinking was fluid and sophisticated, drawing nimbly on an ad hoc selection of visualization techniques that allowed them to mix and merge disparate realms of thought, sources of information, and claims to truth into a corpus of images that was both coherent and capacious in its references, techniques, and styles.

In the vignettes concerned with missionary work and in those describing flora and fauna, the makers of the Capuchin central-African didactic manuscripts demonstrated a sophisticated approach to images paired with a belief in their power to shape minds and convert souls. In other parts of their practical guides, the friars tackled the challenge of identifying and representing the religious practices and instruments of one culture with the visual tools of another. When depicting objects and rituals linked to non-Christian central-African religious life, they reckoned with the culturally relative nature of seeing, representation, and the material manifestations of the numinous. This was an issue at the center of their work as extirpators of what they deemed idolatry, or worship directed to any other recipient but the Christian God. They hoped the pictorial means they devised to present central-African idols and idolatrous practices to European viewers would convey the objects' and practices' true, and sometimes indiscernible, nature.

The task proved difficult. The friars faced a conundrum: they relied on the visual solutions offered by mimetic realism, the prominent early modern European mode of representation, to picture objects that followed, in contrast, a wholly different logic. The connection between central-African religious objects and practices and the invisible forces with which they allowed men and women to interact followed a conceptual logic that stood in sharp contrast to the mechanics of Catholic cult images. In 1563, in response to the Protestant Reformation, the Council of Trent had reaffirmed the nature and role of images in the Roman Church. "Images of Christ, of the Virgin Mother of God, and of the other saints," its decree explains, represent the actual object of worship, that is, God, or

his intercessors, the saints. But, crucially, the visual creations merely referred the honor and veneration the devotee directed at them to the proper recipients, that is, the prototypes "whose similitude they bear."[1] In central Africa, as the friars came to understand, the link between invisible forces and the objects humans used to access and direct them was of a different nature. Though they did not offer a full account of central-African spirituality, the friars endeavored to decipher, to the extent useful to their apostolate, the lexical and visual vocabulary of ritual practices and instruments they encountered in Kongo and Angola. Their observations yielded a uniquely valuable documentation of the region's visual, material, and religious culture in the early modern period. This chapter outlines the Capuchins' observations of what they called

CHAPTER 5

Images Against Idolatry

idolatry, analyzes the methods they used to make sense of it across cultures, and reflects on the ways the documents and techniques they devised enrich our knowledge and understanding of central-African visual, material, and religious culture in the early modern period.

Defining Central-African Spiritual Objects

What were the material means and practices through which central Africans accessed and harnessed invisible forces in the seventeenth and eighteenth centuries? Some archaeological findings, a small number of extant objects dated from the period, oral history peripherally concerned with material culture, and ethnographies from later centuries offer a spectrum of fragmentary sources with which to decipher the form and function of central-African ritual tools and spiritually empowered objects in the early modern period. The comments and observations of European clerics active in the region complete this loose array of information, albeit with perspectives and understandings of local practices that are markedly skewed and bigoted. Nevertheless, when considered with a critical eye to their relatively easily identified biases, these sources offer precious insight into central-African religion in the seventeenth and eighteenth centuries.[2] The European testimonies archive the challenges the clerics faced in identifying, understanding, and countering elements of material and immaterial culture they deemed contrary to Catholic orthodoxy. In zealously attempting to make sense of the forms of rituals and the nature of the numinous among their apostolic flock, they sketch the contours of central-African spiritual and ritual practices.

The friars' reflections appeared in their writings as commentaries on the concepts of idol and idolatry. The dictionaries and multilingual catechisms they compiled with local scholars as part of their work in central Africa recorded and attempted to translate idioms that related to the two concepts. The circa 1650 "Vocabularium Latinum, Hispanicum et Congense," composed in the Capuchin orbit by a member of the Kongo elite, translates the Latin term *idolum* as *quiteque* (pl. *iteque*) in the Kikongo language.[3] By idol, the dictionary means a pagan god in both its insensible form and its material manifestations. The word appears, for instance, in the entry for *penates*, Roman antiquity's household *dij*, or gods, as *itequé anzo*, literally "*iteque* of the house."[4] *Quiteque* also appears in the definition for Mars, the Roman god of war.[5] Jesuits Francesco Pacconio, an Italian twenty-year veteran of central Africa, and Kongo-born António de Couto compiled in Angola around 1640–42 a bilingual catechism of Portuguese and Kimbundu, a language related to Kikongo, spoken by the Mbundu people living in northwest Angola. The term *iteque* for idols also appears in their volume.[6] Capuchin Bernardo Maria da Canicatti uses the same word in his 1804 dictionary of Kimbundu.[7]

Giovanni Antonio Cavazzi describes these "Itiqui" in the *Istorica descrizione*. While most people in central Africa believed in "Nzambiampungú," a single, all-powerful divinity, he explains, they also had faith in "many other gods, inferior, but still disserving veneration." "In fact," he continues, "to them also a cult is given; to this effect, they display a quantity of idols, for the most part made of wood, roughly made, each with its own name."[8] The Italian friar uses the term "idols" to refer both to the divinities and their material manifestations.

"In general, Ganga Itiqui is the name of the one who, with the authority of Minister, receives the gifts and the victims from the hands of the givers, and places them on top of the Altars in front of the Statues of the Idols, among which many have human semblance, of Men, and of Women, and many others of animals, Beasts, Monsters, and Demons, according to the different customs of each Province, Population, and Community."[9] It is Cavazzi's understanding that *iteque* are at once the divinities and their statues. In fact, it is not clear from his writings or those of his colleagues to what extent one existed outside of the other in central-African thought.

For Cavazzi and his brothers in religion, central Africans worshipped "the most extravagant things."[10] In the course of their apostolate, they identified a multitude of items of all sizes and shapes as objects of idolatry. They wrote about deformed and misshapen figures that included elements they considered monstrous, such as horns, or else about nonfigurative compositions that combined different components "according to each person's form of madness."[11] They noticed minute items hanging around the necks of infants, small figures "in the shape of a man with horns and a savage look,"[12] and larger wooden, "poorly made statues."[13] One of the most detailed descriptions talked about figures "who had the exact appearance of a mountebank puppet, dressed just like it, with a red hood on the head."[14] They also occasionally encountered architectural structures devoted to spiritual practices, "particular houses in which [central Africans] [had] many Idols, and where they gather[ed] to invoke them and give them sacrifices, offering them money or else something to eat."[15] The dense devotional furnishings of these temples, which gathered many objects and figures, reminded them of "the crèches of [their own] country."[16]

What Did the Capuchins See?

What were the *iteque* that Capuchins saw? The extant record of visual productions from early modern central Africa is relatively sparse. However, a substantial number of finely worked textiles and decorated ivories sent from the Kongo to Europe between the sixteenth and eighteenth centuries form an eloquent record of elite aesthetics and techne in the region (figs. 71, 88, 104).[17] Stylistic and iconographic analyses paired with archaeological findings have placed some examples of Christian arts from the Kongo in the chronological context of the early modern period (figs. 62, 100).[18] Investigations into rock painting and engravings and associated material have yielded important but few insights on the figurative practices of Kongo and Angola in that same period.[19] Non-Christian figurative productions in central Africa dated to the time of the Capuchin mission, however, number only two, a pair of wooden figures now in the Museo Pigorini in Rome that entered European collections in the seventeenth century.[20] Otherwise, most figurative works from central Africa in museum collections were collected at the height of the struggle over colonial takeover of the region in the late nineteenth and twentieth centuries, and no record was made of their local history in the often violent process. It is likely that a number of these objects, now kept for the most part in Europe and North America, as well as some of the ones still in the hands of local communities, were made and used in the early modern period. However, collection research and art-historical scholarship do not currently provide systematic information in this regard. Dating and chronology of central-African material culture before the twentieth century are far from established.

For this reason, the Capuchin corpus is an invaluable resource, offering crucial, but so far largely overlooked, documentation and insight on the visual culture of central Africa in the early modern period. However, the written descriptions and, above all, the visual images the friars created of what they deemed idols are eminently difficult documents with which to reckon. The central-African figurative objects featured in complex paintings that took form through cross-cultural interactions, in the fraught yet sustained relationships established between the friars and the central Africans alongside whom they worked. The images were at once eyewitness testimonies by Europeans laden with their homegrown preconceptions, attempts at conveying the unexpected nature and form of central-African spirituality to an audience of future missionaries, and the products of an emerging discourse about central-African religious culture that emerged between the friars and the local scholars and specialists with whom they officiated (as discussed in chapters 6 and 7 below). Some of these multilayered painted images in turn became prints that took new form in the hands of artists who brought their own interpretations to bear on the *disegni* they translated into etchings. Still, through multiple veils of translations from one medium to another, from one visual tradition to a wholly different one, and from the realm of central-African religion to that of European Catholicism, the Capuchin images made visible objects and rituals from early modern central Africa that would otherwise remain largely unseen.

The small number of images and the equally limited geographically and temporally close comparative material demand an approach that relies on a nimble methodology and capacious eye. I anchor my investigation of the Capuchin images of early modern central-African spiritual practices in the associated written evidence, drawing from textual commentaries on objects and happenings echoing those pictured, from friars in the same orbit as the image-makers. I also bring to bear on the early modern images and texts visually compelling comparanda. In the absence of contemporary objects from the exact region depicted in the Capuchin corpus, I mobilize from a broad geography and chronology examples that are visually as well as spatially or temporally connected to the ones depicted. Because of the disconnect in time or space, none of the comparisons, even the most evocative ones, are meant to establish identity or claim specific connections between a Capuchin image and a particular object. Instead, the comparisons function on a more general level as a way to define a broad visual, material, and religious field to which the objects depicted and the comparanda give contours. A rigorous analysis of the images that does not dismiss them as idiosyncratic and beyond interpretation emerges by bringing together an array of resonances, similarities, and connections in traits and practices among a range of examples that define a grid within which to consider central-African visual culture from the seventeenth to the twentieth centuries. This methodology does not allow for considerations of historical change, regional variations, or stylistic preferences, or for identification of moments and areas of creative efflorescence or obsolescence, innovation or conservatism. But it begins to sketch a schematic portrait of central-African visual culture since the early modern period, a first and necessary step toward addressing these questions.

Two images extant as prints in Friar Giovanni Antonio Cavazzi's *Istorica descrizione* offer a firmly dated record of the anthropomorphic figures that the Capuchins encountered in central Africa in the mid-seventeenth century (figs. 64, 65). They are among the earliest known visual documents of figurative objects from the region, to my knowledge preceded only by the representation of the "broken idols" of Kongo's heathen past in the coat of arms of the kingdom in a Portuguese armorial of 1548.[21] The first one is in the background of plate number 6 of the printed volume, titled "Pianta del Conde ordinaria" (fig. 64). Behind the print's eponymous tree, a scene unfolds that involves a devotee and an anthropomorphic figure. Legs firmly together, one hand on a hip and the other slightly extended to the side, the figure in the nook of the trunk stands hieratically. The extended arms and solicitous comportment of the person walking toward it from the left suggest that what the etcher somewhat ambiguously rendered was an anthropomorphic image awaiting worshippers. The scene is set under the fronds of a large tree, a space of well-known local significance. Large flora such as *nsanda* (*Ficus psilopoga Welwitsch*) formed sites, symbols, materials, and landscapes for spiritual and political rituals.[22] The Parma Watercolors feature several such trees on their pages. One of them serves as the setting for a local aristocrat's reception of his vassal in a vignette the painter composed to be reminiscent of iconic scenes of French king Saint Louis rendering justice under an oak (plate 16). On another page, "a tree consecrated to idols" receives the blow of a Capuchin's axe, in a gesture of zealous extirpation (plate 65). The background scene in figure 64 thus

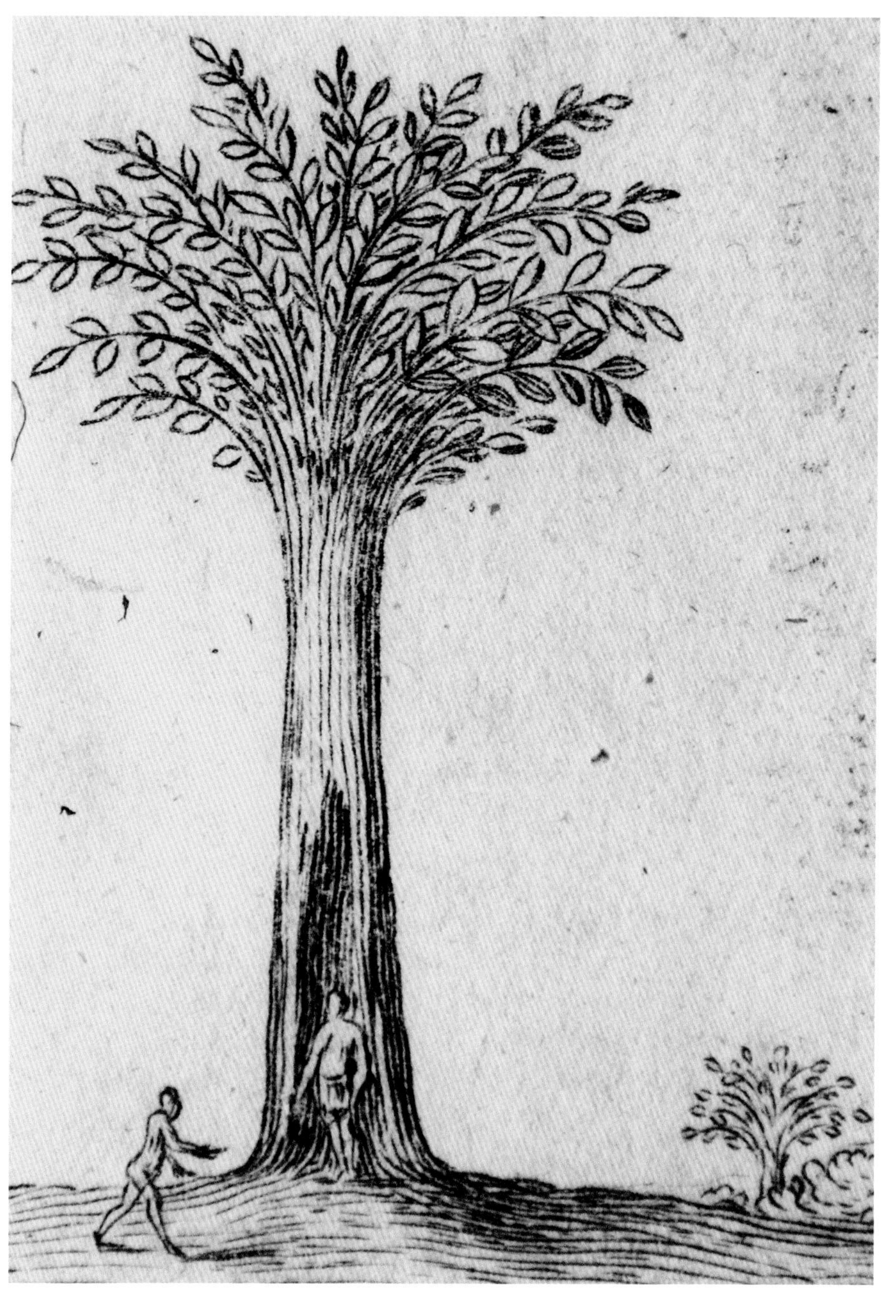

Figure 64

Fortunato Alamandini, *Figure and Devotee* (fig. 18 detail).

depicts a ritual interaction of the type Capuchins showcased in their practical guides.

The engraving in which the detail features is one of the compositions that Alamandini, the final editor of the *Istorica descrizione*, who did not travel to central Africa, created in order to, in his view, correct the images Cavazzi had first commissioned for the book.[23] His etchings are several steps removed from eyewitness accounts of central Africa, but the motifs he used consistently were derived from precedents within the Capuchin eyewitness corpus or earlier travel literature. In this case, the representation of a large hollow tree, hosting in its core a hieratic figure, almost certainly came from one of the Capuchin images Alamandini could consult, possibly one of the Parma Watercolors. The composition, which brings together a person and a figure in a spare landscape, fits well with the images of ritual practices in the Parma group. In fact, it would, for instance, fit neatly in the sequence of the corpus as folio 82 or 84, just before or after another illustration of what the friars understood as an instance of idolatrous worship (fig. 69 / plate 54).

The second image recording central-African figurative objects is plate number 46 of the *Istorica descrizione*, which presents a ritual scene taking place in a circular enclosure (fig. 65). It is one of the prints that Cavazzi himself commissioned, and the numbers 760, 764, and 765 labeling three of its main components likely refer to paragraphs or page numbers in his unfortunately lost manuscript of the book. Alamandini, in his reworking of the text and its illustration program, chose to insert the image within the part of the narrative dealing with feasting at Angolan queen Njinga's court. No doubt the bowls in the hands of some of the protagonists led him to interpret the image as a banquet.

Alamandini, as noted earlier, had not traveled to central Africa.

The scene transpiring within a circular enclosure is undoubtedly ritual in nature. It likely corresponds to the part of Cavazzi's original draft for the book titled, according to the extant table of contents, "Of the Feast they give to their idols."[24] A crowd of men and youths have gathered in an enclosure meeting the friars' description of those used by ritual associations such as Kimpasi.[25] To the left and right of the enclosure's entrance, devotees kneel with their toes firmly planted in the ground, a ritual attitude typical of central Africa, seen in the early modern period, for example, on ancillary figures surrounding Christ on Kongo crucifixes.[26] They hold offerings of food or drink in bowls or cross their arms across their chest in a gesture of respect and salutation.[27] They direct their attention toward the central figure in the image, sitting cross-legged on a large mat or pillow. It is larger in scale than the gathered men and wears a crown of feathers that echoes that of two other larger-than-life figures to the right and left of the enclosure. The three towering characters are the main subject matter of the print and were once discussed in a numbered gloss. The larger scale that gives them more visibility is a visual technique that would be fit for the didactic goals of a practical guide such as the Parma Watercolors, from which the print may derive. Although the printmaker has rendered them ambiguously as lifelike characters, their specific bodily attitudes, placement, size, and labeling with numbers indicate that they are the "Itiqui" Cavazzi describes, "Statues of the Idols, among which many have human semblance, of Men, and of Women."[28] In fact, for each of the three figures, comparanda abound among the central-African anthropomorphic

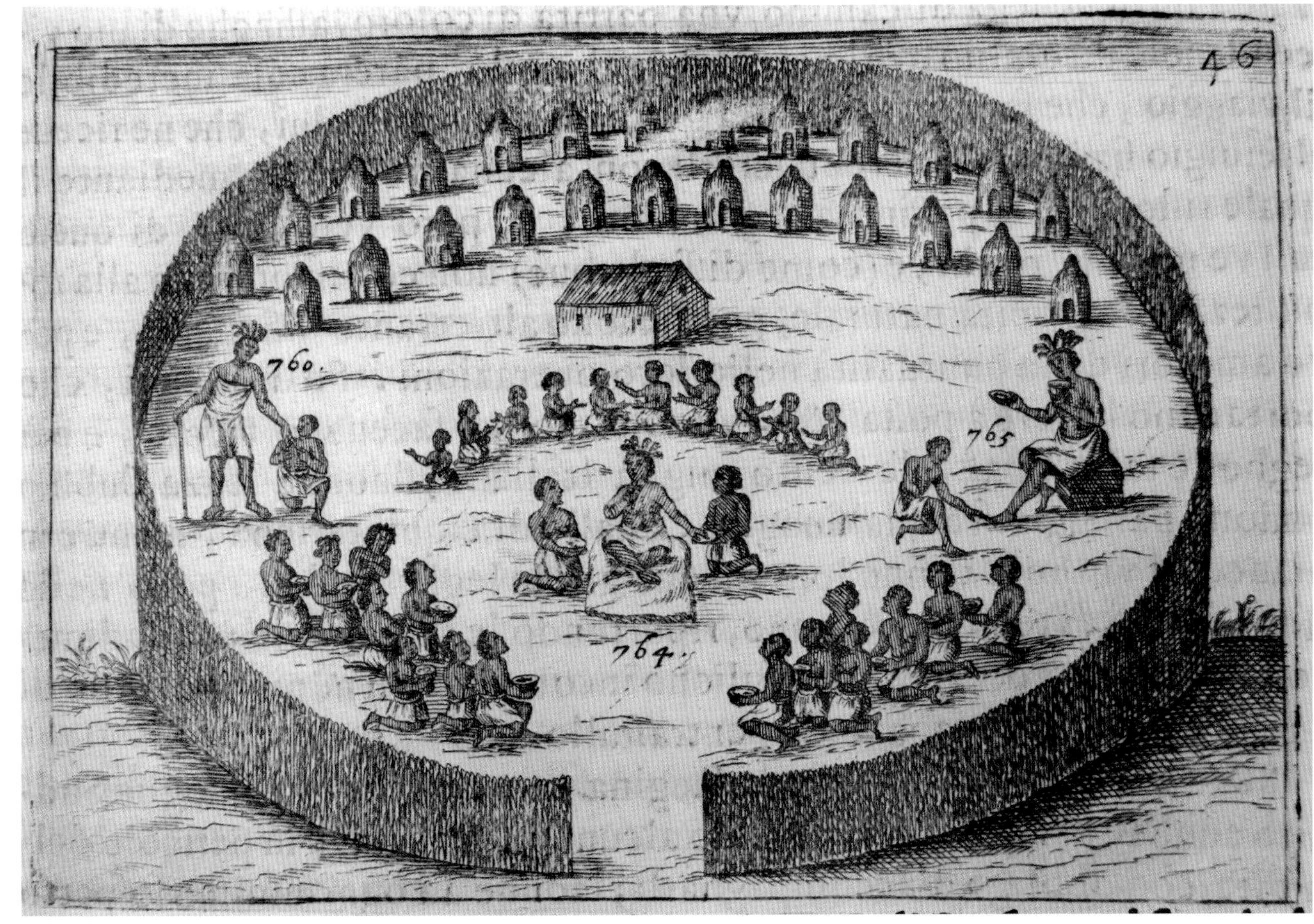

Figure 65

Paolo da Lorena (attr.), *Ritual Enclosure*. Engraving, 10 × 14 cm (plate mark). Plate 46 from Giovanni Antonio Cavazzi and Fortunato Alamandini, *Istorica descrizione de' tre' regni Congo, Matamba, et Angola* (Bologna: Giacomo Monti, 1687), 699. Bibliothèque nationale de France, FOL-H-3133. Photo: author.

objects collected or documented in the nineteenth and twentieth centuries. Considered together, the seventeenth-century printed images and the more recent figures, though evidently unrelated in specific terms, highlight resonances, similarities, and connections that give contours and lend historical depth to central-African visual and material culture.

A seating male figure now in the Metropolitan Museum in New York, in spite of its modest scale, less than a foot high, is a striking cognate to the print's central protagonist (fig. 66). Each man sits cross-legged on a rectangular base and raises his right hand to his chin, slightly turned to the right in an iconic gesture of Kongo's figural tradition.[29] One head is decorated with feathers, the other with a cap, both symbols of spiritual and temporal might. They both sit on textile-inspired bases. The print has rendered it as a mat or cushion, and geometric motifs evocative of weaving patterns inscribe the wood base. Royal portraits associated with an eighteenth-century artistic efflorescence from the Kuba people, to the east of Kongo and Angola, if

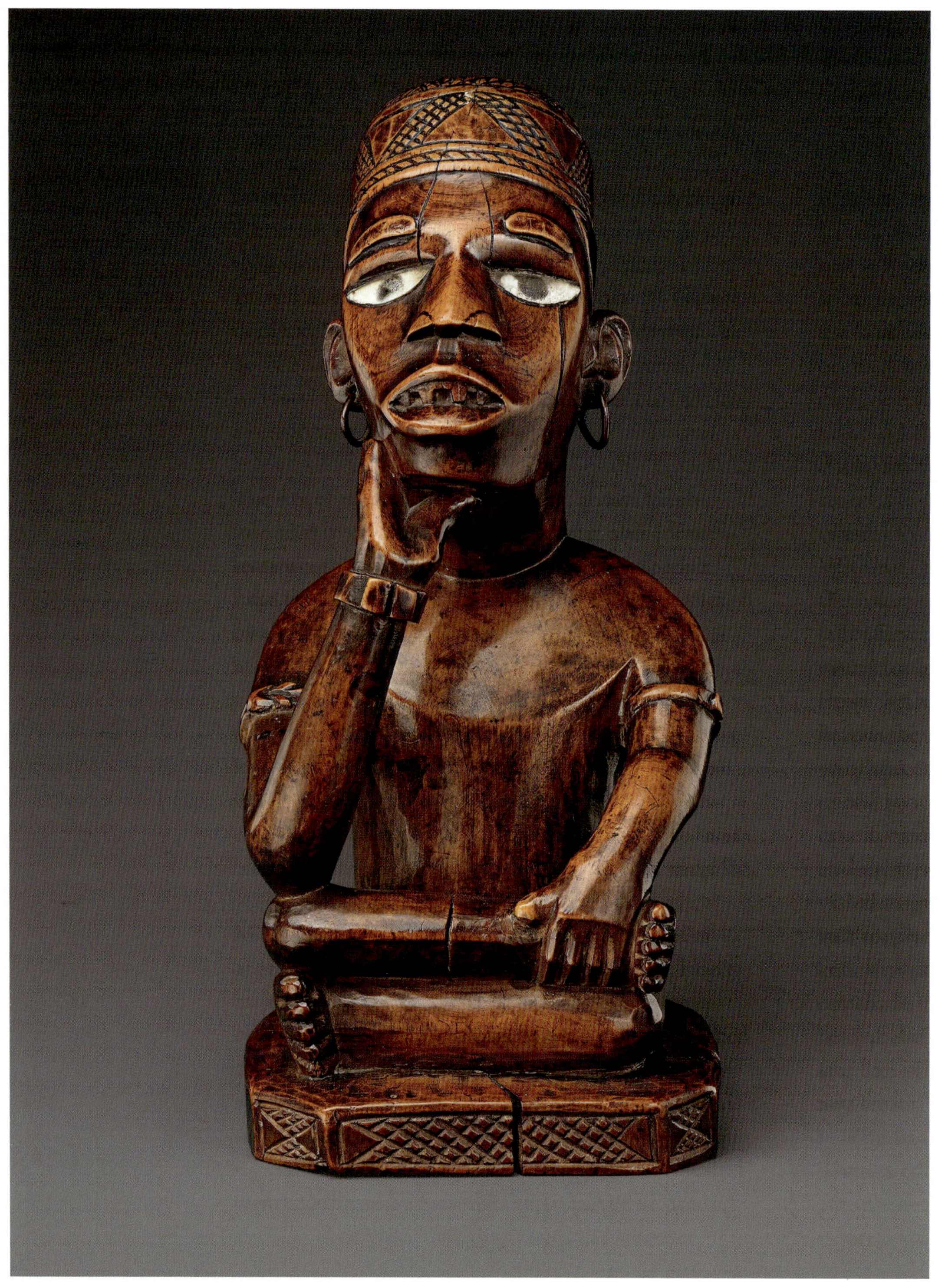

Figure 66

Unknown Kongo artist,
seated male figure,
Kakongo group, mid to
late nineteenth century.
Wood, glass, metal, kaolin,
29.2 × 12.1 × 12.1 cm. The
Metropolitan Museum of
Art, New York. Purchase,
Louis V. Bell Fund, Mildred
Vander Poel Becker
Bequest, Amalia Lacroze de
Fortabat Gift, and Harris
Brisbane Dick Fund, 1996,
1996.281. Photo courtesy of
the Metropolitan Museum
of Art.

Figure 67 (opposite)

Unknown Kongo artist,
scepter, Lower Congo,
Democratic Republic of
the Congo, nineteenth
century. Ivory, resin, oil,
29 × 4.5 cm. Collection
of the Royal Museum for
Central Africa, Tervuren,
Belgium, EO.0.0.43708.
Photo: R. Asselberghs,
RMCA Tervuren ©.

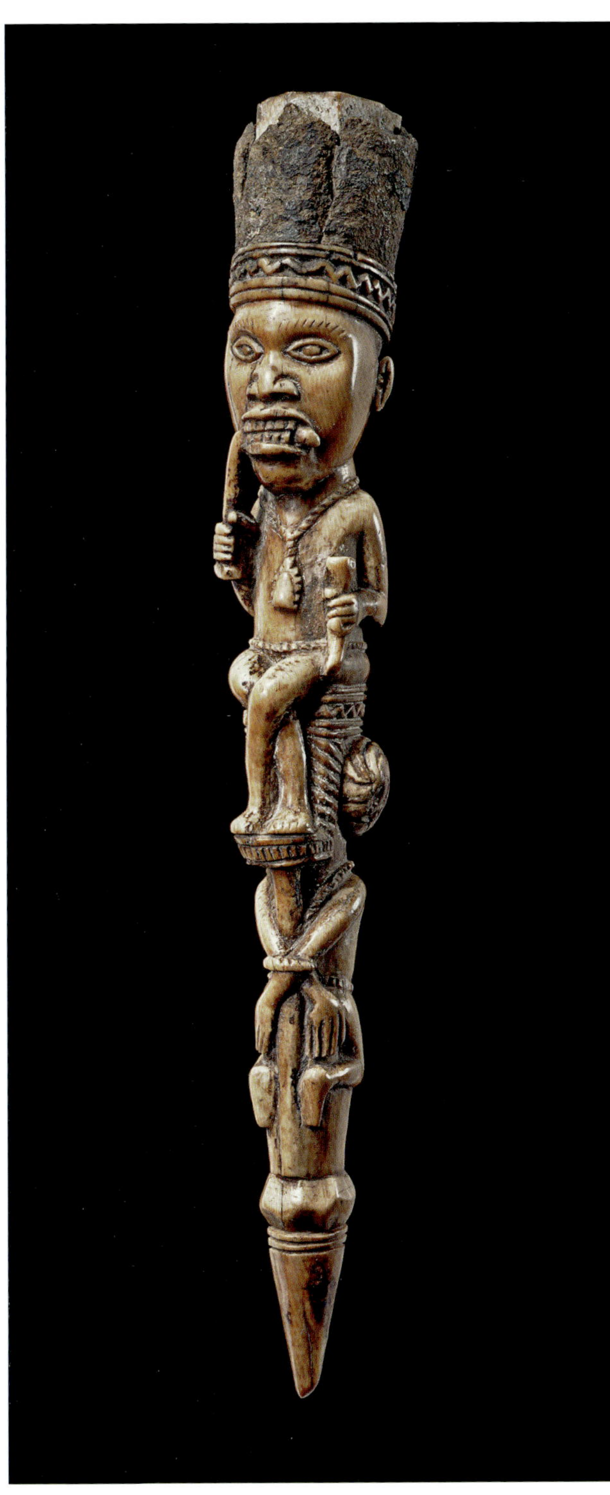

geographically distant, give examples of the same attitude and attributes of composed leadership that bridge the chronological gap.[30]

The man on the right of the print sits, imposing, on a higher stool and receives homage from a crouching attendant lightly touching his foot. The scene recalls the compositions of a tight-knit group of ivory scepters documented in nineteenth- and twentieth-century central Africa. In the example in figure 67, a mighty figure sits, legs crossed, on a high seat, towering over a subdued subaltern in a statement of absolute power. Some resin at the top of the ivory scepter encloses empowered material around the head of the ruler, a privileged part of the body enhanced in the print with a feather crown. In ink or ivory, each stately figure raises one hand toward his mouth, while holding in the other a ritual container: a tusk filled with empowered material in the scepter and a bowl in the print.

The higher garment on the figure on the left of the enclosure, covering the chest, suggests a female body, like those the friars sometimes pictured, each wearing a cloth wrapped around her upper body— for instance, on plates 50, 52, 72. The figure's staff and forward-leaning stand follow the characteristic vocabulary of might and intimidation in central-African visual culture. This is an attitude found in male and female empowered *minkisi* and other types of mighty characters collected since the nineteenth century in the western part of central Africa but mentioned by name in the early modern sources (fig. 74). Heroic leaders of the Chokwe realm, to the east, also stand, staff in hand, leaning forward in alert stances of dynamic repose.[31] Though seated rather than upright, the female Kongo ruler in figure 68 gives concrete

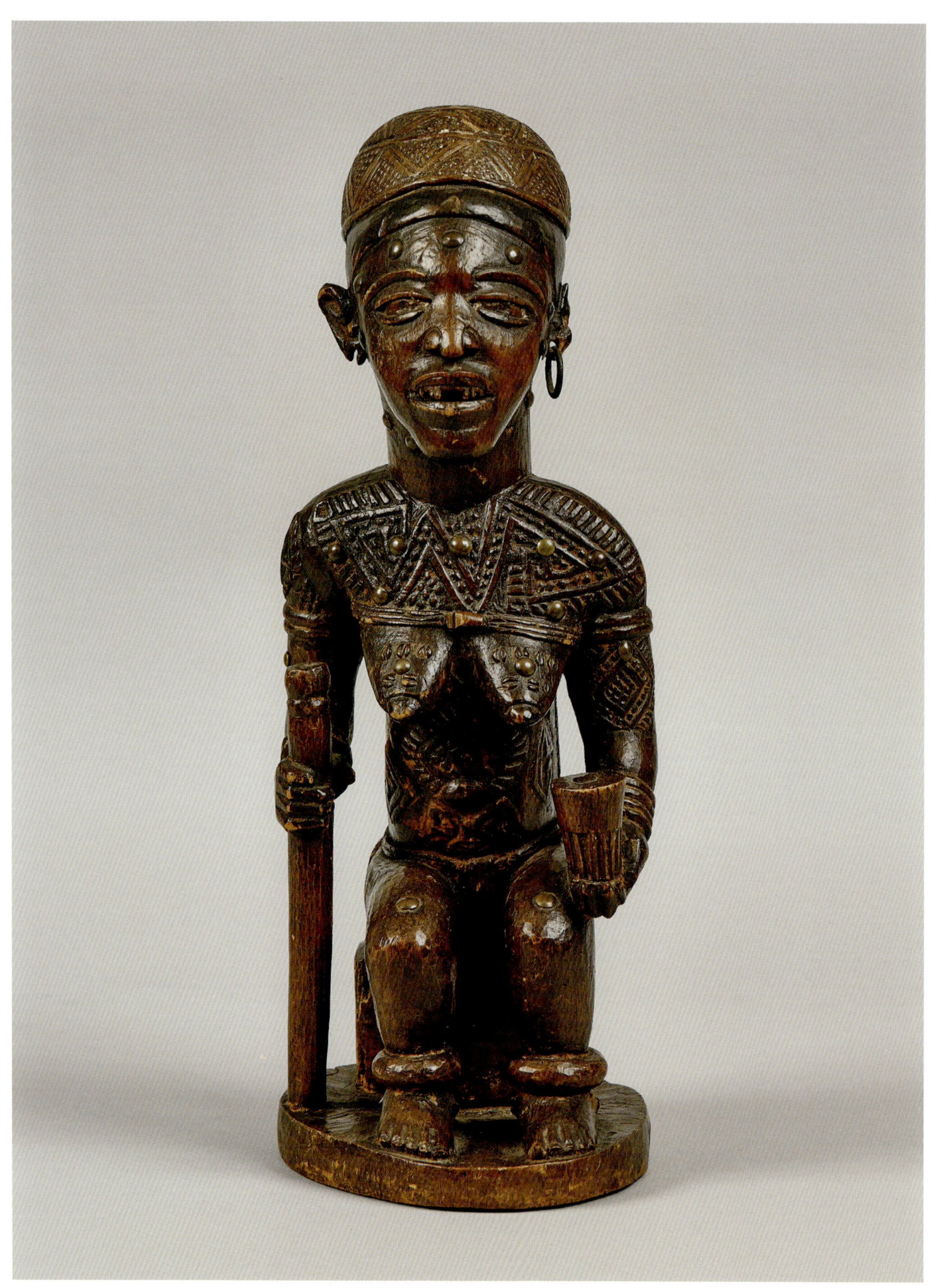

Figure 68

Unknown artist, seated figure of a chieftainess, Zaire or Congo Republic (Yombe), late nineteenth to early twentieth century. Wood, 135 × 375 × 145 mm. Robert and Lisa Sainsbury Collection, Sainsbury Center for Visual Arts, University of East Anglia, Norwich, United Kingdom. Acquired by Robert and Lisa Sainsbury, 1968, UEA 253. Photo courtesy of the Sainsbury Center for Visual Arts.

form to some of her printed counterpart's features, from the staff to the cord tied about the breasts, a detail that could have been read by the printmaker as the edge of a garment. The cup the sitting figure holds in her left hand also parallels containers in the print. And she, too, is coiffed with a cap of status, much as each of the three "Itiqui" of the *Istorica descrizione* wears a crown of feathers, an insignia of political and spiritual power mentioned and depicted in the early modern sources (for instance, in plate 69) and a frequent attribute of central-African empowered figures and figures of power (fig. 74).[32]

Completing the scene, a group of ten youths in a half circle behind the central figure animatedly converse, discussing perhaps the new knowledge senior members of the association have revealed to them in what looks like a tableau of initiation rites. In their texts Capuchin friars discussed at length enclosures of this kind, which they associated with initiatory groups such as the Kimpasi. The surrounding fence and the round and orthogonal architectural structures fit the descriptions of the spaces that hosted the events and housed the ritual tools of these organizations. Friars also encountered buildings of this type, which they identified as idol houses, outside of such compounds (figs. 72, 73). The printmaker rendered the group of smaller seated characters as a gathering of people, although this part of the image could be read as another set of figurative objects. Elsewhere in the *Istorica descrizione*, Cavazzi includes an evocative description of the "enclosures" and "idols" of the Kimpasi, which could be the passage the image originally illustrated. Members of the association, he writes, "in front of the houses plant in semicircular shape many poles roughly carved and painted, which look like shapeless statues." There,

he further explains, "in front of these simulacra, they feast in a bizarre shamelessness."[33] The ambivalent representation of idols, hovering between the animate and the inanimate, may not wholly be a product of the printmaker's misunderstanding. In their descriptions the friars were adamant that devotees related to their idols as if they were people, possibly family members, whom they fed. "They have idols in their houses," writes Serafino da Cortona, and "they call some Father, others sons, and when we want to burn them, they defend them with all their might, and mourn them as if we were burning their children."[34] The ambivalent image efficiently captured and conveyed the nature of the idols as more than inanimate objects in their interactions with their devotees. The ambiguity may have been unintended on the part of the printmaker, but the dexterous use of European form to depict central-African objects in ways that convey elements of their nature otherwise incongruous with European thought is a core characteristic of the Capuchin vignettes dealing with the central-African spiritual environment.

At the Limit of Images

If the friars noted and described in words and images "idols" taking the form of anthropomorphic figures, they also were keenly aware that objects and practices that did not fit their preconceived ideas of religious material could prove idolatrous. In the context of central Africa, as the writers of the practical guides explained, the evidence of the eye was not reliably adequate to identify heathen idolatry and superstition. Luca da Caltanisetta gives one example of such shortfall, having dismissed too quickly as innocuous the pendant a child wore.

The youth "had around the neck two little idols, which at first sight [Friar Luca] thought to be only simple pieces of wood" until a more experienced cleric pointed to his mistake and identified them as protective charms.[35] Serafino da Cortona, too, in his description of the "heathen rites" of central Africa, warns his colleagues that the *quirica* (pl. *iruca*) small children wore around the neck should be removed before baptism. He further notes how specific knowledge, along with a trained eye, was needed to differentiate between things such as the seemingly indistinguishable bracelets women wore, among which copper-colored ones were witchcraft, while brass-hued models were simple ornaments.[36]

The difficulty Europeans had in identifying objects and practices central Africans used to access and manage invisible forces is at the core of the part of the didactic manuscripts dedicated to apostolic work. Though aware of the limitations of observation, the makers of the watercolors still turned to images to convey their knowledge of central-African rituals and religious practices to European novices. As seasoned missionaries, they understood the nature of local rites and knew the importance of being attentive not only to their appearance but also to their underlying worldview. At times, problematic activities could be uncovered by observation, but in other circumstances, only previous knowledge could help identify them. The friars strategically used European forms of visual representation to translate central-African religious thought and communicate to the future missionaries both categories of information. They combined in their images central-African rituals and objects with European conventions for the representation of idolatry and superstition to create an efficient portrayal of central-African thought and its correct

interpretation. The result is images weaving European and central-African visual forms and religious conceptions in deeply cross-cultural creations, images not only *of* but also *from* central Africa.

In a landscape of desolate, bare hills evoking a desert area, three people have come together around a cracked, ancient stone altar on which stands a live goat (fig. 69 / plate 54). A man with a blue cloak is kneeling in the middle of the page, arms extended toward the animal. On the left of the scene, another man walks toward the center, with a bow and arrows and an axe. In the bottom left corner, a woman with large breasts sits on a stone or a stool, holding on her lap a gourd-shaped long-necked basketry-covered vessel. The animal is distinctly alive; its feet are pounding, and its mouth is open, as if bleating. "Many and infinite are the idols of these deserts, and their names are extravagant," explains the text under the vignette:

I only represent this one because it seems to me the most ridiculous. It is a live goat, very large, with very long horns, black and wooly, possessed by the demon. It talks and answers and is adored by all the Jaga people as a god with the name of Zumbi. On the first three days of the new moon it jumps by itself on an altar made of stone, and there it stands to be adored. In all, it is a wondrous thing that it stands immobile, as if it were of stone, until the function is over, then goes to graze wherever it pleases.[37]

The written annotations then carry on describing the many ways in which the devil "deceives these poor blind people," using the animal. As in the natural-history vignettes, the author includes a numbered key to the image. "1: Zumbi goat 2: altar, 3: servant of the Idol, 4: gourd full of

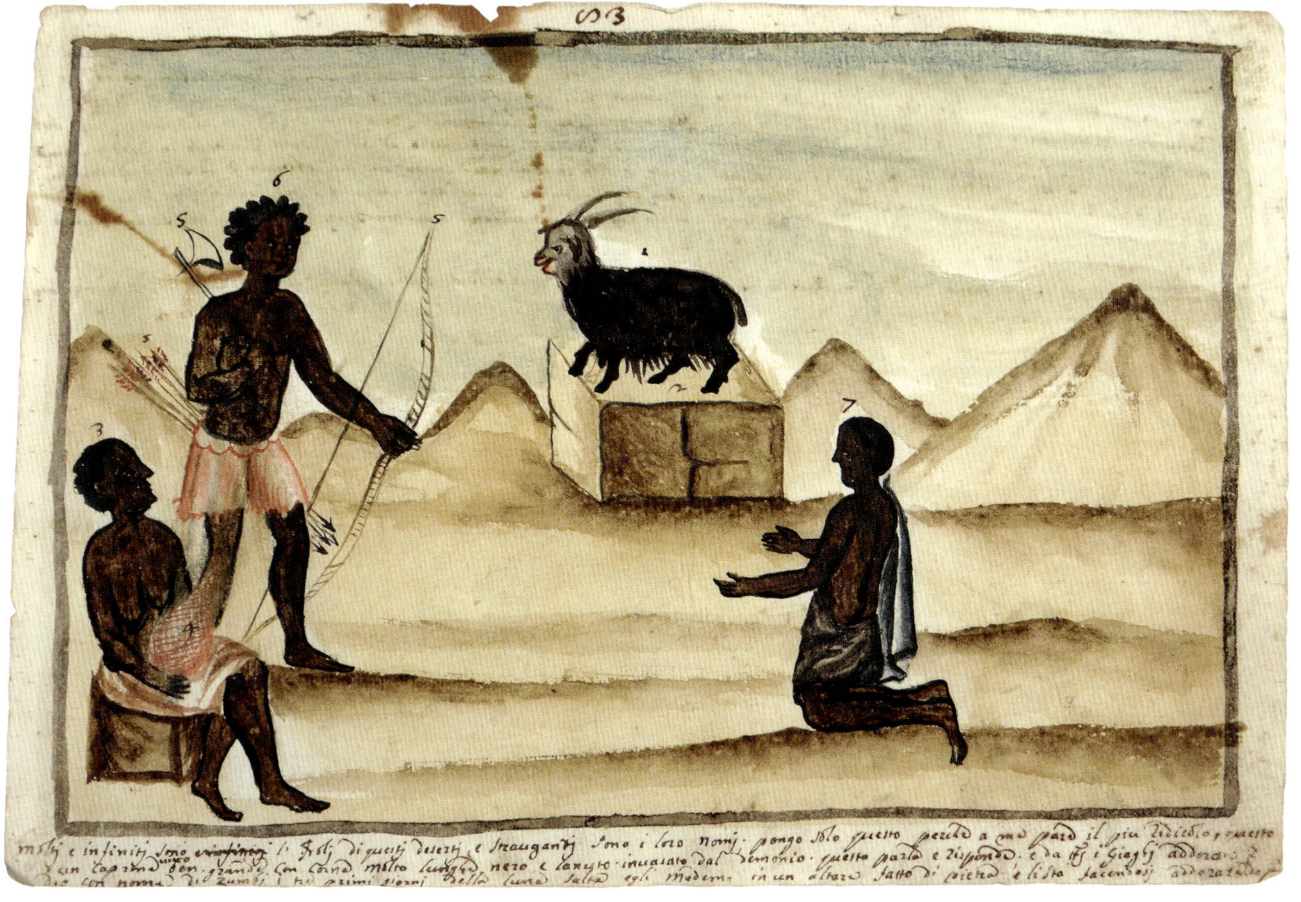

Figure 69

Unknown Capuchin artist, "Many and infinite are the Idols of these deserts," late seventeenth century. Watercolor on paper, 34 × 24 cm. Parma Watercolors, Virgili Collection, fol. 83. Photo: author.

human milk to give to the idol to drink and to wash its mouth as soon as it has spoken, 6: guardian of the Idol, 5: weapons, 7: worshipper."

The writer of the gloss places the scene among "the Jagas," a term that referred to marauding groups known and feared for their military might.[38] In the late seventeenth century, at the time of the composition of the watercolor, the friars' writings depicted the Jagas as a distinctively heathen people, a violent enemy of the converted Kongo kingdom and fiercely resistant to the advances of the Portuguese from their neighboring *conquista* of Angola. They had allied with the fierce Queen Njinga, who adopted their violent mores and military tactics. The image offers to the viewer a range of ethnographic details it ascribes to the group. The characteristic axe with a convex blade carried by the "guardian" and the long-neck flask made of a vessel decorated with woven vegetal fibers are both typical and well-documented central-African objects.[39] Fan-shaped blades are quintessential artifacts of the broad central-African region, recorded in

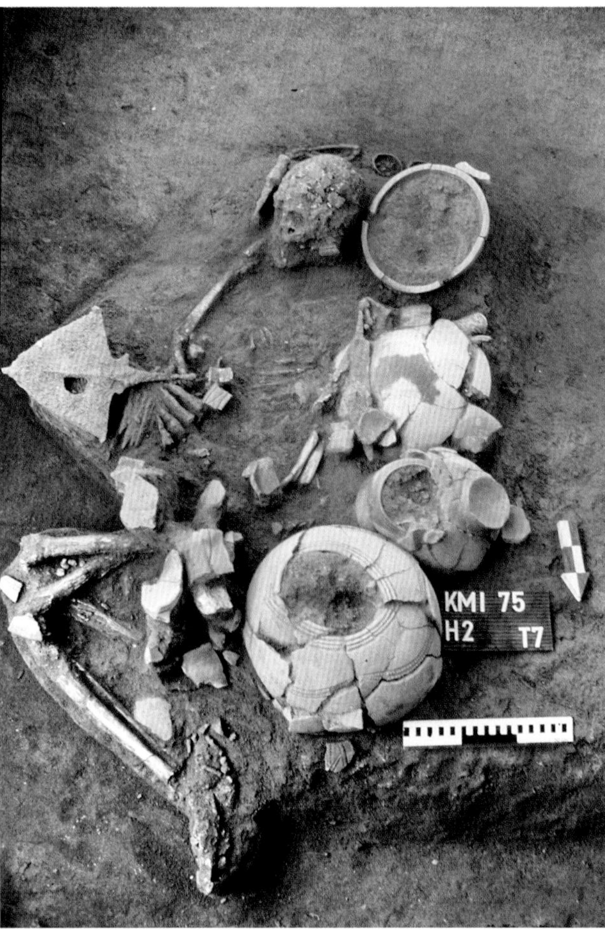

visual keys to render his image efficient as a didactic tool explaining the nature of the ceremony. European viewers could easily interpret, for instance, the attitude of the worshipper, kneeling with his arms outstretched, as a gesture of prayer. The stone altar on which the animal stands was another powerful visual key. Rectangular and proportionate to the body of the goat, it became what a pedestal would be to a statue in European contexts and powerfully suggested the idea of a graven image. With this cue, the author introduced the concept of idolatry and attached it to the live animal, conveying to viewers that the goat itself was the object of worship "as a god." The reference is, of course, to the biblical story of the Golden Calf, but here the friar made clear visually that idolatry had taken a different form. It was a live animal, rather than the image of an animal, that received devotion, and awareness of this possibility was crucial for missionary work in Angola. The image made the object and nature of worship understandable from Europe by presenting them under the guise of the more readable template of idolatry as image worship. With elements drawn from European iconography, such as the gesture of prayer, and visual clues, such as the altar turned pedestal, the author bridged the gap between central-African practices and European visual vocabulary in an elaborate effort at cross-cultural translation.

From Idolatry to Orthodoxy

Armed with their knowledge of local idolatry and superstition, the Capuchins worked in central Africa on different fronts. On the one hand, they faced still-unconverted peoples such as the Jagas, and on the other hand, they worked among populations

archaeological settings since the first millennium CE (fig. 70).[40] A gourd with a basketry covering in the Ulmer Museum, catalogued in the mid-seventeenth century as a vessel used for palm wine in Angola, is cognate with the ritual object in the watercolor (fig. 71).

The painter of the watercolor presented the rest of the objects and actions, including the stone altar and the speaking goat, with the same matter-of-fact documentary verisimilitude as he did the axe and vessel. He also introduced subtle yet powerful

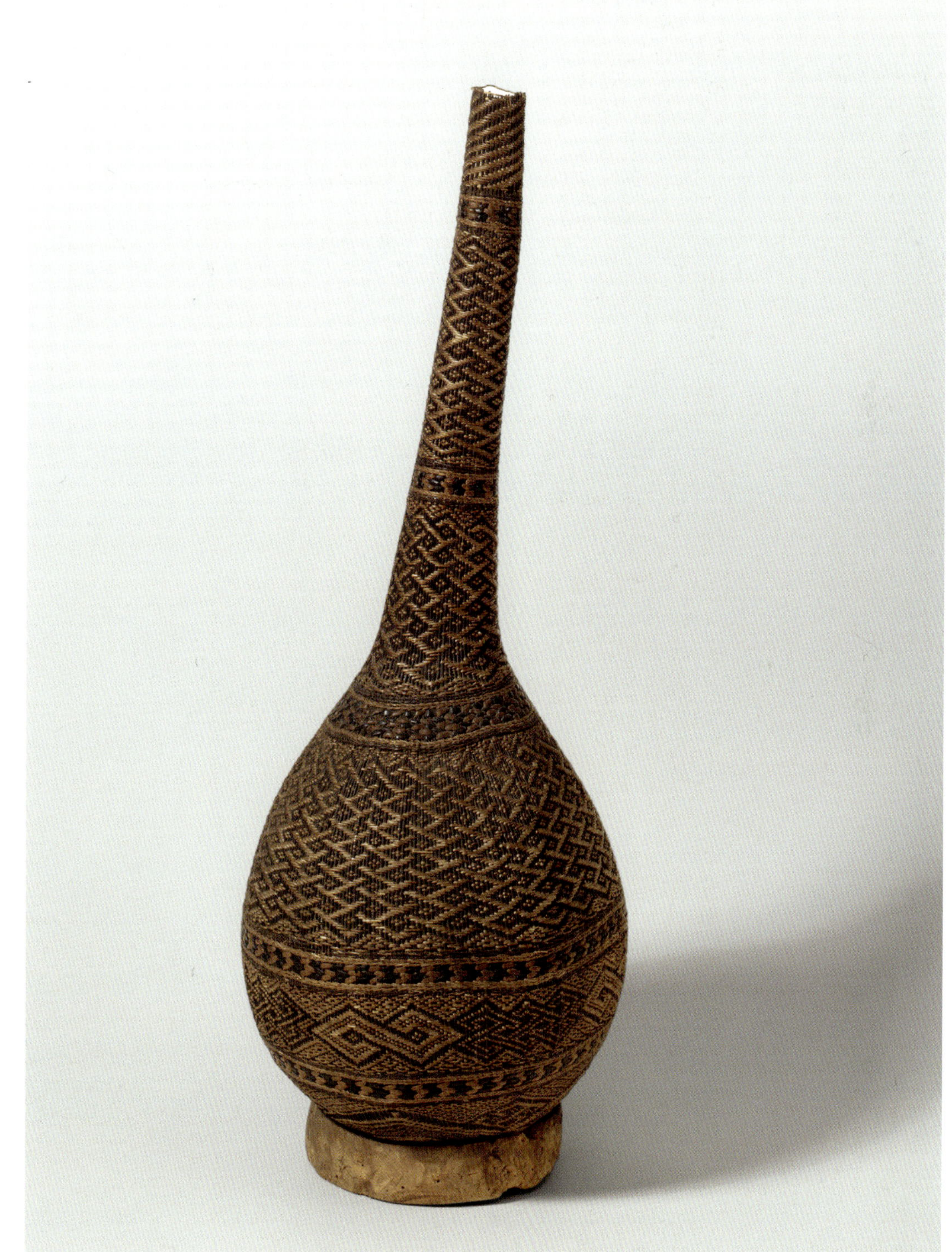

Figure 71

Unknown central-African
artist, basketry-decorated
gourd, before 1659. Gourd,
cork, bast fibers, palm rib,
height 52 cm. Museum
Ulm. © Museum Ulm—
Weickmann Collection.
Photo: Bernd Kegler, Ulm.

within the Kingdom of Kongo and Angola who already professed Catholicism. Their ambition, with respect to the latter, was to reinforce their Christian faith and counter their superstitious ways. Bernardino d'Asti, the author of the "Missione in prattica," admittedly among the most optimistic Capuchins commenting on central Africa, explicitly compares the friars' work in the Kongo to their labors in Italy. If in Europe, he opines, in spite of centuries of zealous apostolic work and the rule of the Church, heresies, schisms, and "errors" still abound, it is no wonder that, in central Africa, faith would be so fragile, being recently introduced and sustained by so few clerics.[41] This is why "idolatries, vain observances, superstitions, and other errors and uses against our Holy Faith are not yet totally extirpated."[42] "One could not expect," he warns his readers, that "given the small number of priests working at propagating the Holy Faith, heathenry could be totally extirpated."[43]

As part of their apostolic work, the friars devoted great time and attention to discovering and understanding local ritual practices in order to establish their efficacy and potential demonic dimension. For this all-important task, they used "well-paid secret informants,"[44] spied in person under cover of night, and remained on alert during every interaction.[45] In their reports they made every effort to describe, analyze, and classify the ways in which local populations called upon the numinous. Their perception of religious practices in Kongo and Angola was shaped by the belief they shared with central Africans in the agency of invisible forces over the course of everyday life. Obtaining divine intervention through prayer and the intercession of the saints was a routine part of early modern Catholicism. However, since not only God but also the devil had the ability to manipulate the natural

order of things, seeking numinous intervention demanded taking the utmost precautions. Only by channeling one's demands through the prayers, objects, and rituals the Catholic Church sanctioned could one be sure to summon the right kind of help. Outside of the Church's rituals, attempts could prove vain, or they could, most nefariously, prove efficacious thanks to demonic intervention. Ineffective appeals to invisible forces or vain observances were not of great danger to Catholicism. The absence of effects proved their lack of connection to superhuman agency. Efficacious calls to the numinous, however, were cause for great concern, as their demonstrated powers could be the work of the devil. In all cases, worship directed to anything but the Christian God was unacceptable to Catholic orthodoxy.

Whether a given object, practice, or habit was innocuous or dangerous, however, was disputable. For example, Central-African *quixilla*, or taboos, that centered primarily on food and were transmitted within families through a patrilineal succession were the topic of intense controversies among the friars.[46] For some, they did not cause any threat. For others, such as Bernardo da Gallo, the tradition betrayed a demonic origin. The consequences transgressors suffered were at the core of the debate. Should a person eat a proscribed food, knowingly or unknowingly, he or she would immediately contract a serious and debilitating disease. The friars, in concert with central Africans, recognized the connection between the ingestion of the prohibited food and the ailment that ensued. But they disagreed among themselves on the cause of the illness. Some attributed it to an inherited family predisposition transmitted from one generation to the other, a hereditary intolerance from a "complexion coming from the blood of the parents."[47] Others,

Friar Bernardo among them, refused to see a natural, that is, acceptable, explanation. "I thus say," he concludes, "that the above effects cannot be caused naturally by one's transgression of such a proscription, eating a forbidden meat, but indeed comes about in a superstitious manner, through some tacit or explicit pact with the Demon."[48] Determining the nature of causality as either God's will or that of the devil was key to the work of the missionary.

Vain observances, which were powerless to change the natural course of things, however, still represented danger and warranted extirpation. They left the door open for the devil to impose his bidding surreptitiously, and should be monitored closely. Medical practices in this regard were particularly risky. Healers used their knowledge of plants and natural remedies to cure patients. But their interventions often led to observances that, though vain, might nonetheless be inspired by the devil, who often tricked the people involved in the healing into believing—wrongly—in his agency. "One should be very well warned," Friar Antonio da Gaeta advises, that "when [the healers] apply the said herbs . . . they habitually make use of diabolical superstitions, taught to them by the demon, so that the credit for all [of the cure] is given to the superstitious treatment that they do," rather than to the herbal medicines themselves. Furthermore, "it is public knowledge, and notorious, that the blacks never start the cure of a sick person without first invoking the demon by offering it animal sacrifices."[49] Even a cure that did not rely upon demonic powers thus became an occasion for idolatry. Friars as a whole found healing, as well as all highly skilled or knowledge-based activities, at very high risk of demonic intervention. The missionaries had to open the eyes of central Africans, "this blind people,"[50] to the manipulations of the devil, who, in divination

rituals or ordeals, told "the truth once in a while, to cover up the many lies that he want[ed] to profess and veil afterward."[51]

The suspicion of local episteme and techne that the friars expressed in their practical guides masked a much more ambivalent stand, as the missionaries relied on the knowledge and know-how of local practitioners at every level of the conduct of their mission. The friars owed their ability to secure food, build shelter, maintain and recover health, and orient themselves geographically to the teachings and cooperation of central Africans. Friar Bernardino had much to say, for instance, about the abundant "simples, roots, woods, and other things of great medicinal virtue" the region held, as well as about its distinguished medical practitioners, able to cure "certain ailments that are given in Europe as incurable."[52] The practical guides themselves and the dictionaries the friars used consisted to a large extent of compilations of knowledge and information gathered from, but also in fact often formulated by, largely unnamed and unacknowledged local scholars (as discussed in chapter 7 below).

Nevertheless, the friars approached local knowledge with unease, all the more so when it dealt with the sensitive issue of the manipulation of causality, in the areas of social, spiritual, or physical well-being. The friars called the trained specialists they encountered *fattucchieri*, who were, in the words of Bernardino d'Asti "the directors, fomenters, that is, the ministers, of every diabolical practice."[53] Unlike those peddling vain observances or divination, who were simple "vagabonds," "crooks," and "felons," the great *fattucchieri* could summon the intervention of the devil. The term *fattucchiera* had appeared in the Florentine Accademia della Crusca's vocabulary of the Italian language since its first edition,

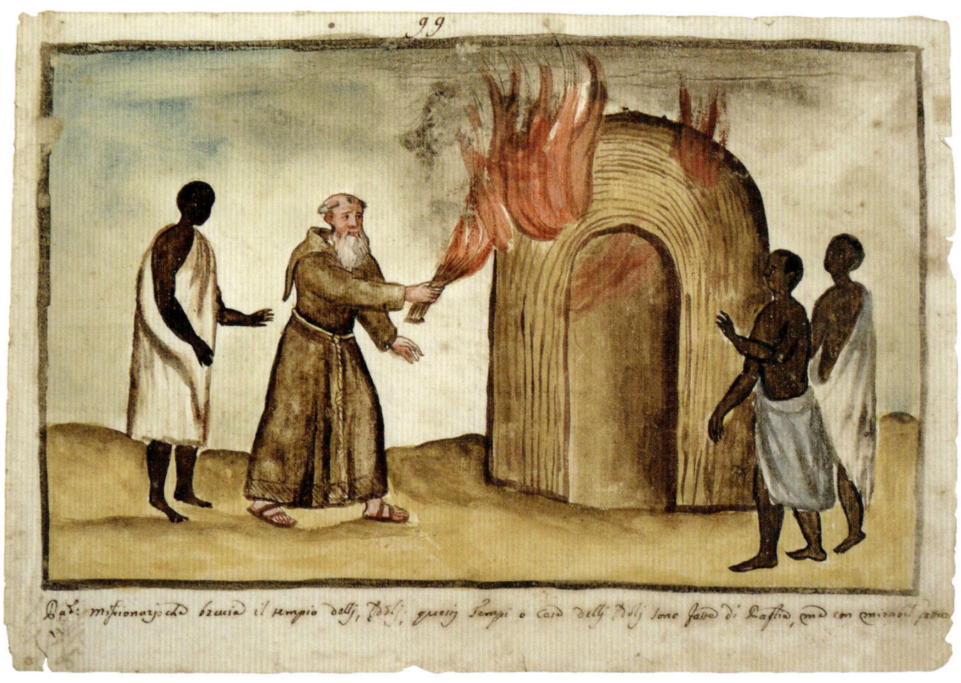

Figure 72

Unknown Capuchin artist, "Missionary Father who burns the temple of the Idols," late seventeenth century. Watercolor on paper, 34 × 24 cm. Parma Watercolors, Virgili Collection, fol. 99. Photo: author.

of 1612, to refer to a female witch and received the Latin definition of *venefica* or *saga* and the Italian synonyms *strega*, *facimola*, and *maliarda*. The Crusca translated *fattucchieria*, in turn, as *veneficium*, a term that refers both to witchcraft and its instruments.[54]

Both categories of ritual specialists—charlatans and real witches—used "instruments" of all kinds, "superstitious things," musical implements, "Idols, some in the figure of formidable men, others of beasts."[55] The friars endeavored to find and destroy these items, often by fire. The burning of central-African ritual paraphernalia occupies two vignettes in the Capuchin corpus. In the Parma Watercolors, a friar sets aflame a rounded structure (similar to those depicted in fig. 65) with a torch (fig. 72 / plate 64). Fire engulfs the straw construction, and smoke darkens the blue sky. The open arched door does not reveal any of its interior or contents. Two *mestres*, with their typical white

outfits, and another man in a blue loincloth witness the scene. "Missionary Father who burns the temple of the Idols," reads the text; "these temples or Idol houses are made of straw, but of remarkable facture."

The corresponding scene in the Turin "Missione in prattica" gives more detail (fig. 73). It illustrates Friar Bernardino's destruction of the paraphernalia he seized from a repentant "Fattochiero" who had received baptism as an infant but had lived henceforth outside of the Church. Brought back to the faith by the friar, he relinquished "many superstitious things, which he gave [him] to burn, namely animal horns, frightful figures, dried-up snakes, knotted woods, animal skulls, lion and tiger claws, etc."[56] In a clearing at the edge of dense vegetation, the missionary lights on fire a small gabled house with a single rectangular door, resembling the central structure in figure 65. Snakes or snake skins and animal horns suspended on the façade around the entrance advertise the purpose of the construction as a repository of ritual paraphernalia. The friar's entourage, two *mestres* and three other men, including the repentant witch, gesture dramatically, pointing at the contents of the house spread on the ground in front of it. They are shocked either at the sight of the objects or at the prospect of their imminent destruction. Two men "full of fear" run away from the arson as the wind teases up the flames eating away the roof of the house and cracking open its façade.

More than a dozen items brought out from the cabin lie on the ground. Among them are, from left to right, long and short animal horns, an anthropomorphic oblong dark shape with white spots, a small upright basket and a larger one turned on its side, emptying its black and white contents. Between the two baskets, the head of a black goat

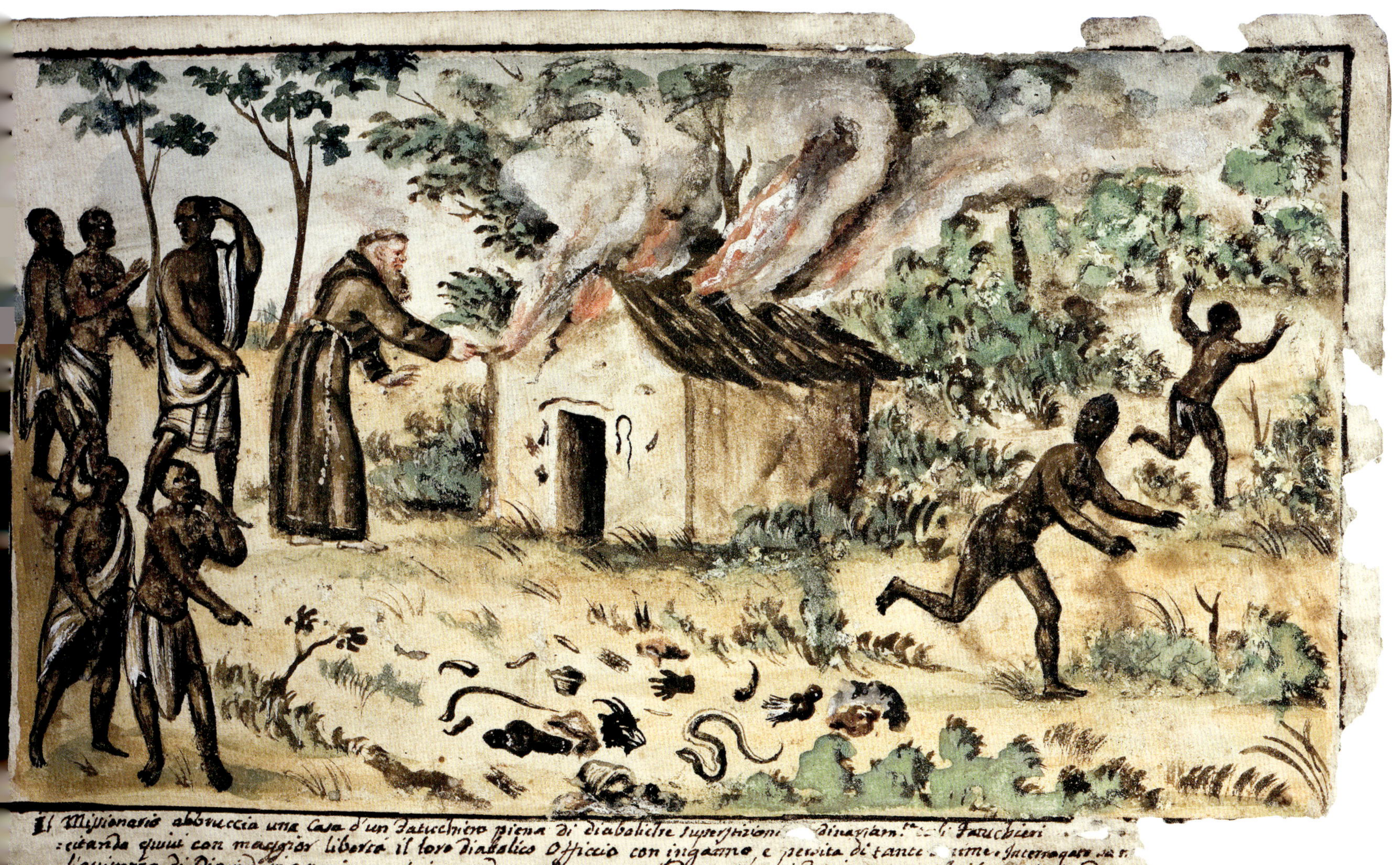

Figure 73

Bernardino Ignazio da Vezza d'Asti, "The Missionary burns
the House of a Witch," ca. 1750. Watercolor on paper,
19.5 × 28 cm. From "Missione in prattica," Biblioteca civica
Centrale di Torino, MS 457, fol. 10r. Photo courtesy of the
Biblioteca civica Centrale, Turin.

faces a human or primate hand, below a brown twisted root.[57] A black-and-white snake undulates next to another horn; to its right lies one more anthropomorphic figure, with bright white eyes and a black-and-white tuft of feathers, leaves, or porcupine spikes on its lower half. A brown spot and a gray spot to the right may be spilled powders, liquids, or a smoking container. As discussed earlier, few examples of material culture from Kongo and Angola firmly dated to the seventeenth and eighteenth centuries have survived to serve as *comparanda* for these items, but written accounts from the period provide good documentation that Friar Bernardino depicted the types of objects one would expect in the hands of a ritual practitioner.[58] The illustration closely echoes the list of paraphernalia obtained from the *fattucchiero* in the Vatican version of the "Missione in prattica."

The anthropomorphic representations described in words as "frightful figures" and in watercolors as dark wooden carvings with contrasting bright details are exceedingly rare documents of eighteenth-century central-African figurative objects. The pictured figures display some of the traits characteristic of later anthropomorphic figures from the region. Wide-open white eyes capture the gaze of beholders. Starkly contrasting, richly textured materials enhance the wooden carvings, forming multisensory accumulative assemblages. Necks and legs are enhanced with additional material. Both figures' upper bodies form rounded cavities that could serve as receptacles for ingredients or empowering materials. The anthropomorphic carvings in fact lie among other types of containers, baskets and horns, in a juxtaposition that suggests that they too are vessels.

A human-shaped power figure collected in the Kongo in the later nineteenth century and now in the Ethnological Museum in Berlin exemplifies the striking visual effects summarily pictured in the anthropomorphic objects about to be destroyed in the watercolor (fig. 74). Feathers, animal skins, vegetal threads, pigments and resins of contrasting colors and textures surround the wooden structure as bundles, ties, belts, braces, and crown. The brilliant wide eyes and glass front of the box on the abdomen shine in bright contrast to the dark hue of the carving itself. Apart from the vibrantly colored, smooth face, the human features of the figure have all but disappeared under the surrounding materials, the box over the abdomen that the arms frame, and the thick layer of resin stuck with feathers at the top of the head. The object is constructed, on a formal level, as a receptacle for ingredients of various sorts, in a striking visual metaphor for its role as a vessel for invisible forces a specialist ensnared within its body.

The watercolor's caption is difficult to read. It explains how "The Missionary burns the House of a Witch [*fatucchiero*] filled with diabolical superstitions." These witches, it continues, "exercise with major freedom their diabolical office, with trickery and loss of many souls." Pushing his investigation further, the friar reports interrogating the repentant witch about his practice. "He answered that he had never seen or heard the devil speak and that he merely exercised such diabolical office . . . ," presumably for reasons articulated in the part of the text now missing. The longer version of the story, told in the Vatican copy of the "Missione in prattica," explains that the motivation of the *fattucchiero* was to "make himself revered, feared, and earn money to sustain himself."[59] With bravado contrary to his colleagues' sentiments about local witchcraft, the friar finally concludes that "in [his] opinion, if the devil appeared in any form, or talked to them,

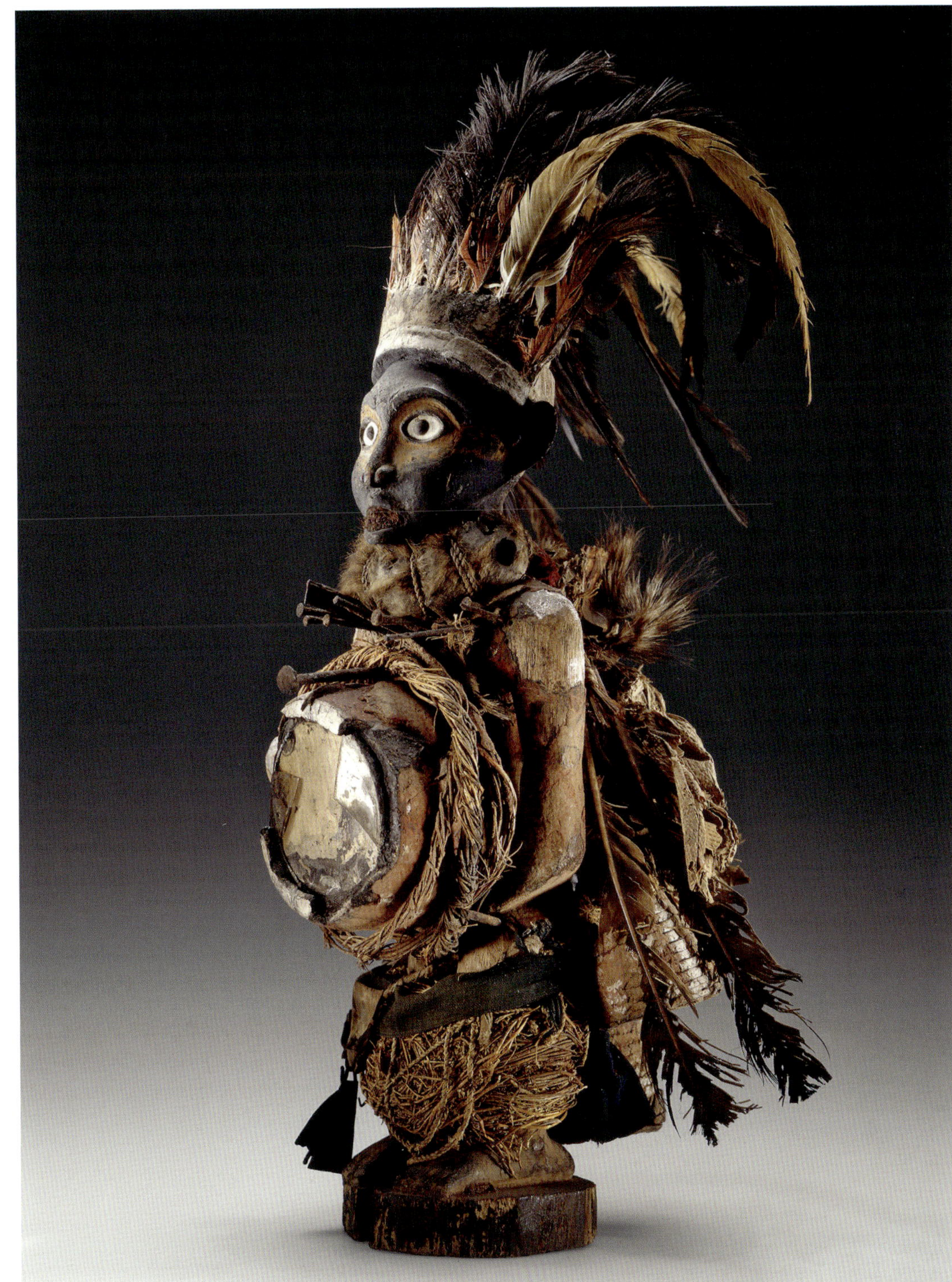

Figure 74

Unknown Kongo artist,
power figure (*nkisi lumweno*),
Republic of Congo, Congo
River, Vili (Bawili) people,
nineteenth century. Wood,
glass, feathers, fibers,
resin, iron, height 60 cm.
Collection of Robert Visser,
Ethnological Museum
of Berlin, III C 8105.
Photo: bpk Bildagentur /
Ethnologisches Museen zu
Berlin / Erik Hesmerg / Art
Resource, New York.

because these Africans [*ethiopi*] are so pusillanimous, they would ran away,"[60] and none would dare exercise "the art of witchcraft" anymore.[61]

The confidence with which Friar Bernardino advises his readers to destroy the temples "with apostolic zeal by fire" is the same as that with which Giovanni Belotti da Romano had recommended a similar treatment to future missionaries in an earlier manuscript of "very beneficial advice."[62] As for the contents of the temple, they could be saved from immediate destruction and remain in the possession of the missionary, available for the staging of a later spectacular sermon and public bonfire.[63] Luca da Caltanisetta reports storing on the floor "behind the door" of the convent the ritual paraphernalia he seized, waiting, sometimes for several weeks, for the occasion to put them to fruitful use in dramatic preaching.[64]

Once the idols were destroyed, the missionaries' strategy consisted in replacing them with Catholic items. They replaced condemnable local practices and paraphernalia with Christian rituals and objects. Merolla recommended relics as a substitute for the bark-cloth belts pregnant women wore. Ties made of consecrated palm leaves, and medals used at the time of baptism, should take the place of strings attached to young children for their protection.[65] Luca da Caltanisetta suggested that crosses and blessed palm branches could substitute for protective amulets.[66] The friars set out to win minds and souls by taking up arms on the battlefield of visual and material culture. They destroyed nefarious items and replaced them with Catholic images and objects that promoted an orthodox approach to the numinous and proper devotion to their one, true God. These visual tools, they believed, infused minds and molded souls with orthodox devotions

and acted efficiently as vectors of conversion and channels of Catholic piety.

Conclusion

Images were hard at work in the Capuchin central-African mission. The agents of that apostolate, as extirpators of idolatry and fighters of superstitions, were necessarily preoccupied with understanding the nature and form of local spiritual practices and instruments. They learned to identify what they called idols, grappling with the culturally relative nature and manifestations of the numinous. They then tackled the challenges of presenting the conceptual religious tools of central Africans through the visual strategies offered by European illusionistic realism to instruct future missionaries. Veterans taught novices that recognizing idolatry and replacing it with orthodoxy was an important goal of their mission that entailed finding and destroying the problematic objects, then replacing them with Catholic devotional paraphernalia.

However, although part of their work was aimed at changing local practices, the Capuchins' activities unfolded within the firm bounds of local structures of power, knowledge, and faith. They worked in central Africa at the invitation of local leaders and had to act according to the preexisting social, political, and religious mores, Christian or otherwise, which they had little latitude to change. In the background of these confident exposés of zealous extirpation and efficacious apostolic methods were many more stories of deep engagement and sustained collaboration between the friars and the local scholars and specialists on whom they relied in all aspects of their apostolate.

A central-African man and a European friar stroll together in an eerily peaceful landscape, engaged in conversation. They gently turn to each other to share thoughts about the awesome cliff they are approaching (figs. 41 and 97). No hint of power dynamics, let alone conflict, disturbs the balance of the carefully calibrated pair. The two men are similar in height, stand with equal confidence, and speak with uniform conviction. This is an unusual pairing of an African and a European in an image created in seventeenth-century Italy. At that time, the inhabitants of the African continent routinely appeared under the brush, burin, or etching needle of European image-makers as savages, subservient or laboring figures, biblical or anonymous characters, or decorative motifs, not as fully realized protagonists.[1] Yet this vignette is typical, maybe even emblematic, of the images that Capuchin friars created to showcase their relationship with the elite of Kongo and Angola, where they officiated as priests and missionaries in the seventeenth and eighteenth centuries.

In parts of their central-African visual and written chronicles not concerned with the elite or apostolic work, the friars portrayed men and women from Kongo and Angola under different, less even-handed guises. A page from the Parma Watercolors depicting life in Portuguese-controlled Angola includes central Africans as slaves (fig. 75 / plate 2). The six dark-skinned men wear striped liveries and what the text identifies as "silver collars," following the iconography of slavery in early modern European visual culture, which portrayed enslaved men, women, or children as emblems of status and refinement of those they served.[2] Central Africans here are not only laborers carrying hammocks and umbrellas, but dehumanized accessories adorning

CHAPTER 6

With "the Consent of the People, and the Secular Arm of the Prince"

and lending prestige to the Portuguese men who claimed them as their property alongside powdered wigs, tricorn hats, silver-pommel canes, and fashionable cassocks.

Elsewhere, the Capuchins sometimes expressed merely negative, at times truly odious, views of their central-African interlocutors.[3] Even the Word of God, one of them wrote, "is of little profit to these people [of the Kongo], for they are so engrossed in these errors and . . . so barbarous and of so little ability that in truth it seems that they only have the appearance of humanity."[4] Giovanni

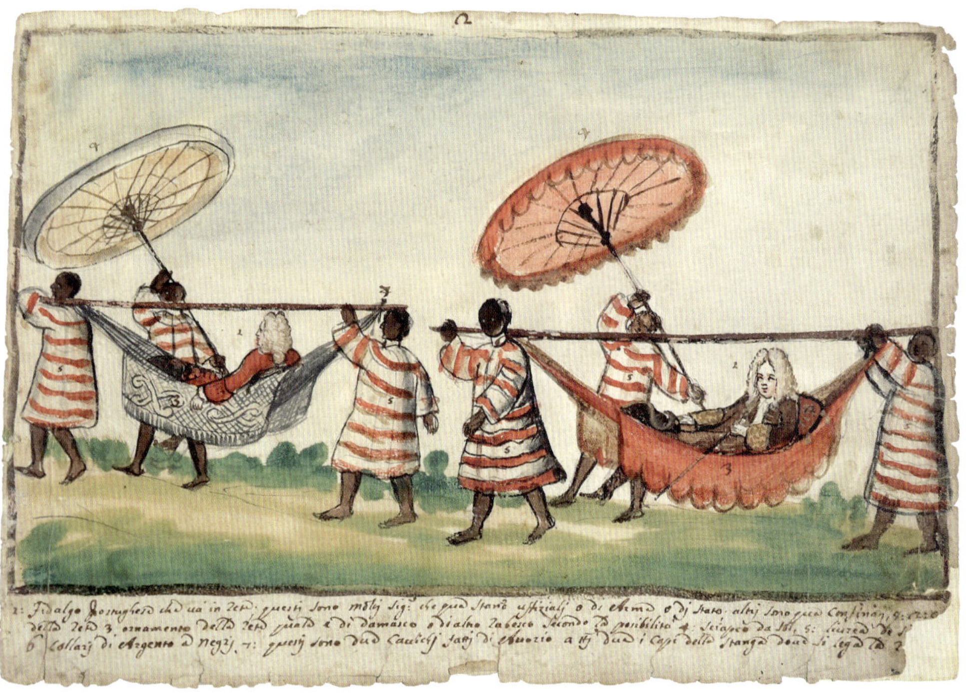

Figure 75

Unknown Capuchin artist, "Portuguese aristocrat[s] traveling in nets," late seventeenth century. Watercolor on paper, 34 × 24 cm. Parma Watercolors, Virgili Collection, fol. 2. Photo: author.

Antonio Cavazzi's fiery paintings about the Jagas in his "Missione Evangelica" manuscript revel with equal bite in scene after scene of human sacrifice and cannibalistic rituals (fig. 14). On a page titled "Sacrifice among the Jagas," the friar has pictured a man crouching on the ground being quartered alive by an axe-wielding man to the sound of a drum (fig. 76). A "caldron with human meat" already full of blood and limbs stands at the ready to the side. Two further captives await their fate in a pen, arms tied behind their backs, with too clear a view of the gruesome scene. In contrast to such bafflingly violent compositions or clichéd portrayals of black subservience in the colonial enclave of Portuguese Angola, the images of the practical guides depicting interactions between Capuchins and central Africans adopted a different tone. Even the presentation of potentially hair-raising topics such as witchcraft

or human sacrifices remained remarkably sober in the didactic compendia (figs. 69, 77, 78, plates 54–58, 68).

Some of the illustrations Cavazzi commissioned for his published *Istorica descrizione* book, which features the Pedras Negras landscape print, were to follow the templates of the exalted paintings he had made for his "Missione Evangelica" manuscript. But the vista, like the volume's other illustrations addressing Capuchin apostolic work in central Africa, follows the more even-keeled tone of the practical guides. There, in images directly concerned with the relationships between friars and local populations—in particular the elite—the friars consistently strive to suggest even standing between central-African greats and themselves. Of course, such texts and images describing a benevolent cooperation between Africans and Europeans are idealized views of what was often a dire, conflictual reality. By the time of the arrival of the friars in the mid-seventeenth century, participation in the commercial, religious, and diplomatic networks of the Atlantic world had shaken the central-African social, material, and spiritual environment to its core. Civil and foreign wars and the related encroachment of the Atlantic slave trade made violence and sociopolitical strife rampant. Friars were not impervious to this embattled landscape, which could at times impede, for instance, their safe passage from one locale to another. They also had a destabilizing role themselves as sometimes-overzealous proselytizers and not rarely as active participants in the slave trade.[5] And though they reported on conflicts in their written chronicles, their peaceful watercolors shied away from representing discord. Only two scenes show physical violence perpetrated against the friars: the martyrdom *in odium fidei* of

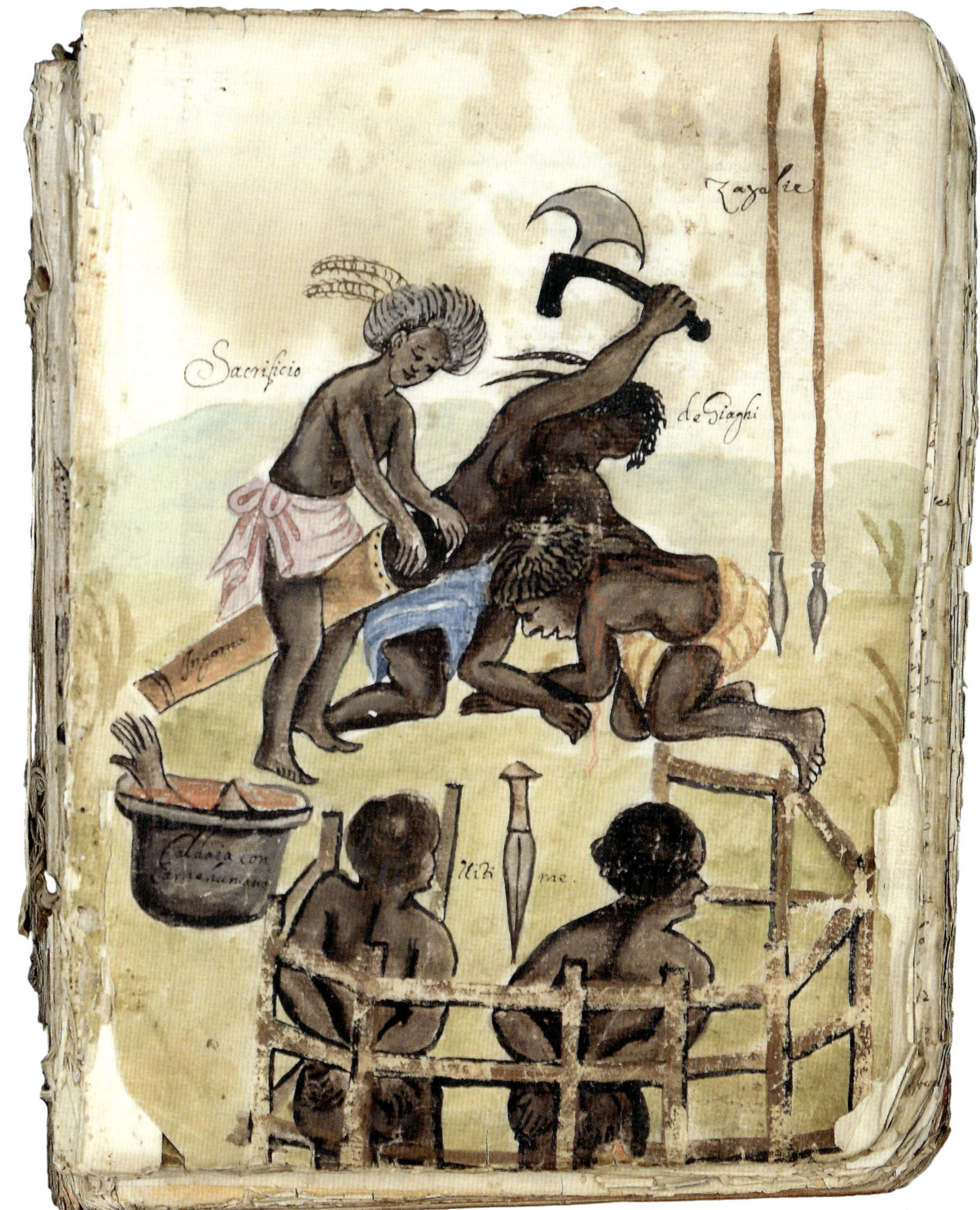

Figure 76

Giovanni Antonio Cavazzi, "Sacrifice among the Jagas." Watercolor and ink on paper, 17 × 21 cm. From Giovanni Antonio Cavazzi, "Missione Evangelica al Regno del Congo" (the Araldi manuscript), vol. A, front matter, p. iii. Gallerie Estensi, Biblioteca Estense Universitaria, Modena. Reproduced by permission of the Italian Ministry for Cultural Heritage and Activities and for Tourism.

Joris van Gheel in the Museo Franciscano ink panel, and Queen Njinga's capture of Buenaventura de Corella and Francisco de Veas in the Parma Watercolors (fig. 26 / plate 1 and plate 66).[6] Reciprocally, just three vignettes explicitly depict violent behavior on the part of the friars, all in scenes of idol-smashing zeal (figs. 72, 73, plates 64, 65).

In their idealized views of the apostolate in Kongo and Angola, Capuchins consistently downplayed the violence of the missionary environment as well as the difficulties they encountered in enjoining the deference they considered themselves due as men of the Church. In fact, the explicit goal of several of the practical-guide images was to teach novices how to command respect from their African hosts, hinting at the difficulty obtaining such deference presented. The zealous attempts at constructing a smooth account of the mission were not only marketing ploys to enlist future missionaries, or falsely modest glorification of Capuchin apostolic success. They were also expressions of the particular relationship that existed between the friars and central Africans in the early modern period. The views of Kongo and Angola they constructed, I argue in this chapter, reflected a unique sociopolitical missionary environment within the two regions and formed a genre of missionary images without parallel in the early modern world.

Picturing Fraught Cooperation

Friar Bernardino d'Asti explains repeatedly in his circa 1750 practical guide to the central-African mission, the "Missione in prattica," the importance of insisting on key elements of etiquette and precedence, which will ensure a missionary's standing among central Africans. When the missionary arrives at a new locale, for example, villagers should come meet him on the road and welcome him with a procession.[7] Before the friar enters a town or village, the local leader himself should come greet him (figs. 77, 78). Only the ruler should use a carpet for kneeling during Mass (plate 70 top).[8] Both the friar and the ruler, and only they, should have seats, and, the Parma Watercolors text adds, friars should always carry one with them because, "when one preaches or catechizes or goes to visit one of those princes, he who does not bring his own chair does not get one."[9] In their vignettes, the friars paint rulers and missionary figures almost as mirror images of one another. As in the landscape print, the image-makers show them in similar bodily attitudes and on a par in height, entourage, and regalia (plate 60; figs. 60, 77, 78).[10] Friars stand or sit on the same level as their African counterparts; they are, like them, surrounded by a retinue and walk protected by an umbrella, albeit of a plain color, in a nod, no doubt, to the humility their Franciscan rule demanded.

This contrived mise-en-scène reflects the delicate balance on which the Capuchin mission depended. If the central-African elite could see the friars' presence as beneficial—it was, after all, Kongo rulers themselves who sought from the pope the dispatch of the Franciscan mission—they also keenly perceived its drawbacks. They welcomed the friars with the hope of benefiting from their stay in many ways, including spiritually. In the Kongo, Christianity and its material culture played a central role in the assertion of political legitimacy, and provincial as well as central rulers saw their powers reinforced by direct access to ordained clerics and the rituals they could perform. Priests remained a rarity in the kingdom, where a seminary never opened in spite

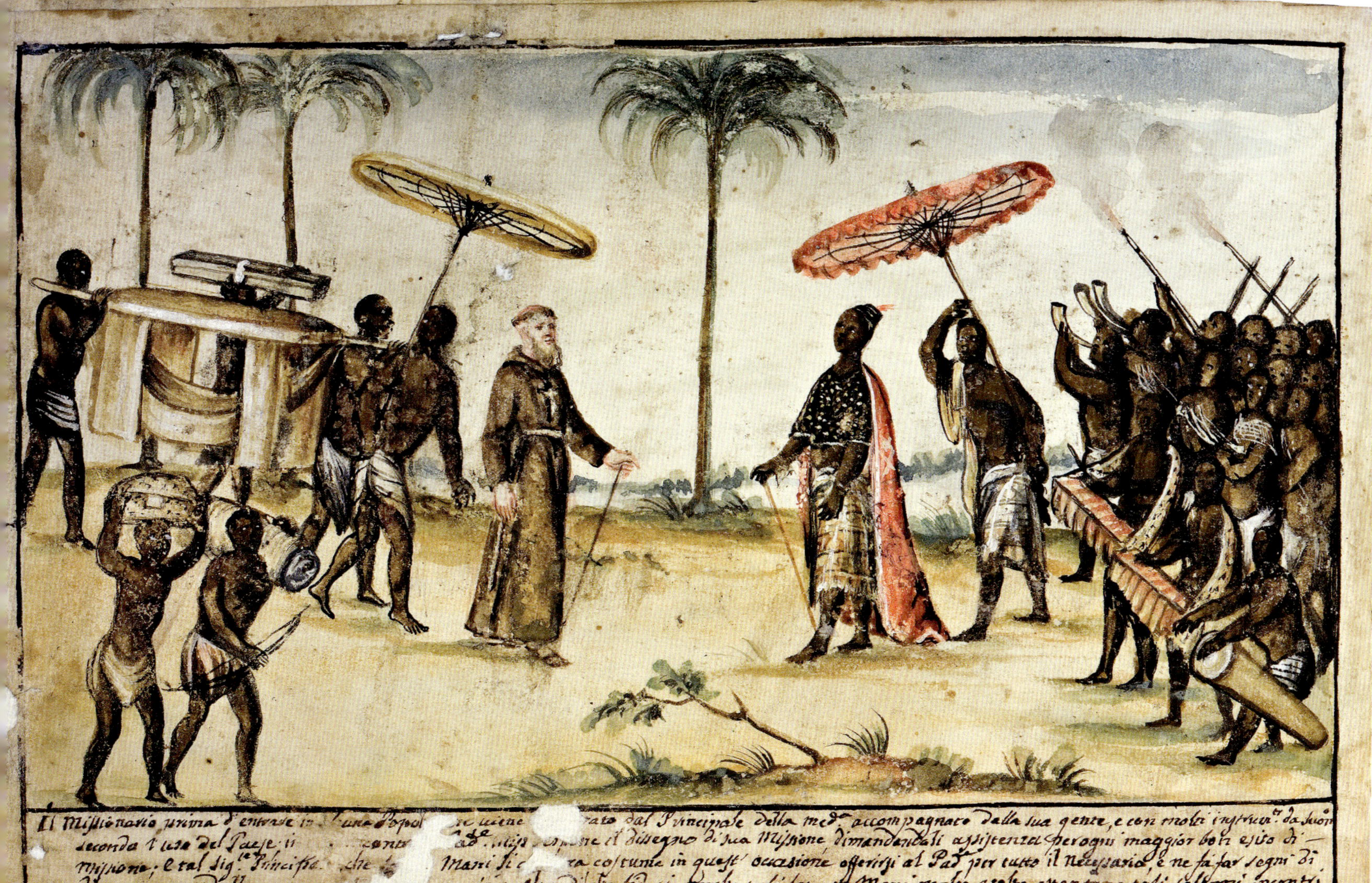

Il Missionario prima d'entrare in [...] una Popol[azio]ne viene [incont]rato dal Principale della med.ᵃ accompagnato dalla sua gente, e con molti instrum.ᵗⁱ da suon'
seconda l'uso del Paese; il [...] ad [...] esporre il disegno di sua Missione dimandandoli assistenza; per ogni maggior bon esito di
missione; e tal sig.ᵉ Principe [...] che [...] Mani si c[...]ra costume in quest'occasione offerisi al Pad.ᵉ per tutto il Necessario, e ne fa far segni di
dimostrazione dalla sua [...] non v'è molto di che fidarsi perche tali Sova[ni] ò Mani molte volte ostentano tali solenni incontri
al missionario per loro fini [...] ma sti[...] e per [...] temporali convenienze ———

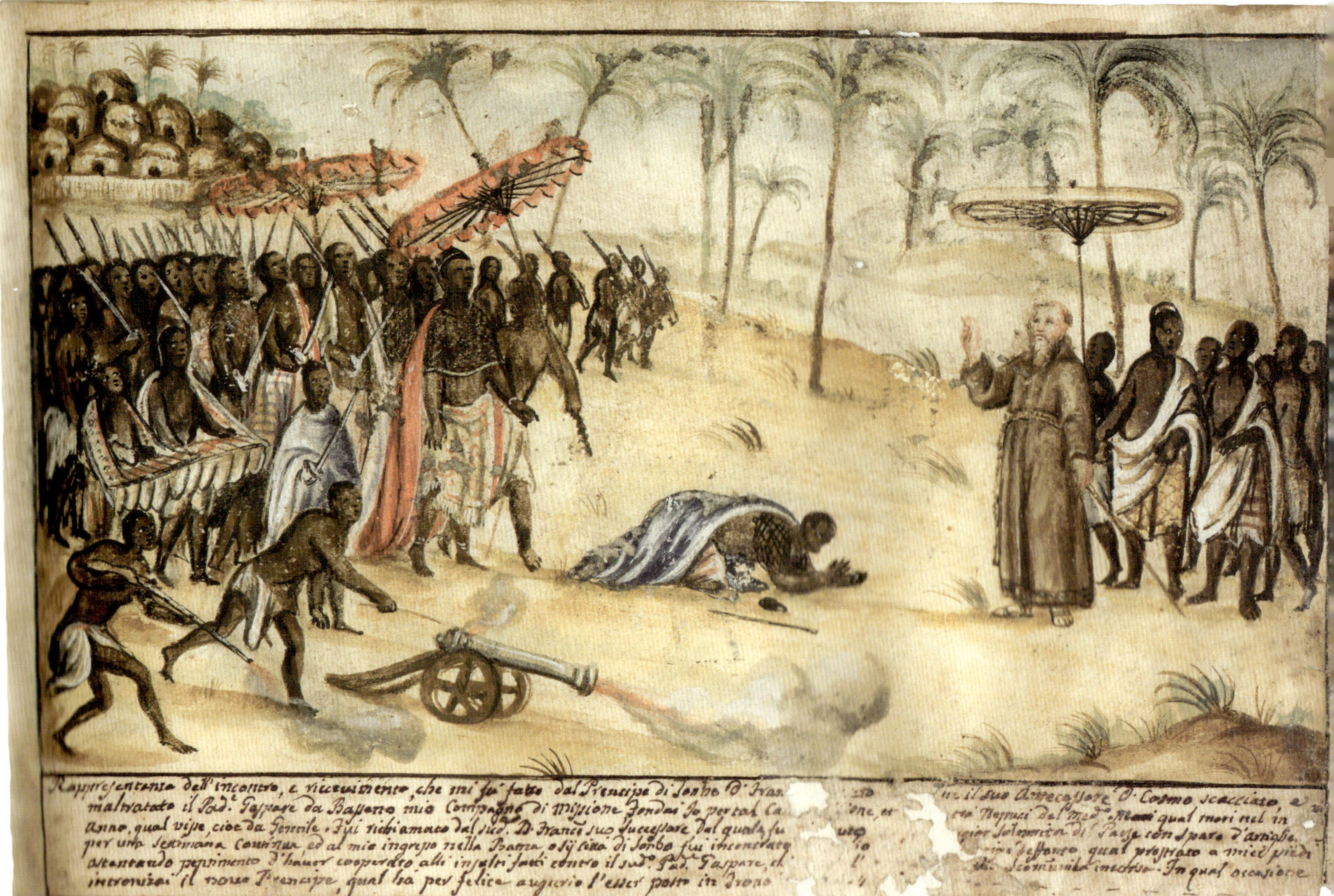

Rappresentanza dell'incontro, e riceuimento, che mi fu' fatto dal Prencipe di Sonho D. Fran...
maltratato il Pad.e Gaspare da Bassano mio Compagno di missione Fondai Io per tal Ca...
anno, qual visse, cioè da Gentile. Fui richiamato dal sud.o D. Francu suo successore dal quale fu...
per una settimana continua ed al mio ingresso nella Boatta o sij sito di Sorbo fui incontrato...
attestando pentimento d'hauer cooperato alli insulti fatti contro il sud.o Pad. Gaspare, et
intronizai il noue Prencipe, qual ha per felice augurio l'esser posto in Trono
...il suo Antecessore D. Cosmo scacciato, e
...Nemici del med.o Mani qual morì nel in
...gior solennità del Paese con spare d'artigliarie
...desteuro qual prostrato a miei piedi
...scomunita incorsa. In qual occasione

of many attempts, and it was mainly local religious leaders called *mestres* (as discussed below) who kept the Church and its teachings alive.[11] However, these important figures in Kongo Christianity did not perform sacraments. What is more, the symbolic weight that ordained clerics could impart to such events as the coronation of the king of Kongo or the enthronement of leaders was unequaled, and aspiring princes would go to great lengths to ensure the presence of priests in these rituals.[12] Outside of the Kongo, the friars' welcome waxed and waned according to local political priorities, as best illustrated in Queen Njinga's cold reception of the friars pictured in plate 66 (fig. 27), followed by her warm embrace of their apostolate. Plate 60 (fig. 105), in turn, displays the welcome a ruler of the Ndembu area, a cluster of polities between Kongo, Angola, and Ndongo—including, for example, Mbwila—gave a friar.[13]

Committed Catholics, recent converts, or heathens, central Africans derived great prestige from hosting friars as a demonstration of their access to long-distance networks, but also as a means to secure much-sought-after Christian paraphernalia. Capuchins brought with them thousands of medals (e.g., that in fig. 59), rosaries, crosses, and devotional images, which they distributed strategically as spiritual gifts or used as bargaining tools to smooth the path of the mission. "Necessity," one of the friars explains, could dictate that "a rosary with a thread of red silk with a medal" be traded for a hen. "Alms for the love of God being little known among [central Africans]," the same friar continues, it was, "in a nutshell, thanks to the rosaries and chaplets [that] I could provide for myself as best as I could."[14] The devotional items in fact functioned as efficiently as *nzimbu*, the shell currency used in the region. "For the rest of the way," the Minorite finally admits, "with *zimbi* [*sic*], rosaries, medals, and chaplets I could get myself carried ahead."[15] Seventeenth-century historian of the Capuchin mission Mateo de Anguiano also comments on this monetized dynamic between the mendicants and their flock. "These people do not usually offer food to [those] whom they do not know; instead, when asked for something, they immediately answer *pagamento, pagamento*, a word they have learned from the Portuguese who trade around there; and it was even necessary to give them some medal or Caravaca cross when they gave the Fathers even the smallest thing."[16]

The arrival of the missionaries was thus often a welcome occasion in central-African towns and villages, particularly within the Christian Kongo. Rulers gladly received the friars with pomp and circumstance, in ceremonies that, in fact, increased their own prestige as much or even more than that of the friars. Yet this mutually advantageous relationship could quickly become fraught, and the delicate balance of power on which it depended easily fell apart. For the friars, local rulers often took too many liberties with the teachings of the Church. Central-African rulers, on their end, thought that the Capuchins fast became onerous and overstepped their position. The friars' main bargaining chips in these situations were the prestige-enhancing sacraments and imported objects they could bestow upon their hosts, which they could as easily withhold as proffer.

A vignette of the Turin "Missione in prattica" records a tense face-off between a friar and a ruler (fig. 78), bringing into focus the tenuous situation addressed implicitly in the rest of a corpus, dedicated to conferring generic advice rather than

Figure 78 (opposite)

Bernardino Ignazio da Vezza d'Asti, "Meeting and Reception I was given by the Prince of Soyo," ca. 1750. Watercolor on paper, 19.5 × 28 cm. From "Missione in prattica," Biblioteca civica Centrale di Torino, MS 457, fol. 9r. Photo courtesy of the Biblioteca civica Centrale, Turin.

Figure 79 (opposite)

Léonard Gaultier, frontispiece to Claude d'Abbeville, *Histoire de la Mission des Pères Capucins en l'Isle de Maragnan* (Paris: Imprimerie de François Huby, 1614). Engraving, 15.3 × 9.4 cm (plate mark). National Library of Portugal, Lisbon, D.S. XVII—24. Photo courtesy of the National Library of Portugal.

reporting on specific events. The page depicts the aftermath of a dispute that unfolded in 1743 between the ruler of the coastal Kongo province of Soyo, Cosme Barreto da Silva, and Bernardino d'Asti, the maker of the vignette, about the prince's right to marry the sister of his deceased wife, against Catholic kinship rules. The disagreement had tested the relative power of the two parties in the Capuchins' oldest mission in central Africa. Faced with Bernardino's refusal to grant him a dispensation for the marriage, Dom Cosme devised a stratagem to fool the friar. With the help of some of his subjects, he planned to bring the woman he chose in front of the priest, pretending she was another, more acceptable match, and have him perform the ceremony. It is worth noting here the weight that the prince of Soyo gave to having an ordained priest preside over the ritual, even if it involved scheming and deception. Bernardino eventually discovered the plot and, with great anger, excommunicated the ruler, "who died as he had lived, that is to say, a heathen."[17] He threatened whoever else might be an accessory to the ploy with the same fate, and left the province.[18]

The vignette in figure 78 records the first encounter between the successor of Dom Cosme and Bernardino. The friar and the new prince lock eyes in a haughty exchange of gazes. Each ostentatiously displays the attributes of his office and showcases his resolve. It is a key moment in which the temporal and spiritual leaders silently negotiate power and hierarchy in the new regime. Because of the damage to the text, it is difficult to know who the prostrated man in the middle of the page may be, but he is likely a repentant associate of the former prince. Part cautionary tale, part proud testament to the friar's hard-won victory over an impious ruler, the

vignette provides valuable perspective from which to approach the other watercolors in the manuscript that directly deal with the relationship between friars and local elite. These images, as direct complements and adamant correctives to the fraught interactions behind the Soyo vignette, offer views of smooth, peaceful dealings between friars and rulers in which the egalitarian mirroring between the two is almost perfect (plate 60, figs. 60, 77).

Envisioning European Missionaries and Local Populations Elsewhere in the Early Modern World

The representation of the relationship between friars and local populations in Kongo and to a large extent Angola as even and cooperative, albeit for reasons of necessity and mutual interest, strikingly differs from depictions of European missionary activities elsewhere in the early modern world, especially compositions regarding contemporaneous Franciscan or Jesuit endeavors. Few of the documents about European missions abroad are as profusely visual as the central-African Capuchin corpus, but a number, in particular from the seventeenth century onward, include at least an illustrated frontispiece announcing the contents of the book. These opening plates for missionary chronicles of the 1600s often feature their main protagonists depicted in monumental, protohagiographic form. More rarely, they include depictions of local people, in attempts to characterize the nature of the relationship that the missionaries claimed to have established with them, whether or not that report was anything more than fantasy.

The 1614 frontispiece to Capuchin Claude d'Abbeville's history of his mission in the Brazilian region of Maranhão is among the examples that provide a counterpoint to the even relationship between Africans and Europeans presented in the pages of Capuchin books and manuscripts about central Africa (fig. 79).[19] In Friar Claude's frontispiece, small, barely clad Indigenous men and women flank monumental, ceremoniously dressed European figures. At the top of the page's architectural frame, Indians implore the allegory of "France, the eldest daughter of the Church," pictured as a large, seated, and crowned woman holding the insignia of French kingship, the heraldic lily and the hand of justice. Below, on either side of the title cartouche, a haloed saint towers in heroic scale over a diminutive Indigenous figure kneeling at his feet. To the left, Saint Peter or his successor, the pope, looks down at the Brazilian man summarily dressed with three feathers attached to the front of a belt, hands joined in prayer and face lifted up. The crowned saint offers him the keys to heaven with one hand, while lifting his right fingers in blessing or admonition. His paternalistic stance and gesture echo the text flowing out of his mouth, the words of Saint Peter himself from the Acts 10.34: "In very deed I perceive that God is not a respecter of persons [i.e., treats all people alike]."[20] The following verse, not included on the page but clearly implied in the scene, further explains how, "in every nation, he that feareth him and worketh justice is acceptable to him." This statement, addressing the generosity of God and the Roman Church personified in the image of the pope, takes on an additional, sensationalistic dimension in its juxtaposition to the vignette directly under the two men, picturing the cannibalistic appetites of three Indigenous people. The chilling tableau of a Garden of Eden gone awry both enhances the generosity and inclusivity

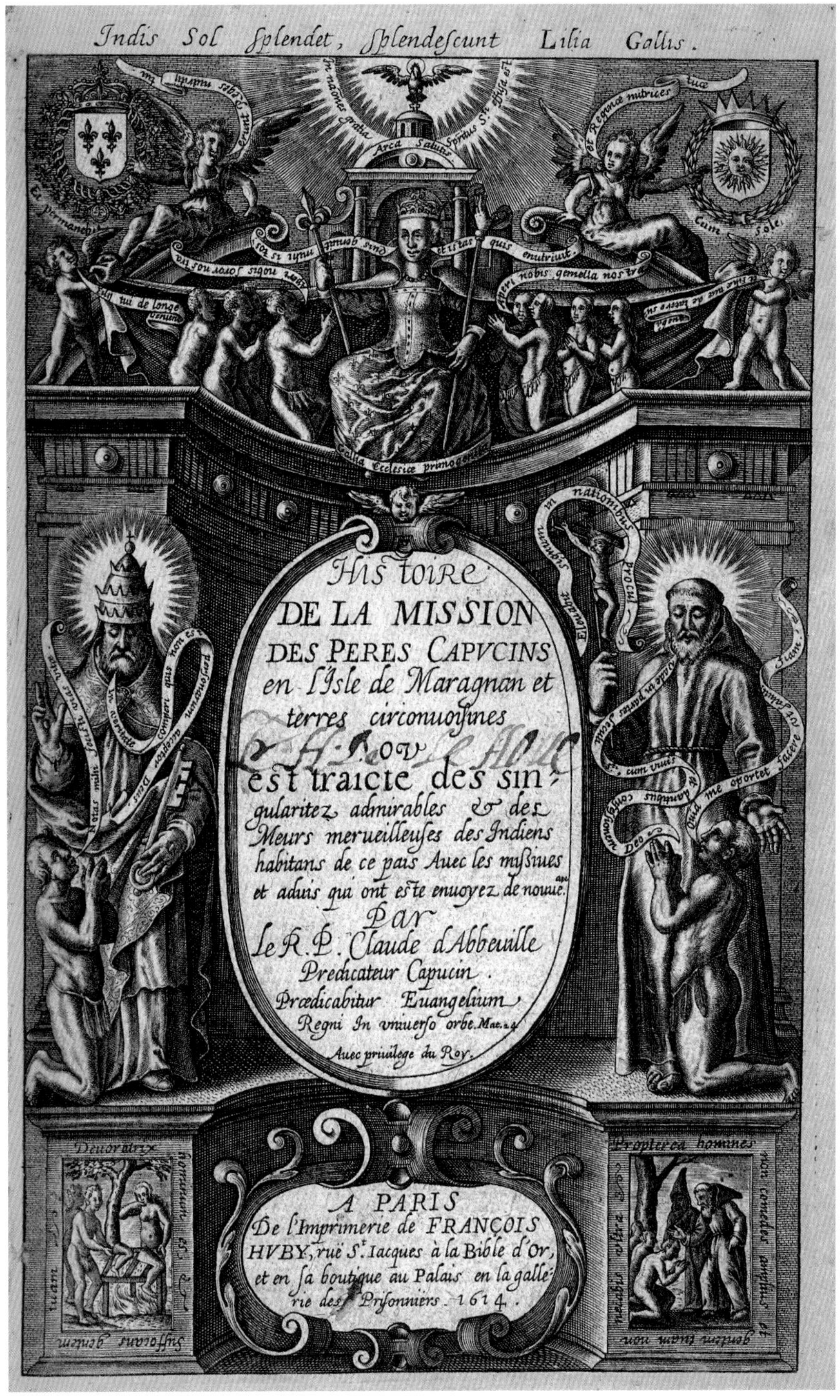

of the Church and justifies its takeover of the Indigenous people. Pacified and docile, the Brazilian man has taken refuge almost between the legs of Saint Peter and, kneeling on top of his robes, coyly replies, "Thou hast made known to me the ways of life."[21]

Other biblical passages link this side of the composition to its pendant to the right. Phrases from Ezekiel 36:13 label the anthropophagous scene to the bottom left: "Thou art a devourer of men, and one that suffocatest thy nation."[22] The Scriptures then carry over to the parallel vignette to the right, presumably showing the same three figures receiving baptism from two friars, framed with the next verse: "Therefore thou shalt devour men no more, nor destroy thy nation any more" (Ezekiel 36:14).[23] The conversion scene, in turn, serves as a base for the figure of a triumphant haloed figure in the same garb as the friars, probably Saint Francis, holding his crucifix high in his right fist as his standard, while extending his left hand to cup the head of a kneeling Indigenous man clad in a thin belt of feathers.[24] "What must I do, that I may be saved?"[25] asks the Brazilian. "Go to the side of the holy age," the friar replies, "with them who live and give praise to God."[26]

The frontispiece makes abundantly clear the hierarchy at play in the Capuchin imaginary of their Brazilian mission in Maranhão. Europeans dominate the scene as monumental, hallowed, and haloed figures towering over the Indigenous people. The domination is presented in symbolic and iconographic terms as well as in physical ones. Indigenous bodies are not only placed within an architectural frame that stands almost as an arch of triumph, but also explicitly controlled and tamed. The saintly garbed figure standing for the Capuchin

missionaries physically dominates the man before him. He holds him still behind his muscular right leg and foot, blocking him from the front. His left hand, extended in a gesture of invitation, is also ready to cup and hold the neophyte's head, should the visual spell in which the crucifix ostensibly holds him break.

Another type of composition for missionary frontispieces to works about the Americas illustrates the relationship between clerics and local populations in equally unambiguous hierarchical terms by isolating the two groups in distinct, starkly delineated parts. On the opening page for Recollect Franciscan friar Gabriel Sagard's account of his voyage in Huron-Wendat country, published in Paris in 1632, two friars stand firmly in an architectural frame (fig. 80). They look up toward the name of God spelled in Hebrew letters at the top of the page, staring past three pairs of Indigenous men and women, situated above them in a register of their own. Initials identify the haloed friars as "S.F.," for Saint Francis, and "B.F.M.D.V.," possibly for Sagard's illustrious predecessor in the American missions, the "Bienheureux Frère Martin de Valence," one of the apostolic twelve responsible for the establishment of the Franciscan mission in Mesoamerica.[27] Above the saint and the blessed man, six men and women, the inhabitants of the "land of the Hurons," stand in a sparse landscape rather than a classical architectural frame. They use simple tools, display blunt weapons, or dance while holding implements of various sorts. Feathers and scant clothing would have marked them as savages in the eyes of the intended European readers of the book.[28] So would have their position on the page, dwelling in a world of their own, oblivious to the friars. The contradistinction the image makes between Europeans and "Hurons," civilization and savagery, carries on to the bottom of the print. The classical architectural elevation enshrining the two Franciscans also frames, in the front panels of its base, a "hut [*cabane*]," a "tomb [*sepulcra*]," and a "canoe [*canot*]." These objects illustrate Indigenous building, religion, and technology while drawing a stark contrast between their ephemeral materials and simple shapes and European architecture and technologies of knowledge and communication. The hut has a single room, one door, no windows, and the very name *cabane* suggests a construction of impermanent material. The tomb, in turn, is a gable roof atop four pillars, open to the four winds. Without any indication of scale, the canoe resembles more an empty nutshell than an impressive feat of design. In counterpoint, the perspectival rendering of a classical stone façade suggests permanence, refinement, and historical depth. The stone construction frames the Indigenous group as well as the products of their manufacture. Alphabetic writing further encloses them in a vise of its own, the canoe held between the split syllables of the word *canot*, and the oblivious three couples at the top between the name of God in Hebrew letters above and the monogram of Christ in Roman letters below.

The ways in which these gestures of contrast and opposition between self and Others created and enshrined notions of savagery and civilization in early modern European discourse is well known (on which, see further in chapter 7 below). The visual rhetoric that these images deploy to characterize the relationship between European missionaries and non-European peoples envision a rapport based on separation, rather than collaboration, and hierarchy, rather than parity, contrary to the interactions portrayed in Capuchin images of central Africa.

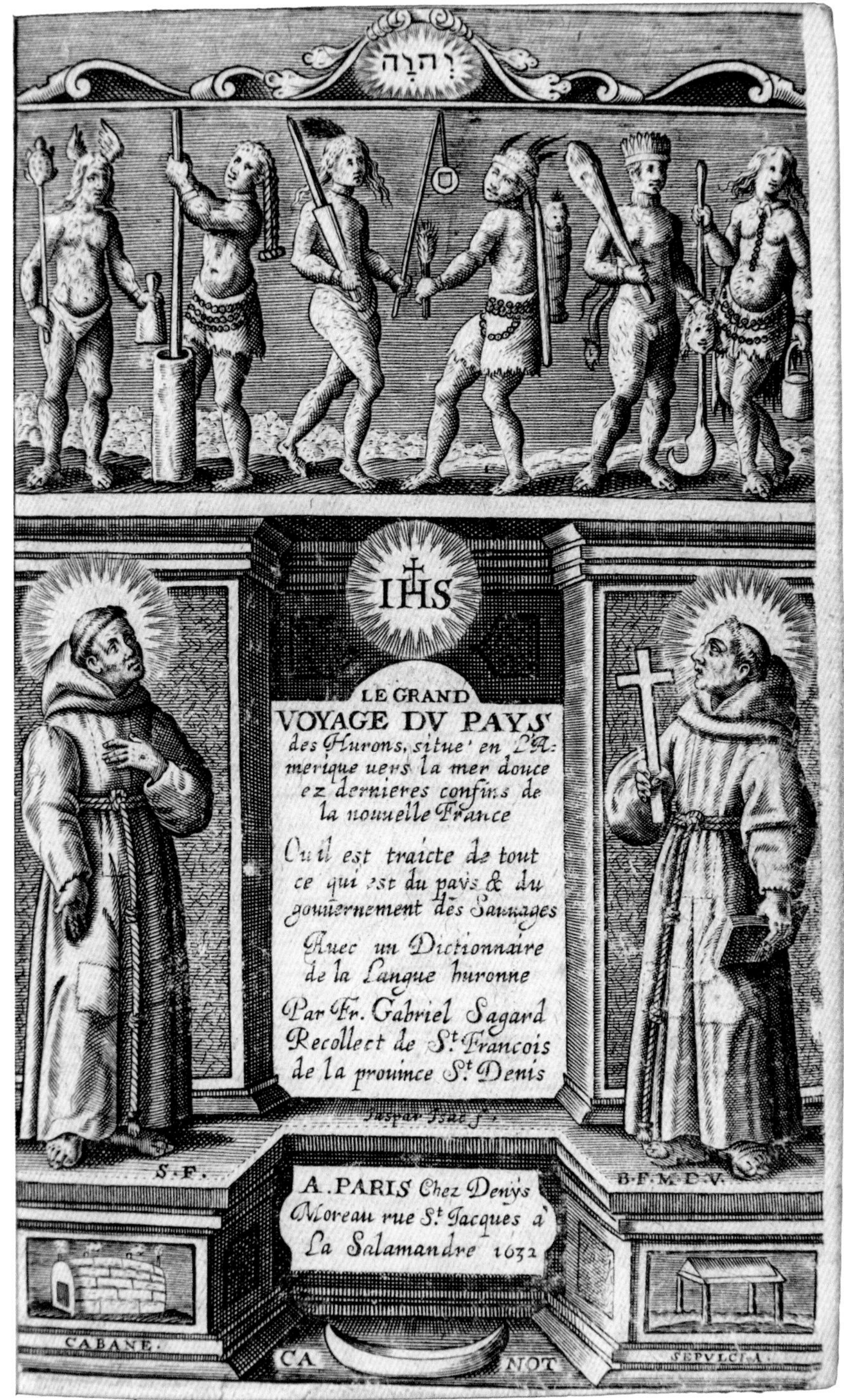

The works of Jesuit Alonso de Sandoval, active in the early seventeenth century in the Caribbean port of Cartagena de Indias among women and men caught in the machinery of the Atlantic slave trade, offer rare comparanda for the central-African images that feature illustrations of missionary work among Africans. The frontispiece for the first (and only) volume of the second edition of his treatise on Africans and apostolic work among the enslaved in the Americas repeats some aspects found in the two types of compositions discussed above (fig. 81).[29] It presents two heroic figures of Jesuit missionary history in monumental scale flanking the title cartouche at the center of the page: Saint Francis Xavier, the famed apostle of the Indies, to the left, and Andrés de Oviedo, missionary to Ethiopia, to the right.[30] Two rondels in the upper corners show them, or perhaps generic missionary figures, baptizing small crowds of kneeling converts.[31] Only in the imaginary space of a biblical scene does an African under the guise of a Magus fully inhabit the pictured space on a par with European-looking characters in the Flemish-born, Madrid-based engraver Juan de Noort's vignette at the center top of the frontispiece. Unlike the kneeling figures in the rondels, pictured in starkly diminutive scale and barely clad, the black king is of equal size to the other protagonists and dressed in equally lavish regalia. The black magus has been a well-known figure in Flemish and Iberian visual culture at least since the sixteenth century and features here as part of Alonso de Sandoval's complex and fundamentally paradoxical argumentation in support both of Africans' spiritual standing and of the institutions that destined them to chattel slavery.[32] Sandoval, literary historian Larissa Brewer-García has argued, conceived of blackness as "an immutable

visible *and* moral stain to black bodies due to Ham's sin," a stain that marked them as natural slaves. Yet he also vehemently argued in favor of the possibility of their salvation for, he writes, "what is impossible for nature is easy for grace."[33] The frontispiece opens a volume containing a geographic and cultural description of the African continent. A second volume, which never appeared but was, like tome 1, to elaborate on Sandoval's earlier 1627 publication, would have formed a manual for ministry among the Africans recently arrived in South America and destined to live there in enslavement.[34]

The whitening of Africans' and other dark-skinned people's souls through baptism is one of the themes of the frontispiece, and a topos ambiguously rendered in the binary white-and-black print medium.[35] Neither the African magus nor the crowds receiving baptism are shown in tones or shading simulating dark complexion. Hair texture and facial features alone suggest physical difference between them and Europeans. This very well may be a visual evocation of the whitening of their souls through Christian redemption. Radiating saintly haloes around the head of Jesus or Saint Francis Xavier further the trope of light and brightness as visible manifestations of godliness. However, it is common to see Africans pictured in early modern prints in light shading or none at all, either in representations eschewing any physical markers of race or in ones that do not rely on skin color.[36] The second half of the seventeenth century did see more instances of dark complexion figured in print, but compared to such representations and in contrast to Sandoval's frontispiece, the appearance of central Africans in Capuchin prints as visibly dark skinned is notable, a deliberate choice marking racial identity in figures otherwise pictured in pious, Christian attitudes.

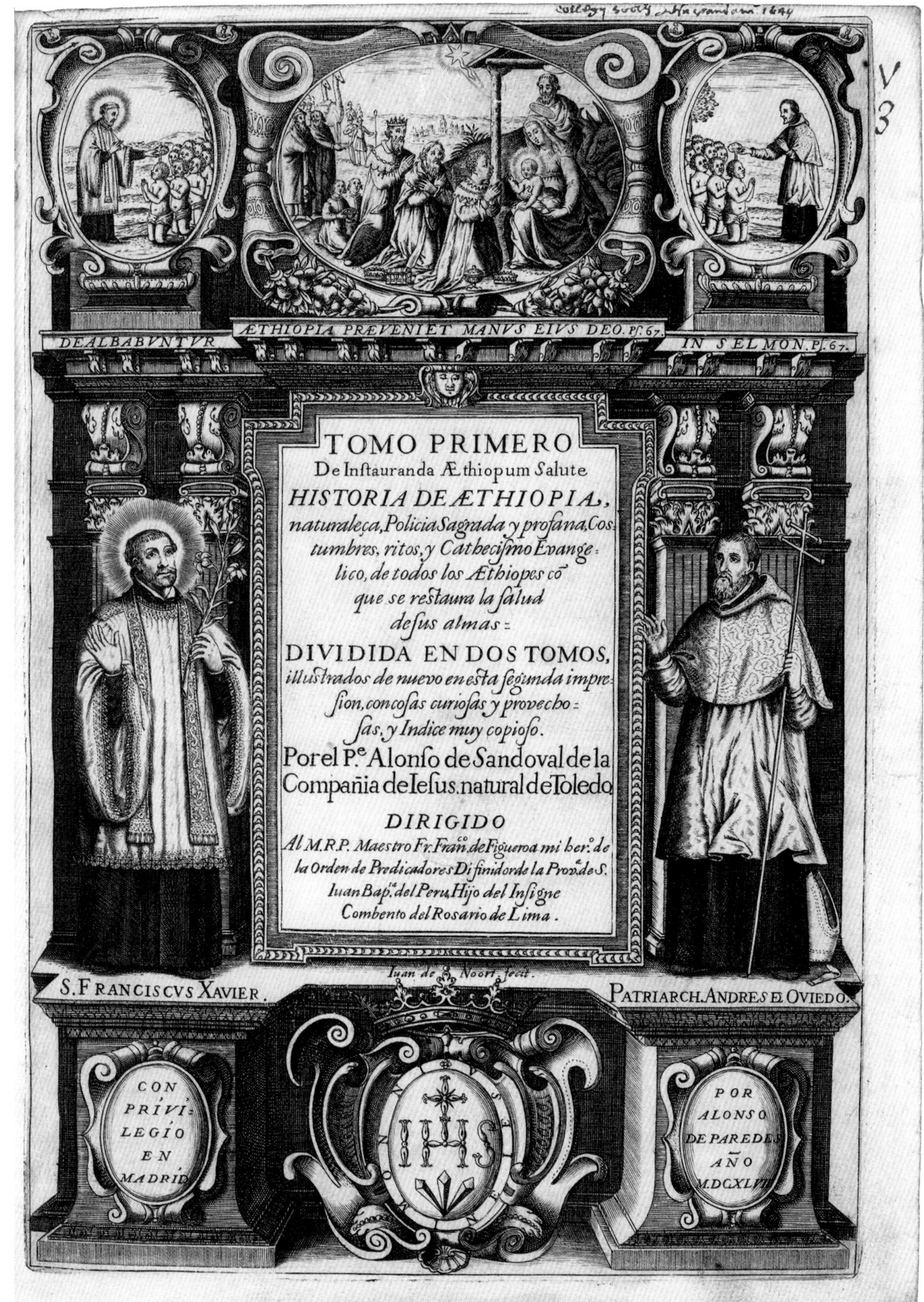

Figure 81

Juan de Noort, frontispiece to Alonso de Sandoval, *De Instauranda Aethiopum Salute* (Madrid: Alonso de Paredes, 1647). Copperplate engraving on paper, 28 × 20 cm. Heidelberg University Library, B 9620 Folio RES:1. Photo courtesy of the Heidelberg University Library.

Beyond considerations of skin color, the visual tropes illustrating the relationship between missionaries and catechumens within Sandoval's frontispiece unfold like those in Claude d'Abbeville's or Gabriel Sagard's opening illustrations. In *De Instauranda Aethiopum Salute* and the *Histoire de la Mission . . . en l'Isle de Maragnan*, missionaries stand in heroic scale and hieratic stance. Converts of diminutive size and in minimal clothing kneel sheepishly at the feet of their spiritual saviors (figs. 79 and 81). In the *Voyage du pays des Hurons*, clerics and potential converts dwell in separate realms, the former aware of the latter, but not vice versa (fig. 80). The saint and the blessed man turn their gazes to the Indigenous group, ready to see their followers irrupt into the Americans' realm. At play in all three compositions is the mechanics of Europe's creation of Otherness, ushering in newly defined conceptions of difference couched as inferiority and instrumentalized as justification for spiritual and colonial takeover as well as enslavement. Europe's encounters with distant peoples as a result of seaborne voyages starting in the fifteenth century yielded intense debates on its own shores about the nature and diversity of mankind, which took visual form, for instance, in the multifaceted illustrations incorporated in maps of faraway lands.[37] These reckonings and their visual manifestations were politicized into statements naturalizing European ambitions of control over and exploitation of peoples now framed as Others and inferiors in ever-increasing numbers of chronicles about European dealings with lands and peoples overseas.[38] By the seventeenth century, European artists and patrons had established a full-fledged iconography of Otherness as savagery or, at best, imperfect civilization, which effloresced into a robust visual culture whose impact continuously grew, for profit not only political but commercial, in the hands of enterprising editors.[39]

The seventeenth-century missionary frontispieces discussed here participated in this visual culture and drew heavily from what was by then the established iconography of Otherness as savagery. Their makers used heroic scale, architectural framing, and written inscriptions—the latter two emblems par excellence of European civilization—in eminently readable statements about the role of missionaries in the project of empire-making within colonial and protocolonial contexts. Spaniard Alonso de Sandoval and Frenchmen Claude d'Abbeville and Gabriel Sagard hailed from countries with definite colonial stakes or ambitions, and their missionary efforts depended on their respective Crowns for funding and support.[40] Their visual statements of an asymmetric power relationship and racialized conceptions of social, cultural, and political backwardness or advancement fully participated in the colonial projects.

Jarringly plain in their presentation of Europeans as different from and superior to the people they encountered overseas, the frontispieces seem almost comically naïve. Europeans are large, individualized, clad, Christian, and standing on classical stone architecture; Others are smaller scaled, indistinct, near-naked, heathen, and dwelling in spaces barely defined by a barren landscape here or a lonely tree there. With their heavy-handed rhetoric, these images are efficient visual statements, representative of deep, formative currents in early modern Europe's conception and representation of itself and its place in the world as civilized, superior, and rightfully dominant. This perception emerged in a deliberate translation of overseas landings as discoveries and of encountered people as Others and savages (as discussed further in chapter 7). Europe's modern subject as well as its overseas imperial projections arose from and reinforced this mode of envisioning novelty and managing difference, in an ever-strengthening worldview that would have deep cultural, political, and social consequences globally from the early modern period onward. The Capuchin central-African images, however, do not fit this historical arc.

Missionary Images Beyond the Colony

While the missionary images opening the works of Sagard, Sandoval, and Claude d'Abbeville presented overseas catechization as part of a European project of territorial conquest and political takeover paired with a rapidly solidifying ideology of racial supremacy, works derived from the Capuchin central-African missions, and most clearly their frontispieces, featured compositions illustrating a markedly different position. At the core of the distinction was the political situation within which the central-African missions took place. Apart from stays within the Portuguese *conquista* of Angola, friars acted in central Africa within polities that remained independent from European colonial control. The Capuchin mission in central Africa, Giuseppe Monari da Modena warned, could not operate "without the consent of the people, and the secular arm of the Prince."[41]

The *Istorica descrizione* opens with an image in which kneeling Capuchins in Franciscan garb and dark-skinned African men in short, ragged loincloths marvel together at the apparition of the Immaculate Conception (fig. 82). The Virgin, standing on a crescent moon supported by the heads of two

angels, appears alongside flying putti in a resplendent beam of light. On the ground, friars and Africans kneel, faces turned up to the heavenly vision. Between sky and earth, a ribbon bears the words of Isaiah 18 from the Vulgate: "Go, ye swift angels, to a nation rent and torn in pieces: to a terrible people, after which there is no other: to a nation expecting and trodden under foot, whose land the rivers have spoiled."[42] Cavazzi chose a passage of Scriptures he deemed appropriate to introduce a book about missionary activity in central Africa. The Kongo fit particularly well the description as a (once) powerful and expanding kingdom, and certainly a land traversed by many rivers, including the great Congo and its many tributaries.

Cavazzi had already used the quote in his "Missione Evangelica" manuscript, on a frontispiece-like image tucked, in the latest state of the manuscript, between the pages of the third of the opus's three codices (fig. 83). In this instance he had taken some liberty with the text, which he might have quoted from memory while penning the image in Angola: "Under the protection of the Holy Virgin Mary, go swift messengers to the ends of Ethiopia, to a scattered nation and to a people waiting. Chapter XVIII." The image itself is very similar to its published counterpart, with the floating Virgin and the congregated missionaries and Africans. In fact, Cavazzi himself had commissioned the prints for the *Istorica descrizione* from Paolo da Lorena and had provided him with sketches on which to base his compositions (see chapter 1 above). For the frontispiece, Friar Paolo drew from Cavazzi's design but also from one of his earlier compositions for Ignazio Carnago's 1655 volume on Marian cults, the *Città di Refugio* (fig. 84). In this earlier plate, the pope, clerics, friars, and crowned heads all kneel

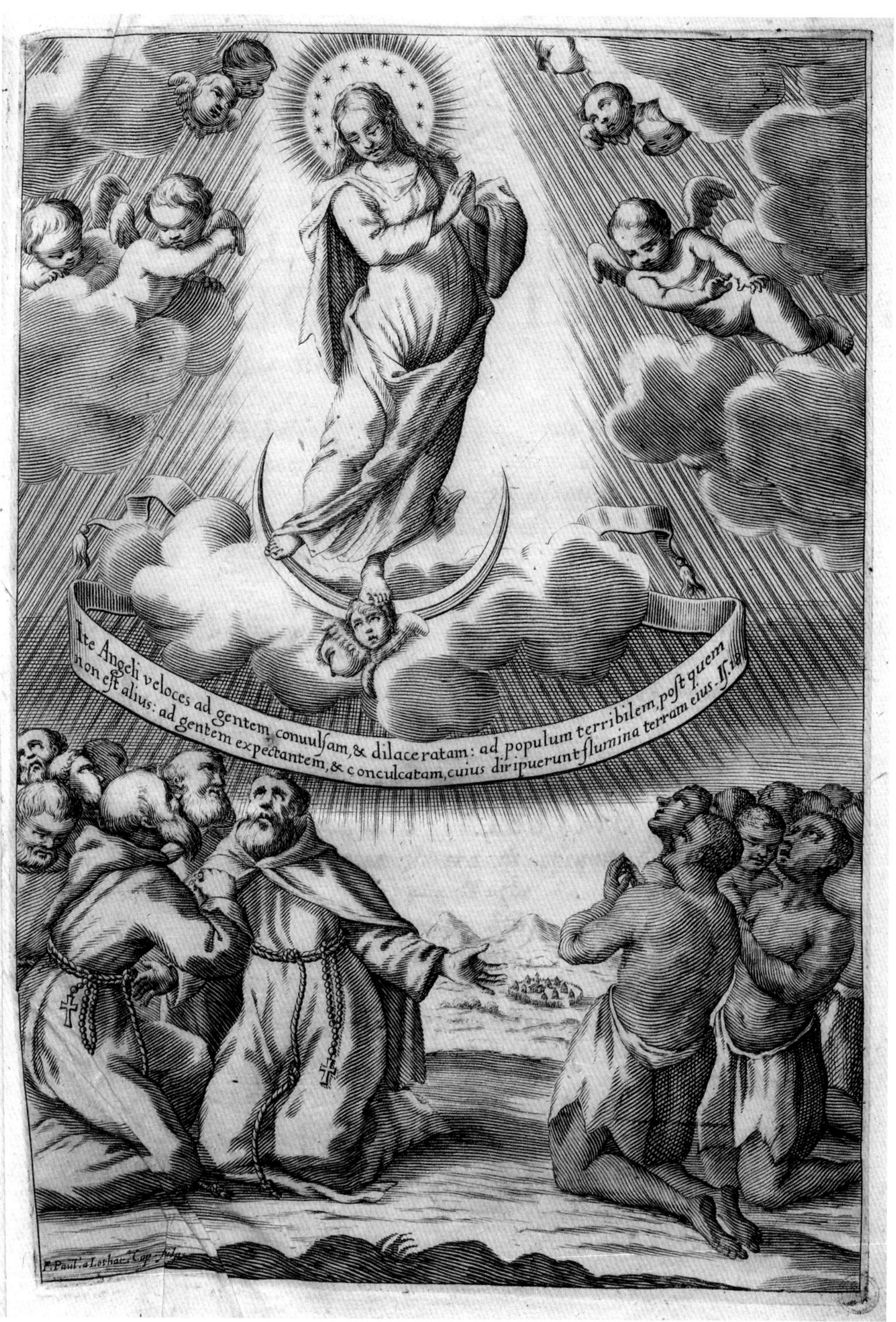

Figure 82

Paolo da Lorena (attr.), frontispiece to Giovanni Antonio Cavazzi and Fortunato Alamandini, *Istorica descrizione de' tre' regni Congo, Matamba, et Angola* (Bologna: Giacomo Monti, 1687). Engraving, 25.3 × 17.1 cm (plate mark). Bibliothèque nationale de France, FOL-H-3133. Photo: author.

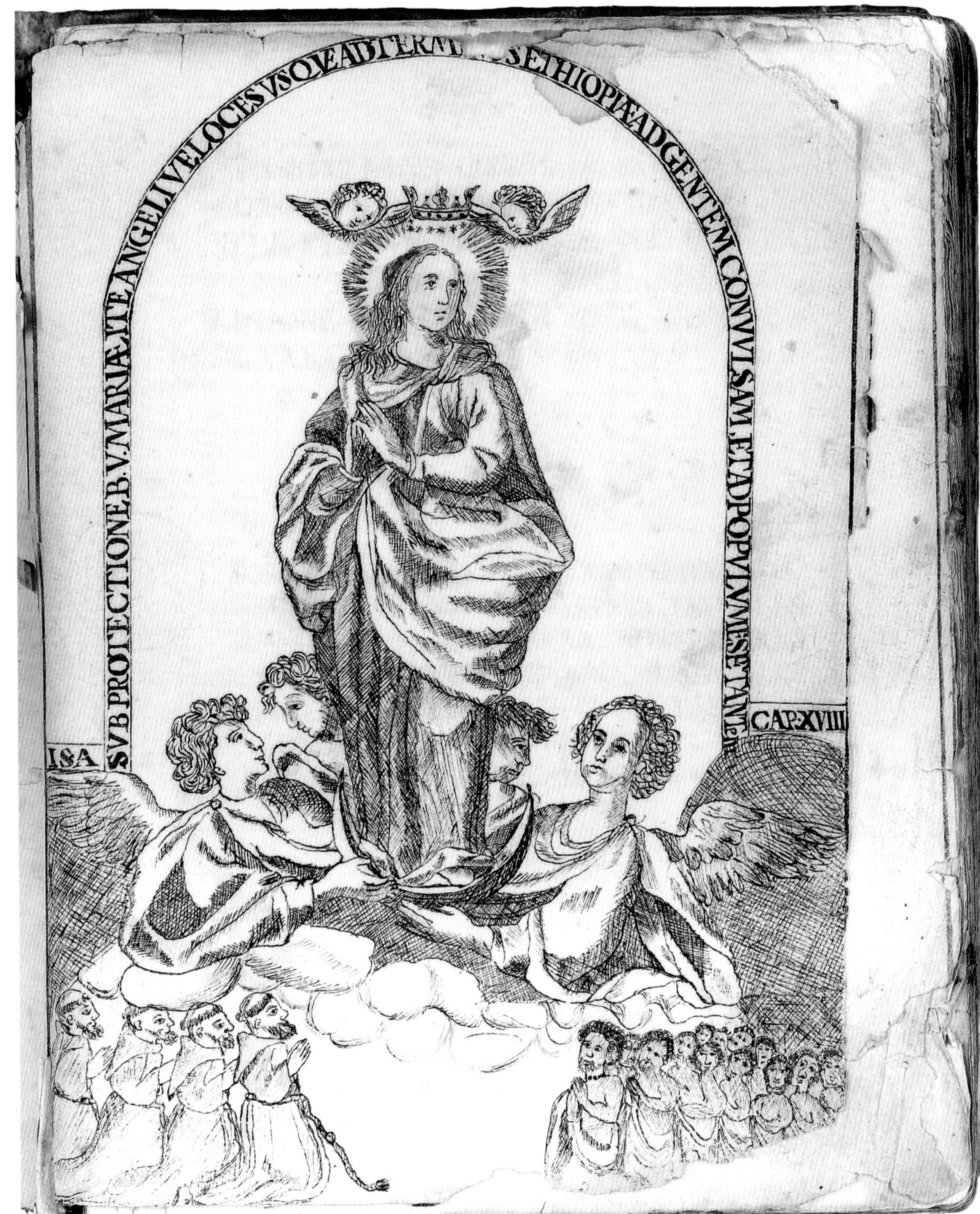

Figure 83

Giovanni Antonio Cavazzi, frontispiece to Giovanni Antonio Cavazzi, "Missione Evangelica al Regno del Congo" (the Araldi manuscript), vol. C, 1665–68. Ink on paper, 17 × 21 cm. Gallerie Estensi, Biblioteca Estense Universitaria, Modena. Reproduced by permission of the Italian Ministry for Cultural Heritage and Activities and for Tourism of Modena.

Figure 84

Paolo da Lorena, plate
in Ignacio Carnago,
Città di Rifugio (Milan:
Appresso Lodovico Monza,
1655), 450. Engraving,
15 × 20 cm (plate mark).
Photo: Convento dei Frati
Cappuccini di Santa Maria
di Bigorio (Svizzera).

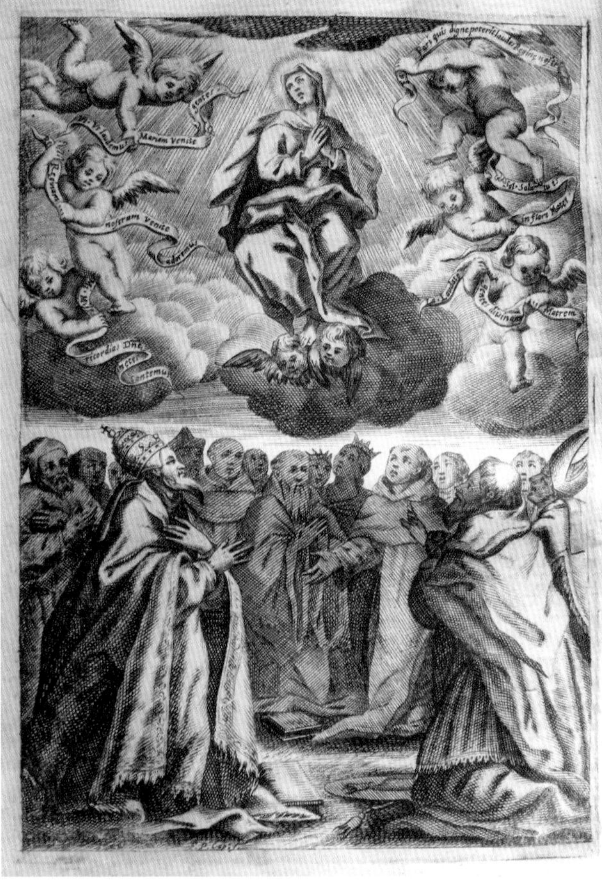

under a Virgin loftily floating on a cloud above
their heads. Neither Friar Paolo nor Cavazzi shied
away from transposing scenes of gathered European
elites such as the one in Carnargo into ones featuring members of the central-African ruling class, as
in figures 82 and 83. On these pages, Capuchins and
Kongo nobles not only inhabit the same pictured
space but experience the Marian apparition on an
equal footing. The illuminated opening page of
the Vatican "Missione in prattica" of the mid-
eighteenth century renewed the *Istorica descrizione*'s
iconography. The painted page provides even

greater symmetry between the friars, portrayed as
individuals, and the central Africans, a ruler identified with a long staff, red headgear, and crimson
mantel surrounded by his followers (plate 69).

This explicit parallel between friars and Africans
in the composition, unusual in comparison to missionary images from elsewhere in the early modern
world, is not unique to Cavazzi. It also appears
in several other Capuchin publications regarding
the central-African mission. The frontispiece to
Antonio da Gaeta's *La maravigliosa conversione . . .
della regina Singa*, published in Naples in 1669, shows
the friar, kneeling at the foot of Christ on the
Cross, facing and only slightly higher placed than
Queen Njinga and her female attendants (fig. 85).
A crown and scepter at the foot of the queen
clearly mark her royal status. Girolamo Merolla
da Sorrento's 1692 *Breve, e succinta relatione* opens
with a baroque frontispiece in which the Trinity
and the Virgin Mary float over Capuchin friars to
the left and Kongo nobles to the right, placed at
equal height and in similar postures (fig. 86). Psalm
95—"Say ye among the Gentiles, the Lord hath
reigned"—offers a sober banner for Merolla's opening scene. It could be an invitation directed at both
the Capuchins and the Kongo nobility to heed the
apostolic call to stretch Christianity beyond the
frontiers of the already Catholic kingdom. The
royal crown and scepter appear here again, in between the two groups. It is now placed on a cushion
similar to the ones illustrated as attributes of Kongo
kings—for example, on the baldachin seat of the
ruler in the *Istorica descrizione* (fig. 87) or holding
the crown at the feet of the throne in Olfert Dapper's illustration of Kongo's royal coronation in his
1668 *Naukeurige beschrijvinge*.[43] Several examples of
this type of cushion from the Kongo were prized

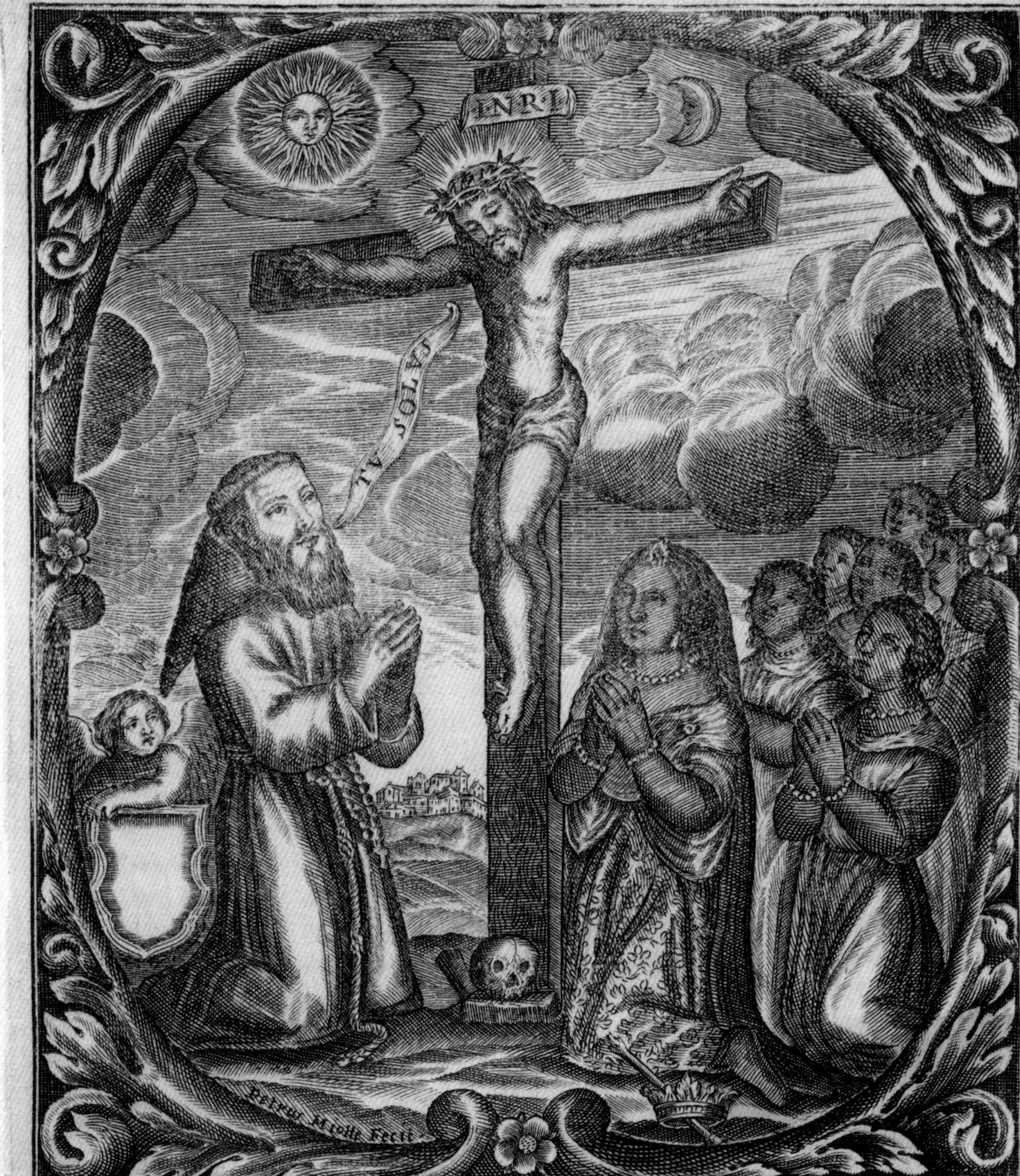

Figure 85

Unknown artist,
frontispiece to Antonio
da Gaeta and Francesco
Maria Gioia, *La maravigliosa
conversione alla santa fede
di Cristo della regina Singa*
(Naples: G. Passaro, 1669).
Engraving, 19 × 14 cm (plate
mark). Houghton Library,
Harvard University,
Cambridge, Massachusetts,
Afr 7306.69. Photo courtesy
of Houghton Library.

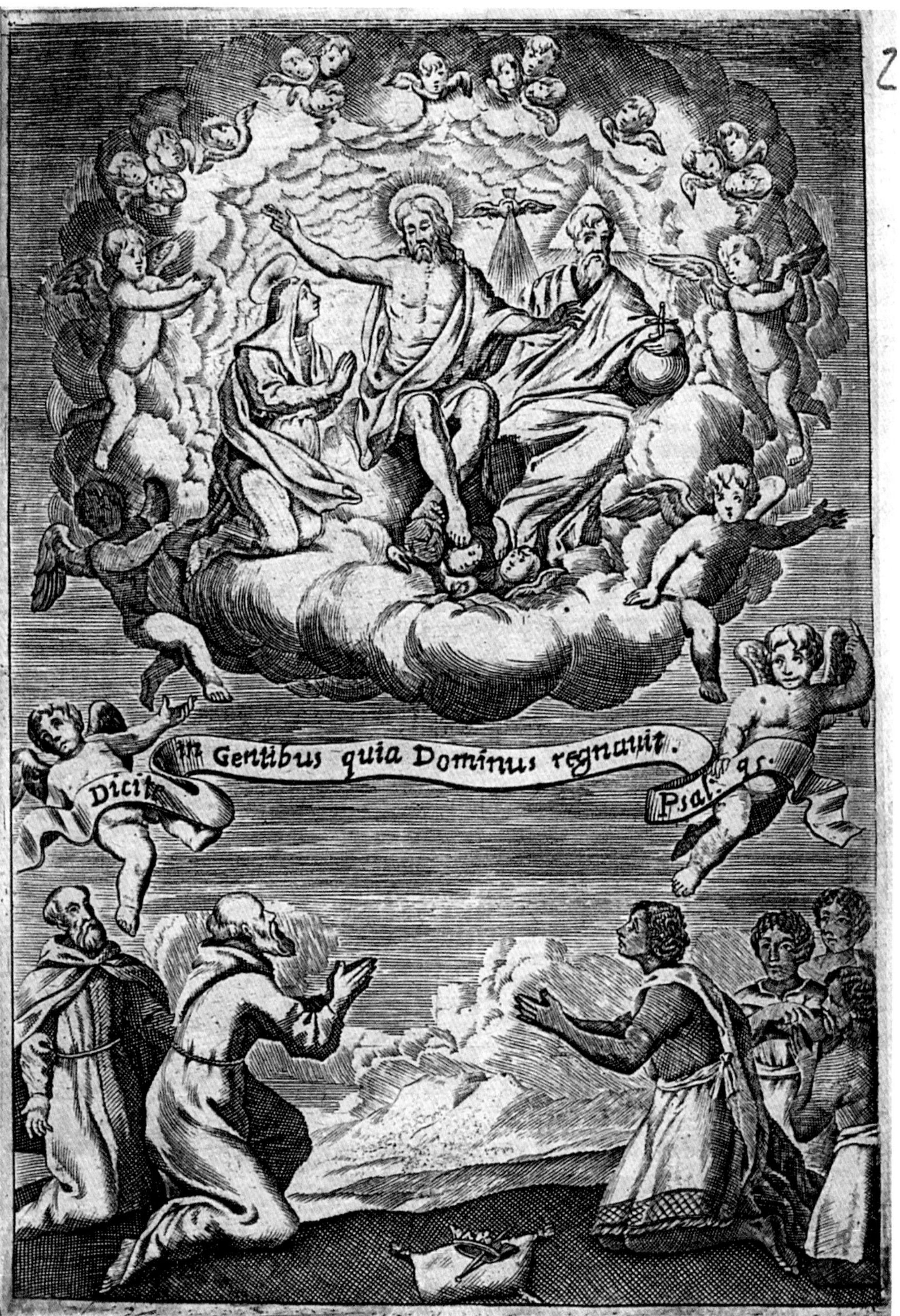

Figure 86

Unknown artist, frontispiece to Girolamo Merolla da Sorrento and Angelo Piccardo, *Breve, e succinta relatione del viaggio nel Regno di Congo* (Napoli: Francesco Mollo, 1692). Copper-plate engraving, 14.5 × 10 cm (plate mark). Biblioteca Nazionale Centrale di Roma, 6.25.H.8. Photo courtesy of the Biblioteca Nazionale Centrale di Roma.

Figure 87 (opposite left)

Paolo da Lorena (attr.), *Reception of Capuchin Friars by the King of Kongo*. Engraving, 10 × 14 cm (plate mark). Plate 41 from Giovanni Antonio Cavazzi and Fortunato Alamandini, *Istorica descrizione de' tre' regni Congo, Matamba, et Angola* (Bologna: Giacomo Monti, 1687), 336. National Library of Portugal, Lisbon, H.G. 9174 A. Photo courtesy of the National Library of Portugal.

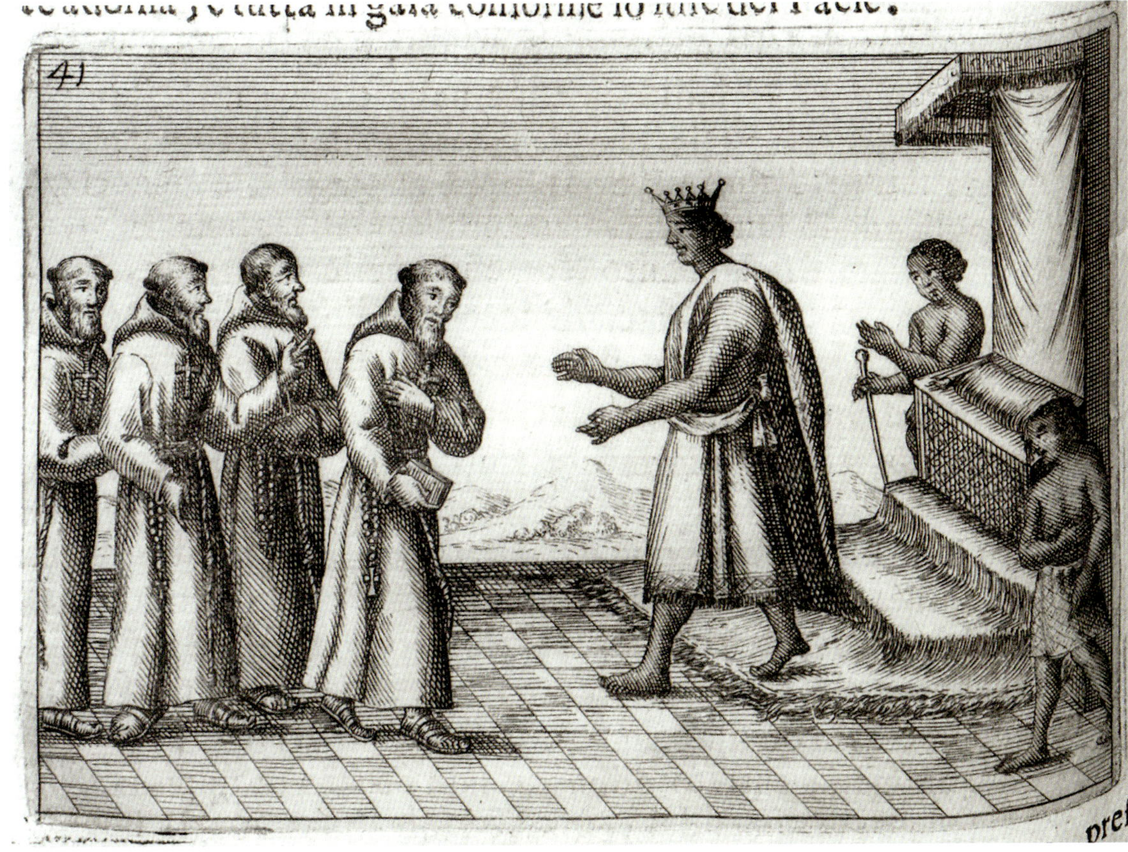

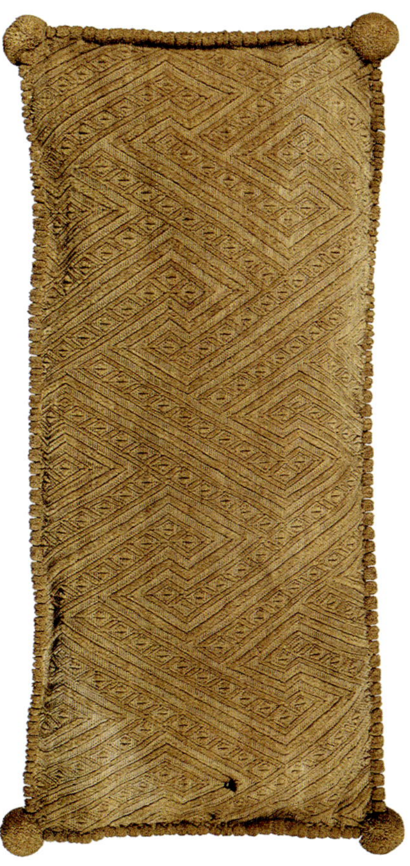

Unknown Kongo artist, cushion cover, sixteenth to seventeenth century. Inventoried 1737. Raffia, 23 × 53 cm. British Museum, London, Af.2822. Photo © The Trustees of the British Museum.

possessions of European collectors of the seventeenth and eighteenth centuries, such as the one in figure 88, inventoried in 1737 in Danish royal collections and now in the British Museum.[44]

The frontispiece for a German translation of one of the Capuchins' chronicles offers a striking opportunity to measure the distance between the visual organization of images found in the Capuchin works, both in manuscript and in print editions closely connected to their authors, and other visual strategies European editors adopted to illustrate encounters between Europeans and Africans. The travelogue of Friar Antonio Zuchelli da Gradisca that first appeared in Venice in 1712 without a frontispiece came out in 1715 in Frankfurt am Main with an opening illustration that places the presumed figure of the author in the midst of a composition dense with exotic clichés (fig. 89).[45] The friar at the bottom right, standing between a banana tree and a coconut tree, with a cross resting nonchalantly on his left shoulder like the rifle of a soldier at ease, blesses with his right hand a pair of kneeling people. Smaller than the cleric in scale, scantily clad with feathered crowns and skirts of leaves, they are generic savages in the visual language of early eighteenth-century Europe. Banana and palm trees

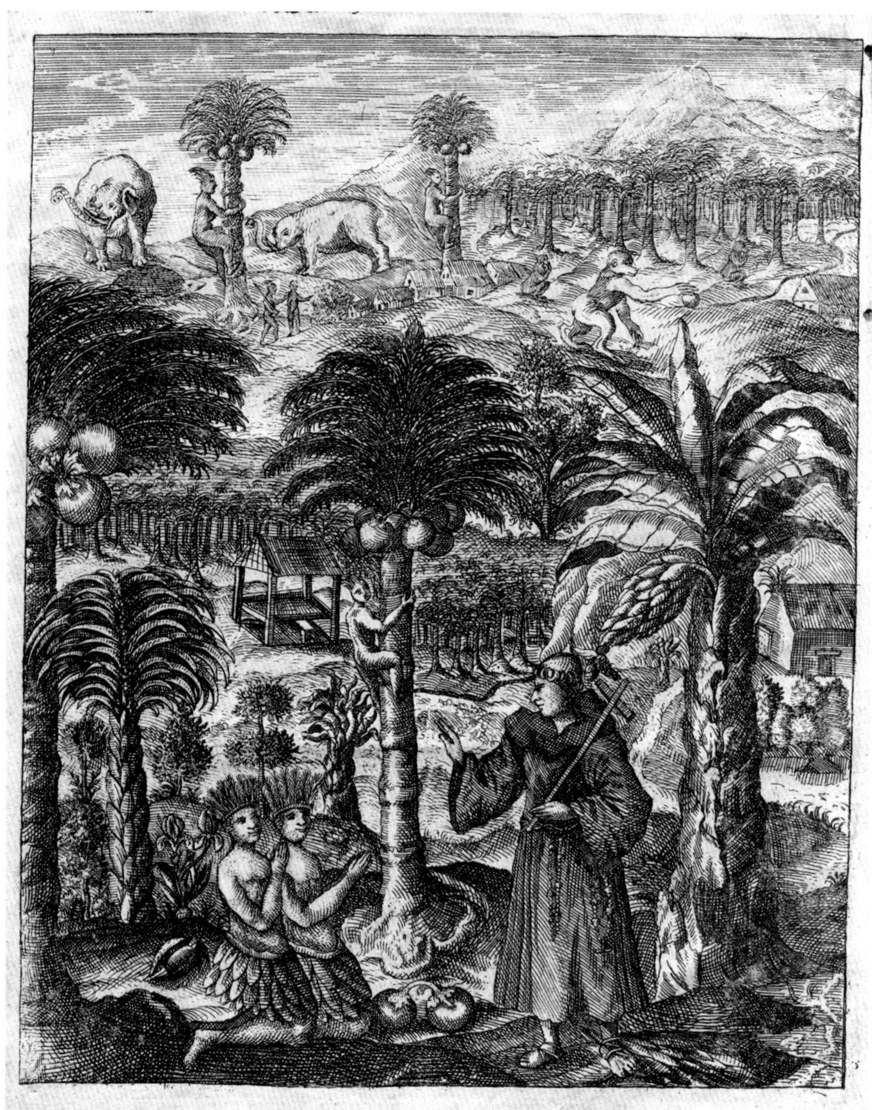

Figure 89

Frontispiece to Antonio Zucchelli, *Merckwürdige Missions- und Reise-Beschreibung nach Congo in Ethiopien* (Frankfurt am Main: Johann Ludewig Gleditsch, Moritz Georg Weidmann, and Mary Lowell Putnam, 1715). Etching, 17.5 × 13.8 cm (plate mark). Bayerische Staatsbibliothek München, 4 It.sing. 317, urn:nbn:de:bvb:12-bsb10366798–5. Photo courtesy of the Bayerische Staatsbibliothek München.

populate the landscape that readers of travel literature might have recognized as a reworking of an image about coconut trees in Asia from Linschoten's 1596 *Itinerario* published by Cornelis Claesz. Johann Ludewig Gleditsch, the editor responsible for the German edition of Zucchelli, seems to have drawn from the *Itinerario* to illustrate a work topically related to another of Claesz's successful products, his 1596 Dutch edition of Duarte Lopes's *Relatione del reame di Congo*.[46] The savages kneeling in front of the towering friar in the foreground, and the jarring reversal between human or humanlike figures climbing trees and apes walking or sitting upright on the ground in the background, are far indeed from the cautiously even representations of clerics and their local interlocutors in the Capuchin central-African corpus.[47]

The Capuchin images of Kongo and Angola were not the only examples of missionary illustrations picturing an even relationship between European clerics and their non-European flock. Another important corpus in this regard belongs to the literature on Jesuit endeavors in China. Active in a mighty realm in which they were little more than tolerated, European clerics still appeared in the frontispieces of works about their missionary efforts in China as dignified saints in the making. Their heroic stance, however, was deeply embedded within local mores and customs. The frontispiece to Matteo Ricci's *De Christiana expeditione apud Sinas Suscepta ab Societate Jesu*, published in Augsburg in 1615 and many times translated and republished in the following years, shows the great protagonist of the Jesuit China mission, to the right, wearing the garb of a Chinese scholar, as a pendant of Saint Francis Xavier, the Jesuit apostle of the Indies, to the left (fig. 90). Both men stand hieratically on either side of the book's title and a map of East Asia.

Jesuit scholar and collector Athanasius Kircher's frontispiece for the later *China Illustrata*, of 1667, adopts a similar composition, featuring Matteo Ricci dressed as a Chinese *literato* opposite the portrait of another member of the company, Adam Schall von Bell, in the dress of a civil official of the Qing bureaucracy.[48] Another print in the body of the text shows Ricci and Chinese scholar and Catholic convert Xu Quangxi standing alongside each other and conversing in front of a Catholic altar (fig. 91).

The iconography related to the Chinese mission formed an alternate template for images picturing relationships between European missionaries and inhabitants of extra-European regions. Unlike their counterparts in the Americas, Asian missions did not go hand in hand with colonialism. In fact, the extent to which the Jesuits were willing to adapt Catholicism to the local mores and customs of Japan, then China, was both remarkable and the subject of intense controversy. The so-called Chinese Rites that Jesuits such as Matteo Ricci elaborated around 1600 proposed a mode of catechization that accommodated, rather than strove to change, local practices not directly in conflict with Church doctrine. Most visibly, according to these principles, clerics such as Ricci took on, as fit for learned and literate men in China, the garb and function of mandarin scholars, a gesture the images above illustrate.

In 1645 the Propaganda Fide, the papal agency in charge of overseas missions, declared its firm opposition to the Chinese Jesuits' accommodationist practices. But its position rapidly changed, and what first had been deemed unacceptable received the Congregation's sanction in 1656. In fact, the Propaganda's own recommendations regarding the conduct of overseas apostolates articulated in the

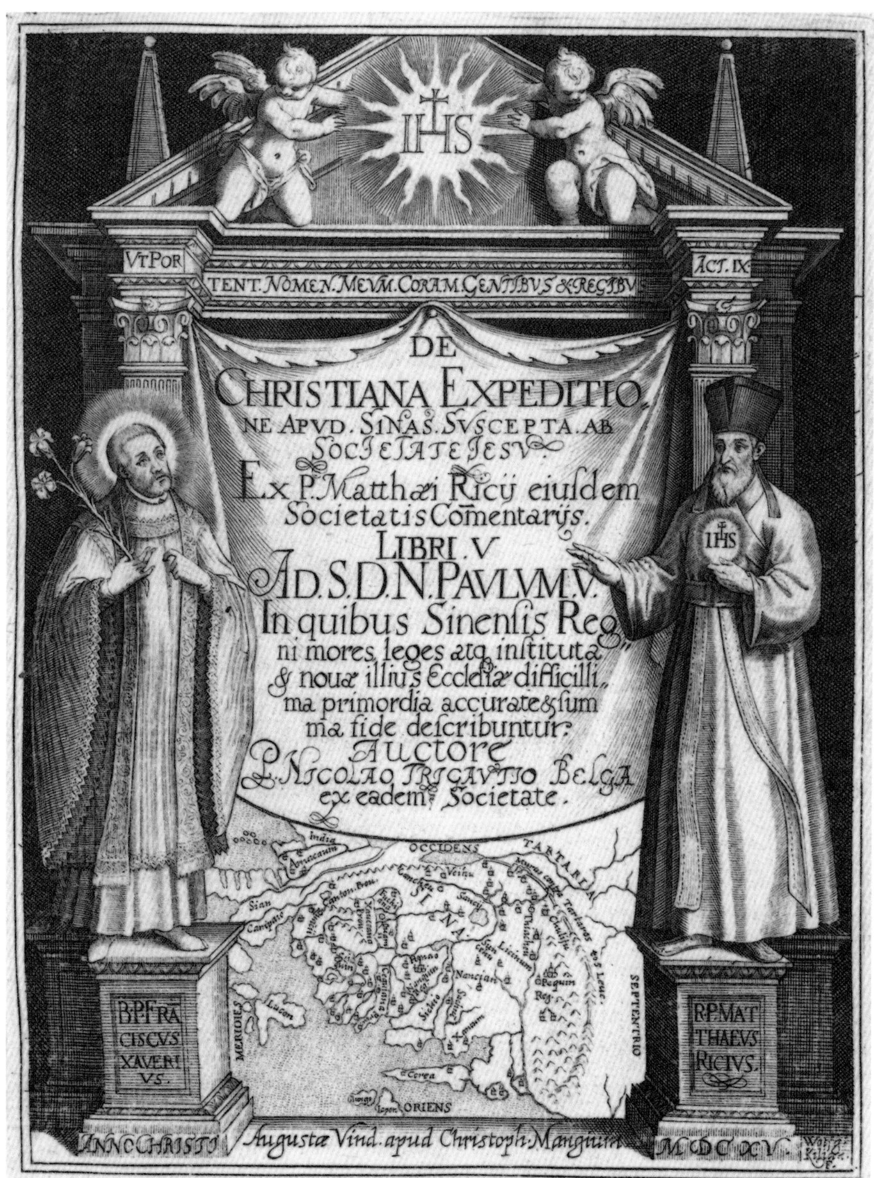

Figure 90

Wolfgang Kilian, frontispiece to Matteo Ricci, *De Christiana expeditione apud Sinas Suscepta ab Societate Jesu* (Augsburg: Christoph. Mangium, 1615). Engraving, 12.2 × 16.6 cm (plate mark). National Library of Portugal, Lisbon, RES. 3479 V. Photo courtesy of the National Library of Portugal.

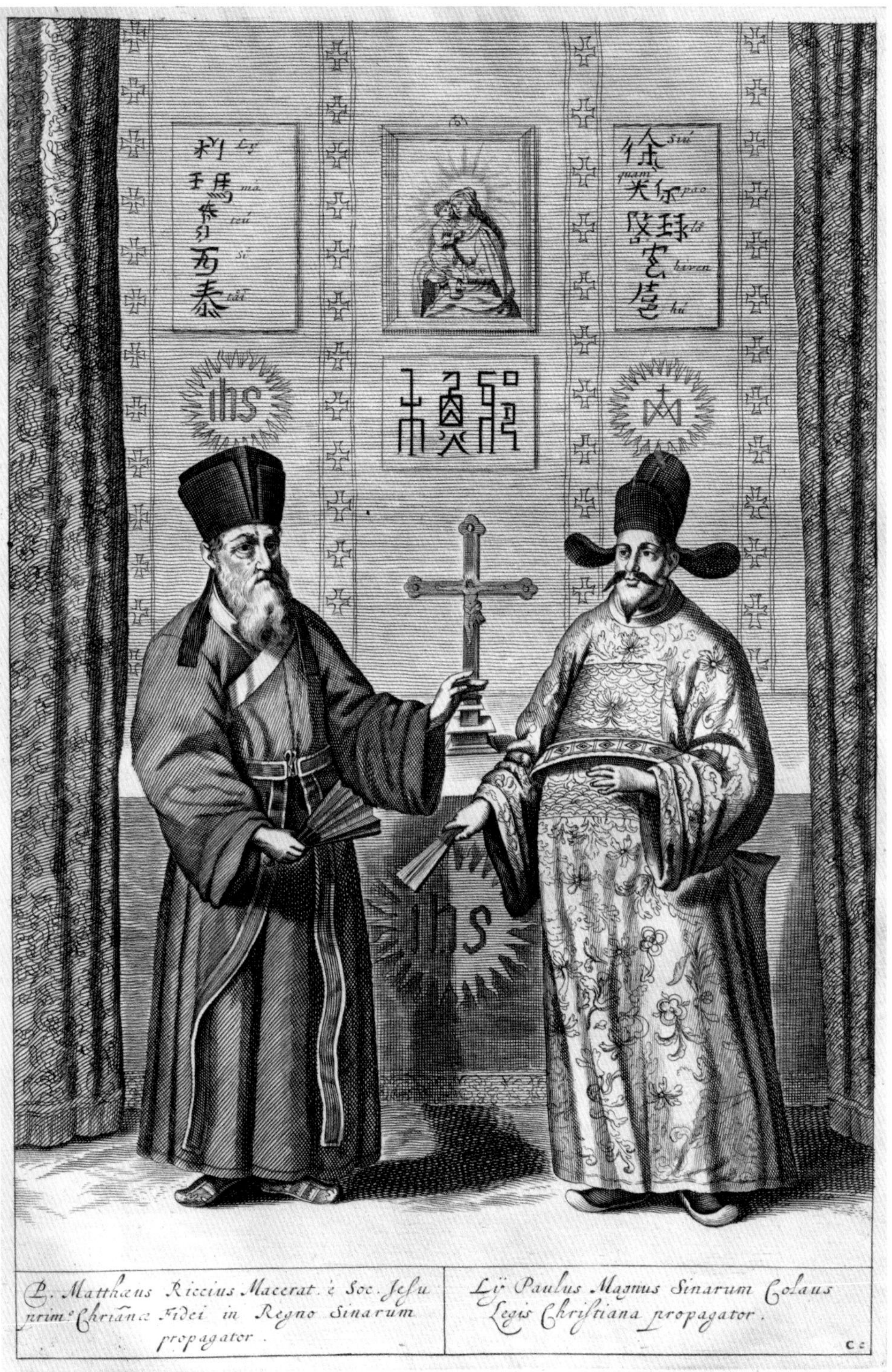

Figure 91

Athanasius Kircher, *Matteo Ricci and Li Paul*. Engraving, 28 × 18 cm (plate mark). From Athanasius Kircher, *China Illustrata* (Amsterdam: Jacobum à Meurs, 1667), plate facing p. 114. McGill University Library, Montreal, folio DS708 K5 1667. Photo courtesy of Rare Books and Special Collections, McGill University Library.

late 1650s closely echoed the methods Jesuits had developed in Japan and China. In preparation for sending its own missionaries to Asia, the Propaganda Fide endeavored to compile the best practices from its past missions through a systematic study of the documentation it had gathered in its archives. The result of the project was a set of "instructions for apostolic vicars departing for the Chinese kingdoms of Tonkin and Cochinchine" disseminated in 1659. The instructions first circulated as manuscripts. Several copies remain in the archives of the Missions étrangères in Paris, and a published version appeared in the same city in 1676.[49] The guidelines instructed missionaries to stay away from involvement in political matters, to accommodate cultural difference when not in opposition to the Christian faith and its moral edicts, that is, practice inculturation, and to promote the creation of a local clergy.

This moment of reckoning on missionary practice of the 1650s was also a formative time for the Capuchin mission to central Africa, under the auspices of the Congregation. Although planned to begin in the 1620s, it only started in earnest in the late 1640s and 1650s, at precisely the moment in which debates over accommodation raged in missionary circles.[50] It is evident from documents relative to their central-African apostolate that the Capuchins were aware of missionary practices elsewhere in the world and thoughtfully considered their applicability to their own field. The vice-prefect Luca da Caltanisetta, for instance, at the end of the seventeenth century compared the rules governing his work in Kongo to those he experienced while passing through Brazil and those of "French missionaries in the Americas."[51]

In another commonality, the Propaganda Fide fought in Asia as in central Africa to establish its missions in spite of and against the patronage rights Portugal and Spain enjoyed over the Church in the overseas territories they claimed as colonies or protectorates. In a series of bulls starting in the mid-fifteenth century, the papacy had conferred to Portugal and, later, Spain the rights and responsibilities of the administration of the Church in their realms.[52] The Church therefore operated in Spanish and Portuguese overseas possessions in concert with political power and served as an arm of the colonization process. The Propaganda Fide, an organization whose purpose was to implement the papacy's claims to global oversight over spiritual matters, thus had to negotiate its activities carefully in lands under the direct or indirect control or even loose purview of Spain or Portugal. The relationship between Rome and Portugal was thus tense in central Africa and Asia, regions that the Iberian realm jealously considered as belonging to the sphere of its patronage even if in effect they remained largely out of reach of its colonial ambitions.

Because of this situation, and in contrast to the policies of forced acculturation implemented in colonial areas, the Propaganda Fide advocated accommodation in its missions to Asia and central Africa. It also explicitly asked for political neutrality from its envoys vis-à-vis local rulers.[53] The spirit of the 1659 instructions, written for Asia but intended for all Propaganda Fide missionaries, resonates in the writings and methods of the Capuchins in Kongo and Angola. The following passage from the "instructions for apostolic vicars" resonates with the words of admonition several friars penned in their guides to the central-African missions, warning novice missionaries against excessive zeal in opposing local customs: "Do not under any pretext try to change or persuade these people to change their rites, customs, and mores, unless they are evidently against the Religion and good mores. What indeed could be more absurd than to introduce France, Spain, or Italy or other parts of Europe to the Chinese? Introduce there Faith and not your country, [that Faith] which does not reject or belittle the rites or customs of any nation as long as these rites are not evil, but rather desires that they be preserved in their integrity and fostered."[54] Bernardino d'Asti, for instance, wrote in the introduction to the Turin "Missione in prattica": "I observed that some new missionaries arriving in these missions, thinking that they were promoting in them major progress by reforming what until then had been practiced, did what should not be done in these kingdoms, and on the contrary caused more destruction than edification."[55] His longer manuscript now in the Vatican Library elaborated on the idea, including a chapter on "the honest laws and good customs of the Congolese and Angolans, which help the missionary in the progress of the mission," and another on "indifferent customs of the Congolese that the missionaries must tolerate."

However, for the friars as for the Propaganda, a bright line separated tolerable practices from "evil" ones, and practices that stood "against the Religion and good mores" crossed that line and excited their extirpating passions.[56] It is thus with matter-of-fact clarity and a keen sense of his words' implications that Bernardino penned a chapter with the blunt title "The Heathens Adore the Devil; How; and Why," which he placed in his manual before the two sections dedicated to accommodation.[57] Friar Bernardino was not an outlier in the history of the Capuchin central-African mission. On the contrary, his methods echoed the ones already established in

the seventeenth century by his predecessors, such as Giovanni Belotti da Romano, writing in 1680–81.[58]

In practice, the friars in central Africa sent their "doubts" about the proper conduct of their apostolate to Rome, as did their colleagues in Asia. They inquired in particular about the difficulties in perceiving the boundaries between acceptable cultural differences and unacceptable behaviors. Another area of interrogation concerned the administration of sacraments. In a 1650 document, for example, the Propaganda Fide answered the questions of Bonaventura da Sorrento.[59] The correspondence sheds light on the dilemmas the Capuchin faced while acting among a population he judged "very tough, with rough brains, so that they cannot understand or learn the Mysteries." It also illustrates the Roman hierarchy's relative flexibility. Baptism emerges as its first priority. Adults, Rome instructed, even those lacking the ability to understand the precepts of the Church, should receive the sacrament, which could be given *in fide ecclesiae*, that is to say, in the same manner as for children unable to grasp the meaning of the ritual. In a similar form of expediency, the Congregation waived the obligation for godparents to be knowledgeable of the teachings of the Church. Other sacraments could also be adapted as needed. For confessions, in the absence of an interpreter, absolution could be granted to penitents only able to communicate one or two sins for lack of linguistic competence. Rome also considered that the Eucharist should be given even when the priests had serious doubts about the person's ability to comprehend the meaning of the Mystery of transubstantiation, as long as the person "[did] what he [could] on his side."[60] On the other hand, Rome rejected the Capuchin's suggestion to instate a process for two people to join in matrimony with each other in the absence of a priest.[61]

These relatively accommodating instructions did not prevent friars from perpetrating in the course of their apostolate great rhetorical and actual violence against central Africans and the rituals they performed outside of the perimeter of the Church. It is also clear that the Capuchins did not have the same admiration and respect for central Africans as their counterparts had for many of the peoples they encountered in Asia. Yet the social and political context of their mission in Kongo and to some extent Angola mitigated their prejudiced views and their ire against "evil" practices because they had to operate within the fabric of central-African society. The relationship between central Africans and Capuchins fell somewhere between the eager inculturation the Jesuits practiced in Asia and the forceful Europeanization the Church aimed to implement in Iberian colonies of the Americas. Accordingly, images of friars in Kongo and Angola show them cultivating a relationship with local populations and, in particular, their elite, in which cooperation depended on a strategically negotiated, delicate balance of power. A particular figure within Kongo society stood at the core of this modus vivendi between Capuchins and central Africans: the worldly and powerful *mestre da igreja*.

Mestres da igreja

Two Kongo men elegantly dressed with colorful wrappers, conspicuous, large white cloths draped over their left shoulders, one of them with a *mpu* cap of status, stand a few steps behind Friar Bernardino in figure 78 as he meets the new prince of Soyo. They are *mestres da igreja*, or church masters, members of the most elite circles of the Kongo, trained since childhood in Portuguese, Latin, and Catholic doctrine by older holders of the office, who formed the backbone of the Kongo Church's organization. Like many of the institutions and symbols of the central-African Church, the position of *mestre* emerged in the first half of the sixteenth century during the reign of the inventor of Kongo Christianity, King Afonso I (r. 1509–42). First mentions of *mestres* appear in early sixteenth-century descriptions of the educational system Afonso put in place as part of the great reforms he implemented in his kingdom after its official conversion under his reign. By 1529 King João III of Portugal considered that sending four schoolmasters to Kongo, in response to a request of its king, would be sufficient, since, he wrote, "I am told there are in your Kingdom men qualified for this task."[62] Although early in the reign of Afonso women taught girls in schools and in subsequent centuries elite females continued to receive education in religion and letters, I have found no mention of female *mestres* in the documentary record.

The word *mestre*, of course, in the context of Manueline-era Portugal, was a generic term designating a trained specialist in any given trade or skill. The *mestres da ler*, or masters of reading, and *mestres da escola*, or schoolmasters, that appear in documents about the Kongo in the early decades of the sixteenth century probably fulfilled functions not entirely like those of the position as it would later solidify. The role, if not yet the name, of *mestre da igreja* acquired its specific tenor by the middle of the century, when figures appear in the documentation fulfilling the role for which *mestres da igreja* would later be well known in the idiosyncratic Kongo method for confession.[63] By 1583 Spanish Carmelite missionaries had described the function of *mestres* at length in a narrative of their encounter with a polyglot and well-mannered "clerigo del evangelio," or deacon, named João (whom they call Juan, in Spanish), who took the lead in organizing their voyage through the kingdom. They also recorded the presence of an "interpreter, whom [central Africans] call maestro. He teaches the doctrine and hears confessions when a priest [is present]."[64]

By the beginning of the seventeenth century, *mestres* could be salaried civil servants or receive a commission on Church services such as burials, or a fee for writing letters, as evidenced in the personal papers of António Manuel, an ambassador of the king of Kongo to the pope, who served as a *mestre* between 1591 and 1600.[65] Chosen from the members of the highest elite, they served in the inner circles of Kongo political power. The late seventeenth-century portrait of a "Black lord or prince" in the Parma Watercolors (plate 16), pictures them close to a Kongo ruler, as one of the trappings of his status. A member of the central-African elite whose powers and insignia encompassed broad, cosmopolitan horizons, the main protagonist of the painting leans on an imported crimson carpet, wears draped bright Indian cotton cloth, and holds a scepter inspired by European turned-wood objects. A *mpu* cap, coral bracelets, and metal anklets, as well as the location of the reception under a large tree, also demonstrate his political and economic might following locally grounded symbolism. Finally, the retinue of three *mestres* completes the classicizing portrait the friar painted of an impressive, worldly central-African leader adjudicating under a tree, like another Saint Louis.

Capuchin watercolors illustrate the special status the *mestres* held among the many Africans in the entourage of the friars. In a vignette demonstrating how to "travel around the country," ten central Africans accompany a friar riding in a hammock (fig. 92, plate 72 top). Among them, two modestly attired, tall and muscular men carry the loaded net hanging on a pole and hold in their hands Y-shaped stands to rest the vehicle when at a stop. Six more men bring along provisions and other materials, while ensuring the safety of the traveling party with their bows and arrows. Two of them, in the front and center of the image, wear an insignia of the elite, the *nkutu* shoulder net. As members of the elite, they have the privilege of carrying precious loads, the portable altar and the umbrella, thanks to which the father can give sacraments with proper decorum while on the road. At the bottom right corner of the vignette, two *mestres* tread lightly in front of the group, leading the way. Unlike the rest of the men, they do not carry much, merely small bags swung over their shoulders. Each wears the *mpu* cap of the elite, a white cloth draped over the shoulders, and carries a staff topped with a cross, a combination that models the typical outfit of their office. Differences in insignia, cargo, and position mark a clear hierarchy within the group and unequivocally place the *mestres* at its top. Lest the distinction escape viewers, the gloss for the image restates it in writing, describing the scene as featuring, in order, "the Father missionary traveling the land, accompanied by two *mestres*, or interpreters, and by the blacks of the convent."[66] Later in the manuscript, hierarchy keeps the *mestres*, in a river-crossing scene, safely sitting in a canoe poled by two standing ferrymen, alongside a friar (fig. 93). The rest of the group crosses the waters on foot,

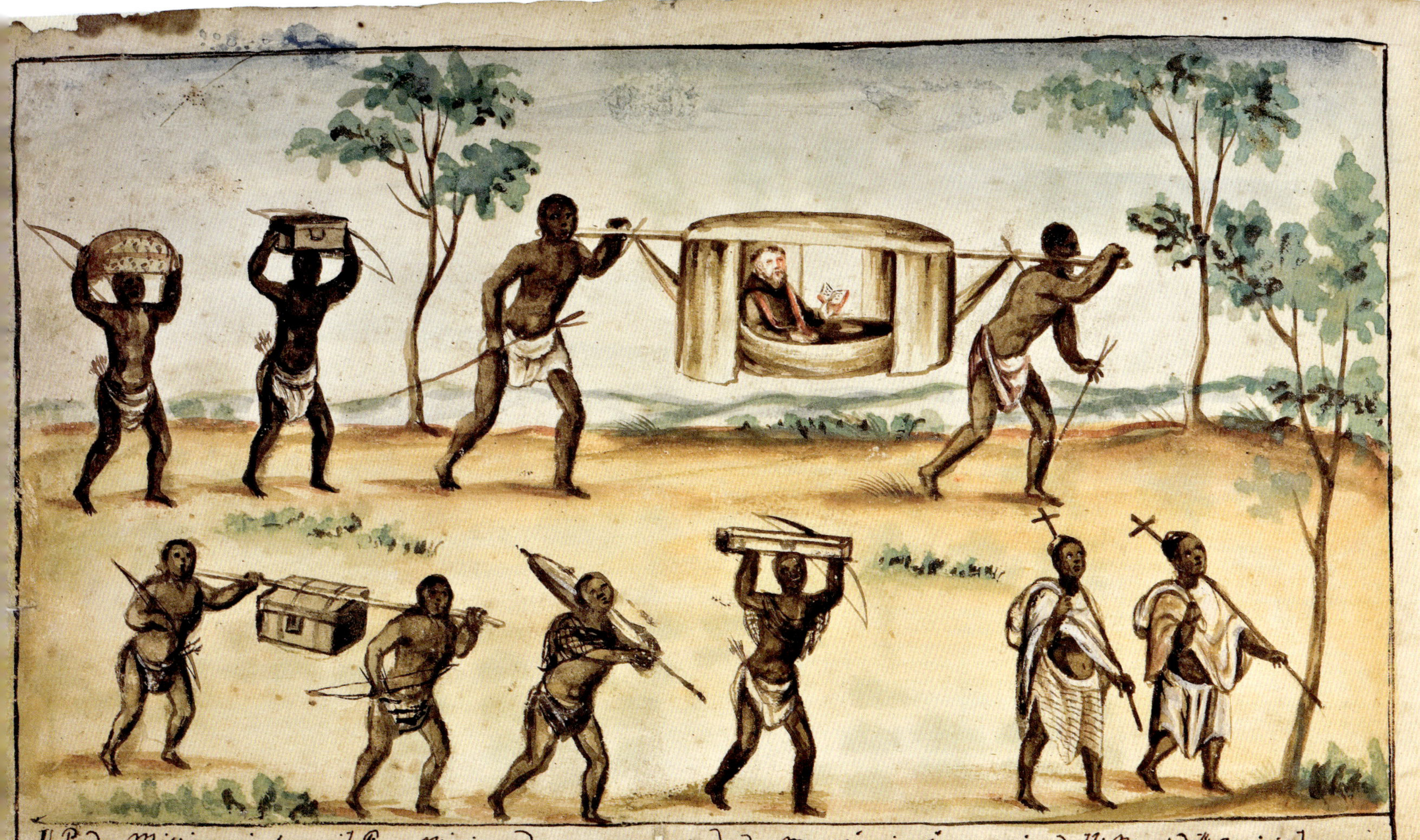

Il Padre Missionario scorre il Paese Missionando, accompa[gn]ato da due Maestri, o sian Interpreti, e dalli Negri dell' Ospizio che carregano le cose necessarie per Missionare, Cioe Altar portabile della Mess[a], un Bauglio con Cera, et altre cose necessarie per l'Administracion de' sacramenti, V[na] Cascia da Cuccina con prouision di Vito e suoi utensili, Un Straportino per dormire, Un Umbrela per riparassi dall' arsure del Sole, quando massime administra li Sacramenti in Campo aperto; ordinariam[en]te seguitano altri quattro Carregatori per la Rete, quando l'Uscita in Missione e intentionata a più mesi di Viaggio, n[e] si trouano altri Carregatori V.

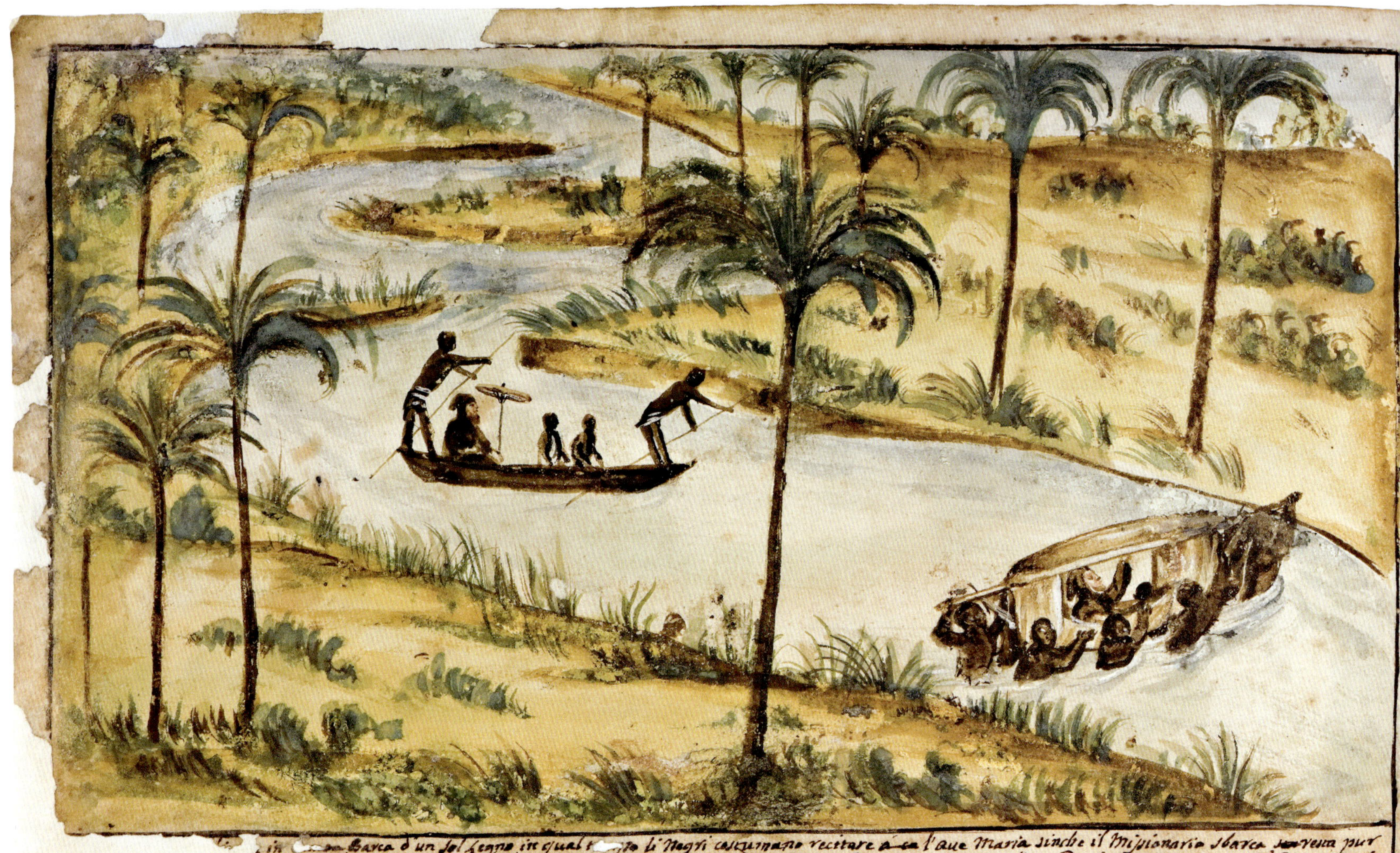

in ... Barca d'un sol Legno, in qual t...go li Negri costumano recitare a ... l'aue Maria sinche il Missionario sbarca ... vena pur in Rete, e si osserui che questi Ethiopi dipinti nell'aqua su alcuna Lagune profonde sollevando la Rete passano sopra d'un picolo ...eso dentro dell'aqua, cosi che il Bilancio per il beso della Rete e della gente fà spasimare il pouero Missionario. Pure conuiensi ed esporsi anche à tali pericolosi cimenti per saluar anime. In questo passaggio il Missionario si ha da lasciar gouernar da Negri ... per diuina prouidenza hanno per grande affronto, che per loro colpa succeda male al miss.o

carrying in a hammock another friar, who holds on uncomfortably to the hammock's support pole and cloth against the currents of white water.

Capuchins, like their Carmelites predecessors, often refer to *mestres* in their writings as interpreters, but their role in the conduct of the mission far exceeded that of mere linguistic intermediaries. The makers of the watercolors gave them a modest, demure presence in the vignettes, where they stand a few steps behind an officiating friar or eagerly converse with him. As the friars intended when picturing their relationship with rulers, they meant to present in these scenes what they deemed proper interactions between clerics and *mestres*. Yet even in these explicitly idealized views, it is clear that the church masters were all but subordinates of the friars. Present in almost every scene of apostolic activity across the corpus, the *mestres* do not so much accompany the friars as watch over their every move. Here again the relationship of power between the missionaries and their African hosts relies on a delicate balance in which friars preside over ritual activities, preach, or catechize, always surveilled and controlled by the local elite through the indispensable *mestres*. "The missionary always must have with him an interpreter [i.e., *mestre*]"[67] who "assists" in the sacraments, Friar Bernardino euphemistically reports.[68]

The most telling example of the compulsory mediation *mestres* conducted between friars and local populations appears in the descriptions of confession methods, in an idiosyncratic arrangement recorded in the Kongo since the mid-sixteenth century.[69] Although many of the Europeans learned to speak the local languages, Capuchins had to hear confessions with the assistance of a local "interpreter" whether or not they could understand the

penitents.[70] In his book of advice on missionary practice, Giovanni Belotti da Romano explains that this unorthodox practice is necessary because "the Blacks are distrustful of the white Europeans . . . so that with the presence of men from their nation as interpreters, and almost as witnesses and advocates in their defense, thus reassured, they remain more content in particular in the act of the sacramental confession."[71] Several vignettes in the visual guides correspond to this written admonition. One, in the Vatican Library version of the "Missione in prattica," shows a Capuchin seated on a stool, listening to the sins of a man kneeling next to him (fig. 94 / plate 71). A *mestre* in his white garb, staff in hand and cross around the neck, sits behind the two men, overlooking the scene from a short distance. The text directly under the image, however, corrects the painting, saying that confession "is here not well represented, the interpreter having to sit next to the Father. See page 43 et s."[72] On page 43, Bernardino d'Asti echoes Belotti's warning that "the missionary should not risk hearing confession in this country, without the help of the interpreter."[73] The Turin version of the manuscript presents the correct arrangement in a slightly different composition (fig. 95). The friar and the interpreter are side by side, and the penitent addresses his confession to the *mestre*, while the priest overlooks the conversation. The accompanying text explicitly states that this unorthodox method for hearing confession is "the custom of the land," to be used even in the absence of a language barrier.[74]

Like confession, catechizing and sermonizing were areas of missionary work that the clerics did not fully control. The friars marveled at the ability of *mestres*, often working in teams of seniors and apprentices, to recall and retell entire speeches. Yet the

Bernardino Ignazio da Vezza d'Asti, *River Crossing*, ca. 1750. Watercolor on paper, 19.5 × 28 cm. From "Missione in prattica," Biblioteca civica Centrale di Torino, MS 457, fol. 10v. Photo courtesy of the Biblioteca civica Centrale, Turin.

Capuchins also worried that the *mestres* changed or elaborated on the original discourse, which became longer in their tongue. "It is not rare," Bernardino warns, "that such Interpreters for their own convenience, or seduced [by the devil], maliciously pass over some phrases of the missionary, either interpreting them or making up altered repetitions that would be against the intention of the [priest]."[75] It was not linguistic need but local customs and power structure that prescribed *mestres*' mediation in

ministry. Friars could merely strive to mitigate the potential risks of unfaithful translation by acquiring proficiency in local languages. "In these moments," Bernardino resignedly concludes in his text on the treacherous river crossing in figure 93, but in a formulation that readily extends to his apostolic endeavors as a whole, a missionary "has to let himself be governed by the blacks."[76]

Images of dialogue between *mestres* and friars fill the Capuchin central-African corpus, and it

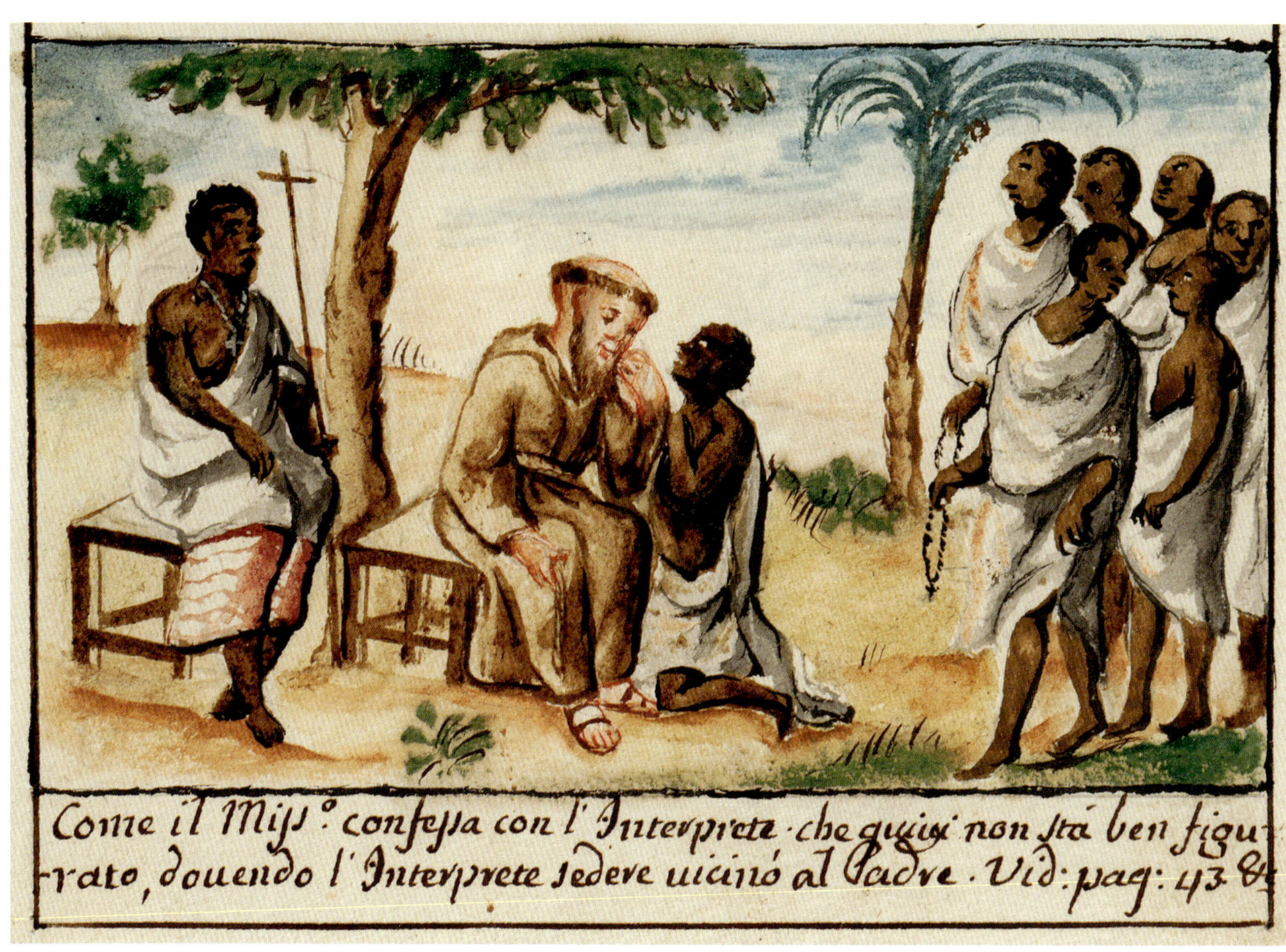

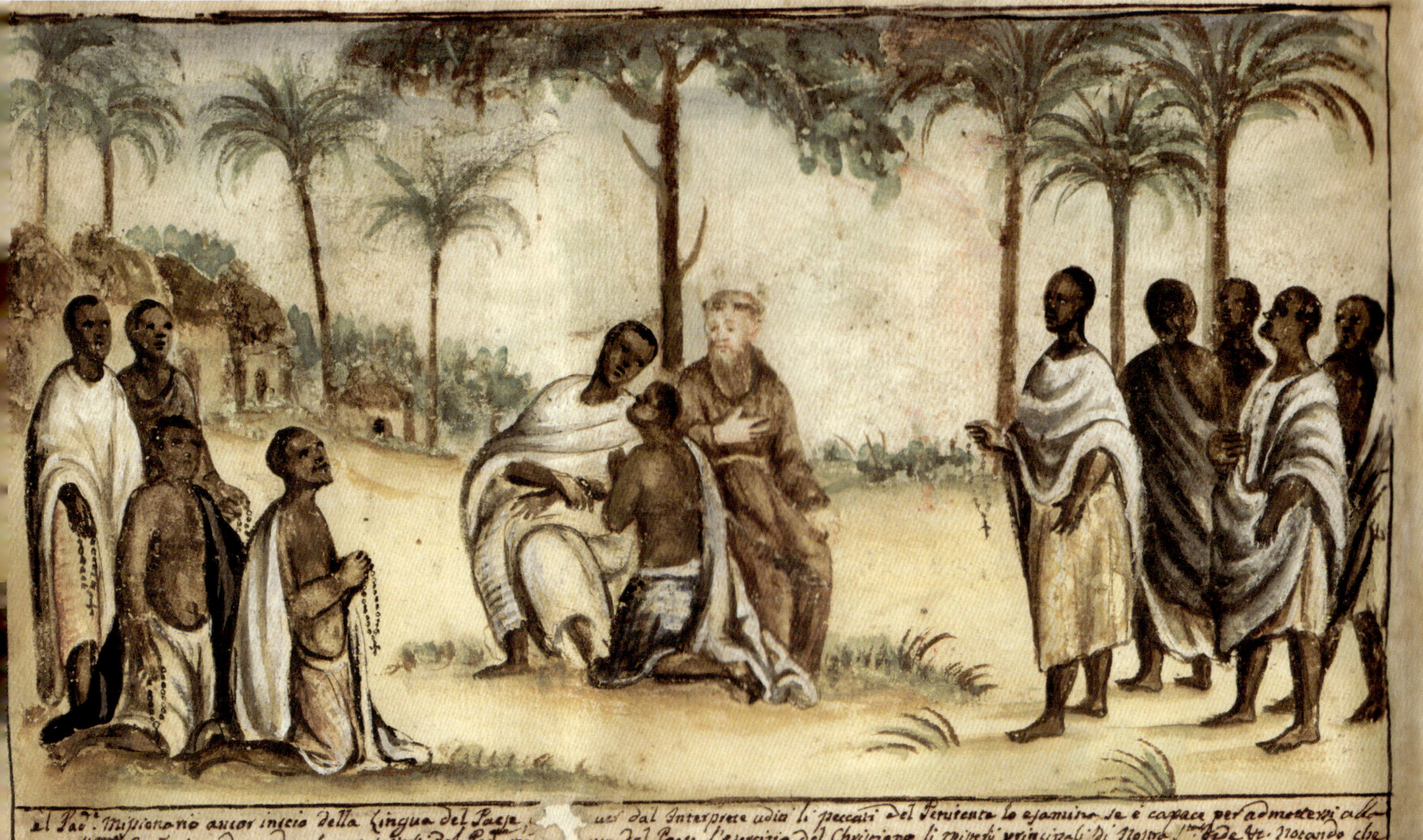

el Pad.ᵉ Missionario ancor incio della Lingua del Paese, ués dal Interprete udia li peccati del Penitente lo esamina se è capace per admettersi alla
li med.ᵐ Comunione dovendo almeno sapersi dal Pad.ᵉ no. ua del Paese l'esercitio del Christiano, li misterj principali di Nostra S.ᵗᵃ fede &c. Notando che
L'interprete deve ascoltare li peccati del Penitente sol... chij dal Missionario, qual ha de osservare attentam.ᵗᵉ se fa Diligentem.ᵗᵉ il suo Officio. Peroche
alcuni di questi Interpreti, perche ricevono da Penitenti in Elemosina: per cumularne molte, presentano tall'hora à piedi del Missionario Penitenti
senza haver ditta la loro Confessione, così dice rippeto una Confessione finta, e composta à loro capriccio - - - - - - - - -

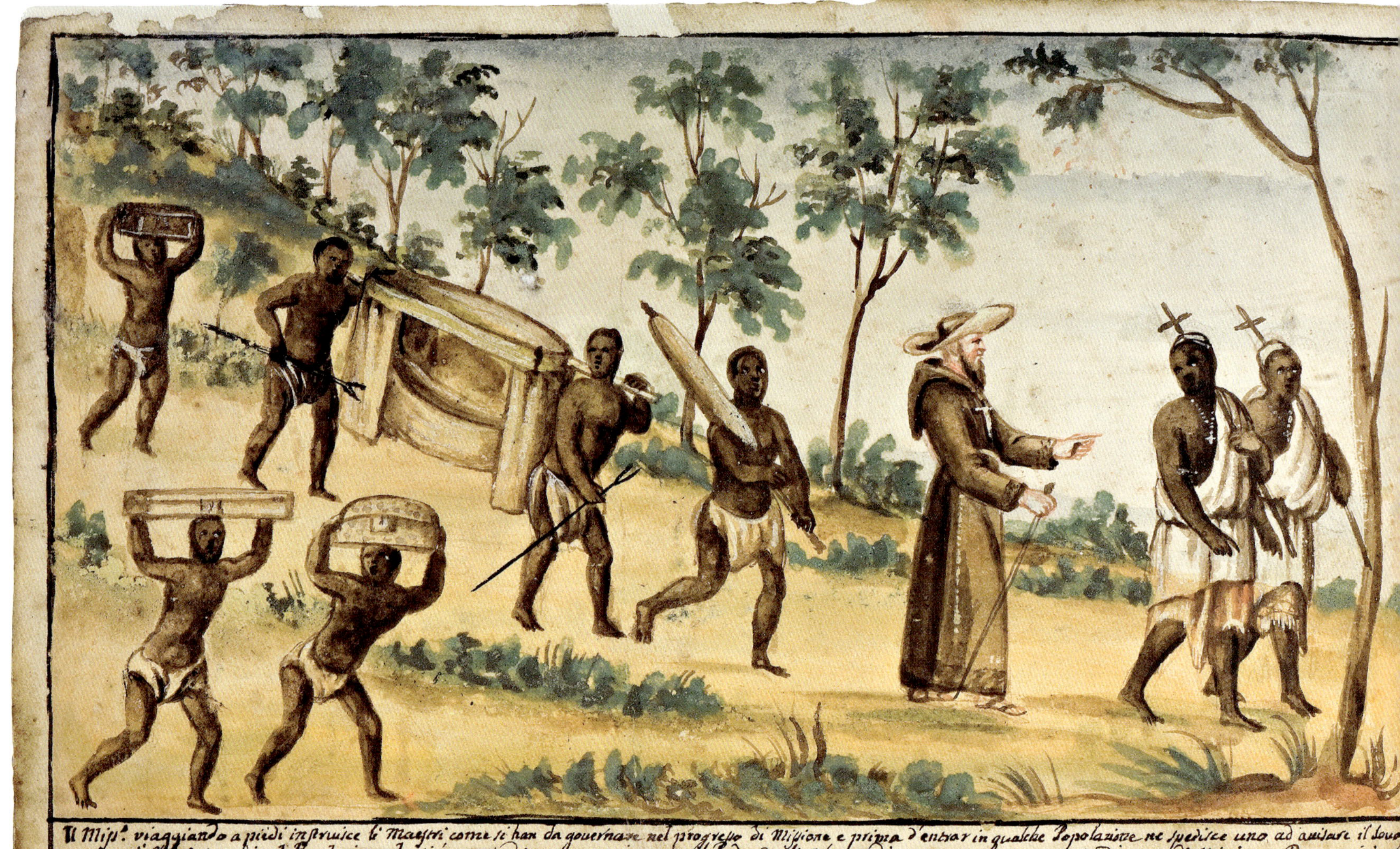

Figure 96

Bernardino Ignazio da Vezza d'Asti, "The Missionary walking," ca. 1750. Watercolor on paper, 19.5 × 28 cm. From "Missione in prattica," Biblioteca civica Centrale di Torino, MS 457, fol. 6v. Photo courtesy of the Biblioteca civica Centrale, Turin.

is precisely such a scene that features in Cavazzi's great landscape (fig. 41). The print almost certainly derived from a watercolor featuring a friar alongside a *mestre* in the manner of the pairs pictured in the "Missione in prattica." A comparison between the figures in one of Bernardino's vignettes and the etched pair makes the visual kinship clear. In the painting and the print alike, a friar walks one step behind one or two *mestres* who turn their heads back toward him in conversation, their hands extended in attitudes of speech (figs. 96, 97). The local men carry the emblems of their status, the white cloth draped on the left shoulder and a staff topped with a cross, two elements the etcher transformed into a bow and loincloth. In fact, the bright, light-colored cloth around the body of the etched African man is draped too high and too loosely to adequately picture a leg wrapper, betraying its origins in the now-missing painting at the source of the print, in which the friar's companion wore his *mestres*' garb. Similarly, the arrow awkwardly held in the left hand likely emerged in the etcher's mind as the logical complement to the bow he placed in the man's right hand, having misread the staff church masters carried on that side. The printmaker may have misunderstood or misrepresented the attributes of the African figure for artistic effect, or because of his biased understanding of Africa and Africans, but his composition still closely fits within the iconography of dialogue and cooperation present all through the Capuchin central-African corpus at large. Placed in this context, the pair ably

Figure 97

Paolo da Lorena (attr.), *Pungu a Ndongo, or Fortress of the Pedras Negras* (fig. 41), detail.

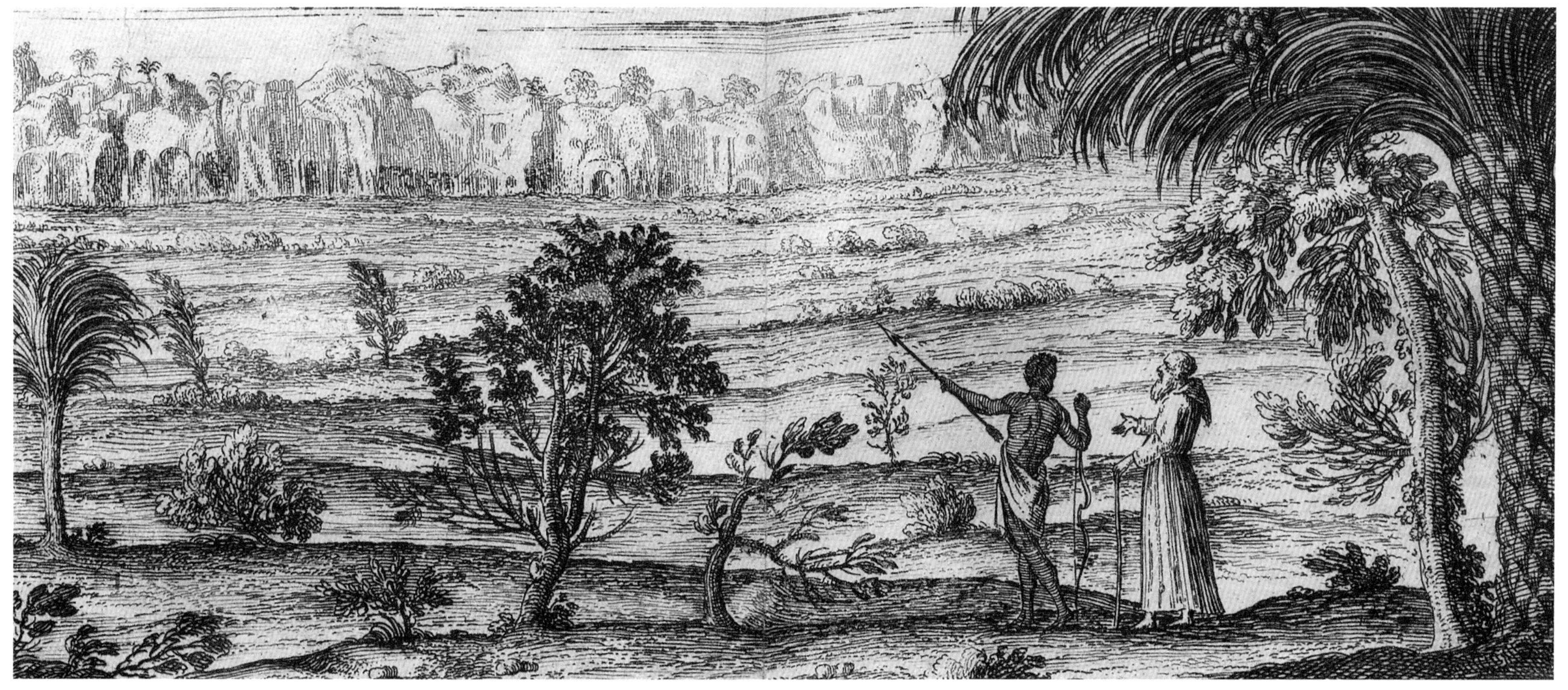

illustrates the particular relationship between friars and local elite, a relationship made remarkably even by a precarious balance of mutual respect and mistrust, common interests and diverging goals.

Conclusion

Following neither the templates of colonial proselytism in the early modern Americas nor the controversial inculturation policies of Asian missions, the relationship between Capuchin missionaries and the populations of Kongo and Angola followed a pattern of its own. Fraught cooperation based on a delicate balance of power underlies the Capuchins' activities in the region. The visual corpus they created in the wake of these interactions both echoed and reflected on this situation, featuring images of carefully calibrated interplay between the clerics and their elite Kongo hosts. Outside of the Christian realm, the friars encountered a broader range of reactions, from violence leading to martyrdom (plate 1) to gracious welcome (plate 69). The vignettes also include in their frames the key figure of the *mestre*, on whom the relationship between local populations and European friars hinged. Though in many regards as biased and idealized as other European representations of overseas polities, the Capuchin central-African images nevertheless form a category of their own within that larger corpus. The visual work Capuchin central-African images performed stands in revealing contrast to the better-known imagery of early modern European missions conducted in the midst of colonial assaults on Mesoamerica or of admiring inculturation in Asia. When addressed not as idiosyncratic oddities but as documents of another kind of interaction between Europeans and those they called their Others, the Capuchin central-African images broaden our understanding of the spectrum of cross-cultural transactions that shaped the early modern world.

Going back to the landscape print, consider the friar's companion, a dark-skinned man clad in a short loincloth (fig. 97). One step in front of the cleric, he stands in a classical pose. He is an Apollo Belvedere seen from the back, with the Roman marble's sweeping drapes, muscular body, and dramatic head and arm gestures made famous by Bolognese engraver Marcantonio Raimondi in a circa 1510–27 print (fig. 98). The etched African man, standing under the palm tree, often associated with the Greco-Roman god, also shares his main attributes: heroic nudity and the bow and arrow. He also recalls for readers of early modern travel literature the imagery of Indigenous American men popularized since the late sixteenth century in the de Bry family editions (fig. 99). Unlike the Apollo, however, who once held his weapon at arm's length in his left hand, as does de Bry's Algonquian man, the African man rests his bent right arm on the tip of his strung bow, while his left hand lifts a long arrow to point toward the impressive mountains in the background of the scene (fig. 41). Turning his head back to speak with the friar standing behind him, he holds as a schoolmaster's stick more than a projectile the arrow that elongates his index finger. A bold, dark diagonal intersecting the thinly etched lines of the rolling hills, the dart is conspicuous in the image. That it is indeed a focal point rather than a detail is clear because the African man points with the left arm, whereas in the Kongo, as elsewhere, most would hold the bow with the left hand and direct the arrow with the right. A telling concession to the composition, and a hint about the original design that inspired it, the placement leaves ample space for and draws attention to the thin shaft. The long arrow thus demands to be read not as a documentary detail or an early modern iconographic

CHAPTER 7

Penned by Encounter

Capuchins, Central Africans, and the Making of a Cross-Cultural Discourse

commonplace connoting savagery but as a feature that directs a certain reading of the image, a reading in which pointing arrow and dark-skinned man play a central role.

Small figures pointing and gazing aloft at the corner of expansive landscapes are common features of early modern Arcadian scenes, imperial tableaux (colonial or otherwise), and exotic vignettes alike. At the edge of vast views, their suggestive presence fulfills a variety of visual functions. In some images, they rehearse the aesthetic pleasure viewers will derive from the depicted scene. In others, they

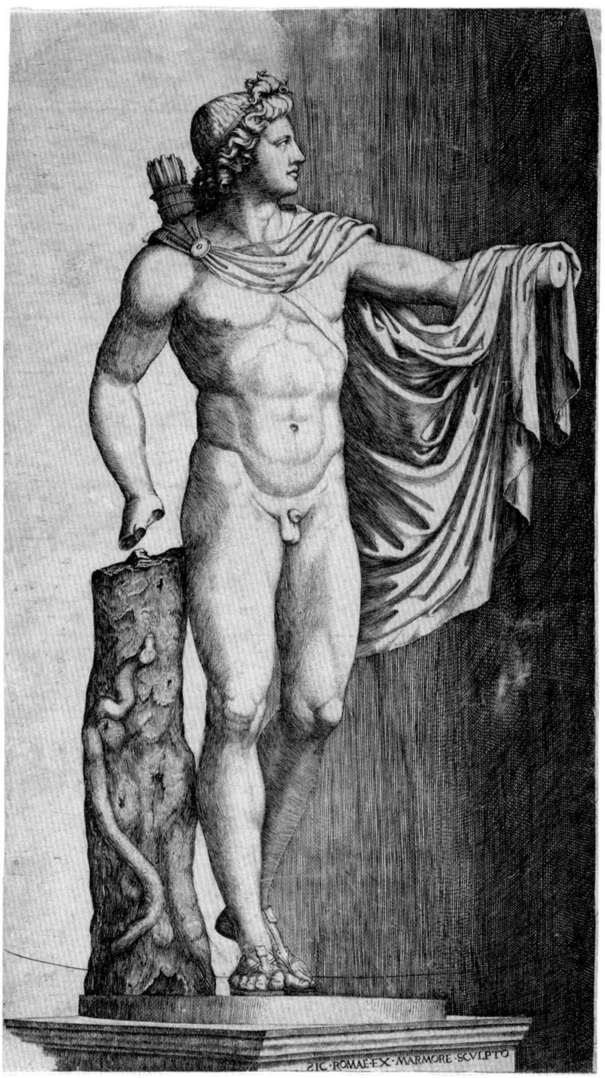

the depicted European friar, the motif of the two
men takes on yet another role. The pair formed by
the Franciscan and the African walking alongside
each other, conversing, and, I argue here, reckoning
together about the landscape around them illustrate and rehearse a process of discourse-making
and a form of relationship typical of the Capuchin
central-African mission. As a clearly self-conscious
image, the print points to its own origins in the
encounter (even if fraught) and in the conversation
(even if messy) between friars and central-African
men and women. It not only records the unfolding
of cross-cultural dialogue and negotiations but also
gives visual form to what these interactions are producing: a specific view of and discourse about early
modern central Africa. As such, the image points to
its character not only as a European-conceived and
executed picture *of* central Africa and its inhabitants
but also—and, I would argue, primarily—as a picture *from* central Africa and molded *by* the dialogue
between central Africans and Europeans. It reveals
how African and European subjectivities shaped
each other and the image in a process of cross-
cultural discourse-making honed in a sociopolitical
context that was neither colonial nor devoid of
prejudice and conflict. Ultimately, the sustained
encounter between the two men and the dialogue
woven between them are, I argue in this chapter,
the image's very authors.

The political and social context of the Capuchins' apostolic endeavors in Kongo and Angola (as
I showed in chapter 6 above) was exceptional within
the early modern world. Far from serving as the
religious arm of a colonial takeover, as clerics did
in the Americas, the friars acted in most of central
Africa at the behest and under the control of local
powers. Even in the enclaves of the Portuguese

embody imperial desires and plans for territorial
possession. Elsewhere, they complete Arcadian
fables, their presence breaking the spell of bucolic
simplicity with reminders of human guile. In this
picture of central Africa in which (as discussed in
chapter 3 above) viewers are expected to immerse
themselves and virtually stand in the position of

conquista of Angola, the European presence remained thin and highly contested. What is more, the core of their mission was in the Kingdom of Kongo, a realm that had professed Christianity and engaged with Europeans and the Atlantic world for a century and a half before the onset of their apostolate.[1] In fact, the rulers of Kongo had themselves requested from the papacy non-Portuguese priests in response to their rapidly deteriorating relationship with the ever more territorially aggressive Iberian realm.[2] The political situation of the Capuchin mission to central Africa resembled that of Catholic missions in Asia, which operated under the purview of local powers. However, it also differed from them in many ways, not least in the violently negative opinion friars had of the populations who hosted them in Kongo and Angola.[3] The immersive Capuchin images of central Africa thus invited viewers to plunge into a pictured space that was shaped by and illustrated a social, natural, and political landscape wrought on the anvil of fraught cross-cultural dialogue, exchange, and negotiation and in which Europeans did not have the upper hand.

Capuchin central-African images possessed an iconographically implemented and theologically driven permeability to the world of their viewers (as discussed in chapter 3 above). The scenes depicted created a relationship between beholder and image, involving the former in the latter. Narrative and formal elements created paths that invited their intended viewers to consider pictured and real worlds as concurrent and connected and to immerse themselves in the depicted space. I take my cue in this chapter from this fluid conception of the close connection and porous relationship between form, content, and visualization at the time of reception.

I explore the parallel ways in which the central-African natural, social, and religious environments in which the friars' vignettes emerged percolated into the images and characterized their form and content in the broadly conceived moment of inception. I argue that this *poesis*, or process of coming into being, actually held authorial agency over the Capuchin corpus.[4]

At the source of the images are moments of cross-cultural encounters from which multiple types of dialogues, negotiations, and attempts at mutual understanding emerged that shaped the pictures' form and content. The Capuchin central-African vignettes proved as permeable to the interactions and cross-cultural reckonings that formed the loam from which their imagery sprouted and flourished as they were openly and actively porous to their viewers. The stakes in considering their authorship in this expansive way are high, for it demands a reading of this and other documentary compendia, nominally created in cross-cultural contexts by one set of hands, that recognizes their emergence not as the expression of a single perspective but rather as the result of encounters, dialogues, and negotiations. It would be, for instance, erroneous to consider the Capuchin central-African corpus as made of exclusively European views and commentaries on Kongo and Angola. In spite of being European images, following a European format, and created for a European audience, they were not the result of one-sided, isolated reckonings and representation by Europeans. Instead, they derived from dialogues and negotiations between the friars and their central-African hosts, they encompassed in their frames multiple perspectives, and they can be fully understood only as cross-cultural productions. In chapter 3 the landscape print serves as a gateway through which to approach and analyze the mechanics of the central-African Franciscan images at the moment of reception. In this chapter it guides further inquiry into their inception in the meeting of African and European subjectivity.

Europe's Great Discovery

Figure 41's printmaker depicted the African man holding his dart as a pointing stick, stepping forward assuredly but also looking back to converse with the friar, as an active participant in the scene. While his presence in the image alongside the cleric is to some extent an index of Capuchin apostolic activities in central Africa, he is also the one whose own elongated pointed finger determines the deictic center of the image. Such a position is of great significance in the representation of a non-European figure as a subject, as well as an object, in the print. Pointing and speaking, the African man is able to determine his own here and now, his own position within the world that he inhabits alongside the European figure. This depiction is particularly meaningful because the absence of subjectivity is precisely one of the recurrent distinguishing features differentiating the savage from the civilized in the early modern European discourse of Otherness.[5]

"According to a central Western myth," art historian Joseph Koerner observes, "savages are defined . . . by their possessing not just a different view of the world, but no proper 'view' at all."[6] Visually, this idea has yielded representations such as Theodor de Bry's sixteenth-century engravings of Indigenous Americans, images that use as their sources the watercolors cartographer John White

made during his 1585–86 visit to the nascent English colony of Virginia in North America.[7] In his study of these prints, art historian Michael Gaudio has identified a range of strategies through which the early modern image-makers figured what they perceived as the Indigenous peoples' lack of perspective. First among these schemes was the insistence on the technological inferiority of people outside of Europe. "What defines the savage as such" in these images, Gaudio writes, "is his inability to undertake a subject position from which he might wield the very instruments" that supposedly gave Europeans their superiority, instruments "for positioning oneself within the universe."[8]

To a large extent, the idea of the newly encountered savage's lack of perspective was the actual Great Discovery Europeans made in what they would later term the age of exploration and overseas expansion.[9] The mental construction emerged in Europe and found narrative form in travel literature, where it appeared as an empirical observation or, in other words, a discovery. And it was a discovery that would prove foundational for and fundamental to European modernity. A supposed lack of perspective became the cornerstone for its definition of the Other as savage and the foundation on which early modern Europeans constructed a newfound and contradistinctive awareness of their world as mutable and their individual worldviews as contingent.

Theodor de Bry's depiction of the American man in "The Marckes of sundrye of the Chief mene of Virginia" (fig. 99) is paradigmatic of that moment. Engraved into being by a European artist confidently picturing a corner of the world other than his own, the American man stands, in contrast, his back turned to European viewers. Even if he

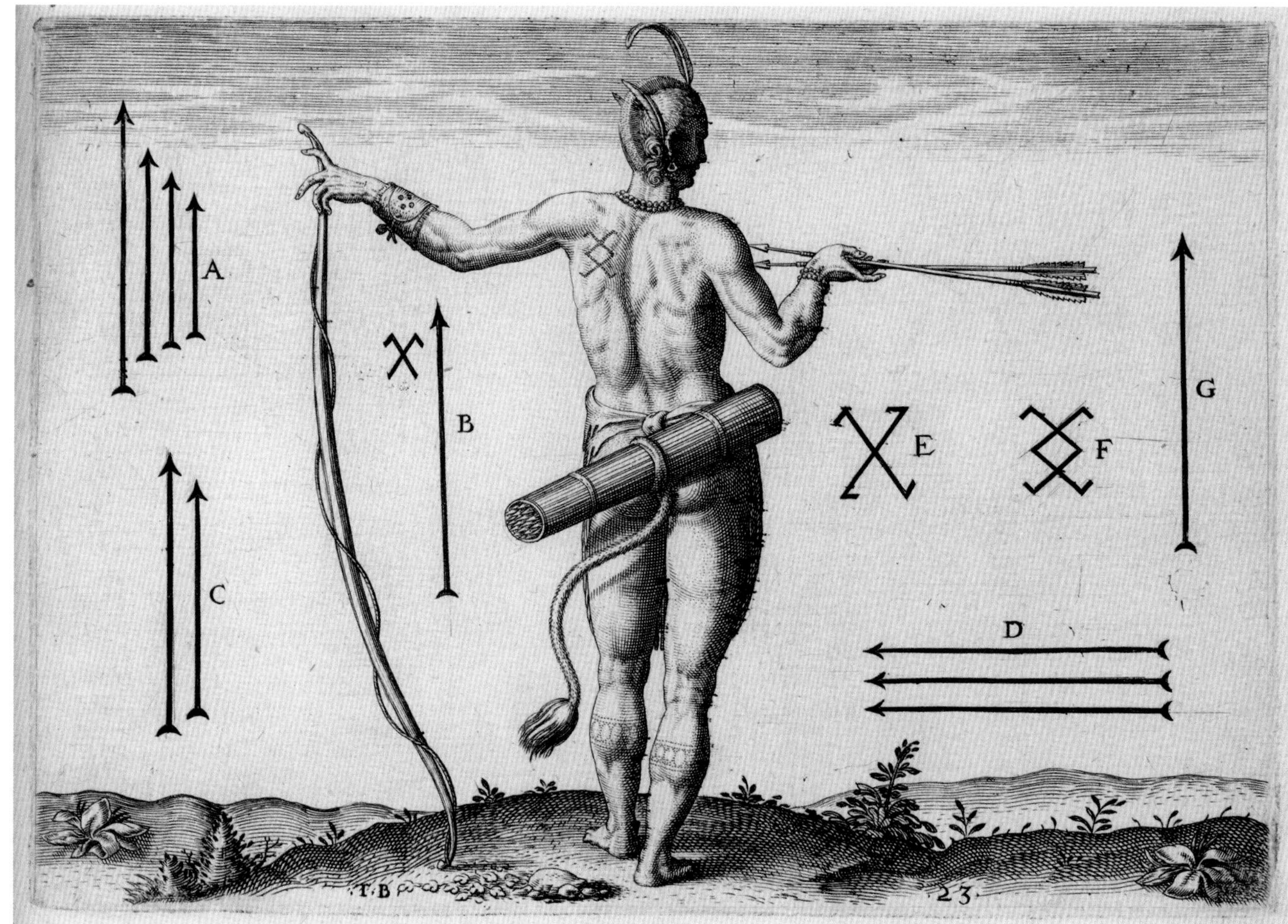

Figure 99

Theodor de Bry, "The Marckes of sundrye of the Chief mene of Virginia." Engraving, 16.2 × 22.2 cm (plate mark). Plate xxiii from Thomas Harriot, *A briefe and true report of the new found land of Virginia* (Frankfurt am Main: Typis Ioannis Wecheli, sumtibus vero Theodori de Bry, 1590). General Collection, Beinecke Rare Book and Manuscript Library, Yale University, Taylor 194. Photo courtesy of the Beinecke Rare Book and Manuscript Library.

holds two arrows, which Gaudio suggests could be read as akin to the engraver's burin, their tips are awkwardly turned inward toward his own body, firmly placing the would-be American instruments of inscription back into the hands of the European image-maker. Furthering the visual rhetoric, the engraver pictures the Indigenous man staring at an empty horizon, on an almost blank page he occupies alongside abstract signs and alphabetic letters that European readers know to combine to form explanations for the tattoos on his body. Though to some extent similar to the "marks" on the Indigenous man's skin, the letters are, Gaudio argues, foremost signs of another kind, belonging to what Europeans considered the chief technology of civilization: alphabetic writing.[10] While the engraver pictures the Other and inscribes him in his own epistemic realm of alphabetic writing and iconographic references, the tattooed Indian man, a savage, is merely pointing to himself in a weak gesture of self-awareness. He stands alone in a world closed onto itself, his body the only canvas and measure of his self-enclosed, perspectiveless world.

Picturing Dialogue in Kongo and Angola

In the landscape print, in contrast, the African man stands firmly on the grounds he is in the process of defining and inscribing, in words within the image as well as ink on the page, by wielding his arrow-cum-stylus with authorial authority and subjectivity. The view of Pungu a Ndongo is in part his, that of an African who has entered into dialogue with the European man and, beyond him, with Europe's linguistic, scientific, and religious epistemologies, as well as technologies of inscription and communication. What the scene so strikingly stages is a shared early modernity in which both men are plunged into a common experience of the paradigmatically modern uncertainty derived from the multiplication of worldviews. Immersed together in the landscape and in the arduous process of cross-cultural meaning-making, the two men confront ideas and exchange points of view and together partake in the construction of an early modern central-African discourse about nature, culture, and faith. This collaboratively honed discourse is the subject matter of the Capuchin didactic corpus, and the dialogue from which it emerges is its author.

European viewers would certainly have seen the African man as an informant, a source for local information about the region. It is also clear that in this context of a missionary image they would have read the friar's response to him as preaching or delivering a revelatory Christian exegesis of the conversation. The African man shows and tells,

provides facts, but the friar brings into the conversation his Christian views on the true source and purpose of nature's wonders—testaments of grace, the work of the Christian God—turning the African facts and thoughts into a form of knowledge with wholly different referents and frames. It is, after all, to the wondrous cliffs, the work of God, that the arrow and with it the image itself point. But it is precisely this picturing of an exchange of points of view that separates the print from many other early modern European images of non-European peoples and reveals its particular cross-cultural inception. Instead of depicting a horizonless savage, as in Sagard's frontispiece or de Bry's engraving (figs. 80, 99), or even an encounter between a worldly European and an Indigenous man pictured as his inferior, as in Claude d'Abbeville's opening page (fig. 79), the landscape print depicts a dialogue between peers. It suggests within its frame the molding of a cross-cultural discourse, here ostensibly about nature, as a dynamic exchange. In the conversation between the two men, two streams of thought about the mountain, the object of their gaze, flow, meet, and, in this eerily peaceful scene, seem to combine effortlessly. The white cliff offers a concrete space of commensurability for the two men's culturally diverse ideas, a common ground on which to build a common or at least mutually intelligible discourse.

Without naïvely and inaccurately suggesting that a series of benign encounters underlay the Capuchin corpus and the missionary activities it was meant to reflect, I want to underline the significance of the corpus's depiction of dialogue between interlocutors of different cultural backgrounds. It is a motif that encourages broad thinking about the multiple perspectives that are present in the images

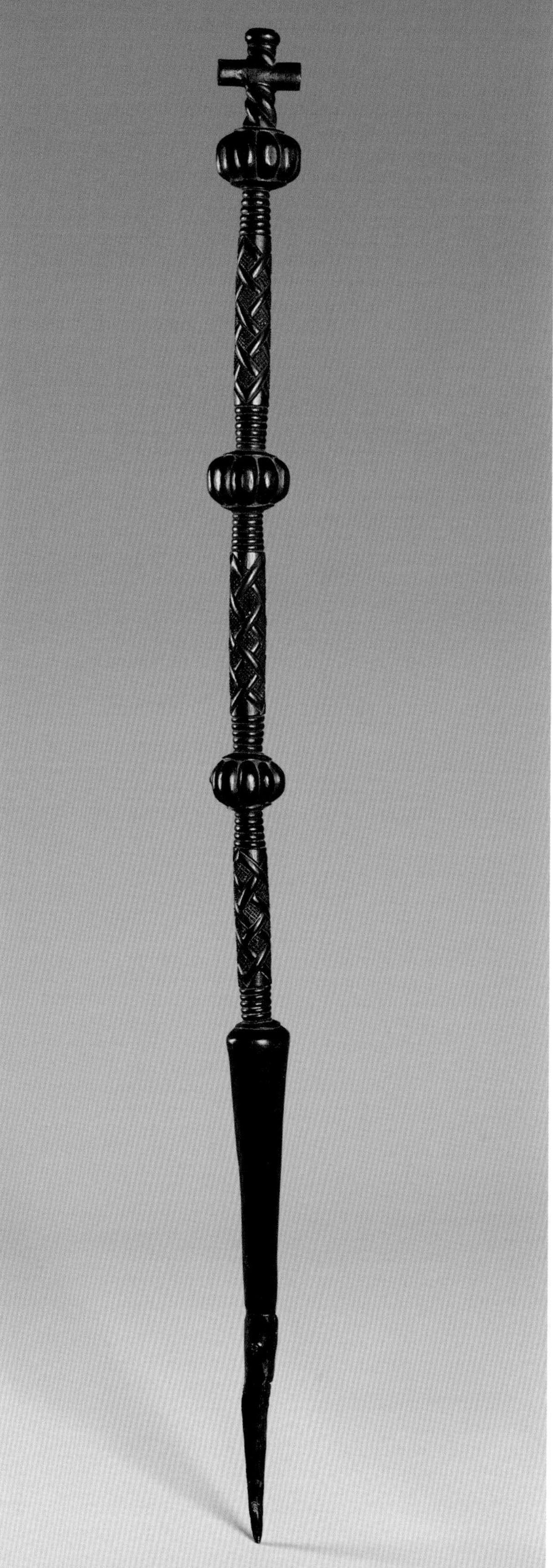

Figure 100

Unknown Kongo artist, *mestre*'s staff, Kongo Kingdom, possibly sixteenth to nineteenth century. Wood, height 118 cm. Museo Nacional de Etnologia, Lisbon, AI 206. Photo courtesy of Direção-Geral do Património Cultural / Arquivo e Documentação Fotográfica (José Paulo Ruas, 2013).

of the corpus. The preceding chapter outlined how the social and religious context of the Capuchin mission yielded carefully calibrated images of cooperation and balanced power between Capuchins and central Africans. Acting at the demand and under the control of the Kongo and Angolan elite, the friars had to work within the fabric of central-African societies. A core visual component of this environment is the conspicuous presence in the Capuchin vignettes of the *mestre*, clad in his easily recognizable white cloak and holding a staff topped with a cross, looming over the friars' every move in the course of their apostolic work. Although the maker of the landscape print misinterpreted the emblematic white cloak and staff of holders of the office, it is clear that the African man in this composition is precisely one of these figures, working alongside the friar and guiding him through the region's natural, social, and political landscape.

Implicit in the print, and even more so when the African man is read as a *mestre*, is the deep background that made possible the encounter and lively conversation it pictures. That the two men talk to each other demonstrates that at least one has learned the language of the other. That the African is a church master points to his status as a member of a sophisticated Christian society. That he holds the staff and white cloth that emblematize his function as *mestre* shows how he inhabits a world with broad religious, artistic, and commercial horizons. The staff and the cloth were two items that local artists and artisans created by recasting once-European and once wholly local emblems into new objects of Kongo Christian visual culture. The luminous white cloth of the *mestres* mixed and merged local and imported religious symbolism. It drew from the deep-rooted cosmological currency of whiteness in central Africa, as well as from Portuguese liturgical garb worn by clerics who traveled to Kongo or featured in the panel paintings imported into the region since the early years of contact between the two realms.[11] Kongo artists created the *mestres'* staffs of office and other objects such as crucifixes, rosaries, and medals in a similar correlation of local and imported ideas and symbols. The staff in figure 100, for instance, articulates central-African textile-inspired surface decoration with a cross at its top and bulbous knobs inspired by European baroque turned wood. Its provenance precludes a definitive dating to the early modern era, but it belongs to a category of objects whose form emerged in that period.[12] In other words, the print, as well as the Capuchin corpus at large, pictures several dimensions of cross-cultural dialogue. It not only captures the confrontation and exchange of ideas between friars and central Africans at the time of the mission but also records, indirectly but significantly, the history of cross-cultural engagement from which central-African visual, religious, and political culture took its form in the early modern period, since well before the Capuchin presence.

This *mestre*-friar pair that features in almost every Capuchin vignette picturing missionary work is also present, albeit less visibly, in every image of the corpus. The observations and interpretations of central-African nature, culture, and religion that the images depict emerged from the close interactions between friars and *mestres*. Precedents and parallels for this collaborative image-making process existed in the production of dictionaries and catechisms, endeavors of linguistic and cultural translation similar to those at play in the watercolors' depictions of natural and cultural landmarks. The earliest of these works still extant today, a catechism titled *Doutrina*

Christaã, which Jesuit Mattheus Cardoso compiled in 1624, relied on the knowledge of *mestres* with whom the nominal author discussed not only lexical details but also larger questions of etymology.[13] Similarly, the 1651 Kikongo-Latin-Spanish dictionary "Vocabularium Latinum, Hispanicum et Congense" was the work of Manuel Roboredo, born in the central-African capital of São Salvador / Mbanza Kongo of a Portuguese father and a sister of the Kongo king. A member of the aristocratic elite, he trained in the Kongo educational system put in place by the *mestres* in the sixteenth century and animated by them since, and may have served as a *mestre* himself.[14] In an unusual trajectory, he became an ordained cleric in 1637, served as the chaplain for King Garcia II, and eventually took the Capuchin habit in 1653 under the name of Francisco de São Salvador, after his birthplace.[15] The "Vocabularium" is a useful parallel to the watercolors. Both works to a large extent follow a European template: some version of Nebrija's Spanish-language dictionary for the "Vocabularium," natural-history or mores and customs albums for the watercolors. They both use European modes of recording, alphabetic writing or post-Renaissance illusionism, to document and translate information about central Africa. They also similarly leave largely unnoted the contributions of central Africans to their compositions, and more broadly the extent to which they are products as well as records of African knowledge.

The "Vocabularium" does not note the name of Roboredo, and the *Doutrina Christaã* explicitly mentions the *mestres* who effectively wrote the catechism in a dedicatory letter to the king of Kongo present only in some copies of the printed book, presumably destined to be sent to central Africa.[16]

There are nonetheless several moments in their texts in which their dialogic genesis comes to the fore. For instance, in his preface to the reader Cardoso talks briefly about moments of dialogue with Kikongo speakers. He explains that his decision not to translate key terms such as "Cross" or "Holy Spirit" resulted from conversations he had with native speakers. *Monho Auquissi*, he notes, was the term "the naturals of the Congo" used for Holy Spirit. He also reports that his findings about the etymology of the term literally "mean[ing] holy soul [*alma santa*]" led him to reject it, for "one can call any of the Blessed [*bemaventurados*] holy souls."[17] In this moment of the *Doutrina*, the otherwise obscured dialogue between the cleric and learned local experts at the basis of the book comes to the fore.

In another of his works, the "História do Reino do Congo," Cardoso further outlines his research methods.[18] Describing his attempts to trace the origins of the practice of circumcision in the region, he "decided, moved by [his] own curiosity, to see if [he] could find out from the native themselves the origin of this affair." At first frustrated by the silence of oral history on the topic, he finally got his answer from Dom Felix do Espirito Sancto, the *mestre* with whom he worked while a curate in the town of Mbanza Nsundi. Dom Felix explained to him that "this custom of circumcision that is spread over all of West Africa [Ethiopia Occidental] must have been introduced as an invention of the devil, since the reason to do it was to increase sexual pleasure because it delays the spilling of semen in the venereal act."[19] In other words, Dom Felix did not merely provide information on the practice, he also brought to the conversation, as a true scholar, an entire thesis about its purpose, origins, and moral significance. The passage then continues in a way

that truly captures the nature of the exchange as an ongoing conversation, an exchange of perspectives. The *mestre* must have used the word *Cariampemba* for devil, and the Jesuit evidently followed up, in vain, with an inquiry about the word: "I tried to learn the etymology of this term *Cariampemba*." The indirect speech with which Cardoso records the explanations of Dom Felix suggests that he considered him not as a mere informant, but as a person whose words rose to the status of arguments of authority. The Jesuit also made clear that he considered the central-African man "very intelligent" and, like himself, possessed of great curiosity, the quintessential quality of mind of early modern intellectuals.

Another learned Kongo man, Dom Calisto Zelotes dos Reis Magos, appears in the writings of several Capuchin missionaries. Like his contemporary Roboredo, Dom Calisto trained in the Kongo educational system and perhaps at the Jesuit College of Mbanza Kongo / São Salvador. He was literate in both Portuguese and Latin.[20] Chroniclers mentioning his name called him an "interpreter" or a "*mestre*" acting in the orbit of the Capuchins in the 1640s and 1650s.[21] He famously fell prisoner to Queen Njinga, who would free him, then elevate him to her intimate circle as secretary and councilor. His rise to favor would also be his demise, as one of the queen's successors beheaded him in 1666 because of his close association with her.[22] It is often mentioned in the secondary literature that he was an ordained priest, but I have not seen mention of his priesthood in primary documents. The confusion may come from Cavazzi's use of the Kongo aristocratic prefix *Dom* to refer to Calisto Zelotes, which readers seemingly understood as the Italian polite form of address for Catholic priests,

Don. Instead, he consistently appears in the sources in roles closely associated with *mestres*. Portuguese chronicler Cadornega identifies him as "mestre da Missão."[23] Cavazzi and Antonio de Teruel call him "an interpreter trained in our school."[24] Significantly, the friars not only refer to him in his role as an interpreter but also quote him as a source of local information and knowledge. Cavazzi, for instance, includes in his text "a very beautiful event" that Dom Calisto reported to him.[25] Antonio da Gaeta turns to him to ascertain an observation, starting a conversation in which the African man brings indispensable light to events witnessed.[26]

That the clerics sought and recorded orally communicated knowledge was not surprising. The history of European early modern science has often focused on the circulation of knowledge through written texts and images, but oral discourse also played a central role in the formation and communication of scientific facts and opinions.[27] The learned men of Europe counted on interviews with informants but also conversations with authorities (so distinguished in any number of ways) and colleagues as sources. Traces of this method pervade the Capuchin corpus. The glosses for the Parma Watercolors routinely record, but never explicitly acknowledge, the conversations the friars had with local informants and scholars. On one level, the note the vignettes take of local vocabulary in Portuguese (*fidalgo*), Kikongo (*mbanza*), Kimbundu (*libata*), as well as creolized or pidgin terms mixing several lexicons (*dembo*) and even terms from Brazilian Indigenous languages (*cagiú* from Tupi *acajú*), bears witness to the dialogical process of translation and language acquisition.[28] On another level, the friars discuss what they learned in central Africa about fruits and animals in the same breath as the

information they mobilize from European oral and written sources. They report the antihemorrhagic use of manatee ribs by central-African "surgeons" and the antivenom benefits of the "snake called *buta*" just as they write about whaling in Brazil or about the Franciscan trope of seeing a crucifix in the flesh of bananas.[29]

Visually, the corpus of Capuchin images illustrate specific moments of dialogue between friars and *mestres*. As in the landscape print, so in the Turin "Missione in prattica" a pair is shown deep in conversation while on the road (fig. 96), or they may be pictured in more animated poses, perhaps in disagreement, as in a scene of temple burning in the Parma Watercolors (fig. 72 / plate 64). These visual and written episodes, albeit relatively few and far between, call attention to the role central Africans played in the projects these documents record. They demonstrate how the European clerics who formally fulfilled the role of authors in these works of cross-cultural invention and translation in fact worked with often unnamed, seldom acknowledged central-African interlocutors who were not merely informants or bearers of local information but essential and, in some cases, principal actors in the knowledge-making enterprise of the Capuchin central-African corpus. The vignettes not only depict evenhanded power relations and cooperation, they also explicitly and implicitly record the active participation of central Africans in the creation of the early modern central-African discourse about nature, culture, and faith that the images picture.

In fact, much of the interest of the Capuchin images lies in their nature as both documents and products of the ongoing process through which common ideas about nature, culture, and faith emerged and took shape in central Africa on the anvil of cross-cultural dialogue and negotiation. The centuries-long presence of the Capuchins in the region, and their activities, even if sporadic, in a vast geography, meant that this shared discourse formed a significant episode in central-African cultural and intellectual history. Franciscan motifs and objects that appeared in the visual and material culture of Kongo and Angola, inside and outside of the geographic and temporal area of Capuchin missionary activity, testify to its sizable impact. To mention but one example, figurines of Saint Anthony, a Franciscan saint whose cult the friars promoted and whose iconography echoed their own garbed look, remained a visual genre in central Africa through at least the nineteenth century (fig. 62). Similar images even continued to bring spiritual and political empowerment to men and women forcefully taken from central Africa to Brazil through the slave trade.[30]

It is also important to bear in mind that the intense and lasting dialogue between central Africans and Capuchins formed only one part of the much broader engagement that the region's men and women maintained with Europe and its visual, material, and religious cultures. The Kongo had declared itself Christian since the beginning of the sixteenth century, that is, more than a century and a half before the arrival of the friars. Its visual culture, Christian and otherwise, thus developed in interaction with Europe through objects and artworks imported into the region by clerics as well as traders over the decades.[31] The region's worldly visual culture also emerged in the late fifteenth century from the experience of many local youth sent to Portugal—and beyond—to study and from that of the realm's ambassadors who toured the courts of Europe. Both groups of mostly men but

also women brought back with them memories and souvenirs from their stays. The experience of Dom Miguel de Castro in the mid-seventeenth century illustrates the process. A Kongo ambassador to the Dutch, who traveled to Brazil and Holland, he commissioned a portrait of himself while in the Low Countries in 1643. He brought back the painting to central Africa along with a range of other items, such as a mirror he purchased and the sword and beaver-felt hat the governor of Dutch Brazil gifted to him during his stay in Recife.[32] The latter two items feature prominently in one of his portraits that remained in Europe and is perhaps similar to the one that traveled back with him to Kongo.[33] Engagement with overseas culture also took the form of object collections of imported luxury items and artworks. In the mid-seventeenth century, for instance, the king of Kongo could draw from his royal estate to dispatch as a diplomatic gift a gilded platter made in Potosí, Peru.[34]

The self-assured pointing gesture of the African man in the landscape print illustrates this larger context of central-African engagement in cross-cultural conversations, long-distance material and political exchange, and confident embrace of broad horizons. It is a reflection of the geopolitical status of the Kongo and many of its neighboring polities as independent entities, outside of Europe's colonial reach and conversant in its technologies of communication and warfare, such as writing and firearms, as well as its religious views and debates.[35] Such a portrayal of an African man engaged in lively dialogue with a European friar is an oddity in the seventeenth- and eighteenth-century repertoire of European images of faraway people in general and of Africans in particular. Contemporary depictions of inhabitants of the continent sooner relied on analogic modes of description that reshaped even empirical observations to fit within preexisting European templates. This mode of early ethnography exoticized faraway people, placing them within the describer's own epistemic realm.[36] The transformation of the *mestre* into an Apollo in the hands of the etcher of the landscape followed exactly such logic. However, exoticism and emblematic conceptions of savagery only played a limited role in the construction of the Capuchin central-African images.

Not a Blank Page

The African man pictured in the print is not a generic savage. He is a *mestre*, an essential intermediary and guide on whom the friars relied and depended in every endeavor. *Mestres* orchestrated the friars' movements, controlled their interactions with local populations, and even voiced their words. It was indeed the practice, no matter how fluent friars would become in local languages, that the *mestre* repeat sermons on their behalf and intercede in the giving of sacraments. The production of a discourse made of multiple interlacing voices was a central aspect of the relationship between *mestres* and friars. The pair repeated, adapted, and redeployed each other's words, essentially making them their own in the process. *Mestres* conveyed their own versions of clerics' speeches and sermons to central-African audiences. Friars wrote down central-African oral argumentation and ideas in their manuscripts for their European audiences. The extent to which the exchange formed a "dialogue of the deaf" has been the subject of much debate.[37] Some scholars have argued that central Africans largely integrated the Christian message into a preexisting cosmology.[38] Others, often missionaries themselves, judged the conversion of the kingdom

as sincere and unproblematic.[39] Still others considered the history of Christianity in central Africa as a sophisticated form of syncretism.[40] In my own analysis of the deep and lasting engagement of central Africans with Christian doctrine and visual culture, I have focused on the complex and evolving ways in which the elite of the Kongo mixed and redeployed local and foreign ideas, objects, and images into a new Kongo Christian discourse.[41] I see the interactions of friars and *mestres* as iterations of this process of cross-cultural reckoning and invention at the level of individuals. *Mestres* adapted the Capuchins' words and actions to local ideas and customs, including those about the nature and practice of Christianity honed over more than a century and a half before the friars' arrival in the region. In turn, in the vignettes concerned with missionary methods, but also in those about flora, fauna, or local customs, the Capuchins recorded and transcribed the knowledge that formed over the course of their conversations with *mestres* and others.

To put things slightly differently, the African man in figure 41's landscape engraving is not Michel de Certeau's "blank (savage) page" on which Europeans inscribe their desires and will through colonization.[42] The French Jesuit scholar coined his famous 1975 formulation in a visual analysis of a print by Jan van der Straet in which Amerigo Vespucci encounters a nude female allegory of America (fig. 101).[43] The Latin caption glosses the scene as the moment in which Amerigo names the continent. He calls out what henceforth will be her name, awakening her into a new world under the political and epistemic purview of Europe. In the blatantly erotic scene, the European man steps off his boat and onto the shore, his hands embarrassed with the instruments of navigation and conquest: a flag, a cross, a compass. He comes face to face with

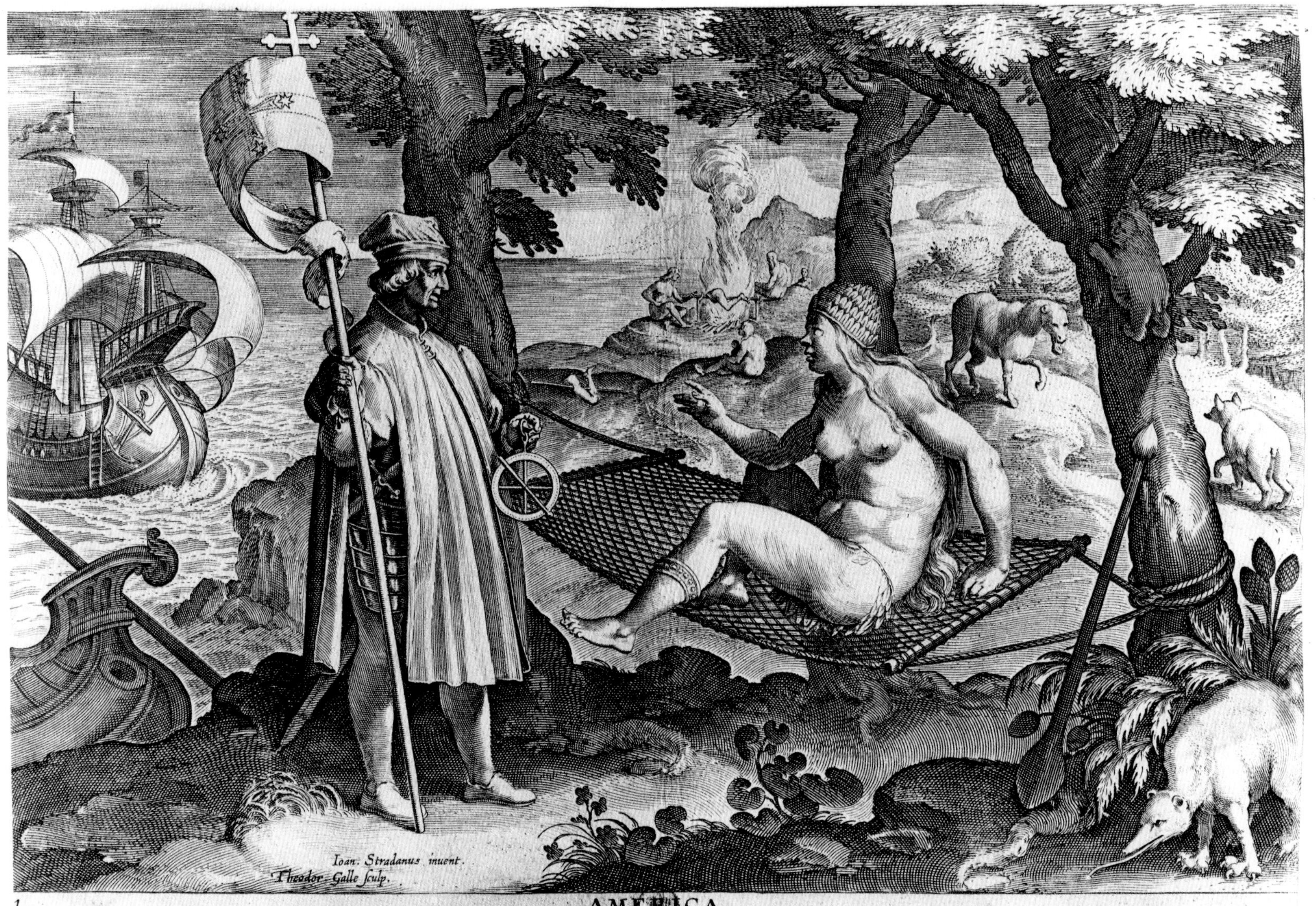

AMERICA.

1. *Americen Americus retexit, ⸺ Semel vocauit inde semper excitam⸺ .*

Ioan. Stradanus inuent.
Theodor Galle sculp.

the beguiling figure of the new-to-him continent, reaching out from her hammock to invite him to step closer. The astonished, perhaps bashful man, stepping onto novel ground, is apparently about to both discover and conquer America, in a rehearsal of male sexual coming of age, given here mythical, allegorical dimensions.

Van der Straet's image is emblematic of early modern European thinkers', artists', and rulers' conceptions and representations of distant Others as inferior, exotic, and prime for political and epistemological conquest. Certeau's interpretation, in turn, is a flagship moment in the questioning of this ideology and the visual apparatus at its service. The composition of the landscape print, revolving around the defining presence of the European-African pair, could easily invite mistaken interpretations of the scene as another example of the type of encounter images Certeau critiqued. Yet, although similar in its setting in sylvan wilderness and its organization around a moment of close interaction between a European and a figure indigenous to the landscape, the central-African print is strikingly different from Van der Straet's image and others of that ilk (fig. 41). The landscape in fact unfolds in full contrast to the scene of European takeover and epistemological appropriation and imposition. There, no hint of conquest either sexual or territorial. No European instruments suggest an inscription of European will or history on the new land. And indeed, politically, central Africa remained independent throughout the early modern period except for the thin Portuguese *conquista* of Angola. Neither does the African man appear to belong to the realm of nature, guileless, raw, and as yet uncultured as the allegory of America. He is a self-possessed protagonist, and the worldview that the print captures is

at least in part his. On the inked paper, the point of the African's arrow and the tip of the etcher's needle meet and together re-create the line once drawn at the nib of the quill in a friar's original *disegno*. Composed through the efforts of many minds and hands, the self-aware central-African image gives visual form to the circumstances of its inception. Its composition, though European in form, emerged within a political and intellectual geography that Africans controlled even in the face of persistent European pressures on their social, political, and spiritual affairs, through the slave trade, Portuguese and Roman proselytism, and outright colonial ambitions. It is an image born at the nexus of European and central-African reckonings, conversations, and negotiations about the world that their relationship, at times fraught and at others amicable, was in the process of shaping. Instead of a "blank page" waiting for inscription, the African is here a link in a chain through which knowledge about and from central Africa and central Africans is mobilized, reworked in dialogue with Europeans, then recorded and communicated to Italian viewers.

This reading of the landscape print is to some extent parallel to Gaudio's interpretation of de Bry's "Marckes of sundrye of the Chief mene of Virginia" (fig. 99). In the opening pages of his *Engraving the Savage*, Gaudio invites readers to consider the engraved arrows in the hand of the Indigenous man not as documentary elements, the weapons he actually used, or as an iconographic feature, the emblem of the savage, but as "opaque signifiers" pointing to the image itself and, through it, to early modern European practices of engraving in particular and image-making in general.[44] He sees in the arrows a moment of European doubt in the possibility of apprehending and making sense of the New World that makes the engraving as a whole "a sixteenth-century example of what W. J. T. Mitchell has called a 'metapicture.'"[45] Metapictures, or self-aware images, are compositions that explicitly call attention to their own production or take it as their main topic.[46]

An analogous reading of the Pungu a Ndongo landscape brings to the fore its own self-awareness. Here the arrow neither factually describes central-African weaponry nor allegorically refers to the man's savagery in any meaningful way. It is in fact but a misreading of a *mestre*'s insignia. Further, African savagery in European images of the time took on a much more graphic guise that relied more on anthropophagy or conflations with the animal realm than on emblematic displays of bows and arrows.[47] The projectile in this print points to the landscape's etched lines, putting what Gaudio calls the "labor of inscription" in the hands of the African man, a key detail that, in the particular context of Capuchin central-African images, points to the inception of the image in the dialogue between several voices hailing from different horizons.

While for Gaudio at stake in the American metapicture is the possibility for Europeans to "construct meaning about the New World," this issue of the construction of meaning and knowledge across cultures takes on another dimension in the central-African print. Here the African stands alongside the European. They are both inscribed and inscribers, subjects and authors, and their intense dialogue suggests shared, if not quite equal, authority over the description and interpretation of the scene. Gaudio saw in the Indigenous man's self-inscription a sign of the "incomplete nature of [the concepts of] civility and savagery" available to

sixteenth-century Europeans. I see in the ambivalent representation of the African as both object and maker of the seventeenth-century image a trace that makes evident the encounter and molding of African and European subjectivity at the core of the shared construction of a cross-cultural discourse. It is this very process that the print both captures and participates in shaping.[48]

Nature as Culture: Pineapples

Not all Capuchin central-African images showcase the contribution of multiple points of view to their construction as explicitly as the landscape print. There, a conversation between a friar and an African interlocutor about central-African nature is both the subject matter of the image and the source from which the information the image brings to viewers about the mountain range of Pungu a Ndongo originates. Other vignettes are more circumspect about the sources of their contents yet emerged from the same dynamics.

A tall pineapple plant features among the fruits and vegetables included in the ordered compendium of central Africa's natural and cultural landscape in the circa 1650 Museo Francescano drawing (plate 1). "Pineapple," the text reads, "best of fruits. It is like the quintessence of melon. Its water [is said to] break [kidney] stones" (fig. 102). The ink-on-paper drawing shows a bulbous fruit topped with small leaves. Two zigzag lines render scaly, uneven skin. It grows from a tall stalk out of a cluster of long, thick, thorny leaves that emerge from the ground. The *ananasso* does not appear in the extant Parma Watercolors, although there is room for it as number 34 in the series, as part of the sequence on fruits, between the cola nut and the bananas. The

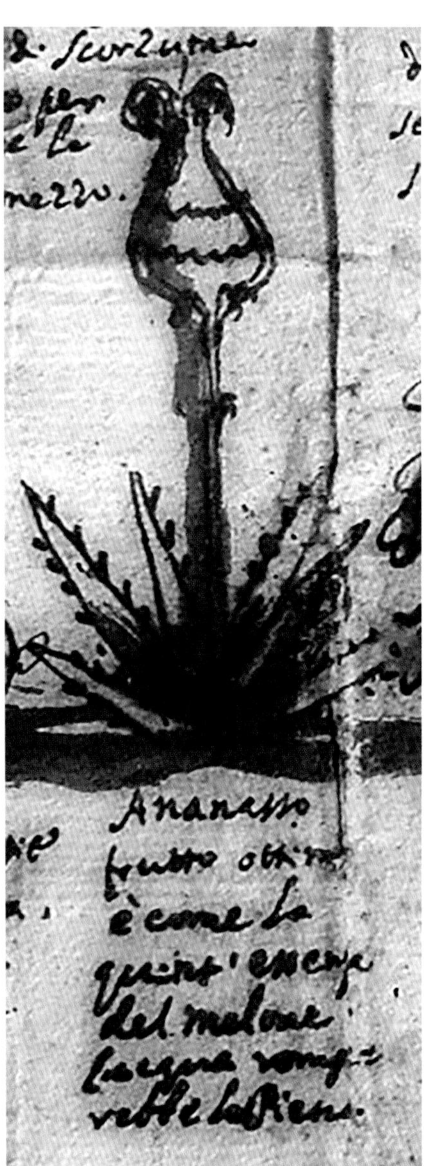

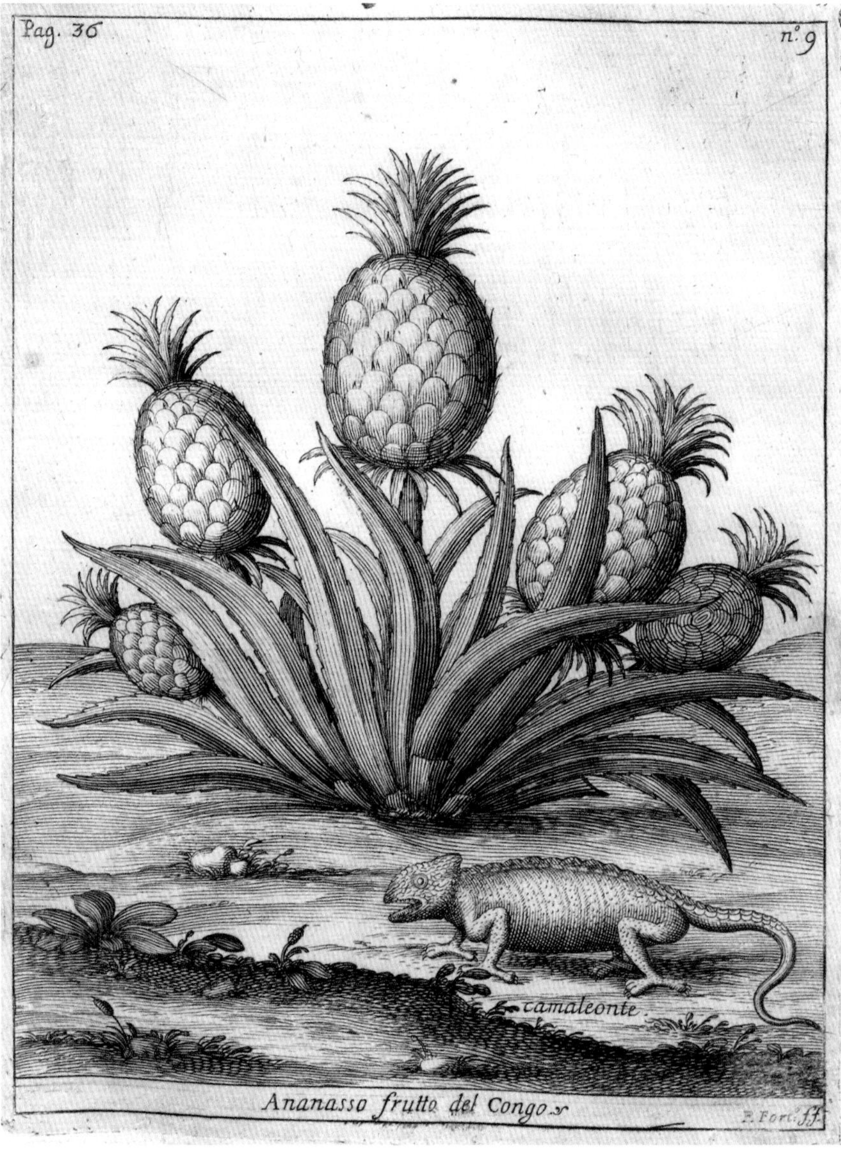

print of the fruit that editor Alamandini created for Cavazzi's *Istorica descrizione* gives an idea of what the Parma Watercolor design may have been (fig. 103). Several scalier, plumper pineapples emerge from less thorny leaves alongside a chameleon, possibly gleaned from another plate prepared by Cavazzi and once in the Parma Watercolors too.[49] Friar Merolla also included a version of the plant in plate 16 of his 1692 *Breve, e succinta relatione,* whose illustrations drew from Cavazzi's book or shared with it a common source.[50] Both printed works comment in their text on the good taste of the fruit, on the ways in which its crown of leaves, when put in the ground, sprout another plant, and draw the same analogy between its leaves and that of a succulent, or "sempreviva."

This analogic approach to the plants in the text, paired with attempts at naturalistic description in the image, is typical of the Capuchin project. Word and image play their parts in the Capuchins' cataloguing of central-African nature as purveyor of food, wondrous Godly creations, and "remarkable" curiosities.[51] Yet the images that appear in the Capuchin compendia also tell a rich, if less immediately visible, story about their inception in the encounter between the friars' worldview and that of their central-African interlocutors. The wording of the glosses, and the confident representations, speak authoritatively of their subject matter, and this authority derived from the convergence of multiple sources. The friars explicitly or implicitly drew from other European writings, but their compendia also speak, as do their dictionaries and catechisms, in the largely unacknowledged but distinguishable voices of individual or collective holders of local knowledge. The pineapple, which is not indigenous to the region, only appears in the Capuchin manuscripts and prints because the inhabitants of Kongo and Angola had adopted and adapted it when it reached their shores with the Portuguese in the sixteenth century. Its very inclusion in the corpus derives from and records this history of central Africans' engagement with novelty and with agricultural, medicinal, and technological innovation.

Opinions about the pineapple as "best of fruits" and able to "break [kidney] stones" appear in European writings of the sixteenth and seventeenth centuries in the broad orbit of the friars. Cristóbal Acosta's 1578 *Tractado delas Drogas* is a possible source for some of the information recorded about the pineapple, including its great taste and beneficial properties for kidney stones.[52] Merolla's description has close kinship to Acosta's, particularly in the observation that the unripe fruit could melt away the blade of a knife. Franciscan *capucho* friar Cristóvão de Lisboa's "Historia dos animaes, e árvores do Maranhão," composed in the 1620s, describes the plant as "the best fruit of this land," its juice "very powerful for the [kidney] stone pain."[53] He had been the guardian of Lisbon's Convent of Santo António, where the Capuchins in transit to Kongo and Angola would reside a couple of decades later. Though elected bishop of Angola and Congo, he never traveled to the region. He died in the Lisbon convent in 1652.[54]

Did the Capuchins hear about the plant's properties from central Africans or from the Portuguese, from books or from word of mouth? Whether their mention of the plant's qualities derived from local experimentation through which central Africans would have identified its properties or from outside knowledge brought to the region, it shows that early modern central Africa was a place where new plants and new knowledge sprung, took root, circulated, and thrived. The pineapple is far from the only example of botanical transfer featuring in the Capuchin corpus. In fact, many of the plants the friars represented because of their usefulness as food sources originated in the Americas. They pictured the potato (plates 1 and 17), the cashew and the purple mombin (plate 24), the guava (plate 25), the papaya (plates 1, 26), as well as peanuts, corn, and manioc (all in plate 1). Only in some cases did the friar note their origins, labeling, for instance, the papaya tree "Arbore dell'America" in the Museo Francescano drawing. The many American crops included in the images are records of central-African technological, gastronomical, agricultural knowledge and innovation whether or not the friars perceived them as such. Although early modern Europeans rarely recognized it, the flora, fauna, and foods they encountered in faraway lands were not inherent features of the natural world but products of human endeavors.[55] Capuchin vignettes of pineapples, which took the guise of natural-historical vignettes, in fact portrayed a long history of central-African engagement with once-foreign crops and with innovation in agricultural techniques.

Along with domesticating the pineapple plant, developing its use as foodstuff, and perhaps discovering its medicinal applications, central Africans also conducted further experimentation that led to the use of its fiber in the making of cloth. Highly textile-literate central Africans probed and identified the fiber-making possibilities of the pineapple plant following a technique similar to the one they used to extract fibers from palm leaves.[56] Many central-African textiles produced in the early modern period are still extant, but further material analysis is needed to determine the nature of their vegetal fiber as either raffia or pineapple. It is clear, however, that at least by the second half of the eighteenth century, the use of pineapple in textile making and its association with prestige items was well established in the region. A 1775 French-Kikongo dictionary from Kakongo, north of the Congo River, gives the translation for pineapple as *infubu* (pl: *zimfubu*: *ananas*). It proposes as an example of the term's use the following phrase: "teva kia nfubu," which the dictionary translates as "sorte de natte brodée" (i.e., type of embroidered mat).[57] The entry for *teva*, translated as "mat," further clarifies the status of the pineapple textile as an elaborate, sophisticated item in drawing a contrast between the "ordinary mat [*natte commune*]" and the "teva kia infubu," or "embroidered mat [*natte brodée*]."[58]

It is easy to perceive how the imaginative central-African textile makers would have relished the seductive interplay of design and material the plant afforded. The patterns and textures of pineapple skin and leaf clusters echo in myriad ways the geometric elaborations and rich textures that have made central-African textiles famous in Europe since the early modern period (figs. 88, 104). The plant's textured spikes and repetition of geometric shapes, often adding up to diamonds, on the fruit's skin are particularly reminiscent of the designs and cut pile surfaces in early modern central-African vegetal-fiber cloth. The example in figures 88 and 104 showcases the diamond-shaped, richly textured geometric elaborations whose details as well as overall effect evoke the look of the pineapple's scaly shell and the interlace of its crown and leaves. The Parma Watercolors also allude to these designs in several of their depictions of clothing (plates 4, 52, 59). This intricate play between material and design particularly befits luxury cloth. It is likely that well before the first clue I have identified in the documentary record in the form of the 1770s dictionary entry, the most sophisticated items of prestige, such as the caps and exquisite textile wrappers of the region's elite, already used the once-new fiber.[59]

The frontispiece to António de Cadornega's 1680 history of Angola provides a clue in this regard. It associates the pineapple with the king of Kongo and the king of Angola, the former possibly wearing the fiber in his hat and wrapper (fig. 20).[60] The

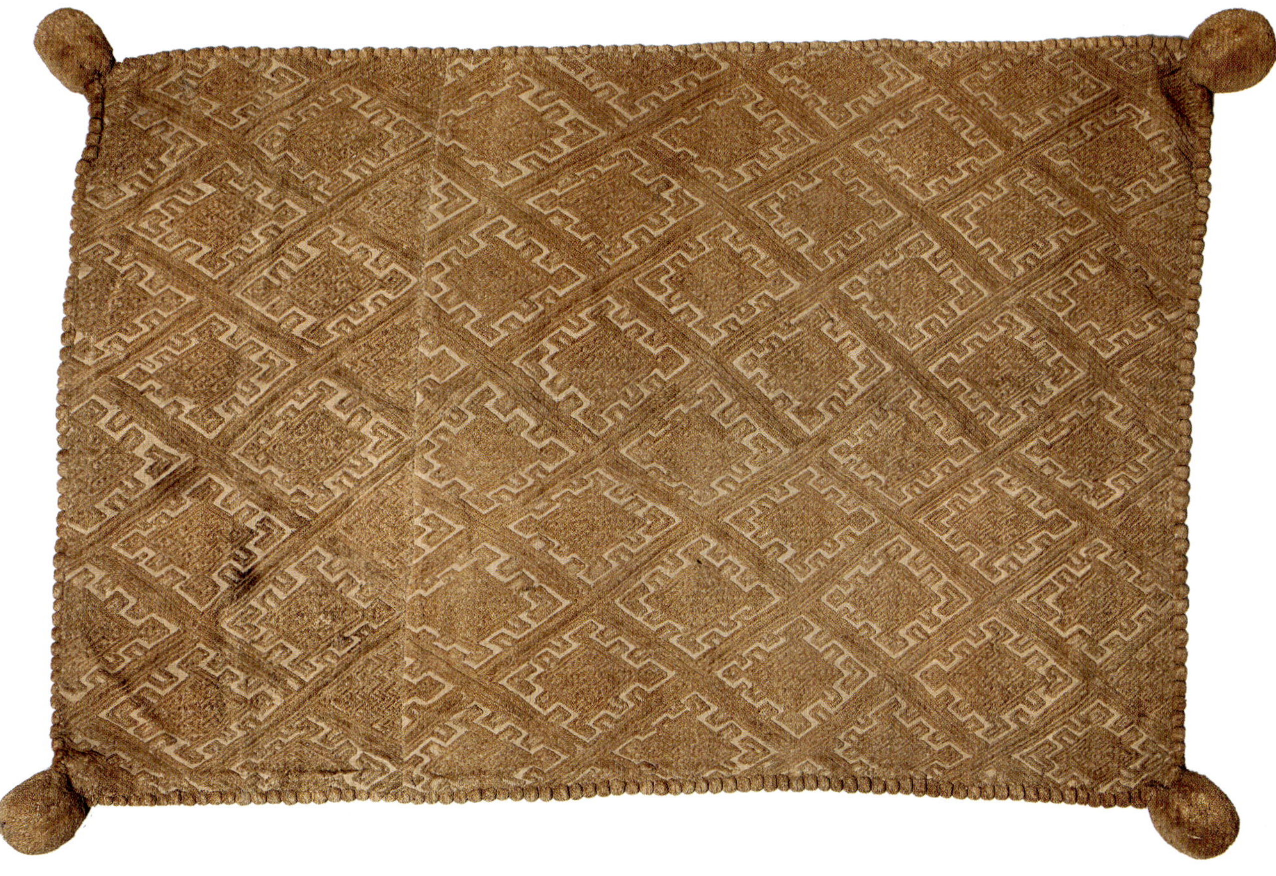

Portuguese chronicler also pictures other rulers from the region, but only these two are associated with European-style crowns and scepters at their feet, as well as a pineapple, the king of fruit, above each of their heads, atop a label announcing "fruit of Angola." He places the other great leaders portrayed in the manuscript under kernels of palm nuts or large cups of woven basketry holding assortments of fruits.[61] The juxtaposition of the once-foreign, yet domesticated pineapple and the rulers of two central-African kingdoms that intensely engaged with the networks of the Atlantic world is particularly evocative.

A seemingly simple image of a plant can reveal itself to be a node in which practical botanical information crosses paths with histories of central Africans' engagement with novelty and involvement in experimentation in ecological change, medical knowledge, and technology. Reading the image as the result of the friar's isolated observation of nature would be either naïve or careless, an uncritical acceptance of an ideology of European epistemological independence and superiority to which even the Capuchins did not fully ascribe. It is a "fallacy," historian Marcy Norton writes about similar material from another continent, to claim "that early modern Europeans encountered American 'nature' without mediation from native communities and practices" and as an untouched world rather than the cultural production of these communities.[62] A more accurate interpretation of the vignette is to recognize its inception in the meeting of central-African and Capuchin perspectives and modes of knowledge, and to consider it more fully as the product and implement of the cross-cultural discourse-making process that unfolded between friars and central Africans.

Conclusion

The landscape print presents an emblematic tableau of the peculiar relationship between the friars and the elite of Kongo and Angola who had invited them to the region and under whose control they served. Unlike most representations of Africans in European seventeenth- and eighteenth-century visual culture, the dark-skinned man pictured in lively conversation with the friar at the bottom right corner of the vista is not figured as a subservient character, a barely human being, or a violent heathen. He is not etched either in the template used at the time to picture the savage, that is, as a guileless, horizonless character about to see European political and epistemological will take over his or her world. Rather, he stands as a full subject involved in an exchange of perspectives with the friar, whom he addresses as a foreigner in his land and a fellow Christian. The self-aware print points to its origins and its role in the construction of the

cross-cultural discourse about nature, culture, and faith that emerged in early modern central Africa at the intersection of the two men's worldviews.

At the source of the image is a history of cross-cultural encounters, dialogues, negotiations, and attempts at mutual understanding that determined and shaped its form and content. It would be erroneous to consider it as the exclusive expression of a friar's views and commentaries on Kongo and Angola. In spite of being an image of European format, created for a European audience, it is not a representation derived from one-sided reckonings. Instead, its authorship lay in the dialogues and negotiations that unfolded between the Capuchins and their central-African hosts. Other images in the corpus are less explicit about their inception and participation in an exchange of points of view and the making of a cross-cultural discourse. Botanical plates, such as images of pineapples, look deceptively wholly European, suggesting erroneously that they were the products of the friars' independent, one-sided observation. Rather, they emerged at the intersection of Capuchin and central-African bodies of knowledge.

The landscape print, the pineapple images, and the Capuchin central-African didactic corpus at large described and emerged from a mode of interaction specific to the region, in which a discourse about nature, culture, and faith grew out of a dialogue, even if imperfect, and cooperation, even if fraught, between the friars and their local hosts and interlocutors, first among which were the *mestres*. European in format, style, and audience, the Capuchin images should nonetheless be approached as cross-cultural productions. They are more than purely European representations of Otherness or imperfect attempts at silencing local voices or disavowing local knowledge on which the friars relied. They are documents and agents of the tense, unresolved, and ongoing conversations between the friars and central Africans about the shape of nature, the makeup of society, and the contours of and connections between the visible and the invisible worlds. They are sites from which to excavate a record of collective reckoning about change, novelty, and the confrontation of world-views in seventeenth- and eighteenth-century central Africa. They give expressive form to a mode of cross-cultural engagement different from the ones observed and analyzed elsewhere in the early modern world. They differ, for instance, from the visual modes of expression arising out of the force-ful religious impositions of the Iberian colonial projects of Latin America. They did not function as gestures of imperial appropriation of form and content from multiple distant visual traditions, such as those at the core of Kalender Paşa's single seventeenth-century album that functioned as a mirror of the vast and varied horizons over which the Ottoman "World Emperor Sultan Ahmed Khan" ruled.[63] They did not operate either as part of an enthusiastic adoption of local culture as in the Jesuits' Asian missions. Instead, the relationship be-tween the Capuchin friars and their central-African hosts, as well as the visual discourse that emerged from it, followed a path of its own, bringing a new dimension to our understanding of the nature, workings, and visibility of cross-cultural interac-tions and of the role these interactions played in shaping the early modern world.

Conclusion

Myriad are the ways in which the Capuchin images from Kongo and Angola published for the first time in this book will affect views of central Africa and the early modern world. Their portrayal of the environment and inhabitants of Kongo, Ndongo, Matamba, Luanda, Ilamba, Kisama, Ndembu, and beyond forms a dense and largely unparalleled documentary source. New horizons for ecological and biological inquiries arise from their descriptions of animal types, locations, and behaviors and depictions of plant species and characteristics. The implements, musical instruments, carved figures, clothing practices, and performances they picture push back the timeline for the study of central-African visual and material cultures, at times by several centuries. The objects they present in use in specific locations map a unique geography of their creation, use, and occurrence.

Archaeological findings and period written accounts from outsiders and Africans have offered illuminating historically-grounded information on some categories of objects and practices from early modern Kongo and Angola.[1] Yet knowledge about large parts of central-African visual and material culture still relies predominantly on oral histories and ethnographies collected in the nineteenth and twentieth centuries that provide only limited insights into the deeper past. The Capuchin central-African corpus changes these epistemic conditions. A great number of cultural productions with well-known manifestations in the 1800s and 1900s gain historical depth in the watercolors and drawings of the Minorite mission. From an Atlantic-wide perspective, the vignettes also sketch a chronologically specific background against which to study the visual and material culture created in Europe and the Americas by men and women of central-African origins or descent caught in the Atlantic slave trade and slave systems. They enable studies that can avoid the pitfalls of anachronic comparisons and build rigorous, historically and geographically anchored circum-Atlantic arguments.

It is a primary goal of this book to bring to scholarly attention the newly uncovered watercolors along with closely related images I gathered from collections and archives around the world.

The conscientious introduction to the set and to its local and global resonances in the preceding chapters has not only outlined how this exceptional newly surfaced documentary compendium greatly enriches our knowledge of Kongo and Angola and literally multiplies the European-format visual record about the African continent before 1850. It has also demonstrated that the corpus transforms our understanding of early modern global interactions in several ways. First, it brings to the fore the Capuchin missionary project of the seventeenth and eighteenth centuries that has remained largely unstudied, although it was every bit as broad and ambitious as the contemporaneous, robustly investigated Jesuit and Franciscan apostolic ventures. Further, it highlights a set of spiritual and intellectual interactions between Africans and Europeans unfolding outside of a colonial context. Analyzing the fraught yet collaborative relationships between friars and central Africans pictured in the images deepens our understanding of religious exchange, enriches our grasp of the cross-cultural dimension of early modern (visual) natural-historical knowledge, and, ultimately, highlights the role of Africa and Africans in shaping the early modern world.

Beyond the scholarly realm, the Capuchin corpus's vivid depictions are poised to shatter preconceptions about Kongo and Angola. How better to counteract the enduring pernicious portrayal of the region as the backward, sinister "heart of darkness," an image that emerged in the late nineteenth century in ideological support of European colonial ambitions, than to display the bright, multifaceted showcase of sophisticated societies in the pages of the Parma Watercolors and "Missione in prattica"? Redressing misconstrued ideas the friars' religious brothers held about Kongo and Angola was after all one of the explicit goals of the Capuchin visual corpus. Instead of exotic pictures of heathen or noble savages, the vignettes showed protagonists of complex sociocultural character such as the Ndembu ruler in figure 105 (plate 60). The leader of a polity located between Kongo and Angola, he wears an imported crimson cloak on his shoulders and walks, cane in hand, followed by a conspicuously self-flagellating entourage, to greet a friar as his equal with an elegant wave of his black beaver-felt hat. Outfitted with the luxurious accessories he shared with late seventeenth-century fashionable men from around the Atlantic world, the Ndembu titleholder stands at the crosscurrents of global networks of trade and material exchange. His cloak likely came from Europe. His hat was made from the fur of North American beavers. If his cane had a silver pommel, the metal would likely trace back to Peru. His blue-and-white striped leg covering could be of indigo-dyed cloth made in west Africa or India. He is anything but the emblematic, naked, and perspectiveless savage in contradistinction to which post-Renaissance Europe constructed its modern self. The new windows the Ndembu's hat and the Capuchin corpus open into the early modern global networks widen the perspective of even the broadest accounts of the first globalization, such as Timothy Brooke's *Vermeer's Hat*, a best-selling panorama of the material connections that tied together far-flung regions of the planet in the seventeenth century. Notably, Africa and Africans only feature modestly in the otherwise geographically capacious book. In contrast, the history of global entanglements the Capuchin images capture does not overlook Africans or reduce them to purveyors of primary resources or unfree labor. It presents them as multifaceted, sophisticated protagonists

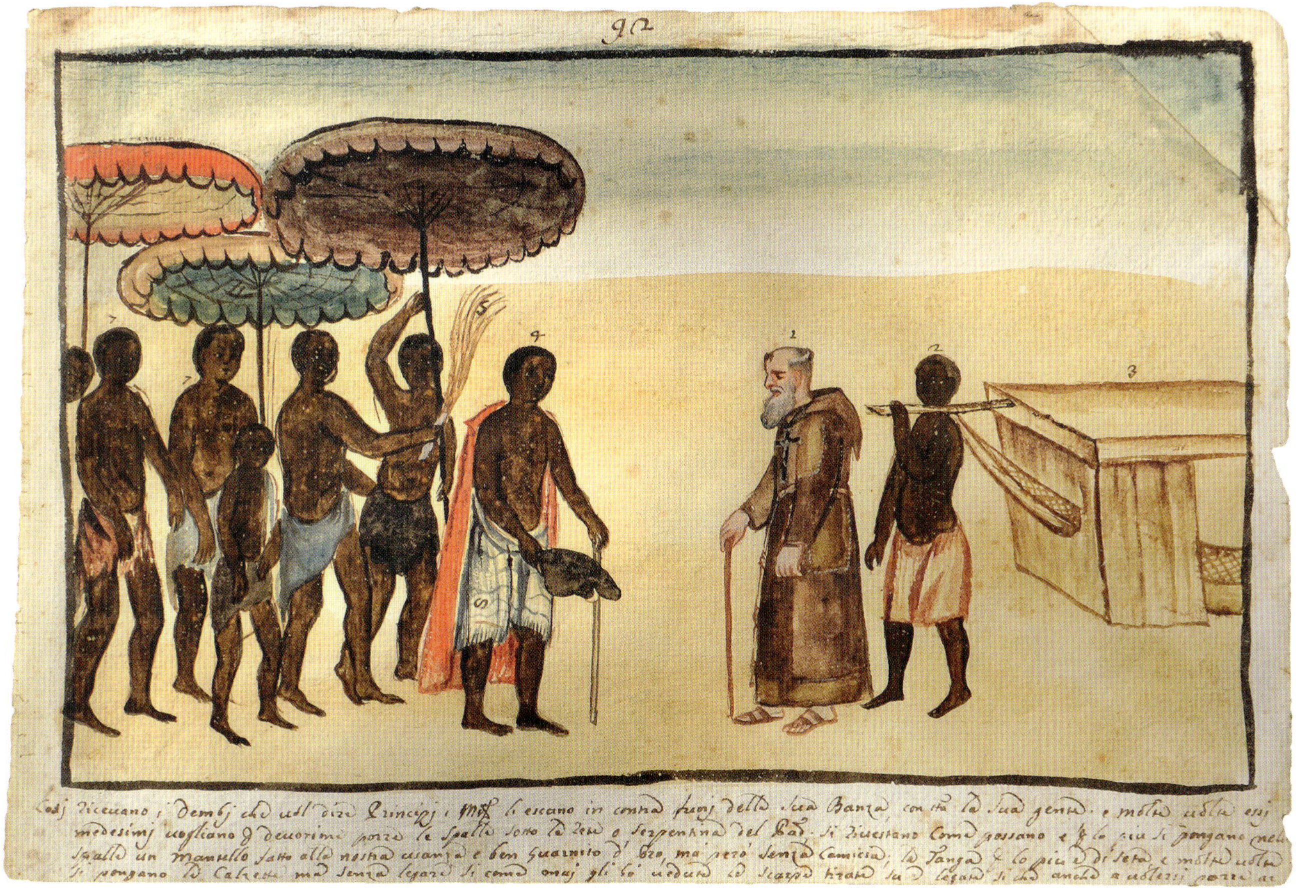

Figure 105

Unknown Capuchin artist, "In this manner the Dembi [Ndembu rulers], which means Princes, receive the Missionaries," late seventeenth century. Watercolor on paper, 34 × 24 cm. Parma Watercolors, Virgili Collection, fol. 92. Photo: author.

in the early modern mechanics of commerce and diplomacy, and as proactive agents in the dynamics that ushered in the circulation of images, objects, and aesthetic sensibilities in the seventeenth and eighteenth centuries.

The Capuchin corpus also makes clear that central Africa's openness to the world meant different things to different groups, each mobilizing or rejecting access to global networks for its own purposes, political or otherwise. In another page of the Parma Watercolors, the manner in which Angolan elites use items acquired from afar for prestige is strikingly different from that of their Ndembu neighbors (fig. 106 / plate 45). Two warrior figures armed with bows and arrows and a semicircular blade axe are dressed in full regalia with cotton leg coverings, wildcat pelts at the waist, red bark ribbons tied around the arms, and large panaches of feathers on the head. Red face paint on the temples enhances their gaze. Their polished, spectacular outfits make for an impressive sight. Because of the feathers and the bows and arrows, emblems par

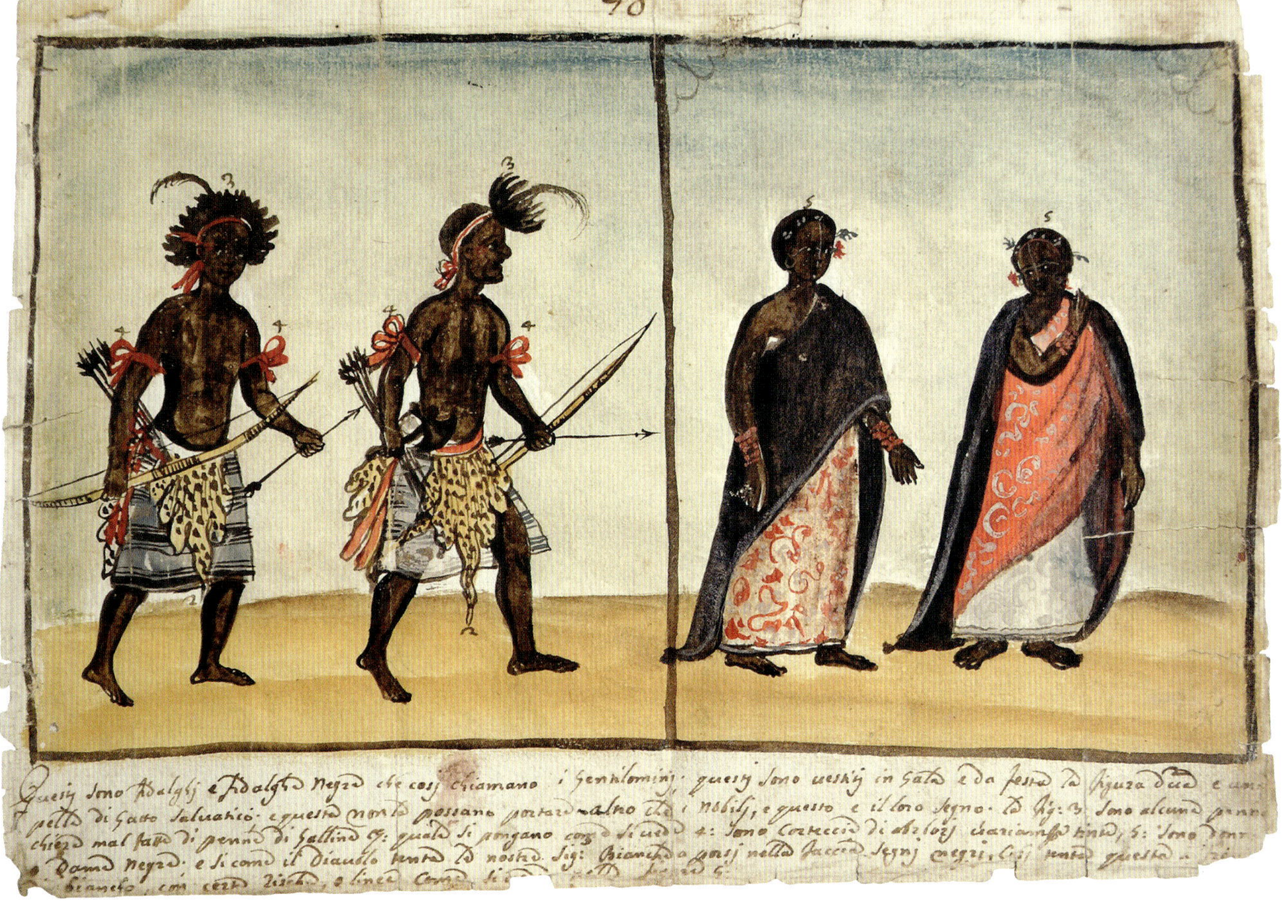

Figure 106

Unknown Capuchin artist, "Black male and female aristocrats," late seventeenth century. Watercolor on paper, 34 × 24 cm. Parma Watercolors, Virgili Collection, fol. 70. Photo: author.

excellence of savagery in European visual culture of the early modern period, they could easily be construed as quintessential savages, living an isolated existence, ignorant of the world outside of their immediate surroundings. But even the stark black line added to the page at a later moment cannot separate them from their female consorts in the vignette, whose appearance breaks the spell of exotic savagery and firmly portrays both men and women as actors on a worldly stage of vast

horizons. The two poised ladies are magnificently dressed and adorned. Flowers and beads in their hair frame their faces, enhanced with thin white lines. The writer of the gloss compares the white traces that highlight the central-African ladies' features to European women's *mouches*, black cosmetic patches meant to highlight fair complexion. Metallic earrings, stacks of red-bead or coral bracelets, and several necklaces rendered in now-faded paint on their one bare shoulder speak to their access to precious commodities. The red jewelry at their wrists, the layers upon layers of colorful floral textiles wrapped about their bodies, the lace trim skimming their ankles, the dark cloaks on their shoulders—all demonstrate the cosmopolitan reach associated with their social status. They wear imported coral, floral textiles from India, European lace, and dark indigo-dyed cloaks that may be the silklike cotton *panos pretos* from Senegambia that were prized imports in Angola.[2] The two women are clothed and adorned with a cosmopolitan mixture of items that speak loudly of their participation in the commercial, material, but also aesthetic networks of the global early modern world. The outfits of their male counterparts thus are not composed of the attributes of the untouched savage but the insignia of two members of a central-African elite whose broad access to goods from around the globe played very little part in the expression of their prestige. The blue-and-white striped cloth covering their legs could be either a locally produced cotton cloth or one imported from other shores.

The flagellant entourage of the Ndembu ruler in figure 105, like the many protagonists pictured in the midst of Christian pious practices elsewhere in the Capuchin corpus, also underlines another prominent dimension of the central-African contribution to the trajectory of the early modern world: the form that Roman Catholicism took in this non-European context. Since the beginning of the sixteenth century, and throughout the early modern period, the region stood as a center of Catholicism. The faith, its precepts, and its institutions held a vibrant place in the various polities of west central Africa, where they followed many different paths. The political elite of the Kingdom of Kongo robustly embraced Roman Catholicism

and made it its disputed, but enduring, state religion. Queen Njinga of Ndongo and Matamba adopted and repudiated it during her lifetime for political and diplomatic expediency. Populations whom the colonial administration of Portuguese Angola strove to control had the religion imposed upon them with the limited means of a relatively weak *conquista*. Through these various modes of engagement and different levels of familiarity with the Christian faith, Church, and paraphernalia, central Africans, as the Capuchin vignettes make plain, shaped the nature, contours, and trajectory of early modern Christianity. They made Catholicism a central-African religion, one whose objects, practices, and precepts would travel to Europe and the Americas with the millions of enslaved men and women who embarked from its shores via the Atlantic slave trade. From deep faith passed down through generations to distant rituals merely glimpsed on one or two memorable occasions or only known through hearsay, the varied experiences of Catholicism central Africans brought across the waters would profoundly shape African diasporic religious tradition.[3]

Beyond Postcolonial

The Capuchin central-African corpus also has an impact on methods. The vignettes disrupt interpretative trends for images created in cross-cultural environments in the early modern period. Emerging from a social and political context in which friars acted at the demand and under the control of local populations, the Capuchin central-African visual corpus did not reflect colonial ambitions or visualize European fantasies about a savage or exotic Other. Rather, it grew at the nexus of fraught but deep and lasting encounters and exchanges between clerics and central Africans, during which both sides saw their knowledge and perspectives transformed. I have argued in this book that it is erroneous to consider the Capuchin images of central Africa as one-sided views of Kongo and Angola seen and represented from the single perspective of the friars. Although ostensibly European in style and format, they were not exotic representations bending observations and information on faraway lands and people to fit early modern Europeans' wide-ranging preconceived ideas about a world whose countless curiosities and riches they deemed within reach, ripe, if not for them to outright conquer, at least for them to envision and consume.

By creating a discourse characterizing difference as alterity, and alterity as formative of a contradistinctive self, such conceptualizations of geographically and culturally distant lands played a central role in the definition of European modernity.[4] The recognition and critique of these fundamental conceptions of a Eurocentric modernity have been at the core of the postmodern and postcolonial projects, and they continue to animate the political and scholarly conversation on decoloniality.[5] In the realm of visual studies, postcolonial readings have guided many interpretations of images created as a result of cross-cultural encounters in the early modern period. Emblematic of these readings are the multiple takes, inside and outside of art history, on Jan van der Straet's *Vespucci Discovering America* as an announcement of Europe's territorial and epistemological conquest of what it considered a new world (fig. 101).[6] The gendered encounter was seen to iterate the dichotomies foundational to Europe's imagined contradistinctive modernity: the clothed male figure endowed with the attributes and instruments

of civilization and scientific thinking against the barely clad female, surrounded with the markers of a primitive existence and of an enchanted, mythical worldview. Scholars have elaborated on and refined this interpretation over the years. Some have brought to bear on the image the lens of invention alongside the idea of conquest. Others have demonstrated the complexities and uncertainties of the European point of view and of its illustration in the print.[7] Developments in scholarly approaches to images such as this one, as well as many others emphatically unlike it, have made increasingly clear that, though enduring and powerful, the postcolonial mode of reading does not illuminate fully or with equal clarity every early modern visual project.[8] For instance, analyzing the creation or form of the Capuchin central-African images through the lens of some of its most critical interventions proves of limited use. At best peripheral to the Capuchin corpus's main concerns are desire for conquest of an Other and contradistinction between that Other and a self it defines; Europe's projections of its own worldview upon faraway lands and people; the couching of difference, racial and otherwise, between Europe and the people and lands across seas or continents—or living in Europe's own midst—as natural rather than historically constructed.[9]

The preceding pages have shown that while the friars drew heavily on European motifs, style, and genres, their didactic vignettes rarely followed the emerging templates of exotic representation and did not operate as colonial imagery. They did not freely conflate distant places and cultures, have recourse to often sensationalistic iconographic clichés, or embrace vagueness as a visual strategy. On the contrary, they were committed to specificity and tellingly made relatively little use of the commonplace iconography of savagery. Their images did not participate, either, in a strongly defined colonial or imperial project presenting people and nature as ripe for takeover and exploitation. That is not to say that the Capuchins were devoid of ambitions to make sense of central Africa on their own terms or did not harbor abhorrent preconceptions about its inhabitants as their inferiors. In fact, the tension between desire and inability to bring to bear a familiar lens on their observations and experiences was a central structuring element of their vignettes. It created many moments in which the images overflowed or challenged the boundaries of the European image types they seemingly followed. Many vignettes, for instance, attempted to present the missionary in control of the social, political, and religious setting of his apostolate but pictured instead fraught encounters, partial understanding, and messy interactions between friars and Africans.

The presence of the crucial figure of the central-African church master, or *mestre*, behind each friar in vignettes of missionary work is a key motif in this regard. In the compositions, these figures feature close to the Capuchins, in positions that easily and purposefully invite readings of them as subalterns. Yet, in fact, the *mestres* did not assist the friars. Socially, they enabled their presence. Politically, they made their activities in the region possible. Intellectually, they imparted to the mission essential religious, practical, scientific, and linguistic knowledge. Although the surface of the page attempts to present them as the friars' subordinates, they stood firmly in the visible and invisible structuring lines of the vignettes not as aides but as the people whose prestige the friars' presence bolstered and without whom the images simply would not have come to life.

Literary scholar Leo Cabranes-Grant has argued that intercultural exchange increases the legibility of *poesis* understood as the coming into being of a cultural object.[10] I have shown in these pages the reverse to be equally true: that attention to the Capuchin images' processes and conditions of creation increases the legibility of intercultural exchange as one of their originative and constitutive features. In other words, the book's attention to *poesis* has demonstrated how, although the Capuchin vignettes were made by Europeans for Europeans, in an almost exclusively European style, they are nonetheless cross-cultural in their sources, formulation, and operation.

Art historians Carolyn Dean and Dana Leibsohn have eloquently warned against the "deception of visibility" in approaches to objects and images crafted at the nexus of cultures. Identifying and analyzing the traces of cross-cultural interactions that are visible in artworks, they write, may lead interpreters astray, encouraging them "to find that the mixings that matter the most are those we can see."[11] They have also warned against the pendant pitfall, if focusing on production rather than appearances, of "fetishizing" the color of the hand that created a cultural object as a sign of its mixing. This book heeds their warning by not falling prey to the deception of the invisibility of mixing in the Capuchin central-African images at a formal level or in the identity of their immediate producers. Though nominally European in style and format, as well as crafted by European hands, they are, in fact, as I have shown in this book, visual documents born from and participating in the cross-cultural encounters and negotiations of knowledge and world-views that unfolded between the friars and central Africans. The Capuchin corpus provides eloquent examples of early modern European-style images that are cross-cultural productions and not one-sided, exoticizing, or hegemonic representations, or the result of an outright dialectical struggle between oppressors and resisting subalterns.

In considering the inception, or *poesis*, of these representations as a deep domain of inquiry in itself, I found a way to shed light on the otherwise hardly visible cross-cultural dimension of the vignettes as expressions of a discourse about nature, culture, and faith that Capuchins and central Africans co-constructed in the course of their interactions. The Capuchin images are not European-conceived and -executed pictures *of* Kongo and Angola and their inhabitants, but pictures *from* central Africa and molded *by* the dialogue that unfolded between the friars and central Africans. To be clear, this is not—or not only—about reading against the grain or uncovering subaltern agency hidden within the images. It is an attempt at seriously considering the origins of their representations in cross-cultural collaboration, albeit one that, in this case, did not leave visible traces in their style, iconography, or modes of production.

The central-African images challenge art-historical inquiry not to fall prey to the deception of the invisibility of their mixing, which does not appear on their surface or emerge from considerations of the identity of who drew their lines or painted their washes. They make clear the seemingly obvious: the claim that Europeans could invent in splendid isolation visual and conceptual solutions to every challenge that depicting and making sense of the world posed to them is unconvincing. It would suggest that Europeans could maintain steadfast control over the production of

a purely European discourse in the course of their interactions with the many people they encountered at home and abroad in the early modern period—to say nothing of the erroneous suggestion that Europe formed a homogeneous as well as an impervious entity.

Literary scholar Stephen Greenblatt has articulated a position of this kind in his 1991 *Marvelous Possessions*: "We can be certain only that European representations of the New World tell us something about the European practice of representation."[12] This seemingly modest approach to contact texts and the related "blunted-impact" theory has been amply and rightly challenged for dismissing even the possibility of identifying, and thus in effect silencing in its own ways, the Indigenous voices associated with such European representations.[13] Historians, ethnohistorians, and cultural historians since the 1990s have proposed different takes on these contact, or colonial, texts that "give voice to the historically silent."[14] In fact, it has been one of Edward Said's central postcolonial interventions in his 1993 *Culture and Imperialism* to point out that traces of the colonized world animated in profound ways Europe and the works considered as the core of its literary canon.[15] Nearly thirty years later, calls to decolonize the perspectives articulated by institutions exerting great power over the public and academic spheres (scholarship, museums, university curricula, and the monumental outfitting of public spaces in Europe, the United States, and elsewhere) demonstrate the continuing intellectual and sociopolitical relevance of such questioning of Europe's modernity project and the epistemic and political violence it has inflicted within and beyond the continent's shores.[16]

Art historians have challenged the same notions of "blunted impact" and looked for subaltern agency from a different angle. Scholars of visual and material culture in the early modern period have focused their attention on the emergence of novel cultural forms in cross-cultural spaces, and on what they reveal about the multivalent human interactions that led to their creation.[17] Inquiries into the circulation of motifs, pigments, materials, but also images have explored entangled histories of visual practices.[18] I add in this book another approach to probe the cross-cultural dimension of images. Instead of looking at formal novelty or material provenance, I focus on the broadly considered conditions and trajectories of their creation, that is, their *poesis*, as a terrain in which to identify and interrogate the visual, epistemological, and political cross-cultural entanglements they both captured and expressed within their frames.

The stakes in recognizing cross-cultural *poesis* as a key dimension of at least some early modern European images, a dimension that falls outside of European cultural and epistemological (as well as political and economic) hegemony and demonstrates their nature as the product of multiple perspectives, are high. On the one hand, it helps to provincialize Europe and to stress how its engagement with the world beyond its shores shaped its own visual core in ways that have been both visible and invisible, in early modern times and in ours, because of ideological disavowal or interpretative shortsightedness.[19] On the other hand, it responds to a fundamental challenge scholars face in the study of early modern global interactions in the disproportion—for many, but by no means not all, regions—between the large archive of documents produced by Europeans and the limited number of sources authored by the historical actors Indigenous to many areas of the globe. This discrepancy is born from the history and structures of archives and is heightened by a historiography that has given outsized emphasis to certain types of documents over others as authoritative sources. Research looking anew into existing depositories, expanded methodologies, theoretical innovations, and attention to Indigenous knowledge are steadily closing that gap, though these endeavors often remain dependent for access, funding, and validation on the backing of institutions created for and in support of the archives and forms of knowledge they aim to complement or outright challenge.[20]

This book charts a path in that direction. It shows that there are many ways in which the European archive holds more than it readily avows.[21] New sets of documents exist, still overlooked. Nominally European texts and images hold a plurality of voices ready to rise from their pages in spite of past and present disavowals and scholarly blindness. Attention to *poesis* can reveal the cross-cultural dimensions of seemingly wholly European visual and textual sources. The Capuchin central-African images demonstrate beyond a doubt that the role of cross-cultural interaction and the impact of the confrontation of perspectives on the conception of images routinely considered as wholly European has been largely underestimated. The approach I propose here allows looking anew at a range of visual and written documentation about the four corners of the world, records produced, nominally, by Europeans and without immediately visible non-European traits, as cross-cultural productions. Identifying and analyzing the multiple, complex forms of interactions that gave shape to the documents in the European archive concerned with the world beyond its shores—or, in other words, considering their cross-cultural *poesis*—not only directs a decolonial lens at their content and opens the door for counter-hegemonic interpretations; it also holds the promise of a richer, more nuanced understanding of the intricacies, range, and complexity of the human interactions and cultural productions that shaped the early modern world.

INTRODUCTION

1. The number twelve, of course, made reference to Christ's apostles, eleven of whom the Holy Spirit visited on the Feast of Pentecost, giving them the gift of tongues, a moment that marked the beginning of their apostolate. A dozen, too, officially opened the Franciscan missionary enterprise in Mexico in 1524, although they were not the first friars to step onto Mesoamerican soil. About the "epochal twelve" Franciscans in early sixteenth-century Mexico, see Edgerton, *Theaters of Conversion*, 19–20, 38–59, and León-Portilla, *Franciscanos*.

2. "For centuries the most common official term for the Portuguese overseas possessions was *As Conquistas*, 'The Conquests'"; see Boxer, *Race Relations*, 2. The word *conquistas* strongly resonates with the Iberian *Reconquista* and its religious dimension. Portugal saw its overseas endeavors not only as lay territorial expansion but also as spiritual conquest of heathen lands on behalf of Christendom; see Blackmore, *Moorings*, xxii.

3. Ratelband, *Os Holandeses*; Demaret, "Portugais, Néerlandais et Africains," 249–350.

4. About the mission from Soyo to Brazil and the resulting portraits, see Fromont, *Art of Conversion*, 114–21.

5. Several friars report this episode, including Juan de Santiago, in "Breve Relacion," 44–60, and

Bonaventura d'Alessano, in his letter to the secretary of the Propaganda Fide of June 4, 1645, Archivio Storico di Propaganda Fide (hereafter APF), Scritture Originali Riferite nelle Congregazioni Generali (hereafter SOCG), vol. 247, fols. 122r–125v, in Brásio, *Monumenta*, 1st ser., 9:256–62. See also Filesi and Isidoro de Villapadierna, *Missio antiqua*, 21–22.

6. One close parallel would be the Capuchin mission in Tibet, which also yielded the production of images. See Beligatti, "Teologia de' Tibetani," and Beligatti, "Giornale."

7. About the Jaga and their embattled historiography, see Heintze, "Extraordinary Journey of the Jaga." See also Thornton, *History of West Central Africa*, 14, 74–76, and Lopes and Pigafetta, *Royaume de Congo*, 291–95. About the foundation of Luanda, see Madeira Santos, "Écrire le pouvoir."

8. About Portugal's patronage rights, or *padroado régio*, in overseas territories, see Rego, *Patronage portugais de l'Orient,* and Sá, "Ecclesiastical Structures and Religious Action," 257–59.

9. Bontinck and Nsasi, *Catéchisme kikongo*, 17–36.

10. Filesi and Isidoro de Villapadierna, *Missio antiqua*; Saccardo, *Congo e Angola*.

11. About the negative views Capuchins held of Africans, see Almeida, "Entre gente 'aspra e dura.'"

12. Monari, "Viaggio al Congo," 172, as cited in Piazza, *Prefettura apostolica*, 246.

13. Fromont, "Tecido estrangeiro."

14. Heywood, *Njinga of Angola*.

15. See ibid., chapter 1 below, and Antonio da Gaeta and Gioia, *Maravigliosa conversione*.

16. The Dembos region is named after *ndembu*, the title of its leaders. About the other polities, see Madeira Santos, "Écrire le pouvoir," and Ferreira, *Kisama em Angola*.

17. Piazza, *Prefettura apostolica*, 130–64.

18. About the end of the Capuchin mission, see Kabolo Iko Kabwita, *Royaume kongo*.

19. The requirement to compose and convey relations was not strictly followed. See Cardinal Rospigliosi's letter from Rome dated March 14, 1665, enjoining the friars to write memoirs of their apostolate, in Cavazzi and Alamandini, *Istorica descrizione*, 769 (book 7, para. 28).

20. "Missione in prattica," accessed July 20, 2021, https://bct.comune.torino.it/manoscritti-e-rari /missione-prattica.

21. Fromont, "Depicting Kongo and Angola," and Fromont, "Nature, Culture, and Faith."

22. For the publication history of the images, see chapter 1 below. For examples of images used as illustrations or covers rather than analyzed sources, see, among others, the otherwise excellent studies Breen, *Age of Intoxication*, 79, 84, and Gómez, *Experiential Caribbean*, cover, 177.

23. See the luxurious edition Collo and Benso, *Sogno*.

24. I am indebted to Padre Giacomo Carlini at the Capuchin Provincial Archives for mentioning the Parma Watercolors, to Fra Romano Mantovi for his help in locating them, and to the Virgili family for generously opening their doors for my study of the watercolors in their collection.

25. See, in particular, Fromont, "Collecting." This book updates and complements the findings published in that essay.

26. "The most important knowledge that we as teachers can convey to our students (and we as Africanists can impart to 'others') is . . . the discerning of the unfamiliar in what has long been familiar, . . . moving beyond, through, behind, and under both customary and new theoretical frames into unchartered seas." Blier, "Truth and Seeing," 140.

27. I derive the definition of *poesis* used here from Cabranes-Grant, *From Scenarios to Networks*.

28. Foucault, "Qu'est-ce qu'un auteur?"

29. "Early modernity was marked by elite, male Europeans' dependence upon subaltern technologies and their 'disavowal' of this dependence." Norton, "Subaltern Technologies," 20.

30. Dean and Leibsohn, "Hybridity and Its Discontents." About history, archives, and their silences, see Trouillot, *Silencing the Past*.

CHAPTER I

1. He appended the drawing of the November 1673 shipwreck to a letter he sent to the Propaganda Fide. Archivio Storico de Propaganda Fide, SOCG (Scritture originali riferite nelle congregazioni generali) 457, fol. 375. The drawing is published in Faria, "João António Cavazzi," L.

2. The rules were later published in Urban VIII, *Decreta Seruanda*. See Schutte, "*Ecco la santa!*," 113–15.

3. Zucchelli, *Relazioni del viaggio*, "Protesta dell'Autore."

4. Letter of Fortunato Alamandini da Bologna to the Propaganda Fide, 1679, in Pistoni, *Fra Giovanni Antonio Cavazzi*, 39–40.

5. Letter of Bonaventura da Montecuccolo to Giacomo Isolani, April 10, 1675, in ibid., 28. About the limits of the friars' mental tools in the face of central-African reality, see Madeira Santos, "Monde excessivement nouveau."

6. Biblioteca Pública de Évora, MS CXVI-2-1. See Toso, *Congo*.

7. Cavazzi, "Missione Evangelica." John Thornton has published a partial translation online: http://www.bu.edu/afam/faculty/john-thornton /cavazzi-missione-evangelica.

8. Faria, "João António Cavazzi," xxxv.

9. See the table of contents in Pistoni, *Fra Giovanni Antonio Cavazzi*, 15–24.

10. See ibid. and Faria, "João António Cavazzi."

11. I.e., "Descrizione de' tre' grandi Regni."

12. See the transcription of the letter in Pistoni, *Fra Giovanni Antonio Cavazzi*, 27–28.

13. See Alamandini's observations to the Propaganda Fide in ibid., 42.

14. Cavazzi and Alamandini, *Istorica descrizione*, preface to the reader.

15. For Paolo da Lorena's letter, see Archiginnasio de Bologna, Raccolta Carrati B 939, fol. 154r.

16. The letter was in APF, Scritture Riferite nei Congressi (herafter SRC), Congo Angola, vol. 1, fol. 289. It is now kept in the iconography section of the archive under the same shelf mark. See Bassani, *Cappuccino nell'Africa nera*, 32, and Toso, *Congo*, 14.

17. Bassani, *Cappuccino nell'Africa nera*.

18. Pistoni, "Manoscritti 'Araldi.'" About Cavazzi and the Araldi manuscript, see also Previdi, *Frate Giovanni Antonio Cavazzi*.

19. Pistoni, "Manoscritti 'Araldi,'" 157, mentions it.

20. See Bassani, *Cappuccino nell'Africa nera*; Cavazzi, "Missione Evangelica"; Levi, "Padre Giovanni Antonio Cavazzi"; and John Kelly Thornton's general introduction to "Cavazzi, Missione Evangelica," John Thornton's African Texts, 2011, accessed May 18, 2020, http://www.bu.edu/afam/people/faculty/john -thornton/john-thorntons-african-texts.

21. About the Jaga and their turbulent historiography, see Heintze, "Extraordinary Journey of the Jaga." See also Thornton, *History of West Central Africa*, 14, 74–76, and Lopes and Pigafetta, *Royaume de Congo*, 291–95.

22. Readers can consult the prints from the *Istorica descrizione* in the online image collection complementing this publication in Fromont, "Depicting Kongo and Angola." About the prints in the Lopes and Pigafetta volume, see Tedeschi, "Natale Bonifacio."

23. Cavazzi and Alamandini, *Istorica descrizione*, 9, 181.

24. Fromont, "Under the Sign of the Cross."

25. About Cavazzi's borrowing from textual sources, see Faria, "João António Cavazzi," xxiii–xxxiii.

26. Cavazzi and Alamandini, *Istorica descrizione*, plates 16–19.

27. Ibid., foreword, n.p., 3rd page of foreword.

28. Ibid., plates 3, 4, 5, 6, 7, 9, 10, 12. The "f.f." in the signature is unclear but could stand for *fecit fare* or *frater franciscanus*. The remaining illustrations are unsigned, except for the frontispiece, which is signed in the lower left corner "F. Paul.ˢ a Lothar.ᵃ Cap. Sculp.," i.e., "Engraved by Friar Paul of Lorraine, Capuchin."

29. Number 3, page 32; number 4, page 33; number 5, page 34; number 6, page 35; number 7, page 35; number 9, page 36; number 10, page 37; number 12, page 52.

30. Pistoni, *Fra Giovanni Antonio Cavazzi*, 15–16.

31. Such as the *Lexicon Capuccinum*.

32. Carnago, *Città di rifugio*.

33. About Boetto and his links to the Capuchins, including his four *eaux-fortes* of friars from 1634, *Le stagioni*, see Vertova, "Per Giovenale Boetto pittore."

34. Ferrerius, *Rationarium Chronographicum Missionis Evangelicae*. The copper-plate map (370 × 740 mm) is signed "F.P. a Lothar. Cap. Sculp." and shows Piedmont and Savoy. Boetto may have painted frescoes in the Garbolli (or Gerbaldi) house in Fossano. See Lanzi, *Histoire de la peinture en Italie*, 5:195. See also Baudi di Vesme, *Peintre-graveur italien*, 52–53.

35. Guimarães, "Mais ilustre capuchinho portugués," 49. As Paolo da Lorena worked on the Capuchin central-African images, Boetto worked on a mission-inspired project, the construction of the Church of San Francesco Saverio in Mondovì, built between 1665 and 1678.

36. Cavazzi and Alamandini, *Istorica descrizione*, 51.

37. Ibid., 46.

38. For Capuchin artists in the Kongo, see, for example, the letter from painter Félix del Villar to the Propaganda Fide, January 20, 1650, in Brásio, *Monumenta*, 1st ser., 10:474–75.

39. Pistoni, *Fra Giovanni Antonio Cavazzi*, 15.

40. Cavazzi and Alamandini, *Istorica descrizione*, plate 8, p. 35.

41. Ibid., plates 11, 13, 14, 15.

42. See also Bry et al., *Americae Tertia Pars*, 179. For a discussion of the imagery of cannibalism, see Zika, "Cannibalism and Witchcraft," 88–90, and Davies, *Renaissance Ethnography*, 65–108.

43. See also Merolla and Piccardo, *Breve, e succinta relatione*, plate 14.

44. Ibid., plate 18. About Merolla, see Sarzi Amade, "Réédition, contextualisation et analyse." For a discussion of some correspondences between Merolla, Dapper, and Cavazzi, see Hirschberg, "Early Historical Illustrations."

45. Cavazzi and Alamandini, *Istorica descrizione*, plate 22; Merolla and Piccardo, *Breve, e succinta relatione*, unnumbered plate labeled "pag. 27," between pp. 26 and 27.

46. Cavazzi and Alamandini, *Istorica descrizione*, 34–35.

47. See, for example, the discussion of cannibalism in Schreffler, "Vespucci Rediscovers America." See also chapter 5 below.

48. See Bleichmar, *Visible Empire*, 151–61, for a discussion of botanical pages' blankness. See also Neri, *Insect and the Image*.

49. Cavazzi and Alamandini, *Istorica descrizione*, plate 41, p. 336.

50. Latour, "Visualisation and Cognition."

CHAPTER 2

1. For examples of discussions of Capuchin images, see Brito, "On Mermaids and Manatees," and Rocha, "Imagens da diplomacia."

2. Fromont, "Under the Sign of the Cross"; Fromont, "Collecting." The Capuchin Historical Institute in Rome (Istituto Storico dei Cappuccini) and Provincial Archive in Florence had been alerted of the existence of the images in the late 1990s. Personal communication.

3. Eyewitness images of Africa in the early modern period are relatively rare but include, for example, journals from merchants such as Jean Barbot ("Description des Côtes d'Afrique").

4. About painting and engraving, featuring foreign objects in central Africa, see Heimlich, *Massif de Lovo*, 55–57, 125–26; Bastian, *Besuch in San Salvador*, 160; and Tuckey and Smith, *Narrative of an Expedition*, 379–83.

5. In Fromont, *Art of Conversion*, I have discussed at length the visual culture central Africans created as their horizons opened to the early modern Atlantic world.

6. Lopes and Pigafetta, *Relatione del reame di Congo*.

7. Lopes and Pigafetta, *Regnum Congo*, in both German and Latin.

8. Volumes 1 and 3 of the original manuscript are in the Academy of Sciences in Lisbon; a fragment of volume 2 is in the British Library. An eighteenth-century copy of all three tomes is in the Bibliothèque nationale de France, Paris. For a modern printing, see the edition by José Matias Delgado. See also Boxer, "Background to Angola"; Boxer, "'História' de Cadornega'"; Heintze, "António de Oliveira de Cadornega"; Weber, "'Angola' como conceito"; Demaret, "Portugueses e Africanos em Angola"; Júnior, *História geral das guerras Angolanas*.

9. Boxer, "'História' de Cadornega."

10. Cadornega, "Historia general das guerras Angolanas," vol. 2 (Portugais 3), frontispiece, 444bis, 444ter.

11. Heintze, "António de Oliveira de Cadornega," 78.

12. Cadornega, "Historia general das guerras Angolanas."

13. Cadornega, *História geral das guerras angolanas* (1940–42). It had been published only partially in 1902.

14. The book had first appeared in 1591 with a title page of a different design that did not include human

figures. See, by Lopes and Pigafetta, *Relatione del reame di Congo* and *Regnum Congo*, both the Latin and German editions. For a bibliography of the many-times translated work, see Hutchinson, "Bibliography of Pigafetta."

15. Heintze, "Unbekanntes Angola."

16. Cadornega, *História geral das guerras angolanas* (1940), 2:191. Heintze, "António de Oliveira de Cadornega," 80. About Cavazzi, see chapter 1 above. Antonio Romano, or da Roma, also known as Antonio da Gaeta or Gaetano Romano, was the prefect of the Capuchins; see Brásio, *Monumenta*, 1st ser., 12:89.

17. Cadornega, *História geral das guerras angolanas* (1942), 3:16, 68.

18. About Kafuxi Ambari, the great ruler figure of Kisama, see Ferreira, *Kisama em Angola*.

19. Pistoni, "Manoscritti 'Araldi.'" The Araldi manuscript remains unpublished and without systematic study, but John Thornton has published online a general introduction to the work and a translation of the front matter of its first volume; see John Kelly Thornton, "Translation of the Araldi Manuscript." My thanks to Dr. and Mrs. Luigi Araldi for allowing me to study the manuscript in person.

20. Bassani, *Cappuccino nell'Africa nera*. See also chapter 1 above.

21. The drawing is now missing from the Propaganda Fide historical archives but is published in Jadin, "Clergé séculier," 260.

22. Édouard d'Alençon, "Essai de Bibliographie capucino-congolaise," 261–62; Fromont, "Collecting."

23. See McAllen, "Jesuit Martyrdom Imagery," and Brockey, "Books of Martyrs." About Jesuit martyrdom cycles outside of the missionary context, see Herz, "Imitators of Christ."

24. After eighteen months in the field, Joris van Gheel was not a novice anymore, but the message about the risks of the mission remains clear. About Friar Joris, see Hildebrandus ab Hooglede, "Père Georges de Gheel."

25. Two partial publications of its images appeared in the late twentieth century: Collo and Benso, *Sogno*; Guattini and Carli, *Viaggio nel Regno del Congo*.

26. Bernardino d'Asti, "Missione in prattica," MS 457. For an online publication and short introduction to the manuscript, see "Missione in prattica," accessed July 20, 2021, https://bct.comune.torino.it/manoscritti-e-rari /missione-prattica.

27. Biblioteca Nacional de Portugal, Lisbon, MS 1432 FG, and Biblioteca Apostolica Vaticana, MS Borg. Lat. 316. The Lisbon and Vatican versions are not published. See also Toso, "Relazioni inedite," 138n18; Jadin, "Survivances chrétiennes au Congo," 139n4; and Cuvelier, "Vénérable André de Burgio," 98n53.

28. Quotes are from the Turin manuscript, MS 457, fol. 2r.

29. On folio 4v of the Lisbon copy, the copyist even refers to a page 99 that does not exist in the non-paginated Lisbon version.

30. Italian Capuchins in 1691 opened a house in Lisbon affiliated with the province of Genoa; see Faria, "Tentativas frustradas," 244–46. The French Capuchins, involved in the missionary activities in Brazil, since 1640 had also had a house in Lisbon, affiliated with the order's Brittany province. The order did not take root in Portugal before the twentieth century.

31. Compare paragraph 5 of page 3 of the Vatican manuscript to the APF SOCG Africa-Angola volume 5, 1736–1780, fol. 180 and following.

32. For my translation of the Parma Watercolors text, see Fromont, "Nature, Culture, and Faith."

33. The Portuguese glosses are on folios 9v, 12v, 20v, 47v, 54v, 56v, 57r, 64v, 65v, 71v, 72v, 76v, and 77v.

34. About the musical instruments in early modern Africa, including those in Cavazzi's prints, see Hirschberg, "Early Historical Illustrations." See also Bassani, *Cappuccino nell'Africa nera*.

35. For a scientific description of the fruit, see Morton, "Purple Mombin."

36. The author mentions the Arno River in the text of folio 22, describing the whale as "as big as one of *our* boats from the Arno," revealing his familiarity with and attachment to the Tuscan river. Parma Watercolors, Virgili Collection, fol. 22, emphasis mine.

37. About whalebone and corsets, see Moheng, "Corps à baleines et paniers."

38. Salvadorini, "Relazione sul Congo," 447–48. About the episode, see Heywood, *Njinga of Angola*, 166–68.

39. Parma Watercolors, Virgili Collection, fol. 101. The event is reported from various sources, among which are Antonio de Teruel, "Descripcion Narrativa," 89, and Antonio da Gaeta and Gioia, *Maravigliosa conversione*, 298. See also Heywood, *Njinga of Angola*, 166–67.

40. About the baptism of Njinga, see Heywood, *Njinga of Angola*, 50–52. I think the story as it is told also fits well the purpose of the text to exalt the Capuchin missions.

41. See Cavazzi and Alamandini, *Istorica descrizione*, 728–29.

42. John K. Thornton also reminded me in a personal communication that the queen was not first baptized following the encounter with the two friars. She had indeed received baptism decades earlier and merely returned to Catholicism on that occasion. According to Thornton, this suggests that the author of the text was rather removed in time from the date of these events.

43. Cavazzi and Alamandini, *Istorica descrizione*, 604–5.

44. A note in the margin adds to the description of the living-chair episode: "Il seguente caso mi é stato referito da varie persone, e per havere io cognesciuto e praticato la Regina Ginga nessuna difficolta ho in crederlo, et anco in farle credere." Cavazzi, "Missione Evangelica," vol. A, book 2, p. 25.

45. About borrowing from printed sources, see Faria, "João António Cavazzi," xxiii–xxxiii.

46. Serafino da Cortona had also urged Friar Girolamo in 1653 to write about his experience; see Piazza, *Prefettura apostolica*, 314.

47. Cuvelier, Olivier de Bouveignes, and Girolamo da Montesarchio, *Jérôme de Montesarchio*, 39; Girolamo da Montesarchio, "Viaggio al Gongho"; Piazza, *Prefettura apostolica*.

48. Simonetti, "P. Giacinto Brugiotti da Vetralla."

49. Letter of Michelangelo Guattini to his father from Loanda (Luanda), 1668; see Guattini and Carli, *Viaggio nel Regno del Congo*, 188.

50. Serafino da Cortona in Filippo da Firenze, "Ragguagli del Congo," 79–80.

51. Bernardino d'Asti, "Missione in prattica," MS 457, fol. 2r.

52. Édouard d'Alençon, "Essai de Bibliographie capucino-congolaise," 252. See also de Jonghe and Simar, "Archives congolaises (suite)," 28n2. Both works are now lost.

53. Belotti's title translates as "Beneficial advice to the apostolic missionaries, especially on the Kingdoms of Congo, Angola, and neighboring places"; Bernardino d'Asti's "Missione in prattica" translates as "Practical guide to the mission, Capuchin fathers in the kingdoms of Congo, Angola, and neighboring places." Other such guides include Giuseppe Monari da Modena's "Avvertimenti necessarissimi á P.P. Missionarij," or "Very necessary advice to the Capuchin fathers," book 2, chap. 5, of his "Viaggio al Congo," although copied for the most part from Belotti. See Monari, "Viaggio al Congo," 272–337.

54. Belotti, "Avvertimenti Salutevoli," p. 2 of "Alli benigni Lettori Missionari."

55. Belotti, "Giornate Apostoliche," "Lettera al benigno lettore."

56. Bernardino d'Asti, "Missione in prattica," MS Borg. Lat. 316, 14.

57. The notice of the failed attempts to sell the Jesuit library appeared in Coimbra, *Livros de "Ofícios para o reino,"* 1:89. About the Jesuit library, see also Cadornega, *História geral das guerras angolanas* (1942), 3:38–39.

58. The German edition, of 1597, has a frontispiece similar to that of the 1598 Latin edition, but a Latin

book is more likely than a German one to have been in Portuguese-speaking Luanda.

59. Groesen, "De Bry Collection of Voyages."

60. Renaissance scholars of rhetoric and the arts (oratory but also dancing and painting) discussed the connection between bodily temperament and quality of the mind, after Plato and Quintilian: "The temper of the mind can be inferred from the glance and the gait." Quintilian, *Insitutio oratoriae* 11.3.105. See Alberti, *"On Painting" and "On Sculpture,"* 80–81, and Boyle, "Deaf Signs," 167–68. About dancing, see Nevile, *Dance*, 87. About gait and noble carriage of the body in early modern Italy, see Gage, *Painting as Medicine*, 76. For the link between movement of the body and movement of the soul since the early Middle Ages, see Kolsky, "Graceful Performances," 14–16.

61. Harriot, *Briefe and true report*, plate XI.

62. Arcangeli, "Dancing Savages."

63. Burke, "Nakedness and Other Peoples." About the *moresca* dance in Italy and the controversies around its interpretation, see Cummings, "Dance and 'The Other.'" Notably, Lopes and Pigafetta's description of Kongo uses the term *morescha* to describe a courtly dance; see Lopes and Pigafetta, *Relatione del reame di Congo*, 69.

64. Leitch, "Burgkmair's *Peoples of Africa and India*," 136.

65. John White's drawings. Hulton and Quinn, *American Drawings of John White*.

CHAPTER 3

1. "Stones" translates the title's *Pietre*, Italian for *Pedras*.

2. The toponym appears in the historical documents and literature as Maopongo, Pedras de Maopungo, Matadi Maupungo, and Pungo Andongo, which amount to different abbreviations of the phrase *matadi ma up-ungu a ndongo*, literally "tall rocks of Ndongo." The site

acquired the epithet of Ndongo when Ngola-a-Ari, resident ruler of Maopungo, became its Portuguese-supported king as Felipe I in 1626, displacing Queen Njinga. It was conquered and incorporated into Portuguese Angola in 1671. Cavazzi visited the site periodically from 1655 to 1664. See Heintze, *Fontes para a história de Angola*, 96, 101, 202. About the Jesuits, see Brásio, *Monumenta*, 1st ser., 7:419. About the name, see Delgado in Cadornega, *História geral das guerras angolanas* (1940), 1:167–68nn. See also Heintze, "Unbekanntes Angola," 768–69, and Cavazzi, *Descrição histórica*, 2:220n71.

3. Belotti, "Giornate Apostoliche," 173–74.

4. Saccardo, *Congo e Angola*, 2:105–6.

5. Cavazzi and Alamandini, *Istorica descrizione*, 799–800.

6. About the wayfaring draftsman in Dutch prints, see Schmidt, *Inventing Exoticism*, 104.

7. See, for example, the works of Claude Lorrain or the Dutch landscapists of the seventeenth century such as Jan Frans van Bloemen and Gaspar van Wittel. About the colonial gaze in landscape, see Bleichmar, *Visible Empire*, 149–51.

8. For a discussion of a similar pattern in the European encounter with the Americas, see Greenblatt, *Marvelous Possessions*.

9. Juan de Santiago, "Breve Relacion," 36. The same paragraph appears in the manuscript composed by Antonio de Teruel, "Descripcion Narrativa," 13. Berchorius, or Pierre Bersuire, was a fourteenth-century commentator on and translator of Ovid, among others. A Benedictine, he was originally a Franciscan. His encyclopedic works touch upon Africa in several parts. See Medeiros, *L'Occident et l'Afrique*, 252–53.

10. Psalm 103:24–26, 31, 34: "quam magnificata ss. opera tua, Domine omnia in sapientia fecisti hoc mare magnum, et spatiosum manibus illic reptilia quorum non est numerus. animalia pusilla cum magnis, illic naves pertransibunt. . . . Sit gloria Domini in saeculum ego vero delectabor in Domino. Excellente modo de contenplar a

Dios en las criaturas gozandose en el y no en ellas." From the Vulgate, modified by Juan de Santiago. My translation with wording from Douay-Rheims.

11. Pacheco, *Arte de la pintura*, 140–41.

12. Merolla and Piccardo, *Breve, e succinta relatione*, 74. See also Antonio de Teruel, "Descripcion Narrativa," 19. *Spalliere* are painted panels in early modern Italy; see Barriault, *Spalliera Paintings*. Pallas Athena, the goddess of crafts, is a weaver.

13. Merolla repeats the word *spalliere* below, referring to the same scene at each bend of the river. It even appears in his index under "Zaire": "Zairo: fiume famosissimo adornato da verde spalliere, e d'Alberi singulari." Merolla and Piccardo, *Breve, e succinta relatione*, indice alfabetico. About the convergence of art and nature in the seventeenth century, see Daston and Park, *Wonders*, 290–301.

14. Marcellino d'Atri, "Giornate Apostoliche," 65, published in Toso and Marcellino d'Atri, *Anarchia congolese*, 17–18.

15. Geronimus, *Piero di Cosimo*, 80; Barriault, *Spalliera Paintings*, 2.

16. Alberti, *"On Painting" and "On Sculpture,"* 55.

17. Hennepin, *Description de la Loüisiane*.

18. Hennepin, *Nouvelle decouverte*, penultimate page of the "Avis au lecteur."

19. Ibid., 446.

20. Sagard, *Histoire du Canada*, 11.

21. Panofsky, *Studies in Iconology*, 3.

22. The banana with the cross is the only illustration in the Middle East travelogue of Capuchin friar Pacifique de Provins, *Relation du voyage de Perse*, 117. Mandeville's mention of the feature probably draws from Dominican friar Wilhelm von Boldensele, but his travelogue is broadly understood as a compilation of Franciscan and Dominican sources. Niccolò da Poggibonsi in the fourteenth century also mentions this feature of the fruit; see Niccolò da Poggibonsi, *Libro d'oltramare*, 2:193. For Mandeville and further discussion, see Howard, *Writers and Pilgrims*, 56–57 and 57–58n6.

23. Capuchin Constitutions of 1608, chap. 2, para. 17. The Capuchin Constitutions count several early modern versions, from the 1529 founding Constitutions of Albacina to those approved in 1643 by Urban VIII. Paul Hanbridge, O.F.M. Cap., has translated into English the Capuchin Constitutions from the Capuchin General Archives in the Colegio San Lorenzo da Brindisi, Rome. In this study, unless otherwise noted, I use his translation.

24. Capuchin Constitutions of 1608, chap. 2, para. 18.

25. It is most probable that Paolo da Lorena produced the foldout print alongside the others in the *Istorica descrizione*, but the print itself is not signed.

26. Saint Bonaventure's *Legenda maior*, the official biography of the saint, was first printed in Italian translation in Milan in 1477. The parables collected in *I fioretti* are based upon popular stories in circulation during the second half of the thirteenth century. Compiled between 1322 and 1328, *I fioretti* was first published in Vicenza in 1476, together with the *Considerazioni sulle stimmate*, a text on the stigmata.

27. "Stare ginocchioni colla faccia e colle mani levate al cielo," in Cesari, *Fioretti di San Francesco*, 180.

28. See prints designed by Ligozzi and etched by Schiamossi in Moroni, *Descrizione del sacro monte*.

29. Bonaventure, *Soul's Journey into God*, 7.3, 112–13.

30. The idea of *Franciscus alter Christus* and his *conformitas* to Christ is articulated in Bartolomeo de Pisa's *Liber de conformitate vitae Beati Francisci ad vitam Domine Jesu*, composed circa 1390, and Ubertino da Casale's *Arbor vitae crucifixi Jesu*, from 1485. About Francis as *alter Christus* and his artistic representation, see Van Os, "St. Francis of Assisi."

31. See Largier and Brett, "Logic of Arousal."

32. Capuchin Constitutions of 1608, chap. 1, para. 5.

33. The Capuchin rule states: "For this reason his life and that of his blessed companions shall be read frequently." Capuchin Constitutions of 1608, chap. 1, para. 5. About the book's presence in the Americas, see Herrejón Peredo, "Marcel Bataillon."

34. Camille, "Before the Gaze," quote on 209.

35. About Renaissance Franciscan optical theory, see Flanigan, "Ocular Chastity." For a broader social history of vision, see Clark, *Vanities of the Eye*, 15. See also Camille, "Before the Gaze."

36. Matthew 28:19: "euntes ergo docete omnes gentes: baptizantes eos in nomine Patris, et Filii, et Spiritus Sancti" (Go ye therefore, and teach all nations, baptizing them in the name of the Father, and of the Son, and of the Holy Ghost, KJV).

37. Other similar formations of bare rocks rising dramatically over the savanna exist in central Africa—for example, the Lovo Massif in the Democratic Republic of the Congo. See Heimlich, "Art rupestre du massif de Lovo."

38. The *Considerazioni* only appeared in print in the twentieth century; see Mancini, *Considerazioni sulla pittura*. "Modo e regola di far viaggio p[er] ridurlo all'atto della prudenza, et eruditione, deve esser tale, e farsi in q[ue]sto modo," Barb. Lat. 4315, Biblioteca Apostolica Vaticana. See Gage, "Exercise for Mind and Body," 1186, and Gage, *Painting as Medicine*.

39. See Gage, "Exercise for Mind and Body," 1192.

40. Ibid., 1194.

41. Gage, *Painting as Medicine*, 77.

42. Gage, "Exercise for Mind and Body," 1195; Jones, *Federico Borromeo and the Ambrosiana*, 82.

43. Conigliello, "Jacopo Ligozzi"; Tongiorgi Tomasi and Hirschauer, *Flowering of Florence*.

44. Baglione, *Vite de' pittori*, 222; Fletcher, "Filippo Napoletano's Museum."

45. Freedberg, *Eye of the Lynx*, 55–59.

46. About Cardinal Borromeo's association with the Accademia dei Lincei and his interest in their botanical studies, see Baldriga, *Occhio della lince*, 21–31, and Jones, "Federico Borromeo as a Patron."

47. Borromeo, *Sacred Painting*, 179, para. 42.

48. Borromeo, "Pro suis studiis," MS G310inf, no. 8, 1628, Biblioteca Ambrosiana, Milan, fols. 252r–253r, cited in Jones, "Federico Borromeo as a Patron," 268.

49. Voigt and Brancaforte, "Traveling Illustrations."

50. Thevet, *Singularitez de la France antarctique*, 144r.

51. Leitch, *Mapping Ethnography*.

52. "Landscapes and still lifes," art historian Pamela Jones writes, "were seen by Borromeo as visual means to spiritual ends." Jones, "Federico Borromeo as a Patron," 271.

53. See the inventory of the Capuchin libraries, http://rici.vatlib.it/Ricerche.asp, and Bellarmino, *De Ascensione Mentis in Deum*.

CHAPTER 4

1. See chapter 3 above.

2. The immense majority of Capuchin missionaries to central Africa came from Italy, with the notable exception of a Spanish mission in the early years. Flemish, French, or Hungarian friars occasionally joined the Italians. For a list of missionaries, including their geographical origins, see the third volume of Saccardo, *Congo e Angola*.

3. About the readership of the Capuchin corpus, see chapter 1 above.

4. Davies, *Renaissance Ethnography*, 10.

5. See, respectively, Parma Watercolors, Virgili Collection, fols. 29, 35, and 53.

6. In the famous formulation of classicist Jean-Pierre Vernant, it is the goal of Western representation to "inscribe absence in presence, to insert the other, the elsewhere in our familiar universe." Vernant, "From the 'Presentification,'" 153. For the original French, see Vernant, *Mythe et pensée chez les grecs*.

7. Freedberg, *Eye of the Lynx*; Ogilvie, *Science of Describing*.

8. Freedberg, *Eye of the Lynx*, 397.

9. Letters of Michelangelo Guattini to his father from Pernambuco, Brazil, September 12 and 17, 1667, published in Guattini and Carli, *Viaggio nel Regno del Congo*, 65–69.

10. Zanoni, *Istoria botanica*, 42.

11. Davies, *Renaissance Ethnography*, 4.

12. Primates' harassing predators is a documented behavior. The animals depicted in the vignettes could be mangabeys. I thank Professor Meg Crofoot from the Max Planck Institute of Animal Behavior and the University of Konstanz for giving me a primer on primates. About primate mob behavior, see Crofoot, "Why mob?"

13. Francesco da Pavia, "Animali quadrupedi," 2v. About apes and sensuality in the early modern period, see Lurati, "'To Dust the Pelisse'"; in the Enlightenment, see Sebastiani, "'Monster with Human Visage.'"

14. Zucchelli, *Relazioni del viaggio*, 260.

15. Findlen, "Early Modern Things."

16. Letter of Guattini to his father, in Pernambuco, September 17, 1667, reproduced in Guattini and Carli, *Viaggio nel Regno del Congo*, 168–69.

17. Ibid., 70.

18. Filippo da Firenze, "Ragguagli del Congo," 157.

19. Cadornega, *História geral das guerras angolanas* (1942), 3:348. Cadornega included a painting of the wild boar in the third volume of his manuscript, "Historia general das guerras Angolana," v.

20. Boccone, *Osservazioni naturali*, 217. See Olmi, "Science, Honour, Metaphor," 11.

21. Ibid., 14.

22. About cabinets of curiosity in general and Aldrovandi in particular, see Findlen, *Possessing Nature*, and Impey and MacGregor, *Origins of Museums*.

23. Almeida, "Infelicidade feliz," 218.

24. Antonio de Teruel, "Descripcion Narrativa," 172.

25. Marcellino d'Atri, "Giornate Apostoliche," 65, published in Toso and Marcellino d'Atri, *Anarchia congolese*, 17–18.

26. Andrea da Pavia, "Viaggio Apostolico," fol. 126r; Filippo da Firenze, "Ragguagli del Congo," 157.

27. See Shepard, *Lore of the Unicorn*; Duffin, "'Fish,' Fossil, and Fake"; Fischer and Cossu Ferra Fischer, "Licorne"; and Gerritsen, "Unicorn and the Pharmacists."

28. See Clarke, *Rhinoceros*. About Abada, see also Gschwend, "Emperor's Exotic and New World Animals," 90–92.

29. See the use in Portuguese India reported by a Discalced Carmelite, Filippo della Santissima Trinità, *Viaggi Orientali*, 404–5.

30. For example, in Thevet, *Cosmographie universelle*, 1:95v.

31. Francesco da Pavia, "Animali quadrupedi."

32. Ibid., 1v.

33. About the lore surrounding the properties of the horn, see Duffin, "'Fish,' Fossil, and Fake," 211–12.

34. See also the explanation from a Portuguese text in the Biblioteca Nacional de Portugal, Lisbon, Caixa 29, doc 25—"E acerca do corno do Unicorne q[u]e em Benguela dizẽ auer m[ui]tos E eu creio são Abadas, mas tẽ a mesma uirtude q[ue] o Unicorne"—as quoted in Parreira, *Dicionário glossográfico e toponímico*, 27.

35. Margócsy, "Camel's Head."

36. Ibid., 76.

37. Elkins, "On Visual Desperation."

38. Thevet, *Cosmographie universelle*, 1:130v.

39. Merolla and Piccardo, *Breve, e succinta relatione*, 62.

40. Ibid., 63.

41. Bernardino d'Asti, "Missione in prattica," MS Borg. Lat. 316, 41.

42. About textiles and baroque liturgical spectacle in a non-European context, see Stanfield-Mazzi, "Weaving and Tailoring."

43. About the elite use of carpets, local and imported, see Merolla and Piccardo, *Breve, e succinta relatione*, 170, 176, and Thornton, *Kongolese Saint Anthony*, 60, 64, 187. See also plates 27 and 101.

44. About the visual program in Kongo churches, see Fromont *Art of Conversion*, 198–201.

45. Hermenegildo de Vilaplana, *Historico, y sagrado novenario*, 22.

46. Ibid., 25. See the analysis in Gonzalez, "From Conversion to Reconversion."

47. Toso and Marcellino d'Atri, *Anarchia congolese*, 289–90.

48. See, for instance, the image of their Soyo convent in Bernardino d'Asti, "Missione in prattica," MS 457, fol. 4r.

49. Merolla and Piccardo, *Breve, e succinta relatione*, 148.

50. Juan de Santiago, "Breve Relacion," 160–61.

51. "Compendio delle vite," fol. 79r.

52. Ibid., fols. 79r–80r. See also Giovanni Francesco [da] Romano, *Breve Relatione*, 93–96.

53. Luca da Caltanisetta, *Diaire congolais*, 170, 209. Note that papier-mâché refers to a range of techniques used to obtain devotional images from molds, a process that allowed for a cheap and rapid production of objects.

54. Statues of the Virgin were dressed with local textiles for example in Kibenga; see Bernardo da Gallo's report in Jadin, "Congo," 499.

55. Mateo de Anguiano, *Misiones capuchinas en Africa*, 1:58.

56. Bernardino d'Asti, "Missione in prattica," MS Borg. Lat. 316, 15.

57. Fromont, *Art of Conversion*, 150–52, 200–201; Fromont, "From Image to Grave." See the list of devotional objects brought to Kongo and Angola by the Capuchins, in Archivio Storico de Propaganda Fide, SOCG 250, fol. 528r (the list appears twice, once on a floating page and once on folio 528r). Tourneur, "Médailles religieuses."

58. Clist et al., "Elusive Archaeology of Kongo Urbanism."

59. They also, for instance, asked for funds from Rome for devotional objects to bring on their ill-fated mission to the Kingdom of Benin in West Africa in 1664. Letter of April 29, 1664, signed by the general procurator of the Capuchins, Archivio Storico de Propaganda Fide, SOCG 255, fol. 111r. Capuchin missionaries to Benin needed a stipend for the trip and devotional objects to give once in Benin to win over the local people.

60. Letter of Felix de Villar to the Propaganda Fide, January 20, 1650, in APF, SOCG 249, fol. 76r, in Brásio, *Monumenta*, 1st ser., 10:474–75.

61. About the Rosary Confraternities in Kongo, see Lorenzo da Lucca and Filippo da Firenze, "Relazioni," 1700–1717, fols. 75–76, in Lorenzo da Lucca, *Relations sur le Congo*, 57. Mutanda wa Mukendi, "Institution." Central Africa counted many confraternities dedicated to the rosary, a devotion that the friars promoted in the region.

62. The ceremony unfolding is a *sangamento*, a martial dance used by leaders to affirm their authority in the Christian Kongo. See Fromont, "Dance."

63. See, for instance, the brass Saint Anthony pendant, possibly from the seventeenth or eighteenth century, in the Metropolitan Museum of Art, inv. 1999.295.1. See Mello e Souza, "Santo Antônio," and Fromont, *Art of Conversion*, 269–71.

64. Fromont, *Art of Conversion*, 206–12; Thornton, *Kongolese Saint Anthony*.

65. The color is faded, but the stole must have been purple.

66. To my knowledge, *mestres* were adults. Since the short stature of the figure suggests a child, I hypothesize that it represents a youth training to become a *mestre*. About the function of the *mestre* in Kongo, see Fromont, "Common Threads," and Brinkman, "Kongo Interpreters."

67. Vansina, "Communications," 130, mentions that cotton weaving on raffia looms arrived in Angola in the 1400s. About *ngele*-type ingots, see Nikis, "Métallurgie du cuivre."

68. The seventeenth-century Latin-Kikongo dictionary records them as *fax: ncandia eanene*. "Vocabularium Latinum," 37r. The fan-shaped blades are illustrated in many of the Araldi-manuscript paintings (1, 7, 8, 13, 18, 20, 22, 32). See Bassani, *Cappuccino nell'Africa nera*, figs. 58–60. Examples of such blades are found in museum collections of artifacts from the region. They are associated with several different groups from today's Democratic Republic of the Congo and Angola but for the most part do not have precise creation dates. See, for

example, the Songye axe in the Metropolitan Museum of Art, inv. 1978.412.370.

69. See Maret and Smith, "Who's Who?," 209–11.

CHAPTER 5

1. "On the Invocation, Veneration, and Relics, of Saints, and on Sacred Images" (*De invocatione Sanctorum*), second decree, Council of Trent, Sess. xxv, December 3–4, 1563.

2. About the sources and their biases, see Hilton, "European Sources," and Gonçalves, "África indômita," 100–131.

3. About the "Vocabularium," see chapter 7 below; De Kind, de Schryver, and Bostoen, "Pushing Back the Origin," 163–64; and the entry for *Idolum* in the "Vocabularium Latinum," fol. 44r.

4. "Vocabularium Latinum," 74r (about *penates*).

5. Ibid., 55r (about Mars).

6. Pacconio, *Gentio de Angola*, 8v–9r, 51v–52r, 73r–v; Doke, "Early Bantu Literature," 51–52. Serafino da Cortona, in "Breve relatione de i riti gentilichi," 4r, also defines "quiteque, pl iteque" as "roughly made statues" and "decorated sticks."

7. Bernardo da Canicatti, *Diccionario da lingua Bunda*, 453.

8. Cavazzi and Alamandini, *Istorica descrizione*, 70–71.

9. Ibid., 71. On the linguistic dimension of religious interactions between Capuchins and central Africans, see Nsondé, "Christianisme et religion traditionnelle," and Nsondé, *Langues, culture et histoire Koongo*, 1.

10. Parma Watercolors, Virgili Collection, fol. 83.

11. Cavazzi, "Missione Evangelica," vol. A, book 2, chap. 11, p. 171. Translation by Thornton, "Translation of the Araldi Manuscript."

12. Luca da Caltanisetta, *Diaire congolais*, 107.

13. Serafino da Cortona, "Breve relatione de i riti gentilichi," 4r.

14. Merolla and Piccardo, *Breve, e succinta relatione*, 281.

15. Serafino da Cortona, "Breve relatione de i riti gentilichi," 4r.

16. Marcellino d'Atri, "Giornate Apostoliche," 118.

17. See, for example, Coote, "Text-Book Textile," and Bassani, "Ivoires et tissus kongo."

18. Fromont, *Art of Conversion*; Fromont, "From Image to Grave"; Volper, *Du Jourdain au Congo*.

19. Heimlich, *Massif de Lovo*.

20. About the Museo Pigorini figures (inv. 4525 and 4526), see Bassani, *African Art and Artefacts*, 157–58. An anthropomorphic fragment in the Fondation Dapper (inv. no. 5250) has been carbon-dated to between the fifteenth and seventeenth centuries. Without further context or complementary material, it does not lend itself to interpretation; see Falgayrettes-Leveau, *Angola*, 40–42.

21. Fromont, *Art of Conversion*, 58–59.

22. See Slenes, "Arbre nsanda replanté," and Janzen and Arkinstall, *Quest for Therapy*, 163–68. For use of *nsanda* for fertility, see Serafino da Cortona, "Breve relatione de i riti gentilichi," 4v.

23. See chapter 1 above.

24. Pistoni, *Fra Giovanni Antonio Cavazzi*, 17.

25. For a seventeenth-century description of Kimpasi, see Girolamo da Montesarchio, "Viaggio al Gongho," 61r–66v. Published with original pagination in Piazza, *Prefettura apostolica*. See also Cavazzi and Alamandini, *Istorica descrizione*, 85–87.

26. See Fromont, *Art of Conversion*, 94–95. For other examples of the attitude, see Falgayrettes-Leveau and Dapper, *Geste kôngo*, 108–19.

27. An early item featuring a variation of the gesture is the ivory box in the Detroit Institute of Arts, inv. 25.183.

28. Cavazzi and Alamandini, *Istorica descrizione*, 71.

29. For other examples of figures displaying this gesture, see Falgayrettes-Leveau and Dapper, *Geste kôngo*, 92, 95, 105.

30. See the Kuba *ndop* portraits in Vansina, "*Ndop*," and LaGamma, *Heroic Africans*, 153–81.

31. See, for example, the heroic Chokwe figure of Chibinda Ilunga (inv. AP1978.05) in the Kimbell Art Museum.

32. See, for example, the Parma Watercolors texts on folios 70 and 89. For figures with crowns of feathers, see Quai Branly, inv. 71.1892.52.5, and Metropolitan Museum 1978.412.533, among many others.

33. Cavazzi and Alamandini, *Istorica descrizione*, 85.

34. Serafino da Cortona, "Breve relatione de i riti gentilichi," 4r.

35. Luca da Caltanisetta, *Diaire congolais*, 104–5.

36. Serafino da Cortona, "Breve relatione de i riti gentilichi," 7v.

37. Parma Watercolors, Virgili Collection, fol. 83.

38. Historiography on the identity of Jaga is long and contentious; see the summary and synthesis of the debate in the long footnotes in Lopes and Pigafetta, *Royaume de Congo*, 291–95.

39. See Bassani, *African Art and Artefacts*, object no. 451.

40. Maret, *Fouilles archéologiques*, vol. 3.

41. The Capuchins had been very active in Europe in the catechization of rural areas and in the fight against Protestantism. The Capuchin missionaries to the Kongo often had previous experiences of missionary work in Europe; for instance, Luca da Caltanisetta worked in the mission of the Abruzzi in central Italy before going to the Kongo. See Luca da Caltanisetta, *Diaire congolais*, xi.

42. Bernardino d'Asti, "Missione in prattica," MS Borg. Lat. 316, 95–96.

43. Ibid., 58. He also notes that the constant contact of the Kongo people with their heathen neighbors made it even more difficult to maintain good Christianity.

44. Jadin, "Andrea de Pavia au Congo," 445.

45. See, for example, Belotti, "Giornate Apostoliche," 215.

46. See the description of the *quixilla* kept by Queen Njinga in Cavazzi, "Missione Evangelica," book 2, chap. 9. About *quixilla*, see Merolla and Piccardo, *Breve,*

e succinta relatione, 145–47; Jadin, "Congo," 459–62; and Toso and Marcellino d'Atri, *Anarchia congolese*, 145. Parma Watercolors, Virgili Collection, fol. 100v.

47. Jadin, "Congo," 460.

48. Ibid., 461.

49. Antonio da Gaeta and Gioia, *Maravigliosa conversione*, 76. Bernardo da Gallo shares Antonio da Gaeta's suspicion of surgeons and medics; see Jadin, "Congo," 460.

50. Luca da Caltanisetta, *Diaire congolais*, 103–4. The trope of blindness recurs in the description of superstition in the Capuchins' accounts.

51. Ibid., 27, 104.

52. Bernardino d'Asti, "Missione in prattica," MS Borg. Lat. 316, 63. See also the discussion of medicinal practices in Batumanisa and Nkasa, "Homme blanc," 41–45.

53. The term appears in a variety of spellings, as the orthography was not fixed. Bernardino d'Asti, "Missione in prattica," MS Borg. Lat. 316, 60.

54. See the online version of the vocabulary at http://www.lessicografia.it.

55. Bernardino d'Asti, "Missione in prattica," MS Borg. Lat. 316, 59.

56. Ibid., fol. 62. The quoted text from the Vatican version of the manuscript clearly refers to the scene illustrated in the Turin version.

57. See a carbon-dated example of such a root in Heimlich, "Kongo Cross," 25.

58. See the most extensive catalogue of objects from Africa before 1800, Bassani, *African Art and Artefacts*. For a description of ritual paraphernalia, see, for example, Luca da Caltanisetta, *Diaire congolais*, 70; Cavazzi and Alamandini, *Istorica descrizione*, 171; and Filesi, *Nazionalismo e religione nel Congo*, 105. For a radiocarbon-dated set of ritual objects, see Heimlich, "Kongo Cross," 25.

59. Bernardino d'Asti, "Missione in prattica," MS Borg. Lat. 316, 62.

60. Ibid., MS 457, fol. 10r.

61. Ibid., MS Borg. Lat. 316, 62.

62. Belotti, "Avvertimenti Salutevoli," 151.

63. Luca da Caltanisetta, *Diaire congolais*, 223.

64. Ibid., 211.

65. Merolla and Piccardo, *Breve, e succinta relatione*, 143–44.

66. Luca da Caltanisetta, *Diaire congolais*, 71.

CHAPTER 6

1. See Sutton, *Early Modern Dutch Prints*; Earle and Lowe, *Black Africans*; and Bindman and Gates, *Image of the Black*, vol. 3, part 1. The depiction of ambassadors is a notable exception; see Fromont, *Art of Conversion*, chap. 3, and Lowe, "Visual Representations of an Elite."

2. About the early modern European iconography of the slave, see Earle and Lowe, *Black Africans*; Lowe, "Lives of African Slaves"; and Fracchia, *"Black but human."* About slave collars and the intersection between the iconography of the slave and ideas of refinement, see Gikandi, *Slavery*, and Bindman and Gates, *Image of the Black*, vol. 3, part 2.

3. About Capuchin negative views on central Africans, see Almeida, "Infelicidade feliz."

4. Serafino da Cortona, "Breve relatione de i riti gentilichi," 4r.

5. About the Capuchins' role in the slave trade, see, for example, Mutanda wa Mukendi, "Question." See also Fromont, *Art of Conversion*, 220–23.

6. See chapter 2 above.

7. Bernardino d'Asti, "Missione in prattica," MS 457, fol. 5v.

8. See also ibid., 7r.

9. Parma Watercolors, Virgili Collection, fol. 90r; Bernardino d'Asti, "Missione in prattica," MS 457, fol. 11v.

10. Bernardino d'Asti, "Missione in prattica," MS 457, fols. 9r, 9v, 11v.

11. About the lack of seminaries in the Kongo, see Jadin, "Clergé séculier."

12. Marcellino d'Atri, "Giornate Apostoliche," 131.

13. About the Dembos, or Ndembu, see Cadornega, *História geral das guerras angolanas* (1942), 3:200–207, and Madeira Santos, "Écrire le pouvoir."

14. Carli and Guattini, *Viaggio*, 130–31.

15. Ibid., 169–70. The author uses here an Italianized, plural version of the Kikongo word *nzimbu*: *zimbo*, pl. *zimbi*.

16. *Pagamento* means "payment" in Portuguese. Mateo de Anguiano, *Misiones capuchinas en Africa*, 1:189.

17. Bernardino d'Asti, "Missione in prattica," MS 457, fol. 9r.

18. Bernardino d'Asti, "Missione in prattica," MS Borg. Lat. 316, 53–54; Archivio Storico de Propaganda Fide, SOCG 721, fols. 298–201.

19. Each of the following Capuchin works on central Africa include an illustrated frontispiece. Manuscripts: Cavazzi, "Missione Evangelica"; Bernardino d'Asti, "Missione in prattica," MS Borg. Lat. 316; Bernardino d'Asti, "Missione in prattica," MS 457. Printed volumes: Antonio da Gaeta and Gioia, *Maravigliosa conversione*; Cavazzi and Alamandini, *Istorica descrizione*; Merolla and Piccardo, *Breve, e succinta relatione*; Zucchelli, *Relazioni del viaggio*.

20. "In veritate *comperi quis* [*sic*] non est personarum acceptor Deus" (Acts 10:34). Translation from the Douay-Rheims Bible, as are the translations of the following verses.

21. "Notas mihi fecisti vias vitae." From Acts 2:28.

22. The Latin labels from Ezekiel 36:13: "Devoratrix hominum es"; "Suffocans gentem tuam."

23. Ezekiel 36:13–14 (Vulg.): "haec dicit Dominus Deus pro eo quod dicunt de vobis devoratrix hominum es et suffocans gentem tuam propterea homines non comedes amplius et gentem tuam non necabis ultra ait Dominus Deus."

24. The ribbon around the cross reads: "Elevabit signum in nationibus procul" (God will raise a signal to a nation from far away). Isaiah 5:26.

25. Acts 16:30: "quid me oportet facere ut salvus fiam."

26. Ecclesiasticus 17:25: "in partes vade saeculi sancti cum vivis et dantibus confessionem Deo."

27. About Mexico's "apostolic twelve," see Edgerton, *Theaters of Conversion*, 38–59.

28. About feathers, see Dean, *Inka Bodies*, 170–75.

29. Sandoval, *De Instauranda Aethiopum Salute*. It was first published in 1627 in a shorter edition without an illustrated frontispiece. The 1647 edition was planned for two volumes, but only the first one appeared. About the two editions of Sandoval, see Restrepo, "*De Instauranda Aethiopum Salute*."

30. About Andrés de Oviedo and the early Jesuit endeavors in Ethiopia, see Alòs-Moner, "Birth of a Mission."

31. Sandoval, *Naturaleza, policia sagrada i profana*. About the print, see, for instance, Brewer-García, "Imagined Transformations."

32. About the black magi, see Kaplan, *Rise of the Black Magus*, and Koerner, "Epiphany of the Black Magus."

33. Brewer-García, "Imagined Transformations," 134. Sandoval, *De Instauranda Aethiopum Salute*, book 1, chap. 4, 24. See also Brewer-García, *Beyond Babel*.

34. Sandoval, *De Instauranda Aethiopum Salute*, "Prologo al letor."

35. About the topos of salvation as whitening, see Harpster, "Color of Salvation," and Spicer, "European Perceptions of Blackness."

36. About black skin in print during the seventeenth century, see Kolfin, "When Africans Became Black," and Kolfin, "Tradition and Innovation."

37. About early European images of extra-Europeans, see Davies, *Renaissance Ethnography*.

38. Leitch, "Burgkmair's *Peoples of Africa and India*"; Gaudio, *Engraving the Savage*.

39. Schmidt, *Inventing Exoticism*.

40. Vaumas, *Éveil missionnaire*.

41. Monari, "Viaggio al Congo," 172, in Piazza, *Prefettura apostolica*, 246.

42. Translations, here and below, are from the Douay-Rheims Bible.

43. Dapper, *Naukeurige beschrijvinge*, 583; Cavazzi and Alamandini, *Istorica descrizione*, plate 41, p. 336.

44. Bassani, *African Art and Artefacts*, 16–17.

45. Zucchelli, *Relazioni del viaggio*; Zucchelli, *Merckwürdige Missions- und Reise-Beschreibung*.

46. Linschoten, *Itinerario*; Lopes and Pigafetta, *Beschryvinghe*. Note that another German-language version of Zucchelli appeared in 1723, without a frontispiece, as *Der Geistliche Robinson*.

47. About the conflation of Africans and apes in seventeenth- and eighteenth-century European discourse, see Sebastiani, "'Monster with Human Visage,'" and Sutton, *Early Modern Dutch Prints*, 113–17.

48. See the discussion of the Jesuit Chinese-mission frontispieces in Hsia, *Sojourners*, chaps. 2 and 3, and Kircher, *China monumentis*.

49. "Instructio Vicarum Apostolicorum ad regna Sinarum Tonchini et Concincinaes proficiscentium." The instructions, which circulated mostly in manuscript form, are extant in several hand-copied versions dated 1659. The published version is titled *Constitutiones Apostolicae Brevia, Decreta, &c.* See Jacqueline, "Instructions." For a modern publication, see "Instructio vicariorum."

50. For the history of the long preparations for the Capuchin mission to central Africa, see Faria, *Primeira tentative*, and Filesi and Isidoro de Villapadierna, *Missio antiqua*.

51. Letter of Luca da Caltanisetta, vice-prefect of the Congo Mission, undated, in Archivio Storico de Propaganda Fide, SOCG Africa 1, fol. 65r.

52. Rego, *Patronage portugais de l'Orient*.

53. Metzler, "Orientation," 167.

54. *Constitutiones Apostolicae*, part IV, 14. See also Metzler, "Orientation," 180.

55. Bernardino d'Asti, "Missione in prattica," MS 457, fol. 2r.

56. See chapter 4 above.

57. See the table of contents of Bernardino d'Asti, "Missione in prattica," MS Borg. Lat. 316, 132–33.

58. Belotti, "Giornate Apostoliche," "Al benigno Lettore."

59. [Jordão], *Historia do Congo*, 217–24.

60. "Si deve dar sempre quando la persona fà quello che può dal canto suo." Ibid., 220.

61. Note that the officiating of the wedding ceremony in a church and with a priest present for validity was an innovation from the Council of Trent, before which the promise of the two spouses sufficed. See Kamen, *Phoenix and the Flame*, 275–85. About marriage in the Portuguese Atlantic world, see Castelnau-L'Estoile, *Catholicisme colonial*.

62. Brásio, *Monumenta*, 1st ser., 1:524.

63. "Carta do Padre Jorge Vaz (1-8-1548)," in Brásio, *Monumenta*, 1st ser., 2:183–85; "Devassa de D. Diogo Rei do Congo, (10-4-1550)," in ibid., 253–54. About *mestres*, see Brinkman, "Kongo Interpreters."

64. *Maestro* is the Spanish version of the Portuguese word *mestre* used in Kongo. "Relação de Frei Diogo do Santíssimo Sacramento (1583)," in Brásio, *Monumenta*, 1st ser., 4:362–64, quote on 64.

65. See Thornton, "Afro-Christian Syncretism," 64. The personal papers of António Manuel have been conserved in the papal archives in Rome, where he died; Vatican Apostolic Archive (formerly Vatican Secret Archive), Miscellanea, Armadio II, vol. 91, fols. 124–58.

66. Bernardino d'Asti, "Missione in prattica," MS 457, fol. 4v.

67. Ibid., 6v.

68. Ibid., 5r, 8r.

69. "Carta do Padre Jorge Vaz (1-8-1548)," in Brásio, *Monumenta*, 1st ser., 2:185.

70. A discussion of the linguistic competence of the Capuchins can be found in Adalberto da Postioma, "Méthodologie missionaire," 368–71.

71. Belotti, "Avvertimenti Salutevoli," 73.

72. Bernardino d'Asti, "Missione in prattica," MS Borg. Lat. 316, plate II.

73. Ibid., 43.

74. Ibid., 44.

75. Bernardino d'Asti, "Missione in prattica," MS Borg. Lat. 316, 39; Bernardino d'Asti, "Missione in prattica," MS 457, fol. 6r.

76. Bernardino d'Asti, "Missione in prattica," MS 457, fol. 10v.

CHAPTER 7

1. Fromont, *Art of Conversion*.

2. See the decision of June 1, 1618, from the general chapter of the Capuchins: "At the demand of the king of Kongo, it is decided in the general chapter to send into this kingdom a visitor general and six other Spanish brothers." Archivio Generale dei Cappuccini, Rome, MS AG-I, fol. 282v, in António Brásio, *Monumenta*, 1st ser., 6:307. See also the letters from the king of Kongo asking for and eagerly awaiting the arrival of the friars. Brásio, *Monumenta*, 1st ser., 6:392, 402, 505. About the long history of the preparations for the mission, see Filesi and Isidoro de Villapadierna, *Missio antique*, and Faria, *Primeira tentative*.

3. See the extensive analysis on the subject in Almeida, "Infelicidade feliz."

4. Cabranes-Grant, *From Scenarios to Networks*, 3.

5. The image functions very differently from the "allochronic" strategy of representation of the Other in many early modern images. See Fabian, *Time and the Other*. See also Schmidt, *Inventing Exoticism*, 105. Schmidt sees the allochronic dimension of seventeenth-century Dutch prints as a commercial strategy to allow for re-use, but an intriguing consequence of this commercial strategy is the propagation, in readers' minds, of the idea that the cultures represented dwell outside of time and history. It was a commercial scheme with broad civilizational consequences.

6. Koerner, "Hieronymus Bosch's World Picture," 299.

7. Hulton and Quinn, *American Drawings of John White*.

8. Gaudio, *Engraving the Savage*, xix.

9. Koerner, "Hieronymus Bosch's World Picture," 299. In this worldview, the early modern explorer is a male figure; discourses of race and gender are intimately entwined; see, for example, Hall, *Things of Darkness*.

10. Rama, *Lettered City*; Rappaport and Cummins, *Beyond the Lettered City*.

11. Fromont, "Common Threads."

12. Fromont, *Art of Conversion*, 148–49.

13. Cardoso, *Doutrina Christaã*; Thornton, "Afro-Christian Syncretism," 69.

14. For a biographical notice on Roboredo, see Brásio, *Historia e missiologia*, 896–97. About *mestres* and the education system, see chapter 6 above; Brinkman, "Kongo Interpreters"; and Thornton, "Afro-Christian Syncretism."

15. De Kind, de Schryver, and Bostoen, "Pushing Back the Origin," 163–64; "Vocabularium Latinum." See Thornton, "Roboredo, Kikongo Sermon."

16. Cardoso, *Doutrina Christaã*, dedicatory letter to the king of Kongo, Dom Pedro II present in the copy of the book at the Biblioteca Nacional de Portugal under call number RES 268. See also Bontinck and Nsasi, *Catéchisme kikongo*, 12.

17. Cardoso, *Doutrina Christaã*, last page of the preface to the reader.

18. The 1624 "História do Reino do Congo" manuscript, though anonymous, is firmly attributed to Cardoso. It has been published with original pagination in [Cardoso], *História do Reino do Congo*.

19. For modesty, Cardoso reports the last part of the indirect speech, about the sexual explanation, in Latin.

20. About the Kongo educational system, see "Carta do Vigário Rui de Aguiar a El-Rei D. Manuel (25-5-1516)," in Brásio, *Monumenta*, 1st ser., 1:361–63, and Serafino da Cortona quoted in Jadin, "Clergé séculier," 223. About the Jesuit college, see Franco, *Synopsis annalium*, para. 15, p. 245. About Dom Calisto, see Antonio da Gaeta and Gioia, *Maravigliosa conversione*, 52, 97–98, 224, 434; Jadin, "Clergé séculier," 226; Mello e Souza,

"Catolicismo e poder no Congo"; Brásio, *Historia e missiologia*, 897–98; and Mello e Souza, "Missionários e mestres," 11–22.

21. Cavazzi and Alamandini, *Istorica descrizione*, 99, 438, 627; Cadornega, *História geral das guerras angolanas* (1940), 2:188, 223; Cavazzi, "Missione Evangelica," vol. A, book 2, pp. 77–78.

22. Cadornega, *História geral das guerras angolanas* (1940), 2:223.

23. Ibid., 2:188, 223.

24. Antonio de Teruel, "Descripcion Narrativa," 74.

25. Cavazzi and Alamandini, *Istorica descrizione*, 99.

26. Antonio da Gaeta and Gioia, *Maravigliosa conversione*, 252.

27. About orality in early modern natural history, see Azzolini, "Talking of Animals." About Mesoamerican knowledge in European science, see De Renzi, "Writing and Talking of Exotic Animals."

28. See my translation of the text: Fromont, "Nature, Culture, and Faith." The examples are respectively from Parma Watercolors, Virgili Collection, fols. 2 and 70, 45, 90, 98, 39.

29. Respectively, Parma Watercolors, Virgili Collection, fols. 20, 68, 22, 35.

30. See Fromont, *Art of Conversion*, 269–70, and Mello e Souza, "Santo António."

31. See Fromont, "Veränderung und Austausch."

32. Whitehead and Boeseman, *Portrait*, 173–74.

33. Jaspar Beckx, *Portrait of Dom Miguel de Castro*, 1643, oil on panel, Statens Museum for Kunst, Denmark, Inv. KMS7.

34. Fromont, *Art of Conversion*, 165; Phipps, Hecht, and Martín, *Colonial Andes*, 211–12.

35. Tavares and Santos, *Africae Monumenta*.

36. Mason, *Infelicities*, 3; Sutton, *Early Modern Dutch Prints*, 88.

37. MacGaffey, "Dialogues of the Deaf."

38. MacGaffey, *Religion and Society*, 189–216; Hilton, *Kingdom of Kongo*, 62–64; Sweet, *Recreating Africa*, 113–17.

39. Baesten, "Jésuites au Congo"; Rinchon, "Capucins au Congo"; Eucher de Roy, *Congo*.

40. Thornton, "Afro-Christian Syncretism"; Brown, *African-Atlantic Cultures*; Young, *Rituals of Resistance*.

41. Fromont, *Art of Conversion*.

42. Certeau, *Écriture de l'histoire*, avant propos à la seconde édition, 3.

43. The image also opens Hulme, *Colonial Encounters*. See also Lia Markey's discussion of the print in Markey, "Stradano's Allegorical Invention," and Markey, *Renaissance Invention*, 31–32.

44. Gaudio, *Engraving the Savage*, 7.

45. Ibid., 7–9, quote on 9. W. J. T. Mitchell calls a metapicture one of the kinds of "pictures that show themselves in order to know themselves: they stage the 'self-knowledge of pictures.'" See Mitchell, *Picture Theory*, 48. See also the earlier discussion of metapictures in Wu Hung, *Double Screen*, 246–59.

46. See also Stoichita, *Self-Aware Image*.

47. See the conflation in print and image of men and monkeys or apes, discussed, for instance, in Sutton, *Early Modern Dutch Prints*, 113–17, and Sebastiani, "'Monster with Human Visage.'" About entrails-eating Africans, see Van Wyk Smith, "'Most Wretched.'" See also the discussion of figure 89 in chapter 6 above.

48. Gaudio, *Engraving the Savage*, 7.

49. See also chapters 1 and 2 above.

50. Merolla and Piccardo, *Breve, e succinta relatione*, 183.

51. "Remarkable," or *mirabile*, is the ubiquitous adjective used in the Parma Watercolors texts. See my translation of the texts: Fromont, "Nature, Culture, and Faith."

52. Acosta, *Tractado delas Drogas*, 346–50. Much of this information also appeared in Linschoten, and some of Merolla's images, such as the mangrove and canoe, seem inspired by Linschoten; see Merolla and Piccardo, *Breve, e succinta relatione*, plate 14; compare to Linschoten, *Itinerario*, 58–59, 74–77.

53. Cristóvão de Lisboa, "Historia dos animaes," fols. 177v, 83v. See the facsimile edition, edited by Jaime Walter, *História dos animaes e árvores do Maranhão*. See also Palomo, "Ascetic Tropics," 6–7.

54. Amorim, *Franciscanos no Maranhão*, 68.

55. Norton, "Subaltern Technologies," 20, 23, 26.

56. About raffia-fiber making, see Vansina, "Raffia Cloth."

57. Descourvières and Cuénot, "Dictionnaire congo et françois," 94.

58. Ibid., 367.

59. Gibson and McGurk, "High-Status Caps."

60. Cadornega, "Historia general das guerras Angolanas," frontispieces of tomes 1 and 3.

61. Ibid., frontispieces of parts 2, 3, and 4 of tome 3.

62. Norton, "Subaltern Technologies," 23.

63. Fetvacı, *Album of the World Emperor*.

CONCLUSION

1. Object types that have been studied with historical depth through pluridisciplinary approaches include pipes, items of personal adornment, and Christian artworks. See Clist, "From America to Africa," and Bostoen and Brinkman, *Kongo Kingdom*.

2. About imports of red beads or coral (two items often conflated in the primary sources) and textiles to central Africa, see Jadin, "Rivalités luso-néerlandaises," 228. About the *panos pretos*, see Kriger, "'Guinea Cloth,'" 115. Joachim John Monteiro, British traveler to Angola in 1858, described the black cloaks as still a conspicuous part of Angolan women's outfits. Monteiro, *Angola and the River Congo*, 2:35–36. See also Pantoja, "Women's Work," 86–93, images on 274–75.

3. Fromont, *Afro-Catholic Festivals*; Fromont, "Dancing for the King of Congo."

4. This idea, which Foucault first outlined in *Madness and Civilization*, has served as a core theoretical model for postcolonial studies—for instance, in Edward Said's key text *Orientalism*. Foucault, *Folie et déraison*, 169. In his 2015 book *Inventing Exoticism*, historian Benjamin Schmidt has breathed new life into the idea of a dynamic

relationship between the construction of the idea of Otherness and the construction of the idea of Europe in the early modern era.

5. Mignolo and Walsh, *On Decoloniality*; Quijano, "Coloniality of Power"; Cohen-Aponte, "Decolonizing the Global Renaissance."

6. For a discussion of the historiography about the print since its influential use in Michel de Certeau, *Écriture de l'histoire*, see Markey, "Stradano's Allegorical Invention," 387–89, 388n6 in particular.

7. Bleichmar, *Visual Voyages*, 12–15; Markey, "Stradano's Allegorical Invention." The idea of the invention of America harks back to O'Gorman, *Invención de América*.

8. For theoretical proposals for the analysis of cross-cultural images not fully illuminated through postcolonial analysis, see Russo, *Untranslatable Image*; Shaffer, *Grafted Arts*; and Fromont, *Art of Conversion*.

9. About the presence of Europe's Others in its midst, see Otele, *African Europeans*, and Spicer, *Revealing the African Presence*.

10. Cabranes-Grant, *From Scenarios to Networks*, 3.

11. Dean and Leibsohn, "Hybridity and Its Discontents," 13.

12. Greenblatt, *Marvelous Possessions*, 7. Closer to my topic, historian Anne Hilton has articulated the related opinion about central Africa that "we cannot, except in the most exceptional circumstances, overcome the problem of the Euro-centricity of the data." Hilton, "European Sources," 310.

13. The phrase and notion of "blunted impact" comes from John Huxtable Elliott, *Old World and the New*. For

a discussion and rebuttal of this theory, see Rubiés, "Travel Writing and Humanistic Culture," and Norton, "Subaltern Technologies." For postcolonial critiques, see, for example, White, "Invisible Tagkanysough," 752.

14. The phrase is from Merrell, "Some Thoughts," 114.

15. Said, *Culture and Imperialism*, 80–97. See also Fraiman, "Jane Austen and Edward Said"; Spivak, "Three Women's Texts."

16. Mignolo and Walsh, *On Decoloniality*.

17. See, among others, Leibsohn, *Script and Glyph*; Singh, *Real Birds in Imagined Gardens*; Kotani, "Studies in Jesuit Art"; Wang, "Global Perspective"; Boone and Cummins, *Native Traditions*.

18. Silva Santos, *Marfim no mundo moderno*; Phipps, Hecht, and Martín, *Colonial Andes*; Hamann, "Mirrors of Las Meninas"; Padilla and Anderson, *Red Like No Other*; Roberts, *Transporting Visions*; Porras, *First Viral Images*.

19. Chakrabarty, *Provincializing Europe*.

20. For examples of pluridisciplinary, methodological, or theoretical scholarship that have challenged, expanded, and rewritten the archive, see Bostoen and Brinkman, *Kongo Kingdom*; Hartman, "Venus in Two Acts"; Taylor, *Archive and the Repertoire*; and Newman, *On Records*.

21. By "European archive" I mean all documents and information that have been created and conserved in support and as a result of Europe's social, economic, and political projects within or beyond its continental limes, wherever their current location may be.

Bibliography

Note: Franciscan and other known religious authors are listed under their first names unless primarily known by their secular patronymics.

Acosta, Cristóbal. *Tractado delas Drogas, y medicinas de las Indias Orientales, con sus Plantas debuxadas al biuo por Christoual Acosta [. . .]: En el qual se verifica mucho de lo que escriuio el doctor Garcia de Orta.* Burgos: Martin de Victoria impressor de su Magestad, 1578.

Adalberto da Postioma. "Méthodologie missionaire des Capucins au Congo-Matamba-Angola, 1645–1834." *Revue du clergé africain* 19 (1964): 359–86.

Alberti, Leon Battista. *"On Painting" and "On Sculpture": The Latin Texts of "De Pictura" and "De Statua."* Edited and translated by Cecil Grayson. New York: Phaidon, 1972.

Almeida, Carlos José Duarte [José Carlos]. "Entre gente 'aspra e dura': Advertências de um missionário no Congo e Angola (1713–1723)." *Revista lusófona de ciência das religiões* 7, nos. 13–14 (2008): 463–83.

———. "Uma infelicidade feliz: A imagem de África e dos Africanos na Literatura Missionária sobre o Kongo e a região mbundu (meados do séc. XVI–primeiro quartel do séc. XVIII)." Doctoral dissertation, Universidade de Lisboa, 2009.

Alòs-Moner, Andreu Martínez. "The Birth of a Mission: The Jesuit Patriarchate in Ethiopia." *Portuguese Studies Review* 10, no. 2 (2002): 1–14.

Amorim, Maria Adelina. *Os franciscanos no Maranhão e Grão-Pará: Missão e cultura na primeira metade de seiscentos.* Lisbon: Centro de Literatura de Expressão Portuguesa, Universidade de Lisboa; Centro de Estudos de História Religiosa, Universidade Católica Portuguesa, 2005.

Andrea da Pavia. "Viaggio Apostolico alle Missioni dell'Africa del P.re Andrea da Pavia Pred.re Capuccino, 1685–1702" [1692–1702]. MS 3165, fols. 68r–132v, Biblioteca Nacional de España.

Antonio da Gaeta and Francesco Maria Gioia. *La maravigliosa conversione alla santa fede di Cristo della regina Singa e del svo regno di Matamba nell'Africa meridionale, descritta con historico stile.* Naples: G. Passaro, 1669.

Antonio de Teruel. "Descripcion Narrativa de la Missión serafica de los Padres Capuchinos y sus Progressos en el Reyno de Congo" [ca. 1646]. MS 3533, Biblioteca Nacional de España.

Antonio Zucchelli da Gradisca. *Der Geistliche Robinson, oder Lustige angenehme und wahrhafftige Beschreibung einer sehr weiten Reise: So ein Capuciner in viele Lande von Europa und Africa gethan.* Erfurt: Johann Heydolph, 1723.

———. *Merckwürdige Missions- und Reise-Beschreibung nach Congo in Ethiopien: Worinnen nicht allein alles das-jenige, was sich auf dieser Reise aus Steyermarck, durch Italien, Spanien, Portugall und Indien biss nach Ethiopien denckwürdiges zugetragen, sondern auch die Sitten und Gebräuche der heydnischen Indianer, ihre Abgötterey und Aberglauben, ihre Regiments-Verfassung [. . .] des glei-chen wie die Verfassung der Mission in diesem Lande bes-chaffen, und wie eine grosse Menge Einwohner durch den Autorem von dem heydnischen Unglauben zur Christlichen Catholischen Religion bekehrt und getaufft worden, nebst unzehlich vielen andern curiösen und lesenswürdigen Sachen beschrieben werden.* Translated from the Italian. Frankfurt am Main: Johann Ludewig Gleditsch, Moritz Georg Weidmann, and Mary Lowell Putnam, 1715.

———. *Relazioni del viaggio e Missione di Congo nell'Etiopia Inferiore Occidentale del P. Antonio Zucchelli da Gradisca, Predicatore Capuccino della Provincia di Stiria, e già Missionario Apostolico in detto Regno.* Venice: Bartolomeo Giavarina, 1712.

Arcangeli, Alessandro. "Dancing Savages: Stereotypes and Cultural Encounters Across the Atlantic in the Age of European Expansion." In *Exploring Cultural History: Essays in Honour of Peter Burke*, edited by Melissa Calaresu, Filippo de Vivo, and Joan-Pau Rubiés, 289–308. London: Routledge, 2010.

Azzolini, Monica. "Talking of Animals: Whales, Ambergris, and the Circulation of Knowledge in Seventeenth-Century Rome." *Renaissance Studies* 31, no. 2 (2017): 297–318.

Baesten, V[incent]. "Les Jésuites au Congo (1548–1759)." *Précis historiques: Bulletin mensuel des missions belges de la Compagnie de Jésus* 41 (1892): 529–46; 42 (1893): 55–75, 101–22, 241–58, 433–57; 44 (1895): 465–81; 45 (1896): 49–60, 145–57.

Baglione, Giovanni. *Le vite de' pittori, scultori, architetti, ed intagliatori: Dal Pontificato di Gregorio XIII. del 1572. fino a' tempi di Papa Urbano VIII. nel 1642.* Naples, 1733.

Baldriga, Irene. *L'occhio della lince: I primi lincei tra arte, scienza e collezionismo (1603–1630).* Rome: Accademia Nazionale dei Lincei, 2002.

Barbot, Jean. "Description des Côtes d'Afrique depuis le Cap Bojador, jusque au Cap de Lopo Gonzalves" [1688]. 2 vols. ADM 7/830A and ADM 7/830B, National Archives, Kew.

Barriault, Anne B. *Spalliera Paintings of Renaissance Tuscany: Fables of Poets for Patrician Homes.* University Park: Pennsylvania State University Press, 1994.

Bassani, Ezio. *African Art and Artefacts in European Collections: 1400–1800.* Edited by Malcolm D. McLeod. London: British Museum, 2000.

———. *Un Cappuccino nell'Africa nera del Seicento: I disegni dei Manoscritti Araldi del Padre Giovanni Antonio Cavazzi da Montecuccolo.* Quaderni Poro 4. Milan: Associazione "Poro," 1987.

———. "Ivoires et tissus kongo: L'Italie, le Portugal et le Congo aux XVe–XVIe siècles." In *La nouvelle histoire du Congo: Mélanges eurafricains offerts à Frans Bontinck, C.I.C.M.*, edited by Pamphile Mabiala Mantuba-Ngoma, 61–72. Paris: Editions l'Harmattan, 2004.

Bastian, Adolf. *Ein Besuch in San Salvador, der Hauptstadt des Königreichs Congo.* Bremen: Druck und Verlag von Heinrich Strack, 1859.

Batumanisa, Makwanza, and Yelengi Nkasa. "L'homme blanc en Afrique centre-occidentale: Quelques témoignages d'échanges interculturels (XVIe–XIXe siecles)." *Africa: Rivista trimestrale di studi e documenta-zione dell'Istituto italiano per l'Africa e l'Oriente* 42, no. 1 (1987): 29–50.

Baudi di Vesme, Alessandro. *Le peintre-graveur italien: Ouvrage faisant suite au "Peintre-graveur" de Bartsch.* Milan: U. Hoepli, 1906.

Beligatti. See Cassiano Beligatti da Macerata.

Bellarmino, Roberto. *De Ascensione Mentis in Deum: Per Scalas Rerum Creatarum Opusculum.* Douai: Baltazaris Belleri, 1615.

Belotti. See Giovanni Belotti da Romano.

Bernardino d'Asti. See Bernardino Ignazio da Vezza d'Asti.

Bernardino Ignazio da Vezza d'Asti. "Missione in Pratica de PP. Cappuccini Italiani ne Regni di Congo, Angola, e adiacenti brevemente esposta p: lume, e guida de Missionari a quelle Sante Missioni destinati" [ca. 1750]. MS 1432 FG, Biblioteca Nacional de Portugal, Lisbon.

———. "Missione in prattica de RP cappuccini italiani ne regni di Congo, Angola, et adiacenti" [ca. 1750]. MS Borg. Lat. 316, Biblioteca Apostolica Vaticana.

———. "Missione in prattica: Padri cappuccini ne' Regni di Congo, Angola, et adiacenti" [ca. 1750]. MS 457, Biblioteca civica Centrale di Torino. https://bct.comune.torino.it/search /node?keys=Missione+in+prattica.

Bernardo da Canicatti. *Diccionario da lingua Bunda, ou Angolense, explicada na Portugueza, e Latina, composta por Fr. Bernardo Maria de Cannecattim, Capuchinho Italiano da Provincia di Palermo, Missionario Apostolico, e Prefeito das Missões de Angola, e Congo.* Lisbon: Impressão Regia, 1804.

Bindman, David, and Henry Louis Gates Jr., eds. *The Image of the Black in Western Art.* Vol. 3, *From the "Age of Discovery" to the Age of Abolition.* Part 1, *Artists of the Renaissance and Baroque.* New ed. Cambridge: Belknap Press of Harvard University Press, 2010.

———. *The Image of the Black in Western Art.* Vol. 3, *From the "Age of Discovery" to the Age of Abolition.* Part 2, *Europe and the World Beyond.* New ed. Cambridge: Belknap Press of Harvard University Press, 2011.

Blackmore, Josiah. *Moorings: Portuguese Expansion and the Writing of Africa.* Minneapolis: University of Minnesota Press, 2009.

Bleichmar, Daniela. *Visible Empire: Botanical Expeditions and Visual Culture in the Hispanic Enlightenment.* Chicago: University of Chicago Press, 2012.

———. *Visual Voyages: Images of Latin American Nature from Columbus to Darwin.* New Haven: Yale University Press in association with the Huntington Library, Art Collections, and Botanical Gardens, 2017.

Blier, Suzanne Preston. "Truth and Seeing: Magic, Custom, and Fetish in Art History." In *Africa and the Disciplines: The Contributions of Research in Africa to the Social Sciences and Humanities,* edited by Robert H. Bates, V. Y. Mudimbe, and Jean O'Barr, 139–66. Chicago: University of Chicago Press, 1993.

Boccone, Paolo. *Osservazioni naturali.* Bologna: Manolessi, 1684.

Bonaventure. *The Soul's Journey into God; The Tree of Life; The Life of Saint Francis.* Translated by Ewert H. Cousins. Classics of Western Spirituality. New York: Paulist Press, 1978.

Bontinck, François, and D. Ndembe Nsasi. *Le catéchisme kikongo de 1624: Réédition critique.* Mémoires— Académie royale des sciences d'outre-mer, n.s., 44-5. Brussels: Koninklijke Academie voor Overzeese Wetenschappen, 1978.

Boone, Elizabeth Hill, and Tom Cummins, eds. *Native Traditions in the Postconquest World: A Symposium at Dumbarton Oaks, 2nd Through 4th October 1992.* Washington, DC: Dumbarton Oaks, 1998.

Borromeo, Federico. *Sacred Painting; Museum.* Edited by Kenneth S. Rothwell Jr. and Pamela M. Jones. I Tatti Renaissance Library. Cambridge: Harvard University Press, 2010.

Bostoen, Koen, and Inge Brinkman, eds. *The Kongo Kingdom: The Origins, Dynamics, and Cosmopolitan Culture of an African Polity.* Cambridge: Cambridge University Press, 2018.

Boxer, Charles Ralph. "Background to Angola: Cadornega's Chronicle." *History Today* 11 (1961): 665–72.

———. "A 'História' de Cadornega no Museu Britânico." *Revista Portuguesa de História* 8 (1959): 291–98.

———. *Race Relations in the Portuguese Colonial Empire, 1415–1825.* Oxford: Clarendon Press, 1963.

Boyle, Marjorie O'Rourke. "Deaf Signs, Renaissance Texts." In *Perspectives on Early Modern and Modern Intellectual History*, edited by Joseph Marino and Melinda W. Schlitt, 164–92. Rochester: University of Rochester Press, 2001.

Brásio, António. *Historia e missiologia: Inéditos e esparsos*. Luanda: Instituto de Investigação Científica de Angola, 1973.

———. *Monumenta missionaria africana: África ocidental*. 15 vols. Lisbon: Agência Geral do Ultramar, Divisão de Publicações e Biblioteca, 1952–88.

———. *Monumenta missionaria africana: África ocidental*. 2nd ser. Lisbon: Agência Geral do Ultramar, Divisão de Publicacões e Biblioteca, 1958–.

Breen, Benjamin. *The Age of Intoxication: Origins of the Global Drug Trade*. Philadelphia: University of Pennsylvania Press, 2019.

Brewer-García, Larissa. *Beyond Babel: Translations of Blackness in Colonial Peru and New Granada*. Cambridge: Cambridge University Press, 2020.

———. "Imagined Transformations: Color, Beauty, and Black Christian Conversion in Seventeenth-Century Spanish America." In *Envisioning Others: Race, Color, and the Visual in Iberia and Latin America*, edited by Pamela A. Patton, 111–41. Leiden: Brill, 2015.

Brinkman, Inge. "Kongo Interpreters, Traveling Priests, and Political Leaders in the Kongo Kingdom (15th–19th Century)." *International Journal of African Historical Studies* 49, no. 2 (2016): 255–76.

Brito, Cristina. "On Mermaids and Manatees: A First Approach to the Evolution of Natural History Images in Early Modern Times." Paper presented at the European Cetacean Society workshop From Nature to Science: Scientific Illustration on Marine Mammals Throughout the Centuries; Old Challenges and New Perspectives, Setúbal, Portugal, 6 April 2013.

Brockey, Liam Matthew. "Books of Martyrs: Example and Imitation in Europe and Japan, 1597–1650." *Catholic Historical Review* 103, no. 2 (2017): vi–223.

Brook, Timothy. *Vermeer's Hat: The Seventeenth Century and the Dawn of the Global World*. New York: Bloomsbury Press, 2008.

Brown, Ras Michael. *African-Atlantic Cultures and the South Carolina Lowcountry*. Cambridge Studies on the American South. New York: Cambridge University Press, 2012.

Bry, Theodor de, Hans Staden, Jean de Léry, Nicolas Barré, Johann Dryander, Johann Adam Lonicerus, and Carolus Clusius. *Americae Tertia Pars Memorabile[m] Provinciae Brasiliae Historiam Contine[n]s*. Frankfurt am Main: Apud Matthiam Beckerum, impensis Theodori de Bry, 1592.

Burke, Jill. "Nakedness and Other Peoples: Rethinking the Italian Renaissance Nude." *Art History* 36, no. 4 (2013): 714–39.

Cabranes-Grant, Leo. *From Scenarios to Networks: Performing the Intercultural in Colonial Mexico*. Evanston: Northwestern University Press, 2016.

Cadornega, António de Oliveira de. "Historia general das guerras Angolanas" [1680]. [Vols. 1 and 3.] Manuscrito Vermelho 77, Academia das Ciencias, Lisbon.

———. "Historia general das guerras Angolanas escrita por Antonio de Oliveira Cadornega, capitaõ reformado e cidadaõ da cidade de Saõ Paulo da Assumpçaõ, natural de Villa-Viçoza" [1701–]. 3 vols. Manuscript portugais 2–4, Bibliothèque nationale de France.

———. "Historia geral das guerras Angolanas" [1680]. [Vol. 2.] Add MS 15183, fols. 231ss, British Library, London.

———. *Historia geral das guerras Angolanas*. Vol. 2. Lisbon: Typographia da Companhia Nacional Editora, 1902.

———. *História geral das guerras angolanas, 1680[–1681]*. Edited by José Matias Delgado. 3 vols. Lisbon: Agência-Geral das Colónias, Divisão de Publicações e Biblioteca, 1940–42.

Camille, Michael. "Before the Gaze: The Internal Senses and Late Medieval Practices of Seeing." In *Visuality Before and Beyond the Renaissance: Seeing as Others Saw*, edited by Robert S. Nelson, 197–223. New York: Cambridge University Press, 2000.

Cardoso, Mattheus. *Doutrina Christaã [. . .]: De novo traduzida na lingoa do Reyno do Congo*. Lisbon: Geraldo da Vinha, 1624.

[———]. *História do Reino do Congo: Ms. 8080 da Biblioteca Nacional de Lisboa*. Edited by António Brásio. Lisbon: Centro de Estudos Históricos Ultramarinos, 1969.

Carli. See Dionigi de Carli da Piacenza.

Carnago, Ignazio. *Città di rifugio a' mortali, che contiene le divotioni dell'altissima signora Madre di Dio e Vergine Immaculata praticate da' suoi servi [. . .] opera non men utile, e dilettevole per la varietà delle divotioni*. Milan: Lodovico Monza, 1655.

Cassiano Beligatti da Macerata. "Giornale di Fra' Cassiano da Macerata nella Marca d'Ancona Missionario Apostolico Capuccino nel Tibet" [ca. 1760]. MS 362, Biblioteca comunale Mozzi Borgetti, Macerata.

———. "La Teologia de' Tibetani" [ca. 1775]. MS 372, Biblioteca comunale Mozzi Borgetti, Macerata.

Castelnau-L'Estoile, Charlotte de. *Un catholicisme colonial: Le mariage des Indiens et des esclaves au Brésil, XVIe–XVIIIe siècle*. Paris: Presses universitaires de France, 2019.

Cavazzi. See Giovanni Antonio Cavazzi da Montecuccolo.

Certeau, Michel de. *L'écriture de l'histoire*. Bibliothèque des histoires. Paris: Gallimard, 1975.

Cesari, Antonio. *Fioretti di San Francesco con otto capitoli aggiunti, le Considerazioni sulle stimmate, le due Regole e il Cantico del sole*. Florence: Libreria editrice fiorentina, 1922.

Chakrabarty, Dipesh. *Provincializing Europe: Postcolonial Thought and Historical Difference*. Princeton: Princeton University Press, 2000.

Clark, Stuart. *Vanities of the Eye: Vision in Early Modern European Culture*. Oxford: Oxford University Press, 2007.

Clarke, T. H. *The Rhinoceros from Dürer to Stubbs, 1515–1799*. London: Sotheby's Publications, 1986.

Claude d'Abbeville. *Histoire de la Mission des Pères Capucins en l'Isle de Maragnan et terres circonuoisines*. Paris: Imprimerie de François Huby, 1614.

Clist, Bernard. "From America to Africa: How Kongo Nobility Made Smoking Pipes Their Own." In Bostoen and Brinkman, *Kongo Kingdom*, 197–215.

Clist, Bernard, Els Cranshof, Gilles-Maurice de Schryver, Davy Herremans, Karlis Karklins, Igor Matonda, Caroline Polet, Amanda Sengeløv, Fanny Steyaert, Charlotte Verhaeghe, and Koen Bostoen. "The Elusive Archaeology of Kongo Urbanism: The Case of Kindoki, Mbanza Nsundi (Lower Congo, DRC)." *African Archaeological Review* 32, no. 3 (2015): 369–412.

Cohen-Aponte, Ananda. "Decolonizing the Global Renaissance: A View from the Andes." In *The Globalization of Renaissance Art*, edited by Daniel Savoy, 65–94. Leiden: Brill, 2017.

Coimbra, Carlos Dias. *Livros de "Ofícios para o reino" do Arquivo Histórico de Angola, 1726–1801*. 2 vols. in 1. Luanda: Imprensa Nacional de Angola, 1959–65.

Collo, Paolo, and Silvia Benso, eds. *Sogno: Bamba, Pemba, Ovando e altre contrade dei regni di Congo, Angola e adiacenti*. Guide impossibili. Milan: F.M. Ricci, 1986.

"Compendio delle vite de R.di Missionari Apostolici mandate della sacra cong.e di propaganda fide alle missioni dell'Africa meridionale ne Regni di Congo, Angola e Zinga" [1716]. Archivio Generale Cappuccini—Collegio Internazionale San Lorenzo da Brindisi, Roma-Bravetta.

Conigliello, Lucilla. "Jacopo Ligozzi tra turchi, fantolini e disegni di architetture." *Paragone, Parte arte*, no. 84 (2009): 49–57.

Constitutiones Apostolicae Brevia, Decreta, &c.: Pro Missionibus Sinarum, Tunquini, &c.; Ad Usum R.R. D.D. Episcoporum, Sacerdotumque à Summis Pontificibus, ab Eminentissimis D.D. Cardinalibus S. Congregationis de Propaganda Fide Respective in Orientem Missorum. Paris: Charles Angot, 1676.

Coote, Jeremy. "A Text-Book Textile at the Pitt Rivers Museum: Historiographical Notes on a Kongo Cushion-Cover, Its Canonical Status, Dating, and Provenance." *African Arts* 48, no. 1 (2015): 66–77.

Cristóvão de Lisboa. *História dos animaes e árvores do Maranhão.* Edited by Jaime Walter. Lisbon: Comissão Nacional para as Comemorações dos Descobrimentos Portugueses: Instituto de Investigação Científica Tropical, 2000.

———. "Historia dos animaes, e árvores do Maranhão pelo muito Reverendo Padre Fr. Christovão de Lisboa Calificador do Santo Officio, e fundador da Custodia do Maranhão da Recolecção de Santo António de Lisboa" [ca. 1625–31]. Códice 1660, Arquivo Histórico Ultramarino.

Crofoot, Margaret C. "Why Mob? Reassessing the Costs and Benefits of Primate Predator Harassment." *Folia Primatologica* 83, nos. 3–6 (2012): 252–73.

Cummings, Anthony M. "Dance and 'The Other': The *Moresca.*" Paper presented at the international interdisciplinary symposium Seventeenth-Century Ballet, a Multi-Art Spectacle, King's College London, 7 August 2010.

Cuvelier, Jean. "Le vénérable André de Burgio et la situation religieuse au Congo et dans l'Angola au temps de son apostolat (1745–1761)." *Collectanea Franciscana* 32 (1962): 87–115.

Cuvelier, Jean, Olivier de Bouveignes, and Girolamo da Montesarchio. *Jérôme de Montesarchio, apôtre du vieux Congo.* Collection Lavigerie 39. Namur: Grands Lacs, 1951.

Dapper, Olfert. *Naukeurige beschrijvinge der afrikaensche eylanden; als Madagaskar, of Sant Laurens, Sant Thomee, d'eilanden van Kanarien, Kaep de Verd, Malta en andere, vertoont in de benamingen, gelegentheit, steden, revieren, gewassen [. . .].* Amsterdam: Jacob van Meurs, 1668.

Daston, Lorraine, and Katharine Park. *Wonders and the Order of Nature, 1150–1750.* New York: Zone Books, 1998.

Davies, Surekha. *Renaissance Ethnography and the Invention of the Human: New Worlds, Maps, and Monsters.* Cambridge Social and Cultural Histories 24. Cambridge: Cambridge University Press, 2016.

Dean, Carolyn. *Inka Bodies and the Body of Christ: Corpus Christi in Colonial Cuzco, Peru.* Durham: Duke University Press, 1999.

Dean, Carolyn, and Dana Leibsohn. "Hybridity and Its Discontents: Considering Visual Culture in Colonial Spanish America." *Colonial Latin American Review* 12, no. 1 (2003): 5–35.

de Jonghe, Édouard, and Théophile Simar. "Archives congolaises (suite)." *Revue congolaise* 4 (1913): 1–29.

De Kind, Jasper, Gilles-Maurice de Schryver, and Koen Bostoen. "Pushing Back the Origin of Bantu Lexicography: The Vocabularium Congense of 1652, 1928, 2012." *Lexikos* 22, no. 1 (2012): 159–94.

Demaret, Mathieu. "Portugais, Néerlandais et Africains en Angola aux XVIe et XVIIe siècles: Construction d'un espace colonial." Doctoral thesis, EPHE, 2016.

———. "Portugueses e Africanos em Angola no século XVII: Problemas de representação e de comunicação a partir da *História Geral das guerras Angolanas.*" In *Representações de África e dos africanos na história e cultura: séculos XV–XXI,* edited by José Damião Rodrigues and Casimiro Rodrigues, 107–30. Ponta Delgada: Centro de História de Além-Mar, 2011.

De Renzi, Silvia. "Writing and Talking of Exotic Animals." In *Books and the Sciences in History,* edited by Marina Frasca-Spada and Nick Jardine, 151–67. Cambridge: Cambridge University Press, 2000.

Descourvières, J. J., and P.-F. Cuénot (copyist). "Dictionnaire congo et françois" [1775]. MS 524, Bibliothèque municipale de Besançon.

Dionigi de Carli da Piacenza and Michael Angelo de Guattini da Reggio. *Viaggio del Padre Michael Angelo de Guattini da Reggio, et del P. Dionigi de Carli da Piacenza Capuccinic, Predicatori, & Missionarij Apostolici nel Regno del Congo.* Bologna: Gioseffo Longhi, 1674.

Doke, Clement Martyn. "Early Bantu Literature—the Age of Brusciotto." *African Studies* 18, no. 2 (1959): 49–67.

Duffin, Christopher J. "'Fish,' Fossil, and Fake: Medicinal Unicorn Horn." *Geological Society, London, Special Publications* 452, no. 1 (2017): 211–59.

Earle, Thomas Foster, and Kate J. P. Lowe, eds. *Black Africans in Renaissance Europe.* Cambridge: Cambridge University Press, 2005.

Edgerton, Samuel Y. *Theaters of Conversion: Religious Architecture and Indian Artisans in Colonial Mexico.* Albuquerque: University of New Mexico Press, 2001.

Édouard d'Alençon. "Essai de Bibliographie capucino-congolaise." *Neerlandia Franciscana* 1, no. 1 (1914): 33–42, 251–65.

Elkins, James. "On Visual Desperation and the Bodies of Protozoa." *Representations* 40, no. 1 (1992): 33–56.

Elliott, John Huxtable. *The Old World and the New, 1492–1650.* Cambridge: Cambridge University Press, 1970.

Eucher de Roy. *Le Congo: Essai sur l'histoire religieuse de ce pays depuis sa découverte (1484) jusqu'à nos jours par le P. Eucher Frère mineur récollet de la Province Belge de Saint Joseph.* Huy: Imprimerie-Librairie Charpentier & Emond, 1894.

Fabian, Johannes. *Time and the Other: How Anthropology Makes Its Object.* New York: Columbia University Press, 1983.

Falgayrettes-Leveau, Christiane. *Angola: Figures de pouvoir.* Paris: Musée Dapper, 2010.

Falgayrettes-Leveau, Christiane, and Musée Dapper. *Le geste kôngo.* Paris: Musée Dapper, 2002.

Faria, Francisco Leite de. "João António Cavazzi: A sua obra e a sua vida." In Cavazzi and Alamandini, *Descrição histórica*, 1:xi–lviii.

———. *A primeira tentativa para os Capuchinhos missionarem no Congo.* Separata de Itinerarium, ano II, no. 8. Braga: Montariol, 1956.

———. "Tentativas frustradas para uma casa de Capuchinhos italianos em Lisboa." *Miscellanea Melchor de Pobladura* 2, no. 1 (1964): 243–77.

Ferreira, Aurora da Fonseca. *A Kisama em Angola do século XVI ao início do século XX.* Ciências humanas e sociais, Série história de Angola, nos. 7–8. Luanda: Kilombelombe, 2012.

Ferrerius, Mathias. *Rationarium Chronographicum Missionis Evangelicae ab Apostolicis Operarijs, praesertim Capuccinis, pro Ecclesiastico Catholico Regno propagando in quatuor Mundi partibus, signanter in Gallia Cisalpina exercitae.* 2 vols. Turin: Carlus Ianellum, 1659.

Fetvacı, Emine. *The Album of the World Emperor: Cross-Cultural Collecting and the Art of Album-Making in Seventeenth-Century Istanbul.* Princeton: Princeton University Press, 2020.

Filesi, Teobaldo. "Nazionalismo e religione nel Congo all'inizio del 1700." *Africa* 26, no. 3 (1971): 267–303; 26, no. 4 (1971): 463–508; 27, no. 1 (1972): 645–68.

Filesi, Teobaldo, and Isidoro de Villapadierna. *La missio antiqua dei cappuccini nel Congo (1645–1835): Studio preliminare e guida delle fonti.* Subsidia scientifica Franciscalia 6. Rome: Istituto storico cappuccini, 1978.

Filippo da Firenze. "Ragguagli del Congo" [1711]. Archivio provinciale dei Cappuccini, Florence.

Filippo della Santissima Trinità. *Viaggi Orientali del Reverendiss. P. Filippo della SS. Trinità Generale de' Carmelitani Scalzi: Da lui composti nella lingua Latina e nuouamente tradotti nell'Italiana da vn Padre del medesimo Ordine; Ne' quali si descriuono varij successi, molti Regni dell'Oriente, Monti, Mari, e Fiumi, la successione de' Prencipi dominanti, i Popoli Christiani & Infedeli che stanno in quelle parti; . . . Con alcune cose di nuouo aggiunte per consiglio dell'Autore.* Rome: Filippo M. Mancini, 1666.

Findlen, Paula. "Early Modern Things: Objects in Motion, 1500–1800." In *Early Modern Things: Objects* and Their Histories, 1500–1800, edited by Paula Findlen, 3–28. New York: Routledge, 2013.

———. Possessing Nature: Museums, Collecting, and Scientific Culture in Early Modern Italy. Studies on the History of Society and Culture 20. Berkeley: University of California Press, 1994.

Fischer, Louis-Paul, and Véronique Cossu Ferra Fischer. "La licorne et la corne de licorne chez les apothicaires et les médecins." Histoire des sciences médicales 45, no. 3 (2011): 265–74.

Flanigan, Theresa. "Ocular Chastity: Optical Theory, Architectural Barriers, and the Gaze in the Renaissance Church of San Marco, Florence." In Beyond the Text: Franciscan Art and the Construction of Religion, edited by Xavier Seubert and Oleg Bychkov, 40–60. St. Bonaventure, NY: Franciscan Institute Publications, 2013.

Fletcher, Jennifer. "Filippo Napoletano's Museum." Burlington Magazine 121, no. 919 (1979): 649–59.

Foucault, Michel. Folie et déraison: Histoire de la folie à l'âge classique. Paris: Plon, 1961.

———. "Qu'est-ce qu'un auteur?" Bulletin de la Société française de philosophie 63, no. 3 (1969): 73–104.

Fracchia, Carmen. "Black but Human": Slavery and Visual Art in Hapsburg Spain, 1480–1700. Oxford: Oxford University Press, 2019.

Fraiman, Susan. "Jane Austen and Edward Said: Gender, Culture, and Imperialism." Critical Inquiry 21, no. 4 (1995): 805–21.

Francesco da Pavia. "Animali quadrupedi, Volatili, Aquatili, che ne Regni del Congo, Angola, Dongo, Matamba, Ghanghella, Chignaca, Ongo, Omba, e Zenze, io fra Fran.co da Pavia Capuccino Missionario Apostolico per più anni ne sudetti Regni vidi vivi, e morti, alcuni de qualli hebbi anche in mio potere." Filza 6381 ins. 7, Archivio di Stato di Firenze, Mediceo del Principato.

Franco, Antonio. Synopsis annalium Societatis Jesu in Lusitania ab anno 1540 usque ad annum 1725. Augsburg: Philippi, Martini, & Joannis Veith, 1726.

Freedberg, David. The Eye of the Lynx: Galileo, His Friends, and the Beginnings of Modern Natural History. Chicago: University of Chicago Press, 2002.

Fromont, Cécile, ed. Afro-Catholic Festivals in the Americas: Performance, Representation, and the Making of Black Atlantic Tradition. Africana Religions. University Park: Pennsylvania State University Press, 2019.

———. The Art of Conversion: Christian Visual Culture in the Kingdom of Kongo. Chapel Hill: University of North Carolina Press, published for the Omohundro Institute of Early American History and Culture, Williamsburg, Virginia, 2014.

———. "Collecting and Translating Knowledge Across Cultures: Capuchin Missionary Images of Early Modern Central Africa." In Collecting Across Cultures: Material Exchanges in the Early Modern Atlantic World, edited by Daniela Bleichmar and Peter C. Mancall, 134–54, 311–15. Philadelphia: University of Pennsylvania Press, 2011.

———. "Common Threads: Cloth, Colour, and the Slave Trade in Early Modern Kongo and Angola." Art History 41, no. 5 (2018): 838–67.

———. "Dance, Image, Myth, and Conversion in the Kingdom of Kongo, 1500–1800." African Arts 44, no. 4 (2011): 52–63.

———. "Dancing for the King of Congo from Early Modern Central Africa to Slavery-Era Brazil." Colonial Latin American Review 22, no. 2 (2013): 184–208.

———. "Depicting Kongo and Angola in the Seventeenth and Eighteenth Centuries." Collection. MAVCOR Journal 6, no. 1 (2022). DOI: 10.223322 /mav.coll.2022.1. https://mavcor.yale.edu/mavcor -journal/collections/depicting-kongo-and-angola -seventeenth-and-eighteenth-centuries.

———. "From Image to Grave, and Back: Multidisciplinary Inquiries into Kongo Christian Visual Culture." In Bostoen and Brinkman, Kongo Kingdom, 143–64.

————. "Nature, Culture, and Faith in Seventeenth-Century Kongo and Angola: The Parma Watercolors Texts." Essay. *MAVCOR Journal* 6, no. 1 (2022). DOI: 10.223322/mav.ess.2022.1. https://mavcor.yale.edu /mavcor-journal/essays/nature-culture-and-faith -seventeenth-century-kongo-and-angola-parma.

————. "Tecido estrangeiro, hábitos locais: Indumentária, insígnias Reais e a arte da conversão no início da Era Moderna do Reino do Congo." *Anais do Museu Paulista: História e cultura material* 25, no. 2 (2017): 11–31.

————. "Under the Sign of the Cross in the Kingdom of Kongo: Shaping Images and Molding Faith in Early Modern Central Africa." PhD diss., Department of History of Art and Architecture, Harvard University, 2008.

————. "Veränderung und Austausch: Zentral-afrikanische Kunst und visuelle Kultur in der Frühen Neuzeit / Changes and Exchanges: Central African Art and Visual Culture in the Early Modern Era." In *Kunstgeschichte der vier Erdteile, 1300–1650: Positionen und Austauschprozesse (Art History of the Four Continents, 1300–1650: The Dynamics of Cultural Exchange)*, edited by Matteo Burioni and Ulrich Pfisterer. Darmstadt: Wissenschaftliche Buchgesellschaft, in press.

Gage, Frances. "Exercise for Mind and Body: Giulio Mancini, Collecting, and the Beholding of Landscape Painting in the Seventeenth Century." *Renaissance Quarterly* 61, no. 4 (2008): 1167–207.

————. *Painting as Medicine in Early Modern Rome: Giulio Mancini and the Efficacy of Art*. University Park: Pennsylvania State University Press, 2016.

Gaudio, Michael. *Engraving the Savage: The New World and Techniques of Civilization*. Minneapolis: University of Minnesota Press, 2008.

Geronimus, Dennis. *Piero di Cosimo: Visions Beautiful and Strange*. New Haven: Yale University Press, 2006.

Gerritsen, W. P. "The Unicorn and the Pharmacists: Early Modern Views on the Presumed Anti-Toxic Effects of Unicorn Horn." *Gewina* 30, no. 1 (2007): 1–10.

Giacinto Brugiotti da Vetralla. "Infelicità felice o vero Mondo alla roversa, Delle Qualità Costumi e Maniere di Vivere dell'Habitatori del Regno del Congo e Paesi Vicini" [1650]. Current location unknown.

Gibson, Gordon D., and Cecilia R. McGurk. "High-Status Caps of the Kongo and Mbundu Peoples." *Textile Museum Journal* 5, no. 4 (1977): 71–96.

Gikandi, Simon. *Slavery and the Culture of Taste*. Princeton: Princeton University Press, 2011.

Giovanni Antonio Cavazzi da Montecuccolo. *Descrião histórica dos três reinos do Congo, Matamba e Angola*. Translated by Graziano Maria da Leguzzano. 2 vols. Estudos de cartografia antiga, série memórias, pub-licações 2–3. Lisbon: Junta de Investigações do Ultramar, 1965.

————. "Missione Evangelica al Regno del Congo [Araldi manuscript]" [1665–68]. Biblioteca Estense, Modena.

Giovanni Antonio Cavazzi da Montecuccolo and Fortunato Alamandini da Bologna. *Istorica descrizione de' tre' regni Congo, Matamba et Angola sitvati nell' Etiopia inferiore occidentale e delle missioni apostoliche esercitateui da religiosi Capuccini*. Bologna: Giacomo Monti, 1687.

Giovanni Belotti da Romano. "Avvertimenti Salutevoli agli Apostolici Missionari, Specialmente Ne Regni del Congo, Angola, e circonuicini Espressi da F. Gio: Belotti da Romano Pred.ᵉ Capuc.º della prov.ᵃ di Brescia Giá Miss.º Apos.º ne sudetti Regni" [1680]. Biblioteca del Clero, Bergamo.

————. "Le Giornate Apostoliche Con varij, nuoui e diletteuoli Successi, descritte dal P. F. Giovanni Belotti da Romano, predicatore capuccino della Provincia di Brescia, gia missionario apostolico ne Regni del Congo, Angola e circonuicini: Opera dis-tinta in tre parti; Con un copioso Indice delle case piu memorabili; Dedicata all'Ill.mo Sig.re Conte Carlo

Vincenzo Giouanelli" [1680]. Capuchin General Archives in Rome.

Giovanni Francesco [da] Romano. *Breve Relatione del Successo della Missione de Frati Minori Capuccini del Serafico P.S. Francesco al Regno del Congo e delle qualità, costumi, e maniere di viuere di quel Regno, e suoi habitatori.* Rome: Nella Stampa della Sacra Congregazione de Propaganda Fide, 1648.

Girolamo da Montesarchio. "Viaggio al Gongho" [ca. 1668]. Fondo Missioni Estere, Archivio provinciale dei Cappuccini, Florence.

Girolamo Merolla da Sorrento and Angelo Piccardo. *Breve, e succinta relatione del viaggio nel Regno di Congo nell' Africa Meridionale, fatto dal P. Girolamo Merolla da Sorrento . . . : Continente variati Clima, Arie, Animali, fiumi, frutti, vestimenti con proprie figure, diuersità di costumi, e di viueri per l'vso humano.* Naples: Francesco Mollo, 1692.

Giuseppe Monari da Modena. "Viaggio al Congo, fatto da me fra Giuseppe da Modena Missionario Apostolico e Predicatore Capuccino, incomentiato alli 11 del mese di Novembre del anno 1711, e terminato alli 22 di Febraro del anno 1713 . . ." [1723]. Alfa.n.09.07, Biblioteca Estense, Modena.

Gómez, Pablo F. *The Experiential Caribbean: Creating Knowledge and Healing in the Early Modern Atlantic.* Chapel Hill: University of North Carolina Press, 2017.

Gonçalves, Rosana Andréa. "África indômita: Missionários capuchinhos no Reino do Congo (século XVII)." Master's diss., Universidade de São Paulo, 2008.

González, Cristina Cruz. "From Conversion to Reconversion: Assessing Franciscan Missionary Practices and Visual Culture in Colonial Mexico." In *Beyond the Text: Franciscan Art and the Construction of Religion*, edited by Xavier Seubert and Oleg Bychkov, 125–46. St. Bonaventure, NY: Franciscan Institute Publications, 2013.

Greenblatt, Stephen. *Marvelous Possessions: The Wonder of the New World.* Chicago: University of Chicago Press, 1991.

Groesen, Michiel van. "The De Bry Collection of Voyages (1590–1634): Early America Reconsidered." *Journal of Early Modern History* 12, no. 1 (2008): 1–24.

Gschwend, Annemarie Jordan. "The Emperor's Exotic and New World Animals: Hans Khevenhüller and Habsburg Menageries in Vienna and Prague." In *Naturalists in the Field: Collecting, Recording, and Preserving the Natural World from the Fifteenth to the Twenty-First Century*, edited by Arthur MacGregor, 76–103. Emergence of Natural History 2. Leiden: Brill, 2018.

Guattini, Michelangelo, and Dionigi Carli. *Viaggio nel Regno del Congo.* Edited by Francesco Surdich. Il fascino dell'ignoto 15. Cinisello Balsamo (Milan): San Paolo, 1997.

Guimarães, Francisco de. "O mais ilustre capuchinho portugués no estrangeiro: O beato Cassiano de Nantes." *Boletim Oficial do Comissariado Geral dos Frades Menores Capuchinhos em Portugal* 2, no. 5 (1956): 43–50.

Hall, Kim F. *Things of Darkness: Economies of Race and Gender in Early Modern England.* Ithaca: Cornell University Press, 1995.

Hamann, Byron Ellsworth. "The Mirrors of Las Meninas: Cochineal, Silver, and Clay." *Art Bulletin* 92, nos. 1–2 (2010): 6–35.

Harpster, Grace. "The Color of Salvation: The Materiality of Blackness in Alonso de Sandoval's *De Instauranda Aethiopum Salute.*" In *Envisioning Others: Race, Color, and the Visual in Iberia and Latin America*, edited by Pamela A. Patton, 83–110. Leiden: Brill, 2015.

Harriot, Thomas. *A briefe and true report of the new found land of Virginia, of the commodities and of the nature and manners of the naturall inhabitants.* Frankfurt am Main: Typis Ioannis Wecheli, sumtibus vero Theodori de Bry, 1590.

Hartman, Saidiya. "Venus in Two Acts." *Small Axe* 12, no. 2 (2008): 1–14.

Heimlich, Geoffroy. "L'art rupestre du massif de Lovo (République démocratique du Congo)." Doctoral thesis, Université libre de Bruxelles and Université Paris I–Panthéon Sorbonne, 2014.

———. "The Kongo Cross Across Centuries." *African Arts* 49, no. 3 (2016): 22–31.

———. *Le massif de Lovo, sur les traces du royaume de Kongo.* Cambridge Monographs in African Archaeology 95. Oxford: Archaeopress, 2017.

Heintze, Beatrix. "António de Oliveira de Cadornega e a sua 'História geral das guerras angolanas': Um historiador e etnógrafo do séc. XVII, natural de Vila Viçosa." *Callipole: Revista de cultura*, nos. 3–4 (1995–96): 75–86.

———. "The Extraordinary Journey of the Jaga Through the Centuries: Critical Approaches to Precolonial Angolan Historical Sources." Translated by Katja Rieck. *History in Africa* 34 (2007): 67–101.

———. *Fontes para a história de Angola do século XVII.* Vol. 1. Veröffentlichungen des Frobenius-Instituts an der Johann Wolfgang Goethe–Universität zu Frankfurt am Main. Stuttgart: F. Steiner Verlag Wiesbaden, 1985.

———. "Unbekanntes Angola: Der Staat Ndongo im 16. Jahrhundert." *Anthropos* 72, nos. 5–6 (1977): 749–805.

Hennepin, Louis. *Description de la Loüisiane: Nouvellement decouverte au Sud' Oüest de la Nouvelle France, par ordre du roy; Avec la Carte du Pays; Les Moeurs & la Maniere de vivre des Sauvages.* Paris: Chez la veuve Sebastien Huré, 1683.

———. *Nouvelle decouverte d'un tres grand pays situé dans l'Amerique, entre le Nouveau Mexique, et la Mer Glaciale.* Utrecht: Guillaume Broedelet, 1697.

Hermenegildo de Vilaplana. *Historico, y sagrado novenario de la milagrosa imagen de Nuestra Señora del Pueblito, de la Santa Provincia de Religiosos Observantes de San Pedro, y San Pablo de Michoacan.* Mexico City: Bibliotheca Mexicana, 1761.

Herrejón Peredo, Carlos. "Marcel Bataillon y el humanismo mexicano en el siglo XVI." *Relaciones: Estudios de historia y sociedad* (Zamora) 21, no. 81 (2000): 187–99.

Herz, Alexandra. "Imitators of Christ: The Martyr-Cycles of Late Sixteenth-Century Rome Seen in Context." *Storia dell'arte*, no. 62 (1988): 53–70.

Heywood, Linda M. *Njinga of Angola: Africa's Warrior Queen.* Cambridge: Harvard University Press, 2017.

Hildebrandus ab Hooglede. "Le père Georges de Gheel (†1652): Missionnaire, philologue et martyr." *Études franciscaines* 42, no. 238 (1930): 76–81.

Hilton, Anne. "European Sources for the Study of Religious Change in Sixteenth and Seventeenth Century Kongo." *Paideuma* 33 (1987): 289–312.

———. *The Kingdom of Kongo.* Oxford Studies in African Affairs. Oxford: Clarendon Press, 1985.

Hirschberg, Walter. "Early Historical Illustrations of West and Central African Music." *African Music* 4, no. 3 (1969): 6–18.

Howard, Donald Roy. *Writers and Pilgrims: Medieval Pilgrimage Narratives and Their Posterity.* Berkeley: University of California Press, 1980.

Hsia, Florence C. *Sojourners in a Strange Land: Jesuits and Their Scientific Missions in Late Imperial China.* Chicago: University of Chicago Press, 2009.

Hulme, Peter. *Colonial Encounters: Europe and the Native Caribbean, 1492–1797.* London: Methuen, 1986.

Hulton, Paul, and David Beers Quinn. *The American Drawings of John White, 1577–1590, with Drawings of European and Oriental Subjects.* 2 vols. Chapel Hill: University of North Carolina Press, 1964.

Hutchinson, Margarite. "Bibliography of Pigafetta." In *A Report of the Kingdom of Congo, and of the Surrounding Countries; Drawn out of the Writings and Discourses of the Portuguese, Duarte Lopez, by Filippo Pigafetta, in Rome, 1591; Newly Translated from the Italian, and Edited with Explanatory Notes, by Margarite Hutchinson; with facsimiles of the Original Maps, and a Preface by Sir Thomas Fowell Buxton . . . ,* 145–48. London: John Murray, 1881.

I fioretti di San Francesco. Vicenza: Giovanni Leonardo Longo, 1476.

Impey, Oliver, and Arthur MacGregor, eds. *The Origins of Museums: The Cabinet of Curiosities in Sixteenth and Seventeenth-Century Europe*. Oxford: Clarendon Press, 1985.

"Instructio vicariorum ad Regna Sinarum, Tonchini et Cocincinae proficiscentium 1659." In *Sacrae Congregationis de Propaganda Fide Memoria Rerum: 350 Jahre im Dienste der Weltmission 1622–1972*, edited by Josef Metzler, vol. 3, documents appendix 3, 697–712. Rome: Herder, 1976.

Jacqueline, Bernard. "Les instructions de la S. C. 'de Propaganda Fide' aux vicaires apostoliques des royaumes du Tonkin et de Cochinchine (1659)." *Revue historique de droit français et étranger* 48 (1970): 624–31.

Jadin, Louis. "Andrea da Pavia au Congo, à Lisbonne, à Madère: Journal d'un missionnaire capucin, 1685–1702." *Bulletin de l'Institut historique belge de Rome*, no. 41 (1970): 375–592.

———. "Le clergé séculier et les capucins du Congo et d'Angola aux XVIe et XVIIe siècles: Conflits de juridiction, 1700–1726." *Bulletin de l'Institut historique belge de Rome* 36 (1964): 185–483.

———. "Le Congo et la secte des Antoniens: Restauration du royaume sous Pedro IV et la 'Saint Antoine' congolaise (1694–1718)." *Bulletin de l'Institut historique belge de Rome*, no. 33 (1961): 411–615.

———. "Rivalités luso-néerlandaises au Sohio, Congo 1600–1675." *Bulletin de l'Institut historique belge de Rome* 37 (1966): 137–359.

———. "Les survivances chrétiennes au Congo au XIXème siècle." *Études d'histoire africaine* 1 (1970): 137–85.

Janzen, John M., with William Arkinstall. *The Quest for Therapy: Medical Pluralism in Lower Zaire*. Berkeley: University of California Press, 1978.

Jones, Pamela M. *Federico Borromeo and the Ambrosiana: Art Patronage and Reform in Seventeenth-Century Milan*. Cambridge: Cambridge University Press, 1993.

———. "Federico Borromeo as a Patron of Landscapes and Still Lifes: Christian Optimism in Italy, ca. 1600." *Art Bulletin* 70, no. 2 (1988): 261–72.

[Jordão, Levy Maria], viscount of Paiva Manso. *História do Congo*. Lisbon: Typographia da Academia Real das Ciências, 1877.

Juan de Santiago. "Breve relación de lo suçedido a doçe religiosos cappuchinos que la Santa Sede Apostólica enbió Por missionarios Apostólicos al Reyno de Congo: Recopilada por uno y el más mínimo Indigno totalmente de tan Sublime ministerio; Dedicada a Nr.º Rm.º Pe. Fr. Inoçençio de Catalagirona, Ministro General de los frailes menores capuchinos de Nr.º Seráfico Pe. S. Francisco" [ca. 1650]. MS II/772, Real Biblioteca del Palacio Madrid.

Júnior, Miguel. *Análise da história geral das guerras Angolanas, 1575–1680, de António Oliveira de Cadornega*. Luanda: Mayamba, 2011.

Kabolo Iko Kabwita. *Le royaume kongo et la mission catholique, 1750–1838: Du déclin à l'extinction*. Mémoire d'églises. Paris: Karthala, 2004.

Kamen, Henry. *The Phoenix and the Flame: Catalonia and the Counter Reformation*. New Haven: Yale University Press, 1993.

Kaplan, Paul H. D. *The Rise of the Black Magus in Western Art*. Ann Arbor, MI: UMI Research Press, 1985.

Kircher, Athanasius. *China monumentis qua Sacris quà Profanis, nec non variis naturae & artis spectaculis, aliarumque rerum memorabilium argumentis illustrata*. Amsterdam: Jacobum à Meurs, 1667.

Koerner, Joseph Leo. "The Epiphany of the Black Magus Circa 1500." In *The Image of the Black in Western Art*, edited by David Bindman and Henry Louis Gates Jr., vol. 3, *From the "Age of Discovery" to the Age of Abolition*, part 1, *Artists of the Renaissance and Baroque*, 7–92. Cambridge, MA: Harvard University Press, 2010.

———. "Hieronymus Bosch's World Picture." In *Picturing Science, Producing Art*, edited by Caroline

A. Jones and Peter Galison, 297–323. New York: Routledge, 1998.

Kolfin, Elmer. "Tradition and Innovation in Dutch Ethnographic Prints of Africans c. 1590–1670." *Zeventiende eeuw* 32, no. 2 (2017): 165–84.

———. "When Africans Became Black: Dürer, Rubens, and the Changing Image of Africans in Northern Europe." *Print Quarterly* 34, no. 4 (2017): 379–92.

Kolsky, Stephen. "Graceful Performances: The Social and Political Context of Music and Dance in the Cortegiano." *Italian Studies* 53, no. 1 (1998): 1–19.

Kotani, Noriko. "Studies in Jesuit Art in Japan." 2 vols. PhD diss., Department of Art and Archaeology, Princeton University, 2010.

Kriger, Colleen E. "'Guinea Cloth': Production and Consumption of Cotton Textiles in West Africa Before and During the Atlantic Slave Trade." In *The Spinning World: A Global History of Cotton Textiles, 1200–1850*, edited by Giorgio Riello and Prasannan Parthasarathi, 105–26. Oxford: Oxford University Press, 2009.

LaGamma, Alisa. *Heroic Africans: Legendary Leaders, Iconic Sculptures*. New York: Metropolitan Museum of Art, 2011.

Lanzi, Luigi. *Histoire de la peinture en Italie, depuis la renaissance des beaux-arts, jusques vers la fin du XVIIIe siècle*. 5 vols. Paris: H. Seguin, 1824.

Largier, Niklaus, and Jeremy Brett. "The Logic of Arousal: Saint Francis of Assisi, Teresa of Avila, and Thérèse Philosophe." *Qui parle* 13, no. 2 (2003): 1–18.

Latour, Bruno. "Visualisation and Cognition: Drawing Things Together." In *Knowledge and Society: Studies in the Sociology of Culture Past and Present*, edited by H. Kuklick, 1–40. Greenwich: Jai Press, 1986.

Leibsohn, Dana. *Script and Glyph: Pre-Hispanic History, Colonial Bookmaking, and the "Historia Tolteca-Chichimeca."* Washington, DC: Dumbarton Oaks Research Library and Collection, 2009.

Leitch, Stephanie. "Burgkmair's *Peoples of Africa and India* (1508) and the Origins of Ethnography in Print." *Art Bulletin* 91, no. 2 (2009): 134–59.

———. *Mapping Ethnography in Early Modern Germany: New Worlds in Print Culture*. Basingstoke, UK: Palgrave Macmillan, 2010.

León-Portilla, Miguel. *Los franciscanos vistos por el hombre náhuatl: Testimonios indígenas del siglo XVI*. Mexico City: Universidad Nacional Autónoma de México, 1985.

Levi, Joseph Abraham. "Padre Giovanni Antonio Cavazzi (1621–1678), nos reinos do 'Congo, Matamba et Angola': Primeiros contatos europeus com a África." *Estudos portugueses e africanos* 33–34, nos. 1–2 (1999): 29–47.

Lexicon Capuccinum: Promptuarium Historico-Bibliographicum Ordinis Fratrum Minorum Capuccinorum (1525–1950). Rome: Bibliotheca Collegii Internationalis S. Laurentii Brundusini, 1951.

Linschoten, Jan Huyghen van. *Itinerario, Voyage ofte Schipvaert van Jan Huygen van Linschoten, naer Oost ofte Portugaels Indien inhoudende een corte beschryvinge der selver Landen ende Zee-custen, met aenwysinge van alle de voornaemde principale Havens, Revieren, hoecken ende plaetsen*. Amsterdam: Cornelis Claesz, 1596.

Lopes, Duarte, and Filippo Pigafetta. *De beschryvinghe vant groot ende vermaert Coninckrijck van Congo, ende de aenpalende oft ommegheleghen Landen, met verclaringhe van veel sonderlinghe saken, ende gheschiedenissen vanden selfden Coninckrijcke: . . . Ghenomen wt deschriften ende mondelicke t'samen spraecken, van Edoart Lopez Portegijs; Beschreven door Philips Pigafetta in Italiaens, ende overgheset in ons Nederlantsche spraecke; Deur Martijn Everart B.* Amsterdam: Cornelis Claesz, 1596.

———. *Regnum Congo, hoc est vera descriptio regni Africani, quod tam ab incolis quam Lusitanis Congus appellatur*. Illustrated by Johann Theodor de Bry and Johann Israel de Bry. Frankfurt am Main: Wolfgang Richter, 1598.

———. *Regnum Congo, hoc est Warhaffte und Eigentliche Beschreibung deß Königreichs Congo in Africa, und* deren angrentzenden Länder, darinnen der Inwohner *Glaub, Leben, Sitten und Kleydung . . . angezeigt wirdt.* Illustrated by Johann Theodor de Bry and Johann Israel de Bry. Frankfurt am Main: de Bry, 1597.

———. *Relatione del reame di Congo et delle circonvicine contrade, tratta dalli Scritti & ragionamenti di Odoardo Lopez Portoghese per Filippo Pigafetta.* Rome: Appresso Bartolomeo Grassi, 1591.

———. *Le royaume de Congo & les contrées environnantes (1591).* Translated and edited by Willy Bal. Collection Magellane. Paris: Chandeigne; UNESCO, 2002.

Lorenzo da Lucca. *Relations sur le Congo du père Laurent de Lucques (1700–1717).* Translated and annotated by Jean Cuvelier. Brussels, 1953.

Lowe, Kate. "The Lives of African Slaves and People of African Descent in Renaissance Europe." In Spicer, *Revealing the African Presence,* 13–33.

———. "Visual Representations of an Elite: African Ambassadors and Rulers in Renaissance Europe." In Spicer, *Revealing the African Presence,* 99–115.

Luca da Caltanisetta. *Diaire congolais: 1690–1701.* Translated and edited by François Bontinck. Publications de l'Université Lovanium de Kinshasa 27. Louvain: Éditions Nauwelaerts; Paris: Béatrice-Nauwelaerts, 1970.

Lurati, Patricia. "'To Dust the Pelisse': The Erotic Side of Fur in Italian Renaissance Art." *Renaissance Studies* 31, no. 2 (2017): 240–60.

MacGaffey, Wyatt. "Dialogues of the Deaf: Europeans on the Atlantic Coast of Africa." In *Implicit Understandings: Observing, Reporting, and Reflecting on the Encounters Between Europeans and Other Peoples in the Early Modern Era,* edited by Stuart B. Schwartz, 249–67. Cambridge: Cambridge University Press, 1994.

———. *Religion and Society in Central Africa: The Bakongo of Lower Zaire.* Chicago: University of Chicago Press, 1986.

Madeira Santos, Catarina. "Écrire le pouvoir en Angola: Les archives ndembu (XVIIᵉ–XXᵉ siècles)." *Annales: Histoire, sciences sociales* 64, no. 4 (2009): 767–95.

———. "Un monde excessivement nouveau: Savoirs africains et savoirs missionnaires; Fragments, appropriations et porosités dans l'œuvre de Cavazzi di Montecúccolo." In *Missions d'évangélisation et circulation des savoirs: XVIᵉ–XVIIIᵉ siècle,* 295–308. Collection de la Casa de Velázquez 120. Madrid: Casa de Velázquez, 2011.

Mancini, Giulio. *Considerazioni sulla pittura.* Fonti e documenti inediti per la storia dell'arte. Rome: Accademia nazionale dei Lincei, 1956.

Marcellino d'Atri. See Marcellino Canzani d'Atri.

Marcellino Canzani d'Atri. "Giornate Apostoliche Fatte a me Fra Marcellino d'Atri predicatore Cappucino nelle missioni de Regno d'Angola e Congo, nella Etiopia inferiore parte occidentale nell'Africa 1690" [1690–1708]. Archivio provinziale dei Cappucini, L'Aquila.

Maret, Pierre de. *Fouilles archéologiques dans la vallée du Haut-Lualaba, Zaire, III: Kamilamba, Kikulu et Malemba-Nkulu, 1975.* Vol. 3. Annales du Musée royal de l'Afrique centrale 131. 2 vols. Tervuren, Belgium: Musée royal de l'Afrique centrale, 1992.

Maret, Pierre de, and Alexandre Livingstone Smith. "Who's Who? The Case of the Luba." In *Ethnic Ambiguity and the African Past: Materiality, History, and the Shaping of Cultural Identities,* edited by François G. Richard and Kevin C. MacDonald, 192–216. Institute of Archaeology Publications 65. Walnut Creek, CA: Left Coast Press, 2015.

Margócsy, Dániel. "The Camel's Head: Representing Unseen Animals in Sixteenth-Century Europe." *Netherlands Yearbook for History of Art / Nederlands kunsthistorisch Jaarboek Online* 61, no. 1 (2011): 61–85.

Markey, Lia, ed. *Renaissance Invention: Stradanus's "Nova Reperta."* Evanston: Northwestern University Press, 2020.

———. "Stradano's Allegorical Invention of the Americas in Late Sixteenth-Century Florence." *Renaissance Quarterly* 65, no. 2 (2012): 385–442.

Mason, Peter. *Infelicities: Representations of the Exotic.* Baltimore: Johns Hopkins University Press, 1998.

Mateo de Anguiano. *Misiones capuchinas en Africa.* Vol. 1, *La misión del Congo.* Biblioteca "Missionalia Hispanica" 7. Madrid: Consejo Superior de Investigaciones Científicas, Instituto Santo Toribio de Mogrovejo, 1950.

McAllen, Katherine. "Jesuit Martyrdom Imagery Between Mexico and Rome." In *The New World in Early Modern Italy, 1492–1750,* edited by Elizabeth Horodowich and Lia Markey, 143–65. Cambridge: Cambridge University Press, 2017.

Medeiros, François de. *L'Occident et l'Afrique (XIIIe–XVe siècle): Images et représentations.* Hommes et sociétés. Paris: Karthala, 1985.

Mello e Souza, Marina de. "Catolicismo e poder no Congo: O papel dos intermediários nativos, séculos XVI a XVIII." *Anos 90* 21, no. 40 (2014): 51–63.

———. "Missionários e mestres na construção do catolicismo centro-africano, século XVII." Paper presented at the twenty-sixth Simpósio Nacional de História, ANPUH, São Paulo, 2011.

———. "Santo Antônio de nó-de-pinho e o catolicismo afro-brasileiro." *Tempo* 6, no. 11 (2001): 171–88.

Merolla. See Girolamo Merolla da Sorrento.

Merrell, James H. "Some Thoughts on Colonial Historians and American Indians." *William and Mary Quarterly* 46, no. 1 (1989): 94–119.

Metzler, Josef. "Orientation, programme et premières décisions (1622–1649)." In *Sacrae Congregationis de Propaganda Fide Memoria Rerum: 350 Jahre im Dienste der Weltmission 1622–1972,* edited by Josef Metzler, 1:146–96. Rome: Herder, 1971.

Mignolo, Walter D., and Catherine E. Walsh. *On Decoloniality: Concepts, Analytics, Praxis.* Durham: Duke University Press, 2018.

Mitchell, W. J. Thomas. *Picture Theory: Essays on Verbal and Visual Representation.* Chicago: University of Chicago Press, 1994.

Moheng, Anne-Cécile. "Corps à baleines et paniers, la mécanique du maintien au XVIIIème siècle." In *La mécanique des dessous: Une histoire indiscrète de la silhouette,* 109–27. Paris: Les arts décoratifs, 2013.

Monari. See Giuseppe Monari da Modena.

Monteiro, Joachim John. *Angola and the River Congo.* London: Macmillan, 1875.

Moroni, Lino. *Descrizione del sacro monte della Vernia.* Florence, 1612.

Morton, Julia Frances. "Purple Mombin." In *Fruits of Warm Climates,* edited by Curtis F. Dowling Jr., 242–45. Miami: self-published, 1987.

Mutanda wa Mukendi, Mukuna. "L'institution et le rôle des confréries dans la mission capucine du royaume du Kongo et de l'Angola de 1645 à 1765." *Revue africaine de théologie* 19, no. 37 (1995): 37–51, 149–65.

———. "La question des 'esclaves d'église' détenus par les pères capucins au Kongo et en Angola (1645–1835)." *Revue africaine de théologie* 15, no. 30 (1991): 163–79.

Neri, Janice. *The Insect and the Image: Visualizing Nature in Early Modern Europe, 1500–1700.* Minneapolis: University of Minnesota Press, 2011.

Nevile, Jennifer, ed. *Dance, Spectacle, and the Body Politick, 1250–1750.* Bloomington: Indiana University Press, 2008.

Newman, Andrew. *On Records: Delaware Indians, Colonists, and the Media of History and Memory.* Lincoln: University of Nebraska Press, 2012.

Niccolò da Poggibonsi. *Libro d'oltramare.* Edited by Alberto Bacchi della Lega. 2 vols. Scelta di curiosità letterarie inedite o rare dal secolo XIII al XIX. Bologna: Gaetano Romagnoli, 1881.

Nikis, Nicolas. "La métallurgie du cuivre en Afrique centrale: Résultats préliminaires des recherches archéologiques en République du Congo." Paper presented at the First Young Researchers' Overseas Day, Brussels, Belgium, 16 December 2014. http://doi.org/10.5281/zenodo.48062.

Norton, Marcy. "Subaltern Technologies and Early Modernity in the Atlantic World." *Colonial Latin American Review* 26, no. 1 (2017): 18–38.

Nsondé, Jean de Dieu. "Christianisme et religion traditionnelle en pays koongo aux XVIIe–XVIIIe siècles." *Cahiers d'études africaines* 32, no. 128 (1992): 705–11.

———. *Langues, culture et histoire Koongo aux XVIIe et XVIIIe siècles.* Vol. 1, *Textes.* Paris: Harmattan, 1995.

Ogilvie, Brian W. *The Science of Describing: Natural History in Renaissance Europe.* Chicago: University of Chicago Press, 2006.

O'Gorman, Edmundo. *La invención de América: El universalismo de la cultura de Occidente.* Mexico City: Fondo de Cultura Económica, 1958.

Olmi, Giuseppe. "Science, Honour, Metaphor: Italian Cabinets of the Sixteenth and Seventeenth Centuries." In *The Origins of Museums: The Cabinet of Curiosities in Sixteenth- and Seventeenth-Century Europe,* edited by Oliver Impey and Arthur MacGregor, 5–16. Oxford: Clarendon Press, 1985.

Otele, Olivette. *African Europeans: An Untold History.* London: Hurst, 2020.

Pacconio, Francisco. *Gentio de Angola sufficientemente instruido nos mysterios de nossa sancta Fé.* Lisbon: Domingo Lopes Resa, 1642.

Pacheco, Francisco. *Arte de la pintura, su antiguedad, y grandezas: Descrivense los hombres eminentes que ha auido en ella, assi antiguos como modernos; del dibujo y colorido; del pintar al temple, al olio, de la iluminacion, y estofado; del pintar al fresco; de las encarnaciones, de polimento, y de mate; del dorado, bruñido, y mate; Y enseña el modo de pintar todas las pinturas sagradas.* Seville: Simon Faxardo, 1649.

Pacifique de Provins. *Relation du voyage de Perse faict par le R. P. Pacifique de Provins.* Paris: Nicolas & Jean de la Coste, 1631.

Padilla, Carmella, and Barbara C. Anderson, eds. *A Red like No Other: How Cochineal Colored the World; An Epic Story of Art, Culture, Science, and Trade.* New York: Skira/Rizzoli, 2015.

Palomo, Federico. "Ascetic Tropics: Franciscans, Missionary Knowledge, and Visions of Empire in the Portuguese Atlantic at the Turn of the Eighteenth Century." *Culture and History Digital Journal* 5, no. 2 (2016): e013.

Panofsky, Erwin. *Studies in Iconology: Humanistic Themes in the Art of the Renaissance.* New York: Harper & Row, 1972.

Pantoja, Selma. "Women's Work in the Fairs and Markets of Luanda." In *Women in the Portuguese Colonial Empire: The Theatre of Shadows,* edited by Clara Sarmento, 81–94. Newcastle upon Tyne: Cambridge Scholars, 2008.

Parma Watercolors [ca. 1666–90]. Virgili Collection, Parma.

Parreira, Adriano. *Dicionário glossográfico e toponímico da documentação sobre Angola, séculos XV–XVII.* Imprensa universitária 79. Lisbon: Editorial Estampa, 1990.

Pellicer de Ossau y Salas y Tovar, José. *Mission Evangelica al Reyno de Congo por la Serafica Religion de los Capuchinos.* Madrid: Domingo Garcia i Morras, 1649.

Phipps, Elena, Johanna Hecht, and Cristina Esteras Martín. *The Colonial Andes: Tapestries and Silverwork, 1530–1830.* New York: Metropolitan Museum of Art; New Haven: Yale University Press, 2004.

Piazza, Calogero. *La prefettura apostolica del Congo alla metà del XVII secolo: La relazione inedita di Girolamo da Montesarchio.* Milan: A. Giuffrè, 1976.

Pistoni, Giuseppe. *Fra Giovanni Antonio Cavazzi da Montecuccolo: Documenti inediti.* Modena: TEIC, 1972.

———. "I manoscritti 'Araldi' di padre Giovanni Antonio Cavazzi da Montecuccolo." *Atti e memorie, Academia nazionale di scienze, Lettere e arti di Modena,* 6th ser., 11 (1969): 152–65.

Porras, Stephanie. *The First Viral Images: Maerten de Vos, Antwerp Print, and the Early Modern Globe.* Forthcoming.

Previdi, Carlo. *Frate Giovanni Antonio Cavazzi: Montecuccolo di Pavullo (MO), 1621–Genova, 1678;*

Scrittore, illustratore e missionario per Congo, Matamba ed Angola. Pavullo (Modena): Adelmo Iaccheri, 2012.

Quijano, Anibal. "Coloniality of Power, Eurocentrism, and Latin America." *Nepentla: Views from the South* 1, no. 3 (2000): 533–80.

Rama, Angel. *The Lettered City*. Latin America in Translation / En Traducción / Em Tradução. Translated by John Charles Chasteen. Durham: Duke University Press, 1996.

Rappaport, Joanne, and Tom Cummins. *Beyond the Lettered City: Indigenous Literacies in the Andes*. Narrating Native Histories. Durham: Duke University Press, 2012.

Ratelband, Klaas. *Os Holandeses no Brasil e na costa africana: Angola, Kongo e São Tomé, 1600–1650*. Translated by Tjerk Hagemeijer. Edited by Carlos Pacheco. Documenta histórica 29. Lisbon: Vega, 2003.

Rego, António da Silva. *Le patronage portugais de l'Orient: Aperçu historique*. Lisbon: Agencia Geral do Ultramar, 1957.

Restrepo, Eduardo. "*De Instauranda Aethiopum Salute*: Sobre las ediciones y características de la obra de Alonso de Sandoval." *Tabula Rasa*, no. 3 (2005): 13–26.

Ricci, Matteo. *De Christiana expeditione apud Sinas Suscepta ab Societate Jesu*. Edited by Nicolas Trigault and Wolfgang Kilian. Augsburg: Christoph. Mangium, 1615.

Rinchon, Dieudonné. "Les capucins au Congo." *Etudes franciscaines*, no. 35 (1923): 615–31.

Roberts, Jennifer L. *Transporting Visions: The Movement of Images in Early America*. Berkeley: University of California Press, 2014.

Rocha, Denise. "Imagens da diplomacia de Nzinga Mbandi Ngola, em Luanda, no ano de 1621: História, gravuras, e narrativa (Pepetela)." Paper presented at the III Encontro Nacional de Estudos da Imagem, Londrina, Brazil, 2011.

Rubiés, Joan-Pau. "Travel Writing and Humanistic Culture: A Blunted Impact?" *Journal of Early Modern History* 10, no. 1 (2006): 131–68.

Russo, Alessandra. *The Untranslatable Image: A Mestizo History of the Arts in New Spain, 1500–1600*. Austin: University of Texas Press, 2014.

Sá, Isabel dos Guimarães. "Ecclesiastical Structures and Religious Action." In *Portuguese Oceanic Expansion, 1400–1800*, edited by Francisco Bethencourt and Diogo Ramada Curto, 255–82. New York: Cambridge University Press, 2007.

Saccardo, Graziano Maria da Leguzzano. *Congo e Angola: Con la storia dell'antica missione dei cappuccini*. 3 vols. Mestre (Venice): Curia provinciale dei cappuccini, 1982–83.

Sagard, Gabriel. *Histoire du Canada et voyages que les frères mineurs recollects y ont faicts pour la conuersion des infidelles*. Paris: Claude Sonnius, 1636.

Said, Edward. *Culture and Imperialism*. New York: Vintage, 2012.

———. *Orientalism*. New York: Pantheon, 1978.

Salvadorini, Vittorio A. "La relazione sul Congo di Bonaventura da Corella, 1654." *Annali della Facoltà di scienze politiche dell'Università degli studi di Pisa* 3 (1973): 421–48.

Sandoval, Alonso de. *De Instauranda Aethiopum salute: Historia de Aethiopia; Naturaleça, Policia Sagrada y profana, Costumbres, ritos y Cathecismo Evangelico de todos los Aethiopes cõ que se restaura la salud de sus almas*. Madrid: Alonso de Paredes, 1647.

———. *Naturaleza, policia Sagrada i Profana, Costumbres i ritos, disciplina i Catechismo Evangelico de todos Etiopes*. Sevilla: Francisco de Lira, 1627.

Sanson, Nicolas. *L'Afrique en plusieurs cartes nouvelles, et exactes; & en divers traicte's de geographie, et d'histoire: Là où sont descripts succinctement, & auec vne belle methode, & facile: Ses empires, ses monarchies, ses estats, &c.; Les moeurs, les langues, les religions, le negoce, et la richesse de ses peuples, &c. et ce qu'il y a de plus beau, & de plus rare dans toutes ses Parties, & dans ses Isles*. Paris: self-published, 1656.

Sarzi Amade, José. "Réédition, contextualisation et analyse de la Breve e Succinta Relatione del Viaggio nel Regno di Congo [. . .] (1692) de Girolamo Merolla da Sorrento." 2 vols. Doctoral thesis, Université d'Aix-Marseille, 2016.

Schmidt, Benjamin. *Inventing Exoticism: Geography, Globalism, and Europe's Early Modern World*. Material Texts. Philadelphia: University of Pennsylvania Press, 2015.

Schreffler, Michael J. "Vespucci Rediscovers America: The Pictorial Rhetoric of Cannibalism in Early Modern Culture." *Art History* 28, no. 3 (2005): 295–310.

Schutte, Anne Jacobson. "*Ecco la santa!* Printed Italian Biographies of Devout Laywomen, Seventeenth–Eighteenth Centuries." In *Devout Laywomen in the Early Modern World*, edited by Alison Weber, 112–32. New York: Routledge, 2016.

Sebastiani, Silvia. "A 'Monster with Human Visage': The Orangutan, Savagery, and the Borders of Humanity in the Global Enlightenment." *History of the Human Sciences* 32, no. 4 (2019): 80–99.

Serafino da Cortona. "Breve relatione de i riti gentilichi e ceremonie diaboliche e superstitioni del infelice Regno di Congo tradotti in Italiano dal P. fra Serafino da Cortona Predicatore Capucccino e missionario Apostolico" [1652–53]. Fondi Missioni Estere, Archivio provinciale dei cappuccini di Firenze.

Shaffer, Holly. *Grafted Arts: Art Making and Taking in the Struggle for Western India, 1760-1820*. New Haven: Yale University Press, 2022.

Shepard, Odell. *The Lore of the Unicorn*. New York: Barnes & Noble, 1967.

Silva Santos, Vaniciéia. *O marfim no mundo moderno: Comércio, circulação, fé e status social (séculos XV–XIX)*. Curitiba: Editora Prismas, 2017.

Simonetti, Giuseppe. "P. Giacinto Brugiotti da Vetralla e la sua missione al Congo (1651–1657)." *Bollettino della Società geografica italiana*, 4th ser., 8, no. 4 (1907): 305–22, 369–81.

Singh, Kavita. *Real Birds in Imagined Gardens: Mughal Painting Between Persia and Europe*. Los Angeles: Getty Research Institute, 2017.

Slenes, Robert W. "L'arbre nsanda replanté: Cultes d'affliction kongo et identité des esclaves de plantation dans le Brésil du Sud-Est entre 1810 et 1888." *Cahiers du Brésil contemporain*, nos. 67–68 (2007): 217–313.

Spicer, Joaneath. "European Perceptions of Blackness as Reflected in the Visual Arts." In Spicer, *Revealing the African Presence*, 35–59.

———, ed. *Revealing the African Presence in Renaissance Europe*. Baltimore: Walters Art Museum, 2012.

Spivak, Gayatri Chakravorty. "Three Women's Texts and a Critique of Imperialism." *Critical Inquiry* 12, no. 1 (1985): 243-61.

Stanfield-Mazzi, Maya. "Weaving and Tailoring the Andean Church: Textile Ornaments and Their Makers in Colonial Peru." *Americas* 72, no. 1 (2015): 77–102.

Stoichita, Victor Ieronim. *The Self-Aware Image: An Insight into Early Modern Meta-painting*. Cambridge Studies in New Art History and Criticism. New York: Cambridge University Press, 1997.

Sutton, Elizabeth A. *Early Modern Dutch Prints of Africa*. Transculturalisms, 1400–1700. Farnham, Surrey: Ashgate, 2012.

Sweet, James H. *Recreating Africa: Culture, Kinship, and Religion in the African-Portuguese World, 1441–1770*. Chapel Hill: University of North Carolina Press, 2003.

Tavares, Ana Paula, and Catarina Madeira Santos. *Africae Monumenta: A apropriação da escrita pelos africanos*. Lisbon: Instituto de Investigação Científica Tropical, 2002.

Taylor, Diana. *The Archive and the Repertoire: Performing Cultural Memory in the Americas*. Durham: Duke University Press, 2003.

Tedeschi, Letizia. "Natale Bonifacio, illustratore del Pigafetta." *Critica d'arte* 57, nos. 9–10 (1992): 119–31.

Thevet, André. *La cosmographie universelle d'André Thevet cosmographe du roy: Illustrée de diverses figures des choses plus remarquables veues par l'auteur, & incogneues de noz anciens & modernes*. 2 vols. Paris: P. L'Huillier, 1575.

———. *Les singularitez de la France antarctique, autrement nommée Amerique: & de plusieurs Terres & Isles decouuertes de nostre temps*. Paris: Heritiers de Maurice de la Porte, 1557.

Thornton, John Kelly. "Afro-Christian Syncretism in the Kingdom of Kongo." *Journal of African History* 54, no. 1 (2013): 53–77.

———. *A History of West Central Africa to 1850*. New Approaches to African History. Cambridge: Cambridge University Press, 2020.

———. *The Kongolese Saint Anthony: Dona Beatriz Kimpa Vita and the Antonian Movement, 1684–1706*. Cambridge: Cambridge University Press, 1998.

———. "Roboredo, Kikongo Sermon." John Thornton's African Texts. http://www.bu.edu /afam/people/faculty/john-thornton/roboredo -kikongo-sermon/.

———. "Translation of the Araldi Manuscript." John Thornton's African Texts. http://www.bu.edu /afam/people/faculty/john-thornton/john -thorntons-african-texts/.

Tongiorgi Tomasi, Lucia, and Gretchen A. Hirschauer. *The Flowering of Florence: Botanical Art for the Medici*. Washington, DC: National Gallery of Art, 2002.

Toso, Carlo. *Il Congo, cimitero dei cappuccini, nell'inedito di P. Cavazzi (sec. XVII)*. Rome: L'Italia francescana, 1992.

———. "Relazioni inedite di P. Cherubino Cassinis da Savona sul 'Regno del Congo e sue Missioni.'" *L'Italia francescana* 45 (1974): 135–214.

Toso, Carlo, and Marcellino d'Atri. *L'anarchia congolese nel sec. XVII: La relazione inedita di Marcellino d'Atri*. Studi di storia delle esplorazioni 15. Genoa: Bozzi, 1984.

Tourneur, Victor. "Médailles religieuses du XVIIIème siècle, trouvées au Congo." *Revue belge de numismatique et de sigillographie* 91 (1939): 21–26.

Trouillot, Michel-Rolph. *Silencing the Past: Power and the Production of History*. Boston: Beacon Press, 1995.

Tuckey, James Hingston, and Christen Smith. *Narrative of an Expedition to Explore the River Zaire, Usually Called the Congo, in South Africa, in 1816*. London: John Murray, 1818.

Urban VIII. *Decreta Seruanda in Canonizatione, & Beatificatione Sanctorum*. Rome: Typographia Reu. Cam. Apost., 1642.

van Os, H. W. "St. Francis of Assisi as a Second Christ in Early Italian Painting." *Simiolus: Netherlands Quarterly for the History of Art* 7, no. 3 (1974): 115–32.

Vansina, Jan. "Communications Between Angola and East Central Africa Before c. 1700." In *Angola on the Move: Transport Routes, Communications, and History = Angola em movimento: Vias de transporte, comunicação e história*, edited by Beatrix Heintze and Achim van Oppen, 130–44. Frankfurt am Main: Lembeck, 2008.

———. "*Ndop*: Royal Statues Among the Kuba." In *African Art and Leadership*, edited by Douglas Fraser and Herbert M. Cole, 41–56. Madison: University of Wisconsin Press, 1972.

———. "Raffia Cloth in West Central Africa, 1500–1800." In *Textiles: Production, Trade, and Demand*, edited by Maureen Fennell Mazzaoui, 263–81. Aldershot, Hants: Ashgate, 1998.

Van Wyk Smith, Malvern. "'The Most Wretched of the Human Race': The Iconography of the Khoikhoi (Hottentots), 1500–1800." *History and Anthropology* 5, no. 3 (1992): 285–330.

Vaumas, Guillaume de. *L'éveil missionnaire de la France au XVIIe siècle*. Paris: Bloud & Gay, 1959.

Vernant, Jean-Pierre. "From the 'Presentification' of the Invisible to the Imitation of Appearance." In *Mortals and Immortals: Collected Essays*, edited by Froma I. Zeitlin, 151–63. Princeton: Princeton University Press, 1991.

———. *Mythe et pensée chez les grecs: Études de psychologie historique*. Paris: Éditions La Découverte, 1996.

Vertova, Luisa. "Per Giovenale Boetto pittore." *Studi piemontesi / Centro Studi Piemontesi* 27, no. 1 (1998): 33–49.

"Vocabularium Latinum, Hispanicum et Congense"
[1651]. MS Varia 274, Fondi minori 1896, Biblioteca
Nazionale Vittorio-Emanuele II di Roma.

Voigt, Lisa, and Elio Brancaforte. "The Traveling
Illustrations of Sixteenth-Century Travel Narratives."
PMLA 129, no. 3 (2014): 365–98.

Volper, Julien. *Du Jourdain au Congo: Art et christianisme en
Afrique centrale*. Paris: Flammarion, 2016.

Wang, Cheng-hua. "A Global Perspective on
Eighteenth-Century Chinese Art and Visual
Culture." *Art Bulletin* 96, no. 4 (2014): 379–94.

Weber, Priscila Maria. "'Angola' como conceito: Uma
análise da obra *História geral das guerras* angolanas de
Oliveira de Cadornega (século XVII)." Doctoral thesis, Pontifícia Universidade Católica do Rio Grande
do Sul, Porto Alegre, Brazil, 2018.

White, Ed. "Invisible Tagkanysough." *PMLA* 120, no. 3
(2005): 751–67.

Whitehead, Peter James Palmer, and Marinus Boeseman.
*A Portrait of Dutch 17th Century Brazil: Animals, Plants,
and People by the Artists of Johan Maurits of Nassau.*
Verhandelingen Afd. Natuurkunde, tweede reeks, 87.
Amsterdam: North-Holland, 1989.

Wu Hung. *The Double Screen: Medium and Representation
in Chinese Painting*. Chicago: University of Chicago
Press, 1996.

Young, Jason R. *Rituals of Resistance: African Atlantic
Religion in Kongo and the Lowcountry South in the Era
of Slavery*. Baton Rouge: Louisiana State University
Press, 2007.

Zanoni, Giacomo. *Istoria botanica di Giacomo Zanoni
semplicista, e Sopraintendente all'Horto publico di Bologna:
Nella quale si descriuono alcune Piante de gl'Antichi,
da moderni con altri nomi proposte; e molt'altre non piu
osseruate, e da varie Reggioni del Mondo venute, con le
virtù, e qualità della maggior parte di esse, & in figure al viuo
rappresentate*. Bologna: Gioseffo Longhi, 1675.

Zika, Charles. "Cannibalism and Witchcraft in Early
Modern Europe: Reading the Visual Images." *History
Workshop Journal*, no. 44 (1997): 77–105.

Zucchelli. See Antonio Zucchelli da Gradisca.

Index